Lecture Notes in Computer Science 10144

Commenced Publication in 1973
Founding and Former Series Editors:
Gerhard Goos, Juris Hartmanis, and Jan van Leeuwen

More information about this series at http://www.springer.com/series/7410

Dooho Choi · Sylvain Guilley (Eds.)

Information Security Applications

17th International Workshop, WISA 2016
Jeju Island, Korea, August 25–27, 2016
Revised Selected Papers

 Springer

Editors
Dooho Choi
ETRI
Daejeon
Korea (Republic of)

Sylvain Guilley
Secure-IC, S.A.S.
Paris
France

ISSN 0302-9743   ISSN 1611-3349   (electronic)
Lecture Notes in Computer Science
ISBN 978-3-319-56548-4   ISBN 978-3-319-56549-1   (eBook)
DOI 10.1007/978-3-319-56549-1

Library of Congress Control Number: 2017935962

LNCS Sublibrary: SL4 – Security and Cryptology

Printed on acid-free paper

This Springer imprint is published by Springer Nature
The registered company is Springer International Publishing AG
The registered company address is: Gewerbestrasse 11, 6330 Cham, Switzerland

Preface

The 17th International Workshop on Information Security Applications (WISA 2016) was held at Ramada Plaza Hotel, Jeju Island, Korea, during August 25–27, 2016. The workshop was hosted by the Korea Institute of Information Security and Cryptology (KIISC) and sponsored by the Ministry of Science, ICT and Future Planning (MSIP). It was also co-sponsored by the Korea Internet and Security Agency (KISA), the Electronics and Telecommunications Research Institute (ETRI), the National Security Research Institute (NSR), Jeju National University, and Kona.

The excellent arrangements were led by the WISA 2016 general chair, Prof. Im-Yeong Lee, and organizing chair, Prof. Ho-won Kim. This year WISA 2016 provided an open forum for exchanging and sharing of ongoing hot topics and results of research, development, and applications in information security areas.

The Program Committee prepared for an interesting program including four invited talks, from Dr. Ludovic Perret of Jussieu University (UPMC), Dr. Stjepan Picek of COSIC, KU Leuven, Prof. Beng Jin Teoh of Yonsei University, and Dr. Sangjoon Park of ETRI. The technical program also included an industrial session and a special event about technology exchange.

The workshop had seven tracks, namely, Cryptography (sessions 1 and 2-A), Authentication and ICT Convergent Security (session 2-B), Network Security (sessions 3-A and 4), Threats Analysis (sessions 3-B and 4), and Network and Application Security (session 5). We would like to thank all authors who submitted papers. Each paper was reviewed by at least three reviewers. External reviewers as well as Program Committee members contributed to the reviewing process from their particular areas of expertise. The reviewing and active discussions were hosted by a Web-based system, EDAS. Through this system, we could check the degree of similarity between the submitted papers and previously published papers to prevent plagiarism and self-plagiarism. Following the strict reviewing processes, 31 outstanding papers from nine countries were accepted for publication in this proceedings volume.

Many people contributed to the success of WISA 2016. We would like to express our deepest appreciation to each of the WISA Organizing and Program Committee members as well as the paper contributors. Without their endless support and sincere dedication and professionalism, WISA 2016 would have been impossible.

August 2016

Dooho Choi
Sylvain Guilley

Organization

General Chair

Im-Yeong Lee   Soonchunhyang University, Korea

Organizing Committee Chair

Ho-won Kim   Pusan National University, Korea

Organizing Committee

ByungHoon Kang   KAIST, Korea
Ikkyun Kim   ETRI, Korea
Sangchoon Kim   Kangwon National University, Korea
Yongdae Kim   KAIST, Korea
Changhoon Lee   Seoul National University of Science and Technology,
                            Korea
Heejo Lee   Korea University, Korea
Ok yeon Lee   Kookmin University, Korea
HyungGeun Oh   NSR, Korea
NamJe Park   Jeju National University, Korea
Young-Ho Park   Sejong Cyber University, Korea
Jung-Taek Seo   Soonchunhyang University, Korea
Kyung-Hoo Son   KISA, Korea
YooJae Won   Chungnam National University, Korea

Program Co-chairs

Dooho Choi   ETRI, Korea
Sylvain Guilley   Telecom ParisTech and Secure-IC, France

Program Committee

Man Ho Au   Hong Kong Polytechnic University, SAR China
Selcuk Baktir   Bahcesehir University, Turkey
Sang Kil Cha   KAIST, Korea
Young-Tae Cha   KISA, Korea
Yue Chen   Florida State University, USA
Seong-je Cho   Dankook University, Korea
Hyoung-Kee Choi   Sungkyunkwan University, Korea
Yoon-Ho Choi   Pusan National University, Korea
Viktor Fischer   Laboratoire Hubert Curien, France

Dong-Guk Han	Kookmin University, Korea
Jinguang Han	Nanjing University of Finance and Economics, China
Swee-Huay Heng	Multimedia University Malaysia
Yong-Sung Jeon	ETRI, Korea
Seung-Hun Jin	ETRI, Korea
Yousung Kang	ETRI, Korea
Geon Woo Kim	ETRI, Korea
Huy Kang Kim	Korea University, Korea
Ikkyun Kim	ETRI, Korea
Jong Kim	POSTECH, Korea
Soohyung Kim	ETRI, Korea
Daesung Kwon	NSR, Korea
Junho Kwon	Pusan National University, Korea
Taekyoung Kwon	Yonsei University, Korea
Donggeon Lee	Attached Institute of ETRI, Korea
Jong-Hyouk Lee	Sangmyung University, Korea
Mun-Kyu Lee	Inha University, Korea
Sung-Jae Lee	KISA, Korea
Zhen Ling	Southeast University, Bangladesh
Zhe Liu	University of Waterloo, Canada
Kirill Morozov	Kyushu University, Japan
Jung-Chan Na	ETRI, Korea
Kihyo Nam	Umlogics Inc., Korea
Elizabeth O'Sullivan	Queen's University Belfast, UK
Raphael Phan	Multimedia University, Malaysia
Stjepan Picek	KU Leuven, Belgium
Junghwan Rhee	NEC Laboratories America, USA
Kouichi Sakurai	Kyushu University, Japan
Seungwon Shin	KAIST, Korea
Tsuyoshi Takagi	Kyushu University, Japan
Chung-Huang Yang	National Kaohsiung Normal University, Taiwan
Jongwon Yoon	Hanyang University Korea
Dae Hyun Yum	Myongji University, Korea
Cong Zheng	Palo Alto Networks, USA

Contents

Does Query Blocking Improve DNS Privacy?
Quantifying Privacy Under Partial Blocking Deployment

Aziz Mohaisen$^{(\boxtimes)}$, Ah Reum Kang, and Kui Ren

University at Buffalo, State University of New York, Buffalo, NY, USA
{mohaisen,ahreumka,kuiren}@buffalo.edu

Abstract. DNS leakage happens when queries for names within a private namespace spread out to the public DNS infrastructure (Internet), which has various privacy implications. An example of this leakage includes the documented [1] leakage of .onion names associated with Tor hidden services to the public DNS infrastructure. To mitigate this leakage, and improve Tor's privacy, Appelbaum and Muffet [2] proposed the special use .onion domain name, and various best practice recommendations of blocking of .onion strings (hidden service addresses) at the stub (browser), recursive, and authoritative resolvers. Without any form of analysis of those recommendations in practice, it is very difficult to tell how much of privacy is provided by following them in various deployment settings. In this paper, we initiate for the study of those recommendations by analyzing them under various settings and conclude that while the unlikely universal deployment will naturally improve privacy by preventing leakage, partial deployment, which is the case for early adoption, will degrade the privacy of individuals not adopting those recommendations.

1 Introduction

The domain name system (DNS) is an essential protocol used for naming and addressing of resources in private networks and on the public Internet. In private networks as well as the public Internet, DNS is used—among other purposes—for mapping domain names to IP addresses. In private networks, however, one does not need to use a delegated top level domain (TLD) for naming hosts and services, and can use pseudo-TLDs, TLDs that are only recognizable within the private network. For example, pseudo-TLDs such .i2p, .onion, and .exit, among others, have been used as a standard suffix for naming services in various private networks. Among them, .onion has been used as the standard pseudo-TLD for naming hidden services in Tor. Queries initiated in the Tor network to .onion second level domains (SLDs) are routed within the Tor network, to aid the goal of hidden services, and are not intended for external use. If one is to query a .onion domain in the public DNS infrastructure, the query will be answered with an NXDOMAIN response (*i.e.*,nonexistent domain) from the root, because .onion is not delegated in the root DNS zone. In reality, under no circumstances, a private network query should be allowed in the public DNS infrastructure.

© Springer International Publishing AG 2017
D. Choi and S. Guilley (Eds.): WISA 2016, LNCS 10144, pp. 1–14, 2017.
DOI: 10.1007/978-3-319-56549-1_1

However, reality somewhat differs: it has been recently reported and systematically demonstrated [1] that queries for .onion strings, among other pseudo-TLDs, leak to the DNS root (public DNS infrastructure) for various reasons, including potential misconfiguration, misuse of .onion strings, and systematic browser prefetching, among other plausible root causes [1]. Even worse, such leakage has been on the rise [3], calling for further exploration.

Given the special nature of some of the pseudo-TLDs like .onion, special considerations need to be taken into account to prevent their leakage. For example, given that .onion names are used for querying hidden services, an eavesdropper on the DNS resolution system (on various links) can associate the .onion query with a user, or reduce the potential number of users associated with that query to a tractable set size, thus breaching the privacy of the user. Roughly speaking, the privacy leakage here means that the adversary will be able to tell that a user $u \in U$ (the set of all users) is interested in $q \in Q$ (a query among all queries), or a user $u \in U'$ (where $U' \subset U$) is interested in q, where (potentially) $|U'| << |U|$. Here we are assuming that the adversary is residing on the public Internet, and does not have any control over the private network (*i.e.*, Tor).

To address this real scenario of leakage, Appelbaum and Muffet proposed in RFC 7686 [2] the special use .onion domain name, and various best practice recommendations of blocking of .onion strings (hidden service addresses) at (i) the stub (browser), (ii) recursive, and (iii) authoritative resolvers (among other equally important best practice recommendations). The hope is that the deployment of such recommendations will improve the privacy of the users using Tor in general and hidden services in particular. No work, however, is done to assess the validity of such hope under any settings, let alone realistic deployment scenarios.

Contributions. In this paper we set out to analyze the privacy implications of blocking of the leaked DNS queries as a mean of improving the privacy of users. We initiate for such study by formalizing the adversary of a DNS system as a collection of capabilities on various links in the DNS resolution structure, as informally argued by Mohaisen and Mankin [4]. We use a well-defined advantage of the adversary to quantify the breached privacy of users over their queries with and without blocking and under various deployment scenarios captured by a parameterized model. We find out that while a universal deployment of such blocking strategies will naturally result in a great privacy benefit to users, such universal deployment is unlikely to happen immediately. As a result, a realistic analysis is drawn from partial deployment, in which we highlight the consequence of shared infrastructure like the DNS resolution system: the privacy of an individual does not only depend on his actions but also the actions of other users. In other words, we highlight scenarios where blocking by some users would make the matters worse for others who do not block.

Organization. The organization of the rest of this paper is as follows. In Sect. 2, we introduce the background of this work. In Sect. 3, we review a framework for the evaluation of privacy in the studied context in this paper. In Sect. 4 we review the results and findings, including discussion. We present the related work in Sect. 5. In Sect. 6 we draw concluding remarks.

2   Background

Domain Names and their Resolution. The DNS is a hierarchical naming system by design [5]. A typical domain name, such as www.example.com. consists of a TLD (com), an SLD (example) and a third level domain, or subdomain (www). The natural hierarchical structure of DNS facilitates manageability, especially of large zones, and involves various entities in resolution. When the above example is queried for resolution (perhaps using a query minimization technique [6]), one of 13 root name servers is queried for the address of com—those servers operate in anycast setting, where queries are routed to the geographically closest server among them. Upon receiving the address of com's authoritative name server, it is queried for the address of the authoritative name server of example, and so forth until the IP of the resource of interest for the full domain name is returned. In the plain DNS (*i.e.,*no security in place), a query for a name that does not exist is answered by NXDOMAIN response. Such response could be returned at any round of resolution of a hierarchical name, including by the root name server.

Resolution System. The above resolution procedure is only conceptual and does not take into account DNS optimizations geared towards improving the response time and manageability of the DNS resolution process by incorporating other entities. In particular, the DNS resolution system typically consists of three entities: *stub resolvers* (also called clients), *recursive resolvers*, and *authoritative name servers* (to simplify the analysis, one could view the authoritative name servers collectively as one of such servers). The stub resolver resides on the host, and forwards queries on behalf of a user to the recursive resolver, which is responsible for the iterative process of resolution above by querying the various authoritative name servers for addresses of names in a full domain name. The recursive resolver may also have *caching capabilities*, thus improving the latency for subsequent requests of previously resolved domain names.

DNS Blocking for Privacy. As mentioned earlier in Sect. 1, Appelbaum and Muffet proposed in RFC 7686 [2] proposed blocking as a means for improving privacy of Tor due to DNS leakage. DNS blocking proposed by them in the afore-mentioned work includes blocking at the stub resolver, blocking at the recursive, and blocking at the authoritative name server.

3   Evaluation Framework

The privacy of DNS is typically analyzed under an eavesdropper, a passive adversary that does not interfere with the resolution or try to change its outcomes, but is rather interested in associating a query with a user, or a set of users that is (typically) smaller than the total number of users in the system. The adversary is also characterized by the "scope" of eavesdropping[1], which determines the number of DNS links such adversary can observe.

In the system defined in Sect. 2 with the three entities involved in the resolution of a DNS query, we also specify various notations. We assume that the set of stubs in the system is S, and the set of recursive is R, where the total number of stubs $|S| = n$ and the total number of recursive is $|R| = k$. The set S is partitioned into non-overlapping subsets[2], denoted by $S_1, \ldots, S_k$, where stubs in each subset are associated with only one recursive resolver $r \in R$. We define the set of links between stubs and their corresponding recursive as $L_{s_i r_j}$ for $1 \leq i \leq S_j$, and $1 \leq j \leq k$. The total number of links is denoted by n, the total number of stubs. Similarly, we define the links between the recursive servers and authoritative name server as $L_{r_j a}$, where the total number of such links is k, which is also the number of recursive resolvers in the system. Similarly, we define the set of stub-to-recursive and recursive-to-authoritative links under the control of the adversary by $L^A_{s_i r_j}$ and $L^A_{r_j a}$ for some i, j.

Definition 1 *(Abstract Adversary). The adversary in our settings is defined as an eavesdropper $A(\alpha, \beta)$. In this adversary model, α is the ratio of the total number of links between the stub and recursive observed by the adversary ($|L^A_{sr}|$) to the total number of links in $L_{s_i r_j}$ (i.e.,$|L_{s_i r_j}| = n$). Furthermore, β is the ratio between the total number of links between the recursive resolvers and the authoritative name server that are observed by the adversary (i.e.,$|L^A_{ra}|$) to the total number of links in $L_{r_j a}$ (i.e.,$|L_{r_j a}| = k$).*

The above definition of the adversary is generic, and can be used to define various instances of adversaries based on actual capabilities (in what we call a concrete adversary; c.f. Sect. 3.1). Such concrete adversaries may include an eavesdropper on links between stub-recursive, recursive-authoritative, or both.

An important aspect of the adversary is his advantage in breaching the privacy in DNS setup. We define the privacy of the user simply as follows, then use that and the abstract adversary above to define the adversary's advantage.

Definition 2 *(User Privacy). for a set of n users, we say that the adversary succeeds in breaching the privacy of a user iff the adversary can associate a DNS query to a given user with probability $P_r[U = u|Q = q] > 0$. We call P_r as the adversary's advantage and use P_r^* to refer to advantage under capabilities $*$.*

---

[1] While it is also theoretically possible to view such adversary as a universal adversary that can see everything at any point in time, such assumption is perhaps unrealistic since meaningful adversaries to study are usually characterized by *bounded resources*. We follow such theme of characterizing the adversary in this paper.

[2] While it is possible in reality to have stub resolvers associated with multiple recursive resolvers over time, we consider the case of many-to-one mapping. This is, however, for simplification, and findings in this work hold even with many-to-many mappings.

3.1 Advantage Under No Blocking

Notice that the above notion of privacy has two cases of analysis and evaluation: (1) the case where the adversary can directly eavesdrop on links between the stub resolver and the recursive (*i.e.*, $A(\alpha, 0)$), thus directly observing queries, and (2) the case where the adversary indirectly eavesdrop on links between the stub and recursive by inferring association between queries and users using a given recursive when eavesdropping on a link between that recursive and the authoritative name server (*i.e.*, $A(0, \beta)$). Using such definition, we now proceed to describe the advantage of the adversary using both cases under no blocking:

– **Advantage of $A(\alpha, 0)$:** for this adversary, the advantage is basically α, since, on average, the adversary can associate queries between stubs and recursive resolvers for α fraction of stub-to-recursive links in the system. This is,

$$P_r^\alpha[U = u | Q = q] = |L_{sr}^A| / |L_{s_i r_j}| = \alpha \tag{1}$$

– **Advantage of $A(0, \beta)$:** for a given link in $L_{r_x a}^A \in L_{ra}^A$, we define the advantage of the adversary of associating a user using the recursive r_x to a query coming out of that recursive on the link $L_{r_x a}^A$ as

$$P_r^\beta[U = u | Q = q] = \frac{1}{|r_x|} = \frac{1}{|S_x|} \tag{2}$$

However, given that A has a number of those links, we generalize the advantage as the average advantage over all links seen by the adversary. This is, we define the average probability as $\overline{P_r^\beta}$ given as:

$$\overline{P_r^\beta} = \frac{1}{|L_{sr}^A|} \sum_{\forall r_x \in L_{sr}^A} \frac{1}{|r_x|} \tag{3}$$

Advantage of $A(\alpha, \beta)$. We notice that the above two advantages in (1) and (3) only capture a partial adversary. Thus, we generalize the advantage to an adversary that eavesdrops on both types of links simultaneously. This is, we define $A(\alpha, \beta)$, for which the advantage is defined as $P_r^{\alpha, \beta}[U = u | Q = q]$, as follows:

$$P_r^{\alpha, \beta}[U = u | Q = q] = P_r^\alpha + P_r^\beta - P_r^\alpha \times P_r^\beta \tag{4}$$

Notice that the subtracted term in (4) is due to the inclusion-exclusion principle, where we want to account for the likelihood that some of the links between recursive and stubs. By substituting from (1) and (3) into (4), we obtain:

$$P_r^{\alpha, \beta}[U = u | Q = q] = \alpha + \frac{1}{|L_{sr}^A|} \sum_{\forall r_x \in L_{sr}^A} \frac{1}{|r_x|} - \alpha \times \frac{1}{|L_{sr}^A|} \sum_{\forall r_x \in L_{sr}^A} \frac{1}{|r_x|}$$

$$= \alpha + (1 - \alpha) \frac{1}{|L_{sr}^A|} \sum_{\forall r_x \in L_{sr}^A} \frac{1}{|r_x|} \tag{5}$$

3.2   Advantage Under Blocking

The assumption for the analysis in the previous section is that no entity in the DNS resolution system performs blocking. Now we turn our attention to the case of the analysis under blocking, where one or more entities in the system do not allow unintended DNS queries to the public DNS infrastructure.

In the following, we assume that either the stub or recursive, or both, perform blocking[3]. To facilitate our analysis, we assume two parameters ψ_1 and ψ_2, corresponding to the ratio of stub resolvers and recursive resolvers that perform blocking, respectively. We also assume that those resolvers are chosen **uniformly at random** among all stub and recursive resolvers in the system, including those under the control of the adversary. We define the advantage under blocking at the stub as $P_r^*[U = u|Q = q]_{\psi_1}$ and the advantage under blocking at the recursive as $P_r^*[U = u|Q = q]_{\psi_2}$, respectively, where $*$ is used for emphasizing the capabilities of the adversary; $i.e., \alpha$, β, or both. With that in mind, we extend the model of the adversary and advantage under blocking as follows:

– **Advantage of $A(\alpha, 0)$ under blocking.** We treat this case with blocking at either the stub or the recursive. First, given that the adversary only controls a number of links between stubs and recursive resolvers, blocking at the recursive does not affect the advantage of the adversary, thus,

$$P_r^\alpha[U = u|Q = q]_{\psi_2} = \alpha \tag{6}$$

However, blocking at the stub resolver when the adversary only controls links between stubs and recursive resolvers reduces the advantage of the adversary, compared to the advantage in (1); given that $0 < \psi_1 \leq 1$, into:

$$P_r^\alpha[U = u|Q = q]_{\psi_1} = (1 - \psi_1)\alpha \tag{7}$$

– **Advantage of $A(0, \beta)$ under blocking.** Similarly, we treat the case with blocking at either the stub or recursive with an adversary $A(0, \beta)$ and formulate the corresponding advantage. When blocking is performed at the recursive, i.e., with $0 < \psi_2 \leq 1$, we have the advantage in (3) reduced into:

$$P_r^\beta[U = u|Q = q]_{\psi_2} = (1 - \psi_2)P_r^\beta = (1 - \psi_2)\frac{1}{|L_{sr}^A|}\sum_{\forall r_x \in L_{sr}^A}\frac{1}{|r_x|} \tag{8}$$

However, the advantage of the adversary in (3) is formulated as follows when blocking is performed at the stub resolvers:

$$P_r^\beta[U = u|Q = q]_{\psi_1} = \frac{1}{|L_{sr}^A|}\sum_{\forall r_x \in L_{sr}^A}\frac{1}{(1 - \psi_1)|r_x|} \tag{9}$$

---

[3] While blocking at the authoritative could serve other purposes, it does not help with privacy under the eavesdropper model treated in this paper; the authoritative name server falls out of the boundaries of the links of interest to our adversaries.

Notice that the assumption used in reaching the result in (9) is that blocking at the stub results in uniformly random blocking of stubs associated with the various recursive resolvers. Thus, on average, the fraction of stubs associated with a given recursive that are blocked due to ψ_1 is also ψ_1. Also, notice that the overall advantage of the adversary in (9) is greater than the adversary's advantage in (3) for any properly defined $\psi_1 < 1$.

Finally, and same as above, one can also generalize the advantage of the adversary for inclusive cases of both types of blocking at the same time, and using both capabilities. For the lack of space, we defer such analysis to the full version of this work, since it does not contribute to the main findings and conclusions.

4 Results and Discussion

We evaluate the various adversaries characterized in this paper on a real-world topology obtained from DNS operations of a large DNS recursive resolution provider. The dataset is not intended for characterizing DNS usage, but rather for demonstrating and comparing various models studied in this paper. We use this data to mainly understand various adversaries and their advantage (based on capabilities) with and without blocking.

4.1 Dataset and Evaluation Criteria

High-Level Statistics. Table 1 provides high-level statistics of our dataset.

In our dataset, and as shown in the Table above, we use traces collected at 180 recursive resolvers, serving over 176,991 stub resolvers, and forwarding queries to various authority servers (collectively viewed as a single sink, as in our framework). The goal of this evaluation is to relatively understand the advantage of the various adversaries discussed in this paper, under a real-world topology (using a simulated adversary). The CDF of the number of stubs associated with the various recursive resolvers (on the y-axis) is shown in Fig. 1(a). Figure 1(b) shows the cumulative distribution of the number of queries associated with the various stub resolvers (on the y-axis): the distribution is strongly heavy-tailed, with only 0.78% of all stub resolvers receiving more than 1000 queries, 5.36% receiving more than 100 queries, and 80.98% receiving less than 10 queries. In the rest of this section, *the advantage is used as the evaluation criteria.*

Table 1. Dataset

Feature	#	Avg. #	Max #
Stubs	176,991	51 queries per stub	77,332
Recursive	180	983 stubs per recursive	5,949
Queries	9,135,311	-	-

Selection Criteria of Links. There are multiple possibilities for the links that the adversary controls (or the stubs that he can observe, if queries are to be taken into account for analysis). Namely, and based on the number of stubs associated with a recursive resolver, the adversary may control the set of links serving the largest number of stubs, the smallest number of stubs, or a random set of links with respect to the number of stubs they carry traffic for. We name those strategies as **largest, smallest,** and **random**, respectively. We, however, believe that an opportunistic adversary would be best represented by the random strategy, which we emphasize in most of this paper. Such adversary would select his links or stubs uniformly at random.

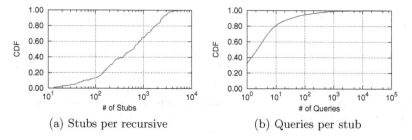

(a) Stubs per recursive   (b) Queries per stub

Fig. 1. Dataset. (a) CDF of the number of stubs and their recursive resolvers. (b) CDF of the number of queries and their stub resolvers.

Advantage Without Blocking. First we evaluate the advantage of the adversary under no blocking, to demonstrate the relative order of the various adversaries. We notice that $A(\alpha, 0)$ is rather a linear function (straight line) in the number of links between the stub and recursive observed by the adversary (results omitted) and moves steadily from 0 to 1 as L_{sr}^A grows to cover all links in L_{sr}. For $A(0, \beta)$, the results are shown in Fig. 2, where Fig. 2(a) shows $A(0, \beta)$ under various strategies of the adversary: smallest, largest and random (as described above) and Fig. 2(b) for various random strategies by $A(0, \beta)$.

We notice that the advantage of the adversary in both figures, while greater than 0 (thus the privacy is breached to some extent), it is small essentially because the advantage herein measures the inferential power of the adversary; when $\beta = 1$, the advantage of the adversary, as defined above, converges to $\frac{1}{|R|}$, where $|R|$ is 180 as shown in Table 1. We also notice from the same figure that the advantage of the adversary over the range of β greatly depends on the strategy of the adversary, where the smallest strategy yields higher advantage, and the largest strategy yields a smaller advantage: when $\beta = 0.5$, the smallest strategy yields an advantage that is more than order of magnitude higher than the largest strategy. The random strategy mimics an average case of both strategies (falls roughly in between both strategies). The difference between various runs of the random strategy is also clear in Fig. 2(b), although indicating the general trend of the advantage towards the average case.

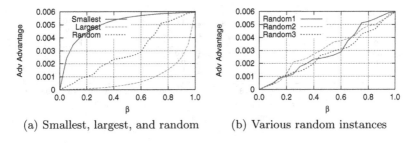

(a) Smallest, largest, and random   (b) Various random instances

Fig. 2. Advantage of the adversary for various values of β. (a) under various strategies: smallest, largest and random. (b) various random strategies by $A(0, \beta)$.

Advantage with Blocking at the Stub. Figure 3 shows the advantage of the adversary under blocking at the stub resolver with various values of α and β for the adversaries $A(\alpha, 0)$ and $A(0, \beta)$. In this evaluation, we use the random strategy highlighted above. In the first figure (*i.e.*, Fig. 3(a)), and as highlighted in the analytical results, we notice that the increase in α corresponds to increase in the initial advantage. However, as ψ_1 increases, the advantage sharply decays and approaches to 0 when all stub resolvers perform blocking.

However, more interestingly, the advantage of the adversary, as shown in Fig. 3(b) is shown to grow by more than an order of magnitude as ψ_i grows. Eventually, the advantage approaches 0 when $\psi_1 = 1$, though. We notice also from the same figures that a larger α and β for the same value of ψ_1 corresponds to the higher advantage of the adversary, which is in line with the prior analysis.

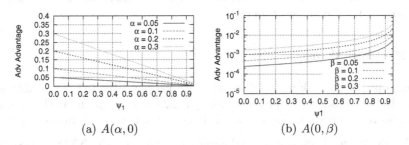

(a) $A(\alpha, 0)$ (b) $A(0, \beta)$

Fig. 3. The advantage of the adversary under blocking at the **stub resolvers** with various values of α and β for the adversaries $A(\alpha, 0)$ and $A(0, \beta)$.

Advantage with Blocking at the Recursive. Figure 4 shows similar results as above when blocking at the recursive resolver (using the parameter ψ_2). From Fig. 4(a) we notice that the advantage of the adversary is not affected by the blocking at the recursive since the recursive falls out of the scope of the adversary's capability. However, based on Fig. 4(b), we notice that the advantage of the adversary decays as ψ_2 increases, suggesting that perhaps blocking at the

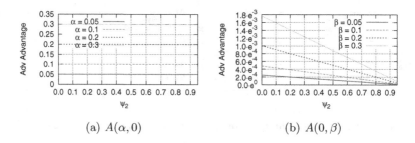

(a) $A(\alpha, 0)$ (b) $A(0, \beta)$

Fig. 4. The advantage of the adversary under blocking at the recursive with various values of α and β for the adversaries $A(\alpha, 0)$ and $A(0, \beta)$.

recursive when the adversary controls links to the authoritative resolver is the best strategy to address leakage.

Which Adversary? A natural question to ask is "which adversary is more realistic than the other?" given the various settings of adversaries, and how they are affected by blocking. Answering such question would allow us to draw a conclusion concerning the effect of blocking in practice. The consistent narrative of the industrial work, as in [4,7–9] indicates that $A(0, \beta)$ is a more likely adversary in practice since it is not easy to mount an attack on DNS between the stub and recursive, in general. For example, for an enterprise setup, the adversary has to be within the same enterprise to mount the attack, which is generally difficult and limiting to the adversary. With such adversary and associated advantage, we notice that blocking at the stub resolver is considered harmful: the advantage of the adversary increases as the number of blocking users increases (as long as it is not the total number of users).

5   Related Work

There is plenty of work on DNS security and privacy, although none addressed understanding blocking for privacy under partial deployment and in the presence of pervasive adversaries. We review a sample of the prior work in the following.

DNS Blocking. Thomas and Mohaisen [10] examined the NXD request patterns observed within the DITL data and A and J roots to better gauge the effectiveness of such a collision blocking technique. Appelbaum and Muffett [2] proposed blocking special queries (*i.e.*, .onion names; supposed to be used and routed within a private network) to improve Tor's privacy.

Modeling DNS Adversaries. Even though previous works have focused on various aspects of DNS security and privacy, including (data-driven) modeling and informal descriptions [4] (for confidentiality [11]), there is no study on formalizing the notion of pervasive adversaries, let alone evaluating them. Our research provides multiple scenarios of such adversaries and quantifies their advantage on DNS topology, and studies the advantage under various DNS behaviors [2]. Bau *et al.* [12] formally modeled the cryptographic operations in DNSSEC and discovered a forgery vulnerability. Herzberg *et al.* [13] presented a comprehensive overview of challenges and potential pitfalls of DNSSEC, including vulnerable configurations, vulnerabilities due to incremental deployment, and interoperability challenges. Goldberg *et al.* [14] demonstrated zone-enumeration vulnerabilities in NSEC and NSEC3, and proposed NSEC5.

DNS Privacy Leakage. Konings *et al.* [15] collected a one-week dataset of mDNS announcements at a university and showed that queries and device names leak a lot of information about users. Krishnan *et al.* [16] demonstrated privacy leakage by prefetching and showed that it is possible to infer the likelihood of search terms issued by clients by analyzing the context obtained from the prefetching queries. Zhao *et al.* [17] analyzed the complete DNS query process and discussed privacy disclosure problems in each step: client side, query transmission process, and DNS server side. Paxson *et al.* [18] developed a measurement procedure to limit the amount of information a domain can receive surreptitiously through DNS queries to an upper bound specified by a security policy. Castillo-Perez and Garcia-Alfaro [19] evaluated DNS privacy-preserving approaches, and pointed out the necessity of additional measures to enhance their security. Jeong *et al.* [20] analyzed the leaked .i2p requests of the public DNS to outline various potential directions of addressing such leakage.

Understanding DNS Behavior. Callahan *et al.* [21] passively monitored DNS and related traffic within a domestic network to understand server behavior. Shcomp *et al.* [22] presented a characterization of DNS clients for developing an analytical model of client interactions with the larger DNS ecosystem. Banse *et al.* [23] studied the feasibility of behavior-based tracking in a real-world setting. Schomp *et al.* [24] presented methods for efficiently discovering the complex client-side DNS infrastructure. They further developed measurement techniques for isolating the behavior of the distinct actors in the infrastructure. Shulman and Waidner [25] explored name servers that use server-side caching, characterized the operators of the server-side caching resolvers and their motivations. Kang *et al.* [26] summarized various works on DNS operation, security, and privacy, and outlined open research directions.

DNS Vulnerability. Schomp *et al.* [27] measured the Internet's vulnerability to DNS record injection attacks and found that record injection vulnerabilities are fairly common even years after some of them were first uncovered. Dagon *et al.* [28] studied and documented how attackers are using Internet resources: the creation of malicious DNS resolution paths. Xu *et al.* [29] described and quantitatively analyzed several techniques for hiding malicious DNS activities. Jackson *et al.* [30] evaluated the cost-effectiveness of mounting DNS rebinding attacks. Schomp *et al.* [31] addressed vulnerabilities in shared DNS resolvers by removing them entirely and leaving the recursive resolution to the clients. Hao *et al.* [32] explored the behavioral properties of domains using the DNS infrastructure associated with the domain and the DNS lookup patterns from networks who are looking up the domains initially. Spaulding *et al.* [33] studied the landscape of domain name typosquatting and highlighted models and advanced techniques for typosquatted domain names generation.

Designs for DNS Privacy. Zhao *et al.* [17] propose to ensure the DNS privacy by concealing the actual queries using noisy traffic. Castillo-Perez *et al.*[19] evaluated this approach and demonstrated that the privacy ensured by added queries is difficult to analyze and that the technique introduces additional latency and overhead, making it impractical. An extended algorithm to ensure privacy while improving the performance is also introduced by Castillo-Perez *et al.*[19], using both noisy traffic and private information retrieval (PIR) techniques.

Standards. The Internet Engineering Task Force (IETF) has recently established a working group dedicated solely to addressing DNS privacy concerns (called DNS PRIVate Exchange, DPRIVE). The working group proposed various techniques that are currently being under consideration [4]. Zhu *et al.* [7] (based on [34]) proposed a connection-oriented DNS transport over TCP, which uses TLS for privacy. Reddy *et al.* [8] proposed to use the DTLS for DNS exchange. To address side-channel attacks, Mayrhofer [9] proposed a padding scheme.

6   Conclusion

DNS blocking of unintended queries is proposed as a technique for improving privacy. In this paper, we analyzed blocking under various adversarial settings and demonstrated that partial blocking at stub resolvers would result into negative privacy outcomes under certain adversary models. However, the same analysis shows that blocking at the recursive for the same adversary setting would result in improved privacy seen in a decaying adversary's advantage. In the future, we would like to explore the impact of queries and take them into account on the adversary's advantage, both analytically and empirically. Furthermore, we would like to analyze the privacy of DNS under blocking and active adversary (physically controlling a subset of the resolvers). Finally, we would like to consider analytical results blocking at multiple entities simultaneously.

Acknowledgement. This work is supported by NSF under grant CNS-1643207.

References

1. Thomas, M., Mohaisen, A.: Measuring the leakage of onion at the root: a measurement of tor's.onion pseudo-tld in the global domain name system. In: Proceeding of WPES (2014)
2. Appelbaum, J., Muffett, A.: The ".onion" special-use domain name. RFC 7686, October 2015
3. Gallagher, S.: Whole lotta onions: Number of Tor hidden sites spikes—along with paranoia, March 2016. Online
4. Mohaisen, A., Mankin, A.: Evaluation of privacy for DNS private exchange (2015). IETF Internet Draft
5. Mockapetris, P., Dunlap, K.J.: Development of the domain name system. In: Proceeding of ACM SIGCOMM (1988)

6. Bortzmeyer, S.: DNS query name minimisation to improve privacy. IETF Draft (2015)
7. Hu, Z., Zhu, L., Heidemann, J., Mankin, A., Wessels, D., Hoffman, P.: DNS over TLS: initiation and performance considerations (2015). IETF Internet Draft
8. T. Reddy, D.W., Patil, P.: DNS over DTLS (DNSoD) (2015). IETF Internet Draft
9. Mayrhofer, A.: The EDNS(0) padding option (2015). IETF Internet Draft
10. Thomas, M., Labrou, Y., Simpson, A.: The effectiveness of block lists in preventing collisions. In: Proceeding of WPNC (2014)
11. Barnes, R., Schneier, B., Jennings, C., Hardie, T., Trammell, B., Huitema, C., Borkmann, D.: Confidentiality in the face of pervasive surveillance: a threat model and problem statement. IETF RFC 7624 (2015)
12. Bau, J., Mitchell, J.C.: A security evaluation of DNSSEC with NSEC3. In: NDSS (2010)
13. Herzberg, A., Shulman, H.: DNSSEC: security and availability challenges. In: CNS (2013)
14. Goldberg, S., Naor, M., Papadopoulos, D., Reyzin, L., Vasant, S., Ziv, A.: NSEC5: provably preventing DNSSEC zone enumeration. In: NDSS (2015)
15. Konings, B., Bachmaier, C., Schaub, F., Weber, M.: Device names in the wild: investigating privacy risks of zero configuration networking. In: Proceeding of IEEE MDM (2013)
16. Krishnan, S., Monrose, F.: Dns prefetching and its privacy implications: when good things go bad. In: Proceeding of USENIX LEET (2010)
17. Zhao, F., Hori, Y., Sakurai, K.: Analysis of privacy disclosure in DNS query. In: Proceeding of MUE (2007)
18. Paxson, V., Christodorescu, M., Javed, M., Rao, J.R., Sailer, R., Schales, D.L., Stoecklin, M.P., Thomas, K., Venema, W., Weaver, N.: Practical comprehensive bounds on surreptitious communication over DNS. In: Proceeding of USENIX Security (2013)
19. Castillo-Perez, S., Garcia-Alfaro, J.: Evaluation of two privacy-preserving protocols for the DNS. In: Proceeding of ICIT (2009)
20. Jeong, S.H., Kang, A.R., Kim, J., Kim, H.K., Mohaisen, A.: A longitudinal analysis of .i2p leakage in the public DNS infrastructure. In: Proceeding of ACM SIGCOMM (2016)
21. Callahan, T., Allman, M., Rabinovich, M.: On modern DNS behavior and properties. ACM CCR **43**(3), 7–15 (2013)
22. Schomp, K., Rabinovich, M., Allman, M.: Towards a model of DNS client behavior. In: Karagiannis, T., Dimitropoulos, X. (eds.) PAM 2016. LNCS, vol. 9631, pp. 263–275. Springer, Heidelberg (2016). doi:10.1007/978-3-319-30505-9_20
23. Banse, C., Herrmann, D., Federrath, H.: Tracking users on the internet with behavioral patterns: evaluation of its practical feasibility. In: Proceeding of AICT (2012)
24. Schomp, K., Callahan, T., Rabinovich, M., Allman, M.: On measuring the client-side DNS infrastructure. In: Proceeding of ACM IMC (2013)
25. Shulman, H., Waidner, M.: Towards security of internet naming infrastructure. In: Pernul, G., Ryan, P.Y.A., Weippl, E. (eds.) ESORICS 2015. LNCS, vol. 9326, pp. 3–22. Springer, Heidelberg (2015). doi:10.1007/978-3-319-24174-6_1
26. Kang, A.R., Spaulding, J., Mohaisen, A.: Domain name system security and privacy: old problems and new challenges. CoRR (2016)
27. Schomp, K., Callahan, T., Rabinovich, M., Allman, M.: Assessing DNS vulnerability to record injection. In: Faloutsos, M., Kuzmanovic, A. (eds.) PAM 2014. LNCS, vol. 8362, pp. 214–223. Springer, Heidelberg (2014). doi:10.1007/978-3-319-04918-2_21

28. Dagon, D., Provos, N., Lee, C.P., Lee, W.: Corrupted DNS resolution paths: the rise of a malicious resolution authority. In: NDSS (2008)
29. Xu, K., Butler, P., Saha, S., Yao, D.: Dns for massive-scale command and control. IEEE TDSC **10**(3), 143–153 (2013)
30. Jackson, C., Barth, A., Bortz, A., Shao, W., Boneh, D.: Protecting browsers from DNS rebinding attacks. ACM Trans. Web **2**(1–2), 26 (2009)
31. Schomp, K., Allman, M., Rabinovich, M.: DNS resolvers considered harmful. In: Proceeding of ACM HotNets (2014)
32. Hao, S., Feamster, N., Pandrangi, R.: Monitoring the initial DNS behavior of malicious domains. In: Proceeding of ACM IMC (2011)
33. Spaulding, J., Upadhyaya, S., Mohaisen, A.: The landscape of domain name typosquatting: techniques and countermeasures. In: Proceeding of ARES (2016)
34. Zhu, L., Hu, Z., Heidemann, J., Wessels, D., Mankin, A., Somaiya, N.: Connection-oriented DNS to improve privacy and security. In: Proceeding of IEEE S&P (2015)

Measuring and Analyzing Trends in Recent Distributed Denial of Service Attacks

An Wang[1(✉)], Aziz Mohaisen[2], Wentao Chang[1], and Songqing Chen[1]

[1] George Mason University, Fairfax, USA
{awang10,wchang7,sqchen}@gmu.edu
[2] SUNY Buffalo, Buffalo, USA
mohaisen@buffalo.edu

Abstract. Internet DDoS attacks are prevalent but hard to defend against, partially due to the volatility of the attacking methods and patterns used by attackers. Understanding the latest of DDoS attacks can provide new insights for effective defense. But most of existing understandings are based on indirect traffic measures (e.g., backscatters) or traffic seen locally (e.g., in an ISP or from a botnet). In this study, we present an in-depth study based on 50,704 different Internet DDoS attacks directly observed in a seven-month period. These attacks were launched by 674 botnets from 23 different botnet families with a total of 9026 victim IPs belonging to 1074 organizations in 186 countries. In this study, we conduct some initial analysis mainly from the perspectives of these attacks' targets and sources. Our analysis reveals several interesting findings about today's Internet DDoS attacks. Some highlights include: (1) while 40% of the targets were attacked only once, 20% of the targets were attacked more than 100 times (2) most of the attacks are not massive in terms of number of participating nodes but they often last long, (3) most of these attacks are not widely distributed, but rather being highly regionalized. These findings add to the existing literature on the understanding of today's Internet DDoS attacks, and offer new insights for designing effective defense schemes at different levels.

Keywords: DDoS attack characteristics · Attack distribution and affinity

1 Introduction

That nature of Distributed Denial of Services (DDoS) attacks on the Internet has evolved in the last ten years due to their increasing complexity. Today's attacks are more prevalent due to the rise of botnets, large pools of infected machines that are well incentivized to pursue persistent criminal activities. Based on a recent report [1], an average DDoS attack is not detected until 4.5 h after its commencement and mitigation efforts do not start until 4.9 h after that. Furthermore, the operational impact, size, and consequences of DDoS attacks on large services on the Internet are widely reported. Recently, 3,000 open domain name

D. Choi and S. Guilley (Eds.): WISA 2016, LNCS 10144, pp. 15–28, 2017.
DOI: 10.1007/978-3-319-56549-1_2

service (DNS) resolvers were capable of generating 300 Gbps DDoS traffic [11], and taking down Spamhaus, a popular spam tracking service. More recently, an amplification attack utilizing 4,529 network time protocol (NTP) servers was capable of generating a 325–400 Gbps of persistent attack traffic [31].

Efforts have been made continuously from both academia and industry to understand the DDoS attacks and defend against them. With ever-improving defenses, the attack strategies are constantly changing. Understanding the latest attack strategies is a key to successful defenses. The most recent literature on the problem is outdated, and utilizes measurements and analyses on DDoS attacks by means of inference from indirect traffic, such as backscatters, or from traffic collected locally, such as in a single Internet service provider (ISP) network or a university, or by infiltration into a botnet. While of a very high interest, a timely and large scale view of today's Internet DDoS attacks is missing from the literature.

We present a timely measurement study of recent DDoS attacks launched by botnets. Our measurement is based on directly observed attack artifacts through anchor points deployed at a large number of major ISPs in a seven-month period. The attack workloads are collected by the monitoring and attribution unit in a commercial DDoS mitigation company located in the United States with global operational footprint. In this seven-month period, a total of 50,704 different DDoS attacks were observed, which were launched by 674 different botnets coming from 23 different botnet families. These attacks targeted 9026 different IPs that belong to 1074 organizations in 186 countries.

Our detailed analyses reveal several interesting observations about today's Internet botnet DDoS attacks. While details are provided in the paper, some highlights include: (1) while 40% of the targets were attacked only once, 20% of the targets were attacked more than 100 times This clearly highlights the inefficiency of defenses deployed by targets; (2) most of the attacks are not massive in terms of number of participating nodes but they often last long. This attacking strategy makes attacks stealthier and more difficult to detect; (3) most of these attacks are not widely distributed, but rather being highly regionalized. This may motivate some more effective DDoS defense development.

While there have been various studies on this topic [5,36,37] that admittedly compete with our study in the size of the utilized data, and the nature of the findings, we believe that our study is distinguished from the prior studies in two aspects. First, our study revisits the topic with a timely dataset obtained from operational mitigation and defense efforts. To our knowledge, the most recent operational look at the problem is based on a dataset that is at least five years older than ours [36], and many are based on datasets that are even more than ten years old [5,37]. Second, as the trends of attacks evolve over time, the new dataset and findings obtained upon analyzing it offer new and unique insights that can be utilized for designing effective and customized defenses.

The rest of the paper is organized as follows. In Sect. 2, we describe out dataset including the overall data statistics and the data fields we utilized to do our analysis. In Sect. 3, we present some basic characterizations of DDoS attacks.

We discuss related work in Sect. 4 and conclude with a concise summary of our analyses and their implications in Sect. 5.

2   Data Collection

Our dataset is provided by the monitoring and attribution unit in a very large DDoS detection and mitigation company that is located in the United States, with partnerships of monitoring with a large number of ISPs for the sole purpose of attack detection and mitigation. The unit constantly monitors attack traffic to aid the mitigation efforts of its clients, using both active and passive measurement techniques [6, 34, 35]. For active measurements and attribution, malware families used in launching the various attacks are reverse engineered, and labeled to a known malware family using best practices [21]. A honeypot is then created to emulate the operation of the reverse-engineered malware sample and to enumerate all bots across the globe participating in the particular botnet. As each botnet evolves over time, new generations are marked by their unique hashes. The enumerated list of bots is then vetted on the participants in the active attacks.

Traces of traffic associated with various DDoS campaigns are then collected at various anchor points located at the aforementioned ISPs across the globe: North and South America, Asia, Europe, and Africa. The traces are then analyzed remotely to attribute and characterize attacks on various targets of interest. The collection of traffic is guided by two general principles: (1) that the source of the traffic is an infected host participating in a DDoS campaign, and (2) the destination of the traffic is a targeted client, as concluded from eavesdropping on C&C of the campaign using a live sample, or where the end-host is a customer of the said DDoS mitigation company.

2.1   High-Level Characteristics

The analysis is high level in nature to cope with the high volume of ingest traffic at peak attack times– on average there were 243 simultaneous verified DDoS attacks launched by the different botnets studied in this work. High level statistics associated with the various botnets and DDoS attacks are recorded every one hour. The workload we obtained ranges from August 28, 2012 to March 24, 2013, a total of 209 days (about seven months of valid and marked attack logs). In the log, a DDoS attack is labeled with a unique DDoS identifier, corresponding to an attack by given DDoS malware family on a given target. Other attributes and statistics of the dataset are shown in Table 1. We cannot reveal the capability of the capturing facility because attackers would learn such information, which is also critical to the business of the data source.

An interesting feature in Table 1 is the attack category, which refers to the nature of the DDoS attack by classifying it into different types based on the protocol utilized for launching it, including HTTP, TCP, UDP, Undetermined,

Table 1. Information of workload entries

Field	Description
ddos_id	A global unique identifier for the specified DDoS attack
botnet_id	Unique identification of each botnet
category	Description of the nature of the attack
target_ip	IP address of the victim host
timestamp	The time when the attack started
end_time	The time when the attack ended
botnet_ip	The IP address of botnets involved in the attacks
asn	Autonomous system number
cc	Country in which the target resides (ISO3166-1 alpha-2)
city	City and/or state in which the target resides
latitude	Latitude of target
longitude	Longitude of target

ICMP, Unknown, and SYN. Different from *Unknown*, *Undetermine* means that the attack type could not be determined based on the available information.

Among the fields listed in Table 1, the *longitude* and *latitude* of each IP address are obtained using a highly-accurate industrial geo-mapping service during trace collection. The mapping of the IP addresses happens in real time, making it resistive to IP dynamics. Beside the longitude and latitude, we also generate the individual *city* and *organization* of each IP address involved in an attack using a highly-accurate commercial grade geo-mapping dataset by Digital Envoy (Digital Element services [2]). We use such information for geographical analysis as presented in later sections.

Table 2 sums up some statistics of our dataset, including information from both the attacker and the target sides. Target statistics are illuminating. Over a

Table 2. Summary of the workload information

Summary of attackers		Summary of victims	
Description	Count	Description	Count
# of bot_ips	310950	# of target_ip	9026
# of cities	2897	# of cities	616
# of countries	186	# of countries	84
# of organizations	3498	# of organizations	1074
# of asn	3973	# of asn	1260
# of ddos_id	50704		
# of botnet_id	674		
# of traffic types	7		

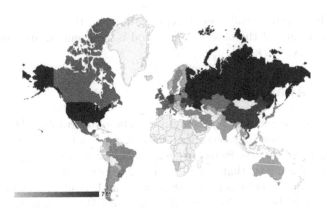

Fig. 1. Geographical distribution (The density is the log of the number of victims in each country).

period of 28 weeks, 50,704 different DDoS attacks were observed. These attacks are launched by 674 different botnets. These attacks targeted victims located in 84 different countries, 616 cities, involving 1074 organizations, residing in 1260 different ASes.

Based on the geographical information, Fig. 1 shows the popularity of DDoS targets at the country level. The color density indicates the number of attacks on each country. Clearly, and as widely believed, the US and Russia are the two most popular targets.

2.2   Discussions of the Dataset

Various related works are focused on radiation and port scanning [4,5,19,24,36] concerned with a single network (e.g., Tier-1 ISP [19] and sinkhole traffic [4,36]), rather than DDoS attacks characterizations in a similar context to ours, thus preventing us from making a fair comparison with our data size and methodology for data collection. However, some of the recent studies show the relevance of our dataset in size. In comparison with [19], our study characterizes more than 50,000 verified attacks over 7 months observation period (compared to 31,612 alarms over a 4 weeks period in [19]). Note the fundamental difference between attacks and alarms, since a large number of triggered alarms in anomaly detection could be false alarms, while attacks are verified.

Nonetheless, the limitation of our dataset is that it does not cover all ISPs on the Internet, suggesting various forms of bias and incompleteness. We note that, however, our data collection also incorporates at-destination data collection, thus all statistics of interest and relevance are gathered in the process. We note that our data collection method is not subject to the shortcoming of locality bias highlighted in [5]: all malware families used for launching attacks that we study are well-understood and reversed engineered, and traffic sources utilized for launching the attacks are enumerated by active participation. To that end, we believe that our data collection is representative to the characterized events, and that the length of the observation period is sufficient to draw conclusions on today's DDoS attacks.

3   Attack Analysis

In this section, we present our analysis results across various DDoS attacks observed in our dataset. Through the analysis, we aim to understand the new trends of these attacks. We focus our analysis on the attack targets and sources in this study. We notice that not all of the 23 botnets logged in our dataset are active, and only 10 of them exhibit patterns and trends; we focus our study on those 10 active botnets. Namely, we study the DDoS attacks by the following families: Aldibot, BlackEnergy, Colddeath, Darkshell, DDoSer, DirtJumper, Nitol, Optima, Pandora, and YZF.

3.1   Botnet and Target Affinity

To take down a victim's site (target), DDoS attacks could be launched continuously. To avoid being detected, some attacks could be split into multiple stages, and individual staged attacks could be launched periodically. Therefore, we first study how many attacks a victim received in our dataset. Along this line, we can identify those long-term targets and short-term targets for some DDoS malware families.

Figure 2 shows the popularity of targets distributions for all active families representing in Cumulative Distribution Function (CDF). There are 9026 unique targets in total. This figure shows that while 40% of the targets were attacked only once, 20% of the targets are attacked more than 106 times. The most

Fig. 2. Target popularity: the number of attacks a victim received over the period of 28 weeks.

popular target was attacked 940 times over the same period. After looking up the most popular target IP address, we found that this IP address belongs to the domain of HostGator, which is a Houston-based web hosting service, indicating that the real target could be an organization hosted by this service.

Table 3 summarizes some statistics of these targets by each botnet family. The second row shows the number of targets that were attacked multiple times by each family, the third row shows the number of unique targets attacked by each family, and the last row shows the percentage of repeatedly attacked targets by each family. This table shows that YZF and Ddoser often focus their attacks on some selected targets while the targets of Aldibot and Blackenergy are more distributed. This may indicate different attack patterns that *Aldibot* and *Blackenergy* focus on short-term targets while *YZF* and *Ddoser* may focus on long-term targets. Note that the short and long term patterns highlighted here also outline the different economical aspects of the attacks: while long-term persistent attacks highlight higher incentives of an adversary whereas short-term attacks may highlight a "hitman-like" strategy for service abruption.

Table 3. Number of targets attacked multiple times by each botnet family

Family	Aldibot	Blackenergy	Colddeath	Darkshell	Ddoser	Dirtjumper	Nitol	Optima	Pandora	YZF
#targets w/ multiple attacks	12	105	127	486	89	3587	99	53	737	72
#unique targets	48	355	265	1029	131	5823	213	131	1775	72
%	25%	30%	48%	47%	68%	62%	46%	40%	42%	100%

Table 4. Target interest duration (h)

Family	Aldibot	Blackenergy	Colddeath	Darkshell	Ddoser	Dirtjumper	Nitol	Optima	Pandora	YZF
Period (h)	144	303	63	82	12.9	406	70.6	295	362	22

Table 4 further shows the average target interest duration of each family. From previous observations, we know that some of the targets will be attacked multiple times periodically. But this period may not last very long since we know that most DDoS attacks are money-driven. The table indicates that the average target interest also varies significantly across different families, ranging from half a day to half a month. The longest period we found is 200 days, of an attack by Dirtjumper (note that Table 4 only shows the average). It almost spans the whole observation period. The target is a Russian web hosting service company, which is known for hosting various malicious websites, indicating that the consistent attack on it is perhaps a form of retaliation to take those sites down.

Insights and Takeaways: The attack target analysis reveals that while about 40% of the targets were attacked only once, more than half of the targets were attacked more than once. This clearly indicates (1) such DDoS attacks are most likely driven by profit since most retaliatory and political attacks are temporary, and (2) the current defense mechanisms in practice fail to respond to such attacks promptly for efficient protections. On the other hand, each botnet family always has some long-term targets, which hints us to develop specific botnet based defenses. In the long run, the effective and practical defense may be to detect and defend various botnets based on their characteristics, rather than detect and defend DDoS since there is no clear pattern along time (last subsection) or on target selection.

3.2   Attack Size and Distribution

Beside the attack distribution, another factor for assessing attacks' strength is the attack magnitude, which refers to how much DDoS traffic was seen towards a target. However, we did not log the raw packets carrying DDoS traffic—for contractual reasons. Rather, we use the number of unique IP addresses used for launching the attack as an estimator of its magnitude. As suggested in [19], to evade being detected quickly, IP spoofing in DDoS attacks is not very common. Thus, we use the number of unique IPs involved in an attack to estimate one aspect of the corresponding attack magnitude.

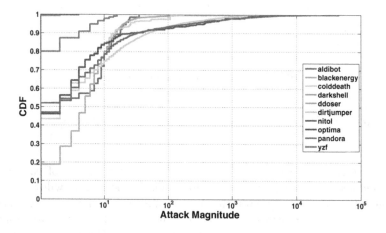

Fig. 3. Attack magnitude of each family

3.2.1   Attack Size – Contrary to the Recent Reports, Most Attacks Are Not Massive

Figure 3 shows the magnitude distributions of the DDoS attack launched by each family. Note that the x-axis is in log scale. Several interesting observations can be found in this figure. First, most of the attacks are not massive in terms of magnitude. As shown in the figure, except some attacks by Dirtjumper and Blackenergy, attacks launched by other botnets typically involve less than 1000 unique IPs. Some botnets, such as Aldibot and YZF, launched a lot of small magnitude DDoS attacks and there are less than 40 unique IPs involved. However, massive DDoS attacks could involve several thousand or tens of thousands unique IPs. For example, the figure shows that the number of unique IPs involved in attacks of *Dirtjumper* and *Blackenergy* could be massive, with the maximum number of unique IPs used in a single *Blackenergy* attack being 2,365 and 37,584 for *Dirtjumper*, respectively.

Taking into consideration the magnitude and the duration of attacks, we aim to infer strategies utilized by botnets. We aggregate the 80% non-massive (small) attacks to calculate the average attack duration and compare it with that of the other 20% attacks—results are shown in Table 5. This table only includes the families that actually launched massive DDoS attacks. We found that 80% of the attacks lasted less than 13882 s in our analysis. But from this table, we can see that, except for family *Dirtjumper*, the 80% non-massive DDoS attacks last longer than 13882 s. This shows that most small attacks are not short-duration attacks.

For those families that didn't launch massive attacks, this is still true: attacks launched by *YZF* involved at most 6 bots; while the average duration of the attacks is 34053 s. The above analysis indicates that most current DDoS attacks utilize a small number of bots with longer duration instead of launching massive DDoS attacks.

Table 5. Attack duration of small and massive attacks

Family	Small attacks	Massive attacks
Blackenergy	5945	7430
Colddeath	16702	38831
Dirtjumper	10222	33568
Optima	31713	27410
Pandora	19121	46428

Figure 3 also indicates that the magnitude of attacks varies across different families, as well as within the same family. As shown in the figure, the attack magnitude of Aldibot and Nitol only slightly changed in 28 weeks, while Blackenergy changed attack magnitude dramatically for different attacks. Notice that on the left corner, there are two families, which are Nitol and Ddoser. The magnitude of their attacks is constantly small.

3.2.2 Attack Distribution – Most DDoS Attacks Are Not Widely Distributed, but Rather Being Regionalized

The attacker's IP enables us to study their distribution as well. According to our data, it is obvious that each botnet family has its own geolocation preferences. Among the four most active families, *Optima* is mostly in Vietnam, India, Indonesia and Egypt; *Dirtjumper* is mostly in India, Brazil, Botswana and Pakistan; *Blackenergy* is mostly in Vietnam, Singapore, Thailand and United States; *Pandora* is mostly in Pakistan, India, Thailand and Indonesia. Generally, the geolocation preference could reflect the current global distribution of botnets. Most of them reside in the countries that lack proper protections like Southeast Asia area [30].

Among all the families, *Dirtjumper* covers the largest number of countries: 164. A comparable coverage is *Optima*'s: 153. Even though these families have very broad country coverages, the average number of country coverage for each attack is small, as shown in Table 6. From this table, we see that only *Pandora* has a very large average number; other families only launched attacks from a few countries. Figure 4 shows the CDF of country coverage of each single DDoS attack for each family. This figure conforms to the result in Table 6.

Table 6. Average number of country coverage for each botnet family

Family	Aldibot	Blackenergy	Colddeath	Darkshell	Ddoser	Dirtjumper	Nitol	Optima	Pandora	YZF
Country coverage	4	3	2	1	1	3	1	9	2	1

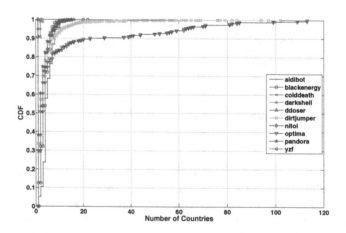

Fig. 4. CDF of country coverage for each family

Insights and Takeaways: The attack size and distribution analysis indicates the change of the attack strategies (resources exhaustion vs. bandwidth attrition), making it challenging to detect such attacks. On the other hand, the highly region-alized nature of most attacks can motivate some new defense strategies: disinfection, if infected hosts are in reach, or early stage filtering at the nearby ISPs connecting those hosts to the Internet [26].

4 Related Work

DDoS attacks have been intensively investigated and numerous countermeasures have been proposed to defend against them. As many DDoS attacks are launched by botnets, a popular approach is to disrupt the C&C channel of the botnet that launches DDoS attacks. However, most of current take-down methodologies are ad-hoc and their effectiveness are limited by the depth of knowledge about the specific botnet family involved in the attack. Nadji et al. [23] proposed a take-down analysis and recommendation system. As a proactive solution to DDoS attacks, several filtering schemes [12,17,25,38,39] are proposed to prevent flooding packets from reaching target victims. Chen et al. [7] proposed a defense that can detect DDoS attacks over multiple network domains. Overlay-based protection systems [15,28] and statistical approaches [9,13,16,18] offer another attractive alternative. Walfish et al. [33] advocated DDoS defense by offense, where attacked servers encourages all clients to send higher traffic volumes to attackers.

Historically, most defense systems such as Cisco IDSM-2 [8] and LADS [27] are deployed at the destination since it suffers most of the impact. Mirkovic et al. [20] proposed D-WARD, a DDoS defense system deployed at source-end networks that autonomously detects and stops attacks originating from these networks. Another detection mechanism [3] is proposed to be deployed at the source to help ISP network to detect attacks. Both studies can benefit from our source characterization to enable their operation. Huang et al. [10] addressed the lack of motivations for organizations to adopt cooperative solutions to defeat DDoS attacks by fixing the incentive chain. Our analysis of the shared fate, and diversity of targets, is a plausible incentive for enabling collaborative defense.

The continuous improvement on detection and defense has caused attackers to be adaptive as well. Thus, it is essential to understand the latest changes of DDoS attacks. In 2006, Mao et al. [19] presented their findings from measurement study of DDoS attacks relying on both direct measurements of flow-level information and more traditional indirect measurements using backscatter analysis, while Moore et al. [22] presented a backscatter analysis for quantitatively estimating DoS activity in the Internet based on a three-week dataset. Due to the growth of network address translation and firewall techniques, much of the Internet was precluded from the study by the traditional network measurement techniques. Thus, in the early days, work [5] proposed an opportunistic measurement approach that leverages sources of spurious traffic, such as worms and DDoS backscatter, to unveil unseen portion of Internet. The monitoring of packets destined for unused Internet addresses, termed as "background radiation", proved to be another useful technique to measure Internet phenomenon.

In 2004, Pang et al. [24] conducted an initial study of broad characteristics of Internet background radiation by measuring traffic from four large unused subnets. In 2010, a more recent study [36] revisited the same topic and characterized the current state of background radiation specifically highlighting those which exhibit significant differences. Our work serves as a revisit to those studies with new insights. Bailey et al. [4] designed and implemented the Internet Motion Sensors (IMS), a globally scoped Internet monitoring system to detect Internet threats, which includes a distributed blackhole network with a lightweight responder and a novel payload signature and caching mechanism. Xu et al. [37] presented a general methodology to build behavior profiles of Internet backbone traffic in terms of communication patterns of end-hosts and services.

In [32], a honey farm system architecture was proposed to improve honeypot scalability by up to six orders of magnitude while still offering quantitatively similar fidelity. Another Internet monitoring system, which primarily targets at early detection of worms, was presented in [40], using a non-threshold based "trend detection" methodology to detect presence of worms by using Kalman filter and worm propagation models.

Finally, theoretical attacks using botnets for "taking down the Internet" are studied in Crossfire [14], CXPST [26], and Coremelt [29]. The size, distribution, and coordination of attacks studied in this work highlight the feasibility of those theoretical attacks.

5   Conclusion

DDoS attacks are the most popular large scale attacks frequently launched on the Internet. While most of the existing studies have mainly focused on designing various defense schemes, the measurement and analysis of large scale Internet DDoS attacks are not very common, mainly due to the data un-availability, although understanding the DDoS attacks patterns is the key to defend against them. In this study, with the access to the dataset on such a large scale, we are able to collectively characterize today's Internet DDoS attacks from different perspectives. Our investigation of these DDoS attacks reveals several interesting findings about today's botnet based DDoS attacks. These results provide new insights for understanding and defending modern DDoS attack at different levels. While this study focuses on the DDoS attack characterization, in the future, we plan to leverage these findings to design more effective defense schemes. A direction is to combine the geolocation affinity information based on the botnet behavior pattern.

Acknowledgement. We would like to thank anonymous reviewers for their comments. This work was supported in part by an ARO grant W911NF-15-1-0262, NSF grant CNS-1524462, and the Global Research Lab. (GRL) Program of the National Research Foundation (NRF) funded by Ministry of Science, ICT (Information and Communication Technologies) and Future Planning (NRF-2016K1A1A2912757).

References

1. A ddos attack could cost $1 million before mitigation even starts, October 2013. http://bit.ly/MUXadv
2. NetAcuity and NetAcuity Edge IP Location Technology, February 2014. http://www.digitalelement.com/
3. Akella, A., Bharambe, A., Reiter, M., Seshan, S.: Detecting DDoS Attacks on ISP Networks. In: ACM SIGMOD/PODS MPDS (2003)
4. Bailey, M., Cooke, E., Jahanian, F., Nazario, J., Watson, D., et al.: The internet motion sensor-a distributed blackhole monitoring system. In: Proceeding of NDSS (2005)
5. Casado, M., Garfinkel, T., Cui, W., Paxson, V., Savage, S.: Opportunistic measurement: extracting insight from spurious traffic. In: Proceeding of ACM Hotnets (2005)
6. Chang, W., Mohaisen, A., Wang, A., Chen, S.: Measuring botnets in the wild: some new trends. In: Proceeding of ACM ASIA CCS (2015)
7. Chen, Y., Hwang, K., Ku, W.S.: Collaborative detection of DDoS attacks over multiple network domains. IEEE TPDS (2007)
8. Cisco: Cisco Catalyst 6500 Series Intrusion Detection System, February 2014. http://bit.ly/1hspyy9
9. Feinstein, L., Schnackenberg, D., Balupari, R., Kindred, D.: Statistical approaches to DDoS attack detection and response. In: DARPA Information Survivability Conference and Exposition (2003)
10. Huang, Y., Geng, X., Whinston, A.B.: Defeating DDoS attacks by fixing the incentive chain. ACM ToIT **1** (2007)
11. Info Security Magazine: Spamhaus suffers largest ddos attack in history - entire internet affected, March 2013. http://bit.ly/1bfx3ZH
12. Ioannidis, J., Bellovin, S.M.: Implementing pushback: router-based defense against DDoS attacks. In: Proceeding of NDSS (2002). https://www.cs.columbia.edu/~smb/papers/pushback-impl.pdf
13. Jin, S., Yeung, D.: A covariance analysis model for DDoS attack detection. IEEE ICC (2004)
14. Kang, M.S., Lee, S.B., Gligor, V.D.: The crossfire attack. In: Proceeding of IEEE S&P (2013)
15. Keromytis, A.D., Misra, A.D., Rubenstein, D.: SOS: an architecture for mitigating DDoS attacks. IEEE JSAC (2004)
16. Lee, K., Kim, J., Kwon, K.H., Han, Y., Kim, S.: DDoS attack detection method using cluster analysis. Expert systems with applications (2008)
17. Li, J., Mirkovic, J., Wang, M., Reiher, P., Zhang, L.: Save: source address validity enforcement protocol. In: Proceeding of IEEE ICCC (2002)
18. Li, M.: Change trend of averaged Hurst parameter of traffic under DDOS flood attacks. Computers and Security (2006)
19. Mao, Z.M., Sekar, V., Spatscheck, O., van der Merwe, J., Vasudevan, R.: Analyzing large DDoS attacks using multiple data sources. In: Proceeding of ACM SIGCOMM LSAD (2006)
20. Mirkovic, J., Prier, G., Reiher, P.: Attacking DDoS at the source. In: Proceeding of IEEE ICNP, November 2002
21. Mohaisen, A., Alrawi, O., Larson, M., McPherson, D.: Towards a methodical evaluation of antivirus scans and labels. In: Information Security Applications (2014)

22. Moore, D., Shannon, C., Brown, D.J., Voelker, G.M., Savage, S.: Inferring internet denial-of-service activity. ACM TOCS **24**(2), 115–139 (2006)
23. Nadji, Y., Antonakakis, M., Perdisci, R., Dagon, D., Lee, W.: Beheading hydras: performing effective botnet takedowns. In: Proceeding of ACM SIGSAC, November 2013
24. Pang, R., Yegneswaran, V., Barford, P., Paxson, V., Peterson, L.: Characteristics of internet background radiation. In: Proceeding of ACM IMC (2004)
25. Park, K., Lee, H.: On the effectiveness of route-based packet filtering for distributed DoS attack prevention in power-law Internets. In: Proceeding of ACM SIGCOMM (2001)
26. Schuchard, M., Mohaisen, A., Kune, D.F., Hopper, N., Kim, Y., Vasserman, E.Y.: Losing control of the internet: using the data plane to attack the control plane. In: Proceeding of NDSS (2011)
27. Sekar, V., Duffield, N., Spatscheck, O., van der Merwe, J., Zhang, H.: Lads: large-scale automated DDoS detection system. In: Proceeding of USENIX ATC (2006)
28. Stavrou, A., Keromytis, A.D.: Countering DoS attacks with stateless multipath overlays. In: Proceeding of ACM CCS (2005)
29. Studer, A., Perrig, A.: The coremelt attack. In: Backes, M., Ning, P. (eds.) ESORICS 2009. LNCS, vol. 5789, pp. 37–52. Springer, Heidelberg (2009). doi:10.1007/978-3-642-04444-1_3
30. Thomas, N.: Cyber security in East Asia: governing anarchy. Asian Secur. **5**(1), 3–23 (2009)
31. Vaughan-Nichols, S.J.: Worst DDoS attack of all time hits french site, February 2014. http://zd.net/1kFDurZ
32. Vrable, M., Ma, J., Chen, J., Moore, D., Vandekieft, E., Snoeren, A.C., Voelker, G.M., Savage, S.: Scalability, fidelity, and containment in the potemkin virtual honeyfarm. ACM SIGOPS **5**, 148–162 (2005)
33. Walfish, M., Vutukuru, M., Balakrishnan, H., Karger, D., Shenke, S.: DDoS defense by offense. In: Proceeding of SIGCOMM (2006)
34. Wang, A., Mohaisen, A., Chang, W., Chen, S.: Capturing DDoS attack dynamics behind the scenes. In: Almgren, M., Gulisano, V., Maggi, F. (eds.) DIMVA 2015. LNCS, vol. 9148, pp. 205–215. Springer, Heidelberg (2015). doi:10.1007/978-3-319-20550-2_11
35. Wang, A., Mohaisen, A., Chang, W., Chen, S.: Delving into internet DDoS attacks by botnets: characterization and analysis. In: Proceeding of IEEE DSN (2015)
36. Wustrow, E., Karir, M., Bailey, M., Jahanian, F., Huston, G.: Internet background radiation revisited. In: Proceeding of ACM IMC (2010)
37. Xu, K., Zhang, Z.L., Bhattacharyya, S.: Profiling internet backbone traffic: behavior models and applications. In: ACM SIGCOMM CCR. No. 4 (2005)
38. Yaar, A., Perrig, A., Song, D.: SIFF: a stateless internet flow filter to mitigate DDoS flooding attacks. In: Proceeding of IEEE S&P (2004)
39. Yaar, A., Perrig, A., Song, D.: StackPi: new packet marking and filtering mechanisms for DDoS and IP spoofing defense. IEEE JSAC (2006)
40. Zou, C.C., Gong, W., Towsley, D., Gao, L.: The monitoring and early detection of internet worms. IEEE/ACM TON **5**, 961–974 (2005)

SD-OVS: SYN Flooding Attack Defending Open vSwitch for SDN

Xinyu Liu[✉], Beumjin Cho, and Jong Kim

Department of Computer Science and Engineering, POSTECH, Pohang, Republic of Korea
{xinyuliu918,beumjincho,jkim}@postech.ac.kr

Abstract. Software defined networking (SDN) is a novel programmable networking paradigm that decouples control and data planes. SDN relies heavily on the controller in control plane that tells the data plane how to handle new packets. Because the entire network may be disrupted if the controller is disabled, many attacks including SYN flooding aim to overload the controller by passing through the ingress switches. In this paper, we propose a security enhanced Open vSwitch (SD-OVS) to protect the controller from SYN flooding. The switch authenticates benign hosts by interchanging cookie packets and generates a short-lived security association (SA). The retransmitted SYN packet from these benign hosts is validated using SA and passed on to the controller. Our evaluation shows that SD-OVS protects the controller from SYN flooding at an acceptable time cost.

Keywords: Software defined networking · OpenFlow · Open vSwitch · SYN flooding

1 Introduction

Software defined networking (SDN) has emerged as a new network paradigm that provides programmability by decoupling the control and data planes [1]. The programmer can manage and control the entire network centrally in a desired manner. The controller of SDN thus becomes the brain of the network because the controller determines the manner in which to deal with the packet; the controller then inserts the flow rules to switches. The switches then handle the packets based on the flow rules stored in the flow table.

Despite these benefits, the rapid emergence of SDN has also generated several types of threats [5–7]. We must ensure the security of SDN when we apply it. In a traditional network, SYN flooding [2] is one of the most common types of attacks that can be launched easily and has powerful effects on its target. The SYN flooding attack exhausts the backlog resource of the destination host by sending SYN packets so that the host generates and stores the half-open connection in a backlog.

To prevent the SYN flooding attack, mitigations such as increasing the backlog, reducing SYN-RECEIVED timer, or using firewalls and proxies must occur [3]. Some researchers have proposed three counter algorithms to ensure that the connection stored in a backlog is benign [4]. However, none of the previous methods can be applied to

© Springer International Publishing AG 2017
D. Choi and S. Guilley (Eds.): WISA 2016, LNCS 10144, pp. 29–41, 2017.
DOI: 10.1007/978-3-319-56549-1_3

SDN directly because SYN flooding can disrupt an entire SDN network rather than just the destination host. For example, if an attacker launches an SYN flooding attack from one compromised host and sets the arrival of new packets to a sufficiently high rate, the attacker can disable the controller by making it busy to respond to packets; which will disrupt the entire network in consequence.

AVANT-GUARD [7] is the first attempt to modify the OpenFlow switch to mitigate an SYN flooding attack in an SDN. However, it has an adaptation problem, as it must modify the controller and switch together. Moreover, it requires additional resources to maintain TCP connections.

In this paper, we propose an SDN switch called SD-OVS, which protects the controller from an SYN flooding attack and enhances the stability of the switch by authenticating benign hosts through security association (SA). When an SD-OVS switch receives an SYN packet and no matching flow exists, the switch sends back an illegitimate SYNACK packet with a cookie. If the switch receives the RST packet with a valid cookie, the switch generates a security association. The SA acts as an identification of the host for the SYN packet and is deleted when the connection is established. The SD-OVS switch utilizes the retry mechanism of the TCP connection establishment. After receiving the retransmitted SYN packet that matches with a stored SA, the switch forwards it to a controller as part of the original process. SD-OVS protects the controller because it does not send a message about a new SYN packet to the controller if the host is not authenticated by the SA. In addition, it does not generate useless flow rules triggered by the SYN flooding attack in the switch.

Our study makes the following contributions:

- We propose a scalable and stable method called SD-OVS, which protects the SDN from an SYN flooding attack in a data plane without requiring any modification to the control plane.
- We evaluate the performance of SD-OVS both in normal operation and when under attack, and the results show that SD-OVS protects SDN from SYN flooding attacks at an acceptable time cost.

The remainder of this paper is organized as follows. In Sect. 2, we provide background information. Section 3 presents the working mechanism of the proposed switch SD-OVS. Section 4 provides details about the implementation of SD-OVS. Section 5 presents evaluation results. Section 6 discusses possible attack issues to be considered in the proposed switch. Section 7 presents related studies and a conclusion.

2   Background

In this section, we briefly introduce the architecture of the software defined networking (SDN), and then describe two components of SDN: OpenFlow Protocol and Open vSwitch (OVS). At the end of the section, we introduce the SYN cookie method.

2.1 Architecture of SDN

SDN consists of at least one protocol and the following three layers: application, control, and data forwarding layers (Fig. 1).

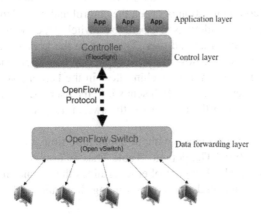

Fig. 1. Framework of SDN.

The protocol used in SDN defines the manner in which the control layer interacts with the data forwarding layer. The innovative applications and protocols are implemented in the application layer. The controller in the control plane communicates with the application layer through its northbound interface. Finally, the controller guides the switches in the data forwarding layer to handle the packets through the secure channel in the switch.

Vulnerability in SDN architecture. Because the network relies heavily on the controller, the entire network could be thrown into chaos or even totally disabled if the controller undergoes a critical attack such as an SYN flooding attack. In addition, because of the limited capacity of the switch, a benign flow rule cannot survive in a switch if several malicious flow rules compete; that is, they either cannot enter or can be dropped from the flow table.

2.2 OpenFlow Protocol

The OpenFlow protocol [1] is a typical and widely used protocol in SDN. The OpenFlow protocol specifies that every time a new packet arrives into the switch, the switch extracts the packet information and determines whether a matching flow exists in the flow table. If no matching flow is present, the switch asks the controller the course of action to take by sending a PACKET_IN message. The controller then creates a flow rule and sends it to all related switches for handling packets associated to the original new packet. Finally, the switch follows the flow rule to handle the packet.

2.3 Open vSwitch

Here, we introduce the OpenFlow switch and Open vSwitch (OVS).

An OpenFlow switch [8] consists of at least a flow table, secure channel, and Open-Flow protocol. The flow table stores the flow rules from the controller, and the secure channel is used for communication between the control and data planes.

Open vSwitch [9] is a widely used OpenFlow switch. Open vSwitch code space is divided into two spaces: kernel and user. The flow in the kernel space is the precise flow, which is set based on the flow in the user space. When a new packet comes into a switch, the switch first looks for a matching flow in the kernel space. If no matching flow is present in the kernel space, OVS sends it to the user space for a second search. If a matching flow exists in the user space, the switch moves the precise flow to the kernel space.

When a new SYN packet exists without a matching flow, the switch performs the action in the "Table Miss." The default "Table Miss Action" is to send the extracted packet to the controller [1]. The controller determines the manner in which to handle the new SYN packet and sends the corresponding flow rule to the user space of all relevant switches.

2.4 SYN Cookie

SYN cookie [10] is one of the mostly used techniques to resist SYN flooding attacks. Our method modifies part of the mechanism of SYN cookie. Thus we explain the working mechanism of it.

SYN cookie is activated if an attack occurs or the backlog queue becomes full. When it is activated, the destination host sends back the appropriate SYNACK packet without storing any information. This is performed to protect the host. When the host receives a subsequent ACK response, it stores the TCP connection into the backlog as a full connection. The sequence number of a SYNACK packet is called a "cookie," which is produced by a hash function with a source IP address, destination IP address, source port number, destination port number, sequence number, maximum segment size (MSS), current time, and random keys.

Drawback of SYN cookie. Although SYN cookie has powerful capabilities, it still possesses a drawback. The destination host can confirm the delivery of SYN cookie when it receives an ACK packet from the source. Otherwise, the destination cannot differentiate whether a SYN cookie from itself or an ACK packet from the source is lost [11]. The destination cannot re-transmit the SYNACK packet because it does not store any information in the backlog. This will produce an unsuccessful connection.

3 SD-OVS

In this section, we provide an overview of our method and explain each stage of SD-OVS in detail.

SD-OVS consists of four stages: auth-cookie generation, SA creation, SA matching, and SA deletion. The first three stages filter malicious SYN packets. The fourth stage provides better performance. The four stages operate as follows. First, a source sends a new SYN packet to a destination through a connected SD-OVS switch. When SD-OVS receives it, it responds with an illegitimate SYNACK packet containing a cookie. The source then responds with an RST packet with the received cookie. When SD-OVS receives the RST packet, it verifies the cookie. If the cookie is valid, SD-OVS creates an SA for this host and stores it. Finally, when the source resends the SYN packet according to the retry mechanism of the TCP/IP protocol, SD-OVS checks whether a matching SA is present. If it finds a matching SA, it sends the PACKET_IN message to the controller. The controller determines whether to set up a flow rule in the switches. SD-OVS then forwards the packet to the destination according to the flow rule to complete the TCP connection (Fig. 2).

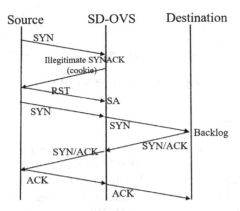

Fig. 2. Workflow of SD-OVS.

We next describe each of the four stages in SD-OVS.

3.1 Auth-Cookie Generation Stage

In Stage 1, SD-OVS sends an illegitimate SYNACK packet that contains a cookie. When the switch receives a SYN packet, the switch looks for a flow that matches it. If a matching flow is found, the switch performs the normal corresponding actions defined in the flow rule. If no matching flow is found, the switch accesses the memory to determine whether a matching SA of the host exists. If no matching SA exists, this means that the sending host (source) has not been authenticated for the packet. The switch then sends an illegitimate SYNACK packet with a cookie to the host (Fig. 3a). The cookie contains TCP/IP information from the SYN packet. In the TCP/IP protocol, the host that receives an illegitimate SYNACK packet must use the ACK sequence number of the SYNACK packet as the sequence number of the RST packet. Thus, in our method, we set the cookie on the ACK sequence number field of the SYNACK packet. In the mean-time, the SYNACK packet becomes illegitimate because of the wrong ACK sequence number.

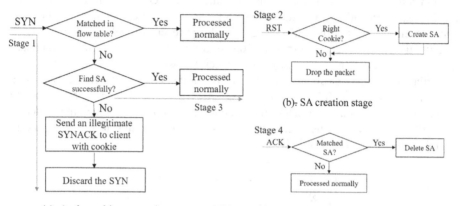

(a). Auth-cookie generation stage and SA matching stage—— (c). SA deletion stage

Fig. 3. Four stages of SD-OVS.

3.2 SA Creation Stage

In Stage 2, SD-OVS verifies the cookie to authenticate the host and creates an SA for the authenticated host (Fig. 3b). In the TCP/IP protocol, when the source receives an illegitimate SYNACK packet, it responds with an RST packet. This RST packet assigns ACK sequence number of the received packet as its sequence number to indicate the corresponding illegitimate packet. When SD-OVS receives the RST packet, it verifies whether the sequence number is the valid response for the cookie generated in Stage 1. If the cookie is legitimate, the switch creates an SA and stores it. An SA consists of the source IP address, destination IP address, and source port number. If the sequence number is invalid or has already been used to create an SA, the switch drops this RST packet.

3.3 SA Matching Stage

In Stage 3, when a corresponding SA for the retransmitted SYN packet exists, SD-OVS sends the extracted TCP/IP information of the SYN packet to the user space as the original OVS does (Fig. 3a).

The benign host resends the same SYN packet to the switch after the RST packet based on the retry mechanism in the TCP/IP protocol. At this time, SD-OVS first deter-mines whether a matching flow is present in the flow table. For the resending benign host, SD-OVS finds a matching SA even though it finds no matching flow. This is because the host is authenticated in Stage 2. The SYN packet is then forwarded to the controller as the original OVS does.

Therefore, we can ensure that the benign packet can be processed correctly and that the controller only handles benign SYN packets for a TCP connection.

3.4 SA Deletion Stage

In the last stage, SD-OVS deletes the SA when it receives the last ACK packet in a TCP connection (Fig. 3c). When an ACK packet is present, SD-OVS searches for a matching SA in memory. If a matching SA is found, the switch deletes this SA and then forwards the ACK packet as the original OpenFlow switch does. The reason for this stage is twofold. First, it is for the purpose of memory management. The SA does not hold the memory space for a long time and has negligible effect on memory. Second, it is to prevent the attacker from exploiting the authenticated port after the benign host closes the TCP connection.

4 SD-OVS Implementation

We first describe our implementation environment and our extension of the original OVS. We then discuss the design of the cookie in detail and the specified management for SA.

4.1 SD-OVS Implementation

SD-OVS is implemented in the datapath of Open vSwitch 2.4.0. We extend OVS without any harm to its functionality, and no modification is required for the controller. We use Floodlight as our controller [12].

We add SD-OVS to the kernel space. Four stages are implemented after the "ovs_flow_tbl_lookup_stats" function and before the "upcall" function. When SD-OVS finds an SA, SD-OVS completes the required information for "upcall" and completes processes as the original OVS does. In Stage 4, after deleting the SA, SD-OVS calls "upcall" as the original OVS does.

4.2 Cookie Detail Design and SA Management

Cookie detail design. If we use the original SYN cookie generation method [10], the proposed method can be vulnerable to an RST flooding attack that consumes all SA tables. To prevent this, we must manage SYN cookies carefully.

The original SYN cookie consists of a minute-scale timestamp, MSS index, and a hash [13, 14] of the source IP/port, destination IP/port, timestamp, and security keys. Malicious attackers can reuse the timestamp and MSS index to generate an RST packet with a forged SYN cookie after finding security keys. To prevent a forged SYN cookie, we must make finding secret keys difficult. Thus, we change secret keys frequently and randomly to avoid an exhaustive search of keys by malicious attackers.

SYN cookie generation. SYN cookie is a 32-bit secure sequence number stored in the ACK sequence number field of a SYNACK packet. The original cookie is generated with the following formula as coded in FreeBSD syncookie.c. In the formula, COOKIEBITS is 24 and COOKIEMASK is $(((\_u32)1 << COOKIEBITS) - 1)$:

"cookie_hash(saddr, daddr, sport, dport, 0, 0) + sseq + (count << COOKIEBITS) + ((cookie_hash(saddr, daddr, sport, dport, count, 1) + data) & COOKIEMASK))"

The system generates a 32-bit cookie. The top 8 bits correspond to a minute-scale cookie timestamp (count<<COOKIEBITS) and the remaining 24 bits are "data" plus cookie-hash of source-destination information with a timestamp and secret key index of 1. The "data" is the index of MSS (MSSIND). That value is then included with the overlapping hash value and "sseq." The "cookie_hash(saddr, daddr, sport, dport, 0, 0)" is the overlapping hash value of source-destination information with a setting timestamp of 0 and a secret key index of 0. The "sseq" is the original source-side packet sequence number. Because we are sending an RST packet with an illegitimate sequence number, "sseq" is meaningless in our scheme.

In the cookie hash function, a secret key indexed by 0 or 1 is added. These secret keys (only two 32-bit values) are crucial and maintained only in the switch. Although an attacker can find these keys after an exhaustive search, a considerable amount of time is required. However, to increase their secrecy, we change these keys frequently and randomly before an attacker finds them. Thus, an attacker is unable to generate packets easily using a forged SYN cookie by reusing information in a valid SYN cookie.

SA management. Because the SA table is another resource of a switch, it should be managed properly to prevent the switch from denying incoming connection requests. The entry in an SA table is generated by receipt of an RST packet with an SYN cookie. The corresponding entry is then deleted after receipt of the last ACK packet from the source. If SD-OVS does not receive a corresponding ACK packet necessary to delete the SA, we call this SA an "incomplete SA." An incomplete SA is removed after a timeout to prevent an attacker from first sending a valid RST packet and then exploiting the existing SA later in launching attacks.

5 Evaluation

In this section, we describe our evaluation results and show that SD-OVS protects the SDN efficiently at an acceptable time cost.

We evaluated SD-OVS on the same computer by using a virtual network namespace. First, we tested SD-OVS with a benign host and evaluated the amount of time consumed. Second, we evaluated the performance of SD-OVS and the original Open vSwitch during an SYN flooding attack.

5.1 SD-OVS for Benign Host and Time Cost

For the benign host, we tested whether SD-OVS can function well and evaluated the amount of time consumed in sending the illegitimate SYNACK packet and creating the SA in Stages 1 and 2.

We used a network namespace to create a virtual network topology to be evaluated (Fig. 4). The h1 represents a receiving host and h2 a benign sending host. The switch is connected with the Floodlight controller. Without considering the amount of time to transmit a packet in the network, we evaluated the amount of time consumed for one TCP connection in Stage 3.

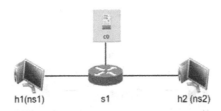

Fig. 4. The virtual network topology used in Sect. 5.1

The benign host (h2) attempts to make a TCP connection with the receiving host (h1). Detailed packet information is captured by Wireshark (Fig. 5). The top circle represents Stages 1 and 2, and the second circle represents Stage 3.

						Stage 1 & 2	Stage 3
Time	Source	Destination	Protocol	Lengtl	Info		
1 0.000000	10.0.0.2	10.0.0.1	TCP	74	45712 > ddi-tcp-1 [SYN] Seq=0 Win=29200 Len=0 MSS=1460 SACK PERM=1 TSval=4294961324 TSecr=0 WS=128		
2 0.000050	10.0.0.1	10.0.0.2	TCP	74	[TCP ACKed unseen segment] ddi-tcp-1 > 45712 [SYN, ACK] Seq=0 Ack=938349147 Win=29200 Len=0 MSS=1460 SACK		
3 0.006242	10.0.0.2	10.0.0.1	TCP	54	45712 > ddi-tcp-1 [RST] Seq=938349147 Win=0 Len=0		
4 0.870381	10.0.0.2	10.0.0.1	TCP	74	[TCP Retransmission] 45712 > ddi-tcp-1 [SYN] Seq=0 Win=29200 Len=0 MSS=1460 SACK PERM=1 TSval=4294961574 T		
5 0.881069	10.0.0.1	10.0.0.2	TCP	74	[TCP Retransmission] ddi-tcp-1 > 45712 [SYN, ACK] Seq=2793790547 Ack=1 Win=28960 Len=0 MSS=1460 SACK PERM=		
6 0.881084	10.0.0.2	10.0.0.1	TCP	66	45712 > ddi-tcp-1 [ACK] Seq=1 Ack=2793790548 Win=29312 Len=0 TSval=4294961574 TSecr=4294961574		
7 5.584787	10.0.0.2	10.0.0.1	TCP	66	[TCP Retransmission] 45712 > ddi-tcp-1 [FIN, ACK] Seq=1 Ack=2793790548 Win=29312 Len=0 TSval=4294962759 TS		
8 5.590070	10.0.0.1	10.0.0.2	TCP	66	ddi-tcp-1 > 45712 [ACK] Seq=2793790548 Ack=2 Win=29056 Len=0 TSval=4294962751 TSecr=4294962750		
9 7.817645	10.0.0.1	10.0.0.2	TCP	66	[TCP Retransmission] ddi-tcp-1 > 45712 [FIN, ACK] Seq=2793790548 Ack=2 Win=29056 Len=0 TSval=4294963308 TS		
10 7.817657	10.0.0.2	10.0.0.1	TCP	66	45712 > ddi-tcp-1 [ACK] Seq=2 Ack=2793790549 Win=29312 Len=0 TSval=4294963308 TSecr=4294963308		

Fig. 5. Packet information when using SD-OVS.

In the top circle, the ACK sequence number of the second packet (the illegitimate SYNACK packet) is the cookie value generated in Stage 1. The sequence number of the third packet (RST packet) sent from the benign host is the same as the sequence number of the SYNACK packet. In this case, the benign host can verify the cookie successfully and create an SA during Stage 2. The second circle shows that the TCP connection is established in Stage 3.

The total amount of time consumed for Stages 1 and 2 is 0.242 ms, and the time for Stage 3 is 2.703 ms. Because the retransmission time gap could be set differently, we evaluated it based on the default time in Linux. The sixth packet shows that the amount of time consumed for one TCP connection is less than 1 s (Fig. 5), which is acceptable.

We recommend setting the transmission time gap to a small value when using SD-OVS to produce better performance.

5.2 SD-OVS Under SYN Flooding Attack

We evaluated the performance for both SD-OVS and the original Open vSwitch during an SYN flooding attack.

A virtual network namespace was used for evaluation. We assumed that the attacker could not compromise the switch but had the ability to compromise the host. The h3 represents the compromised host and, in our experiment, launched the SYN flooding attack (Fig. 6).

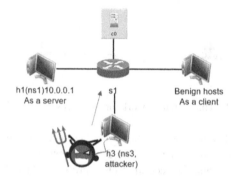

Fig. 6. Virtual network topology used under attack.

When the attack rate was greater than 60 PPS, the original Open vSwitch could no longer respond to the benign new SYN packets. By contrast, the controller connected to SD-OVS could always respond to the new SYN packets with an acceptable time cost (Fig. 7). The time cost incurred during the attack was still less than 1 s (which included the retransmission time gap). This shows that SD-OVS protects the controller at an acceptable time cost (Table 1).

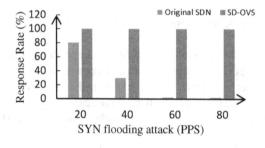

Fig. 7. Response rate compared with original OVS under SYN flooding attack.

Table 1. Time cost comparison for one TCP connection under SYN flooding attack

	TCP connection time (s)
Original SDN	∞
SD-OVS	0.92652

6 Other Possible Related Attacks

In this section, we discuss solutions for some possible attacks that bypass SD-OVS.

First, we defined the incomplete SA in Sect. 4.2 and the management rules for the incomplete SA to prevent the attacker from exploiting the SA by sending a valid RST packet. If the attacker compromises one host and sends an RST with a valid cookie, SD-OVS creates the SA. The attacker then launches an SYN flooding attack instead of following the proposed connection procedure. The malicious SYN packet can complete Stage 3 because of an existing SA. With the proposed timeout scheme for incomplete SA management, SD-OVS deletes the incomplete SA automatically even though the attacker does not send the ACK packet. When the attacker tries to launch the SYN flooding attack, the SYN packet must repeat Stages 1 to 4. Therefore, the SYN flooding attack is not successful.

Second, the Linux kernel can allow a local attacker to obtain sensitive information because of the imperfect secret random value given by the "net_get_random_once" function. Thus, SD-OVS must refresh the secret value frequently to prevent the attacker from acquiring the values, which is most important when we generate the cookie.

Third, if an attacker launches an RST attack by resending the RST packet with valid cookies repeatedly, the switch may create multiple copies of the same SA, which may exhaust the memory. We consider that SD-OVS should check whether the same SA exists before creating a new SA to avoid exhausting memory.

Finally, in the original SYN cookie method, the destination host had an unstable connection when the last ACK packet from the source was lost [10, 11]. The source assumed a connection was established. However, the destination did not have a connection established. In the proposed scheme, TCP handshaking between the source and destination occurs normally without using an SYN cookie. The SYN cookie in our method is used only between the source and ingress switch. The destination receives the SYN packet, which is already authenticated by the SD-OVS switch. The destination stores the information in its backlog. If any packet is lost during the connection establishment, it triggers the retry mechanism as in the original TCP handshaking protocol.

7 Related Work

Our study was inspired by some previous studies that describe the vulnerabilities in SDN [5, 6, 15, 16] and AVANT-GUARD [7]. These studies were the first to attempt to modify the OpenFlow switch and use the SYN cookie method in SDN.

AVANT-GUARD has two shortcomings. First, it must modify both the OpenFlow switch and controller. AVANT-GUARD has two important stages: migration and relay.

These stages are commanded by the controller, and the switch must send a special message, which is defined by AVANT-GUARD for the controller, which is necessary to obtain the command from the controller. Because many different types of controllers exist, AVANT-GUARD requires that all these controllers be modified. Our proposed method does not have this drawback because the SD-OVS switch alone protects against a SYN flooding attack. Thus, our method can provide better scalability. Second, AVANT-GUARD must modify the sequence numbers of TCP packets in an established connection because of the connection relay. AVANT-GUARD must manage two TCP connections as a single connection. Therefore, it must store the value difference between two SEQ numbers of packets as well as change the SEQ number of each packet. Our scheme can avoid this added burden because SD-OVS utilizes the retry mechanism in the TCP protocol. SD-OVS neither needs to manage two TCP connections nor maintain any value to change the packets.

For the same goal of protecting the controller from an SYN flooding attack, SD-OVS is easier to apply with minimal modification to the OpenFlow switch and no modification to the controller. SD-OVS also has a simpler workflow without managing any TCP connection or informing the controller.

8   Conclusion

In this paper, we proposed a SDN switch called SD-OVS to defend against SYN flooding attacks. The mechanism to block malicious SYN packets to protect controller is a host authentication with SYN cookie and TCP retry. We showed a method of establishing a host authentication for an incoming SYN packet and using it for a second attempt with the same SYN packet. Our evaluation results showed that SD-OVS can protect a controller from an SYN flooding attack at an acceptable time cost. The proposed scheme operates effectively against an SYN flooding attack with minimal change to the SDN switch and no modification to the SDN controller.

Acknowledgements. This work was supported by Samsung Research Funding Center of Samsung Electronics under Project Number SRFC-TB1403-04.

References

1. McKeown, N., et. al.: OpenFlow: enabling innovation in campus networks. In: ACM SIGCOMM Computer Communications Review, New York, pp. 69–74 (2008)
2. CERT, TCP SYN Flooding and IP Spoofing Attacks (1996)
3. Eddy, W.: TCP SYN flooding attacks and common mitigations. In: Request for Comments: 4987, pp. 6–10 (2007)
4. Gavaskar, S., Surendiran, R., Ramaraj, E.: Three counter defense mechanism for TCP SYN flooding attacks. Int. J. Comput. Appl. 6(6), 12–15 (2010)
5. Hong, S., Xu, L., Wang, H., Gu, G.: Poisoning network visibility in software-defined networks: new attacks and countermeasures. In: NDSS Symposium on 2015, San Diego (2015)

6. Braga, R., Mota, E., Passito, A.: Lightweight DDoS flooding attack detection using NOX/OpenFlow. In: IEEE 35th Conference on Local Computer Networks (LCN), pp. 408–415. IEEE, Denver (2010)
7. Shin, S., Yegneswaran, V., Porras, P., Gu, G.: AVANT-GUARD: scalable and vigilant switch flow management in software-defined networks. In: ACM SIGSAC Conference on Computer and Communications Security, CCS 2013, New York, pp. 413–424 (2013)
8. OpenFlow Switch Specification. http://www.openflow.org/documents/openflow-spec-v1.0.0.pdf
9. Open vSwitch. http://openvswitch.org/
10. Bernstein, D.J.: SYN cookie, September 1996
11. Kim, T., Choi, Y., Kim, J., Hong, S.: Annulling SYN flooding attacks with whitelist. In: 22nd International Conference on Advanced Information Networking and Applications, Okinawa, pp. 371–376 (2008)
12. Floodlight. http://www.projectfloodlight.org/floodlight/
13. Goldreich, O.: Foundations of Cryptography: Volume II Basic Applications, pp. 498–502. Cambridge University Press, New York (2004)
14. PUB, FIPS, Secure Hash Standard. FIPS PUB 180-4, pp. 18–20 (2012)
15. Scott-Hayward, S., O'Callaghan, G., Sezer, S.: SDN security: a survey. In: Future Networks and Services (SDN4FNS), pp. 1–7. IEEE, Trento (2013)
16. Kloti, R., Kotronis, V., Smith, P.: OpenFlow: a security analysis. In: 21st IEEE International Conference on Network Protocols, pp. 1–6. IEEE, Goettingen (2013)

Slowloris DoS Countermeasure over WebSocket

Jongseok Choi, Jong-gyu Park, Shinwook Heo, Namje Park,
and Howon Kim$^{(\boxtimes)}$

Information Security and IoT Laboratory,
Electrical Electronic Computer Engineering Department,
Pusan National University, Busandeahak-ro 63, Busan, Korea
{jschoi85,pjk5401,shinwookheo,howonkim}@pusan.ac.kr,
namjepark@jejunu.ac.kr
http://infosec.pusan.ac.kr

Abstract. We evaluate security of WebSocket, one of HTML5 APIs, in the view of L7 DoS attack and design the countermeasure against Slowloris attack which is known as difficult to be detected by IDS and IPS. It is easy to disable services based on WebSocket by sending partial request packets slowly. The server no longer provide the service since Slowloris attack makes request buffer full. For the solution, we design a dual-buffer based countermeasure. The main features of countermeasure are separation of buffer according to status of connections and request acceptance without limitation. In this countermeasure, we propose structure of request buffer free from fullness by employing circular buffer. The connections after handshake process move out to another buffer not to be affected from the request attack. In our construction, when the request buffer is full, the oldest request would be overwritten with a new request. Finally, our proposal allows the benign requests to be successful during Slowloris attack. Our construction could be also applied to other applications including HTTP, FTP and etc.

Keywords: Slowloris · WebSocket · DoS · Countermeasure · HTML5

1   Introduction

With popularization of the Internet, World Wide Web has been grown as a platform for software applications run directly on a browser. As connectivity of Internet becomes ubiquitous, Web service which operates over the Internet gets much higher degree of usability and accessibility than ever before. With the growth of Web, HTML evolved from a simple language with small number of tags to a complex markup language which grants all manners of gimmick [1]. With all sorts of innovations, HTML+, HTML2, HTML3.2 and HTML4 have been introduced and finally the first version of HTML5 published in 2008. HTML5 is based on HTML, CSS and JavaScript and reduces the necessity for third-party plugins [2,3]. Its standardization is still a work in progress, just before the finalization, and major browsers (e.g. Safari, Chrome, Firefox, Opera and Internet Explorer) are supporting its new features already [4].

© Springer International Publishing AG 2017
D. Choi and S. Guilley (Eds.): WISA 2016, LNCS 10144, pp. 42–53, 2017.
DOI: 10.1007/978-3-319-56549-1_4

While HTML standards transformed and getting more powerful, the importance of browsers, a software application presenting resources on the Web, and their security became higher. With strenuous effort of browser writers, modern browsers became safer. But to keep that security up-to-date, developers and security experts need to keep their eyes on new standards and find potential threats. It is because of that those movements are also observed from the malicious users. Like security professionals and developers, attackers do research on new standards and find flaws in firmness. In the war of defense and offence, attackers always have found new ways to exploit. In other words, as concern about security increased and wall of defense elevated, attack techniques are branched out and elaborated.

Especially, L7 DoS attack is one of the results of diversification and evolution of attack techniques. Briefly, Denial-of-Service (DoS) attack is an attempt to prevent normal users of a service from using that service by running victims resources out or obstructing the communication between legitimate users and the victim [5]. Originally, the first DoS attacks usually performed by individuals, with handful of resources and its principle and working form was simple. End of eighties, easy-to-use tools for DoS attacks appeared. Anybody who wants to perform DoS attack could leverage them with ease and that contributes to an increase of DoS attacks. DoS attack expanded its territory in the form of embedded routine in malware payload. Using these malware, attackers could assault the target at the specified time with much amplified resources. After mid-2000s, it changed its form as a botnet and attackers regain control on their tools by C&C (command-and-control) server. Not only its appearance became different, but also its method has been evolved. Traditionally, Distributed DoS (DDoS) attacks are performed at the network layer (e.g. SYN flooding, ICMP flooding and UDP flooding). However, a number of protection schemes against simple bulk attacks are proposed and as a result IDS (Intrusion Detection System) appeared as a countermeasure of network layer DoS attacks [6–9]. The IDS conducts monitoring and recognizes anomaly from network traffic or system activities. Anomaly is usually detected by inspection of preconfigured signature on monitored network packets or comparison between activities of monitored network and statistically predetermined normal activities of network. Therefore common volumetric attacks are easily caught by IDSs. Accordingly making a success in DoS attacks based on network layer is getting harder [10].

In order to detour the detection by IDS, attackers shifted their focuses and expanded their attack surface to application layer. Since there is a prone to doing more computations in application layer than in network layer, application-layer DoS (as known as Layer 7 DoS or L7 DoS) attack, a variant of DoS attack, can be done with much less traffic than traditional DDoS [11,12]. Besides, there is a phenomenon called Flash Crowds [13] named after a short story of science fiction. The Flash Crowds occurs when a large number of users simultaneously access a particular website. It is caused by benign users but looks very similar to DDoS attacks. Thus it is difficult to distinguish and stop Layer 7 attacks from normal traffic [14,15]. They usually target HTTP or DNS but the number of attacks targeting HTTPS, SMTP and SIP/VOIP is on the rise. The Slowloris [16,17], the Rudy, the SlowPost, the MyDoom worm and the CyberSlam are representative L7 DoS schemes. In the case of Slowloris attack, this HTTP GET-based attack uses partial HTTP request packets to open and hold the connections with target server. While in the connection stage, it regularly sends subsequent packets to prevent the socket from closing and keeps that states as long as possible like never ending story. Since Slowloris attack employs legitimate traffic, the target server cannot distinguish these malicious connections from normal connections and keeps all connections alive. Not using bad HTTP request makes existing signature-based IDS crippled against Slowloris attack. When the entire connection pool of web server exhausted then server itself becomes utterly inaccessible. Security researchers consider application layer DoS attacks as an area of persistent growth and may supersede network layer attack [18].

WebSocket, one of HTML5 related APIs, provides a novel way to communicate in the manner of asynchronous and bidirectional method. This new protocol enables full-duplex connection between client browsers and server. Since default ports are 80 and 443, there is no need to open additional ports in firewall. It works as a strong point to enterprises to accept this new protocol. Its connection is started with HTTP(S) protocol at first and taken over by WebSocket protocol. Despite a guarantee of interactivity, higher throughput and two-way communication, existence of the known vulnerabilities and the potential new threats make us worry [4,19,20]. Of course there are a variety of potential threats but we need to pay keen attention on fast growing L7 DoS. In this paper, we cover Slowloris attack on WebSocket and propose a countermeasure for Slowloris attack.

1.1 Our Contributions

We have two main contributions: evaluation of WebSocket security and a design of countermeasure against Slowloris attack. First, we performed L7 DoS attacks on WebSocket which is new function of HTML5. Especially, we focused on Slowloris attack and interrupting parsing request packet by sending the request except splitting identification. We know interruption on parsing method would be easily prevented by well-made exception handler. However, detecting and preventing Slowloris attack are difficult even if high price IDS and IPS are equipped. Therefore we propose brand-new countermeasure against Slowloris attack as our second contribution. The main feature which makes our strategy different from existing logic for WebSocket is that our construction splits the buffer into two parts: handshake buffer and connected buffer. In detail, we used circular buffer for handshake packet and after handshake process, the connection is moved out to connected buffer. The main point of the design is that it allows all the client requests to be accepted by employing circular buffer. Namely, the oldest socket stored in handshake buffer would be overwritten by a new request socket. There are two issues to employ circular buffer for request storage: empty memory indexing and overwriting. For those issues, we also can suggest two solutions: stack-based solution and heap-based solution. The solution could satisfy the dynamic feature unlike FIFO (First In, First Out) or LIFO (Last In, First

Out). With these solutions, the server could infinitely accept the requests with fixed memory and the complexity of $O(n)$.

2   Related Works

2.1   Slowloris Attack

Generally, DoS attack makes a target server cannot provide services by depleting the resource of the server. Slowloris attack is a kind of DoS attacks. Unlike most DoS attacks have been based on TCP, Slowloris attack is based on HTTP. An attacker sends GET request with partial http header to the target server after making a session between them. After that, the server waits for the rest part of header but the attacker slowly sends it to keep the connection from closing. Then the connection is active continuously and the server has to stay in wait state. In this state, the attacker sends new http connection requests over and over. Because the server has lots of connections, resources of the server are running out gradually. Up to now, there are no countermeasures on Slowloris attack. As we can see in Fig. 1, WebSocket handshake process is an extended version of HTTP. Therefore same vulnerabilities related to HTTP can be applied to WebSocket. This means WebSocket is threatened with Slowloris attack as well.

2.2   DoS Attack Detection

There are two categories in network based IDS (Intrusion Detection System) for DoS attack detection. The first one is signature based detection methods and the second one is threshold based detection methods. Each method has pros and cons. The signature based detection methods have a high probability of DoS attack detection but it cannot cope with a new kind of DoS attack rapidly. The threshold based detection methods are able to respond a new kind of DoS attack and they can adapt universal statistical methods. However, the reliability of DoS attack detection may be low in the case of special circumstance such as Flash Crowds.

Signature Based Detection. Signature based detection is called by misuse based detection or knowledge based detection. DoS attack traffic is different in the type of attacks. Nevertheless, there are general features when the attack occurred. First, a flow rate imbalance between a source and a target server is observed because an attacker sends mass traffic to the target server. Second, the attacker uses random pattern traffic in order to confuse the origin of traffic. Third, there is a high correlation between abnormal traffic at the source and attack traffic at the target server. These features can be used to detect DoS attack based on signature.

There are several schemes based on signature based detection. MULTOPS (Multi Level Tree for Online Packet Statistics) was proposed by Gil and Poletto [9]. MULTOPS activates a monitor which detects DoS attack. It is based upon the premise that a number of incoming traffic's packets is proportionate to a number of outcoming traffic's packets. It uses a dynamic tree structure for monitoring the packet rate of each IP address. Each node of the tree is composed of 256 records and represents the total amount and bit rates of packets. This information is proportionate to packet rates to pass through the hosts and subnets. Thus, if imbalance of packet flow occurred, the monitor discriminates DoS attack. SYN detection, one of the other detection scheme, was proposed by Wang et al. [21]. The feature of SYN flood attack is that the number of SYN packets is too many in comparison with the number of FIN or RST packets in the process of normal TCP handshakes. In SYN detection, a proper parameter is selected toward incoming traffic and then calculate the ratio between SYN packets and FIN or RST packets. If this ratio is abnormal, the system regards that DoS attack happened.

Threshold Based Detection. Threshold based detection is called anomaly based detection or profile based detection. There are two steps as a training phase in threshold based detection. The first step is to identify effective parameters such as packet length, inter-arrival time, flow size, number of packet per flow and so on. The parameters can be utilized to describe the network traffic which will be used to distinguish the normal traffic from the anomalistic traffic. The second step is to calculate the similarity representing how different the monitoring traffic and expected normal traffic are. Kolmogrov-Smirnov tests [7] have been used to provide similarity metrics [6]. If the similarity between the monitored traffic and the normal traffic profile is less than threshold which is decided in the second step, the system regards whether DoS attack occurred.

3   Our Construction

Slowloris attack is an L7 DoS attack which can be applied to almost every TCP-based services but no countermeasure. Most of the layer 7 applications in OSI (Open Systems Interconnection) model [22] make handshake with their own method before data communication. However handshake can be used to attack the protocol by L7 DoS attack.

For example, assume that an attacker wants to stop the service of the WebSocket server without any illegal packet. The attacker can send partial request packets to the server at intervals a bit shorter than time-out to keep socket from closing. As the result, the server would be tied up on handshake. When the client pool is full due to the reception of the partial handshake packets, the server no longer provides the service because a buffer to accept clients is understaffed. This kind of the layer 7 attack is called Slowloris DoS attack. In the circumstance, server needs the following time to finish handshake.

$$\frac{request\ packet\ size}{partial\ packet\ size} \times time\ interval \tag{1}$$

Although threshold based detection [23] and signature based detection [24, 25] of various detections [12, 26–28] have been used as the major countermeasures on DoS attack, they confront with difficulties in detecting Slowloris attack. In the case of threshold based detection, it is easy to detect the DoS attack using high traffic resources, such as flooding or ping attack, but the Slowloris attack is based on low traffic. In signature based detection, abnormal packets can be detected but Slowloris attack uses no illegal packets. Due to these reasons, there is no practical answer for threats by the Slowloris attack.

In existing implementations for the service over WebSocket, status variable is defined in WebSocket structure because server needs to determine whether selected socket is on handshake process. By usage of the structure, the Web-Socket servers can be implemented with asynchronous communication based on multi-thread. In other words, the implementations for the WebSocket servers are currently using the 1-dementional array for request buffer of the defined structure. Due to the feature, when all the buffers for connected/connecting sockets are full, the server no longer provides services to not only connecting sockets but also connected sockets. In this section we describe the implementation of WebSocket and propose the countermeasure against Slowloris attack.

3.1   Implementation of Websocket Server

Implementation of WebSocket server is similar with implementation of asynchronous TCP sockets based on multi-thread. Specifically, a server and clients establish asynchronous connection with TCP protocol as the first step. At the next step upon receiving a request packet from clients, the server determines whether the packet is for handshake process based on status variable of the socket and fulfills handshakes or services. The point of this construction is implementation of WebSocket structure stating status of the sockets of each client. The structure can be defined as an array of connecting/connected sockets for multi-communication. However the problem is that the Slowloris attacks can abuse the array of WebSocket structure and the server has no choice but to reject and stop providing services to all the clients as a result of those attack.

The following pseudo code illustrates the main part of flow of the WebSocket server. In this code, st_websocket denotes array variable of the WebSocket structure including two statuses: handshakeStat and connectedStat. Those statuses can be used to distinguish if selected sockets is on handshake process or not.

Server Side Implementation of Websocket Service

```
ReceiveCallback
Input : socket ID of receiving packets
    rcIndex=-1
    For i from 0 to length of websocket do
        If(st_websocket[i]=socketID)
            rcIndex=i

    switch(st_websocket[rcIndex].status)
```

```
case handshakingStat:
    handshaking(st_websocket[rcSocket]);
    st_websocket[rcSocket].status <- connetedStat;
    break;
case connectedStat:
    service();
    break;
end.
```

Slowloris attack is performed with handshakeStat of status variable. In the detail of the flow, an attacker slowly sends partial request packets to keep the connection from closing. The server cannot start verification of the request packet before receiving all the partial packets but it takes a long time. In addition, though an attacker sends arbitrary partial packets not to be exact request packet of WebSocket, the server has no alternatives but to wait to finish receiving all the partial packets. Especially, this attack allows one attacker to hold more than one items of the array, st_websocket, by using multi-threads and IP spoofing thanks to the quite long interval among the sent partial packets. For example, if the server sets timeout up to five seconds, an attacker can take idle time about five seconds. As the result, a small server can be halted by only one attacker.

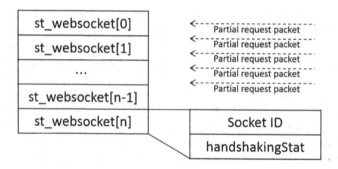

Fig. 1. The servers' stack for WebSocket array assaulted by Slowloris attack. This figure shows the flow of Slowloris attack, which is slowly sending partial packets for handshake request. The server unconditionally wait to finish packet reception. However the status fields of st_websocket structure is set as 'handshakeStat' so that the handshake process is delayed and the waiting could not be ended for long.

The above figure (Fig. 1) shows Slowloris attack. An attacker sends very small partial packets of WebSocket request and can trick the server with spoofed packets of multiple threads. The server sets status field of the st_websocket to handshakeStat until finishing WebSocket handshake process. Thereafter, the server has to wait until finishing to receive the request packet, which is transmitted slowly by the client, and uses all the assigned stack for services over WebSocket. Finally, the server rejects all the clients, who want to get the service, until completion of authenticating the Slowloris packets.

3.2   Countermeasure Against Slowloris Attack over WebSocket

In this section, we describe countermeasure on Slowloris attack. The main idea of the countermeasure is splitting a buffer, which stores sockets of clients, of Web-Socket structure into two buffers according to each status. Basically, it is very difficult to prevent DoS attack by software implementation due to massive traffic. In the case of Slowloris attack, it is possible to prevent it by software implementation because the packets of the Slowloris attack cannot cause any computation overhead to the server; in Slowloris attack, the problem is the delayed packets. Fortunately, it is easy to prevent it if two buffers are used for the WebSocket server.

In short of the problem on Slowloris attack, there are two problems. The first problem is that the servers have no sense about connection status except when receivecallback function is called. Otherwise the server have to confirm the status fields of all WebSocket structures to sense the status of the sockets. However, it causes very high overheads to confirm the fields of entire items in buffer. Therefore, we divided the buffer into connected buffer and handshake buffer. When handshake process is finished, the socket ID move out to connected buffer. The second problem is that if buffer for sockets of clients is full, the server no longer allows all the clients to request services. As the solution, we designed the handshake buffer as circular buffer because normal request quickly finished. As the result, the oldest request has the highest possibility to be the packets for Slowloris attack. Therefore we overwrote the stack with new request.

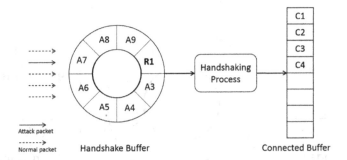

Fig. 2. The architecture of countermeasure on Slowloris attack. This figure shows that partial packets (A series packets) and normal request packets (R series packets) are come in the server. As the first step, all the request is stored in handshake buffer. At the next step, the connections move out to connected buffer after handshake process. The connections in handshake buffer will be overwritten with new requests in time order.

The above figure (Fig. 2) shows how our solution endures Slowloris attack. An attacker sends partial packets at the interval of a bit shorter than time-out, which make the stack of a server full. However, there are no limitation in acceptance of handshake buffer because the buffer was designed as circular buffer. The main point of this is that removing items in the handshake buffer have no influence over connected clients because the socket IDs of the clients, which is completed from handshake process, moved out to connected buffer.

3.3   Consideration

In order to employ circular buffer instead of non-circular buffer, there are some considerations. In this section we describe the considerations and solutions. There are some studies [29–31] on circular buffer but all the studies were based on FIFO (First In, First Out) or LIFO (Last In, First Out) data structure. However, two following issues have to be considered for asynchronous communication.

Empty memory indexing means finding empty spaces in the circular buffer. In general concept of circular buffer, the empty space can be chosen by end pointer and start pointer due to FIFO data structure. However FIFO and LIFO is unsuitable for our construction because the empty spaces can be irregularly occurred unlike general circular buffer over asynchronous communication.

Overwriting means how to determine which spaces in the buffer will be removed. It outwardly seems simple to remove it time by time. However it is difficult to make sense of how old socket is.

For the mentioned issues: empty memory indexing and overwriting, we designed two solution: stack-based solution and heap-based solution. The first solution is based on stack memory. For the stack-based solution, each space in circular buffer is composed of structure including time index.

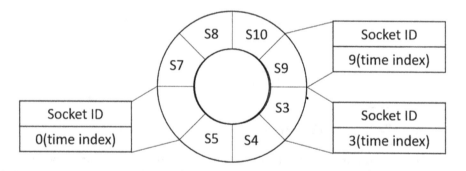

Fig. 3. The structure of circular buffer employed into countermeasure on Slowloris attack. This figure shows that the structure of circular buffer is composed of socket ID and time index. About socket ID is already described in this section. Time index denotes the created time of each socket. What time index is zero means empty. Except zero, as the smaller time index is, the older the socket was created.

The above figure (Fig. 3) shows the structure of circular buffer. Specifically, the construction has to find an empty space in the circular buffer as the first step. It is very simple to find empty space by search zero time index. It needs only complexity of $O(n)$, which is the worst case such as no empty space. Thereafter, it has to find which space will be overwritten; it means that which the oldest socket ID is. The problem can be solved by selecting the space including the smallest time index.

$$\arg \min \mathbb{T} = \{time\ indexs\} \tag{2}$$

As the next solution, we designed heap-based solution. It means binary linked list data structure. When adding a new socket, the head and tail of new socket are connected to a tail of the last socket and a head of the first socket respectively. Then the last socket is changed to the new socket. In addition, when changing the first socket, before the above works, we had to change the first socket to the second socket instead of changing the last socket. The point of the heap-based solution is that you have to stipulate limitation of the count of the list sockets due to the attacks on abusing memory of the server.

4 Conclusion

DoS attacks have changed their form and strategy numerous times since the birth of its concept. Although DoS attacks were started with individual and handful resources, became diverse, delicate and massive with advent of automated tools. There are plenty kinds of DoS attacks (e.g. SYN Flooding, Ping of Death, Peer-to-Peer attack and Slow Read attack) depending on its strategies. They transformed their appearance into routine embedded in virus, worm and botnet recently and work as a part of entire assault. Most recently, it expanded its working area to application layer and is showing steady growth in new territory. For all that transitions, the penetrative concept of DoS attacks has never been changed. It means that the victims always have a buffer of limited capacity and the attacker fills the buffer up.

We evaluated security of WebSocket, a new function of HTML5 for bidirectional communication, on the view of Slowloris DoS attack and then designed the dual-buffer based which separating handshake part and connected part. Main concept of the countermeasure is to allow the request acceptance with no limitation. For that reason, there are two differences between the concept of existing implementation and our countermeasure. The first is that our construction splits a buffer into handshake buffer and connected buffer. It means that the server can distinguish whether the handshake process is completed or not, intuitively. The second is that the design of handshake buffer for the WebSocket requests is based on circular buffer. It does mean that the server can accept all requests from clients with no limitation. In other words, although massive packets of Slowloris attack were assigned in handshake buffer, the buffer would not be full by employing circular buffer.

Our concept, request buffer free from fullness, is important to prevent DoS or DDoS attack because most of them exploit limitation of request acceptance.

Because there was no even concept to accept all the requests without limitation, they couldnt be prevented. If the buffer for request sockets, which stores all the request sockets and connections, is implemented by typical circular buffer then normal connections should be also disconnected by overwriting or the server should require heavy computation to distinguish complete connection and incomplete connection of handshake for avoiding complete connections from overwritten. In our construction, we solve it by splitting a buffer into two parts. This construction could be applied to a variety of countermeasures of DoS attacks including layer 7 and layer 4.

References

1. Raggett, D., Lam, J., Alexander, I., Kmiec, M.: Raggett on HTML 4, 2nd edn. Addison-Wesley Longman Publishing Co., Inc., Boston (1998)
2. Anthes, G.: HTML5 leads a web revolution. Commun. ACM **55**(7), 16–17 (2012)
3. Wang, P.S.: Dynamic Web Programming and HTML5. Chapman & Hall, London (2012)
4. Kuppan, L.: Attacking with HTML5. Webinar, Black Hat Webcast Series (2010)
5. Heron, S.: Denial of service: motivations and trends. Netw. Secur. **2010**(5), 10–12 (2010)
6. Peng, T., Leckie, C., Ramamohanarao, K.: Survey of network-based defense mechanisms countering the DoS and DDoS problems. ACM Comput. Surv. (CSUR) **39**(1), 3 (2007)
7. Manikopoulos, C., Papavassiliou, S.: Network intrusion and fault detection: a statistical anomaly approach. IEEE Commun. Mag. **40**(10), 76–82 (2002)
8. Anderson, D., Frivold, T., Valdes, A.: Next-generation intrusion detection expert system (NIDES): a summary. SRI International, Computer Science Laboratory (1995)
9. Thomer, G., Massimiliano, P.: Multops: a data structure for bandwidth attack detection. In: Proceedings of the Tenth USENIX Security Symposium, pp. 23–29. Washington, DC (2001)
10. Mirkovic, J.: Internet Denial of Service: Attack and Defense Mechanisms. Prentice Hall, Upper Saddle River, NJ (2005)
11. Cambiaso, E., Papaleo, G., Aiello, M.: Taxonomy of slow DoS attacks to web applications. In: Thampi, S.M., Zomaya, A.Y., Strufe, T., Alcaraz Calero, J.M., Thomas, T. (eds.) SNDS 2012. CCIS, vol. 335, pp. 195–204. Springer, Heidelberg (2012). doi:10.1007/978-3-642-34135-9_20
12. Yoon, S.Y.: System and method for determining application layer-based slow distributed denial of service (DDoS) attack. US Patent 20,130,042,322, 14 Feb 2013
13. Jung, J., Krishnamurthy, B., Rabinovich, M.: Flash crowds and denial of service attacks: characterization and implications for CDNs and web sites. In: Proceedings of the 11th international conference on World Wide Web, WWW 2002, pp. 293–304. ACM, New York (2002)
14. Xie, Y., Yu, S.Z.: A novel model for detecting application layer DDoS attacks. In: First International Multi-symposiums on Computer and Computational Sciences, IMSCCS 2006, vol. 2, pp. 56–63. IEEE (2006)
15. Xie, Y., Yu, S.Z.: Monitoring the application-layer DDoS attacks for popular websites. IEEE/ACM Trans. Networking **17**(1), 15–25 (2009)

16. RSnake: Slowloris HTTP DoS
17. Gallagher, S.: High Orbits and Slowlorises: Understanding the Anonymous Attack Tools. Ars Technica (2012)
18. McGregory, S.: Preparing for the next DDoS attack. Netw. Secur. **2013**(5), 5–6 (2013)
19. Koch, R.: On websockets in penetration testing
20. Erkkilä, J.P.: Websocket security analysis
21. Wang, H., Zhang, D., Shin, K.G.: Detecting SYN flooding attacks. In: Proceedings of the IEEE, INFOCOM 2002, Twenty-First Annual Joint Conference of the IEEE Computer and Communications Societies, vol. 3, pp. 1530–1539. IEEE (2002)
22. Briscoe, N.: Understanding the OSI 7-layer model. PC Network Advisor **120**(2) (2000)
23. Choi, Y., Kim, I.-K., Oh, J.-T., Jang, J.-S.: AIGG threshold based HTTP GET flooding attack detection. In: Lee, D.H., Yung, M. (eds.) WISA 2012. LNCS, vol. 7690, pp. 270–284. Springer, Heidelberg (2012). doi:10.1007/978-3-642-35416-8_19
24. Kruegel, C., Toth, T.: Using decision trees to improve signature-based intrusion detection. In: Vigna, G., Kruegel, C., Jonsson, E. (eds.) RAID 2003. LNCS, vol. 2820, pp. 173–191. Springer, Heidelberg (2003). doi:10.1007/978-3-540-45248-5_10
25. Vaidya, V.: Dynamic signature inspection-based network intrusion detection. US Patent 6,279,113, 21 Aug 2001
26. Yi, H.K., Park, P.K., Min, S., Ryou, J.C.: DDoS detection algorithm using the bidirectional session. In: Kwiecień, A., Gaj, P., Stera, P. (eds.) CN 2011. CCIS, vol. 160, pp. 191–203. Springer, Heidelberg (2011). doi:10.1007/978-3-642-21771-5_21
27. Sourav, K., Mishra, D.P.: DDoS detection and defense: client termination approach. In: Proceedings of the CUBE International Information Technology Conference, pp. 749–752. ACM (2012)
28. Giralte, L.C., Conde, C., de Diego, I.M., Cabello, E.: Detecting denial of service by modelling web-server behaviour. Computers & Electrical Engineering (2012)
29. Papworth, D.B., Glew, A.F., Fetterman, M.A., Hinton, G.J., Colwell, R.P., Griffith, S.J., Gupta, S.R., Hegde, N.: Entry allocation in a circular buffer using wrap bits indicating whether a queue of the circular buffer has been traversed. US Patent 5,584,038, 10 Dec 1996
30. Laurenti, G., Djafarian, K., Catan, H.: Circular buffer management. US Patent 6,363,470, 26 March 2002
31. Ogasawara, Y., Ogino, Y., Shimakura, M.: Apparatus for selectively comparing pointers to detect full or empty status of a circular buffer area in an input/output (I/O) buffer. US Patent 5,537,552, 16 July 1996

Detecting Encrypted Traffic: A Machine Learning Approach

Seunghun Cha[✉] and Hyoungshick Kim[✉]

Department of Software, Sungkyunkwan University, Suwon, Republic of Korea
{sh.cha,hyoung}@skku.edu

Abstract. Detecting encrypted traffic is increasingly important for deep packet inspection (DPI) to improve the performance of intrusion detection systems. We propose a machine learning approach with several randomness tests to achieve high accuracy detection of encrypted traffic while requiring low overhead incurred by the detection procedure. To demonstrate how effective the proposed approach is, the performance of four classification methods (Naïve Bayesian, Support Vector Machine, CART and AdaBoost) are explored. Our recommendation is to use CART which is not only capable of achieving an accuracy of 99.9% but also up to about 2.9 times more efficient than the second best candidate (Naïve Bayesian).

1 Introduction

Conventional deep packet inspection (DPI) techniques are ineffective in analyzing encrypted traffic. Therefore, two different procedures could generally be used according to whether the inspected packets are encrypted or not. We first classify network packets into encrypted and unencrypted packets and then inspect only unencrypted ones in real time; encrypted ones are just recorded in log files for offline analysis. This approach might be helpful to improve the performance of intrusion detection systems by avoiding unnecessary efforts to analyze encrypted packets in their DPI engines. Moreover, the use of encryption is one of the important features for distinguishing bot traffic from normal traffic because payload encryption is a popularly used to hide bot communication [9]. Hence, detecting encrypted packets is becoming an essential part of intrusion detection systems.

To identify encrypted traffic, the most widely used techniques are pattern matching in packet payloads [21] and entropy analysis [7,13,20]. Although the entropy model is more effective for new botnet traffic, it also incurs both false positives and false negatives that cannot be ignored when a simple entropy-based approach is used for classification. To make matters worse, those approaches using the entropy estimation alone cannot deal with the distinction between encrypted and compressed traffic since both might have a high entropy measure [18]. In this paper, we will show that the entropy-based detection method performed very poorly on distinguishing encrypted traffic from compressed traffic through experiments with real datasets including a significant proportion of compressed packets (see Sect. 5).

© Springer International Publishing AG 2017
D. Choi and S. Guilley (Eds.): WISA 2016, LNCS 10144, pp. 54–65, 2017.
DOI: 10.1007/978-3-319-56549-1_5

Recently, some researchers [2,3] proposed a more promising approach using machine learning to overcome the limitation of simple threshold models in entropy analysis. However, their designs have mainly focused on developing classification models using flow based features rather than packet based features where temporal information such as inter-arrival time is required. Although the flow-based detection systems have advantage over the packet-based systems because payload inspection is not needed anymore for detecting bot communication [10], a long time interval is required to extract time-based flow features from the network traffic.

Unlike their approach, we aim to develop a real-time classifier even with a single packet (or a few packets). To achieve this goal, we narrow down the problem scope to detecting encrypted traffic only rather than botnet communication. Our proposed technique can be incorporated into a firewall as its pre-filter to screen candidates.

To demonstrate the effectiveness of our approach, we experimented with four well-known machine learning techniques (Naïve Bayesian, Support Vector Machine, CART and AdaBoost) compared with a simple entropy-based detection method. For experiments, we used a real traffic dataset (HTTP: 161,948, FTP: 1,309, Telnet: 205, SSH: 30,185 packets) collected from a honeypot. The experimental results showed that the proposed machine learning based detection methods significantly outperformed the simple entropy-based detection method. In particular, CART produced the best results, which is not only capable of achieving a F-measure of 0.997 but also up to about 2.9 times more efficient than the second best candidate (Naïve Bayesian). Moreover, since the results of CART algorithm can directly be used to generate a series of if-then rules from a binary decision tree representation, we highly recommend using CART for building a high-performance DPI system.

The rest of this paper is organized as follows. In Sect. 2, we survey related work in developing encrypted packet classification techniques. In Sect. 3, we present the proposed detection technique using a machine learning algorithm with randomness tests. In Sect. 4, we briefly explain the classification algorithms used in our experiments. Then, in Sect. 5, we evaluate their accuracy and performance by conducting experiments in real-world environments. Finally, we conclude in Sect. 6.

2   Related Work

A *botnet* is a network of compromised computers controlled by a remote attacker called *botmaster*, which is typically used for performing illegitimate activities such as distributed denial-of-service (DDoS) attacks, spam emails distribution. For botnet communication, the IRC protocol was the most widely used due to its simple construction. Recently, however, attackers are moving towards using encryption (from simple XOR [12] to sophisticated AES-256 [15]), which makes it much harder to detect their communication against firewalls and intrusion detection systems [16,20]. Thus detecting encrypted traffic becomes one of the most challenging issues in designing a bot detection tool.

Entropy-based classification is the most common method to distinguish encrypted parts from plaintexts. Lyda and Hamrock [13] used entropy analysis to identify encrypted and packed malware, but they only focused on offline executable files. Dorfinger et al. [7] proposed a classification method based on entropy estimation to detect encrypted traffic used for Skype and eDonkey. For each packet, their proposed system compares the entropy of the packet with the estimated entropy of uniformly distributed random payload of the same length. If the difference is greater than a pre-defined threshold, the packet is classified as unencrypted traffic. White et al. [19] revisited this problem through intensive experiments to classify opaque traffic including not only encrypted but also compressed communication. They also used entropy-based tests and demonstrated that their technique is able to identify opaque data with about 95% accuracy, on average, while examining less than 16 bytes of payload data. Zhang et al. [20] also proposed a similar technique using the entropy measure and showed that the proposed technique might be effectively deployed to prevent encrypted bot communication. However, those approaches had to ignore the difference between both encrypted and compressed traffic since both might have a similar level of entropy estimation. Wang et al. [18] addressed this limitation in using the entropy estimation alone for detecting encrypted contents and proposed an alternative metric to identify the distinction between encrypted and encoded/compressed data.

We extend their work into a more sophisticated model using machine learning algorithms and several randomness tests; while Wang et al. [18] empirically selected a threshold for the chi-square randomness test result, we build a detector with machine learning algorithms and several randomness tests to improve the accuracy of encrypted communication detection.

Although the idea of using machine learning algorithms is not new in the field of traffic classification, previous studies [1,3] focused on using flow based features rather than packet based features, which inherently requires an observation time interval to monitor time based flow features from the network traffic. The scenario for flow based classification is fundamentally distinct from the setting we explore in this work: for real-time analysis on the network, it is preferred to individually process every packet without requiring the maintenance of state for every connection.

3 Encryption Detection with Randomness Tests

The key idea is simple: When the proposed system receives a packet, the header and payload of the packet are first separated, and the randomness of the payload is analyzed by running several randomness tests. This is because the payload of a packet is only encrypted for hiding bot communication while its header is in the clear (see Fig. 1). Surely, in practical intrusion detection systems, packet header information is generally used before inspecting the payload of packets. The proposed method may be applied only to packets when it is difficult on the packet header alone to decide whether the packets are encrypted or not.

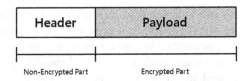

Fig. 1. A typical form of packet

With the randomness test results, we can determine the nature of the packet (i.e., the encrypted payload or not) using a classifier trained with data from previous test results. Unlike previous studies [7,13,20] using a pre-determined threshold of entropy alone, we use machine learning techniques to improve the accuracy of a classifier with the following three randomness tests that are commonly used, particularly for evaluating the randomness of pseudorandom number generation algorithms [17].

- **Entropy:** The Shannon entropy is a traditional estimator of measuring the unpredictability of an information stream. Let X be a random variable that takes on the possible values x_1, x_2, $\cdots$, x_n. Here, x_i is the ith byte value because we calculated the entropy in bytes. The Shannon entropy $H(X)$ is defined by the following formula:

$$H(X) = -\sum_{i=1}^{n} p(x_i) \log p(x_i) \tag{1}$$

  where $p(x_i)$ is the probability that $X = x_i$.

- **Chi-square test:** The chi-square distribution is used to test how well a sample fits a theoretical distribution (e.g., Poison distribution). Here, for ith byte value, the number of the observed values o_i is compared with that of expected values e_i from a uniform distribution. The chi-square distribution χ^2 is defined by the following formula:

$$\chi^2 = \sum_{i=1}^{n} \frac{(o_i - e_i)^2}{e_i} \tag{2}$$

  where n is the number of values.

- **Arithmetic mean:** The arithmetic mean can simply be calculated by summing all of the byte values in the tested data (i.e., a packet) and dividing by the number of those byte values. If the data are generated from a uniform distribution, the arithmetic mean should be about 127.5. The arithmetic mean A is defined by the following formula:

$$A = \frac{1}{n} \sum_{i=1}^{n} x_i \tag{3}$$

  x_i is the ith byte value in a packet.

The results of those randomness tests are used to construct a classifier to detect encrypted traffic. Not surprisingly, a classification method should be carefully selected based on constraints such as the desired level of accuracy, the time available for training and testing, and the nature of classification problems. The classification methods used in our experiments are described in the following section.

4   Applying Classification Methods

We select four different classification methods which are popularly used for many applications. We carried out a number of experiments to evaluate those classification methods and find the best performing one. This section introduces those classification methods as follows:

- **Naive Bayesian:** Naïve Bayesian (NB) classification [6] is one of the most successful learning algorithms for text classification. Based on the Bayes rule, which assumes conditional independence between classes, this algorithm attempts to estimate the conditional probabilities of classes given an observation. The joint probabilities of sample observations and classes are simplified because of the conditional independence assumption. While this Bayes rule assumption is often violated in practice, NB is known to perform well in many security applications such as spam email filtering.
- **Support Vector Machine:** Support Vector Machine (SVM) [5] is known as one of the best supervised learning techniques for classification with high dimensional feature space and small training set size. The idea is to find the optimal separating hyperplanes that classify data by maximising the geometric margin space between the classes' closest points. SVM is receiving great attention due to some excellent performance it has achieved on real-world applications [11].
- **Classification and Regression Trees:** Classification and Regression Trees (CART) [4] is an interesting non-parametric technique to build a binary decision tree based on historical data. CART constructs a binary tree by repetitively splitting the high dimensional space of the objects in the training set into subspaces so that the observations within each subspace are more homogeneous than the high dimensional space.
- **Adaptive Boosting Algorithm:** AdaBoost [8], short for "Adaptive Boosting", is an iterative process that tries to improve the classification results by learning the results from a set of classifiers (often referred to as "weak learners"), in that their weights are adaptively updated according to the errors in previous iterations. The essence of AdaBoost is to combine multiple weak classifiers for constructing a single strong classifier.

5   Experiments

The aim of our experiments was to demonstrate the feasibility and effectiveness of our approach, and determine the best performing classification method.

We tested real network traffic using the four classification methods described above (NB, SVM, CART and AdaBoost).

We collected real packets captured by a honeypot (taken from the "Capture the hacker 2013 competition") and filtered TCP packets only, which consist of 161,948 HTTP, 1,309 FTP, 205 Telnet and 30,185 SSH packets. For plaintexts, we used the packets for HTTP, FTP, and Telnet application protocols while we used only encrypted payload in SSH packets for ciphertexts. Figure 2 shows the distribution of packet sizes, respectively, for those datasets; the y axis is shown in log-scale for improved visualization.

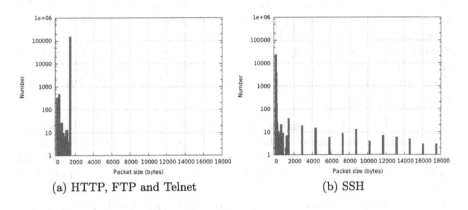

(a) HTTP, FTP and Telnet   (b) SSH

Fig. 2. Histogram of packet sizes in the datasets.

In terms of the packet size, we can see the differences between them; all packets for HTTP, FTP, and Telnet protocols are less than 2,000 bytes while a majority (about 93.6%) of packets for SSH protocol are less than 64 bytes long and large packets were sometimes used. We surmise that the default packet size differences in underlying protocols may explain this. The default Maximum Segment Size (MSS) of 1,460 bytes (which covers about 95.5% of our dataset) is generally used for HTTP, FTP, and Telnet protocols while the minimum packet size of 28 bytes is most popularly used for SSH protocol because the data exchanged might be mostly short commands for botnet communication [14]. Interestingly, the packets used in our experiments include a significant proportion (about 78.15%) of compressed ones (using either `gzip` or `bzip2`) in HTTP, FTP and Telnet packets (see Table 1).

Table 1. Proportions of content types in HTTP, FTP and Telnet packets

Compressed	Octet-stream	Others
78.15%	0.32%	21.53%

We assigned the ciphertexts with 'Positive' answers (P) and the plaintexts with 'Negative' answers (N). True Positive (TP), False Positive (FP), True Negative (TN), and False Negative (FN) can be summarized as below:

- TP: ciphertexts correctly classified as ciphertexts;
- FP: plaintexts incorrectly classified as ciphertexts;
- TN: plaintexts correctly classified as plaintexts;
- FN: ciphertexts incorrectly classified as plaintexts.

To evaluate the performance of classifiers, we use four measures as follows:

- **Accuracy**: the proportion of correctly classified packets; $(TP+TN)/(P+N)$
- **Precision**: the proportion of packets classified as ciphertexts that actually are ciphertexts; $(TP)/(TP+FP)$
- **Recall**: the proportion of ciphertexts that were accurately classified; $(TP)/(TP+FN)$
- **F-measure**: the harmonic mean of *precision* and *recall*; $(2 * Precision * Recall)/(Precision + Recall)$

We also measured the running time of the classifiers to show the relative efficiency of the classification methods. The classifiers were implemented using the `scikit-learn` library in Python. The experiments were conducted with an Intel Core i7 (3.60 GHz), running on the virtual machine of Ubuntu 14.04 LTS with 4 GB RAM.

For classification, we used a 10-fold (stratified) cross-validation where the training samples are partitioned into 10 equal-sized groups with similar class distributions. Table 2 shows the performance of the four classification methods. The running time for training and testing is presented as the mean time using the whole dataset in a group from the 10 independent experiments. Moreover, we compared the tested classification methods with the simple entropy-based detection to show the superiority of the machine learning based detection algorithms over the conventional detection technique. For entropy-based detection, a threshold was chosen to maximize F-measure for each training set.

Table 2. Performance of classification methods.

	Accuracy	Precision	Recall	F-measure	Training	Testing
NB	0.990	0.953	0.987	0.970	0.056 s	1.604 s
SVM	0.997	**0.998**	0.981	0.989	559.097 s	15.034 s
CART	**0.999**	0.997	0.996	**0.997**	0.528 s	0.560 s
AdaBoost	0.998	0.996	0.994	0.995	7.789 s	125.198 s
Entropy	0.159	0.157	**0.998**	0.272	**0.052 s**	**0.006 s**

Overall, except for the entropy-based detection used as a baseline, all methods performed well (see Table 2). The entropy-based detection produced the worst results (0.272 in F-measure). Probably, the performance of entropy-based detection was strongly affected by the significant proportion (about 78.15%) of compressed packets in the dataset. The results confirmed that the entropy estimation only is not sufficient to distinguish encrypted contents from compressed contents even though it is significantly faster than machine learning based detection algorithms in testing time.

Among machine learning based detection algorithms, CART not only produced the best accuracy results (about 0.999 in accuracy and 0.997 in F-measure), but was most efficient in testing (about 0.560 s) which is up to approximately 2.9 times better than the second best candidate (NB). Although AdaBoost also performed well in terms of accuracy and F-measure, when we consider how computationally expensive the testing phase of AdaBoost is (about 125.198 s), we would not recommend using AdaBoost. For the same reason, SVM is not suitable for detecting encrypted traffic in real-time. Therefore, we here focus only on the analysis of CART and NB.

Although the testing time of each classification method is relatively efficient compared with its training time, calculation of the three randomness scores (Entropy, Chi-square test, Arithmetic mean) for testing cannot be easily ignored where the running time of the calculation increases (linearly) with the size of packet observed. Thus, in terms of efficiency, it might be desirable to classify a packet with only a few (front) bytes of the packet instead of using all of the packet data. We performed additional experiments to discuss how the performance of classification methods may change with the size of observed part of the packet for testing and to identify the optimal size. Tables 3 and 4 show the results with variation in the size of the observed part of the packet.

Table 3. Classification results with the first k bytes of each packet.

k	NB		CART	
	Accuracy	F-measure	Accuracy	F-measure
1	0.843	0.001	0.843	0.001
4	0.843	0.000	0.843	0.004
16	0.646	0.248	0.842	0.014
32	0.681	0.362	0.962	0.868
64	0.962	0.869	0.983	0.947
100	0.969	0.893	0.996	0.986
All	0.990	0.970	0.999	0.997

In Table 3, we can see that two classification methods (CART and NB) still performed well even with only a part of the packet (when $k \geq 64$) rather than using all of the packet data. Although those methods produced poor performance results (<0.015) in F-measure with a very few bytes (when $k = 1, 4$ or 16), the detection accuracy of those classification methods dramatically increases when

Table 4. Running time for randomness tests with the first k bytes of each packet (μ: mean, σ: standard deviation). Byte, Entropy, Chi-sq., and Arith. represent the time for analyzing byte frequency distribution, entropy, Chi-square distribution and arithmetic mean, respectively.

k	Byte(μ)	Byte(σ)	Entropy(μ)	Entropy(σ)	Chi-sq.(μ)	Chi-sq.(σ)	Arith.(μ)	Arith.(σ)	Total(μ)	Total(σ)
1	0.018 ms	7.0e−8 ms	0.147 ms	9.2e−7 ms	0.073 ms	3.9e−7 ms	0.019 ms	7.0e−8 ms	0.258 ms	2.0e−6 ms
4	0.019 ms	6.0e−8 ms	0.148 ms	1.1e−6 ms	0.073 ms	3.7e−7 ms	0.019 ms	6.0e−8 ms	0.259 ms	2.2e−6 ms
16	0.019 ms	7.0e−8 ms	0.146 ms	1.2e−6 ms	0.073 ms	4.2e−7 ms	0.019 ms	7.0e−8 ms	0.257 ms	2.6e−6 ms
32	0.021 ms	8.0e−8 ms	0.154 ms	1.0e−6 ms	0.073 ms	3.8e−7 ms	0.019 ms	8.0e−8 ms	0.267 ms	2.2e−6 ms
64	0.023 ms	8.0e−8 ms	0.148 ms	1.1e−6 ms	0.073 ms	5.7e−7 ms	0.019 ms	7.0e−8 ms	0.263 ms	2.6e−6 ms
100	0.025 ms	2.5e−7 ms	0.147 ms	1.2e−6 ms	0.073 ms	4.8e−7 ms	0.019 ms	7.0e−8 ms	0.265 ms	2.9e−6 ms
All	0.10 6ms	2.3e−6 ms	0.148 ms	9.8e−7 ms	0.075 ms	3.8e−7 ms	0.021 ms	7.0e−8 ms	0.349 ms	4.7e−6 ms

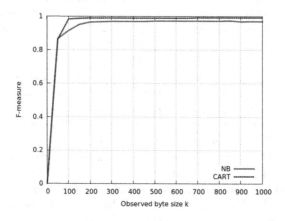

Fig. 3. F-measure of classifiers with randomly selected k bytes of each packet.

$k \geq 32$ (for CART) or $k \geq 64$ (for NB). Moreover, it also led to improvement in running time for randomness tests (see Table 4); the total running time of the randomness tests was reduced from 0.349 ms (millisecond) to 0.263 ms on average, which was significantly affected by the analysis of byte frequency distribution (Byte) rather than other tasks.

To avoid this detection strategy, an attacker's best response is to generate dummy plaintext data and add the data into the first k bytes of each packet if the attacker already knows the system parameter k in a detection system. Therefore it is not enough to simply observe the first k bytes of each packet. Alternatively, we consider using a randomized approach with k bytes randomly selected from the whole packet data. The experimental results in F-measure are shown in Fig. 3. Overall, CART produced the better results compared with NB. Also, we can see that the accuracy of two classification methods (CART and NB) was improved as k increased. In particular, both curves increase rapidly toward 1 until $k < 100$ and then tends to be smooth and flat when $k \geq 100$. This implies that it might be enough to use a randomly chosen part of a packet (e.g., with at least 100 bytes long) instead of using the whole packet data to speed up the detection test procedure for each packet.

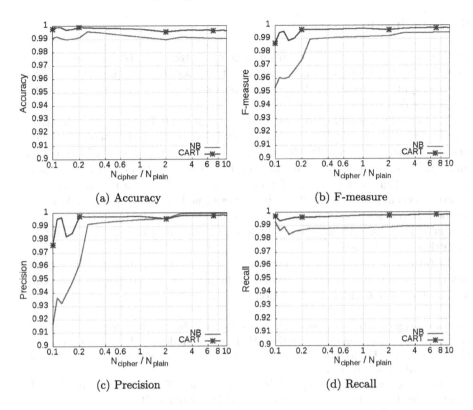

Fig. 4. Performance of classification methods with varying N_{cipher}/N_{plain} ratio.

To examine the influence of ratio of ciphertext (N_{cipher}) to plaintext (N_{plain}), we performed additional experiments with varying N_{cipher}/N_{plain} ratio by artificially controlling the number of generated encrypted packets. However, we still used the fixed ratio of plain to cipher packets. Figure 4 shows how the performance of classification methods were changed over the different ratio of N_{cipher}/N_{plain}.

Overall, two classification methods (CART and NB) are scalable with varying N_{cipher}/N_{plain} ratio except when the ratio of N_{cipher}/N_{plain} is less than 0.2. This is because those methods demonstrate a significant decrease in precision when the number of ciphertexts is greatly less than the number of plaintexts. Hence, we would not recommend using the proposed technique for such conditions. Our recommendation would still be to use CART except those cases, even though NB is slightly better than CART in terms of precision when the ratio of N_{cipher}/N_{plain} is greater than 2.

6 Conclusion

Distinguishing encrypted data from non-encrypted packets still remains an important research problem in the field of network security. We present a machine learning approach based on three randomness tests (Entropy, Chi-square, Arithmetic mean).

For performance evaluation, we used a total of 193,647 packets (163,462 plain and 30,185 encrypted). The packets ware tested with four machine learning based classification methods—Naïve Bayesian, Support Vector Machine, CART and AdaBoost—the simple entropy-based detection method to find the most proper classification method to detect encrypted traffic. The machine learning based detection methods significantly outperformed the entropy-based detection method. In particular, our recommendation would be to use CART that not only produced the best accuracy results (0.997 in F-measure) but was most efficient in testing (about 0.560 s).

In future work, we plan to increase the size of the dataset and investigate any changes in performance. It would also be interesting to deploy the proposed approach on a real intrusion detection system.

Acknowledgements. This research was supported by Institute for Information & communications Technology Promotion (IITP) grant funded by the Korea government (MSIP) (No. B0717-16-0116, Development of information leakage prevention and ID management for secure drone services).

This work was supported by the National Research Foundation of Korea (NRF) grant funded by the Korea government (No. 2014R1A1A1003707).

This research was supported by the MSIP(Ministry of Science, ICT and Future Planning), Korea, under the ITRC (Information Technology Research Center) support program (IITP-2016-R0992-16-1006) supervised by the IITP (Institute for Information & communications Technology Promotion).

This work was supported by Institute for Information & communications Technology Promotion(IITP) grant funded by the Korea government(MSIP) (No.R-20160222-002755, Cloud based Security Intelligence Technology Development for the Customized Security Service Provisioning).

References

1. Alshammari, R., Zincir-Heywood, A.N.: Investigating two different approaches for encrypted traffic classification. In: Proceedings of the 6th IEEE Annual Conference on Privacy, Security and Trust (2008)
2. Alshammari, R., Zincir-Heywood, A.N.: Generalization of signatures for SSH encrypted traffic identification. In: IEEE Symposium on Computational Intelligence in Cyber Security (2009)
3. Alshammari, R., Zincir-Heywood, A.N.: Can encrypted traffic be identified without port numbers, IP addresses and payload inspection? Comput. Netw. **55**(6), 1326–1350 (2011)
4. Breiman, L., Friedman, J., Stone, C.J., Olshen, R.A.: Classification and Regression Trees. CRC Press (1984)

5. Cristianini, N., Shawe-Taylor, J.: An introduction to support vector machines and other kernel-based learning methods. Cambridge University Press (2000)
6. Domingos, P., Pazzani, M.: On the optimality of the simple Bayesian classifier under zero-one loss. Mach. Learn. **29**(2–3), 103–130 (1997)
7. Dorfinger, P., Panholzer, G., John, W.: Entropy estimation for real-time encrypted traffic identification. In: Proceedings of the 3rd International Conference on Traffic Monitoring and Analysis (2011)
8. Freund, Y., Schapire, R.E.: A decision-theoretic generalization of on-line learning and an application to boosting. J. Comput. Syst. Sci. **55**(1), 119–139 (1997)
9. Gu, G., Yegneswaran, V., Porras, P., Stoll, J., Lee, W.: Active botnet probing to identify obscure command and control channels. In: Annual Computer Security Applications Conference (2009)
10. Haddadi, F., Le Cong, D., Porter, L., Zincir-Heywood, A.: On the effectiveness of different botnet detection approaches. In: Proceedings of the 11th International Conference on Information Security Practice and Experience (2015)
11. Hearst, M., Dumais, S., Osman, E., Platt, J., Scholkopf, B.: Support vector machines. IEEE Intell. Syst. Appl. **13**(4), 18–28 (1998)
12. Holz, T., Steiner, M., Dahl, F., Biersack, E., Freiling, F.: Measurements and mitigation of peer-to-peer-based botnets: a case study on storm worm. In: Proceedings of the 1st Usenix Workshop on Large-Scale Exploits and Emergent Threats (2008)
13. Lyda, R., Hamrock, J.: Using entropy analysis to find encrypted and packed malware. IEEE Secur. Privacy **5**(2), 40–45 (2007)
14. Ramachandran, A., Seetharaman, S., Feamster, N., Vazirani, V.: Fast monitoring of traffic subpopulations. In: Proceedings of the 8th ACM SIGCOMM Conference on Internet Measurement (2008)
15. Stover, S., Dittrich, D., Hernandez, J., Dietrich, S.: Analysis of the storm, nugache trojans: P2P is here. ;login: **32**(6) (2007)
16. Thuraisingham, B.: Data mining for security applications: Mining concept-drifting data streams to detect peer to peer botnet traffic. In: International Conference on Intelligence and Security Informatics (2008)
17. Walker, J.: ENT: a pseudorandom number sequence test program (2008). http://www.fourmilab.ch/random/
18. Wang, R., Shoshitaishvili, Y., Kruegel, C., Vigna, G.: Steal this movie - automatically bypassing DRM protection in streaming media services. In: Proceedings of the 22nd USENIX Conference on Security (2013)
19. White, A.M., Krishnan, S., Bailey, M., Monrose, F., Porras, P.: Clear and present data: opaque traffic and its security implications for the future. In: Proceedings of the Network and Distributed Systems Security Symposium. The Internet Society (2013)
20. Zhang, H., Papadopoulos, C., Massey, D.: Detecting encrypted botnet traffic. In: Conference on Computer Communications Workshops (2013)
21. Zhang, Y., Paxson, V.: Detecting backdoors. In: Proceedings of the 9th Conference on USENIX Security Symposium (2000)

Features for Behavioral Anomaly Detection of Connectionless Network Buffer Overflow Attacks

Ivan Homoliak[⊠], Ladislav Sulak, and Petr Hanacek

Faculty of Information Technology,
BUT, Bozetechova 1/2, 612 66 Brno, Czech Republic
{ihomoliak,xsula04,hanacek}@fit.vutbr.cz
http://www.fit.vutbr.cz/.en

Abstract. Buffer overflow (BO) attacks are one of the most danger-ous threats in the area of network security. Methods for detection of BO attacks basically use two approaches: signature matching against packets' payload versus analysis of packets' headers with the behavioral analysis of the connection's flow. The second approach is intended for detection of BO attacks regardless of packets' content which can be ciphered. In this paper, we propose a technique based on Network Behavioral Anom-aly Detection (NBAD) aimed at connectionless network traffic. A sim-ilar approach has already been used in related works, but focused on connection-oriented traffic. All principles of connection-oriented NBAD cannot be applied in connectionless anomaly detection. There is designed a set of features describing the behavior of connectionless BO attacks and the tool implemented for their offline extraction from network traffic dumps. Next, we describe experiments performed in the virtual network environment utilizing SIP and TFTP network services exploitation and further data mining experiments employing supervised machine learning (ML) and Naive Bayes classifier. The exploitation of services is performed using network traffic modifications with intention to simulate real net-work conditions. The experimental results show the proposed approach is capable of distinguishing BO attacks from regular network traffic with high precision and class recall.

Keywords: Buffer overflow · Connectionless traffic · SIP · TFTP UDP vulnerabilities · NBAD · Naive Bayes

1 Introduction

Buffer overflow attacks belong to the category of the most dangerous network attacks. They are typically used for the execution of an attack code remotely by overflowing a piece of memory. It occurs when a program attempts to write beyond the end of an array with the purpose of changing an instruction flow [5]. In the case of vulnerable application running with root privileges, the attacker

© Springer International Publishing AG 2017
D. Choi and S. Guilley (Eds.): WISA 2016, LNCS 10144, pp. 66–78, 2017.
DOI: 10.1007/978-3-319-56549-1_6

will also get root account permissions. As a result, the whole machine may be compromised, which can have very harmful consequences.

There exist various methods for detection of such attacks. One of the approaches is to analyze receiving data from traffic and to search for the known payload signatures of attacks. However, successful detection of unknown threats (zero-day), obfuscated attacks or encrypted data is restrained or not even possible. Also, the whole process can be very time-consuming in this approach. Another approach for detection of mentioned attacks is Network Behavioral Anomaly Detection (NBAD), which will be focused in this paper. NBAD is a technique used for analyzing network traffic without knowledge of transferring data, therefore problems mentioned above may be reduced noticeably. On the other hand, the possibility of evasion (false negatives) and denial of legitimate traffic (false positives) can be increased in NBAD [4].

A connection-oriented communication [7] includes the session initiation phase at the very beginning of each communication and the session destruction phase at the end of a session. TCP is representative of connection-oriented communication where it is possible to track the beginning and the end of a connection thanks to the presence of handshake and endshake. After the successful establishment of a TCP connection, the useful data are delivered and reconstructed to be in the same order as they are sent. Moreover, some protocols are able to determine the current state of connection-oriented communication, like in FTP, Telnet or Samba. It should be noted that some protocols are designed to be primarily connection-oriented, but they can be switched to connectionless mode, too.

This work is primarily focused on connectionless communication, because this problem has been omitted in the past [6,10] and there is little research primarily aimed at this problem. The typical representative of connectionless communication is UDP protocol which does not contain any session establishing or destruction, and thus poses a problem in the assignment of packets to particular connection records. Regarding NBAD, we propose a collection of features which describe the behavior of connectionless buffer overflow attacks in the way which enables us to distinguish between legitimate communications and attack ones. A tool for extraction of the designed features collection is proposed. Gathered data containing features of connections' records serve as the input for the ML process, which is a fundamental step in the data mining phase.

The paper is organized as follows. We describe related work with a focus on NBAD intrusion detection and ML based internet traffic classification in Sect. 2. Next, Sect. 3 characterizes proposed features with a description and categorization of them. Section 4 contains detailed information about our experiments performed in a virtual network environment as well as about vulnerabilities and exploits. In Sect. 5, we describe data processing and the analysis of our collected dataset. Section 6 presents a summary of achieved results and the last part – Sect. 7 – concludes the paper.

2   Related Work

Indeed, there exists hardly any research thoroughly dealing with up-to-date behavioral anomaly intrusion detection in connectionless network traffic. The reason can be the fact that prevalent amount of network services are primarily using TCP and, therefore, are more attractive for attackers. Another reason may be related with unavailable information about the beginning and end of the connectionless flow as discussed above.

2.1   NBAD in Connectionless Network Traffic

The first known work which performs behavioral-based network anomaly intrusion detection primarily aimed at connection-oriented traffic, but including connectionless too, is contained in paper [8]. The approach of this work simplifies the connectionless traffic by treating each UDP packet as one connection record and, therefore, misses all behavioral and statistical characteristics of related packets in the connectionless flow. Also, the data set of this work is not up-to-date. Latter related work [3] dealing with network intrusion detection including connectionless traffic is based on collecting of flows' statistics with accumulation of a concern index value which is assigned to host machines. When a concern index of a host is exceeded, an alert is raised. No results presenting performance of a designed system are available and there is not described any approach of determining a session establishment or destruction.

2.2   NBAD in Connection-Oriented Network Traffic

There exist several papers which discuss and propose various non-payload based behavioral anomaly intrusion detection models for connection-oriented traffic. Most of them evaluate their performance on DARPA dataset. DARPA dataset was considered useful for evaluation of intrusion detectors in 2008 [14], but it is arguably these days. Examples of works using DARPA dataset include: PHAD [9], ADAM [2], APAN [13] etc.

PHAD [9] is anomaly detection algorithm that learns the normal ranges of values for each packet header field at data link, network, and transport layers. It detects 72 of 201 instances (29 of 59 types) of attacks with only approx. 10 false positives per day. It detects some attacks (6 types) based on anomalous IP addresses. ADAM [2] is based on Naive Bayes classifier as supervised machine learning model. It monitors port numbers, IP addresses, subnets, and TCP state. The paper presents its successful improvement using pseudo-Bayes estimators with aim on reduction of false positives and detection of new attacks. Evaluation is performed on DARPA 1998 training data and tested on DARPA 1999. Shin et al. [13] introduced a novel probabilistic approach which uses Markov chain for probabilistic modeling of abnormal events in network traffic. Performance of the proposed approach was evaluated by a set of experiments using the DARPA 2000 dataset. It achieved a high detection performance while representing level of attacks in stages. Bayesian Neural Networks classifier designed in [1] is discussed to be a part of a complete Intrusion Detection System. However, performed experiments were primarily aimed at network traffic classification. The work uses Moore's 2005 datasets discussed in [10]. The paper [6] describes a formal definition of the ASNM features describing various properties of the connection-oriented communication intended for network anomaly intrusion detection. Later, performance is evaluated using the Naive Bayes classifier and CDX 2009 dataset [12]. In contrast to discussed group of non-payload based NBAD there exists group of NBAD whose representatives analyze application payload of packets too, but this group is not considered as related to our approach.

2.3   Network Traffic Classification

One of the related research branches is dealing with network traffic classification. The representative of connectionless traffic classification based on statistical properties of the flows is designed in [16]. The authors do not define handling of beginning and end of the UDP flows, but on the other hand, they mention the UDP flow has to contain at least two packets. Another work which includes connectionless & connection-oriented traffic classification using statistical approach is work [15] dealing with online game traffic classification methods. The authors of the paper define end of the UDP flow as 60 s timeout in the sending of packets. Next example of work in connection-oriented & connectionless traffic classification group is work [11] which uses Linear and Quadratic Discriminate Analysis. A.Moore et al. proposed behavioral-based features for network traffic classification called discriminators [10]. Discriminators designed in this work perform analysis of connection-oriented network traffic only [1]. The authors discuss connectionless classification as future work, but they never performed it because of not easily identified beginning and end of the UDP flow.

3   Design of Features for Connectionless Communications

A collection of features designed for describing the characteristics of connectionless network buffer overflow attacks' behavior is detailed in this section. The input serving for computation of the features include information from packets' headers, packets' lengths and counts, time-arrival measurements and various information about simultaneous traffic, too. Features themselves are computed on UDP connections, because it is the most common connectionless protocol running at the transport layer of the TCP/IP protocol stack. Some of the other basic protocols, such as TCP and ICMP, are processed as well, but only for providing some auxiliary information about the behavior of a given UDP connection. We considered the nature and principles of two UDP based network services (SIP and TFTP) when designing and especially improving the feature set.

3.1   Categorization of the Features

There are 117 features defined and categorized into six groups according to their principles and input data used for their computation:

(a) **Data from packets' headers.** These features are computed from information of network and transport layers headers of UDP packets. Some fields of packets' headers, like MAC and IP addresses, are not taken into account because our NBAD approach is based on analysis of statistical and behavioral properties of UDP flows without considering any host-localization information. Also, port numbers are processed, as they are useful in another group of features.

(b) **Data from packets' counts and sizes.** This category contains various features which are based on statistical information considering the number of packets and payload lengths taken from data packets only. A data packet refers to any packet with a non-zero length application layer's payload.

(c) **Analysis of fragmented packets.** This category is a bit problematic in connectionless traffic because in some cases there is not a 100% assurance that a given fragmented packet belongs to the connection assigned to it. Therefore, only a few features are designed in this category.

(d) **Data from time slope and arrival time of packets.** Analysis of such data makes sense in the field of buffer overflow attacks, because malicious communication does not have to be regular and stable. On the other hand, it is arguable, because the time slope of any particular communication can have various characteristics which depend on the actual network traffic situation or possible obfuscation. Therefore, we will perform network traffic modifications of executed BO attacks in order to simulate real conditions, and thus this group of features will not be favored in data mining phase.

(e) **Analysis of quartile time segments.** This category is basically just a slightly sophisticated version of the previous one. It represents extraction of various features over 4 time segments (quartiles) for a period of each connection's duration.

(f) **Data from related connections in specified time context.** These features examine connections started before the beginning, during the progress and after the end of an analyzed UDP connection. It includes, for example, the presence of TCP connections, ICMP packets, and the detection of destination port change in the time context of analyzed connection. The time context is specified to include packets of connections occurred 30 s before beginning and 30 s after end of analyzed UDP connection. Connections related to the analyzed one are restricted by the time context. This category was designed in order to be useful when backdoor communication occurs or there exists a hidden relation between analyzed communication and another one.

The enumeration of categorized features is depicted in Tables 1 and 2. Almost all the features listed in the tables consider packets from both directions of a connection together during their computation. Exceptional features which are computed for each direction separately are marked in the tables by an asterisk.

Table 1. Summary of designed features (part 1/2)

Source	Group	Features
Type of Service	(a)	• Mode,[a] median,[a] mean[a]
Time to Live	(a)	• Minimum,[a] maximum,[a] sum,[a] median,[a] mode,[a] • Mean,[a] standard deviation[a]
Port numbers	(a)	• Source and destination port numbers
Packet counting	(b)	• The number of all incoming packets,[a] • The number of all outgoing packets,[a] • The ratio of incoming and outgoing packets, • The number of data packets, • The number of non-data packets, • The ratio of data packets and non-data packets counts
Payload lengths	(b)	• Sum, mode, median, mean, standard deviation
Fragmentation	(c)	• The number of fragmented packets, • The number of non-fragmented packets, • The ratio of fragmented and non-fragmented packets counts, • Sum of fragmented packet payload lengths, • The ratio of non-fragmented and fragmented packets' payload lengths
Packets' IAT	(d)	• Minimum,[a] maximum,[a] median,[a] • Mean,[a] Standard deviation[a]

[a]Computed separately for each direction.

The quartile-time flow analysis group contains features regarding one quartile only, but actually, the features are computed on all 4 quartiles. One of the most important issues taken into account during designing and improving features set is a connection searching mechanism which has to consider the fact that there is no exact sign of connections' boundaries in connectionless traffic. Therefore, we created a mechanism based on a time-out value for determining the end of each connection. The beginning of each connection is simply determined by occurrence of a packet with flow parameters (ports, IPs) not contained in the current list of running connections. It turned out that the number of found connections is very sensitive about the time-out value. For example, using our further dataset with the value of 30 s resulted in 900 connections being found, while using the value 180 s resulted in 500 connections being found. The feature extraction process also provided different values in both cases. Therefore, according to some of the Linux-based operating systems[1], Netgear VPN Firewall[2] and MikroTik[3] devices, we decided to utilize an approach respecting the following statements:

---

[1] http://www.iptables.info/en/connection-state.html.

[2] http://documentation.netgear.com/fvx538/enu/202-10062-08/pdfs/FullManual. pdf.

[3] https://www.mikrotik.com/testdocs/ros/2.8/ip/conserv.php.

Table 2. Summary of designed features (part 2/2)

Source	Group	Features
Transfer time	(d)	• Duration of connection, • Bytes per second, • The sum of time without data packets transfer, • The sum of time without data packets transfer – Included into the sum only if higher than 2000 ms, • The ratio of two above features
Quartile-time segments	(e)	• Minimum, maximum, median, mode, mean and standard deviation of Ethernet data lengths, • Ratio of means of Ethernet packets' data length in one quartile and the whole connection, • The number of all incoming packets,[a] • The number of all outgoing packets,[a] • The number of incoming data packets,[a] • The number of outgoing data packets,[a] • The ratio of incoming and outgoing packets counts, • The ratio of incoming and outgoing data packets counts
Related connections	(f)	• Occurrence of at least 1 following TCP packet, • Occurrence of at least 1 following ICMP packet, • Port change detected in the related connection, • The number of previous related connections, • The number of following related connections
Consequent connections	(f)	• The number of packets, • The mean of packets' payload lengths, • The sum of packets' payload lengths, • The sum of packets' sizes, • The mean of packets' sizes, • Standard deviation of packet sizes, • Bytes per second

[a]Computed separately for each direction.

– if the transfer is in progress in one direction only, then the time-out is set to 30 s, as per default,
– if at least 1 packet occurred in the opposite direction, then the value is set to 180 s and the connection is now considered to be established.

4 Network Traffic Simulation Experiments

Experiments were performed in a virtual network environment and were aimed at collecting a dataset containing UDP network buffer overflow attacks. The *VirtualBox*[4] tool was used for safe and legal network vulnerability exploitation.

---

[4] https://www.virtualbox.org/.

The simple scheme of network infrastructure that we used is illustrated in Fig. 1. The only vulnerable virtual machine which was running under operating system Windows XP with Service Pack 3 was utilized. *Wireshark*[5] tool was used for capturing network traffic between the legitimate machine and attacker's machine – the one with operating system Ubuntu 14.10. The Windows XP machine was equipped with vulnerable applications and the firewall was disabled on it. A snapshot of the machine was taken after its initial setup, which served for a quick recovery after successful exploitation of the machine.

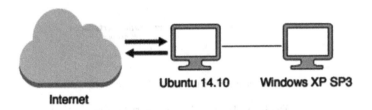

Fig. 1. Network scheme of exploitation environment

Exploits and some vulnerable applications associated with them were obtained by a tool which had been designed for this purpose. A scheme of the tool is illustrated in Fig. 2. *CVE Parser* component builds a relational database from data sheets available at nvd.nist.gov. Consequently, *Vulnerable SW & Exploits Scraper* component utilizes the database by queries specifying UDP buffer overflow vulnerabilities with a high impact score. Then, fetched information is used for web scraping in a public database of exploits *exploit-db*[6] resulting in the download of exploits and vulnerable applications if they are available. We observed that the number of UDP network vulnerabilities present at nvd.nist.gov and exploit-db is not so high as in the case of TCP. Except for exploits downloaded from exploit-db, we used *Metasploit* framework[7] for some attack executions, too. As a result, we successfully executed 223 buffer overflow attacks, performed on various SIP and TFTP network services, which resulted into 433 UDP connection records in total. The attacks utilized various network traffic modifications: spreading out packets in time; segmentation & fragmentation; changing of packets' order; simulation of unreliable network channel; packets' loss; packets' duplication as well as their combinations. The summary of vulnerable applications together with CVEs are listed in Table 6 of Appendix.

Also, we collected legitimate network traffic from several public sources like *pcapr.net*[8] and *wireshark.org*[9] as well as from campus network environment. The final dataset is summarized in Table 3.

---

[5] https://www.wireshark.org/download.html.

[6] https://www.exploit-db.com/.

[7] http://www.rapid7.com/products/metasploit/.

[8] http://pcapr.net/home.

[9] https://wiki.wireshark.org/SampleCaptures.

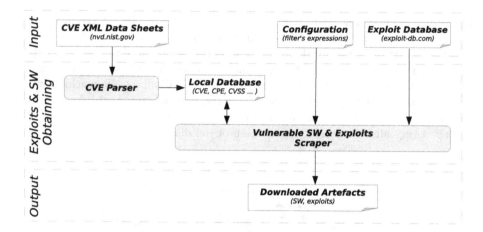

Fig. 2. Collection of exploits and vulnerable SW

Table 3. Testing dataset distribution

Network service	Count of UDP Records		
	Legitimate	Attacks	Summary
TFTP	52	356	408
SIP	65	77	142
Other UDP Traffic	5012	n/a	5012
Summary	5129	433	5562

5   Data Processing and Analysis

Collected dataset was used as an input for the data mining process. A new tool was designed to extract proposed features' values for each UDP communication record. The tool is implemented in Python 2.7 using library *dpkt*[10] for parsing of packet headers. The scheme in Fig. 3 illustrates the whole process which consists of the following three parts:

- The upper segment represents the input of the whole process. It contains files with captured network traffic, which was collected during a simulation of attacks and legitimate communications. Another part of this segment serves for obtaining ground truth (expert knowledge) from metadata of each connection. The ground truth provides information about the type of communication (attack or legitimate) and identification of vulnerability (CVE-ID). Directory structure has been designed specifically for this purpose as well as metadata included in the input with additional files.
- The middle segment performs data processing. The *Communication Extractor* module executes parsing of tcpdump files. It also aggregates UDP packets from

---

[10] https://code.google.com/p/dpkt/.

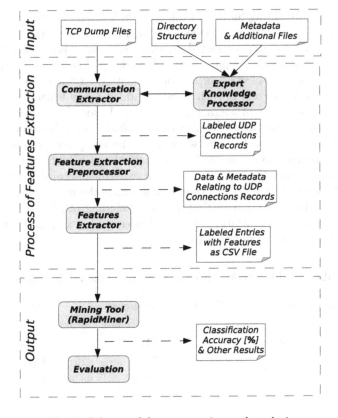

Fig. 3. Scheme of data processing and analysis

input network traffic into connection records. Then, with the use of *Expert Knowledge Processor*, each connection record is labeled by all necessary data. Such objects are passed to *Feature Extraction Preprocessor*, which prepares some of the embedded data for easier and faster processing. The last module in this segment is *Features Extractor* which performs the extraction process itself on each UDP connection record and outputs the CSV file.

- The bottom segment illustrates the mining and assessment process. It produces results based on data stored in the CSV file. In this work we use *Rapid-Miner*[11] tool for machine learning process and for evaluation purposes.

6   Summary of the Results

The purpose of this stage is to perform supervised classification in order to evaluate discrimination properties of proposed features by analyzing feedback of a classifier. All experiments were performed by the Naive Bayes classifier

---

[11] https://rapidminer.com/products/studio/.

employing kernel weighting function for feature-independent estimation of value density distribution, which is considered as non-parametric estimation model. Considering our testing dataset distribution, 5-fold cross validation method was selected for all classification experiments. We performed Forward Feature Selection (FFS) method for selection of the best features. FFS started to run with an empty set of features and in each iteration added a new feature contributing by the best improvement of average recall of all classes. The average recall of all classes was computed using the underlying 5-fold cross validation evaluating the Naive Bayes classifier. In FFS, we allowed the acceptance of one iteration without improvement, as we wanted to alleviate the possibility of the selection process becoming stuck in local extremes. Our experiments consisted of two executions of the FFS. The first execution took as input the whole testing dataset. The second one took as input testing dataset excluding other UDP traffic. We performed only little optimization of Naive Bayes model, and in the result, set fixed bandwidth of kernel function to 0.1.

Table 4. FFS with 5-fold cross validation of the whole dataset

Classification accuracy: 99.75% ± 0.13%		True class		Precision
		Legitimate	Attacks	
Predicted	Legitimate	5122	7	99.86%
Class	Attacks	7	426	98.38%
Recall		99.86%	98.38%	$F_1 = 98.38\%$

The performance result of the first FFS experiment is depicted in Table 4. The confusion matrix obtained in this experiment shows high precision and recall of both classes. Note that F_1 notation represents $F\text{-}measure_1$ which equally balances precision and recall measures for positive class (Attacks).

We excluded other traffic from the second execution of FFS, and thus validated discrimination properties of our features only for TFTP and SIP traffic. The associated confusion matrix is depicted in Table 5. Comparing the result of this experiments to the previous one, we can see that better discrimination property between malicious and legitimate UDP traffic was achieved. Thus, we can observe that explicit training data of specific service comprised of both malicious

Table 5. FFS with 5-fold cross validation of all SIP and TFTP traffic

Classification accuracy: 99.82% ± 0.36%		True class		Precision
		Legitimate	Attacks	
Predicted	Legitimate	117	1	99.15%
Class	Attacks	0	432	100.00%
Recall		100.00%	99.77%	$F_1 = 99.88\%$

and legitimate instances provides a better performance results than training data containing only representatives of one class.

7   Conclusion

The main objective of this work is to design a non-payload based collection of features describing statistical, behavioral and contextual characteristics of connectionless network traffic aimed at anomaly detection of buffer overflow attacks. The work also deals with the connection searching problem taking into consideration the fact that there is no exact sign of the connections' boundaries in connectionless traffic. This problem is resolved using a time-out approach inspired by existing devices and Unix based operating systems.

The performance of the designed feature set is evaluated by Naive Bayes classifier and 5-fold cross validation method. The summary of the presented results shows that our feature set is successfully utilized in classification of UDP network traffic into malicious and legitimate classes.

Acknowledgments. 'This article was created within the project Reliability and Security in IT (FIT-S-14-2486) and supported by The Ministry of Education, Youth and Sports from the National Programme of Sustainability (NPU II); project IT4Innovations excellence in science - LQ1602.

A   Appendix

Table 6. Vulnerable UDP network services

Application	Version	CVE[a]	Attacks
Tftpd32	≤2.21	2002-2226	3
TFTP Server TFTPDWIN	0.4.2	2006-4948	38
3Com TFTP Service	2.0.1	2006-6183	19
Allied Telesyn TFTP	2.0	2006-6184	37
Quick TFTP Pro	2.1 & 2.2	2008-1610	36
TFTPUtil GUI	1.4.5	2010-2028	19
Serva 32 TFTP	2.1.0	2013-0145	18
Distinct TFTP	3.10	2012-6664	17
SIPfoundry's sipXezPhone	0.35a	2006-3524	18
SIPfoundry's sipXphone	2.6.0.27	2006-3524	18
Overall number of attacks			223

[a]http://cve.mitre.org/cve/identifiers/index.html

References

1. Auld, T., Moore, A.W., Gull, S.F.: Bayesian neural networks for internet traffic classification. IEEE Trans. Neural Netw. **18**(1), 223–239 (2007)
2. Barbara, D., Wu, N., Jajodia, S.: Detecting novel network intrusions using bayes estimators. In: SDM, pp. 1–17. SIAM (2001)
3. Copeland III., J.A.: Flow-based detection of network intrusions, US Patent 7,185,368 (2007)
4. Corona, I., Giacinto, G., Roli, F.: Adversarial attacks against intrusion detection systems: taxonomy, solutions and open issues. Inf. Sci. **239**, 201–225 (2013)
5. Cowan, C., Wagle, P., Pu, C., Beattie, S., Walpole, J.: Buffer overflows: attacks and defenses for the vulnerability of the decade. In: DARPA Information Survivability Conference and Exposition (DISCEX 2000), Proceedings, vol. 2, pp. 119–129. IEEE (2000)
6. Homoliak, I., Barabas, M., Chmelar, P., Drozd, M., Hanacek, P.: ASNM: advanced security network metrics for attack vector description. In: Proceedings of the 2013 International Conference on Security & Management, pp. 350–358. Computer Science Research, Education, and Applications Press (2013)
7. ISO Standard IS 8072: Information Processing Systems - Open Systems Interconnection - Transport Service Definition. Technical report, International Organization for Standardization (1986)
8. Lee, W., Stolfo, S.J.: Data mining approaches for intrusion detection. In: Usenix Security (1998)
9. Mahoney, M.V., Chan, P.K.: PHAD: packet header anomaly detection for identifying hostile network traffic (2001)
10. Moore, A.W., Zuev, D., Crogan, M.: Discriminators for use in flow-based classification. Technical report, Intel Research, Cambridge (2005)
11. Roughan, M., Sen, S., Spatscheck, O., Duffield, N.: Class-of-service mapping for QoS: a statistical signature-based approach to IP traffic classification. In: Proceedings of the 4th ACM SIGCOMM Conference on Internet Measurement, pp. 135–148. ACM (2004)
12. Sangster, B., OConnor, T., Cook, T., Fanelli, R., Dean, E., Adams, W.J., Morrell, C., Conti, G.: Toward instrumenting network warfare competitions to generate labeled datasets. In: Proceedings of the 2nd Workshop on Cyber Security Experimentation and Test (CSET 2009) (2009)
13. Shin, S., Lee, S., Kim, H., Kim, S.: Advanced probabilistic approach for network intrusion forecasting and detection. Expert Syst. Appl. **40**(1), 315–322 (2012)
14. Thomas, C., Sharma, V., Balakrishnan, N.: Usefulness of DARPA dataset for intrusion detection system evaluation. In: SPIE Defense and Security Symposium, p. 69730G. International Society for Optics and Photonics (2008)
15. Williams, N., Zander, S., Armitage, G.: Evaluating machine learning methods for online game traffic identification. Centre for Advanced Internet Architectures, C 60410 (2006). http://caia.swin.edu.au/reports
16. Zander, S., Nguyen, T., Armitage, G.: Automated traffic classification and application identification using machine learning. In: The IEEE Conference on Local Computer Networks, 30th Anniversary, pp. 250–257. IEEE (2005)

A Behavior-Based Online Engine for Detecting Distributed Cyber-Attacks

Yaokai Feng[1](✉), Yoshiaki Hori[2], and Kouichi Sakurai[1]

[1] Kyushu University, Fukuoka, Japan
fengyk@ait.kyushu-u.ac.jp, sakurai@csce.kyushu-u.ac.jp
[2] Saga University, Saga, Japan
hori@cc.saga-u.ac.jp

Abstract. Distributed attacks have reportedly caused the most serious losses in recent years. Here, distributed attacks means those attacks conducted collaboratively by multiple hosts. How to detect distributed attacks has become one of the most important topics in the cyber security community. Many detection methods have been proposed, each of which, however, has its own weak points. For example, detection performance of information theory based methods strongly depends on the information theoretic measures and signature-based methods suffer from the fact that they can deal with neither new kinds of attacks nor new variants of existing attacks. Recently, behavior-based method has been attracting great attentions from many researchers and developers and it is thought as the most promising one. In behavior-based approaches, normal behavior modes are learned/extracted from past traffic data of the monitored network and are used to recognize anomalies in the future detection. In this paper, we explain how to implement an online behavior-based engine for detecting distributed cyber-attacks. Detection cases of our engine are also introduced and some actual attacks/incidents have been captured by our detection engine.

Keywords: Cyber security · Distributed attacks · Behavior-based detection

1 Introduction

Both the frequency of cyber-attacks and the damages caused by them have increased greatly in recent years, despite many approaches for avoiding and detecting attacks have been proposed. The basic reason for this is that the technologies used by attackers have also become more and more sophisticated. The most of modern sophisticated attacks are conducted collaboratively by many hosts. Such attacks are called distributed cyber-attacks.

1.1 Distributed Cyber-Attacks

A typical example of distributed attacks is distributed denial-of-service (DDoS) attack, in which many compromised systems (called bots) send a large amount

© Springer International Publishing AG 2017
D. Choi and S. Guilley (Eds.): WISA 2016, LNCS 10144, pp. 79–89, 2017.
DOI: 10.1007/978-3-319-56549-1_7

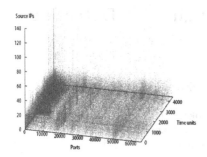
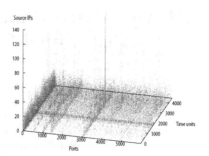

Fig. 1. Traffic data distribution.   **Fig. 2.** Locally enlarged image.

of accesses to the target. The network bandwidth and/or the computer resources may be consumed heavily (even exhaustedly) and the target is forced to deny services even to legitimate users. Distributed attacks have reportedly caused the most serious losses in recent years [1]. It was reported that DDoS attacks could expose 40% of businesses to losses of 100,000 or more an hour at peak times [2].

In order to visualize distributed attacks, we investigated all the TCP packets sent to the /24 darknet of our campus network in one month. There are 2,187,086 TCP packets in total, which are visualized in Fig. 1. In this figure, the x-axis denotes the destination TCP ports (0-65535), the y-axis is the series of the time units (one time unit=10 min) and the z-axis indicates the number of the unique source IP addresses in one time unit. Figure 2 is a locally enlarged one. From Fig. 1, we can see that, at a specific time unit, the number of the unique source hosts accessed some destination port greatly and suddenly increased, which is obviously a suspicious distributed attack.

1.2 Existing Cyber-Attack Detection Technologies

To detect cyber-attacks, many approaches have been proposed, including signature-based methods [3,12–14], volume-based methods [15,16,27], histogram-based methods [4,5], and so on. However, it is well-known that signature-based methods are not efficient for new variants and new kinds of attacks, because they can only detect the anomalies stored in a pre-prepared database. Volume-based methods need to determine the thresholds in advance, which is obviously not easy in most applications. In histogram-based methods, many statistic histograms are built using clean past data and each of the histograms is mapped into one point in a high-dimensional feature space. Then the smallest bounding boxes of those points are regarded as the normal region and are used to detect anomalies. This method, however, often has very high false negative rates [6]. And, clean past traffic data are collected, which is not easy, even is impossible for most cases. At the same time, several methods based on information theory have also been proposed [7,8]. Such methods suffer from the following weak points: their performance is highly dependent on the choice of the information theoretic measure; they are efficient only when a significantly large number of anomalies exist in the data and it is difficult to associate an anomaly score with a test instance [9]. Kim et al. The work [10] proposed a method for finding scan attacks and TCP SYN flood attacks by detecting change-points based on the characteristics of the packets. The session information based on the actions of communication protocols such as TCP and UDP was also used to detect scan attacks [11].

1.3 Behavior-Based Detection

Behavior-based cyber-attack detection, briefly speaking, is such methods that attacks are detected using normal behavior-modes (hereafter normal modes) extracted from past traffics. That is, anomalies are detected by comparing the real-time traffic patterns with normal nodes.

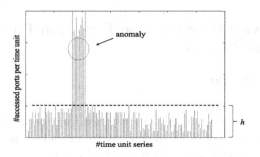

Fig. 3. Example of behavior-based methods.

Figure 3 shows an example of normal modes. In this figure, the horizontal axis represents a series of time units while the vertical axis denotes, for example, the number of unique source hosts who accessed a monitored port in the corresponding time unit. Roughly, h can be regarded as the normal range of the number of unique source hosts accessed the monitored port in one time unit. The traffic in the circle is seemingly an anomaly. Obviously, how to extract correct or roughly correct normal modes from past traffic data is a critical challenge. If we can extract normal mode from past traffic of the monitored network over a relatively long history period, a reasonable result can be obtained. The behavior-based detection has at least the following four strong points.

1. The threshold for distinguishing anomalies from the normal traffic is automatically extracted from the past traffic. That is, we no longer need to decide it manually in advance.
2. The extracted normal modes can reflect the features of the specific monitored networks. This is important because the network traffics in different organizations are perhaps very different from each other.
3. New kinds and new variants of attacks are also able to be detected.

4. Detection is fast because the detection process is only a simple value-comparison between the real-time traffic patterns and the extracted normal mode.

1.4 Our Contributions

1. A behavior-based detection engine for distributed cyber-attacks.
2. This detection engine works in online mode and utilizes a parameterless algorithm with the help of an evaluation function for extracting normal modes.
3. A method to give the alerts quickly even when the time unit is long.
4. A method to decrease the repeated alerts.
5. A concept of global alerts and our detection engine can publish not only the local alerts but also the global alerts.
6. Our detection engine is running in real environment and has successfully captured several actual cyber-attacks.

2 Our Behavior-Based Online Detection Engine of Distributed Attacks

2.1 Problem Definition

A behavior-based detection engine is designed and accomplished in this study. In this engine, all the destination ports are monitored separately and an alert will be given if the number of the unique source hosts accessed some port in a time unit increases greatly and suddenly. Figure 4 shows our scenario.

2.2 General Idea

The normal modes are automatically extracted from past traffic data of the monitored network and are used to find anomalies. The users do no longer need to give predefined thresholds. Moreover, our engine is running in online mode, which is necessary for most applications. That is, the real-time traffic stream

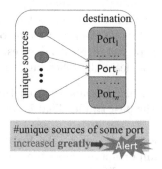

Fig. 4. The destination ports are monitored one by one.

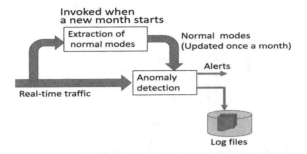

Fig. 5. General idea.

is flowing continuously to the engine and the detection results (alerts) are also published right away once an anomaly has been detected. Moreover, not only the detected alerts but also some important statistical data related to the alerts are logged.

Obviously, the extracted normal modes should not be immutable. That is, they must be updated frequently to reflect the new situation. In our detection engine, the traffic data from the 1st to 28th of the previous month are used to extract the normal mode. For example, when we begin to detect the traffic of Jan. 2016, the traffic data from Dec. 1, 2015 to Dec. 28, 2015 are used to extract the normal mode and the extracted normal mode will be valid until the end of Jan. 2016. That means that, when a new month starts, the learning algorithm is invoked to update the normal mode. Figure 5 is our general idea.

2.3   General Flow

Our detection engine consists of the following four steps.

Step 1. Collecting traffic data for extracting the normal mode. This is done separately for each of the destination ports and spanning a long time period (e.g., four weeks).

Step 2. Building frequency distributions. For each of the monitored destination ports, a frequency distribution is built on the number of the unique source hosts that accessed this port in a time unit. Figure 6 shows an example. In the horizontal axis, the number of unique source hosts is divided into bins, while the vertical axis denotes the number of time units. That is, in how many time units the number of unique source hosts drops to the range indicated by the corresponding bin.

Step 3. Extracting normal behavior modes from the frequency distributions. In Fig. 5, the small bins or bin-group located on far-right from the largest group are regarded as outliers (the anomalies in the past traffics). After all the outliers have been discarded, the x-axis range of the remaining bins is regarded as the normal mode. The normal mode of a destination port indicates the range of the number of the unique source hosts accessing this port in one time unit. Obviously,

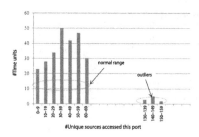

Fig. 6. Frequency distribution and behavior mode.

the biggest challenge and one of the core issues in the detection engine is how to extract correct (or roughly correctly) normal mode from a frequency distribution.

Step 4. Detecting possible distributed attacks using the normal behavior modes. Concretely, in the current time unit, the unique source hosts of every destination port are counted separately. Once a time unit has finished, the counted number of every destination port is compared with its normal mode. An alert is given if the former increased greatly, which indicates that a distributed attack has possibly occurred for this port. Moreover, according to the comparison result, the alert can be associated with a score (attack level), indicating the relative scale of this attack.

2.4 Algorithm for Automatically Extracting Normal Modes

An algorithm for extracting normal mode from past traffic was proposed in our previous study [17]. In this algorithm, two parameters indicating area-threshold and distance-threshold need to be predefined. However, determining the two parameters is not an easy issue for real applications. After that, we proposed an extraction algorithm utilizing an evaluation function [26], in which no parameters are needed.

For one frequency distribution (an example is shown in Fig. 6), the end-point of every bin is regarded as a candidate of the extracting result. Each of the candidates is given a score by a evaluation function and the candidate having the lowest score is reported as the final extracting result. In this way, the extracting result can be decided according to the frequency distribution itself, or say, according to the dataset distribution. Thus, parameters are no longer needed.

The frequency distribution can be denoted by $(f_1, f_2, ..., f_n)$, where f_i $(1 \leq i \leq n)$ is the y-value of the ith bin ; n is the index of the right-most non-zero bin. In addition, the candidates of the extracting result are denoted by $\{r_1, r_2, ..., r_n\}$, where r_i $(1 \leq i \leq n)$ is the x-value of the end position of the ith bin. For example, r_4 is 39 in Fig. 6.

This proposal is based on the basic consideration that, when a bin is examined whether or not it should be discarded as an outlier, its y-value and its distance from the origin should be taken into account. That is, the less its y-value is and the farther it is from the origin, the more the possibility that it is regarded as an outlier should be. If a bin should be regarded as an outlier then, all the bins located its right-hand are also thought as outliers at the same time. Thus, when one bin is checked to decide if it should be regarded as an outlier, all the bins at its right-hand should also be taken into consideration. Based on these considerations, the evaluation function for the candidate r_i $(1 \leq i \leq n)$ is designed as below.

$$Score(r_i) = \frac{\sum_{q=i}^{n} sb(f_q)}{n-i} = \frac{\sum_{q=i}^{n} \frac{f_q}{q}}{n-i}.$$

In this equation, f_q/q is the local score of the q_{th} bin, which considers the current bin only. The final score is the average of all the local scores of the bins located on the right of the current bin. At last, The candidate having the lowest score will be the final extracting result of the normal mode. Ties are resolved by choosing the larger one. That is,

$$Result = \arg\min_{r_i} Score(r_i)$$
$$= \arg\min_{r_i} \frac{\sum_{q=i}^{n} \frac{f_q}{q}}{n-i}.$$

2.5   Global Alerts

We assume that the input online traffic come from multiple sensors, although our engine can also work even for the situation having only one sensor. Thus, several online packet streams come to the engine simultaneously and global alerts also can be detected. Here, *global alerts* means those occurring multiple sensors simultaneously. Global alerts should be paid special attention since the same alerts occurred in different sensors/regions/countries in the same time. The necessary number of sensors to define global alerts can be decided by users. In our engine, this number is set by default to be three, which means that, if an alert occurred simultaneously in at least 3 sensors, it will be reported as a global alert.

2.6   Output

The following data are output as separate files in our detection engine.

- **AlertList file** for every sensor. In this file, each line is an alert including date, time, port-type (TCP or UDP), port-number, alert-level, normal mode and the actual number of the unique source hosts.
- **AlertDetails file** for each sensor. This file has the details of every alert in the mentioned-above AlertList file, including SensorID, Detection date/time, Targeted port-number/port-type, Unique source IP list of this alert. The last number in the parenthesis is the number of the unique source IP addresses of this alert.

- **Global alerts.** In this file, one block is one global attack including date-time, port-number/port-type, the corresponding sensors and the common source IPs of this alert in these sensors. The last number in the parenthesis is the number of the common source IP addresses of this alert.

3 Detection Cases

Some actual detection cases of our engine are reported in this section.

3.1 About Darknet

A darknet is a set of unused IP addresses [18], in which no actual services (web, mail, and so on) exist, since these addresses have not been distributed to any legal users. Real traffic data in many companies and other organizations are often not available to researchers because of the strict rules and laws for protecting personal privacy or the organizations' secrets. Fortunately, it has been confirmed by many studies that global trends in network threats can be observed by monitoring darknets [19–21].

3.2 Online Data

The online darknet traffic data (packet streams) from 10 sensors deployed in different countries are sent to our detection engine. The countries include Singapore, Philippines, Thailand, USA, France, Japan, Malaysia, Maldives and Indonesia. This is a project supported by Japan Government called "Proactive Response Against Cyber-attacks Through International Collaborative Exchange (PRACTICE)".

3.3 Online Incident Detection

A botnet of a large number of digital video recorders using 23/TCP and 53413/UDP was announced on Dec. 15, 2015 [22,23]. Actually, our just-completed detecting engine also successfully captured that botnet in Nov. 2015. The global alerts reported by our engine in the whole Nov. 2015 are shown in Fig. 7(a), in which totally 44 global alerts were reported concentrating on 3 destination ports. Of the 44 global alerts, 14 alerts were on 53413/UDP and 29 alerts on 23/TCP. The similar phenomenon did not occur in other months before or after Nov. 2015. This means that our detection engine captured clearly and accurately the behaviors of the above botnet. From Fig. 7(a), we observed that, a global alert on 32764/TCP was also reported at the same time, which is seemingly a secret backdoor [24] according to the Hacker News, April 20, 2014. The detection result of individual sensors are shown in Fig. 7(b). Six of these 10 sensors got involved in the above botnet and many alerts related to this botnet.

Sensors	Number of alerts
01	48
02	51
03	34
04	19
05	66
06	17
07	88
08	51
09	61
10	46

#global alerts	Details
44	53413/UDP (14 times) 23/TCP (29 times) 32764/TCP (once)

(a)   (b)

Fig. 7. Online detection result in Nov. 2015.

4 Conclusion

Distributed cyber-attacks have caused the most serious security problems in recent years. Among the existing methods for detecting cyber-attacks, the behavior-based detection is thought promising. In most practical detection systems, the network traffic need to be monitored in online mode and anomalies should be reported as soon as possible. In this paper, we introduced our behavior-based online engine for detecting distributed attacks. Our detection engine has been fully accomplished and is running in real environment. The general idea and the general flow were explained. In addition, for efficiently extracting normal modes which is the core of behavior-based detections, an extraction algorithm that need not any predefined thresholds was introduced to this engine. In addition, some specific and important technologies are utilized in this engine. And some actual detection cases of our engine were also introduced. Our engine captured a botnet before it was reported on public. In the future, we will try to use real or imitated traffic data that have labeled anomalies to examine in detail the detection performance of this detection engine. Also, we will try to find the attack groups of distributed cyber-attacks, which is obviously possible if the source IP addresses of the distributed attacks are analyzed carefully. At the same time, we will try to find the relations among the detected attacks on the separated destination ports.

References

1. Xu, S.: Collaborative attack vs. collaborative defense. In: Bertino, E., Joshi, J.B.D. (eds.) CollaborateCom 2008. LNICSSITE, vol. 10, pp. 217–228. Springer, Heidelberg (2009). doi:10.1007/978-3-642-03354-4_17
2. ComputerWeekly News. http://www.computerweekly.com/news/4500243431/DDoS-losses-potentially-100k-an-hour-survey-shows. Accessed 6 Nov 2016

3. Tang, Y.: Defending against internet worms: a signature-based approach. In: Proceedings of 24th IEEE Annual Joint Conference of the Computer and Communications Societies (INFOCOM), pp. 1384–1394 (2005)
4. Eskin, E., Lee, W.: Modeling system call for intrusion detection with dynamic window sizes. In: Proceedings of DARPA Information Survivalility Conference and Exposition (DISCEX), pp. 165–175 (2001)
5. Kind, A., Stoecklin, M.P., Dimitropoulos, X.: Histogram-based traffic anomaly detection. IEEE Trans. Netw. Serv. Manage. **6**(2), 1–12 (2009)
6. Feng, Y., Hori, Y., Sakurai, K., Takeuchi, J.: A behavior-based method for detecting outbreaks of low-rate attacks. In: Proceedings of 3rd Workshop on Network Technologies for Security, Administration and Protection (NETSAP), SAINT 2012, pp. 267–272 (2012)
7. Lee, W., Xiang, D.: Information-theoretic measures for anomaly detection. In: Proceedings of IEEE Symposium on Security and Privacy, pp. 130–143 (2001)
8. Xiang, Y., Li, K., Zhou, W.: Low-rate DDoS attacks detection and traceback by using new information metrics. IEEE Trans. Inf. Forensics Secur. **6**(2), 426–437 (2011)
9. Chandola, V., Banerjee, A., Kumar, V.: Anomaly detection: a survey. ACM Comput. Surv. **41**(3), 1–72 (2009)
10. Kim, M.S., Kang, H.J., Hong, S.C.: A flow-based method for abnormal network traffic detection. In: Proceedings of IEEE/IPIP Network Operations and Management Symposium, pp. 599–612 (2004)
11. Treurniet, J.: A network activity classification schema and its application to scan detection. IEEE/ACM Trans. Netw. **19**(5), 1396–1404 (2011)
12. Snort user's manual. http://www.snort.org/docs. Accessed 6 Nov 2016
13. The Bro internet security monitor. https://www.bro.org/. Accessed 6 Nov 2016
14. Network and Security Manager (NSM). https://www.juniper.net/documentation/en_US/release-independent/nsm/information-products/pathway-pages/nsm/product/index.html. Accessed 6 Nov 2016
15. Gates, C.: The Modeling and Detection of Distributed Port Scans: a Thesis Proposal, Technical Report CS-2003-01, Dalhousie University (2003)
16. Yegneswaran, V., Barford, P., Ullrich, J.: Internet intrusions: global characteristics and prevalence. In: Proceedings of 2003 ACM Joint International Conference on Measurement and Modeling of Computer Systems, pp. 138–147 (2003)
17. Feng, Y., Hori, Y., Sakurai, K., Takeuchi, J.: A behavior-based method for detecting distributed scan attacks in darknets. J. Inf. Process. (JIP) **21**(3), 527–538 (2013)
18. Cooke, E., Bailey, M., Mao, Z.M., Watson, D., Jahanian, F., McPherson, D.: Toward understanding distributed blackhole placement. In: Proceedings of ACM CCS Workshop on Rapid Malcode, pp. 54–64 (2004)
19. Eto, M., Inoue, D., Song, J., Ohtaka, K., Nakao, K.: NICTER: a large-scale network incident analysis system. In: Proceedings of 1st Workshop on Building Analysis Datasets and Gathering Experience Returns for Security (BADGERS), pp. 37–45 (2011)
20. Murakami, K., Kamatani, T., et al.: A proposal of method for detecting synchronized increase of attacks on multiple dataknet sensors. In: Computer Security Symposium in Japan, pp. 32–39 (2014)
21. Bailey, M., Cooke, E., Jahanian, F., Nazario, J., Watson, D.: The internet motion sensor: a distributed blackhole monitoring system. In: Proceedings of 12th ISOC Symposium on Network and Distributed Systems Security (NDSS), pp. 167–179 (2005)

22. National Police Agency of Japan: Internet Report. http://www.npa.go.jp/cyberpolice/detect/pdf/20140328.pdf
23. https://www.npa.go.jp/cyberpolice/detect/pdf/20151215_1.pdf. Accessed 6 Nov 2016
24. Hacker News (2014). http://www.daemonology.net/hn-daily/2014-04.html
25. Nakao, K., Inoue, D., Eto, M., Yoshioka, K.: Practical correlation analysis between scan and malware profiles against zero-day attacks based on darknet monitoring. IEICE Trans. Inf. Syst. **92**(5), 787–798 (2009)
26. Feng, Y., Hori, Y., Sakurai, K.: A proposal for detecting distributed cyber-attacks using automatic thresholding. In: Proceedings of 10th Asia Conference on Information Security (AsiaJCIS) (2015)
27. Yazid, I., Hanan, A., Aizaini, M.: Volume-based network intrusion attacks detection. In: Advanced Computer Network and Security, pp. 147–162. UTM Press (2008)

Influence Evaluation of Centrality-Based Random Scanning Strategy on Early Worm Propagation Rate

Su-kyung Kown[1], Bongsoo Jang[2], Byoung-Dai Lee[3], Younghae Do[4],
Hunki Baek[5], and Yoon-Ho Choi[1(✉)]

[1] School of Electric Electronics and Computer Engineering,
Pusan National University, Busan, Korea
{ksk3579,yhchoi}@pusan.ac.kr
[2] Department of Mathematical Sciences,
Ulsan National Institute of Science and Technology, Ulsan, Korea
bsjang@unist.ac.kr
[3] Department of Computer Science, Kyonggi University, Suwon, Korea
blee@kyonggi.ac.kr
[4] Department of Mathematics, KNU-Center for Nonlinear Dynamics,
Kyungpook National University, Daegu, Korea
yhdo@knu.ac.kr
[5] Department of Mathematics Education, Catholic University of Daegu, Daegu, Korea
hkbaek@cu.ac.kr

Abstract. Smart devices interconnected through Internet became one of everyday items. In particular, we are now able to access Internet anywhere and anytime with our smartphones. To support the ad-hoc access to Internet by using smartphones, the computer network structure has become more complex. Also, a certain network node is highly connected to support the diverse Internet services. In this paper, we note that when a node is infected by malicious programs, their propagation speeds from the node with a high level of centrality will be faster than those from the node with a low level of centrality, which identifies the most important nodes within a network. From experiments under diverse worm propagation parameters and the well-known network topologies, we evaluate the influence of Centrality-based random scanning strategy on early worm propagation rate. Therefore, we show that centrality-based random scanning strategy, where an initial infected node selects the victim based on the level of centrality, can make random scanning worms propagate rapidly compared to Anonymity-based random scanning strategy, where an initial infected node selects the victim uniformly.

Keywords: Worm propagation · Centrality theory · Centrality-based random scanning strategy · Anonymity-based random scanning strategy

1 Introduction

Internet worm refers to a computer program that replicates itself. It is similar to computer virus. However, computer virus is usually executed in conjunction with other executable

© Springer International Publishing AG 2017
D. Choi and S. Guilley (Eds.): WISA 2016, LNCS 10144, pp. 90–101, 2017.
DOI: 10.1007/978-3-319-56549-1_8

programs. In contrast, computer worm is executed independently. That is, it does not need other executable programs [1].

So far, many studies on computer worms have been conducted. A majority of these computer work-related studies have focused on the mathematical models for efficiently propagating worms in specific network topologies [2–5]. Also, many of these studies have examined how to efficiently detect worms for preventing infection propagation [6–8]. The increasing use of smartphone is making our computer network get bigger. Also, the rapid growth of IoT (Internet of Things) market is contributing to the growing complexity of our computer network. As a result, the number of devices connected to a network is on the rise. More importantly, increasing importance is being placed on network equipment. For example, Fig. 1 shows the propagation path based on the node where the propagation begins. Figure 1-(a) shows the case in which the worm propagates from the node that has the fewest number of links. Figure 1-(b) shows the case in which the propagation from the node that has the largest number of links. As shown in Fig. 1-(b), the worm is propagated more quickly from the node that has the largest number of links.

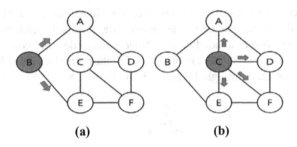

(a)   **(b)**

Fig. 1. Comparison on worm propagation based on the centrality of initial infected node: (a) next infection from the node with the fewest number of links, (b) next infection from the node with the largest number of links.

2   Background

Assuming that graph G is expressed in $G = (v, e)$ that has node v and edge e, Degree Centrality (DC) is then expressed in the number of links that are directly connected to that node as shown in Fig. 2-(a). To express this in a normalized value, we should divide it by $(N - 1)$, where N refers to the total number of nodes. $\deg(v)$ refers to the total number of links connected to the node v:

$$DC(v) = \frac{\deg(v)}{N - 1} \tag{1}$$

Closeness Centrality (CC) is defined as the inverse of farness, which in turn, is the sum of distances to all other nodes. Figure 2-(b) shows the CC of each node. The higher a CC value becomes, the closer a given node is to other nodes. Following is the calculation formula of CC. d_{vj} refers to the shortest distance between node v and node j. It should then be divided by $(N - 1)$ for the normalization of CC:

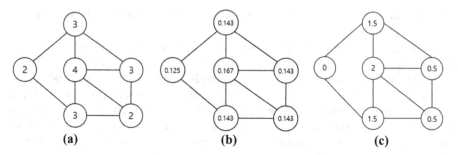

Fig. 2. Centrality value examples for the different centrality types: (a) DC, (b) CC and (c) BC.

$$CC(v) = \frac{1}{\displaystyle\sum_{v \neq j}^{N} d_{vj}} \quad (2)$$

Third, Betweenness Centrality (BC) is ratio of included node v in all shortest path. Denominator is all shortest paths to node s from node t, and numerator is shortest paths that to node s from node t included node v. Node s and node t and node v is not equal. It is graphically expressed as shown in Fig. 2-(c). For the normalization of BC, we should divide the value obtained through the below formula by $\{(N-1) * (N-2)\}/2$ [9–11]:

$$BC(v) = \sum_{s \neq v \neq t, s < t} \frac{\sigma_{st}(v)}{\sigma_{st}} \quad (3)$$

3   Related Work

The previous studies on worm propagation can be broadly divided into two types. The first type is worm propagation modeling and the second is the threat posed by worm in relation to such factors as worm's latent period. Following are the results of some worm propagation related studies.

The study of Cliff et al. [2] proposed the new propagation model as arguing that the conventional code red worm and Kermack-Mckendrick model were not suitable for the current Internet conditions. However, they did not take the network characteristics into consideration. The study of Feng et al. [3] proposed the worm propagation model based on the growing number of smartphones. However, they did not take into consideration the network topology change based on the growing number of devices. The study of Kim et al. [4] proposed and experimented the new propagation model called "SIRS" on the basis of elapsed time. The study called "Network Worm Propagation Model Based on a Campus Network Topology" [5] proposed and verified the new SIR model based on the following two premises: (1) an administrator could plan a measure to address issues associated with worm propagation in a campus network environment, and (2) propagation speed can vary depending on network size.

As such, a majority of the precedent studies have focused on worm propagation model on the basis of Kermack-Mckendrick epidemic model. In contrast, only few studies have focused on actual network nodes and network environment. The size of network topology has increased substantially in recent years. More importantly, a node with high centrality has a large influence on a network. In this regard, we can reasonably expect that propagation speed becomes faster if a worm first infects a node with high centrality. Hence, this study aims to experimentally compare and verify worm propagation speed on the basis of node centrality and relationship between nodes and network.

4 Evaluation Methodology

The three types of network topology are used in this experiment. The first is the random graph that represents random network environment. The second is Barabási–Albert model based graph that represent a network that has a large number of links between nodes. The third is Watts and Strogatz model based graph that represents a network that has a small number of links between nodes [12].

The simulator was designed based on the SI model. It was created in JAVA by using the eclipse mars 2 in Windows 10. GraphStream [13] was utilized as the library related to the graphs.

The propagation process has four steps. First, the nodes in the simulator are placed in order from the highest to the lowest based on the centrality of network nodes. Second, to propagate the infection, the infected nodes scan their surrounding nodes. Third, when infected node selects any node, selected node is infected after a period of time as the link cost. Finally, it repeats as much as parameter C.

The purpose of this simulation is to measure the propagation speed by examining how many nodes can be infected with the assigned number of infection trials. Definitions of the parameters used in the simulation and experiment are as shown in Table 1.

Table 1. Definition of parameters used in the experiment

λ	Scan rate
N	Number of nodes in graph
LC	Link cost
deg	Average degree of network
N_{init}	Number of hosts to be infected at an initial phase
C	Number of trials to infect the entire graph

5 Evaluation Result

5.1 Centrality-Based Random Scanning Strategy *vs.* Anonymity-Based Random Scanning Strategy

A node with high centrality has great importance in a network. To compare the propagation speed between Centrality-based random scanning strategy and Anonymity-based random scanning strategy and to verify the effect of centrality on work propagation, the propagation speed between the Centrality-based random scanning strategy and Anonymity-based random scanning strategy was examined in each network environment on the basis of the parameters described in Table 2.

Table 2. Parameters of comparison between centrality-based random scanning strategy vs. anonymity-based random scanning strategy

λ	0.4
N	10,000
LC	Random number from 1 to 8
deg	10
N_{init}	5
C	40

In Fig. 3, the number of infected nodes in the case of CC increased from 61 (4 trials) to 101 (5 trials). In the case of BC, it increased from 55 (4 trials) to 98 (5 trials). In the case of DC, it increased from 59 (4 trials) to 96 (5 trials). In the case of Anonymity-based random scanning strategy, it increased from 23 (4 trials) to 34 (5 trials). In Fig. 4, the number of infected nodes in the case of CC increased from 667 (4 trials) to 1,246 (5 trials). In the case of BC, it increased from 711 (4 trials) to 1,322 (5 trials). In the case of DC, it increased from 741 (4 trials) to 1,427 (5 trials). In the case of Anonymity-based random scanning strategy, it increased from 35 (4 trials) to 77 (5 trials). In Fig. 5, the number of infected nodes in the case of CC increased from 66 (4 trials) to 93 (5 trials). In the case of BC, it increased from 65 (4 trials) to 105 (5 trials). In the case of DC, it increased from 32 (4 trials) to 49 (5 trials). In the case of Anonymity-based random scanning strategy, it increased from 32 (4 trials) to 44 (5 trials). The increase in the infected nodes in the case of CC is similar to that of BC. However, there was no significant difference in the propagation speed between DC-based random scanning infection and Anonymity-based random scanning strategy.

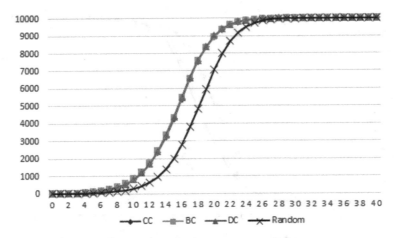

Fig. 3. Propagation speed in the random network in Experiment 5.1

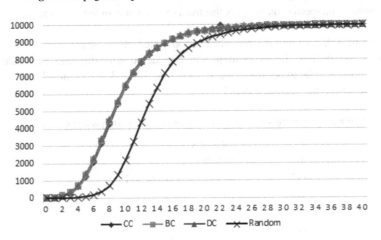

Fig. 4. Propagation speed in the network that has a large number of links in Experiment 5.1 [14]

Moreover, the propagation speed of Centrality-based random scanning strategy was faster than that of the Anonymity-based random scanning strategy. In particular, the difference in the propagation speed became larger in the networks that has a large number of the links whose inter-node connectivity difference was substantial.

The propagation speed was then experimented based on the scan rate for comparing the propagation speed between centralities. However, there was almost no difference in the propagation speed between centralities.

5.2 Influence of Scan Rate on Worm Propagation Speed

A node can have more chances to infect other nodes when it has a high scan rate. That is to say, we can reasonably assume that DC is greatly influenced by a change in scan rate because those nodes with many connections become top priority in DC. To compare

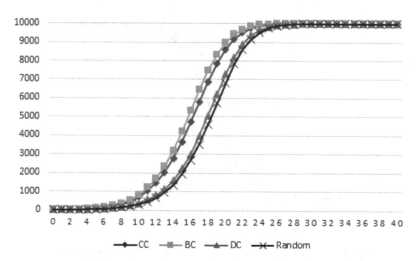

Fig. 5. Propagation speed in the network that has a small number of links in Experiment 5.2 [15]

the impact of link cost and degree when a node attempts to infect other nodes and to verify this assumption, the experiment was conducted with different scan rates. The parameters used in the experiment are as shown in Table 3. You can refer to Sect. 5.1 for the case where the scan rate is 0.4.

Table 3. Parameters of influence of scan rate on worm propagation speed

λ	0.4 or 0.8
N	10,000
LC	Random number from 1 to 8
deg	10
N_{init}	5
C	40

In Fig. 6, the number of infected nodes in the case of CC increased from 318 (4 trials) to 752 (5 trials). In the case of BC, it increased from 413 (4 trials) to 961 (5 trials). In the case of DC, it increased from 319 (4 trials) to 676 (5 trials). In the case of Anonymity-based random scanning strategy, it increased from 126 (4 trials) to 317 (5 trials). In Fig. 7, the number of infected nodes in the case of CC increased from 3,685 (4 trials) to 5,842 (5 trials). In the case of BC, it increased from 3,876 (4 trials) to 6,042 (5 trials). In the case of DC, it increased from 3,916 (4 trials) to 6,026 (5 trials). In the case of Anonymity-based random scanning strategy, it increased from 773 (4 trials) to 2,293 (5 trials). In Fig. 8, the number of infected nodes in the case of CC increased from 260 (4 trials) to 557 (5 trials). In the case of BC, it increased from 303 (4 trials) to 607 (5 trials). In the case of DC, it increased from 196 (4 trials) to 459 (5 trials). In the case of Anonymity-based random scanning strategy, it increased from 109 (4 trials) to 221 (5 trials). The propagation speed became faster than the case where the scan rate was 0.4. However, there was no difference in the

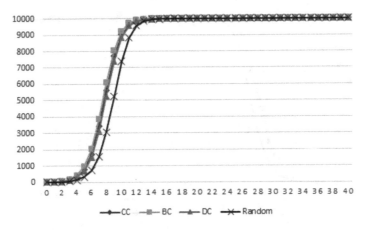

Fig. 6. Propagation speed in the random network in Experiment 5.2

propagation speed between the centralities. There was no substantial increase in DC-based random scanning strategy propagation speed even with an increase in the scan rate.

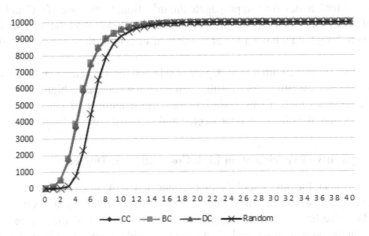

Fig. 7. Propagation speed in the network that has a large number of links in Experiment 5.2 [14]

The average link cost of the edges connected to the nodes were examined. Moreover, the number of connections of the node that has the highest centrality was also examined. The results are as shown in Table 4.

Table 4. Result values of influence of scan rate on worm propagation speed

Centrality	First order node	Avg. LC	deg
DC	2079	4.870	23
CC	411	2.722	18
BC	411	2.722	18

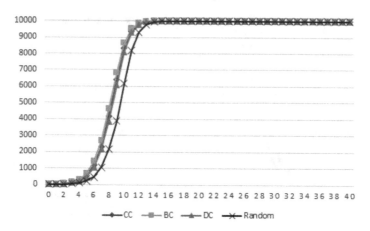

Fig. 8. Propagation speed in the network that has a small number of links in Experiment 5.2 [15]

In the case of DC, the node degree was high. Hence, the number of infection trials has substantially increased. However, it also has some links whose link cost was high. As a result, it took a long time to propagate the infection. In the case of CC and BC, the degree of node can be low. However, their link cost is lower than that of DC. In other words, even though they have a fewer number of infection trials, the propagation at a fast rate.

As for DC, the node with a high degree is selected. In this selection, the link cost is not taken into consideration. As a result, even though a node has a high link cost value, DC value becomes high if this node has the largest number of connections. In the following section, the effects of node degree and link cost were examined.

5.3 Comparative Experiment on Link Cost and Node Degree

In this experiment, the link cost of the links connected to the top 5 highest-degree nodes of DC was set at 5, which was the difference in the degree of the top nodes between DC, CC and BC. The link cost of the remaining links was set at 1. If the degree has great influence on the propagation speed, then the gap would be quickly reduced because the link cost of the surrounding links was high. The parameters are as shown in Table 5.

Table 5. Parameters of comparative experiment on link cost and node degree

λ	0.4
N	10,000
LC	1 or 5
deg	10
N_{init}	5
C	20

As shown in Figs. 9, 10 and 11, the momentary propagation speed were similar to each other. However, DC-based random scanning strategy propagation speed became substantially slower. This is because it generally takes longer for infection to propagate when the link cost is high even though the number of infection trials is high. As a result, link cost has greater influence on propagation speed. In particular, those links with low link cost exercise great influence on propagation speed because they have a wide bandwidth.

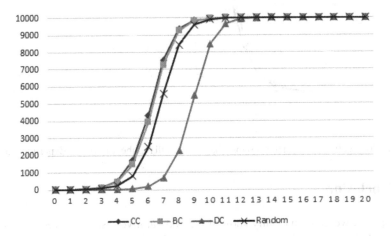

Fig. 9. Propagation speed in the random network in Experiment 5.3

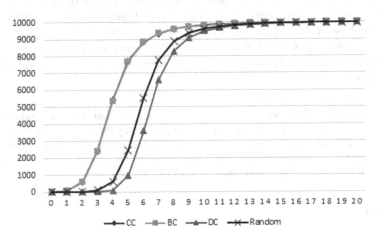

Fig. 10. Propagation speed in the network that has a large number of links in Experiment 5.3 [14]

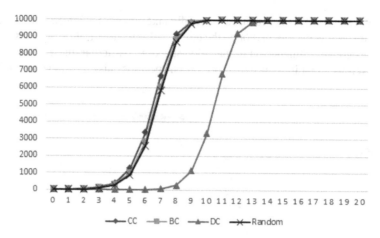

Fig. 11. Propagation speed in the network that has a small number of links in Experiment 5.3 [15]

6 Conclusion

In this paper, we experimentally showed the comparative results between Centrality-based random scanning strategy propagation speed and Anonymity-based random scanning strategy propagation speed through simulation. Basically, we showed that Centrality-based random scanning strategy has a higher propagation speed than Anonymity-based random scanning strategy. Also, we showed that link cost did cause a significant change in CC and BC-based random scanning strategy propagation speed while link cost exercised great influence on DC-based random scanning strategy propagation speed.

Acknowledgments. This work was partly supported by Institute for Information & communications Technology Promotion (IITP) grant funded by the Korea government (MSIP) (No. 10043907, Development of high performance IoT device and Open Platform with Intelligent Software) and basic science research program through national research foundation korea (NRF) funded by the ministry of education (NRF-2013R1A1A1005991).

References

1. Wikipedia. https://ko.wikipedia.org/wiki/%EC%9B%9C
2. Zou, C.C., Gong, W., Towsley, D.: Code red worm propagation modeling and analysis, In: ACM, pp. 138–147 (2002)
3. Chao-shengl, F., Zhi-guang, Q., Ding, Y., Xia, L., Jian-jun, W.: Modeling passive worm propagation in mobile P2P networks. In: ICCCAS International Conference, pp. 241–244 (2010)
4. Kim, J., Radhakrishnan, S., Dhall, S.K.: Measurement and analysis of worm propagation on Internet network topology. In: Proceedings of ICCCN 2004, pp. 495–500 (2004)
5. Mohammed, A., Nor, S.M., Marsono, M.N.: Network worm propagation model based on a campus network topology. In: ITHINGSCPSCOM 2011, pp. 653–659 (2011)

6. Xiaojun, T., Zhangquan, Z., Huimin, S., Zhu, W.: The analysis of worm non-linear propagation model and the design of worm distributed detection technology: In: Ninth International Symposium on DCABES 2010, pp. 219–223 (2010)

7. Chan, Y.-T.F., Shoniregun, C.A., Akmayeva, G.A.: A NetFlow based internet-worm detecting system in large network. In: ICDIM 2008, pp. 581–586 (2008)

8. Yongjian, W., Bin, F., Shupeng, W.: The rapid worm detecting technology in large-scale network. In: Proceedings of the 2011 International Conference on Internet of Things and 4th International Conference on Cyber, Physical and Social Computing, pp. 756–761 (2011)

9. Borgatti, S.P.: Centrality and network flow. Soc. Networks $27(1)$, 55–71 (2005). (Elsevier)

10. Network Centrality. http://cs.brynmawr.edu/Courses/cs380/spring2013/section02/slides/05_Centrality.pdf

11. Kchiche, A., Kamoun, F.,: Centrality-based access-points deployment for vehicular networks. In: 2010 IEEE 17th International Conference on Telecommunications (ICT), pp. 700–706 (2010)

12. Wei, Z., Facheng, Q., Shiqi, C., Ruchuan, W.: The study of network worm propagation simulation. In: ICCASM 2010, pp. 295–299 (2010)

13. GraphStream. http://graphstream-project.org

14. Albert, R., Barabási, A.-L.: Statistical Mechanics of Complex Networks (2002)

15. Watts, D.J., Strogatz, S.H.: Collective dynamics of 'small-world' networks. Nature $\mathbf{393}$, 440–442 (1998)

Analysis on South Korean Cybersecurity Readiness Regarding North Korean Cyber Capabilities

Jeong Yoon Yang[1(✉)], So Jeong Kim[1], and Il Seok Oh(Luke)[2]

[1] National Security Research Institute, P.O. Box 1Yuseong, Daejeon 34188, South Korea
{jyyangrok,sjkim}@nsr.re.kr
[2] Legal Research Institute of Korea University, CJ Law Building 405 Ho, Anam-dong
Seongbuk-gu, Seoul 02481, South Korea
NUSL2006@gmail.com

Abstract. Cyber attacks cause fatal blow by destructing critical infrastructure of nations with relatively small cost. North Korea uses cyber attacks as a major asymmetric strategy along with nuclear weapon. In this situation, South Korea needs to find better way to cope with North Korea's aggressive cyber threats. In the present paper, we shall see North Korean cyber capability including its backgrounds, organization, and personnel. By exploring some key signifying structures consisting North Korean cyber power, it is intended to broaden understanding of the nature of North Korean cyber operations. The purpose of this paper is to come up with appropriate and effective ways to respond North Korean cyber attacks.

Keywords: Cybersecuriy · Cyber attack · Cyber capability · South Korean cybersecurity readiness · Asymmetry

1 Introduction

The First Secretary Kim Jong-un ended the legacy rule, the hereditary succession period, and stabilization in the three-year mourning term after the death of his father Kim-Jong-il and now focuses on establishing his own leadership in North Korea [1]. In order to build up his own dictatorship, he reshuffled power elites and adopted 'Economy-Nuclear Parallel Policy' through strengthening economic construction and national defense capability [2]. However, after the 4th North Korean nuclear test on 6 January 2016 and successive missile launches, North Korea hit with tough sanctions from international society and internal and external crises have increased. It is expected that North Korea's provocations to South Korea, the U.S., and other nations will keep escalating to break the current deadlock.

In the point that cyber attacks cause fatal blow by destructing critical infrastructure of nations with relatively small cost, North Korea uses cyber threats as a major asymmetric strategy with nuclear power [3]. As a way to catch up on its military inferiority and recover recession-bound economy, North Korea has been expanding its cyber capabilities [4]. Cyber attack is difficult to identify the attacker and finding evidence and investigating sophisticated attack are incredibly difficult [5]. In addition, even if one can

© Springer International Publishing AG 2017
D. Choi and S. Guilley (Eds.): WISA 2016, LNCS 10144, pp. 102–111, 2017.
DOI: 10.1007/978-3-319-56549-1_9

trace the attack and spot a person or a country as a culprit, one can deny it arguing for presenting evidence. Also, North Korea's lack of IT infrastructure provides defensive circumstances or shelter room to North Korea for counter attacks [23]. Cyber attacks have become organized and start to target nations beyond their previous targets such as individuals and enterprises.

Recognizing advantages of cyber attacks, the North Korean leader Kim Jong-un once mentioned "Cyber warfare is an all-purpose sword which can guarantee ruthless strikes of the Korean People's Army along with the nuclear weapon and missile." In this situation, South Korea needs to find better way to respond North Korea's aggressive cyber threats. In the present paper, we shall see North Korean Cyber capability including backgrounds, organization, and personnel. By exploring some key signifying structures consisting North Korean cyber power, it is intended to broaden understanding of the nature of North Korean cyber operations. As the rooting theory, realism theory would be taken in order to explain the South and North relations. Mostly, government released reports, think tanks' research papers, news paper articles will be used for the research. The purpose of this paper is to come up with appropriate and effective ways to South Korea against North Korean cyber threats.

2 North Korean Cyber Capability

2.1 Backgrounds

Although North Korea's Internet infrastructure is far lag behind than other nations, it has made significant investment in cyber capabilities [6]. Also North Korea is motivated by wide disparity between North and South Korea's Internet environment. Worldbank data shows that 84.3% of South Korean uses Internet in 2014 while the number of North Korean Internet users is not counted. Using such asymmetric characteristics in cyber space, North Korea is able to have greater cyber attack impact on South Korea from individuals to the whole society.

Table 1. ASPI cyber maturity in the Asia-Pacific Region by weighted scores

	Country	Weighted score
1	United States	90.7
2	Japan	85.1
3	South Korea	82.8
⋮	⋮	⋮
20	North Korea	16.4

[Source: 2015 Cyber Maturity in the Asia-Pacific Region (ASPI)] [9]

In the 2015 Index of U.S. Military Strength Report released by the Heritage Foundation assessed the North Korean cyber threat is 'Limited Capable' since its cyber activities are aggressive, unpredictable, and scattered across the world [7]. In addition, ITU (International Telecommunication Union) assesses 5 categories, Legal, Technology, Organizational, Capacity Building, and Cooperation, to gauge Global

Cybersecurity Index, and North Korea ranked almost the lowest score among 193 countries [8]. Australian Strategic Policy Institute (ASPI) also issued a report on Cyber Maturity in the Asia-Pacific Region in 2015 [9]. In this report, North Korea ranked 20 with 16.4 scores while South Korea ranked 3 with 82.8 scores among 20 Asia-Pacific countries including the U.S. and the United Kingdom (Table 1) [10].

It assessed cyber maturity by 5 indexes, Governance, Cybercrime, Military, Business, Social, and it is remarkable that North Korean military role in cyberspace acquired 8 points while other scores hit bottom (Table 2).

Table 2. ASPI cyber maturity index of South and North Korea by category

Country	Governance	Cybercrime	Military	Business	Social	Total
South Korea	31	7	9	18	18	83
North Korea	6	0	8	1	2	17

[Source: 2015 Cyber Maturity in the Asia-Pacific Region (ASPI)] [9]

Internet access in North Korea is available only with special authorization or for governmental purposes. North Korea has broadband infrastructure, however, online services for individuals and private institutions are provided through a domestic network known as Kwangmyoung (광명). This indicates that it is difficult to reach North Korean people or North Korean institutions via Internet while North Korea is able to access almost all South Korean individuals or institutions using Internet. In other words, North Korea's Internet inferiority makes it much more defendable to cyber attacks while South Korea's developed Internet environment makes it vulnerable to such attacks.

In other assumption, to gain access to Internet in North Korea, one needs to obtain permission from the Postal Service Ministry, the Ministry in charge of postal service, information, and communication [11]. If someone attempts to launch cyber attack, he or she needs to get IP address from the ministry. For that reason, cyber attacks originated from North Korea are impossible to be executed without North Korean government's support [11].

In addition, in North Korea, people use internal Intranet system called 'Kwangmyoung' and Internet access with Kwangmyoung is blocked. North Korea uses its own developed software such as OS called 'Bulunbyeol (붉은별)', firewall called 'Neongra (능라)', vaccine program called 'Clarksae (클락새)', and access control solution called 'Bogum (보검)'. Therefore, although a foreign hacker succeeds in invading North Korea's Internet, it not easy to hack North Korean self-produced computer systems.

North Korea commits cyber attacks towards South Korea and the U.S. mainly in political purposes. The recent remarkable North Korean cyber attack against the U.S is Sony Pictures hack in 2014. On November 24, 2014, Sony Pictures Entertainment is hacked with the malware deleting data and the hackers posting online employee's personal information and unreleased films [12]. An FBI investigation revealed North Korea to be behind the attack and a hacker group "Guardians of Peace" hacked Sony Pictures because of its film "The Interview", a comedy about a plot to assassinate Kim Jong-un.

North Korean cyber threats towards South Korea frequently occur with various techniques such as DDoS, APT, MBR wiper attack, GPS botnet, malicious code, code obfuscation, trace deletion, steganography, and so forth. North Korea not only commits cyber attacks with forementioned techniques but also uses all around ways such as using internet game sites or writing malicious comments in the Internet. The below is the list of cyber attacks associated with North Korea (Table 3).

Table 3. Cyber attack cases associated with North Korea towards South Korea

Date	Event	Technique
Mar. 2016	South Korean officials' smartphone hacking	APT
Oct. 2015	Hacking at the National Assembly, the Ministry of Unification, the Blue House	APT
Dec. 2014	Data exfiltration and extortion on Korea Hydro& Nuclear Power (KHNP)	APT
Sep. 2013	Hacking on think tanks, the Ministry of Defense, and Korean defense industry firms	APT
Jun. 2013	DDoS on 16 government and media websites, targeted DNS servers	APT/DDoS
Mar. 2013	Daily NK, Free North Korea Radio, Nknet, North Korea Intellectuals Society website disrupted. The attack shut down 32,000 computers of banks (Nonghyup, Shinhan, Jeju) and media agencies (YTN, KBS, MBC)	MBR wiper attack
Apr. 2011	Nonghyup Bank server disrupted, data erased	APT
Mar. 2011	DDoS on public, government, military, and private websites	DDoS
Jul. 2010	DDoS on government and private sector websites	DDoS
Jul. 2009	DDoS on public and government websites	DDoS

[Source: Significant Cyber Events(CSIS)] [12]

After 2009, North Korean cyber attacks to South Korea have been increasing and becoming emboldened. South Korean Cyber Warfare Command announced that, from 2009 to 2013, the estimated amount of damage from the North Korean cyber attack is over $860 million and total amount of damage is estimated to $196.3 billion.

2.2 Organization

In 1991, North Korea began to pay attention to cyber tactics when it witnessed the U.S. defeated Iraq in Gulf War by high-tech computer and communications technique [4]. At the time, the North Korean leader Kim Jong-il said "Internet is a gun. Observe South Korean computer network in great detail".

Reconnaissance General Bureau (RGB, 정찰총국) is thought to be the center of North Korean cyber activity. In 2009, North Korea restructured some of its intelligence organs. In the process, units spread between the Korean Worker's Party (KWP) and the Ministry of People's Armed Forces (MPAF) were combined in the RGB [13]. RGB is associated with cyber activity as well as with terrorist, clandestine, and illicit activities and this shows that North Korea would use cyber activities for more provocative purposes.

Under RGB, Bureau 121 (121국) is the most important cyber unit in North Korea. It performs wide range of cyber defensive and offensive operation including cyber espionage, network exploitation, and cyber crime [14]. It is also known that 1st Operations Bureau (작전국), 414 Liaison Office (414연락소), 128 Liaison Office (128 연락소) are major cyber unit in RGB and RGB operates Computer Technology Research Lab as a research and development center [13].

In 1993, North Korea created Cyber Unit under the General Staff Department (총참모부) in the Korean People's Army (KPA, 인민군) [4]. In 1995, it established Cyber terror organization under the South Korean espionage operation unit.

Under the GSD, Operation Bureau (작전국) carries out operational military planning, strategy, and general management. It can be construed Operation Bureau does not directly perform cyber operations but it makes key decisions in North Korean cyber operation. Command Automation Bureau (지휘자동화국) reportedly conducts computer network operations and is responsible for developing malware and searching for exploits. Command Automation Bureau has 50 to 60 officers in Unit 31, responsible for malware development, Unit 32, responsible for software development for military use, and Unit 56 responsible for developing military command and control software. Enemy Collapse Sabotage Bureau (적군와해공작국)'s Unit 204 uses Internet to spread anti-South Korean propaganda in peace time and war time. It is composed of three brigades each with around 600 to 700 personnel, for a total of 2,000 and it is also referred to as the 563th Army Unit. Communications Bureau (통신국) overseas all administration and operations regarding communications within the KPA, including monitoring of domestic and foreign telecommunications and securing KPA communications. Electronic Warfare Bureau (전자전국) oversees and trains all electronic warfare and electronic intelligence assets within the KPA [13].

As a Technology and Industrial Base, Korea Computer Center (조선콤퓨터센터) established in 1990 is a state-run IT R&D center. It performs a wide range of IT-related activities including development of computer hardware and software as well as computer networks. Pyongyang Informatics Center (평양정보센터), established in 1986, focuses primarily on software programming widely used in North Korea with around 520 personnel (Fig. 1) [13].

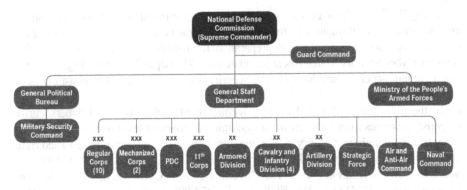

Fig. 1. North Korea's military command structure. [Source: 2014 Defense White Paper (Ministry of National Defense, ROK)] [23]

2.3 Personnel

In 1991, North Korea started to train cyber experts centering to Kim Il Automation University (김일자동화대학), Moranbong University (모란봉대학), Kim Il Sung University (김일성종합대학), and Kim Chaek University of Technology (김책공업종합대학). The number of North Korean hackers has sharply increased from 100 in 2004, 500–600 in 2007, 3,000 in 2012, and 5,900 in 2014. North Korea has strategically nurtured cyber experts in the long term. Young students talented in science and mathematics are educated in Gumseong 1, 2 middle school's computer classes. Students who graduate with honors are privileged with being provided accommodation in Pyeongyang and enter to prestigious universities such as Kim Chaek University of Technology and Kim Il Automation University. After graduating from the university, they study abroad with government support [4]. They receive advanced computer education more than 500 h a year and are allocated to RGB as cyber warriors. In 2015, it is known that the number of North Korean hackers is estimated to 6,800.

3   South Korean Cybersecurity Readiness

3.1 Cybersecurity Response System

Coping with consistent North Korean cyber threats, South Korea is making whole range of efforts. In this part, we shall see South Korea's cybersecurity response system focusing on legislation, responsible organization, and response system.

In South Korea, several legislations and regulations related to cybersecurity have been enacted. Act on Promotion of Information and Communications Network Utilization and Information Protection (정보통신망 이용촉진 및 정보보호 등에관한 법률) focuses on facilitating utilization of information and communications network, protecting information using information and communications services, and developing an environment in which people can utilize information and communication networks in a sounder and safer way. The Act on the Protection of Information and Communications Infrastructure

(정보통신기반보호법) is enacted to operate critical information and communications infrastructure in a stable manner by formulating and implementing measures concerning the protection of such infrastructure, in preparation for intrusion by electronic mean. The National Cyber Security Management Regulation (국가사이버안전관리규정) is a regulation guiding official South Korean cybersecurity response, roles, and responsibilities of various organization [16, 22].

In the policy level, South Korean government officially published cybersecurity response measures in order to ensure a systemic government-level response to various cyber threats to national security. So far, major cybersecurity measures have issued right after national level cyber attacks by North Korea. After 7.7 DDoS attack in 2007, the South Korean government issued 'The Government-wide Cyber Crisis Comprehensive Countermeasure (범정부   사이버위기   종합대책)'. In the countermeasure, KCC (Korea Communications Commission) takes responsibility to report cyber threats against private sector. Also, South Korea established DDoS shelter as well as other response tools. After 3.4 DDoS and Nonghyup Bank attack in 2011, the government announced 'National Cybersecurity Master Plan (국가사이버안보마스터플랜)'. In the plan, South Korea established Private•Public•Military Cyber Threat Joint Response Team, separates networks, and reinforces security of subcontractor companies. In 2013, government announced 'National Cybersecurity Comprehensive Countermeasure (국가   사이버안보종합대책)' after 3.20 and 6.25 cyber terror. In the countermeasure, the Blue House became control tower to the national cybersecurity issue. In 2015, the government built up 'National Cybersecurity Preparation Reinforcement Measure (국가사이버안보태세강화   종합대책)' after hacking on Korea Hydro & Nuclear Power (KHNP). In the measure, National Security Office became a cybersecurity control tower and established Secretary to the Cybersecurity. Also the measure enhanced security to the major information and communications infrastructure [16].

Regarding South Korean cybersecurity response organizations, National Cyber Security Center (NCSC) in South Korea is carrying out major role in dealing with cyber attacks. NCSC is in charge of monitoring and securing public sector computer systems, networks, and critical information infrastructures. In addition, NCSC supports private sectors with technical assistance, public-private partnership programs. It also monitors and coordinates the implementation of South Korean national cybersecurity strategy, policy and roadmap. The Ministry of Science, ICT and Future Planning (MSIP) establishes, supervises, adjusts and evaluates scientific and technological policies, such as on informational security, information culture, ICT convergence promotion and radio wave management. Cyber Warfare Command, established in 2010, is in charge of cyber attacks relating to the national defense (Fig. 2) [19].

3.2 Limits of the Current South Korean Cybersecurity Response System

Although South Korea has made various actions to protect its cybersecurity, still it needs to put forth the necessary efforts to make cyber space much safer. As we reviewed before, South Korea has legal measures, policies, and organizations that could be applied in cyber issues, but they are not complete. First of all, there is no fundamental statute regulating and governing cybersecurity initiatives performed in public and private

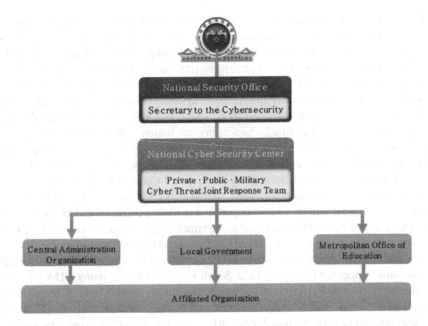

Fig. 2. South Korean cyber attack response system [Source: 2016 National Information Security White Paper (ROKI)] [18]

sector. Under the current cyber attack response structure described in the National Cyber Security Management Regulation, controls shall be limited to public sector since the regulation is a presidential directive which governing only to public sector. The current cyber attack response structure also lacks swiftness and efficiency because several governmental organizations shall have their only authorities on cyber security issues, such as NCSC is in charge of public sector, the Ministry of National Defense in national defense, KCC and KISA (Korea Internet & Security Agency) under the MSIP in the private sector and National Police Agency in investigation. Therefore, the current structure described by presidential directive, shall be prescribed into provisions of Special Act enacted by National Assembly to enrich its application to private sectors to promote South Korean response to cyber attacks. Second, the lack of security management of each public and private sectors aggravate cause problems. The current top-down cybersecurity system is not able to fully operate without voluntary participation of every sector. Third, international cooperation is highlighted in cybersecurity. In many cases, cyber attacks use transit nation in order to conceal origin of attacks. CERTs do have the information sharing system among each other, however, without nation-level cooperation, it is difficult to thwart or investigate cyber attacks [23].

4 Conclusion with Policy Recommendation

Considering the current cyber crises, South Korea needs to seek for better counterplans to cope with North Korean continuous cyber threats.

First of all, South Korea needs to enact the comprehensive Cyber Security Act as soon as possible [20]. The Act should contain provisions describing fundamental structures governing whole stake holders' initiatives protecting South Korean cyber security. The Act should arrange role of cyber security institutions in a better way and be the basis for further grounds in establishing correspondence manual in cyber crisis situation.

Second, autonomous security management system should be strengthened. Every institutions or sectors can be targeted by attackers and although government devises various cyber plans, it is hard to achieve security safe nation without autonomous participation and preparedness by institutions [22]. Every institution is needed to be equipped with cybersecurity or information security plans, division, personnel, and budget.

Third, South Korea needs to actively participate in international consultations on cyber security that create internationally shared cyber norms. Mostly, cyber attacks happen using transfer nation, so it is imperative to have a common understanding that cyberspace should not be utilized as a space to create conflicts among states. Along with international cooperation such as UN and Conference on Cyberspace and regional cooperation such as ARF and OSCE, South Korea needs to enlarge bilateral or multilateral international cooperation on cyber field. South Korea is running many ODA (Official Development Assistance) programs towards developing nations and if Seoul more actively passes on its IT technology into those nations, they will have their own IT ability then they will not be used as a transfer nation by cyber attackers [21]. In order to promote capacity building, South Korea also needs to enhance research and development (R&D) investment, information security industry, threat information sharing system, and cybersecurity experts training.

Forth, the Korean government's constant efforts such as monitoring cyber attacks, strengthening information systems, and establishing policies are in need to respond North Korea cyber attacks [24]. North Korea is well aware of asymmetric advantages of cyber attacks and it will continue to invade South Korea in cyber space. The whole public and private sectors should make their utmost efforts to protect South Korean cybersecurity. North Korea aims to bring economic damage and social chaos, and paralyze C4ISR (Command, Control, Communications, Computers, Intelligence, Surveillance, and Reconnaissance) system. Under the armistice situations, South Korea needs to keep alert to every North Korean provocation using land, sea, air, space, and cyber space.

References

1. KINU North Korea Studies Division: Analysis of North Korea's 2016 New Year's Address and Domestics and Foreign Policy Outlook: Korea Institute for National Unification (KINU) Online Series CO16-01 (2016)
2. Korea Institute for National Unification (KINU): North Korea Domestic and Foreign Policy Evaluation and Outlook after Kim Jong-un seizing the Power: 11th KINU Unification Forum, pp. 1–5 (2015)
3. Feakin, T.: Playing blind-man's buff: estimating North Korea's cyber capabilities. Int. J. Korean Unification Stud. 22(2), 63–90 (2013)

4. Oh(Luke), I.S., Lee, S.Y., Kim, S.J.: Designing effective responding legal and political measures against North Korea's cyber attacks. Institute for National Security Strategy (IISS) Policy Stud. **186** (2015)
5. Kwon, M.T.: A study on countermeasures to the North Korean asymmetric strategy - 'cyber surprise attack'. J. Inf. Secur. **10**(4) (2010)
6. Chanlett-Avery, E., Rinehart, I.E.: North Korea: U.S relations, nuclear diplomacy, and internal situation: Congressional Research service 7-5700, p. 20 (2014)
7. Wood, D.L.: 2015 Index of U.S. Military Strength: The Heritage Foundation (2015)
8. ITU Global Cybersecurity Index & Cyberwellness Profiles (2016)
9. Australian Strategic Policy Institute (ASPI): Cyber Maturity in the Asia-Pacific Region (2015)
10. Bae, S., Park, S., Kim, S.J.: A study on the development for the national cybersecurity capability assessment criteria. J. Korea Inst. Inf. Secur. Cryptology **25**(5), 1293–1314 (2015)
11. Osborne, C.: North Korean tactics in cyberwarfare exposed, CNET
12. Lewis, J.A., Zheng, D.E.: Significant Cyber Events: Center for Strategic & International Studies (CSIS) (2016)
13. Jun, J., LaFoy, S., Sohn, E.: North Korea's Cyber Operations - Strategy and Response: Center for Strategic & International Studies (CSIS) (2016)
14. Choi, H.Y., Jung, H.S.: Analysis of North Korean Cyber Capability, Shindonga, vol. 644 (2015)
15. Korea Institute for National Unification (KINU): North Korea's internal state of affairs. KINU Mon. North Korean Rev. **3**(4) (2009)
16. Robinson, N.: Information Sharing for Cyber-Security: Evidence from Europe: The Asan Institute for Policy Studies, Issue Brief, No. 72 (2013)
17. Jun, Y.O., Yong, B.K., Hong, K.J., Jun, S.H., Tae, S.Y.: A study on measures for strengthening cybersecurity through analysis of cyberattack response. J. Inf. Secur. **15**(4) (2015)
18. National Intelligence Service: Ministry of Science, ICT and Future Planning, Korea Communications Commission. National Information Security White Paper, Ministry of Interior (2016)
19. Park, S., Kim, S.J.: A study on cybersecurity bills for the legislation of cybersecurity act in Korea. J. Inf. Secur. **13**(6) (2013)
20. Jeongyoon, Y., Sangdon, P., Sojeong, K.: Analysis on the U.S Legislation Relation to Cybersecurity: Overview and Discussion of Five Acts Including National Cybersecurity Protection Act: Legislation and Policy, vol. 7, no. 2 (2015)
21. Kim, S.J., Park, S.: A study on cybersecurity policy in the context of international security. J. Inf. Secur. **13**(6) (2013)
22. Park, S., Kim, I.: A study on tasks for the legal improvement for the governance system in cybersecurity. J. Inf. Secur. **13**(4) (2013)
23. Ministry of National Defense, ROK, 2014 Defense White Paper (2014)
24. Morgus, R., Skierka, I., Hohmann, M., Maurer, T.: National CSIRTs and Their Role in Computer Security Incident Response: GPPi, New America, Ministry of Foreign Affairs of the Netherlands (2015)

A Practical Analysis of TLS Vulnerabilities in Korea Web Environment

Jongmin Jeong[✉], Hyunsoo Kwon, Hyungjune Shin, and Junbeom Hur

Department of Computer Science and Engineering, Korea University,
145, Anam-ro, Seongbuk-gu, Seoul 136-701, Korea
{jmjeong,hskwon,hjshin,jbhur}@isslab.korea.ac.kr

Abstract. TLS protocol provides a secure communication environment by guaranteeing the confidentiality and the integrity of transmitted data between two parties. However, there have been lots of vulnerabilities in TLS protocol and attacks exploiting them in aspects of protocol, implementation, and cryptographic tools. In spite of the lessons learned from the past experiences, various attacks on the network systems are being reported continuously due to the lack of care with regard to the proper TLS deployment and management. In this paper, we investigate TLS vulnerabilities in Korea's top 100 websites selected from Alexa global top 500 sites and 291 Korea's public enterprise websites. We compare the analysis results with those of Alexa global top 100 websites. Then, we discuss the lessons learned from this study. In order to analyze TLS vulnerabilities efficiently, we developed a TLS vulnerability scanner, called Network Vulnerabilities Scanner (NVS). We also analyze e-mail security of Korea's top 3 e-mail service providers, which are supposed to be secured by TLS. Interestingly, we found that the e-mail service of them is not so secured by TLS as opposed to the analysis of Google's transparency report.

Keywords: Transport Layer Security · TLS vulnerability · E-mail privacy · Web security

1 Introduction

The Transport Layer Security (TLS) [16] protocol is widely used to establish secure communications which provides confidentiality and integrity of exchanged application data between two communicating parties. Unfortunately, however, TLS protocols have faced lots of security vulnerabilities caused by various reasons such as implementation error, server's misconfiguration, specification design flaws, and so on. For instance, Heartbleed is an implementation bug in TLS protocol which allows attacker to obtain secret information, such as server's secret key. These vulnerabilities are reported on a Common Vulnerabilities and Exposures (CVE) [3] database. Existing vulnerabilities can be solved by applying security patches corresponding to them. However, in practice, lots of security vulnerabilities are not being patched in practical network systems these

© Springer International Publishing AG 2017
D. Choi and S. Guilley (Eds.): WISA 2016, LNCS 10144, pp. 112–123, 2017.
DOI: 10.1007/978-3-319-56549-1_10

days because of many reasons such as inattention of system administrators, late update support of open source library, or irregular and troublesome security inspection.

In this paper, we investigate TLS vulnerabilities in Korea web ecosystems to give awareness to service providers. In order to analyze the TLS vulnerabilities efficiently, we implemented a novel TLS vulnerability scanning tool, called Network Vulnerabilities Scanner (NVS). NVS is a customized scanner, which is specifically designed for efficient detection of the following TLS vulnerabilities: POODLE [17,24], Heartbleed [18,21], SLOTH [14], DROWN [13], and weak cryptographic primitives (that is, RC4 [19,27], MD5 [23,26], and SHA-1 [15,28]) vulnerabilities.

By using NVS, we analyzed TLS vulnerabilities in Korea's top 100 websites selected from Alexa top 500 websites [1], and 291 Korea's public enterprise websites. We, then, compare the investigation results with those of Alexa top 100 websites.

We also analyze e-mail security of Korea's top 3 e-mail service providers, which is the most widely used service in electronic communication on Internet. To protect privacy of the contents of e-mail, it is important to establish secure connection using TLS when sending or receiving an e-mail. If a user sends an e-mail without TLS connection, all communications would be transmitted in a plaintext. This may allow Man-in-the middle (MITM) attackers to hijack and capture original data easily. Therefore, analyzing e-mail security can be seen as another important effort to investigate security vulnerability in Korea web environment in terms of TLS deployment.

The main contributions of this study can be summarized as follows:

1. We investigate TLS vulnerabilities in Korea's websites, and compare the analysis results with those of global websites to inform the status of transport layer security of Korea's web environment. On the basis of the analysis results, we found that lots of server are still vulnerable to specific attacks. Over 30% of all of the websites we investigated are still vulnerable to POODLE attack; but all of them are secure against Heartbleed attack. While none of the Alexa top 100 websites are vulnerable to SLOTH and DROWN, 9% and 19% of Korea top 100 websites, and 16% and 67% of Korea public enterprise websites are vulnerable to SLOTH and DROWN attacks, respectively. For usage of weak cryptographic primitives, 16% of Korea top 100 websites, 36% of Alexa top 100 websites, and 14% of 291 Korea public enterprise websites use RC4; but none of the websites use MD5. While none of the Alexa top websites use SHA-1, 9% of Korea top websites, and 15% of Korea public enterprise websites are still using SHA-1.

2. We analyze security of e-mail service in Korea's top 3 e-mail service providers. According to our study, we found that only one of them supports TLS connection for secure e-mail service. Interestingly, this is an opposite observation to Google's transparency report [5]. This is because Google's transparency report only analyzed TLS connections between e-mail servers. However, TLS connections between client and server should be also considered for e-mail security, which is overlooked by Google's transparency report.

2 Background

In this section, we give a brief introduction to the TLS and its vulnerabilities.

2.1 Transport Layer Protocol (TLS)

TLS is a cryptographic protocol standard for communication security over a computer networks, which was proposed by the Internet Engineering Task Force (IETF) [6]. It's main goals are to provide privacy and data integrity between the client and the server. It prevents malicious adversaries from eavesdropping or tampering private data.

TLS is composed of two layers: the handshake protocol and the record protocol. The handshake protocol enables communicating parties, say client and server, to negotiate the cipher suite and security parameters to generate a session key. Specifically, the handshake protocol progresses as follows. First, the client sends a ClientHello message to the server to provide supported cipher suite list and a random nonce. On receiving ClientHello message, the server sends a ServerHello message including the chosen cipher suite, servers random nonce, and the certificate to the client. If the certificate is validated, the client generates a pre-master secret, encrypts it by servers public key, and sends it to the server over a ClientKeyExchange message. Then, the client and the server can compute a shared master secret using the pre-master secret and the random nonces. Lastly both client and server sends ChangeCipherSpec message specifying that subsequent message will be encrypted by chosen cipher suite and session key.

The record protocol secures application data using the keys created during the handshake protocol.

2.2 TLS Vulnerabilities

In this section, we focus on the up-to-date TLS vulnerabilities, that is POODLE, Heartbleed, SLOTH, and DROWN. Even if POODLE attack can be prevented by disabling support of SSL 3.0, but some servers still support SSL 3.0 for backward compatibility and a variant of the original POODLE attack can exploit by downgrading TLS version from 1.2 to SSL 3.0. Heartbleed, SLOTH, and DROWN are disclosed recently, so we also select these vulnerabilities as useful standards for analyzing security in Korea web environment.

POODLE. Google Security Team discovered Padding Oracle On Downgraded Legacy Encryption (POODLE) and disclosed it on October 14, 2014. POODLE attack [17,24] is started from downgrading TLS version. The servers choose the highest TLS version when connecting with the client, but servers support lower versions because of backward compatibility. Attackers downgrade the version to SSL 3.0. It allows weak cipher suites based on Cipher Block Chaining (CBC) which leads padding oracle attack [29]. The attackers can decrypt messages between the server and the client through this attack.

Heartbleed. Heartbleed [18, 21] was disclosed in April 2014 in the implementation of OpenSSL cryptography library. It results from TLS implementation error in heartbeat extension. In TLS extension, heartbeat is used to check whether the connection is maintained or not between the server and the client. The client and the server exchange the heartbeat messages. But server's improper input validation allows attacker to do buffer over read attack and read more data than should be allowed. Attackers then can obtain critical data such as servers private key.

SLOTH. Security Losses from Obsolete and Truncated Transcript Hashes (SLOTH) [14] was disclosed in 2015. It is a new transcript collision attack caused by insecure hash functions such as MD5 and SHA-1. It incurs authentication failure in secure communication protocol such as TLS and SSH and leads to impersonation attack.

DROWN. Decrypting RSA with Obsolete and Weakened Encryption (DROWN) attack [13] was disclosed in March 2016. It allows attackers to break the confidentiality and reveal sensitive credentials such as passwords, credit card numbers. DROWN attackers can decrypt TLS connections between clients and servers by sending probes to the server that supports SSL 2.0 and uses the same private key.

2.3   Weak Cryptographic Primitives in TLS

In TLS protocol, many cryptographic primitives are supported for flexibility. However some primitives are disclosed vulnerable to specific attacks. We investigate vulnerabilities caused by the insecure cryptographic primitives, that is RC4, MD5, and SHA-1.

RC4. RC4 is a stream cipher which was designed in 1987, and widely used because of its simplicity and speed in software. It is used to encryption function in TLS cipher suite. However, the bias has been discovered in RC4 cipher [19, 27]. Finally, in 2015, IETF published RFC 7465 [25] to prohibit the RC4 cipher in TLS protocol. It can reveal practical key.

MD5. MD5 was initially designed to be used as a cryptographic hash function, however, many vulnerability caused by various collision attack [12, 23, 26] in MD5. According to these vulnerability, MD5 is considered as cryptographically broken and unsuitable for further use.

SHA-1. SHA-1 is cryptographic hash function and it is used to produce message digest in TLS protocol. Cryptanalysts found collision attacks on SHA-1 [15, 28] and it is no longer secure enough. Many organizations recommended its replacement by SHA-2 or SHA-3.

3   Related Work

A survey of TLS vulnerabilities has been presented by Benjamin Fogel [20,22]. They analyzed the top 100,000 sites selected from Alexas Top 1 million global sites in terms of the POODLE attack, and the FREAK attack. They used open-source tools in their survey. In addition, they sorted scanned websites into multiple categories based on ranking, type and security characteristics. Our paper is similar with this work in terms of TLS vulnerability analysis. However, we focus on Korea web environment with more diverse vulnerabilities that is, POODLE, Heartbleed, SLOTH, DROWN, and weak cryptographic primitives. Also, we investigate e-mail security in Korea top 3 e-mail service providers, which is one of the most widely used security application based on TLS in the world.

When it comes to e-mail security, Google provides statistical data that shows whether some enterprise servers encrypt their e-mail or not on inbound and outbound channels in its transparency reports [5]. Even if Google's transparency report analyze how many servers are securing their e-mail using TLS, it only investigates limited part of it, that is server-to-server communication. However, we further analyzed client-to-server connections in e-mail transmission, which could be also important weak point for e-mail security.

4   Analysis of TLS Vulnerability in Korea Web and E-Mail Service

4.1   TLS Vulnerabilities in Web Server

Methodology. In order to scan target servers effectively, we develop a customized scanning tool named Network Vulnerability Scanner (NVS) in JAVA. NVS detects POODLE, SLOTH, Heartbleed, and DROWN vulnerabilities. It also analyzes the usage of weak cryptographic primitives in TLS including RC4, MD5, and SHA-1. In order to detect the vulnerabilities, we designed specific detections rules in NVS for each of them. For instance, if server supports SSL 3.0 and negotiates with weak ciphersuite with CBC mode, that means the target server is potentially vulnerable to POODLE. NVS can scan for specific vulnerability that we defined and take an input websites list and make the scanning result to an excel file. It makes us to analyze the result efficiently. Our tool has been opened to the public as a open-source program in websites [2] and Fig. 1 shows the example of the analysis result. We compare the our scanner's result with Qualys SSL Labs site's analysis [9] to confirm that the detected vulnerabilities are correct. Our result is consistent with the Labs' result.

Data Set. We scanned Korea's top 100 websites from Alexa top 500 sites, and Korea's 291 public enterprises websites. Then, we compare the analysis results with those of Alexa global Top 100 websites. We upload the result of our analysis to the dropbox except target websites' host name. We share the link [10], and you can see the details here.

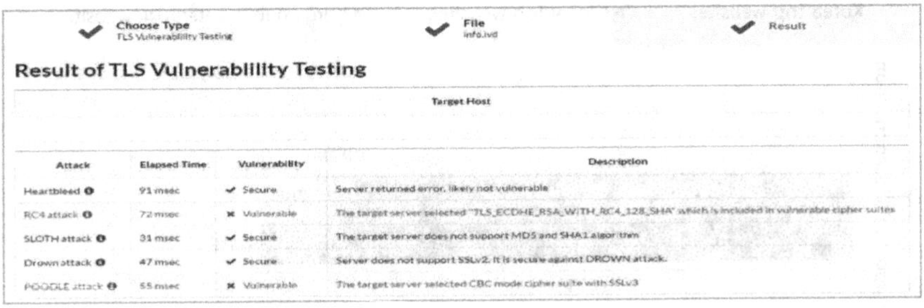

Attack	Elapsed Time	Vulnerability	Description
Heartbleed	91 msec	✓ Secure	Server returned error, likely not vulnerable
RC4 attack	72 msec	✗ Vulnerable	The target server selected "TLS_ECDHE_RSA_WITH_RC4_128_SHA" which is included in vulnerable cipher suites
SLOTH attack	31 msec	✓ Secure	The target server does not support MD5 and SHA1 algorithm
Drown attack	47 msec	✓ Secure	Server does not support SSLv2. It is secure against DROWN attack.
POODLE attack	55 msec	✗ Vulnerable	The target server selected CBC mode cipher suite with SSLv3

Fig. 1. Example of analysis result

4.2 TLS Vulnerabilities in E-mail Service

TLS Connection on E-mail Transmission. Nowadays, many people use an e-mail for electronic communications. If the e-mail contents are exchanged in plaintext, a man-in-the-middle attacker is able to hijack and see the content of the e-mail. In this situation, if the e-mail is encrypted with TLS, eavesdropper cannot read original message. For this reason, TLS connection for the e-mail is an important factor in electronic communication security.

In order to analyze client-to-email server communications (server-to-server communications have been already analyzed by Google's transparency report), we only observe the e-mail transmission from sender's computer to the mail server.

Data Set. We survey Korea's top 3 e-mail service providers: Naver e-mail [8], Daum e-mail [4], Nate e-mail [7].

5 Result of Analysis

5.1 Analysis of the TLS Vulnerability

TLS Vulnerabilities in Korea's Top 100 Websites. We investigate Korea's top 100 websites selected from Alexa top sites list. Figure 2 shows the percentage of websites that supports TLS connection. Among 100 websites, 68% of websites support TLS connection, however, 32% of websites do not support TLS. If website does not offer TLS, TLS vulnerabilities can not exist, however, plaintext would be exchanged between the server and the client. Therefore, the attacker can get or manipulate the original message. Thus, we can consider these websites are vulnerable to all the attacks.

Figure 3 shows another analysis result of vulnerabilities in Korea top 100 websites. According to our investigation, 31% of websites are vulnerable to POODLE. 19% of websites are vulnerable to DROWN attack and 9% of websites are vulnerable to SLOTH. No websites are vulnerable to Heartbleed.

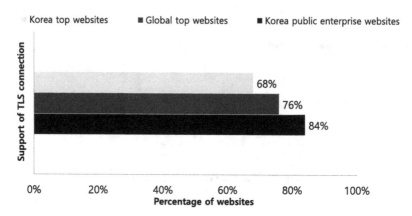

Fig. 2. The percentage of websites that support TLS connection

TLS Vulnerabilities in Global's Top 100 Websites. For comparison purpose, we also investigate global top 100 websites selected from Alexa top sites
list. As we can see in Fig. 2, among 100 websites, 76% of websites support TLS
connection, however, 24% of websites do not support TLS connection.

As shown in Fig. 3, 8% of websites are vulnerable to POODLE. None of the
website has Heartbleed, SLOTH and DROWN vulnerabilities.

TLS Vulnerabilities in Korea Public Enterprise Websites. We investigate 291 Korea public enterprise websites. As shown in Fig. 2, among 291 websites, 84% of websites support TLS connection, however, 16% of websites do
not support TLS. Since public enterprise websites may handle important and

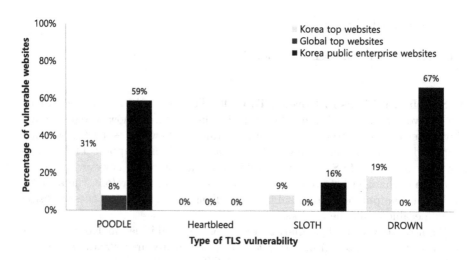

Fig. 3. Percentage of detected vulnerabilities

sensitive information of government, server administrators should make their website support TLS connection.

As shown in Fig. 3, 59% of websites have POODLE vulnerability. 67% of websites are vulnerable to DROWN attack. 16% of websites have SLOTH vulnerability. It presents that many servers are exposed to attack to those latest TLS vulnerabilities, so urgent patches are required.

5.2   Comparison of Korea's Top 100 Websites with Global Top 100 Websites

We compare Korea's TLS web environment with Global's. We compare the percentage of websites that provide TLS connection and weakness to TLS vulnerabilities.

Supporting TLS Connection. 68% of Korea top websites support a TLS connection and 84% of public enterprise websites support a TLS connection. 76% of global websites support a TLS connection. It shows Korea enterprise websites provide comparably more secure communication environment in web service. Despite of importance of TLS connection, still more than 10% of websites do not support TLS in every set.

Weakness to TLS Vulnerabilities. Still over 30% of Korea's top 100 websites are vulnerable to POODLE, while 8% of global top websites are vulnerable. None of the Korea and global websites has Heartbleed vulnerability. While all of the global websites are patched against SLOTH and DROWN, 9% of the Korea websites and 16% of the Korea public enterprise websites are vulnerable to SLOTH and 19% of the Korea websites and 67% of the Korea public enterprise

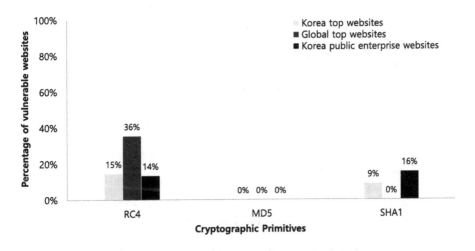

Fig. 4. Usage of weak cryptographic primitives

websites are vulnerable to DROWN, respectively. We can see that Korea websites are relatively more vulnerable to the recent attacks: DROWN and SLOTH. Server administrators for Korea websites should be more circumspective to these vulnerabilities.

5.3   Usage of Weak Cryptographic Primitives in TLS

RC4, MD5, and SHA-1 are recommended to prohibit to use in TLS protocol, since they are vulnerable to several attacks. Figure 4 shows that still 15% of Korea top websites, 36% of global websites, and 14% of Korea public enterprise websites support RC4. For MD5, none of the websites support it. 9% of Korea top websites and 16% of Korea public enterprise websites still support SHA-1. Server administrators should make their server not to support weak cryptographic primitives.

5.4   Analysis of the E-mail Service Providers

We investigate three e-mail service providers. We send an e-mail and check whether the e-mail service provides TLS connection or not. We captured a packet by Wireshark [11] from client to server. According to the results of our investigation, while Naver e-mail supports TLS connection for client-server connection, Daum and Nate e-mail do not. Therefore, we can see the contents of the e-mail that sent from the user. As we can see in Fig. 5, we send an e-mail to

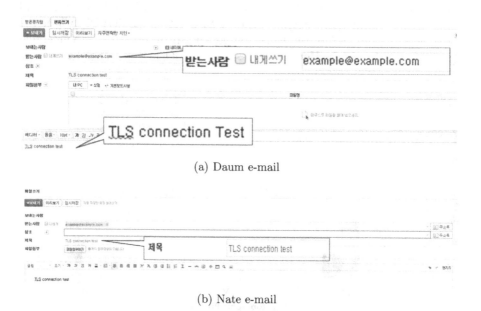

(a) Daum e-mail

(b) Nate e-mail

Fig. 5. An e-mail to example@example.com

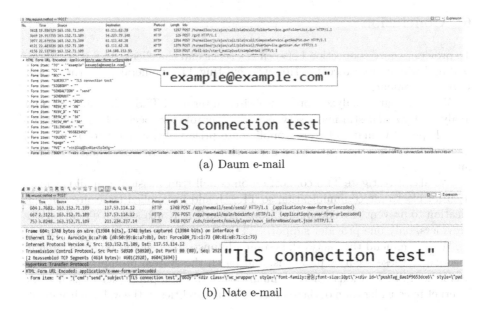

(a) Daum e-mail

(b) Nate e-mail

Fig. 6. Captured HTTP post packet from the user to e-mail server

Table 1. Exposure of content in e-mail

	Naver e-mail	Daum e-mail	Nate e-mail
Receiver	×	○	×
Sender	×	×	○
Title	×	○	○
Body	×	○	×

○: revealed, ×: not revealed

example@example.com with a title 'TLS connection test' and the same e-mail body. Then, we found that the e-mail contents are revealed from HTTP post packet including e-mail address and body in plaintext as we can see in Fig. 6. Table 1 summarizes the results. The receiver is revealed in Daum e-mail, sender is revealed in Nate e-mail, title is revealed in Daum and Nate e-mail, and body is revealed in Daum e-mail. When the e-mail contains secret information such as credit card number or personal information, it may incur huge financial damage to the user by MITM attacker.

According to analysis of Google's transparency report, Nate and Daum e-mail are secure through a TLS connection. However, it is limited to server to server connection. They do not support TLS for client to server connection, so MITM attackers between client and server can hijack the unencrypted packet. It shows that only providing TLS for server to server connection is not enough. Daum and Nate e-mail service should establish client-server TLS connection to secure e-mail content when transmitting the e-mail.

6   Conclusion

To provide secure connection between the sever and the client, TLS is standardized and widely used recently. However, existing TLS vulnerabilities threat safe web environment.

We survey and analyze Korea's websites in terms of TLS vulnerabilities. Our analysis show that still many servers are vulnerable for specific TLS vulnerabilities. Especially, many of Korea public enterprise websites have to be patched immediately, since they may handle important and sensitive governmental information.

We also investigate TLS connection on e-mail transmission. E-mail is widely used for electronic communication so TLS should be applied to secure communication to prevent eavesdropping. However, among Korea's top 3 e-mail service providers, only one provider supports TLS connection when sending an e-mail.

We recommend that network system administrators should be more circumspective to these security problems, and patch the system promptly. Also, web users should be cautious when communicating through public networks like the Internet in consideration of these possible vulnerabilities in the web environment.

Acknowledgments. This work was supported by the National Research Foundation of Korea (NRF) grant funded by the Korea government (MSIP) (No. 2016R1A2A2A05005402). This work was also supported by Institute for Information & communications Technology Promotion (IITP) grant funded by the Korea government (MSIP) (No. R0190-15-2011, Development of Vulnerability Discovery Technologies for IoT Software Security).

References

1. Alexa top 500 sites. http://www.alexa.com/topsites/
2. Center for software security and assurance website. http://iotqv.korea.ac.kr/
3. Common vulerabilities and exposures. https://cve.mitre.org/
4. Daum mail. http://mail.daum.net/
5. Google transparency report about e-mail TLS. https://www.google.com/transparencyreport/saferemail/?hl=ko/
6. The internet engineering task force. https://www.ietf.org/
7. Nate mail. http://mail3.nate.com/
8. Naver mail. http://mail.naver.com/
9. Qualys ssl labs web site. https://www.ssllabs.com/index.html/
10. Target website lists and the result of scanning. https://www.dropbox.com/s/mhr4f7mpioow0hd/Result%20of%20scanning.xlsx?dl=0/
11. Wireshark. https://www.wireshark.org/
12. Aoki, K., Sasaki, Y.: Preimage attacks on one-block MD4, 63-step MD5 and more. In: Avanzi, R.M., Keliher, L., Sica, F. (eds.) SAC 2008. LNCS, vol. 5381, pp. 103–119. Springer, Heidelberg (2009). doi:10.1007/978-3-642-04159-4_7
13. Aviram, N., Schinzel, S., Somorovsky, J., Heninger, N., Dankel, M., Steube, J., Valenta, L., Adrian, D., Halderman, J.A., Dukhovni, V., et al.: Drown: Breaking TLS using SSLv2

14. Bhargavan, K., Leurent, G., Cadé, D., Blanchet, B., Paraskevopoulou, Z., Hriţcu, C., Dénès, M., Lampropoulos, L., Pierce, B.C., Delignat-Lavaud, A., et al.: Transcript collision attacks: breaking authentication in TLS, IKE, and SSH. In: Network and Distributed System Security Symposium-NDSS 2016 (2016)
15. Biham, E., Chen, R., Joux, A., Carribault, P., Lemuet, C., Jalby, W.: Collisions of SHA-0 and reduced SHA-1. In: Cramer, R. (ed.) EUROCRYPT 2005. LNCS, vol. 3494, pp. 36–57. Springer, Heidelberg (2005). doi:10.1007/11426639_3
16. Dierks, T.: The transport layer security (TLS) protocol version 1.2 (2008)
17. Durumeric, Z., Adrian, D., Kasten, J., Springall, D., Bailey, M., Halderman, J.: Poodle attack and SSLv3 deployment (2014)
18. Durumeric, Z., Kasten, J., Adrian, D., Halderman, J.A., Bailey, M., Li, F., Weaver, N., Amann, J., Beekman, J., Payer, M., et al.: The matter of heartbleed. In: Proceedings of the 2014 Conference on Internet Measurement Conference, pp. 475–488. ACM (2014)
19. Fluhrer, S., Mantin, I., Shamir, A.: Weaknesses in the key scheduling algorithm of RC4. In: Vaudenay, S., Youssef, A.M. (eds.) SAC 2001. LNCS, vol. 2259, pp. 1–24. Springer, Heidelberg (2001). doi:10.1007/3-540-45537-X_1
20. Fogel, B.: A survey of web vulnerabilities. Ph.D. thesis, Auburn University (2015)
21. Gujrathi, S.: Heartbleed bug: AnOpenSSL heartbeat vulnerability. Int. J. Comput. Sci. Eng. **2**(5), 61–64 (2014)
22. Fogel, B., Farmer, S., Alkofahi, H., Skjellum, A., Hafiz, M.: POODLEs, more POODLEs, FREAK attacks too: how server administrators responded to three serious web vulnerabilities. In: Caballero, J., Bodden, E., Athanasopoulos, E. (eds.) ESSoS 2016. LNCS, vol. 9639, pp. 122–137. Springer, Cham (2016). doi:10.1007/978-3-319-30806-7_8
23. Liang, J., Lai, X.J.: Improved collision attack on hash function MD5. J. Comput. Sci. Technol. **22**(1), 79–87 (2007)
24. Möller, B., Duong, T., Kotowicz, K.: This poodle bites: exploiting the SSL 3.0 fallback. Google, September 2014
25. Popov, A.: Prohibiting RC4 cipher suites. Comput. Sci. **2355**, 152–164 (2015)
26. Sasaki, Y., Naito, Y., Kunihiro, N., Ohta, K.: Improved collision attack on MD5. IACR Cryptology ePrint Archive 2005, 400 (2005)
27. Vanhoef, M., Piessens, F.: All Your biases belong to Us: Breaking RC4 in WPA-TKIP and TLS. In: 24th USENIX Security Symposium (USENIX Security 15), pp. 97–112 (2015)
28. Wang, X., Yin, Y.L., Yu, H.: Finding collisions in the full SHA-1. In: Shoup, V. (ed.) CRYPTO 2005. LNCS, vol. 3621, pp. 17–36. Springer, Heidelberg (2005). doi:10.1007/11535218_2
29. Yau, A.K.L., Paterson, K.G., Mitchell, C.J.: Padding Oracle attacks on CBC-mode encryption with secret and random IVs. In: Gilbert, H., Handschuh, H. (eds.) FSE 2005. LNCS, vol. 3557, pp. 299–319. Springer, Heidelberg (2005). doi:10.1007/11502760_20

Doppelganger in Bitcoin Mining Pools: An Analysis of the Duplication Share Attack

Yujin Kwon$^{(\boxtimes)}$, Dohyun Kim$^{(\boxtimes)}$, Yunmok Son$^{(\boxtimes)}$, Jaeyeong Choi$^{(\boxtimes)}$,
and Yongdae Kim$^{(\boxtimes)}$

Korea Advanced Institute of Science and Technology (KAIST), 291 Daehak-ro,
Daejeon, Republic of Korea
{dbwls8724,dohyunjk,yunmok00,go1736,yongdaek}@kaist.ac.kr

Abstract. Bitcoin is a cryptocurrency based in peer-to-peer network that uses a blockchain. To maintain the blockchain without trusted third parties, a player called a *miner* proves that he has completed a *proof-of-work*. As the difficulty of *proof-of-work* is increasing, *mining pools*, consisting of a number of miners, have become major players compared with solo miners. Most mining pools consist of a manager and miners. All miners who belong to a mining pool submit their *shares* to the manager and get paid in proportion to the amount of their *shares*. Therefore, the manager has to pay all miners fairly.

However, many Bitcoin mining pools were ruined by an attack called the Duplicate Share Attack (DSA) in 2015. In this paper, we analyze DSA in multiple directions. First, we mathematically analyze DSA against one mining pool and multiple mining pools. As results of our analyses, we derive the optimal attacker's strategy, which shows that DSA can give a large extra profit to an attacker with little computational power. Because the duplicate share vulnerability has been already fixed in a few large mining pools after DSA was introduced, DSA may not be considered a threat any more. However, we show that several small mining pools are still vulnerable to DSA and an attacker can unfairly earn a large extra profit using these unpatched small mining pools. In summary, we argue that honest miners in Bitcoin network are not yet free from DSA.

Keywords: Bitcoin · Mining pool · Duplicate share · Attacker strategy

1 Introduction

Bitcoin is a decentralized cryptocurrency with SHA-256, developed by Satoshi Nakamoto in 2008 [14]. Different from traditional currencies that rely on trusted third parties, Bitcoin uses a peer-to-peer network because of preventing single point of failure. Since Bitcoin's invention, it has been popular, and the current price of 1 BTC (i.e., unit of Bitcoin) has been evaluated to be about 570 USD [7].

In Bitcoin, each exchange of Bitcoin creates a data structure, called a *transaction*. Transactions that are generated in a specific time interval are embedded in a larger data structure, called a *block*. In the header of a block,

© Springer International Publishing AG 2017
D. Choi and S. Guilley (Eds.): WISA 2016, LNCS 10144, pp. 124–135, 2017.
DOI: 10.1007/978-3-319-56549-1_11

information on transactions that are included in the block is also stored using a Merkle tree [17]. In addition, by using a hash chain to headers of all blocks (i.e., a blockchain), the integrity of all blocks can be maintained. To maintain the blockchain without trusted third parties, every block is broadcast to and stored in every peer in a Bitcoin network.

The header of a block includes the Merkle hash value of all transactions in the block, a random number called a *nonce*, and the hash value of the previous block's header. Among these, the nonce is very important in generating a legitimate block. The nonce can be obtained by solving a cryptographic puzzle. On average, every 10 min among the whole Bitcoin network, the puzzle is solved once. Because, for a specific 10 min, all *miners* try to solve the same puzzle, the process for calculate a nonce, called *mining*, is competitive. Additionally, miners that participate in mining take a specific amount of Bitcoin as the subsidy (12.5 BTC in August, 2016) in return for providing computational power to find the nonce.

As the difficulty of the cryptographic puzzle has increased, many *mining pools* have been organized by grouping individual miners. Each miner submits the results of his computation, called a *share*, to the manager of the pool. Then, the manager checks submitted shares and pays the corresponding miners in the pool according to the amounts of their submissions.

However, the payment can be maliciously fabricated by a tricky miner to make unfair profits. In 2015, a technical problem that allows exploitation of duplicated shares was reported [3]. This problem permits an attacker to submit duplicated or crafted shares and be unfairly rewarded for them while providing only a part of her computational power to a mining pool (and, in fact, using the other part of her computational power for solo mining).

In this paper, to the best of our knowledge, we first analyzed the duplicate share attack (DSA) mathematically when a target is one pool. The results of our analyses derive the optimal strategy for maximizing an attacker's profit. The strategy is to send as many duplicate shares as possible while using minimum power. Moreover, if the pool's power is 25%, an attacker can earn a global maximum profit 12.49% of the total 12.5 BTC subsidy with our strategy. We also expand our strategy against one pool to multiple pools. The expanded strategy increases the attacker's profit from the case in which the target is a single pool. To show the feasibility of DSA, we found that multiple small mining pools are still vulnerable to DSA, unlike existing popular ones. According to our analyses, an attacker can earn 4.997% of the total 25 BTC subsidy by trying DSA in multiple small mining pools with a minimum power of 0.24%. This result shows that DSA is more efficient than previous attacks. Therefore, we prove that the Bitcoin system is still unsafe against DSA because of these vulnerable small mining pools. Our contributions are as follows.

- We mathematically analyze DSA for one mining pool and derive the optimal attacker strategy.
- We expand our strategy to target multiple mining pools for maximum profit.

– At the time of submission of this paper, we found that several small mining pools have not patched this vulnerability. We, prove then, that DSA can still allow an attacker to profit unfairly against multiple small, as yet unpatched, mining pools.

This rest of the paper is organized as follows: Sect. 2 provides background knowledge, particularly of mining pools and DSA. Section 3 describes the detailed analyses for DSA against one pool and multiple pools. In addition, the feasibility of our analyses is explained in Sect. 4. Existing related works and our conclusion are presented in Sects. 5 and 6, respectively.

2   Background

In this section, we describe the mining process in a mining pool and the technical problem related to DSA introduced in 2015.

2.1   Mining Process in a Mining Pool

Most mining pools consist of a manager and miners aiming to solve a cryptographic puzzle effectively. To understand this puzzle, it is first necessary to know the components of a *block header*. A block header contains the Merkle hash value of all *transactions* in the *block*, a random number called a *nonce*, and the hash value of the previous block's header. For a given 256-bit number a, the miner tries to find a valid nonce that makes the hash value of the block header smaller than a[1]. Therefore, the probability to find the nonce is $\frac{a}{2^{256}}$; the process of solving this puzzle is called *proof-of-work* [5]. In mining pools, the difficulty of this puzzle can be adjusted more easily. In other words, in order to incentivize the miners to work in pools, a manager can choose to solve this problem using a divide and conquer methodology, by using another 256-bit number b which is larger than a.

Every miner (i.e., honest miner) who belongs to the pool tries to find a valid nonce for target b given by the pool. If one of the miners finds a nonce, he would submit the nonce for his profit to the manager of the mining pool. This nonce is submitted using the Stratum protocol [6,16] which defines a data structure called a *share* for the submission. In general, the Stratum protocol is implemented differently for every mining pool, but the share commonly has five parameters: miner's name, share ID, extra-nonce, current time, and nonce. After a share is submitted, the manager checks it to run the mining pool fairly (e.g., preventing duplicated shares). This checking process is also defined in the mining pool's Stratum protocol, and thus any misimplementation of the protocol can become problematic.

---

[1] Note that for Bitcoin a SHA256-based Hash function is used.

2.2 DSA

In DSA, miners unfairly earn greater profits by submitting duplicate shares to their mining pool manager. This was first noted in Bitcoin Forum [2] in 2015 because it can affect many mining pools [3].

In the Stratum protocol, a mining pool has to detect duplicate shares in order to prevent an attacker from getting paid an unfair profit. Therefore, when an attacker sends a duplicate share to the mining pool, the duplicate share is rejected with a "duplicate share" error. However, the detection processes of many mining pools did not distinguish capital and lowercase letters in data represented as hexadecimal characters (e.g., 0xA versus 0xa). As a result, an attacker could submit duplicate shares by replacing a capital letter with a lowercase letter or vice versa in three parameters of a share: the extra-nonce, current time, and nonce, which are 32-bit hexadecimal values, without "duplicate share" error. For example, nonce 0x01abcdef and 0x01Abcdef are regarded as different nonce even if they are the same value. Using DSA, the attacker can submit on average $(\frac{22}{16})^{24} \approx 2085$ duplicate shares per share.

Currently, the DSA problems of many mining pools have been fixed by replacing all capital letters with lowercase ones in those three parameters in submitted shares before managers check whether shares are duplicate shares. However, some small mining pools have not fixed the problem yet.

3 Mathematical Analysis of DSA

In this section, we mathematically analyze DSA and derive an attack strategy for the maximum profit considering two conditions: first, when an attacker makes an attempt at DSA in only one mining pool and second, in multiple pools. In this paper, *profit* is defined as how much Bitcoin miners can gain in one round on average and *power* refers to the computational power of miners or mining pools which is represented as a relative value between 0 and 1 compared to the total computational power of a Bitcoin network.

In our analysis, we assume as follows.

1. The profit of a solo miner or a mining pool is proportional to their computational power.
2. A manager pays its profit to each miner who belongs to the pool proportionally to his computational power that is used for the pool.
3. The computation power of a mining pool is the sum of all miners in the pool.
4. For simplicity, we also assume that the subsidy is 1 BTC instead of 25 BTC. Therefore, the amount of profit of a mining pool or a solo miner is the value of one's computation power.
5. All managers and miners other than the attacker are honest.

Before analyzing DSA, it is required to show how much an honest miner (without DSA) earns when he divides his power as a solo miner and a participant in a mining pool. If the mining pool and the honest miner have the power α and β, respectively, and the honest miner contributes his power with γ ratio to the mining pool (i.e., the power of the honest miner that is used for the mining pool is $\gamma\beta$), then the profit of the mining pool is $\alpha + \gamma\beta$. Therefore, the honest miner earns not only $\frac{\gamma\beta}{\alpha+\gamma\beta}$ of the pool reward P_{pool} but also $(1-\gamma)\beta$ (P_{solo}) because he can use the rest of his power as solo miner. Finally, his total profit P_h is

$$P_h = P_{solo} + P_{pool} = (1-\gamma)\beta + \frac{\gamma\beta}{\alpha+\gamma\beta} \cdot (\alpha+\gamma\beta) = \beta.$$

This shows that the profit of an honest miner is can still earn profit proportionally to his mining power β. In other words, in a fair and true payoff system, miners' profits are proportional to their own computational power without considering any attack. In this paper, therefore, the goal of an attacker is to earn more profit than an honest miner's profit (i.e., β) by gaining unfair advantage against the mining pool and other honest miners.

3.1   For One Mining Pool

For simplicity, we first analyze the case in which a miner attacks only one pool. The power of a mining pool before an attacker's participation and an attacker are α and β, respectively. If an attacker uses γ ratio of her power in the pool, mining pool power after her participation and her solo mining power are $\alpha + \gamma\beta$ and $(1-\gamma)\beta$ each. We assume that she submits duplication shares k times. Then, she receives $\frac{k\gamma\beta}{\alpha+k\gamma\beta}$ ratio of pool's total profit, and the attacker's total profit P is

$$P = P_{solo} + P_{pool} = (1-\gamma)\beta + \frac{k\gamma\beta}{\alpha+k\gamma\beta} \cdot (\alpha+\gamma\beta)$$

$$= \beta - \gamma\beta + \frac{k\gamma\beta}{\alpha+k\gamma\beta} \cdot (\alpha+\gamma\beta)$$

$$= \beta + f(k,\gamma,\beta).$$

when

$$f(k,\gamma,\beta) = \frac{\alpha\gamma\beta}{\alpha+k\gamma\beta} \cdot (k-1). \quad (k \geq 1) \qquad (1)$$

Equation (1) is an increasing function of k. Therefore, an attacker should copy a share as many as possible to get the maximum profit. If she ideally chooses k as infinity, her total profit P will be

$$\lim_{k\to\infty} P = \alpha + \beta.$$

In other words, an attacker is ideally able to get the maximum $\alpha + \beta$ profit by submitting the same share infinitely. However, k cannot be increased to be infinity in reality because of network delay between the mining pool and an attacker and the possible range of k in technical problem described in Sect. 2. Specifically, the maximum practical k is 2085.

After determining k, an attacker should determine γ in order to get maximal profit. We assume that the an attacker increases his power for mining in a pool

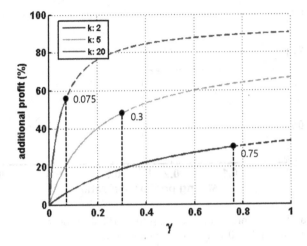

Fig. 1. The x- and y-axes represent γ and %-additional profit, respectively. The percentage additional profit is defined an extra gain compared with the profit P_h of a honest miner and represented as $\frac{P-P_h}{P_h} \cdot 100$. It is also called earnings rate. This figure shows that profit P is an increasing function of γ. Additionally, 0.75, 0.3, and 0.075 are the maximal γ values by Eq. (4) when k is 2, 5, and 20, respectively.

as fake, restricting the fake power of the pool up to 50% of the total substantive power to avoid suspicion of the manager. Hence, γ has to satisfy following condition.

$$k\gamma\beta \leq \min(\frac{1}{2} - \alpha, k\beta) \tag{2}$$

By this condition, an attacker has to choose

$$\beta \geq \frac{1 - 2\alpha}{2k} \tag{3}$$

$$\gamma = \frac{1 - 2\alpha}{2k\beta} \tag{4}$$

so as to earn maximal profit, because profit P is an increasing function of γ, as in Fig. 1. The figure represents the percentage additional profit according to γ when α and β are 0.2. The percentage additional profit is the relative extra profit compared with profit P_h earned by an honest miner, and it is expressed as $\frac{P-P_h}{P_h} \cdot 100$.

Then, an attacker earns profit

$$\beta + \frac{(k-1)\alpha(1 - 2\alpha)}{k}. \tag{5}$$

The second term of Eq. (5) represents extra gain compared to fair profit P_h. It is affected only by the pool's power α, regardless of the attacker's power β. As a result, an attacker can earn a large extra gain with minimal power

$$\frac{1 - 2\alpha}{2k}$$

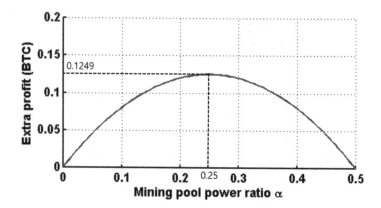

Fig. 2. The x- and y-axes are α and extra profit in BTC, respectively. The extra profit reaches a global maximal of 0.1249 BTC when α is 0.25.

expenditure and, percentage additional profit can increase up to $2(k-1)\alpha \times 100\%$. For example, we assume that one pool has the technical problem described in Sect. 2.2 and the pool's power is 0.2. First, an attacker will choose her maximum k as 2085 per our strategy. Then she needs minimum power 1.4388×10^{-4} by Eq. (3) and can earn maximum 0.1199 BTC additionally. Also, her percentage additional profit will be 83,360% (i.e., approximately 834 times larger) when she uses minimum power 1.4388×10^{-4}.

Moreover, we illustrate Fig. 2 to show the tendency of maximum extra profit according to a pool's power. Figure 2 shows that extra profit is the global maximum when α is 0.25. Therefore, if an attacker tries DSA with minimum computational power in a pool that has 0.25 computational power, she can earn the global maximum extra profit.

3.2   For Multiple Mining Pools

Second, we expand the attacker's strategy from targeted one pool to targeted multiple pools in this section. We assume that the attacker joins in multiple mining pools (pool 1, 2, ... , n), and notations are defined as follows:

α_i : Power of mining pool i

β : Attacker's power

γ_i : The ratio between her power consumed in mining pool i and α_i.

Then her profit $P_{pool\ i}$ gained from pool i is

$$\frac{k\gamma_i\beta}{\alpha_i + k\gamma_i\beta} \cdot (\alpha_i + \gamma_i\beta)$$

if she duplicates a share k times in pool i. She also earns $(1 - \sum_{i=1}^{n} \gamma_i)\beta$ on average by solo mining. Therefore, her total profit P is

$$P = (1 - \sum_{i=1}^{n} \gamma_i)\beta + \frac{k\gamma_i\beta}{\alpha_i + k\gamma_i\beta} \cdot (\alpha_i + \gamma_i\beta)$$

$$= \beta + \sum_{i=1}^{n} f(k, \gamma_i, \beta).$$

when function f is as defined in Eq. (1). Then, we can apply the DSA strategy described in Sect. 3.1 to all mining pools i because the maximization of the attacker's profit in every mining pool is equivalent to maximizing her total profit in the case that targets are multiple pools, as is Eq. (6)

$$\arg\max_{k,\gamma} \beta + \sum_{i=1}^{n} f(k, \gamma_i, \beta)$$

$$= \arg\max_{k,\gamma_i} f(k, \gamma_i, \beta)\ (i = 1 \sim n\,)$$

$$= \arg\max_{k,\gamma_i} \beta + f(k, \gamma_i, \beta)\ (i = 1 \sim n\,). \tag{6}$$

Therefore, an attacker can choose as large k as possible and use the minimal computational power

$$\sum_{i=1}^{n} \frac{1 - 2\alpha_i}{2k} \tag{7}$$

according to Eq. (3) for DSA. Second, she divides her computational power into

$$\gamma_i = \frac{1 - 2\alpha_i}{2k\beta}$$

for pool i so as to get the maximum extra profit. Then she can earn the maximum extra profit

$$\sum_{i=1}^{n} \frac{(k-1)\alpha(1-2\alpha)}{k}.$$

For example, if three mining pools are vulnerable, an attacker can try to apply DSA against three mining pools. If the computational powers of the three mining pools are 0.1, 0.05, and 0.05, respectively, she has to choose k as 2085 and prepare the minimum power 6.235×10^{-4} by Eq. (7). Additionally, she divides her power into 0.3077, 0.3462, and 0.3462, for each of pools 1, 2, and 3 according to our strategy. Then, the attacker can earn the maximum extra profit of 0.1699 BTC. Note that this profit is larger than the 0.1199 BTC that are the maximum extra profit when attacking against one pool with a computational power of 0.2. As a result, we show that an attack against multiple pools is more profitable than one against a single pool, even if the total power of the targets is the same.

4   Feasibility of DSA

At present, most of the popular mining pools have patched the DSA vulnerability described in Sect. 2. Therefore, many people may believe that an attacker cannot earn unfairly a large extra profit but a small extra profit by DSA. However, several mining pools still have this problem, though they are unpopular and have relatively little computing power (i.e., less than 1% of the whole power of the Bitcoin network). For this, we reviewed programs for bitcoin in the Github repository and discovered that at least 28 projects still have the DSA vulnerability. With this, one interesting question is if one can get a significantly large extra profit by utilizing DSA against these small, as yet unpatched mining pools. Before analyzing the extra profit from attacking multiple small mining pools, we first recall the maximum additional profit that an attacker can gain through DSA against one pool with power ratio α:

$$\frac{(k-1)\alpha(1-2\alpha)}{k}. \tag{8}$$

Further, when the target is n pools and each pool i has power α_i, recall that the maximum additional profit is

$$\sum_{i=1}^{n} \frac{(k-1)\alpha_i(1-2\alpha_i)}{k}. \tag{9}$$

Because all α_i (<0.01) are small, Eq. (9) is approximated to

$$\frac{k-1}{k} \sum_{i=1}^{n} \alpha_i. \tag{10}$$

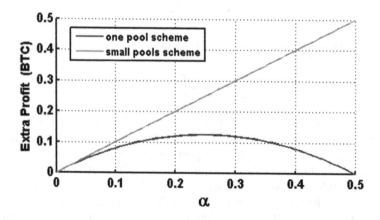

Fig. 3. The x-axis is the total power of target mining pools and the y-axis is additional profit in BTC. The red and blue lines mean extra profits when the target is small pools and one pool, respectively. (Color figure online)

Table 1. Each mining pool's computational power in the last three years (from May, 2013 to May, 2016). We calculated the distribution of their computational powers from [4].

Mining pool	Computational power (%)	Mining pool	Computational power (%)
F2Pool	19.72%	Eligius	6.27%
GHash.IO	16.27%	Slush	5.96%
AntPool	11.93%	BW.COM	4.24%
BitFury	7.77%	KnCMiner	1.97%
BTCC pool	6.71%	The others[a]	19.16%

[a] Includes small mining pools and solo miners.

Equation (10) is always greater than the Eq. (8), in concurrence with what we see in Fig. 3. The x- and y-axes of Fig. 3 represent targeted pools' total power ratio and the attacker's extra profit in BTC, respectively. The scheme for small pools is always more efficient than the scheme for one pool even if the targets' total power is the same as the power of the single target pool.

To show the impact of DSA, we estimate the attacker's extra profit in current pools' computational power distribution according to our strategy. Table 1 is mining pools' power distributions for recent three years and, *the others* includes small pools and solo miners. Assume that the attacker's targets are a set of unpatched small mining pools possibly belonging to *the others*. Further, we assume that the number of vulnerable small pools is 28 and the total computing power of the set is 5% (i.e., $\sum_{i=1}^{28} \alpha_i = 0.05$). In this case, by applying Eq. (10) with these numbers, we can conclude that an attacker can unfairly earn a maximum extra profit of 0.04997 BTC by using a minimum power 0.0067.

We note that DSA is significantly more efficient than other previous attacks. Rosenfeld [15] analyzed the pool-hopping attack and claimed that an attacker can earn 0.02815 BTC more in profit than an honest miner by using a computational power 0.1. Additionally, Luu et al. [13] showed that an attacker's extra profit can be 0.0123 BTC by performing a block withholding attack with a computational power 0.25. In contrast, the DSA attack against a set of small mining pools can let the attacker obtain 0.04997 BTC by using a computational power 0.0067. Therefore, we can conclude that DSA against small mining pools is the strongest attack compared to previous ones.

5   Related Work

In recent years, a number of papers have studied the security of the Bitcoin world, such as double spending for fast payment, anonymity, and selfish mining. Particularly, attacks and a competition among mining pools also have been studied, as pools have become major players in the Bitcoin world.

An attacker can perform selfish mining in a mining pool, which means that the attacker unfairly receives more pay from the pool manager [1,10].

Rosenfeld [15] introduced the most widely known attack to mining pools, called a block withholding attack (BWH). The attack is that miners in the pool do not submit valid a nonce which makes a block legitimate, so as to degrade the mining pool's power. The author argued that an attacker does not earn any benefit from the pool by the BWH attack. However, Courtois et al. [8] proved that the BWH attack allows an attacker to earn more profit in the long term, proposing a practical BWH attack that generalizes the BWH attack introduced by Rosenfeld [15]. Moreover, Luu et al. [13] found an optimal strategy of an attacker, focusing on splitting his power into several mining pools in order to get a maximum profit. At the same time, Eyal [9] introduced a notion called the miner's dilemma, which refers to the decision of whether or not to perform a BWH attack in a game between two pools and estimated a BWH attack's effect on two pools. We do not consider BWH attacks in this paper.

The competition among mining pools has been analyzed based on game theoretic models [8,12]. Johnson et al. [11] considered a competition between two mining pools which can make an attempt at Distributed Denial-of-Service (DDoS) attacks each other. They claimed that managers of two pools can choose mischievous tactics, such as triggering a DDoS attack to lower a competing pool's mining power, and compared the trade-off between mischievous tactic and the benign tactic, which is to perform honest mining in the Bitcoin network, under game-theoretic analysis. Meanwhile, we focus herein on the DSA attack of an miner against mining pools instead of the relation between mining pools.

6   Conclusion

In 2015, DSA introduced in Bitcoin Forum was caused by an implementation problem in many mining pools. In this paper, we first derive the optimal strategy of an attacker for DSA mathematically. Our results show that, considering multiple small unpatched mining pools, an attacker can gain a large amount of unfair profit using minimal computational power by DSA using our optimal strategy. Therefore, we conclude that, as ever, DSA is a practical threat to Bitcoin systems, even if many major mining pools have patched the vulnerability. We also argue that managers or developers of existing mining pools must patch the problem in their Stratum protocols as soon as possible.

Acknowledgments. This work was partly supported by Institute for Information & communications Technology Promotion (IITP) grant funded by the Korea government (MSIP) (No. B0717-16-0116, Development of information leakage prevention and ID management for secure drone services) and Institute for Information & communications Technology Promotion (IITP) grant funded by the Korea government (MSIP) (No. R-20160222-002755, Cloud based Security Intelligence Technology Development for the Customized Security Service Provisioning).

References

1. Bahack, L.: Theoretical Bitcoin Attacks with Less than Half of the Computational Power (draft). arXiv preprint arXiv:1312.7013 (2013)
2. Bitcoin Forum: Bitcoin Forum (2016). https://bitcointalk.org/. Accessed 05 June 2016
3. Bitcoin Forum: Duplicate Shares Exploit - Most Pools Affected (2016). https://bitcointalk.org/index.php?topic=1065576.0. Accessed 05 June 2016
4. BitcoinChain: Bitcoin Mining Pools (2016). https://bitcoinchain.com/pools. Accessed 05 June 2016
5. Bitcoinwiki: Proof of Work (2016). https://en.bitcoin.it/wiki/Proof_of_work. Accessed 05 June 2016
6. Bitcoinwiki: Stratum Mining Protocol (2016). https://en.bitcoin.it/wiki/Stratum_mining_protocol. Accessed 05 June 2016
7. CoinDesk: Bitcoin Price Index Chart (2016). http://www.coindesk.com/price/. Accessed 05 June 2016
8. Courtois, N.T., Bahack, L.: On subversive miner strategies and block withholding attack in bitcoin digital currency. arXiv preprint arXiv:1402.1718 (2014)
9. Eyal, I.: The Miner's dilemma. In: 2015 IEEE Symposium on Security and Privacy (SP), pp. 89–103. IEEE (2015)
10. Eyal, I., Sirer, E.G.: Majority is not enough: bitcoin mining is vulnerable. In: Christin, N., Safavi-Naini, R. (eds.) FC 2014. LNCS, vol. 8437, pp. 436–454. Springer, Heidelberg (2014). doi:10.1007/978-3-662-45472-5_28
11. Johnson, B., Laszka, A., Grossklags, J., Vasek, M., Moore, T.: Game-theoretic analysis of DDoS attacks against bitcoin mining pools. In: Böhme, R., Brenner, M., Moore, T., Smith, M. (eds.) FC 2014. LNCS, vol. 8438, pp. 72–86. Springer, Heidelberg (2014). doi:10.1007/978-3-662-44774-1_6
12. Laszka, A., Johnson, B., Grossklags, J.: When bitcoin mining pools run dry: a game-theoretic analysis of the long-term impact of attacks between mining pools. In: BITCOIN 2015: The Second Workshop on Bitcoin Research. Citeseer (2015)
13. Luu, L., Saha, R., Parameshwaran, I., Saxena, P., Hobor, A.: On power splitting games in distributed computation: the case of bitcoin pooled mining. In: 2015 IEEE 28th Computer Security Foundations Symposium (CSF), pp. 397–411. IEEE (2015)
14. Nakamoto, S.: Bitcoin: A Peer-to-Peer Electronic Cash System (2008)
15. Rosenfeld, M.: Analysis of bitcoin pooled mining reward systems. arXiv preprint arXiv:1112.4980 (2011)
16. SLUSH POOL: Stratum Mining Protocol (2016). https://slushpool.com/help/#!/manual/stratum-protocol. Accessed 05 June 2016
17. Wikipedia: Merkle tree – wikipedia, the free encyclopedia (2016). https://en.wikipedia.org/w/index.php?title=Merkle_tree&oldid=720708959. Accessed 05 June 2016

Detecting Impersonation Attack in WiFi Networks Using Deep Learning Approach

Muhamad Erza Aminanto and Kwangjo Kim[✉]

Cryptology and Information Security Lab, School of Computing,
Korea Advanced Institute of Science and Technology (KAIST),
Daejeon, Republic of Korea
{aminanto,kkj}@kaist.ac.kr

Abstract. WiFi network traffics will be expected to increase sharply in the coming years, since WiFi network is commonly used for local area connectivity. Unfortunately, there are difficulties in WiFi network research beforehand, since there is no common dataset between researchers on this area. Recently, AWID dataset was published as a comprehensive WiFi network dataset, which derived from real WiFi traces. The previous work on this AWID dataset was unable to classify Impersonation Attack sufficiently. Hence, we focus on optimizing the Impersonation Attack detection. Feature selection can overcome this problem by selecting the most important features for detecting an arbitrary class. We leverage Artificial Neural Network (ANN) for the feature selection and apply Stacked Auto Encoder (SAE), a deep learning algorithm as a classifier for AWID Dataset. Our experiments show that the reduced input features have significantly improved to detect the Impersonation Attack.

1 Introduction

In the near future, wireless network traffics will rise drastically. According to Cisco Visual Networking Index report [1], wireless traffics will account for two-thirds of total Internet traffics by 2020. Then, we expect that 66% of IP traffics come from WiFi and mobile devices. For local area connectivity, WiFi networks (so called 802.11 networks) are widely deployed. The increased usage of WiFi network will be followed by unknown attacks and vulnerabilities accordingly. There are several security protocol for WiFi network such as Wired Equivalent Privacy (WEP) and WiFi Protected Access 2 (WPA2) [2]. Our goal is to make these protocols more secure against unauthorized traffic by Intrusion Detection System (IDS) using up-to-date deep learning approach.

This work was partly supported by Institute for Information & communications Technology Promotion (IITP) grant funded by the Korea government (MSIP) (B0101-16-1270, Research on Communication Technology using Bio-Inspired Algorithm) and the National Research Foundation of Korea (NRF) grant funded by the Korea government (MSIP) (No. NRF-2015R1A2A2A01006812).

D. Choi and S. Guilley (Eds.): WISA 2016, LNCS 10144, pp. 136–147, 2017.
DOI: 10.1007/978-3-319-56549-1_12

However, IDS research on WiFi network was difficult since there was no common dataset so for. Recently, Kolias *et al.* [2] published a comprehensive WiFi network dataset, called Aegean WiFi Intrusion Dataset (AWID). This dataset contains 14 distinct attacks categorized by three different attacks. There are a number of previous work that use AWID dataset: Usha and Kavitha *et al.* [8], Alotaibi [4], *etc.* Unfortunately, all the previous publications were unable to improve the Impersonation Attack detection. Impersonation Attack is one of forging activity in order to take an advantage over others. Usually, it masquerades a legitimate device in a WiFi network. So, we try to improve the Impersonation Attack using AWID dataset. Major improvements of the previous IDSs can be achieved by leveraging the latest highly effective machine learning methods [5], so called deep learning. The computations for most of deep learning are heavy. Reducing the dimensionality of input features is one of light candidate solutions.

We leverage Artificial Neural Network (ANN) for the feature selection. The weight from trained models mimics the importance of the correspondence input. By selecting the important features only, the training process becomes lighter and faster than before. To validate our approach, we use *Stacked Auto Encoder* (SAE) as a classifier, which is one of popular deep learning algorithms, since this employs consecutive layers of processing stages in hierarchical manners for pattern classification and feature or representation learning [3]. Our experiment shows that the reduced input features are sufficient for SAE algorithm to achieve better detection rate for Impersonation Attack.

This paper is organized as follows: Sect. 2 reviews related work in brief. We describe our proposed scheme in Sect. 3. Section 4 reports our experimental results and analysis. Conclusion and future work of this paper will be presented in Sect. 5.

2   Related Work

The importance of feature selection for IDS dataset was introduced by Kayacik *et al.* [3]. They investigated the relevance of each feature in KDD 99 Dataset and provided the information gain for each feature. Their conclusion ends with the list of the most relevant features for each class label. Afterwards, there are several publications that employ feature selection method. Zaman and Karray [6] categorized the IDS based on the TCP/IP network model using a feature selection method called Enhanced Support Vector Decision Function (ESVDF). Louvieris *et al.* [7] proposed an effects-based feature identification IDS using Naive Bayes as a feature selection method.

In this paper, we focus on WiFi network. Kolias *et al.* [2] published a comprehensive WiFi network traces that becomes a public dataset for 802.11 networks. They checked various machine learning algorithms to validate their dataset in a heuristic manner. Among all the classification results, Impersonation Attack detection is the most unsatisfactory result. Hence, our goal is to improve the Impersonation Attack detection. We leverage recent deep learning algorithm published by Wang [9]. In 2015, Wang has shown that neural networks especially the deep neural networks can be used for finding features in the raw network flow data. We use AWID dataset [2] for our experimental purpose. Recently, Usha and Kavitha *et al.* [8] leveraged AWID dataset and successfully improved the overall detection rate. However, they didn't focus on improving Impersonation Attack detection which is the one of most concerns by Kolias *et al.* [2].

3 Our Approach

In this section, we briefly describe our approach to improve Impersonation Attack detector. Basically there are two main tasks, feature selection and classification. Figure 1 shows our proposed architecture which starts with data collection task, and then training phase, ends by validation phase. We use a real WiFi networks trace, AWID [2]. The preprocessing should be conducted before using AWID dataset. The preprocessed dataset will be fed into feature selection method. Feature selection method which contains ANN learner results a list of important features to detect Impersonation Attacks. In order to validate this reduced feature list, we employ one of deep learner, SAE.

3.1 Data Preprocessing

AWID dataset [2] not only contains discrete type, but also consists of continuous, and symbolic types with flexible value range. This format will be difficult for most of pattern classification methods to learn [10]. The preprocessing should be conducted in advance. There are two main steps for the preprocessing: the mapping step from symbolic-valued attributes into numeric values and the normalizing step. Target class will be mapped into one of these integer-valued classes: 1 for Normal, 2 for Impersonation, 3 for Flooding and 4 for Injection Attacks. Meanwhile, symbolic attributes such as receiver, destination, transmitter, source address, *etc.*, will be mapped into integer values with scale from 1 to N where N is the number of symbols. Some attributes that have hexadecimal values such

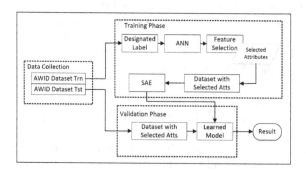

Fig. 1. Our proposed architecture

as WEP Initialization Vector (IV) and Integrity Check Value (ICV) need to be casted into the integer values. Also, there are some attributes with continues values as the timestamp. In addition, AWID dataset also contains the question mark ("?") for those not available value on the corresponding attributes. This question mark can be assigned with zero value. After all attributes values casted into the integer values, each of the attributes linearly normalized between zero and one. Equation (1) shows the normalizing formula.

$$z_i = \frac{x_i - min(x)}{max(x) - min(x)}, \tag{1}$$

where z_i denotes the normalized value, x_i refers to the corresponding attribute value and $min(x)$ and $max(x)$ are the minimum and maximum values of the attribute, respectively.

3.2   Feature Selection

Feature selection belongs to feature learning which contains feature extraction and feature selection [9]. Feature learning is defined as the ability to model the traffic behavior from the most characterizing raw input. Feature learning is very important to show the correlation between the detection performance and the traffic model quality [11]. However, feature extraction and selection are different terms. Feature extraction refers to deriving new features from raw feature space to be informative and non-redundant. Those features in raw feature and new generated features are usually different. On the other hand, feature selection is to select several features from the raw feature space. So, new generated features are just selected from the raw one without transformation. Both feature extraction and selection are aiming the smaller number of new generated features than the raw one. In this paper, *we adopt feature selection using ANN explicitly while feature extraction is deployed in SAE implicitly.*

We apply ANN in order to improve Impersonation Attack detection rate. By using ANN, we are able to choose some features which are important to learn the Impersonation Attack model based on the heuristic weights from ANN learning. We train our ANN with two target classes only, Normal and Impersonation Attack, instead of four target classes. Figure 2 shows the ANN model where $b1$ and $b2$ represent the bias values for the corresponding hidden layer, respectively.

We use the first hidden layer only for feature selection and consider the weight value between the first two layers to choose the important input features. The weight represents the contribution of the input features to the first hidden layer features. Very small or even zero W_{ij} means that the corresponding input feature x_j is meaningless for further propagation. So, one hidden layer is sufficient since we consider the weights in the first hidden layer only. We define the importance value of each input feature, as expressed by Eq. (2).

$$V_j = \sum_{i=1}^{h} |W_{ij}|, \tag{2}$$

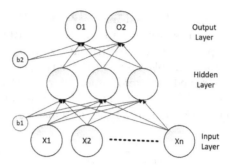

Fig. 2. ANN model

where h is the number of neurons in the first hidden layer. In order to select the most important features, we sort the input features according to V_j value in a descending order. We pick some features that have V_j value bigger than a threshold value.

3.3 Classification

In order to validate the performance of chosen features, we utilize a deep learning algorithm. Deep learning is a class of machine learning methods, which exploits the cascaded layers of data processing stages in hierarchical structure for unsupervised feature learning and for pattern classification. We choose SAE as a classifier because SAE is able to replace original features with unsupervised approach and has hierarchical feature extraction phase. Basically, Auto Encoder (AE) model is similar to ANN as shown in Fig. 3.

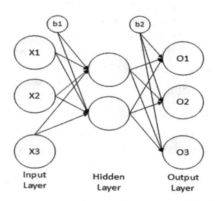

Fig. 3. AE model

Compared with ANN model, AE model is characterized by the same number of the input and output layers. Meanwhile, the nodes in the hidden middle layer represent new features set with lower dimension. This architecture leads to an ability that can reconstruct the data after complicated computations. Since AE aims to learn a compact set of data efficiently, it can be stacked to build deep networks. Each training results of the middle layer can be cascaded. This structure is called SAE, which can learn lots of new features in different depths [9]. Figure 4 shows the proposed SAE architecture used in this paper.

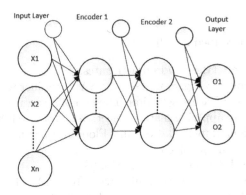

Fig. 4. Proposed SAE architecture

We employ two hidden (encoder) layers. The features that were generated from the first encoder layer used as the training data in the second encoder layer. Meanwhile, the size of each hidden representation is decreased accordingly so that the encoder in the second encoder layer learns an even smaller representation of the input data. We complete our stacked architecture with the supervised learning approach by *softmax* regression function, which is a generalization of logistic regression for classification purposes using labels from training data. The function can take more than two possible classes and is commonly cascaded after any unsupervised learning methods.

4 Evaluation

In this section, we show the detailed steps before conducting our experiments and the results. We first explain our four Tests here and the dataset preparation followed by the experimental results and analysis.

4.1 Experiment Setup

We constructed four Tests in order to show that our proposed scheme can improve Impersonation Attack detection rate. Table 1 shows the summary of our four Tests.

Table 1. Summary of our four tests

Test	Trn dataset	Tst dataset	Attributes	Feature selection	Target classes
(a)	Unbalanced	Unbalanced	154	N/A	4
(b)	Balanced	Balanced	154	N/A	2
(c)	Balanced	Balanced	35	ANN	2
(d)	Balanced	Unbalanced	35	ANN	2

Four Tests are described as follows:

1. Test (a): All target classes and all attributes.
   In Test (a) as shown in Fig. 5, we feed the SAE classifier with the normalized
   dataset without any feature selection. The aim of Test (a) is to show the basic
   performance before applying feature selection method. All four target classes
   (Normal, Injection, Impersonation and Flooding) are included and original
   154 input features are involved.
2. Test (b): Balanced dataset and all attributes.
   Test (b) as shown in Fig. 6 is similar with Test (a). The difference is that
   Test (b) uses balanced dataset and considers two target classes (Normal and
   Impersonation) only. Test (b) aims to show the performance if we focus on
   detecting Impersonation Attack only with the whole original attributes. Two
   target classes are included and 154 input features are involved.
3. Test (c): Balanced dataset and reduced attributes.
   We employ our proposed scheme in Test (c) as shown in Fig. 7. We first generate the balanced dataset that aim to detect Impersonation Attack properly.
   We train our ANN with the balanced dataset and output a list of selected
   important features. Next, balanced test dataset with selected features only
   is fed into SAE classifier. The aim of Test (c) is to show that our proposed
   scheme can outperform Test (a). Two target classes (Normal and Impersonation) are included and selected 35 input features are involved.
4. Test (d): Full dataset test from learned system.
   Test (d) as shown in Fig. 8 is almost same with Test (c). The only difference
   is that Test (d) uses full test dataset which is unbalanced. The goal of Test
   (d) is to show that the learned model by Test (c) is able to work in real
   detection process. In Test (d), two target classes (Normal and Impersonation)
   are included and selected 35 input features are involved.

In addition, we deploy an experiment environment: MATLAB R2016a which
runs in Intel(R) Xeon(R) CPU E-3-1230v3@3.30 GHz, RAM 32 GB. Also, as the
performance evaluation, we use Detection Rate (DR) which is the number of
correctly detected attacks divided by the total number of attacks. On the other
hand, False Positive Rate (FPR), defined as the number of normal instances
that are classified incorrectly as attacks divided by the total number of normal
instances. Intuitively, we should maintain DR as high as possible and FPR as
low as possible.

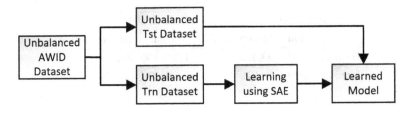

Fig. 5. Test (a)

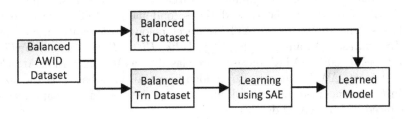

Fig. 6. Test (b)

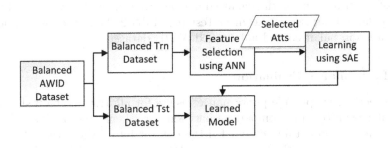

Fig. 7. Test (c)

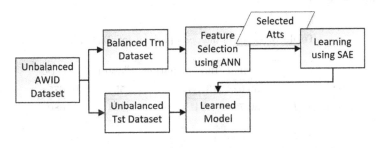

Fig. 8. Test (d)

Table 2. Distribution of each classes in balanced and unbalanced dataset

	Balanced		Unbalanced	
	Normal	Impersonation	Normal	Impersonation
Train	163,319	48,522	1,633,190	48,522
Test	53,078	20,079	530,785	20,079

4.2 Dataset

The AWID dataset [2] contains real trace of WiFi traffic. There are two types of AWID dataset based on the number of target classes. The first type named "CLS" with four target classes and the second named "ATK" with 16 target classes. The 16 classes of "ATK" dataset belong to four attack categories in "CLS" dataset. As an example, *Caffe-Latte, Hirte, Honeypot* and *EvilTwin* attack types listed in "ATK" dataset, are classified as Impersonation Attack in "CLS" dataset. AWID dataset also divided into two types based on the size of data instances included, namely full and reduced dataset. In this paper, we use the reduced "CLS" AWID dataset.

We need to do balancing of the AWID dataset since it contains a huge number of normal instances compared to attack instances, especially Impersonation Attack. We need to take balancing for training purpose. Once the IDS model was successfully trained using the balanced dataset, we can validate the model using the unbalanced dataset as shown in Test (d). Table 2 shows the distribution of each classes in balanced and unbalanced AWID dataset.

4.3 Performance Evaluation

In this section, we provide performance results for all Tests. Table 3 shows the performance of Test (a), comparison between our scheme and original work [2]. In Test (a), we do nothing except fed the dataset into SAE learner. This approach already improves the Impersonation Attack detection with classified 13,087 (65%) instances correctly. Also, this approach has comparable performance in classifying Normal and Injection Attacks. However, the DR for Flooding Attack is still unsatisfactory.

Table 3. Performance comparison for Test (a)

	Normal	Impersonation	Flooding	Injection
Test (a)	530,028	13,087	2,555	16,675
Kolias *et al.* [2]	530,765	4,419	5,974	16,680

Test (b) focuses on detecting Impersonation Attack in balanced dataset. And as expected, it shows the highest DR for both Impersonation Attack and Normal

Table 4. Performance comparison for Tests (b), (c) and (d)

	Normal	DR	FPR	Duration
Kolias *et al.* [2]	530,765 (99.9%)	4,419 (22%)	14,187 (2.75%)	-
Test (b)	52,427 (98.6%)	18,613 (92.7%)	651 (1.23%)	30 min
Test (c)	51,826 (97.6%)	17,033 (85%)	1,252 (2.36%)	5 min
Test (d)	518,237 (97.6%)	17,033 (85%)	12,548 (2.36%)	5 min

classes among all Tests as shown in Table 4. However, it took about 30 min for training and validating process. Meanwhile, Test (c) and (d) took about 5 min only.

In Test (c), we first train our ANN learner as a feature selection method as expressed in Fig. 7. We consider weights on first hidden layer only. Figure 9 shows the distribution of each input feature's weight. In order to get selected important features, we set the threshold value to 15 due to most of attributes have weight value lower than 15. We may adjust the threshold value in order to get optimal result. Hence, 35 features are selected, as listed in Table 5.

We use the balanced dataset in Test (c) in order to learn the Impersonation Attack properties properly. We select 35 attributes only based on previous result, and fed it into SAE learner. Table 4 shows the performance comparison for Tests (b), (c) and (d). The DR for Impersonation Attack in Test (b) is significantly improved compared to Kolias *et al.* [2]. Also, the DR for Normal class is slightly below the original work. Test (b) also shows the significant improvement on FPR.

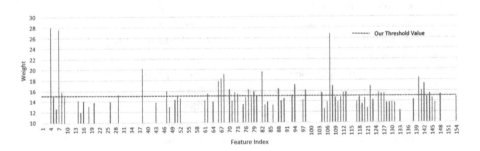

Fig. 9. Distribution of each input feature's weight

Test (d) is the same Test (c) with different test dataset. We use the unbalanced dataset which contains full test instances from AWID dataset [2]. By this approach, we demonstrate that our learned model is able to be used for detecting Impersonation Attack properly in real network traffic. Table 4 shows that the DR for both classes are the same for Tests (c) and (d). This result supports our claim that the learned model by Test (c) can be implemented in real network traffic.

Table 5. Selected features for Impersonation Attack detector

Index	Feature name	Description
4	frame.time_epoch	Epoch time
7	frame.time_relative	Time since reference or first frame
8	frame.len	Frame length on the wire
29	radiotap.present.rxflags	RX flags
38	radiotap.mactime	MAC timestamp
47	radiotap.datarate	Data rate (Mb/s)
62	radiotap.antenna	Antenna
66	wlan.fc.type	Type
67	wlan.fc.subtype	Subtype
68	wlan.fc.ds	DS status
70	wlan.fc.retry	Retry
72	wlan.fc.moredata	More data
73	wlan.fc.protected	Protected flag
77	wlan.da	Destination address
79	wlan.sa	Source address
80	wlan.bssid	BSS Id
82	wlan.seq	Sequence number
88	wlan.ba.bm	Block Ack bitmap
93	wlan_mgt.fixed.capabilities.privacy	Privacy
94	wlan_mgt.fixed.capabilities.preamble	Short preamble
98	wlan_mgt.fixed.capabilities.short_slot_time	Short slot time
104	wlan_mgt.fixed.listen_ival	Listen interval
107	wlan_mgt.fixed.timestamp	Timestamp
108	wlan_mgt.fixed.beacon	Beacon interval
112	wlan_mgt.fixed.auth_seq	Authentication SEQ
113	wlan_mgt.fixed.category_code	Category code
122	wlan_mgt.tim.dtim_period	DTIM period
125	wlan_mgt.country_info.environment	Environment
126	wlan_mgt.rsn.version	RSN version
127	wlan_mgt.rsn.gcs.type	Group cipher suite type
140	wlan.wep.iv	Initialization vector
141	wlan.wep.key	Key index
142	wlan.wep.icv	WEP ICV
144	wlan.ccmp.extiv	CCMP Ext. initialization vector
148	wlan.qos.ack	Ack policy

5   Conclusion and Future Work

We address the limitation of the previous work which was unable to detect
Impersonation Attack properly. We employ feature selection method in order

to select the most important attributes for detecting Impersonation Attack. We selected 35 attributes based on our ANN learning. Our experiments using SAE learner with selected features show significant improvements compared to Kolias *et al.* [2].

In the near future, we will conduct experiments for all attack classes of AWID dataset. In addition, combining several learning methods as an ensemble learning is a challenging issue in order to achieve optimal IDS in WiFi network.

Acknowledgment. The authors are very grateful to anonymous reviewers for their valuable feedbacks and suggestions.

References

1. Cisco Visual Networking Index: Forecast and Methodology, 2015–2020. http:// www.cisco.com/c/en/us/solutions/collateral/service-provider/visual-networking-index-vni/complete-white-paper-c11-481360.html
2. Kolias, C., Kambourakis, G., Stavrou, A., Gritzalis, S.: Intrusion detection in 802.11 networks: empirical evaluation of threats and a public dataset. IEEE Commun. Surv. Tutorials **18**(1), 184–208 (2015). IEEE
3. Kayacik, H., Zincir-Heywood, A.N., Heywood, M.I.: Selecting features for intrusion detection: a feature relevance analysis on KDD 99 intrusion detection datasets. In: Proceedings of the 3rd Annual Conference on Privacy, Security and Trust, PST (2005)
4. Alotaibi, B.: A majority voting technique for wireless intrusion detection systems, University of Bridgeport (2016)
5. Sommer, R., Paxson, V.: Outside the closed world: on using machine learning for network intrusion detection. In: 2010 IEEE Symposium on Security and Privacy (2010)
6. Zaman, S., Karray, F.: Lightweight IDS based on features selection and IDS classification scheme. In: International Conference on IEEE Computational Science and Engineering, CSE 2009, vol. 3, pp. 365–370. IEEE (2009)
7. Louvieris, P., Clewley, N., Liu, X.: Effects-based feature identification for network intrusion detection. Neurocomputing **121**, 265–273 (2013). Elsevier, IEEE
8. Usha, M., Kavitha, P.: Anomaly based intrusion detection for 802.11 networks with optimal features using SVM classifier. Wireless Netw. J. Mob. Commun. Comput. Inf. **22**, 1–16 (2016). Springer
9. Wang, Z.: The Application of Deep Learning on Traffic Identification. BlackHat, USA (2015)
10. Sabhnani, M., Serpen, G.: Application of machine learning algorithms to KDD intrusion detection dataset within misuse detection context. In: Proceedings of the International Conference on Machine Learning: Models, Technologies, and Applications, pp. 209–215 (2003)
11. Palmieri, F., Fiore, U., Castiglione, A.: A distributed approach to network anomaly detection based on independent component analysis. In: Concurrency Computation Practice and Experience, Bd. 26, Nr. 6, S., pp. 1113–1129. Wiley (2013)

Pay as You Want: Bypassing Charging System in Operational Cellular Networks

Hyunwook Hong[(⊠)], Hongil Kim, Byeongdo Hong, Dongkwan Kim, Hyunwoo Choi, Eunkyu Lee, and Yongdae Kim

Korea Advanced Institute of Science and Technology (KAIST),
291 Daehak-ro, Daejeon, Republic of Korea
{hyunwook.h,nagoyam159,byeongdo,dkay,zemisolsol,
ekleez,yongdaek}@kaist.ac.kr

Abstract. Accurate and fair data charging in cellular networks is an important issue because of its large impacts on profits of operators and bills for users. In this study, we analyze the data charging policies and mechanisms for protocols and applications. The analysis shows that all operators in South Korea did not charge the payload of Internet Control Message Protocol (ICMP) echo request/reply messages, as well as the payload attached to Transmission Control Protocol (TCP) SYN and TCP RST packets. In addition, the operators only utilize IP addresses to verify whether the traffic comes from the expected application. By misusing the findings with consideration of Network Address Translator (NAT) in IPv4 cellular networks, we validate with empirical experiments the feasibility of free-riding attack, which enables an adversary to use the cellular data service for free, and propose effective countermeasures.

Keywords: Cellular networks · Mobile data services · Data charging

1 Introduction

As 3G/LTE cellular networks are deployed, the popularity of mobile devices such as smartphones and tablets, increased, enabling a large number of users to enjoy cellular data services. According to a report [14], 64% of adults in the U.S. own a smartphone, and 19% of them rely on a smartphone to access the Internet. However, these cellular data services are not given to users for free. Most operators charge the cellular data based on data usage volume of the user with their policies. Considering the large impacts on profits of operators and bills for users, an accurate and fair data charging has become an important issue for both cellular operators and users. As discovered in previous works [8,11], some operators did not charge the traffic for control purposes in operations of networked systems, such as the Domain Name System (DNS) [11] and Transmission Control Protocol (TCP) retransmission traffic [8]. Furthermore, operators also do not charge the data traffic from a designated mobile application, such as a customer service application. These charging policies open the feasibility of the free-riding

© Springer International Publishing AG 2017
D. Choi and S. Guilley (Eds.): WISA 2016, LNCS 10144, pp. 148–160, 2017.
DOI: 10.1007/978-3-319-56549-1_13

attack, which enables an adversary to use the cellular data service for free. For this reason, we investigated the charging policies for protocols and applications that have not been examined previously.

First, we analyzed the charging policies for two different protocols, namely, Internet Control Message Protocol (ICMP) and Transmission Control Protocol (TCP) in six major operators, three of which are from the U.S. and the other three are from South Korea. We found that all operators in South Korea did not charge ICMP echo request/reply messages, as well as the payload attached to TCP-SYN and TCP- RST packets. On the other hand, only one operator in the U.S. did not charge the payload attached to those TCP packets.

Second, we focused on the charging policies for applications in three major operators of South Korea. The subscribers of optional services can enjoy music and video contents by using the provided mobile applications with additional data volumes. In addition, operators generally provide mobile applications for customer services to request an inquiry of subscriber information; and the data usage from these applications are not charged. To identify the vulnerability of these charging policies, we first analyzed the charging mechanisms for these applications, and found the way for misusing them. We disclosed that operators utilized only IP addresses to verify whether the traffic comes from the expected application. Moreover, we assume an adversary in IPv4 networks (for both the cellular network and the Internet); therefore, we considered Network Address Translator (NAT) in cellular networks. Since NAT drops incoming packets that do not exist on the recorded NAT mapping table, we not only developed two methods so that the downlink traffic can pass through NAT: creation of a real and a fake connection to make a 5-tuple entry on NAT mapping table, but also found the way for identifying the 5-tuple entry. Using these methods, we conducted empirical experiments and obtained result showing that the normally generated data traffic, which masquerades as the data traffic generated from the designated application, was not charged. This finding could validate the feasibility of the free-riding attack.

We propose countermeasures for the free-riding attack. Operators can limit the size of payload or the amount of traffic in the fixed time period for the ICMP traffic, and block uncommon traffic, such as TCP-SYN or TCP-RST packets containing the payload. The free-riding attack that misuses charging policies for the application requires more efforts than other attacks because it is difficult to differentiate between the normal traffic and the misused traffic. The attack can be mitigated by locating the application server inside cellular networks. Furthermore, operators can utilize the anomaly detection and prevention. However, operators should be reminded that the application of these countermeasures can cause unexpected problems such as false positives; therefore, sufficient consideration on their implications should be given.

We summarize our contributions as follows:

– We analyze the charging policies and mechanisms for two different protocols and five applications, and found that these charging policies and mechanisms can be misused.

- We develop and demonstrate free-riding attacks using the analyzed charging policies and mechanisms. In addition, we responsibly disclosed all these vulnerabilities to the operators.
- We propose effective countermeasures that can mitigate the attacks targeting charging policies and mechanisms for protocols and applications.

The rest of the paper is organized as follows. We provide related works in Sect. 2. In Sect. 3, we describe the architecture of cellular network with charging system and the methodology of our experiment. Then, we analyze the charging policies for two protocols in Sect. 4 and examine policies for applications in Sect. 5. Finally, we discuss and propose countermeasures in Sect. 6, and conclude our work in Sect. 7.

2   Related Works

Several studies reported that the data charging systems in cellular networks can suffer from two types of attack: over-billing and free riding attacks [8–12]. Peng *et al.* [11] demonstrated these two attacks in 3G cellular networks. They showed that an adversary could use free data by exploiting the loopholes where data communication using DNS port number is not charged. Furthermore, closing a connection based on the timeout could expose a client to an over-billing attack. Peng *et al.* [12] also reported vulnerabilities of the charging system. They showed that the source IP spoofed data are not charged and an adversary could impose overcharged bills to a victim. Moreover, the adversary can hide inflated data usage volume by adjusting the Time To Live (TTL) value in the IP header. Go *et al.* [8] misused the TCP retransmission for an attack vector. Since a charging system only inspects the IP layer in the middle of the network, it cannot identify the accurate state of TCP context; thus, it is difficult to identify whether the retransmission is malicious or not. Their analysis on the charging policy for TCP retransmission shows that some countries charged the retransmission data while others did not. By exploiting this policy, they showed that over-billing and free-riding attacks were feasible. On the other hand, several studies demonstrate the possibility of over-billing and free-riding attacks by exploiting a voice over LTE (VoLTE) interface newly adopted to LTE networks [9,10]. Li *et al.* [10] disclosed that an adversary could send a large amount of packets from a VoLTE interface to a data interface of a victim. This attack misused the accounting policy that the VoLTE interface is free while the data interface is charged. Kim *et al.* [9] demonstrated that four free data channels were available: direct communication of phone-to-phone and phone-to-Internet and SIP/media tunneling. They also showed that an over-billing attack is possible by spoofing the phone number of the caller.

In this study, we examine the data charging policies for the ICMP and TCP traffic, which is used for control purposes in network operations, and analyze the charging policies and mechanisms for applications used by optional services and customer services. Furthermore, we demonstrate the free-riding attack by misusing the findings from the analysis.

3   Background

3.1   Architecture of Cellular Charging System

Figure 1 shows that the cellular network consists of the Radio Access Network (RAN) [1] and the Core Network (CN) [3]. RAN acts as an intermediary to provide connection between a cellular device and the CN. It transmits data between the cellular device and the CN, and controls information for radio resources. The CN is a major part of the cellular network that provides call control and charging among others. The Serving Gateway (S-GW) and the Packet data network Gateway (P-GW) are the key elements in the CN. The S-GW routes and forwards data packets from and to the base station and the P-GW. The P-GW supports connectivity between a cellular device and external data network, such as the Internet [5].

For the charging system, several components, such as the Billing Domain (BD), the Charging Gateway Function (CGF), and the Online Charging System (OCS), are used [2]. There are two charging modes: offline and online [4]. When a cellular device uses the data service, charging procedures are triggered. In offline charging mode, the S-GW/P-GW initially makes Charging Data Records (CDRs) and records data volume. Charging information comprises as follows: source/destination IP address and port number and protocol ID, such as TCP and UDP. The CGF validates CDRs, and filter the data according to the policy of the operator. Then, the CGF sends CDRs to the BD. The BD generates billing information from the charging ID in the CDRs at the end of the process. In online charging, a user has to pre-pay to acquire their credits for data service. The OCS checks whether a user has sufficient credits or not, and the S-GW/P-GW deducts credits based on his/her data usage. Data service is stopped when the user's credit is depleted.

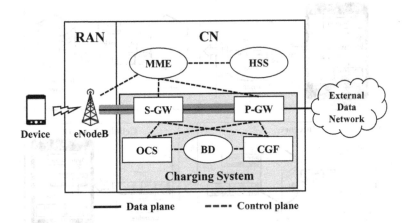

Fig. 1. Charging architecture in LTE network.

3.2 Methodology

In this study, we examine the charging policies at each layer of the cellular network, such as network, transport, and application layer. For network and transport layers, we investigate the ICMP and TCP traffic in six major operators, where three are from the U.S. and the other three are from South Korea. We also analyze the charging policies for applications in three major operators of South Korea. For non-disclosure reason, we anonymized the name of operators by labeling them as US-I, US-II, and US-III for the U.S. and KR-I, KR-II, and KR-III for South Korea operators. Since all operators offer interfaces for the charged data usage, we can check the charged data usage by using web pages or mobile applications provided by the operators. However, because these interfaces do not reflect the data usage in real time, after the sufficient time has passed (at least 1 h later), we check the last applied time for the charged data usage and verify it.

Moreover, all experiments are conducted on IPv4 cellular networks with devices connected to the LTE network. In IPv4 networks, NAT [15] is used to resolve the lack of public IPv4 address resources; thus, our experiments are carried out by considering NAT. Since NAT drops incoming packets that do not exist on the recorded NAT mapping table, we developed two methods for creating the mapping so that the traffic can pass through NAT. (see Sect. 5). On the other hand, in IPv6 networks, all proposed attacks could be launched more easily than in IPv4 networks because NAT is not used in IPv6 networks. Note that our experiments do not affect any other users in cellular networks, and we only conduct the experiments for research purposes and responsibly disclose our finding to operators.

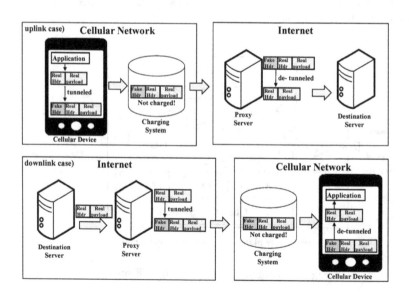

Fig. 2. Free-riding attack process.

In this study, we discover the methods to avoid the charging mechanisms; thereby, users can use the cellular data service for free. In addition, we develop free-riding attacks by misusing the analyzed charging policies and mechanisms. To implement the attack, we utilize similar methods used in previous work [8]. Figure 2 depicts the process of the free-riding attack which requires a collaborating tunneling proxy to relay the tunneled packets and real traffic. Specifically, for uplink traffic (from cellular device to server), packets are tunneled to the proxy and de-tunneled by the proxy and relayed to the destination server. For downlink traffic (from the server to the cellular device), the packets are sent to the proxy which tunnels them to the cellular device, and the device de-tunnels and passes them to the application. In this scenario, the charging system in the cellular core network can only observe the traffic between the cellular device and the proxy, which will not be charged.

4   Charging Policies for Control Traffic of Protocols

In this section, we investigate the charging policies for two different control packets: (1) an ICMP packet, and (2) a TCP control packet for operators in the U.S. and South Korea. Then, we demonstrate the feasibility of the free-riding attack by misusing these charging policies.

4.1   Charging Policies for ICMP Traffic

ICMP messages are used for diagnostic or control purposes in response to errors in IP operations of networked systems [6,13]. Operators usually have different charging policies for this traffic. Figure 3 shows that an ICMP packet comprises an IP header, an ICMP header, and an ICMP payload. ICMP messages are classified by the Type and Code fields in the ICMP header. Among several types of ICMP messages, we focused on an ICMP echo request (Type = 8, Code = 0) message. The ICMP echo message is used for identifying reachability of target hosts by sending an echo request to the target hosts and receiving the response if they reply. In addition, this ICMP echo message could contain any payload that does not exceed maximum transmission unit (MTU) or risk being fragmented. Considering this in our experiment, we sent $30 \times 1,024$ IMCP echo request messages containing 1,024 bytes payload (30 MB traffic) from our mobile device to our server on the Internet. Similarly, our server responded to these messages with ICMP echo reply messages containing 1,024 bytes payload. We repeated this experiment for each operator, and checked whether each operator charged for this traffic. According to the RFC standard [13], the payload in the ICMP echo reply should be the same as the payload in the IMCP echo request. However, in our experiment, we used different payload for each request and reply since our purpose is to check whether the ICMP echo request/reply could be utilized for the free data channel. The result of this experiment is presented in the Table 1.

Table 1 shows that all operators in South Korea did not charge the ICMP echo messages, whereas all U.S. operators charged these messages. Thus, for the

	Bits 0-7	Bits 8-15	Bits 16-23	Bits 24-31
IP Header (20 bytes)	Version / IHL	Type of service	Length	
	Identification		Flags and *offset*	
	Time To Live (TTL)	Protocol	Checksum	
	Source IP address			
	Destination IP address			
ICMP Header (8 bytes)	Type of message	Code	Checksum	
	Header Data			
ICMP Payload (*optional*)	Payload Data			

Fig. 3. Composition of an ICMP packet.

Table 1. The amount of charged traffic of ICMP echo request and reply in Korea and the U.S. operators.

	KR-I	KR-II	KR-III	US-I	US-II	US-III
ICMP echo request	0 MB	0 MB	0 MB	30 MB	30 MB	30 MB
ICMP echo reply	0 MB	0 MB	0 MB	30 MB	30 MB	30 MB

operators in South Korea, an adversary could perform the free-riding attack by utilizing tunneling technique of the ICMP echo message traffic. Consequently, we conducted this attack, and verified that any data traffic through the ICMP tunnel was not charged. This finding validates the feasibility of the free-riding attack.

4.2   Charging Policy for TCP Control Traffic

TCP utilizes various control packets to provide stateful connection by using flags, such as SYN for the synchronization of the sequence number, ACK for the reliability of the data transmission, and FIN and RST for the appropriate termination of the connection. These control packets could be generated by the network condition regardless of the intention of the user and it is unclear whether operators should charge for this traffic. For this reason, we examined the charging policy for TCP traffic for control purposes. We utilized SYN and RST packets for this experiment. As similar with the ICMP case, we sent 30 × 1,024 SYN packets containing 1,024 bytes payload (30 MB) from our cellular device to our server on the Internet. Likewise, on our server, we sent same amount of RST packets to our mobile device on receiving SYN packets. The result of this test is presented in the Table 2.

Table 2 shows that all operators in South Korea did not charge for both SYN and RST packets containing the payload, whereas two of the U.S. operators charged for those traffic. From this experiment, an adversary can also misuse the SYN and RST packets for free data channel. Consequently, we conducted the free-riding attack by utilizing the tunneling technique, and verified that

Table 2. The amount of charged traffic of TCP control packets in Korea and the U.S. operators.

	KR-I	KR-II	KR-III	US-I	US-II	US-III
SYN with payload	0 MB	0 MB	0 MB	30 MB	30 MB	0 MB
RST with payload	0 MB	0 MB	0 MB	30 MB	30 MB	0 MB

any of the data traffic passed the TCP-SYN/RST tunnel was not charged. The finding validates the feasibility of the free-riding attack. Note, IPv4-based cellular networks utilize NAT; therefore, all traffic should be initiated within the cellular network. The details of this issue are introduced in the following section.

5   Charging Policies for Applications

5.1   Mobile Applications for Optional Services and Customer Services

Operators recently provide various optional services as well as charging plans to meet the diverse needs of their customers for data service. Some optional services offer a new type of charging plan for specific mobile applications that provide music and video streaming. Once mobile users subscribe these services, operators apply a different charging policy for these services regardless of the current data usage plan. For example, operators give sufficient (e.g. 2 GB for a day) or even unlimited data as long as the subscriber uses a designated application for content streaming. Another interesting fact is that operators in South Korea do not charge for the data used for inquiry of subscriber information. In other words, mobile users can check their current data usage, change, or join a new usage plan without being charged using a given mobile application for the customer service from their operators. In this context, from security perspective, one may concern whether an adversary could masquerade a normal data traffic as the traffic generated from given applications. To this end, we analyzed the charging mechanisms for these applications and demonstrated how an adversary deceives the charging policy.

5.2   Deceiving Charging Policy

As described in Sect. 3, S-GW/P-GW records the data volume with a CDR that comprises the information in the protocol header (source/destination IP addresses and port number, protocol). An adversary can easily obtain this information by inspecting the traffic generated from the application, thus the adversary is able to bypass data charging for her data usage with the modified header that masquerade as the traffic from the application. To this end, we first examined the traffic generated by the applications, identified the information for the CDR, and developed the method for the free-riding attack. We utilized the mobile applications for the customer service of three major operators in South Korea, and three optional services (two of which for video streaming, one for music streaming) of two operators in South Korea. Consequently, we obtained the server IP address and port number that the applications connect to, and found that all the applications utilized TCP connections for their communication. We describe the steps for deceiving the charging policy of the operators with several considerations.

Considerations. First, an adversary can launch the free-riding attack only for downlink traffic (from the server to the cellular device). In the case of the downlink, the server of the adversary on the Internet can send the data that masquerades as the data from the server that the applications connect to, and the adversary can receive this data at the cellular device of the adversary without being charged. On the other hand, in the case of the uplink (from the cellular device to the server), because the masqueraded data will not arrive at the server of the adversary, but arrived at the server of the service provider; thus, there is no way to receive the data departing from the cellular device of the adversary. For this reason, we focused on the downlink traffic and developed the free-riding attack for downlink. Next, since we assume that all the proposed attacks are launched in IPv4 networks (for both cellular network and the Internet), we considered NAT in cellular networks. When a device inside the cellular network initially connects to an external host, NAT translates the IP address and port number of the device to its own external values, and creates a 5-tuple[1] entry on its external mapping table. The traffic, which does not map on the table, will be blocked by NAT. Thus, to allow the downlink traffic to pass through NAT, we developed two methods for creating a 5-tuple entry on NAT.

Creating a 5-tuple entry on NAT. The first method is creating a real connection between the cellular device and the server, and using the 5-tuple for the connection. This method is quite simple because it requires only identifying the 5-tuple for the connection. However, the connection not used by a client after the TCP three-way handshake can be closed by sending TCP-FIN or TCP-RST from the server of the service provider. In this context, a new connection has to be created whenever the server closes the connection, and this requires frequent identification of the 5-tuple. The other method is creating a fake connection between the cellular device and the server. This method is only valid when the server of the service provider does not respond to any packets from the device. Otherwise, every connection is reset by the server. Thus, creating a fake connection for the running services (port number) is impossible. For this method, the device first sends a TCP-SYN packet to the server of the service provider, and an adversary on the Internet respond to the packet with a TCP-SYN/ACK packet that masquerade as the response of the server. After receiving the TCP-SYN/ACK packet at the device, the device completes TCP three-way handshake by responding to the TCP-SYN/ACK packet with a TCP-ACK packet. The procedures of

---

[1] Protocol, server IP address and port number, External IP address, and port number of NAT.

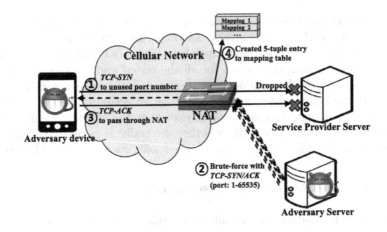

Fig. 4. Procedures of creating a fake connection.

creating a fake connection are presented in Fig. 4. The 5-tuple entry created by the TCP-SYN packet is removed in a short time (according to the test, it took 10 s); therefore, an adversary also needs to identify the created 5-tuple entry within a short time. However, in this case, the adversary does not need to consider the case that the connection is closed by the server of the service provider.

Identifying the connection information. These two methods for creating the 5-tuple entry require identification of the 5-tuple to pass through NAT. Among these five tuples, we could identify the protocol, server IP address, and server port number by inspecting the traffic generated from the target application, but the external IP address and port number of NAT require other techniques. To this end, we analyzed the mapping pattern of NAT by repeatedly re-establishing connections and observing the variation of the external IP address and port number. As a result, we found that the external IPv4 address of NAT is not changed frequently when a new TCP connection is established from the same device (regardless of the server IP address and port number). Therefore, if an adversary creates a TCP connection between her device and the server, and observes the external IP address of NAT at the server, she can predict the external IP address of NAT for the next connection from the same device. On the other hand, the external port of NAT varied randomly whenever a new connection is established. However, because the port number is allocated within the range 1–65,535 (2 bytes), the adversary can brute-force the port number. In other words, she can send packets to all port numbers from 1 to 65,535. The size of a packet is 44 bytes; therefore, it would take around 0.2 s to send to all the ports with a 100 Mbps network (44 bytes × 8 bits/byte(s) × 65,535/100 Mbps = 0.22 s). While sending the packets, the payload containing the current port number is attached to each packet; thus, when the packet passed through NAT and arrived at the cellular device, it can offer the external port number of NAT in the payload.

Attack validation. With these methods, we conducted experiments to verify the feasibility of the free-riding attack. The experiments were performed similar to Sect. 4. While carrying out the experiments, we could utilize two methods: creating a real or a fake connection for all the tested applications. As a result, we found that the downlink traffic using these connections was not charged. The traffic using the fake connection, which utilizes an actual unused port number at the server, was not charged. This implies that the operators only use the server IP address when they verify whether the traffic is generated from target applications or not. This finding validates the feasibility of the free-riding attack.

6   Countermeasures and Discussion

The suggested free-riding attacks misuse charging policies of operators; therefore, operators can easily block the attacks by modifying their charging policies. However, these policies are closely related with the needs of customers, profits of an operator, and recommendations from the government. Thus, operators cannot change their policies without sufficient consideration. For this reason, we can consider mitigation in the technical aspects rather than policy aspects.

For the ICMP traffic, operators can limit the size of the payload or the amount of the traffic in the fixed time period. Furthermore, for TCP control packets, the problem can be alleviated by blocking uncommon traffic, such as a TCP-SYN packet containing the payload. Although a TCP-SYN or a TCP-SYN/ACK packet can include payload [7], these packets are rarely used in networks. Thus, we can expect that blocking these packets does not have significant impact on the operators. On the other hand, the attacks, masqueraded as the traffic from an application, are more difficult to prevent because there is no certain way to differentiate between the normal traffic and the masqueraded traffic. As a countermeasure, the attacks can be mitigated by locating the content server inside cellular networks. However, this is not easy to adopt since the service is usually operated by a third party. Another method is for operators to utilize the anomaly detection and prevention. For example, when the amount of the downlink traffic is significantly more than the acknowledgment traffic of the uplink, or the large amount of traffic using unused port number in the real system is observed at the server of the service provider, it is likely to be an attack. However, this method can cause false positives; thus, it should be given more considerations prior to application.

7   Conclusion

In this study, we analyzed the charging policies for two different protocols, namely, ICMP and TCP, in six major operators of the U.S., and South Korea. We found that all operators in South Korea did not charge ICMP echo request/reply messages, and TCP-SYN and TCP-RST packets. In addition, we also investigated the charging policies and mechanisms for applications used for optional services and customer services, and discovered that operators utilized only the

IP addresses to verify whether the traffic comes from the expected application. By misusing the findings with consideration of NAT in IPv4 cellular networks, we validated the feasibility of the free-riding attack.

Our study provides some insights. Operators should be reminded that unthoughtful charging policies can lead to the free-riding attack. Furthermore, the charging system limitation that lies in the middle of communication allowed the viewing of the information in the protocol header only, making it difficult to handle the charging problems occurring at the end points. Therefore, we recommend that operators adopt additional methods to monitor their core networks and end points.

Acknowledgement. This research was supported by (1) Institute for Information & communications Technology Promotion (IITP) grant funded by the Korea government (MSIP) (No.R-20160222-002755, Cloud based Security Intelligence Technology Development for the Customized Security Service Provisioning), and (2) the MSIP (Ministry of Science, ICT and Future Planning), Korea, under the ITRC (Information Technology Research Center) support program (IITP-2016-R0992-16-1006) supervised by the IITP.

References

1. 3GPP: Access Network (E-UTRAN); Architecture description. TS 36.401, 3GPP (2010)
2. 3GPP: Telecommunication management; Charging management; Charging architecture and principles. TS 32.240, 3GPP (2010)
3. 3GPP: LTE; Network architecture. TS 23.002, 3GPP (2011)
4. 3GPP: Telecommunication management; Charging management; Online Charging System (OCS): Applications and interfaces. TS 32.296, 3GPP (2011)
5. 3GPP: LTE; Interworking between the Public Land Mobile Network (PLMN) supporting packet based services and Packet Data Networks (PDN). TS 29.061, 3GPP (2015)
6. Braden, R.: Requirements for Internet Hosts - Communication Layers. RFC 1122 (INTERNET STANDARD), updated by RFCs 1349, 4379, 5884, 6093, 6298, 6633, 6864, October 1989. http://www.ietf.org/rfc/rfc1122.txt
7. Cheng, Y., Chu, J., Radhakrishnan, S., Jain, A.: TCP fast open. RFC 7413 (Experimental), December 2014. http://www.ietf.org/rfc/rfc7413.txt
8. Go, Y., Won, J., Kune, D.F., Jeong, E., Kim, Y., Park, K.: Gaining control of cellular traffic accounting by spurious TCP retransmission. In: Network and Distributed System Security Symposium (NDSS) (2014)
9. Kim, H., Kim, D., Kwon, M., Han, H., Jang, Y., Han, D., Kim, T., Kim, Y.: Breaking and fixing VoLTE: exploiting hidden data channels and mis-implementations. In: ACM Conference on Computer and Communications Security (2015)
10. Li, C.Y., Tu, G.H., Peng, C., Yuan, Z., Li, Y., Lu, S., Wang, X.: Insecurity of voice solution VoLTE in LTE mobile networks. In: ACM Conference on Computer and Communications Security (2015)
11. Peng, C., Li, C.y., Tu, G.H., Lu, S., Zhang, L.: Mobile data charging: new attacks and countermeasures. In: Proceedings of the 19th ACM SIGSAC Conference on Computer and Communications Security (2012)

12. Peng, C., Li, C.Y., Wang, H., Tu, G.H., Lu, S.: Real threats to your data bills: security loopholes and defenses in mobile data charging. In: ACM Conference on Computer and Communications Security (2014)
13. Postel, J.: Internet control message protocol. RFC 792 (INTERNET STANDARD), updated by RFCs 950, 4884, 6633, 6918, September 1981. http://www.ietf.org/rfc/rfc792.txt
14. Smith, A.: US Smartphone Use in 2015. Pew Research Center (2015)
15. Srisuresh, P., Holdrege, M.: IP network address translator (NAT) terminology and considerations. RFC 2663 (Informational), August 1999. http://www.ietf.org/rfc/rfc2663.txt

Towards Automated Exploit Generation for Embedded Systems

Matthew Ruffell[1]([⊠]), Jin B. Hong[1], Hyoungshick Kim[2], and Dong Seong Kim[1]

[1] Computer Science and Software Engineering, University of Canterbury,
Christchurch, New Zealand
{msr50,jho102}@uclive.ac.nz, dongseong.kim@canterbury.ac.nz
[2] Department of Software, Sungkyunkwan University, Seoul, South Korea
hyoung@skku.edu

Abstract. Manual vulnerability discovery and exploit development on an executable are very challenging tasks for developers. Therefore, the automation of those tasks is becoming interesting in the field of software security. In this paper, we implement an approach of automated exploit generation for firmware of embedded systems by extending an existing dynamic analysis framework called *Avatar*. Embedded systems occupy a significant portion of the market but lack typical security features found on general purpose computers, making them prone to critical vulnerabilities. We discuss several techniques to automatically discover vulnerabilities and generate exploits for embedded systems, and evaluate our proposed approach by generating exploits for two vulnerable firmware written for a popular ARM Cortex-M3 microcontroller.

Keywords: Embedded system · Exploit generation · Software vulnerability

1 Introduction

Embedded systems are small low powered computers that carry out a specific task. To keep costs down, embedded systems typically omit modern security features such as Address Space Layout Randomisation (ASLR) or Data Execution Protection (DEP/W⊕E) [17] which make exploitation of vulnerabilities significantly easier. Most software on embedded systems is also never updated or patched [12], so systems remain vulnerable even when vulnerabilities are found and disclosed. It then becomes important to find vulnerabilities in the development stage.

Unlike personal computers, conventional static and dynamic analysis tools are often ineffective in analysing firmware because non-standard peripherals are typically used in embedded systems. It takes considerable effort to emulate the behaviours of a peripheral which greatly slows the analysis of firmware. Hence, we need an efficient dynamic analysis tool which can automatically detect vulnerabilities and generate possible exploits even with specialized peripherals that the firmware interacts with.

© Springer International Publishing AG 2017
D. Choi and S. Guilley (Eds.): WISA 2016, LNCS 10144, pp. 161–173, 2017.
DOI: 10.1007/978-3-319-56549-1_14

The aim of this paper is to extend an existing dynamic analysis framework, namely *Avatar* [19], to automatically generate exploits on embedded systems. The tool was originally developed to analyse a wide range of firmware without source code since most users have no direct access to the source code of firmware in many embedded systems. Ideally there should be limited human interaction in the vulnerability discovery and exploit generation process, to make the tool useful to even less skilled developers. All codes developed in this paper can be found in [1,2].

The contributions of this paper are as follows:

- We extended a security analysis framework with generic device input communication and automated exploit generation modules to analyse firmware for embedded systems;
- We evaluate the feasibility of the proposed framework with two vulnerable custom firmwares.

The rest of the paper is organized as follows. Section 2 presents the related work. Section 3 presents the design and implementation of our framework. Section 4 presents the evaluation of our proposed framework. Then, discussion is given in Sect. 5, and we conclude our paper in Sect. 6.

2   Related Work

Automated Vulnerability Analysis: The process of automatically discovering security vulnerabilities in a program is referred to generally as *automated vulnerability analysis*. Costin *et al.* [11] implemented a wide scale automated vulnerability analysis service for firmware images. Mulliner *et al.* [15] implemented a fuzzer which automatically sends randomly crafted SMS messages to mobile phones. However, their vulnerability detection engine is not intelligent, and is limited to detecting simple faults which happen to crash mobile phones. An intelligent fuzzing tool, TaintScope, has been built by Wang *et al.* [18], which bolsters fuzzing with dynamic taint analysis and symbolic execution to target fuzzing towards attacker controlled input. Davidson *et al.* [13] implemented FIE, a tool that uses symbolic execution to verify memory safety for the MSP430 microcontroller. Symbolic execution is becoming popular a mechanism to verify memory safety. Intel [5] has also started analysing the firmware for its processors using S2E [10].

Source Code Based Automated Exploit Generation: Source code based automated exploit generation tools can generate exploits with full knowledge of source code. Exploits generated are typically not very reliable as exploits may behave differently when applied to program binaries which are compiled and optimised by different compilers. Avgerinos *et al.* [3] implemented AEG, the first end-to-end system for automated exploit generation.

Binary Code Based Automated Exploit Generation: Binary code based automated exploit generation tools can generate exploits from analysing binary program distributions. Exploits are typically reliable since they are generated specifically for the program binary, but may not necessarily evade memory protection techniques of host operating systems. Automated exploit generation tools have been mainly developed for general purpose computers, as none currently exist for embedded systems. Brumley et al. [7] introduced a method to automatically generate an exploit by analysing a vulnerable binary program P, and the patched binary program P'. Schwartz et al. [17] built Q, a tool which can automatically build ROP [16] exploits for a given binary program. Dynamic taint analysis is performed in conjunction with symbolic execution to find vulnerable program states. If the vulnerability can be exploited by ROP, then *gadgets* [16] are located in the binary and a payload generated. A similar framework, Crax, by Huang et al. [14] uses program crash traces as input. Crash traces can be found from typical static or dynamic analysis tools such as fuzzers, or from normal use. Crash traces are then used as execution traces for concolic symbolic execution within the S2E [10] framework, and if the crash condition is exploitable, an exploit could be produced. Cha et al. [9] developed Mayhem, a tool which automatically generates exploits for a given binary program, with no additional information required. Mayhem was run over all binaries in the Debian Linux distribution, and over 13,000 bugs were found and 150 exploits generated [4].

3   Proposed Approach: Design and Implementation

We extend the Avatar framework to automatically generate exploits for embedded systems firmware. First, we explain features implemented by the Avatar framework in detail in Sect. 3.1, then we describe the implementation in Sect. 3.2.

3.1   Avatar Framework

Avatar [19] is an event driven dynamic analysis framework. On a high level, Avatar is responsible for executing firmware and testing its behaviours based on the emulation of a target device. The overview of the Avatar architecture is shown in Fig. 1.

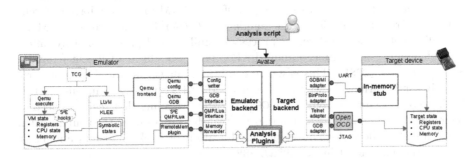

Fig. 1. An overview of the Avatar architecture (adapted from [19])

Avatar provides a concrete wrapper implementation to use the Selective Symbolic Execution (S2E) [10] framework. S2E is a flexible framework that supports emulating applications and firmware in QEMU [6] that is a machine emulator supporting many architectures (e.g., ARM, X86, MIPS and SPARC) while performing symbolic execution with KLEE [8] concurrently. I/O operations can be intercepted and forwarded to the physical device while signals and interrupts can be injected into the emulator.

3.2   Implementation

Avatar Configuration. The Avatar configuration file is the core Python script that controls the operations of the Avatar framework. This file imports all relevant libraries for analysis, and contains configuration parameters required for S2E.

S2E requires considerable configuration for emulating a target device. Firstly, the hardware of the target device needs to be specified in order to create a virtual machine that closely emulates the target processor. Memory ranges also need to be mapped manually, according to the layout of the target device. This is to ensure that the addresses contained in the firmware match with those on the emulator, and memory regions which can be marked as local to the emulator are so. At a minimum the code and RAM regions should be mapped to the processor. Avatar will then forward any operations that involve addresses outside of those regions to the target device. If the code and RAM are not mapped, then all memory operations will be forwarded to the target device.

Plugins that are loaded directly into S2E must also be configured. The most notable plugins are the RawMonitor, ModuleExecutionDetector and Annotation. RawMonitor simply assigns memory regions to modules. ModuleExecutionDetector then keeps track of the program counter in relation to modules, and calls any plugins which register dependency on particular modules. Annotation allows the user to call Lua callback functions to exhibit symbolic execution when a particular address inside of a module is reached.

Custom functions that are too specific to be placed into the framework are also implemented inside the Avatar configuration file. These include call monitors, memory and register state transfer functions. Transferring registers is a specific implementation issue since different ARM processors have different amounts of registers outside of the mandated 12 general purpose registers. Many have different names on different processor families, and provide slightly different behaviour. For example, standard ARM processors have a Current Program Status Register (CPSR). This is where conditional flags are stored such as zero, negative and overflow. However, the Cortex-M3 ARM processor implements this in the xPSR register, and omits the CPSR register. Meaning that registers need to be manually defined in the actual register transfer functions in the configuration file. This also allows for convenient modification of tricky registers and flags, such as the Thumb bit in the CPSR/xPSR.

The remainder of the Avatar configuration file implements the analysis logic. This involves setting up the OpenOCD connections and loading them into the

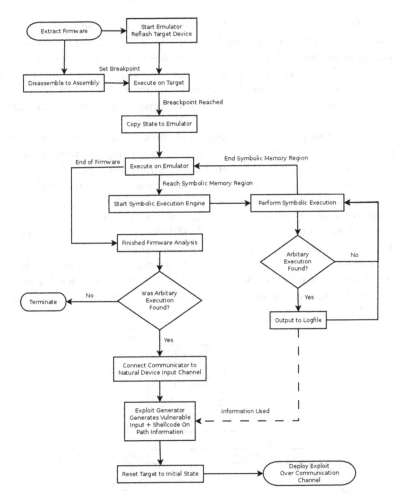

Fig. 2. Methodology behind automated exploit execution on embedded systems

Avatar framework. Each state of the flowchart shown in Fig. 2 represents one or a small group of function calls in the Avatar configuration file.

Generic Device Input Communication. Most frameworks (including Avatar) have no way to communicate with the target device over its real communication channels. If input is needed to be injected into the target device, a debugger is typically used to modify the contents of received data to the injected data. However, the problem is that if exploits are injected into the firmware with a debugger, there is no way of verifying that the injected exploit is really what is sent over real communication channels. That is, we need to assure the integrity of injected data. Take a UART serial port for an example. The data to be injected to the firmware could contain machine codes that are interpreted as ASCII codes for newline and/or carriage return characters. When those data are injected into the firmware via a debugger, all bytes would be loaded into the firmware exactly as contained in the data. However, if those data was to be sent over a real UART serial channel, the UART transmitter would typically interpret the bytes that map to ASCII carriage return characters to indicate the end of transmission. This would cause only parts of the data to be copied, not assuring the integrity of injected data.

To overcome this problem, we developed the Communicator module, which presents a generic interface of abstract functions for implementing channel initialisation, connection, disconnection, reading and writing (which can be found in [1]). The user can simply extend the Communicator class to provide concrete implementations of abstract functions for a specific channel type, making the Communicator class suitable for any communication channel mechanism, such as Ethernet, USB, Bluetooth or serial UART. Since embedded systems receive input from various sources, many concrete communicators may be active at any time. All communicators adhere to the same interface, which enables the developer to quickly and easily switch between different input channels for deploying exploits. The UML diagram in Fig. 3 shows the functionalities of the Communicator module.

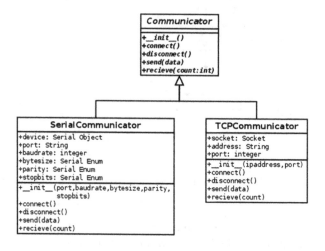

Fig. 3. UML depicting the communicator module

Exploit Generation. We develop the ExploitGenerator module to automate exploit generation. To extend this module to various exploit kits, the ExploitGenerator class presents a generic interface which can be integrated with any exploitation method such as stack buffer overflow, return oriented programming, use after free and null pointer dereference. Figure 4 shows the functionalities of the ExploitGenerator module in the UML diagram form.

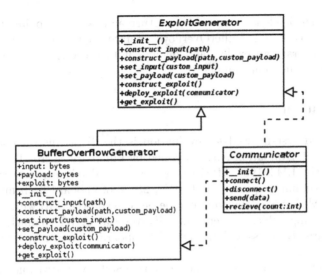

Fig. 4. UML depicting the ExploitGenerator module

The ExploitGenerator module revolves around the notion that an exploit is the concatenation of an input string which places the device into a vulnerable state, and shellcode which acts upon the vulnerable state. In order to automatically generate inputs which place the device into a vulnerable state, Exploit-Generator examines path information output from the ArbitaryExecution S2E plugin. When writing the construct_input() function, a developer must take care to arrange the variables from the path in the correct order that they appear in inputs, as depending on the exploit method selected, the order that S2E provides variables from path information may not be correct. Constructing payloads is a similar matter, as existing shellcode is combined with a referenced address to the buffer found from vulnerable path information. The user also has the option to manually override the automatically generated input and payload variables.

To deploy the exploit to the target device, the ExploitGenerator class sends the exploit down a previously created generic input communication channel, denoted by a concrete implementation of the Communicator class. Since all concrete implementations of Communicator adhere to the same interface, any ExploitGenerator can send constructed exploits down any communication channel.

For simplicity, in this paper, we only focus on automatically generating exploits for stack buffer overflow vulnerabilities. BufferOverflowGenerator is a concrete implementation of ExploitGenerator which implements this feature (which can be found in [1]). However, the developed framework is not limited to this type of attacks as it can be flexibly extended with other exploit generation modules. BufferOverflowGenerator first builds vulnerable input strings by using vulnerable path information to place the device into a state where it will read and store a buffer in a viable location. The payload is constructed such that existing shellcode is extended by a return address which points to the start of the vulnerable buffer. BufferOverflowGenerator concatenates the input and payload to generate an exploit and deploys it to the target device through a specified communication channel.

4   Evaluation

The embedded system used for evaluation is the Texas Instruments Stellaris EKS-LM3S1968 Evaluation Kit, developed by Luminary Micro. The evaluation kit features the LM3S1968 ARM Cortex-M3 embedded microprocessor, which boasts a maximum frequency of 50 MHz, 256 K of onboard flash memory, and 64 K of SRAM. Device debugging can be performed over USB with the popular FTDI 2232D chip, which implements USB to serial UART channels, which can be used to directly access and program the onboard flash memory. JTAG access is also provided.

The communication channel between the Stellaris board and the Avatar framework was achieved over a serial UART line, which is popularly used in real world embedded systems. In order for the host computer to communicate with the target device, an external USB UART TTY was required. A generic off-the-shelf adapter was selected to support the CP2102 UART chip.

The host computer running the Avatar and S2E frameworks has the following specifications: a 3.4 GHz Quad-core Intel i7-4770 processor, 16 GB of DDR3 RAM, running the 64-bit Debian 7.8 Linux distribution.

4.1   Vulnerable Firmware

Two vulnerable firmware versions were developed to show the feasibility of our implementation. Those firmware versions share the common vulnerability but are significantly different in code size. Each of the firmware versions tested utilise two different hardware peripherals, a serial UART and the OLED display. Each of these peripherals must be initialised during initial device setup, even if they are not explicitly used in later stages of firmware execution. This enables the driver objects to be linked with the firmware during compilation, enabling access to those peripherals by any shellcode executed. The firmware developed share a common vulnerability that can be exploitable on some execution paths of the firmware. The vulncpy() function introduces a simple stack buffer overflow vulnerability since it does not perform any length checking of an array passed as a parameter. The vulncpy() function is called after the firmware receives a message over the serial UART line, which contains tainted data which is entirely attacker controlled. In this section, we first briefly describe how those firmware versions work and discuss the annotations for symbolic execution.

Small. *Small* simply initialises hardware peripherals, receives a message over the serial UART line, and immediately passes the message buffer to vulncpy() to potentially trigger the vulnerability. *Small* receives the message by first reading

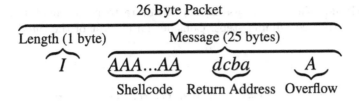

Fig. 5. Small packet structure and example exploit

in a single byte, and converting the byte from ASCII to an integer. This becomes the `length` of the buffer to receive. It then proceeds to read and fill the message buffer with `length` bytes received over the serial UART line.

The inputs required to place *Small* into a vulnerable state is simply a `length` value greater than 20, in order to overflow the buffer found in the vulncpy() function. Since there is only one path through the firmware, this is easily found with symbolic execution. The message presented in Fig. 5 consists of 20 bytes of shellcode to fill the buffer in vulncpy(), 4 bytes to overwrite the return address to the desired value `0xabcd` (represented in little-endian form) and a further byte which overwrites the previous stack frame.

Large. *Large* recreates an in-vivo example of a real world firmware with a complex message passing system, which can craft and display messages sent and received from the Stellaris board. The application contains 5 different views that the user can directly interact with. The application contains a significant amount of control flow logic and various nested loops and other tricky components such as dynamic memory allocation to the heap. The details of *Large* can be found in [2].

Large can be placed into a vulnerable state by sending command 1 to print an attached message to the screen. The message is parsed and vulncpy() is called before the message is printed to the screen. The message shown in Fig. 6 follows the same format used in *Small* firmware.

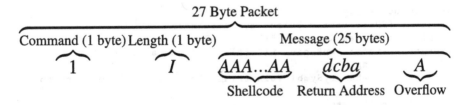

Fig. 6. Large packet structure and example exploit

Annotations. Manually disassembling firmware to place annotations is one of the most time-consuming steps. Consider an excerpt of the *Small* firmware shown in Fig. 7.

```
00000720 <main>:
   720:   b5f0          push      {r4, r5, r6, r7, lr} ; Context Switch
   ...
   744:   f000 fa85     bl        c52 <UARTCharGet>    ; Read length
   748:   b2c4          uxtb      r4, r0               ; r4 = length message
   74a:   3c30          subs      r4, #48              ; Correctly zero length
   74c:   dd0a          ble.n     764 <main+0x44>      ; if < 0 do not read
   74e:   466f          mov       r7, sp               ; r7 is buffer location
   750:   eb04 060d     add.w     r6, r4, sp           ; Allocate length bytes
   754:   4628          mov       r0, r5               ; CALL ANNOTATION HERE
   756:   f000 fa7c     bl        c52 <UARTCharGet>    ; Read 1b of message
   75a:   1e64          subs      r4, r4, #1           ; Decrement counter
   75c:   f807 0b01     strb.w    r0, [r7], #1         ; Store 1b in buffer
   760:   d1f8          bne.n     754 <main+0x34>      ; Loop and read more
```

Fig. 7. Example of annotations in the *Small* firmware

Annotations need to be placed at sections of the firmware where variables or buffers of tainted data are required to be marked symbolic. In the above example, one variable and one buffer needs to be marked symbolic. The length variable can be marked as symbolic by setting the register r0 to a symbolic value since the UART driver library places a received character into register r0, a common return value register. For the buffer, the variable which points to the buffers location in memory is stored in register 7, as seen at 0x74e when the location takes the value of the stack pointer. The buffer is allocated upon the next instruction 0x750. This adds the buffer length to the current stack pointer, placing the address of the end of the buffer in register 6. The buffer consists of the bytes between the addresses of r7 and r6. The idea is to call a Lua callback function to mark those addresses as symbolic before instruction 0x754 is executed. An instruction annotation is used, which calls the required function when the program counter reaches the address 0x754.

```
function buffer_symbolic_all (state, plg)
   print ("[S2E]: making buffer symbolic\n")
   buff = state:readRegister("r7") -- r7 contains buffer address
   length = state:readRegister("r4") -- r4 contains length
   for i = 0,length do
      state:writeMemorySymb("VulnString", buff+i, 1) -- mark symbolic
   end
   -- Write null byte
   state:writeMemory(buff + length, 1, 0)
end
```

Fig. 8. Annotation callback function marking buffer as symbolic

The annotation callback function marking buffer as symbolic (see Fig. 8) takes part inside of S2E, during symbolic execution with KLEE. KLEE reads the address and length of the buffer from the registers of the emulator, and then iteratively marks each byte as symbolic. By utilising similar annotations, two firmware versions were tested with our implementation.

4.2 Exploits Generated

Generating exploits for *Small* is a straightforward process with the extended Avatar framework. The vulnerability is triggered if there are more than 20 bytes copied into the buffer, which means that the first length character must be greater than 20. Since *Small* length in as a printable ASCII character, the length is offset by the character '0', or 0x30. This means that the SMT solver was tasked to find values greater than 20 which include the offset. Two exploits are shown in Fig. 9. In both exploits, the length value satisfies the minimum value of 0x44 (20). Note that the shellcode used is a string of 'a' (0x61) characters acting as placeholders, and the address of the buffer is always the same. If a debugger is consulted at run time, the buffer is allocated between 0x200000B8 and 0x200000D1, which agrees with the generated exploits.

```
Length Shellcode                                        Return    Overflow
4B      616161616161616161616161616161616161616161       b8000020  61
7F      616161616161616161616161616161616161616161       b8000020  61
```

Fig. 9. Exploits generated for Small, shown in hexadecimal form

Unfortunately, our implementation failed to automatically generate an exploit for *Large* within reasonable time. This is because a significant amount of execution paths were explored with various input mechanisms (e.g., push buttons, UART packets, etc.). Moreover, symbolic execution often generated states to explore already explored paths, which finally led to state space explosion in the search field.

5 Discussion

We found that Avatar is not scalable for large complex embedded systems, as demonstrated in Sect. 4. The action of performing symbolic execution and passing all memory-mapped I/O peripheral accesses over USB to the target device is too slow for real systems. For example, firmware for a baseband processor used in cellular phones is typically several megabytes in size, and utilise many nested loops and state machines to implement the GSM protocol. Since symbolic execution would likely tend towards state space explosion, time critical radio peripheral accesses can also fail, and the USB debug channel may exhaust bandwidth to cope with the interrupts generated.

Moreover, Avatar has no mechanism to determine what class of vulnerability has been detected. Avatar simply detects vulnerabilities if a symbolic variable is used as a control flow jump address (i.e., a symbolic variable is loaded to the program counter). A method to automatically distinguish between various vulnerability classes and a feature needs to be implemented in the extended Avatar which would automatically select the required ExploitGenerator. This would remove another decision users need to make when setting up the Avatar configuration file, as it may not be known what class of vulnerability is inside the firmware under test.

We did not evaluate our framework with real world scenarios. However, as we described previously, our custom built firmware allow us to comparatively analyse how our proposed framework can generate exploits for different complexity of firmware. But for our future work, we will investigate the effectiveness of our proposed framework for various types of real world embedded systems firmware.

6   Conclusion

Embedded systems often lack capabilities to support security features. Hence, in embedded systems, finding security flaws is essential in their development stages. In this paper, we extended the Avatar framework to implement an automated exploit generation tool for embedded systems. To show the feasibility of the implemented tool, we used two independent firmware versions that share the same vulnerability but are significantly different in size.

In our experiments, the small-sized firmware was quickly exploited while we failed to automatically generate an effective exploit on the large-sized firmware. This is because a lot of execution paths were inherently generated based on the symbolic execution technique. To overcome this limitation, we will explore various heuristics to prioritize the most important execution paths when it is not feasible to consider all possible execution paths in a target firmware.

References

1. Automatic exploit generation for embedded systems - extended avatar. https://github.com/msr50/avatar-python
2. Automatic exploit generation for embedded systems - vulnerable firmwares. https://github.com/msr50/avatar-stellaris
3. Avgerinos, T., Cha, S.K., Hao, B.L.T., Brumley, D.: AEG: automatic exploit generation. In: NDSS, vol. 11, pp. 59–66 (2011)
4. Avgerinos, T., Cha, S.K., Rebert, A., Schwartz, E.J., Woo, M., Brumley, D.: Automatic exploit generation. Commun. ACM **57**(2), 74–84 (2014)
5. Bazhaniuk, O., Loucaides, J., Rosenbaum, L., Tuttle, M.R., Zimmer, V.: Symbolic execution for bios security1 (2015)
6. Bellard, F.: QEMU, a fast and portable dynamic translator. In: USENIX Annual Technical Conference, FREENIX Track, pp. 41–46 (2005)

7. Brumley, D., Poosankam, P., Song, D., Zheng, J.: Automatic patch-based exploit generation is possible: techniques and implications. In: IEEE Symposium on Security and Privacy (SP 2008), pp. 143–157. IEEE (2008)
8. Cadar, C., Dunbar, D., Engler, D.R.: KLEE: unassisted and automatic generation of high-coverage tests for complex systems programs. In: OSDI, vol. 8, pp. 209–224 (2008)
9. Cha, S.K., Avgerinos, T., Rebert, A., Brumley, D.: Unleashing mayhem on binary code. In: 2012 IEEE Symposium on Security and Privacy (SP 2012), pp. 380–394. IEEE (2012)
10. Chipounov, V., Kuznetsov, V., Candea, G.: S2E: a platform for in-vivo multi-path analysis of software systems, vol. 39. ACM (2011)
11. Costin, A., Zaddach, J., Francillon, A., Balzarotti, D., Antipolis, S.: A large-scale analysis of the security of embedded firmwares. In: USENIX Security Symposium (2014)
12. Cui, A., Costello, M., Stolfo, S.J.: When firmware modifications attack: a case study of embedded exploitation. In: NDSS (2013)
13. Davidson, D., Moench, B., Ristenpart, T., Jha, S.: Fie on firmware: finding vulnerabilities in embedded systems using symbolic execution. In: USENIX Security, pp. 463–478 (2013)
14. Huang, S.K., Huang, M.H., Huang, P.Y., Lai, C.W., Lu, H.L., Leong, W.M.: Crax: software crash analysis for automatic exploit generation by modeling attacks as symbolic continuations. In: 2012 IEEE Sixth International Conference on Software Security and Reliability (SERE), pp. 78–87. IEEE (2012)
15. Mulliner, C., Golde, N., Seifert, J.P.: SMS of death: from analyzing to attacking mobile phones on a large scale. In: USENIX Security Symposium (2011)
16. Prandini, M., Ramilli, M.: Return-oriented programming. IEEE Secur. Priv. 10(6), 84–87 (2012)
17. Schwartz, E.J., Avgerinos, T., Brumley, D.: Q: exploit hardening made easy. In: USENIX Security Symposium (2011)
18. Wang, T., Wei, T., Gu, G., Zou, W.: Taintscope: a checksum-aware directed fuzzing tool for automatic software vulnerability detection. In: 2010 IEEE Symposium on Security and Privacy (SP), pp. 497–512. IEEE (2010)
19. Zaddach, J., Bruno, L., Francillon, A., Balzarotti, D.: Avatar: a framework to support dynamic security analysis of embedded systems firmwares. In: Proceedings of the 21st Symposium on Network and Distributed System Security (2014)

Empirical Analysis of SSL/TLS Weaknesses in Real Websites: Who Cares?

Sanghak Oh[1], Eunsoo Kim[2], and Hyoungshick Kim[1(✉)]

[1] Department of Software, Sungkyunkwan University, Suwon, Korea
hyoung@skku.edu
[2] Department of Computer Science and Engineering,
Sungkyunkwan University, Suwon, Korea

Abstract. As SSL/TLS has become the de facto standard Internet protocol for secure communication in recent years, its security issues have also been intensively studied. Even though several tools have been introduced to help administrators know which SSL/TLS vulnerabilities exist in their network hosts, it is still unclear whether the best security practices are effectively adopted to fix those vulnerabilities in real-world applications. In this paper, we present the landscape of real websites about SSL/TLS weaknesses through an automatic analysis of the possibilities of six representative SSL/TLS attacks—Heartbleed, POODLE, CCS injection, FREAK, Logjam and DROWN—on popular websites. Surprisingly, our experiments show that 45% and 52.6% of top 500 most popular global and Korean websites are still vulnerable to at least one of those attacks, respectively. We also observed several interesting trends in how websites were vulnerable to those attacks. Our findings suggest that better tools and education programs for SSL/TLS security are needed to help administrators keep their systems up-to-date with security patches.

Keywords: SSL/TLS · Vulnerability · Attack · Security patch

1 Introduction

Secure Sockets Layer/Transport Layer Security (SSL/TLS) protocol has become the de facto standard for ensuring confidentiality and data integrity of messages that are exchanged between network parties in the Internet [1]. Due to the popularity of the SSL/TLS protocol, the security of SSL/TLS has also been intensively studied for a long time. Moreover, it is commonly believed that flaws could be fixed rapidly by the community if and when they are found. This belief motivated our study to assess the practical security levels of websites that are using the SSL/TLS protocol.

In this paper, we particularly investigate how many popular websites are vulnerable to the six representative SSL/TLS attacks—Heartbleed [2], POODLE [3], CCS injection [4], FREAK [5], Logjam [6] and DROWN [7] attacks—to understand the gap between academic research and real-world practice in using the SSL/TLS protocol.

© Springer International Publishing AG 2017
D. Choi and S. Guilley (Eds.): WISA 2016, LNCS 10144, pp. 174–185, 2017.
DOI: 10.1007/978-3-319-56549-1_15

In order to perform our experiments on a large scale, we developed an integrated tool to automatically check the possibilities of the six SSL/TLS attacks on websites, respectively. With this tool, we tested the 500 most popular global and Korean websites collected in Alexa (http://www.alexa.com/topsites) and then found that 45% and 52.6% of those global and Korean websites are still vulnerable to at least one of those attacks, respectively. We also observed several interesting trends in how websites were vulnerable to those attacks. For example, we found there exist some positive correlations between those six attacks. This implies that websites may be exposed to an SSL/TLS vulnerability (e.g., Logjam) with a high chance when they are exposed to another SSL/TLS vulnerability (e.g., FREAK). Also, when we observe the changes in the number of vulnerable websites over the four weeks, the overall adoption rates of patches seem slow although the number of vulnerable websites for each attack was rather decreased. We believe that our experiment results are quite impressive because the six tested SSL/TLS attacks and their defense techniques were already reported many times in media coverage as well as academic papers.

We summarize the key contributions of the paper as follows:

- We performed a large-scale quantitative analysis of the six representative SSL/TLS attacks on popular websites and found that many popular websites (more than about 45%) are still vulnerable to at least one of those attacks.
- We developed an integrated tool to automatically check the possibilities of the six tested SSL/TLS attacks on target websites at the same time. This kind of tools can be used for the purpose of identifying SSL/TLS security flaws early in websites.
- We discussed how to narrow down the gap between academic research and real-world practices for using the SSL/TLS protocol.

The rest of paper is organized as follows. Section 2 briefly explains the SSL/TLS protocol and the six SSL/TLS attacks used in our experiments. Section 3 presents our methodology for experiments. Section 4 presents the key experiment results. Section 5 suggests our recommendations to reduce SSL/TLS vulnerabilities in websites. Related work is covered in Sect. 6, and our conclusions are in Sect. 7.

2   Background

In this section, we describe the overall explanation of SSL/TLS protocol and six typical attacks related to SSL/TLS vulnerabilities.

2.1   SSL/TLS Protocol

SSL/TLS, developed by Netscape, is the de facto Internet protocol for ensuring confidentiality and data integrity. The security of SSL/TLS has been studied for a long time, and formally verified [8]—its end-to-end security is equivalent to the cryptographic strength of the underlying algorithms if implemented properly. Surely, however, security proofs are no panacea. The implementations for SSL/TLS may often have bugs although flaws are generally fixed by the community when they are found.

2.2   SSL/TLS Attacks

2.2.1   Heartbleed Attack

Heartbleed vulnerability is a buffer overread due to the bug with the TLS Heartbeat extension which was released in OpenSSL version 1.0.1 on March 13, 2012 [2]. The Heartbeat extension enables each connected peer to determine whether the peer on the other end-point is still present or not by sending a HeartbeatRequest message to verify their connectivity. The request message consists of a type field, payload length field, a payload and random padding. If the payload length is greater than the amount of data in a HeartbeatRequest message, an attacker can read private data from its victim's memory. The latest OpenSSL patch checks whether the received HeartbeatRequest message's payload length field exceeds the length of the payload.

2.2.2   POODLE Attack

POODLE attack is a man-in-the-middle attack which uses SSL requests to downgrade TLS version to older protocol versions (e.g., SSL 3.0). Fogel et al. [9] was able to gather data with TLS_FALLBACK_SCSV flag option using the vulnerability in the OpenSSL toolkit. To prevent POODLE attack, Google security team provided a temporary solution that inserts an extra flag (TLS_FALLBACK_SCSV) into SSL/TLS implementations on clients and servers sides. The flag forbids any attempt to downgrade TLS to SSL, but the vulnerability still exists with the clients with SSL v3.0. Disabling the entire SSL v3.0 can also be another alternative solution.

2.2.3   CCS Injection Attack

CCS injection attack was discovered to be using the vulnerability in OpenSSL library [4]. This attack can be used to exploit the vulnerability to decrypt, extract and modify traffic through a man-in-the-middle attack against an encrypted connection. During the handshake stage, the client or the server could often decide to modify the ciphering strategies of the connection by using a Change-CipherSpec request. Unlike the standards (RFC 5246 [10]), OpenSSL accepted a ChangeCipherSpec request ChangeCipherSpec request which results in the state between both sides being desynchronized. CCS injection vulnerability was already patched in OpenSSL by fixing the way CCS packets and zero-length pre-master secret values are managed.

2.2.4   FREAK Attack

FREAK attack is a technique which uses a man-in-the-middle attack to obatain RSA key by downgrading the key length to 512-bit export-grade length in a TLS connection. Beurdhouch et al. [5] showed that the attack involves factoring RSA_EXPORT keys with only a modest amount of computation, and because many TLS libraries still provide compatibility to handle legacy cipher-suites, it may cause clients to fallback to RSA_EXPORT. In their study, they tested on a number clients and found that most mobile web browsers, such as Android Browser, Safari, Chrome, Blackberry and Opera, were vulnerable to FREAK attack. It was reported that as of March 2015, the vulnerable web browsers were patched by their vendors.

2.2.5   Logjam Attack

Logjam attack is a flaw of TLS protocol with Diffie-Hellman cryptography in a TLS connection. Adrian et al. [6] performed a man-in-the-middle attack to recover the session key by attacking connections between the web browsers and any servers that accept export-grade Diffie-Hellman which allows down-grading connection to export-grade. During this attack, a server would select DHE_EXPORT instead of the regular DHE connection for negotiation when there is an export-grade fallback, and issue a signed ServerKeyExchange message. It is important to note that the structure of this message and the message sent during the standard DHE ciphersuite is the same, meaning that there is no indication of which ciphersuite is chosen by the server. Many popular vendors, such as Apple, Google, Microsoft and Mozilla already released patches to fix the problem.

2.2.6   DROWN Attack

The DROWN attack uses the vulnerability of SSLv2. The latest clients and servers use TLS protocol to perform cryptographic communication, but a lot of servers still provide compatibility with SSLv2. It is even possible that the servers, which do not allow SSLv2 connection by default, may have their options modified unintentionally by the administrators during the server optimization process. Aviram et al. [7] presented a novel cross-protocol attack called special DROWN, which can decrypt passively collected TLS sessions by using a server which supports SSLv2 as a Bleichenbacher padding oracle. The exploitation process includes a chosen-ciphertest attack which can be used to steal a session key for a TLS handshake. Aviram et al. advised to consider two properties when designing a protocol to prevent DROWN attack; to use longer RSA plaintexts, such as 48 bytes, and let server authenticate the client first to check if it has the knowledge of the RSA plaintext.

3   Methodology

To discover SSL/TLS vulnerabilities on a set of websites in a scalable manner, we implemented a tool based on Nmap 7.1.2 [11] to integrate existing Nmap scripts for the five SSL/TLS vulnerabilities (Heartbleed, POODLE, CCS injection, FREAK and Logjam) on each of target websites by iteratively sending predefined packets to the target website and analyzing the response from that website. For DROWN attack, we used the website [12] that offers the interface to check whether a given host appears to be vulnerable to DROWN attack. We also developed another tool based on Selenium WebDriver [13] to perform automated tests with a large scale of websites. Given a set of websites, our tool checks the existence of the DROWN attack vulnerability on those websites and collects all test results.

The developed tools are available on our GitHub (see https://github.com/sanghak/Checking_SSL_attacks/).

4   Experiments

This section presents the experiment results for most popular websites. We checked the possibilities of the six attacks introduced in Sect. 2.2 on Alexa Top 500 websites, respectively, in both the world and South Korea to analyze not only the trends of SSL/TLS security in global websites but also compare the results with those of regional websites in South Korea to understand inter-country differences in keeping SSL/TLS servers up-to-date to deal with known SSL/TLS vulnerabilities.

We note that the main motivation of our experiments was not to damage real websites. We just intended to conduct a threat and risk analysis on websites to understand the SSL/TLS attack trends and evaluate their severity and likelihood. For secure communication over the Internet, we will publish statistics of the SSL/TLS vulnerabilities found on websites tested and suggest how to fix the discovered vulnerabilities.

For experiments, we used a PC (with a 3.2 GHz Intel Core i5 CPU and 8 GB RAM) running the Ubuntu 14.04 version, and equipped with a non-congested 100 Mbit/s LAN that was connected to the Internet. The experimental results are shown in the following sections. We measured the running time of our implementation to show the relative efficiency of the SSL/TLS scanning methods. Table 1 shows performance measurements of our implementation for each of SSL/TLS attacks tested.

We measured the running time of our implementation to evaluate the performance of the SSL/TLS vulnerability scanners with a real dataset. Overall, except for Logjam, all scanning methods were efficiently implemented. For Logjam attack, the standard deviation is very large in comparison with other attacks, which means that the testing time for Logjam attack varied greatly depending on websites.

Table 1. Running time of our implementation for scanning SSL/TLS vulnerabilities on websites (μ: mean, σ: standard deviation).

	Heartbleed	POODLE	Logjam	CCS injection	FREAK	DROWN
Time (μ)	6.58 s	8.18 s	32.03 s	3.2 s	13.17 s	18.64 s
Time (σ)	8.07 s	5.31 s	208.45 s	5.24 s	13.34 s	12.92 s
Tool	Nmap	Nmap	Nmap	Nmap	Nmap	Web

4.1 Ratio of Vulnerable Websites for SSL/TLS Attacks

We first analyzed how many websites are still vulnerable to each of the six SSL/TLS attacks tested. In Fig. 1, we show the ratio of websites vulnerable to each SSL/TLS attack. A significant portion of popular websites is vulnerable to at least one of the SSL/TLS attacks tested in both global websites (about 45%) and Korean websites (52.6%) (see "any" in Fig. 1). These results are quite surprising because the tested attacks were already intensively studied. We found that nearly half of all websites tested have supported legacy protocols (e.g., SSL 3.0), weak encryption algorithms (e.g., EXPORT_DHE and EXPORT_RSA) and/or used an unpatched OpenSSL version without taking proper countermeasures.

Among the vulnerabilities tested, DROWN and POODLE vulnerabilities remain the most popular ones in both global and Korean websites. This is not surprising since DROWN vulnerability is the most recently introduced while POODLE vulnerability cannot be easily fixed—there is the only way to mitigate POODLE vulnerability by disabling SSL 3.0.

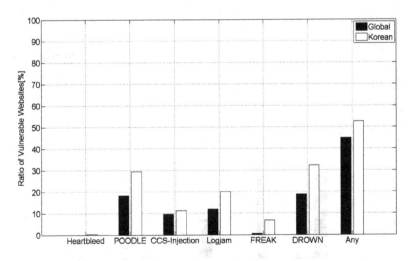

Fig. 1. Ratio of vulnerable websites for each of SSL/TLS attacks.

For Heartbleed attack, there was no vulnerable website in the global websites, which is similar to the results in a technical report [2]. However, although very few, there were still 2 of 500 vulnerable websites in South Korea. Unfortunately, it appears to be a very critical result since one of those websites provides a real name verification service (with "i-PIN") for Korean users where users' sensitive personal data (including user name, password, RRN [14], phone number) could be improperly managed.

Overall, Korean websites (52.6%) are significantly more vulnerable to SSL/TLS attacks than global websites (45%) ($p = 0.019$, Fisher's exact test). This is probably because the latest SSL/TLS attacks might be more popular for global websites compared with Korean ones. Therefore, in South Korea, there is a need to develop a more effective patch management process so as to meet global standards for SSL/TLS protocol implementations.

4.2   Characteristics of SSL/TLS Vulnerabilities

We study the distribution of the number of vulnerabilities per website in order to examine how many websites are vulnerable to multiple vulnerabilities. Figure 2 shows the results for global and Korean websites, respectively. We observed a similar trend in both global and Korean websites—most websites are vulnerable to a small number of SSL/TLS vulnerabilities and considerably skewed to the left. Interestingly, in global websites, the websites vulnerable to a single SSL/TLS attack were dominated (100%) by POODLE attack (see Table 2) while a clear majority is DROWN attack in the case of the websites vulnerable to two or three SSL/TLS vulnerabilities. For the Korean websites with a small number of vulnerabilities, DROWN and POODLE attacks more popular than other attacks (see Table 3).

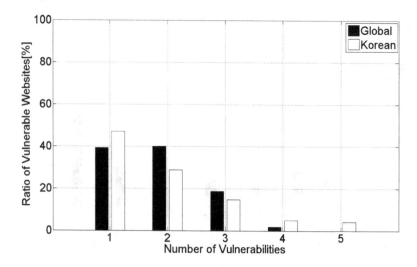

Fig. 2. Number of vulnerabilities per website.

Table 2. Proportions and numbers of SSL/TLS attacks with the number of vulnerable attacks on global websites. Numbers in parentheses indicate the numbers of vulnerable websites for each attack.

# vulner-abilities	Heartbleed	POODLE	Logjam	CCS injection	FREAK	DROWN
1	0% (0)	100% (65)	0% (0)	0% (0)	0% (0)	0% (0)
2	0% (0)	0% (0)	46.96% (31)	53.03% (35)	0% (0)	100% (66)
3	0% (0)	74.19% (23)	83.87% (26)	41.93% (13)	0% (0)	100% (31)
4	0% (0)	100% (3)	100% (3)	0% (0)	100% (3)	100% (3)
5	0% (0)	0% (0)	0% (0)	0% (0)	0% (0)	0% (0)

Table 3. Proportions and numbers of SSL/TLS attacks with the number of vulnerable attacks on Korean websites. Numbers in parentheses indicate the number of vulnerable websites for each attack.

# vulnerabil-ities	Heartbleed	POODLE	Logjam	CCS injection	FREAK	DROWN
1	0% (0)	23.39% (29)	12.90% (16)	9.68% (12)	0% (0)	54.03% (67)
2	1.32% (1)	75% (57)	46.05% (35)	17.11% (13)	2.63% (2)	57.89% (44)
3	0% (0)	94.87% (37)	64.1% (25)	33.33% (13)	30.77% (12)	76.92% (30)
4	0% (0)	100% (13)	100% (13)	53.85% (7)	76.92% (10)	69.23% (9)
5	9.09% (1)	100% (11)	100% (11)	100% (11)	90.9% (10)	100% (11)

We also measured correlations between the six different types of vulnerabilities tested to examine how those attacks are related to each other. To analyze correlations between those vulnerabilities, Pearson's correlation coefficients were calculated. Tables 4 and 5 show the results for global and Korean websites, respectively. For global websites, we found positive correlations between POODLE, Logjam and FREAK. We also found a positive correlation between Logjam and DROWN (see Table 4). For Korean websites, we can see that all SSL/TLS attacks except for Heartbleed are positively correlated. Our findings suggest that the detection of an SSL/TLS vulnerability could be used as an early warning indicator of other SSL/TLS security vulnerabilities since they have positive correlations. Therefore, we first scan only a representative SSL/TLS vulnerability (e.g., DROWN attack) before testing all known vulnerabilities. We note that the vulnerability of DROWN attack was always found in the global websites with multiple vulnerabilities (see Table 2). This approach might be helpful to improve the performance of network scanning systems.

We also analyzed the relationship between the ranks of websites and the number of vulnerabilities to examine whether more popular websites are more likely to be secure against SSL/TLS attacks. However, we failed to find any significant correlations with the websites tested.

Table 4. Correlations between SSL/TLS attacks on global websites. Numbers represent correlation coefficients and p-value (numbers in parentheses). Significant values (p-values < 0.05) are marked with bold font.

Attacks	Heartbleed	POODLE	Logjam	CCS injection	FREAK	DROWN
Heartbleed						
POODLE	NaN					
Logjam	NaN	**0.1608 (p < 0.001)**				
CCS injection	NaN	−0.0657 (p = 0.142)	0.0468 (p = 0.296)			
FREAK	NaN	**0.1647 (p < 0.001)**	**0.2104 (p < 0.001)**	−0.0253 (p = 0.572)		
DROWN	NaN	−0.0014 (p = 0.974)	**0.1059 (p = 0.017)**	0.0517 (p = 0.248)	−0.0374 (p = 0.404)	

Table 5. Correlations between SSL/TLS attacks on Korean websites. Numbers represent correlation coefficients and p-value (numbers in parentheses). Significant values (p-values < 0.05) are marked with bold font.

Attacks	Heartbleed	POODLE	Logjam	CCS injection	FREAK	DROWN
Heartbleed						
POODLE	0.0287 (p = 0.522)					
Logjam	**0.1267 (p = 0.004)**	**0.4346 (p < 0.001)**				
CCS injection	0.078 (p = 0.081)	**0.2441 (p < 0.001)**	**0.2346 (p < 0.001)**			
FREAK	−0.0171 (p = 0.702)	**0.4011 (p < 0.001)**	**0.3813 (p < 0.001)**	**0.2568 (p < 0.001)**		
DROWN	0.0241 (p = 0.590)	**0.2787 (p < 0.001)**	**0.137 (p = 0.002)**	**0.1489 (p < 0.001)**	**0.2049 (p < 0.001)**	

4.3 Changes in the Number of Vulnerable Websites over Time

Lastly, we analyzed how the number of vulnerable websites were changed over time. We repeated the scanning procedure with the same websites tested once a week from March 22nd 2016 to April 19th 2016. The results for global and Korean websites are shown, respectively, in Tables 6 and 7. We note that the number of vulnerable websites can be rather increased compared to previous results since some websites were often unreachable in our test attempts.

We observed a similar trend in both global and Korean websites—the number of vulnerable websites was slightly decreased in all SSL/TLS vulnerabilities tested except for FREAK in global websites. In particular, in global websites, the websites vulnerable to DROWN (18%) attack were more likely to be patched than others while the numbers of POODLE (12.9%) and Logjam (12%) attacks were the most highly reduced vulnerabilities in Korean websites. Although slight improvements among SSL/TLS vulnerabilities may be noted, the adoption rates of patches seem still slow.

Table 6. Changes in number of vulnerable global websites tested over four weeks.

	Heartbleed	POODLE	Logjam	CCS injection	FREAK	DROWN
Week 1	0	91	60	48	3	100
Week 2	0	90	61	41	3	80
Week 3	0	91	61	44	4	80
Week 4	0	85	53	42	4	82

Table 7. Changes in number of vulnerable Korean websites tested over four weeks.

	Heartbleed	POODLE	Logjam	CCS injection	FREAK	DROWN
Week 1	2	147	100	56	34	161
Week 2	2	143	98	57	34	160
Week 3	2	142	97	53	33	148
Week 4	2	128	88	53	32	151

5   Recommendations

In Sect. 4, we can see that a significant number of websites (i.e., 45% of global websites and 52.6% of Korean websites) are still vulnerable to SSL/TLS attacks even though there already exist several vulnerability scanners such as Zmap [15] and Masscan [16]. This implies that the automation of security vulnerability detection is necessary but not sufficient for less-skilled administrators. Most existing tools simply detect vulnerabilities and do not offer actionable advices to fix the problems (see the results in Fig. 3). When vulnerabilities are discovered, less-skilled administrators would lack the security knowledge to understand the dangers of those vulnerabilities and to patch them. Hence, we should develop tools to provide more actionable advices to administrators; if an automated security analysis tool detects a security vulnerability on a target host, it seems

```
                            ...
|       State: LIKELY VULNERABLE
|       IDs:   CVE:CVE−2014−3566   OSVDB:113251
|              The SSL protocol 3.0, as used in OpenSSL through
|              1.0.1i and other products, uses nondeterministic
|              CBC padding, which makes it easier for man−in−the
|              −middle attackers to obtain cleartext data via a
|              padding−oracle attack, aka the "POODLE" issue.
|       Disclosure date: 2014−10−14
|                            ...
```

Fig. 3. Example of detection results in Nmap.

better to show its potential risks and step-by-step instructions that enable an administrator to implement the best security practices to fix the problem.

Here, government could have a role in periodically performing such security checks and publishing the checking results for system administrators to encourage them to keep their systems up-to-date with latest security patches.

6   Related Work

As the SSL/TLS protocol has become the de facto standard for Internet, the security about SSL/TLS has also been intensively studied. CCS injection was first reported on December 2013 [4]. Heartbleed, a notorious vulnerability of SSL/TLS, emerged during April 2014 [2]. POODLE attack, which exploits the vulnerability of supporting SSL 3.0, was reported on October 2014 [3]. During March 2015, FREAK attack caused quite a stir amongst the security administrators as it makes use of the vulnerability of export RSA cipher [5]. Logjam, reminiscent of FREAK attack, was reported to be related to the vulnerability of export DH cipher on October 2015 [6]. Lastly, DROWN attack [7] was reported recently on March 2016.

Benjamin et al. [9] analyzed how many websites were vulnerable to POODLE and FREAK attacks on Alexa's top websites and found that there was a slow patch adoption rate in mitigating those attacks. We extend their work by testing the six representative SSL/TLS attacks—Heartbleed, POODLE, CCS injection, FREAK, Logjam and DROWN—on popular websites. We also compared the analysis results on global websites with those on Korean websites to examine the differences between regional websites and global websites.

7   Conclusion

We analyzed how most popular websites are vulnerable to well-known SSL/TLS attacks to understand the gap between academic research and real-world situations in deploying security practices. We conducted experiments on the top 500 most popular global and Korean websites, respectively. Our results showed that 45% of global websites and 52.6% of Korean websites are still vulnerable to at least one of the six SSL/TLS attacks tested. This is probably because the state-of-the-art of defense methods against SSL/TLS attacks has not been popularly introduced to system administrators (particularly in Korean websites). To bridge the gap between academia and real-world systems, we need better vulnerability scanners and education programs that deal with the SSL/TLS security issues.

Acknowledgements. This work was partly supported by the MSIP/IITP (R0166-15-1041), the ITRC (IITP-2016-R0992-16-1006), and the IITP (No. R-20160222-002755). Authors would like to thank all the anonymous reviewers for their valuable feedback.

References

1. Bhiogade, M.S.: Secure socket layer. In: Proceedings of the Computer Science and Information Technology Education Conference (2002)
2. Durumeric, Z., Kasten, J., Adrian, D., Halderman, J.A., Bailey, M., Li, F., Weaver, N., Amann, J., Beekman, J., Payer, M., et al.: The matter of heartbleed. In: Proceedings of the Conference on Internet Measurement Conference (2014)
3. Möller, B., Duong, T., Kotowicz, K.: This POODLE bites: exploiting the SSL 3.0 fallback. Google, September 2014
4. MITRE. CCS-injection CVE Report(CVE-2014-0224) (2013). http://cve.mitre.org/cgi-bin/cvename.cgi?name=CVE-2014-0224
5. Beurdouche, B., Bhargavan, K., Delignat-Lavaud, A., Fournet, C., Kohlweiss, M., Pironti, A., Strub, P.-Y., Zinzindohoue, J.K.: A messy state of the union: taming the composite state machines of TLS. In: Proceedings of the IEEE Symposium on Security and Privacy (2015)
6. Adrian, D., Bhargavan, K., Durumeric, Z., Gaudry, P., Matthew Green, J., Halderman, A., Heninger, N., Springall, D., Thomé, E., Valenta, L., et al.: Imperfect forward secrecy: how Diffie-Hellman fails in practice. In: Proceedings of the 22nd ACM SIGSAC Conference on Computer and Communications Security (2015)
7. Aviram, N., Schinzel, S., Somorovsky, J., Heninger, N., Dankel, M., Steube, J., Valenta, L., David Adrian, J., Halderman, A., Viktor Dukhovni, D., et al.: Breaking TLS using SSLv2 (2008)
8. Paulson, L.C.: Inductive analysis of the internet protocol TLS. ACM Trans. Inf. Syst. Secur. **2**(3), 332–351 (1999)
9. Fogel, B., Farmer, S., Alkofahi, H., Skjellum, A., Hafiz, M.: POODLEs, More POODLEs, FREAK attacks too: how server administrators responded to three serious web vulnerabilities. In: Caballero, J., Bodden, E., Athanasopoulos, E. (eds.) ESSoS 2016. LNCS, vol. 9639, pp. 122–137. Springer, Cham (2016). doi:10.1007/978-3-319-30806-7_8
10. Dierks, T., Rescorla, E.: RFC 5246: The Transport Layer Security (TLS) Protocol Version 1.2, Updated by RFCs, 5746(5878):6176, August 2008
11. Lyon, G.F.: Nmap network scanning: the official Nmap project guide to network discovery and security scanning. Insecure (2009)
12. Aviram. The DROWN Attack (2016). https://drownattack.com/
13. Huggins, J.: Selenium WebDriver (2016). http://docs.seleniumhq.org/projects/webdriver/
14. Song, Y., Kim, H., Huh, J.H.: On the guessability of resident registration numbers in South Korea. In Proceedings of Australasian Conference on Information Security and Privacy (2016)
15. Durumeric, Z., Eric Wustrow, J., Halderman, A., ZMap: fast internet-wide scanning and its security applications. In: Proceedings of the Usenix Security (2013)
16. Graham, R.D.: MASSCAN: Mass IP port scanner (2014). https://github.com/robertdavidgraham/masscan

Development of Information Security Management Assessment Model for the Financial Sector

Eun Oh[1], Tae-Sung Kim[2(✉)], and Tae-Hee Cho[1]

[1] ArchiSec Consulting, Seoul, Republic of Korea
[2] Chungbuk National University, Chungbuk, Republic of Korea
kimts@cbnu.ac.kr

Abstract. This study integrates the representative information security certification systems such as ISMS, PIMS and PIPL in order to improve efficiency of information security management. It also suggests information security management assessment model for the financial sector by incorporating new control items derived from laws and regulations related to financial IT and information security into the integration model of information security certifications to reflect characteristics of financial industry. The findings have significance in that they solve problems related to duplication of previous information security certification systems and suggest the orientation of information security management system for financial industry enhancing the organizations' ability to cope with security accidents. Moreover, the suggested methodology can be used in study on systematic and specific information security management standard for each industry.

Keywords: Financial security · Information security management system

1 Introduction

In recent years, information security accidents occur in various ways such as service suspension and information breaches. The ensuing threat on information security shows increasingly signs of these accidents being organized and criminalized beyond mere display of force for simple monetary purpose [11]. Especially noteworthy is that these security accidents occur frequently in financial institutions that use, store and manage diverse information of customers as target [2, 19]. In view of the fact that they can cause paralysis of a nation's finance and economy, overlook breaches of personal information, and bring about actual monetary damages. These financial security accidents are very serious matters [1, 10, 14]. Table 1 shows representative breaches of personal information that occurred during the last 5 years to domestic finance companies.

As can be seen in the above Table, in the case of financial industry, financial security accidents keep occurring due to changes in financial and IT environments. Since there is a potential of serious impingement on customers' interest in this industry than in any other industry, these security accidents can cause secondary damages. For this reason, among others, these accidents should be dealt with more strictly than simple risk management as seen in other industries and should be managed systematically [6].

D. Choi and S. Guilley (Eds.): WISA 2016, LNCS 10144, pp. 186–197, 2017.
DOI: 10.1007/978-3-319-56549-1_16

Table 1. Personal information breaches in the financial sector

Year	Related Organization	Cause	Victims
2011.4	Hyundai Capital	Hacking	1.75 million
2011.5	Hanwha Gerneral Insurance	Hacking	160,000
2011.8	Samsung Card	Illegally copied by insider	800,000
2011.12	IBK Capital	Illegally copied by insider	5,800
2012.2	Standard Chartered Bank	Illegally copied by employee of outsourcing partner	10,4000
2013.4	Citi Bank	Illegally copied by insider	3,4000
2013.5	Meriz Fire&Marine Insurance	Illegally copied by insider	16,4000
2014.1	KB Card, Lotte Card, NH Card	Illegally copied by employee of outsourcing partner	104 million

Source: Wikipedia (ko.wikipedia.org) [26]

In order to propose an Information Security Management Level Evaluation Model that is specialized for financial sector, the present research has been carried out in the following fashion. First, an integrative comparison and analysis was carried out for Information Security Management System (ISMS), Personal Information Management System (PIMS), and Personal Information Protection Level (PIPL) which are the representative information security and personal information certification systems of Korea.

Of the laws related to IT and information security which are applicable to domestic financial institutions, the Electronic Financial Transactions Act and the Credit Information Use and Protection Act were reflected to an integrated model of Information Security Certification System and complemented in order to derive an Information Security Management Level Assessment Model for financial sector. The Electronic Financial Transactions Act regulates IT system requirements for financial institutions overall [5], and the Credit Information Use and Protection Act deals with technological, managerial and physical protection measures of credit information computer system [25]. There are contents in these two Acts that overlap with stipulations of the Act on Promotion of Information and Communications Network Utilization and Information Protection, Etc. and the Personal Information Protection Act which are the foundation laws for certification of Information Security Management System of Korea respectively.

2 Research Background

2.1 Importance of Financial Information Security Management

Goodhue and Straub (1991) presented three (3) reasons why finance companies should invest more in the protection of information system information than other companies. First, as finance companies rely more on information system in operating their business, loss caused by misuse or abuse of information system can be quite big, and the corporate image is very important for their business [3]. In order to analyze influences on the selection of information system protection measures, Yeh and Chang (2007) set up as their research target managers' awareness of threat on information system, industry type (general manufacturing, hi-tech industry, banking and finance, and retail and services), and level of computer dependence of the organization. As a result of empirical analysis, not much difference was discovered in the level of computer dependence of the organizations but it turned out that the banking and financing industry as well as retail and service industry depended more heavily on IT in relative terms. Also, as a result of severity measurement of perceived threats for 7 information system categories (software, hardware, data, network, physical facilities, human resources, and regulation), banking and finance industry turned out to be the highest [21]. Randazzo et al. (2004) presented the result of a research on 23 security accidents perpetrated by insiders of the financial sector from 1999 to 2002 as well as its implications. Most of the technologies used in the accidents were not very precise, the insider perpetrators planned the crime in advance, and their main purpose was financial gain rather than any intention to harm a company or information system. Furthermore, the rate of security accidents perpetrated by insiders rather than in-charges of the security business reached 61%. The result also indicated that almost all financial institutions that suffered from security accidents perpetrated by insiders had financial loss. Other damages included a problem of business continuity and damage to reputation of the organization concerned [18]. Humphreys (2008) also stated that especially the financial industry worried out frauds perpetrated by insiders, and argued that for the purpose the company should introduce an enterprise-wide information security management framework [4].

2.2 Information Security Certification System

Information security management system denotes a system that is used to manage various security measures to differentiate confidentiality, integrity, and availability of information assets and to manage and operate information security throughout the entire cycles of construction, implementation, operation, monitoring, review, and improvement based on risk-based approaches [15]. As for international information security management standard, one can think of ISO 27001 first which regulates requirements for establishing, implementing, operating, monitoring, maintaining, and improving information security management systems based on BS7799 that was the information security management system of the U.K. in the past [12]. As for representative information security certification system being operated in Korea, there are ISMS, PIMS, and PIPL.

ISMS (Information Security Management System) certification system, which was introduced in 2002, is a system that, when an organization has constructed and is operating an information security management system, judges whether the information security management system satisfies certification criteria set independently and objectively by an authorized certification organization. Since 2013, major ISPs (Information and communication Service Provider) were designated under this certification system as obligatory targets. The criteria for certification are divided in the main into two categories, Information Security Management Process and Information Security Countermeasures [15]. PIMS (Personal Information Management System) certification is used to check whether a corporation has constructed a system of security measures that are necessary to implement personal information management activities systematically on an on-gong basis. In case a corporation satisfies these criteria, a certification certificate is awarded. The certification criteria are divided into three (3) fields including Management Process, Protection Measures, and Life Cycle [17]. PIPL (Personal Information Protection Level) certification is a system that awards a certification mark when a Personal Information Manager has completed a Personal Information Management System and fulfilled stipulations that are required to implement Personal Information Protection Measures to a satisfactory level. The certification criteria are divided in the main into two categories, Personal Information Management System and Personal Information Protection Measures [20]. Korea Communications Commission has operated PIMS based on Act on Promotion of Information and Communications Network Utilization and Information Protection, Etc., and the Ministry of the Interior has operated PIPL system based on Personal Information Protection Act with public institutions and regular business owners as targets. Companies related to personal information protection have suffered from similar but conflicting requirements of certification system operated by the two Government organizations, and in response to popular demands for unified requirements, Korea Internet & Security Agency started to operate this system from Jan. 1, 2016. As a result, 124 assessment items of PIMS and 65 items of PIPL were integrated into 86 items (Refer to Table 2).

Table 2. Assessment items for integrated certification of PIMS, PIPL

Areas	Assessment items			
	Public institution	Large companies/ Internet communicat ions services providers	Small & medium sized firms	Small enterprise
Personal information management processes	16	16	15	3
Personal information lifecycle and assurance on rights	20	19	19	19
Personal information security countermeasures	50	48	44	22
Total	86	83	78	44

2.3 Status of Information Security in Financial Sector

Due to continuing incidents of personal information breaches including information breaches of card companies, the entire financial sector seems to make concerted efforts to reinforce information security. One of the most representative movements along this line is acquisition of information security management system certification [9]. A close look at the data, status of ISMS certification acquisition in financial industry shows that as of Dec. 9, 2015, a total of 28 financial companies have acquired ISMS, and included in the range of certification turned out to be mostly Internet banking and on-line trading systems [16]. NH Nonghyup Bank (2003), BC Card (2009), and 25 financial companies other than NH Nonghyup Bank (2012) turned out to have acquired ISMS after acquisition of ISMS became mandatory during the early 2013. Of all financial companies, acquisition of ISMS certification by securities companies was most noteworthy. This seems to indicate that securities companies have decided to hasten in reinforcing their security systems partially influenced by a series of financial security accidents that occurred recently in the midst of increasing concern on imminent security vulnerability with regard to on-line trading systems of securities companies [9]. But among card companies, the one that has acquired ISMS certification was BC Card only. This is all the more surprising since after 2014 when personal information breaches occurred en masse, there was no company that acquired ISMS certification. (Reference: Financial Security Institute (FSI) that was newly designated as the authorized ISMS certification organization has awarded the Certificate of ISMS Certification to Samsung Card as of Dec. 10, 2015 [13]. Card companies are half-hearted in acquiring ISMS for the reason that they have already satisfied the requirements of financial authorities, not to mention of the fact that ISMS certification is by no means obligatory [24].

3   Methodology

The method for drawing Information Security Management Assessment Model in view of the characteristics of the financial industry is shown in Fig. 1.

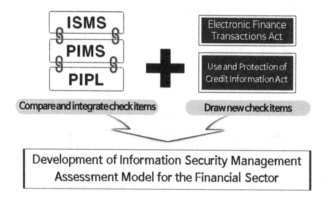

Fig. 1. Methodology and procedure of the study

First, compare detailed control items of ISMS, PIMS, and PIPL and classify identical and similar items into a number of groupings before drawing control items to be added to existing ISMS. Table 3 shows the result of the above procedure, displaying control items (detailed upper level items) that were newly added to ISMS. Ultimately, 32 new detailed control items were drawn and a new integrated Information Security Certification System was developed by adding a life-cycle control field of PIMS that did not exist in existing ISMS.

Table 3. Integration of information security certification systems

Areas			Additional control activities
2	Information security organization	Organizational system	(PIMS) Appointment of the employee responsible for and in charge of personal information by sections
		Role and responsibility	(PIMS) Report and communication system
10	Access control	Access control management	(PIMS) The responsibility of employee in charge of personal information
		Access authority management	(PIMS) Authority management of employee in charge of personal information
11	Operations security	Medium security	(PIPL) Keeping of storage media
		Log management and monitoring	(PIMS) Storage of access records of personal information system
			(PIMS) Designation of output purpose of personal information and protection measure and personal information masking

Through a series of matching operations of legal provisions contained in detailed control items of an integrated ISMS, PIMS, and PIPL model, Electronic Financial Transactions Act [Statute No. 12837; enforced on Oct. 10, 2015], Enforcement Decree of Electronic Financial Transactions Act [Presidential Decree No. 26199; enforced on Oct. 16, 2015], Regulation on Supervision of Electronic Finance [Notification of Financial Services Commission No. 2015-18; enforced on Jun. 24, 2015], Credit Information Use and Protection Act [Statute No. 13216; enforced on Sept. 12, 2015], Enforcement Decree of the Credit Information Use and Protection Act [Presidential Decree No. 26517; enforced on Sept. 12, 2015], Regulation on Credit Information Supervision [Notification of Financial Services Commission No. 2015-31; enforced on Sept. 11, 2015], legal provisions that are not contained in the integrated model were drawn before they are added to detailed control items. In the case of Credit Information Use and Protection Act, related Enforcement Degree, and Regulation on Supervision, certain legal provisions enforced on Mar. 12, 2016 are reflected [5, 7, 8, 22, 23, 25]. Fourteen (14) detailed control items newly drawn are shown in Table 4 below.

4 Verification of Assessment Model

In order to verify appropriateness of Information Security Management Assessment Model for the finance sector, a questionnaire survey was carried out with 21 IT and information security professionals and information security consultants or certification auditors who have consulting experience in certification of information security management system and who personally work in the finance industry and understand well

Table 4. Information security management assessment model for the financial sector

	Areas					Control activities	
(ISMS)IS counter-measures	2	Information security organization	2.1	Organizational system	2.1.1	Appointment of chief information security officer (CISO)
					2.1.2	Organization of working group
	8	System development security	8.3	security for outsour-cing development	8.3.1	Security for outsourcing development
	11	Operations security	11.1	Operation procedure and alteration management	Addition	Establishment of plan on information technology sector
			11.2	System and service operation security	Addition	Analysis and evaluation on weak point of electronic finance infrastructure
			11.3	Electronic business and information transmission security	Addition	Public notice of matters to be attended for users
(PIMS) lifecycle	Areas					Control activities	
	1	Collection of personal information	1.3	Privacy policy	Addition	Credit information utilization status
	2	Use and provision of personal information	2.2	Protection of user 's right	2.2.3	Withdrawal of consent
					2.2.4	Public notification of credit information utilization status
			2.4	Protection of personal information in case of provision to 3rd party	2.4.1	Consent is needed, in case of provision to 3rd party
					Addition	Consent to provision and use of personal credit information
					2.4.2	Management of personal information provided
			2.5	Protection of information in case of personal information transfer	2.5.1	Protective measure in case of personal information transfer
	3	Management and destruction of personal information	3.1	Management and destruction of personal information	3.1.5	Retention after achieving a purpose

business characteristics of the industry as target. Table 5 shows general characteristics of the respondents. All respondents are in charge of information security business, and the number of professionals with longer than 10 years of experience is 14 or 67% of the total respondents.

Of control items (upper level of detailed control items) to which detailed control items drawn from finance related laws (the Electronic Financial Transactions Act and the Credit Information Use and Protection Act) belong, the respondents are supposed to evaluate the

Table 5. Descriptive statistics for the respondents

Type		Frequency	Percentage (%)
Type of industry	Financial public enterprise	1	4.8
	Insurance	1	4.8
	Credit Card	4	19.0
	Security consulting company	6	28.6
	ISMS Assessors	4	19.0
	etc.	5	23.8
Number of employees	Under 100	9	42.9
	100–300	3	14.3
	300–1,000	3	14.3
	1,000–5,000	4	19.0
	5,000–10,000	1	4.8
	Over 10,000	1	4.8
Career	1–5year	2	9.5
	5–0year	5	23.8
	10–15year	9	42.9
	Over 15year	5	23.8
Certifications acquisition or not (Multiple responses possible)	K-ISMS	8	29.6
	PIMS	3	11.1
	PIPL	0	0.0
	ISO 27001	4	14.8
	Not acquired	12	44.4
Ought to acquire ISMS or not	Yes	4	19.0
	No	17	81.0
Total		21	100.0

degree to which he or she feels necessary when evaluating information security management level of financial companies on control items that are added to an integrated model of information security certification system using a 5-point scale (1: Never Needed, 2: Not Needed, 3: Normal, 4: Needed, 5: Much Needed). If the mean value of respondents is 3.0 or above, appropriateness of a control item was regarded as having been satisfied, and the mean values for response results are as shown in Table 6. Value for 'Consent to provision and use of personal credit information' was the highest at 4.20 and 'The public notification of matters to be attended for users' was relatively low at 3.52. The mean values of response results were all 3.0 or above, indicating that appropriateness of control items turned out to be satisfactory.

Table 6. Result of survey on information security management assessment model for the Financial Sector

Questionnaire items	Mean
1. Establishment of plan on information technology sector	3.81
2. The analysis on and evaluation of weak point of electronic finance infrastructure	4.10
3. The public notification of matters to be attended for users	3.52
4. Public notification of credit information utilization status	4.00
5. Consent to provision and use of personal credit information	4.20

Additionally, a questionnaire survey was carried out on the necessity of information security management system in the financial sector and the response results are as shown in Fig. 2. Respondents who answered negatively ('Never Needed', 'Not Needed') and respondents who answered positively ('Needed', 'Much Needed') were all 48% respectively.

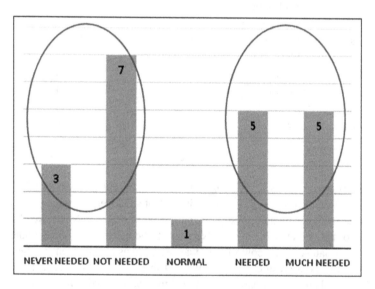

Fig. 2. Opinion on the necessity of information security management system specialized for the financial sector

In order to find out common characteristics of the respondents who answered positively or negatively on the necessity of information security management system specialized for the financial sector, the respondents were divided into two groups and the ratios of their career, business scale, status of ISMS certifications acquisition, and whether they ought to acquire ISMS were examined (Refer to Table 7).

Table 7. Opinion on the necessity of information security management system specialized for the financial sector (Characteristics of respondents)

Opinion on necessity	Business Scale			Career		Certifications acquisition or not		Ought to acquire ISMS or not	
	Small	Medium	Large	Under 10-year	Over 10-year	Yes	No	Yes	No
Yes	70%	10%	20%	40%	60%	40%	60%	10%	90%
No	40%	20%	40%	30%	70%	50%	50%	30%	70%

Note: Small (Having less than 300 employees), Medium (Having less than 1,000 employees), Large (Having more than 1,000 employees)

Most of the respondents who answered that information security management system specialized for the financial sector is necessary belonged to an SMB company that was not required to acquire ISMS. Also, the business type they belonged to was either a security consulting company or a certification auditor. Accordingly, we are going to conduct a group analysis after classifying the security consulting companies and the certification auditors as 'Certification body' and other companies as 'Institution to be inspected for certification'. Table 8 reveals the results of analysis conducted after classifying the two groups as 'Certification body' and as 'Institution to be inspected for certification'. Although the latter exhibited a negative attitude (2.64) on the information security management system specialized for the financial sector, the former exhibited a positive attitude (3.60).

Table 8. Opinion on the necessity of information security management system specialized for the financial sector (Group analysis)

Institution to be inspected for certification		Certification body		Total	
Mean	Standard Deviation	Mean	Standard Deviation	Mean	Standard Deviation
2.64	1.63	3.60	1.17	3.10	1.48

We had the questionnaire respondents choose the degree of necessity on information security management system specialized for the financial sector and state the reasons for selecting it. Common opinions of those who answered positively was that 'there is a need to establish a management system that can satisfy all the requirements of a financial environment as the financial sector views legal compliance more strictly than other industries and as the requirements of the foundation laws of information security certification and requirements of laws related to finance are different in specific contents'. In the case of respondents who answered negatively, there were more opinions that certification criteria should be converted to a direction that differentiate certification criteria to reflect characteristics of the financial sector and improve check items as a separate certification system can result in redundant regulations.

5   Conclusion

As can be seen in a large-scale breaches of personal information of 2014, the necessity of information security management is getting more important especially in financial sector as security accidents can cause not only breaches of personal information but also monetary damage and secondary damages and as their range is very far-reaching.

Hence, in this research, an attempt was made to improve efficiency of information security management job and to draw an information security management level assessment model taking characteristics of the financial security into consideration through integration of redundant information security certification systems. And we have drawn a final information security management level assessment model by adding 14 new detailed control items reflecting the Electronic Financial Transactions Act and the Credit Information Use and Protection Act on the integrated model of ISMS, PIMS, and PIPL certification systems. Furthermore, we have measured reliability of the proposed model through a questionnaire survey with the professionals as the target and were actually able to confirm the necessity of information security management system of the financial sector.

Implications of this research can be summarized as follows: First, we have tried to prove validity of introducing an information security management system (F-ISMS) that reflects characteristics of the financial sector in the midst of a controversy on introduction of certification. As we have seen above, the 'Certification body' and the 'Institution to be inspected for certification' revealed a distinct difference of opinions on the necessity of an information security management system of the financial sector. But both of the two groups also showed an identical opinion in the sense that, with the existing information security certification system alone, all the requirements demanded by the financial sector cannot be satisfied. The feasibility of introducing a separate information security management system specialized for the financial sector can be examined through responses of the industry by adding detailed check items that took characteristics of the financial sector into account while applying the existing information security certification system. Ultimately, what is important is to establish and operate an information security management system specialized for the financial sector, and for the purpose, the position of the industry concerned should be considered sufficiently and diverse exchange of opinions and accommodation processes are needed.

Second, in industrial fields other than the financial industry, introduction of an effective information security management level assessment model is possible which reflects characteristics of the industry concerned by applying the methodology proposed in this research. In the future, in order to propose a systematic and concrete information security management guideline for each industry, on-going researches related to this subject seem necessary.

References

1. Jung, C.Y.: Financial authority's policy and financial institution's response on the latest financial information security related incidents. Credit Union Research, no. 63, pp. 45–82 (2014)

2. Seo, D.J., Kim, T.S.: Influence of personal information security vulnerabilities and perceived usefulness on bank customers "willingness to stay". J. Korean Inst. Commun. Sci. **40**(8), 1577–1587 (2015)
3. Goodhue, D.L., Straub, D.W.: Security concerns of system users: a study of perceptions of the adequacy of security. Inf. Manage. **20**(1), 13–27 (1991)
4. Humphreys, E.: Information security management standards: Compliance, governance and risk management. Inf. Secur. Techn. Report **13**(2), 247–255 (2008)
5. Electronic Finance Transactions Act
6. Oh, E., Kim, T.S., Cho, T.H.: Improvement of the certification model for enhancing information security management efficiency for the financial sector. J. Korea Inst. Inf. Secur. Cryptology **26**(2), 541–550 (2016)
7. Enforcement Decree of the Electronic Financial Transactions Act
8. Enforcement Decree of Use and Protection of Credit Information Act
9. Kim, G.A.: Analysis on the status of ISMS certification acquisition in financial industry … last year, only 15 security companies. The Boannews, 22 January 2015
10. Mun, H.J., Kim, K.S., Um, N.K., Li, Y.Z., Lee, S.H.: Effective access control mechanism for protection of sensitive personal information. J. Korean Inst. Commun. Sci. **32**(7), 667–673 (2007)
11. Kang, H.S.: An analysis of information security management system and certification standard for information security. J. Secur. Eng. **11**(6), 455–468 (2014)
12. ISO, ISO/IEC 27001 - Information security management. http://www.iso.org/iso/home/standards/management-standards/iso27001.html, Accessed 13 Nov 2015
13. Park, J.E.: Financial security institute, start to issue ISMS certification. The Electronic Times, 13 December 2015
14. Lee, J.H., Park, M.H., Jung, S.W.: OTP-based transaction verification protocol using PUFs. J. Korean Inst. Commun. Sci. **38**(6), 492–500 (2013)
15. Korea Internet & Security Agency, Information Security Management System (ISMS) certification guideline (2013)
16. Korea Internet & Security Agency, Status of ISMS certification acquisition in financial industry. http://isms.kisa.or.kr/kor/issue/issue01.jsp?certType=ISMS, Accessed 9 Dec 2015
17. Korea Internet & Security Agency, Personal Information Management System (PIMS) certification guideline (2010)
18. Randazzo, M.R., Keeney, M., Kowalski, E.: Insider threat study: Illicit cyber activity in the banking and finance sector, U.S. Secret Service and CERT Coordination Center, Technical report (2004)
19. Yim, M.S., Jeong, T.S., Lee, J.M.: A suggestion for information security awareness of finance firms. J. Secur. Eng. **11**(6), 479–498 (2014)
20. National Information Society Agency, Personal Information Protection Level (PIPL) guideline (2015)
21. Yeh, Q.J., Chang, A.J.T.: Threats and countermeasures for information system security: a cross-industry study. Inf. Manage. **44**(5), 480–491 (2007)
22. Regulation on Supervision of Credit Information Business
23. Regulation on Supervision of Electronic Financial Activities
24. Park, S.Y.: Cards company still turns away ISMS certification. The Digital Times, 19 January 2015
25. Use and Protection of Credit Information Act
26. Wikipedia, Security accidents in Korea. https://ko.wikipedia.org/, Accessed 25 Oct 2015

A Practical Approach to Constructing Triple-Blind Review Process with Maximal Anonymity and Fairness

Jisoo Jung, Joo-Im Kim, and Ji Won Yoon[✉]

Center for Information Security Technologies (CIST),
Korea University, Seoul, Republic of Korea
{jisoo_kor,jooimkim,jiwon_yoon}@korea.ac.kr

Abstract. Most journals and conferences adopt blind review process to ensure fairness through anonymization. Although the identity of an author is blinded in a manuscript, information about the author is known to the system when an account is created for submission. So, Information leak or the abuse from journal editor, who is able to access this information, could discredit the review process. Therefore, the triple-blind review process has been proposed to maximize anonymity through blinding the author, reviewer and also the editor. However, it has not been widely used compared to single- and double-blind review processes because there is difficulty in selecting the reviewers when the author is not known to the editor. In this paper, we propose a novel scheme to select the adequate reviewers in the triple-blind review process without any disclosure of author information to even the editor. This is done by using machine learning classification and a conflict of interest measuring method.

Keywords: Blind review process · Author identification · Artificial neural network · Multinomial naive Bayes · Conflict Of Interest

1 Introduction

The development of scientific research is led both by sharing academic research and by publishing a novel and advanced articles. To improve the research, it is important to ensure the fairness of publication process, especially in the review process. Accordingly, journals and conferences adopt single or double-blind review process [1]. Single-blind review (SBR) hides reviewers' identities from authors so that the reviewers feel free to make impartial decisions. But still, the evaluation could be biased because of the personal relationship with the author of the manuscript. So, double-blind review (DBR) is used to make the author unknown to the reviewer. It can prevent biased decisions based on information such as whether they are from the same school or they have had a personal relationship beforehand. Therefore, many journals have changed from

© Springer International Publishing AG 2017
D. Choi and S. Guilley (Eds.): WISA 2016, LNCS 10144, pp. 198–209, 2017.
DOI: 10.1007/978-3-319-56549-1_17

SBR to DBR systems. For instance, several journals published by 'Nature' have applied DBR process since March 2015 [2].

However, there are still concerns about the fairness of DBR. In the review process, a journal editor takes charge of the overall process including filtering out irrelevant manuscripts, deciding which articles to reject, and selecting reviewers [3]. To submit a paper, authors are asked to fill their information (e.g., name, affiliation, nationality, and so on.) in the form to create an account. This means that journal editors can access the information in order to decide which reviewers to choose. Therefore, it could negatively influence the overall review process if there is a conflict between the author and the editor. From this point of view, we need the triple-blind review (TBR) which is able to ensure anonymity by blinding even the journal editor in addition to author and reviewers.

Nevertheless, there exist some considerations when applying the TBR. It needs to find the *Conflict Of Interest (COI)* of authors to select appropriate reviewers. If not, a manuscript can be accidentally assigned to the parties that hold interests (e.g., him/herself, his/her advisor, colleague, etc.). It is, unfortunately, hard to measure COI since the editor does not know the author's identity in TBR [4]. For this reason, the reviewer recommendation system needs to have the automatic selection functionality by analyzing the content of the manuscript in order to build successful TBR process with maximal anonymity and fairness.

In this paper, we propose a practical approach to removing the disadvantages of the conventional TBR system. Our approach consists of two folds: (a) an automatic author identification which predicts the author of the paper and (b) a new COI measurement which decides suitable reviewers for the TBR process. Note that this author identification is not used for providing the author's information to the editor but for exploring the COI. That is, author information is hidden to the editor in our proposed approach. Artificial neural network and multinomial naive Bayes classification are utilized as machine learning techniques for identifying the author, and a weighting method is used for COI selection with co-author information.

The remainder of this paper is organized as follows. Sections 2 and 3 provide the requisite related works and technical backgrounds of this paper. In Sect. 4, we propose a scheme which supports TBR process finding fair reviewers. In Sect. 5, we show the prospect of our proposal by accomplishing the proposed scheme. Section 6 concludes the discussion and lists future work to be done.

2   Related Work

The scheme we propose contains the technique of author identification and measuring the COI weights between identified author and potential reviewers. Authorship attribution has been consistently researched. Yankauer [5] did a survey through reviewers whether they could identify the author and the institution in a manuscript. A large number of reviewers in the survey responded that it was possible to identify 30% of the author and/or the institution by self-referencing and personal knowledge. Hill and Provost [6] have identified the author using only citations from KDD Cup 2003 data set, but the accuracy was maximum 45% and had several constraints. The 76% of 20 authors was identified in Luyckx and Daelemans [7] using support vector machine and maximum entropy. Our experiment shows better accuracy than prior works, which is maximum 81% of 20 authors by using simple and fast naive Bayes classifier.

In comparison with prior works, our techniques focused on not only the author identification but also the fair reviewer selection. Regarding the reviewer selection problem, Aleman-Meza et al. [8] measured the weight and level of COI between author and potential reviewer. They used FOAF (Friend of a Friend) information from Semantic Web and co-author information from DBLP (Computer Science Bibliography Website). Our proposed approach embeds the method of weighting the COI between an identified author and potential reviewers by using co-author information from DBLP.

3   Technical Background

Text classification using machine learning technique has been studied steadily. Especially in spam filtering [9], a well-known classification problem, some of the most popular machine learning methods such as Bayesian classification, k-nearest neighbors, artificial neural network and support vector machine have been applied to solve the problem. In the experiment, we compare artificial neural network [10] and naive Bayes classification [11,12] which give good performances in the spam filtering.

3.1   Artificial Neural Network

The artificial neural network is the method imitating human brain structure and operation process. It contains artificial neurons, network structures and learning algorithm. Artificial neurons receive inputs and perform the functional calculation. Network structure sets up the structure of artificial neurons and establishes operation process. Learning algorithm takes charge of artificial neural network learning system.

Every single layer is composed of several artificial neurons. An artificial neuron seen in Fig. 1(a) calculates the weighted sum $u = \sum_{i=1}^{n}(w_i x_i)$ by adding all multiplication of inputs $(x_1, x_2, ..., x_n)$ and weights $(w_1, w_2, ..., w_n)$. Then the weighted sum is put into the activation function and the result is passed as an input to other artificial neurons in other layers. For the activation functions, there are step function, sigmoid function, identity function and hyperbolic tangent function. Sigmoid function and hyperbolic tangent function, which are nonlinear functions, are normally used as an activation function.

After setting the activation function, network structure has to be fixed. One of the simplest structures is the single-layer perceptron which is a type of linear classifier. Since the single-layer perceptron is inappropriate for a nonlinear problem, multi-layer perceptron which contains at least one hidden layer is generally used as a richer model. Multi-layer perceptron containing a single hidden layer

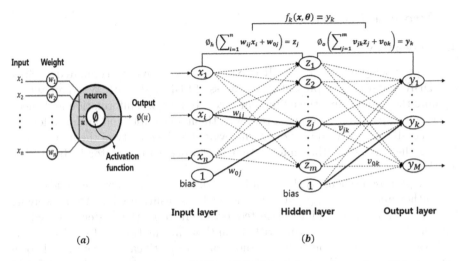

Fig. 1. Structure of artificial neural network in (a) and structure of multi-layer perceptron using single hidden layer in (b)

is utilized in our approach (see Fig. 1(b)). Also, in the experiment, we ran error backpropagation learning algorithm for multi-layer perceptron, which is one of gradient descent methods. It consistently modifies the weight w_{ij} (the weight from input neurons to hidden neurons) and v_{jk} (the weight from hidden neurons from output neurons) in order to reduce the error.

3.2 Naive Bayes Classification

The naive Bayes classification assumes that the attribute values are conditionally independent given the target value. It is extensively used due to its simplicity of the implementation, computational efficiency, and high accuracy. As a result, it is generally used for text classification based on term frequencies.

The naive Bayes classifier is basically based on Bayes' rule

$$p(C_i|\mathbf{w}) = \frac{p(\mathbf{w}|C_i)p(C_i)}{p(\mathbf{w})} \propto p(\mathbf{w}|C_i)p(C_i), \tag{1}$$

where $\mathbf{w}$ represents the terms $(w_1, w_2, ..., w_n)$ which are used as an attribute value, and C_i are the authors used as target values in the experiment. Since the naive Bayes assumes w_ks are independent, we can simply predict the class $\hat{y}$ in a MAP (maximum a posteriori) scheme as follows,

$$\hat{y} = \underset{i \in \{1, ..., I\}}{\text{argmax}} \; p(C_i) \prod_{k=1}^{n} p(w_k|C_i). \tag{2}$$

4   Proposed Scheme

4.1   Overview

As we previously mentioned, TBR maximizes the anonymity compared to SBR and DBR. Figure 2(a) represents the process of SBR and DBR. When an author submits the manuscript, the editor can access to author's information and check the manuscript. After choosing a reviewer, the manuscript (and author information in SBR) is sent to the reviewer who evaluates the quality of the manuscript. During the process, author information is exposed to the editor in both SBR and DBR.

Our proposed scheme is shown in Fig. 2(b). In this case, our system identifies the author and selects appropriate reviewer by measuring COI. After receiving both the manuscript and the selected reviewers from the system, the editor will check only the manuscript without author information and send it to the reviewer. Note that, in our scheme, the result of identification has to be known only to the system. Even editor cannot access or view the author's inferred identification. That is, we need to limit access to the system by people who have an influence on reviewer selection.

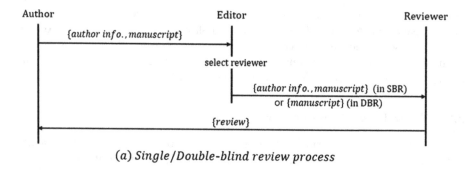

(a) Single/Double-blind review process

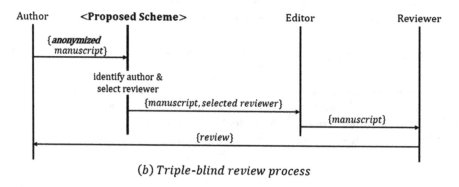

(b) Triple-blind review process

Fig. 2. Overview of Single/Double-blind review process and Triple-blind review process

4.2   Procedure

In this paper, we propose a scheme which identifies the author by machine learning algorithm and finds appropriate reviewers by measuring COI. Figure 3 illustrates the flow of the scheme which supports our proposal. The proposed scheme is achieved by 5 steps as follows:

1. *Data Collection:* First of all, sufficient set of data has to be collected before the experiment. Corpus of published paper by K authors were collected and stored from 'Google Scholar'.
2. *Preprocessing:* Data preprocessing is essential for data analysis process to extract meaningful data. Parsing the paper from introduction to right before the references section, extracting only text data and removing the stopword would fall in the category of preprocessing.
3. *Feature Selection:* This step is important because the result of the classification mostly depends on the feature. In the experiment, term-document matrix is used which represents the term frequencies appearing from each document, basically used in information retrieval. Weighting and thresholding method is combined with the matrix to select valuable features.
4. *Author Identification:* In the last part of the authorship attribution, the classification algorithm is executed to identify the author. In this experiment, we have accomplished and compared artificial neural network and multinomial naive Bayes classification.
5. *Conflict of Interest Measure (COI):* After the author identification, a relationship between identified author and potential reviewers has to be measured to obtain the COI weight. For the experiment, the committee members of a well-known conference were selected as potential reviewers and the value of COI was calculated based on the co-author information extracted from DBLP.

5   Experiment

5.1   Preprocessing and Feature Selection

Preprocessing. Twenty authors were randomly selected from committee members of top information conferences (IEEE Security and Privacy, ACM CCS, NDSS) and their 315 published papers were collected from 'Google Scholar'. Unlike the submission papers, the form of published papers includes author information. Therefore, data preprocessing is essential for the experiment. It is preprocessed according to 3 steps using 'tm' package with a free software environment for statistical computing and graphics R (http://www.r-project.org/).

First of all, we generated a text corpus as input data from introduction to reference section of collected papers by using the text mining package of R. Unlike the previous research using the citation information of papers [6], we have mainly focused on the text content information to identify the author of the paper. After the parsing step, text data was standardized through extracting alphabets except special symbols and then converted to lower case.

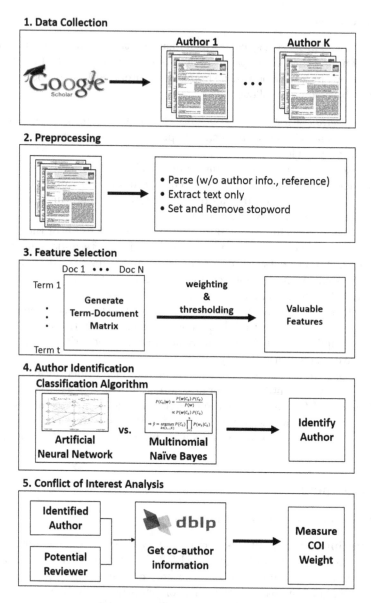

Fig. 3. Flow of the scheme supporting triple-blind review process finding fair reviewer

Finally, stopwords like articles and author information were eliminated from text data. The list of 571 words called "smart stopword list", which was built by Gerard Salton and Chris Buckley for the experimental SMART information retrieval system at Cornell University, was used in the experiment. Furthermore, the sentence including the author's name was removed in case the running author's name showed up repeatedly in every page of paper.

Feature Selection. To select features for classification, a bag of words including 21,549 words was created from 315 preprocessed papers and then the term frequencies of each paper were calculated. In addition, TF-IDF (Term Frequency-Inverse Document Frequency) was used to improve the accuracy of classification considering the fact that the total size of each paper is different. TF-IDF reflects the weight of terms in information retrieval and text mining fields. TF is the number of times that a term t occurs in a document d, and IDF is the rareness of a term t in the entire document D. It is the product of TF and IDF as follows,

$$\text{TF-IDF}(t, d, D) = \frac{f(t, d)}{|\{t : t \in d\}|} \times \log\left(\frac{|D|}{|d \in D : t \in d|}\right), \tag{3}$$

where $f(t, d)$ is the raw frequency of a term in a document, $|\{t : t \in d\}|$ is the number of terms in document d, $|D|$ is the number of documents and $|d \in D : t \in d|$ is the number of documents in which the term t appears.

Finally, the TF-IDF value was multiplied by 1,000 and was put into the term-document matrix as a selected feature. During the training process, only the terms above the threshold were selected to reduce the dimension and to improve the efficiency.

Author Pattern. To check the possibility of author identification, we visualized 21,549 words in 315 papers from 20 authors as simple graphs in Fig. 4. It shows the author pattern and term frequency of the paper. In each graph, x-axis is the index of unique terms and y-axis is the frequency of each term. The thick blue line represents the authors' pattern extracted from their published papers. We can find that each author's pattern is slightly different. The difference includes not only author's field of study but also writing style. The green line is the term frequency of the one random paper from each author. It seems to follow the tendency of thick blue line. For this reason, it is expected to be possible to identity the author using classification methods.

5.2 Classification

Artificial Neural Network. In the experiment, artificial neural networks with the multi-layer perceptron were used to identify the author. The input data was TF-IDF matrix from feature selection and the activation function was the form of a hyperbolic tangent. During the training procedure, the number of nodes in the hidden layer was changed (10, 20, 30, and 40) and the threshold was increased by 0.001 from 0 to 0.01. The results are represented in Fig. 5. The x-axis represents the threshold and y-axis shows the accuracy of the classification. Each line marked with rectangles, diamonds, triangles, and circles represents the result of artificial neural network using 10, 20, 30, and 40 hidden layer nodes. We achieved success rates of 51% to 71% when the number of nodes in hidden layer was more than 20, while the accuracy rate was very low when it was 10. Therefore, the proper number of hidden nodes was 20 in consideration of the speed and efficiency. The highest accuracy was 71.05% with the threshold of 0.003 and 20 hidden nodes.

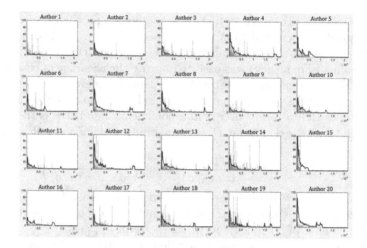

Fig. 4. Pattern of 20 authors: x-axis is the index of unique terms (21,549) and y-axis is the frequency of each term. The thick line is the authors' pattern from their published papers. The thin line is the term frequency of the one random paper from each author. (Color figure online)

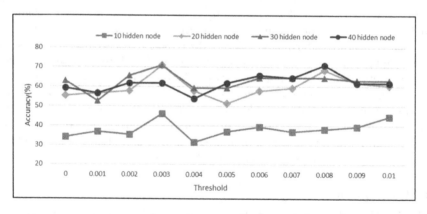

Fig. 5. Accuracy comparison for different threshold and hidden layers

Multinomial Naive Bayes. Multinomial naive Bayes was chosen as the classifier because the features in the experiment were based on term frequency. Using the TF-IDF matrix (made from feature selection step in Sect. 5.1), we conducted the multinomial naive Bayes classification (WEKA version 3.8) and 10-fold cross-validation. Figure 6 shows the classification results of 315 instances with threshold increased by 0.001 from 0 to 0.03. The solid line represents the accuracy of the classification and dotted line represents the number of terms. Since using more terms demands more training time, the optimal threshold has to be selected considering its tradeoff.

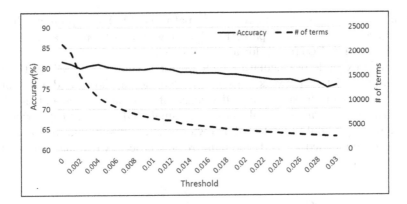

Fig. 6. Result of multinomial naive Bayes classifier with varying a threshold

Result of Classification. We found 71.05% the highest accuracy classifying author by the artificial neural network using 20 hidden nodes and threshold of 0.003. Meanwhile, multinomial naive Bayes classifier mostly gives high classification rate and shows maximally 81.59% accuracy. It seems to give high accuracy because the assumption that each attribute is independent makes relations between each pair of terms weak. On the other hand, the artificial neural network modifies every single weight from terms while running the learning algorithm.

5.3   Conflict of Interest (COI)

After identifying the author, it is necessary to calculate COI weight between identified author and potential reviewers in order to select the fair reviewer. In this paper, a set of potential reviewers is chosen from the committee members of 'USENIX Security 2015'. In the experiment, a ratio of co-author $w(x, y)$ is computed based on co-author information extracted from DBLP (see Eq. 4). For all possible paths between the author a and the reviewer r, COI weights $COI(a, r)_n$ are calculated as Eq. 5. The maximum value among COI weights is chosen to be the final COI weight between the author a and the reviewer r, thereby yielding the reviewer who has the smallest COI weight in potential reviewers set as the most appropriate reviewer for the author a.

The weight of co-authored publications between x and y is calculated as

$$w(x, y) = \frac{2 \cdot |CO(x, y)|}{|P_x| + |P_y|}, \tag{4}$$

where $|CO(x, y)|$ represents a number of co-authored paper by x and y, and $|P_x|$ represents the number of paper published by x. For all possible paths, COI weight of the author and the reviewer is defined as

$$COI(a, r)_n = \frac{1}{\{d(a, r)\}^2} \times \sum_{(x,y) \in (X,Y)_n} w(x, y) \tag{5}$$

where $d(a,r)$ represents the degree of nth path and $(X,Y)_n$ represents the set of all adjacent nodes in n^{th} path. Final COI weight between a and r is the maximum value of $COI(a,r)_n$ for all possible paths.

A simple example of calculating COI weight is shown in Fig. 7. In the left side, there is a virtual network between an identified author a and a potential reviewer r. In the right side, the COI weights of 5 possible paths and the final COI weight are shown. After calculating the final COI weight, people who are having low weight could be selected as reviewers. As a result, suitable reviewers could be recommended in the triple blind review process while maintaining the anonymity of the author.

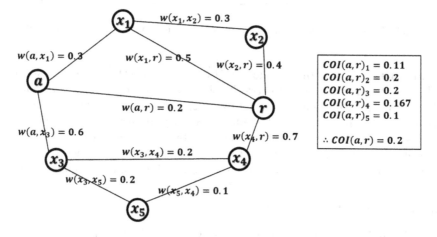

Fig. 7. A simple example of calculating COI weights: A virtual network between a and r (left). $COI(a,r)_1$ to $COI(a,r)_5$ represents COI weights where the possible paths are $\{a, x_1, x_2, r\}, \{a, x_1, r\}, \{a, r\}, \{a, x_3, x_4, r\}, \{a, x_3, x_5, x_4, r\}$ (right).

6   Conclusion

Blind review process attempts to ensure the fairness of reviewing process via protecting the anonymity. Triple Blind Review (TBR) emphasizes the anonymity by blinding not only the author and the reviewer but also the journal editor. However, it has a problem in selecting fair reviewers since it is not easy to distinguish 'Conflict of Interests' (COI). We have shown the applicability of TBR process by choosing the fair reviewers using classification methods and a new COI measurement. In addition, our scheme could maximize anonymity of review process as well as choose appropriate reviewers.

In this paper, we simply demonstrated the applicability of TBR process as a prototype. So, it has to make some improvements in future work. First of all, the current system provides only one author as an output of author identification step. To mitigate the risk of misclassification, it should recommend the list of authors having strong possibilities. For better COI measurement, in addition, we need to use various information such as affiliations and social relationships as well as co-author list. Furthermore, the way to prevent the leakage of author information have to be devised. It would result in improving the robustness of our scheme.

Acknowledgments. We would like to thank Dr. Jun Ho Huh from Honeywell, for his opinion on Conflict of Interests.

References

1. Snodgrass, R.T.: Editorial: single-versus double-blind reviewing. ACM Trans. Database Syst. (TODS) **32**(1), 1 (2007)
2. Nature journals offer double-blind review. Nature **518**, 274 (2015). Nature Publishing Group. http://www.nature.com. Accessed 19 Feb 2015
3. Hall, J., Hundley, V., Van Teijlingen, E.: The journal editor: friend or foe? Women and Birth **28**(2), e26–e29 (2015)
4. Jump, P.: Will double-blind reviewing bring quality into focus? Times Higher Education (2015). https://www.timeshighereducation.com/. Accessed 12 Mar 2015
5. Yankauer, A.: How blind is blind review? Am. J. Public Health **81**(7), 843–845 (1991)
6. Hill, S., Provost, F,: The myth of the double-blind review? Author identification using only citations. ACM SIGKDD Explor. Newsl. **5**(2), 179–184 (2003)
7. Luyckx, K., Daelemans, W.: Authorship attribution and verification with many authors and limited data. In: Proceedings of the 22nd International Conference on Computational Linguistics, vol. 1. Association for Computational Linguistics (2008)
8. Aleman-Meza, B., et al.: Semantic analytics on social networks: experiences in addressing the problem of conflict of interest detection. In: Proceedings of the 15th International Conference on World Wide Web. ACM (2006)
9. Tretyakov, K.: Machine learning techniques in spam filtering. Data Mining Problem-oriented Seminar, MTAT, vol. 3, no. 177 (2004)
10. Christopher, M.B.: Pattern recognition and machine learning. Company New York **16**(4), 049901 (2006)
11. Shimodaira, H.: Text classification using naive Bayes. Learning and Data Note 7 (2014)
12. Raschka, S.: Naive Bayes and Text Classification I-Introduction and Theory. arXiv preprint arXiv:1410.5329 (2014)

GIS Vector Map Perceptual Encryption Scheme Using Geometric Objects

P.N. Giao[1], Suk-Hwan Lee[2], Kwang-Seok Moon[3], and Ki-Ryong Kwon[1(✉)]

[1] Department of IT Convergence and Application Engineering, Pukyong National University,
Pusan, South Korea
ngocgiaofet@gmail.com, krkwon@pknu.ac.kr
[2] Department of Information Security, TongMyong University, Pusan, South Korea
skylee@tu.ac.kr
[3] Department of Electronics Engineering, Pukyong National University, Pusan, South Korea
ksmoon@pknu.ac.kr

Abstract. Recently years, vector map is used in many applications and on/off-line services widely. The cost of production of vector map data is very expensive but it is stolen or copied easily by pirates without permission from the original providers. Therefore, provider desires vector map data should be encrypted before storing and transmitting to ensure the access control and prevent the illegal copying of vector map. In this paper, we proposed a perceptual encryption scheme for vector map using geometric objects. The geometric objects of vector map data is extracted to compute features as bounding boxes and distance vectors. After that, we encrypted those features and use them to compute and obtain encrypted vector map data. Experimental results is verified that the entire vector map is changed after encryption process. The proposed method is very effective for a large of dataset, responsive to requirements of security.

Keywords: Vector map data · Vector map data security · Geometric objects and perceptual encryption

1 Introduction

Vector map is based collection of Geographic Information System (GIS) data about earth at various levels of detail. Vector map is created and developed by the merging system of cartography, statistical analysis, and database technology based on vector model [1, 2]. Due to vector map data is so high value in many applications that any company can buy it, make illegal copies and distribute or sell them easily many times without taking any permission from the original GIS data providers. Moreover, some applications of vector map requires security, and must be kept away from unauthorized users. So vector map data should be encrypted before storing and transmitting to prevent illegal duplication and distribution of it.

Looking for the recent security techniques of vector map, the network security techniques for secure transmission or storage and copyright protection of vector map data have been mainly researched [3–12]. But these methods only mentioned techniques for

© Springer International Publishing AG 2017
D. Choi and S. Guilley (Eds.): WISA 2016, LNCS 10144, pp. 210–220, 2017.
DOI: 10.1007/978-3-319-56549-1_18

the control access and management GIS dataset on Web database. Moreover, some methods encrypted the entire vector map data following data formats or encrypted vector map data directly. They are not also flexible for various data types and high computational complexity. Specially, database management system based security technique is vulnerable by the conversion between data formats. So, the security technique for vector map is must preserve the security in various formats of vector map data, reduce complex computation and change the entire vector map data. Thus, the perceptual encryption is suitable and necessary for vector map protection.

For meeting above requirements, we present a perceptual encryption scheme for vector map in this paper. The main content of proposed scheme is to extract geometric objects from vector map data to compute bounding boxes and distance vectors. Then, it encrypted bounding boxes and distance vectors by secrete key. Encrypted vector map data will be obtained from encrypted bounding boxes and distance vectors. To clarify the detailed contents of proposed scheme, we organize our paper as follows. In Sect. 2, we look into the vector map data security techniques and explain the relation of vector map data to proposed scheme. The detailed scheme is described in Sect. 3. Experimental results and the evaluation of proposed scheme will be shown in Sect. 4. Section 5 shows the conclusion.

2   Related Works

2.1   Vector Map Security

Bertino et al. [3], Chena et al. [4], and Rybalov et al. [5] presented approaches to the definition of an access control system for spatial data on the Web. Similar, Bertino et al. [6], and Ma et al. [7] also presented approaches to manage GIS datasets by using access control on the Web or database in 2008 and 2010. Mostly, authors explained technical challenges raised by the unique requirements of secure geospatial data management such as access control, security and privacy policies. But the access control and management on Web or database do not maintain security in the outflow of an authenticated user. Wu et al. [8] proposed a compound chaos-based encryption algorithm of vector data by considering the storage characteristics and sensitivity of the initial values and parameters of chaos-based systems. This algorithm is not available to various data formats and object indexing. Li et al. [9] encrypted a set of vector data in external Oracle DBMS by using DES and an R-Tree spatial index. This algorithm encrypts the spatial index when the GIS dataset is transmitted to the client and designs the key management of public and private keys on a PKI system. So, this algorithm does not keep the security of the vector map on the DBMS because the length of key is short. Dakroury et al. [10] also proposed better encrypting algorithm which combined AES and RSA cryptography with a simple watermarking technique for the copyright protection of vector maps in on/off line service. This algorithm encrypts all parts of a shape-file format using an AES block cipher operator of 256 bits. Previously, we also proposed the selective encryption algorithm in DCT domain for vector map [11, 12]. This selective algorithm selects polyline, polygon and transform them to the frequency of discrete cosine transform. After that, it encrypts them in DCT domain. It is also effective but it is also general, simple and not originality. The disadvantages of this method is the computational time of it be dependent on the number of group in clustering and the size of matrix in DCT process.

2.2 Vector Map Based Perceptual Encryption

Vector map data is stored in layers. Each layer is a basic unit of geographical objects be described, managed in a map and represented by point, polyline and polygon. Point is used to represent simple objects while polygon and polyline are used to represent complex objects. Polyline is an ordered set of vertices, has starting point and ending point be different. It is used to represent objects as road, contour line, river and railway. Polygon is a set of connected polylines, has starting point is the ending point, is also called the closing polyline. It is used to represent objects as building, area, lake and boundaries [13]. Thus, polyline and polygon are very important components of vector map. And vector map encryption should use them as encrypting targets.

Beside geographical information, vector map also consists of attribute information as header, text and notation. This information is used to describe, manage and note other information on map. And it is called as attributed data while geometric objects is considered content data. Figure 1 shows data components of vector map data. Because, the attribute data does not contain geographical information. Thus, it does not determine the shape of object, and we only need to extract geometric objects to perform perceptual encryption process.

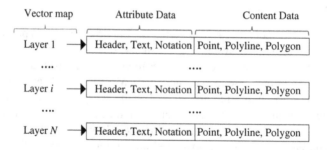

Fig. 1. Classification of vector map data.

3   The Proposed Algorithm

3.1 Overview

The proposed algorithm is shown detailed in Fig. 2. Polyline and polygon are encrypting targets and extracted from vector map to perform perceptual encryption. With each extracted object, we compute the bounding box and center of bounding box corresponding to that object to calculate a set of distance vectors. Distance vector is the distance from center to the vertex of object. After that, bounding box and distance vectors will be encrypted using secret key which is generated from user key by hashing function.

Next, we compute the center of encrypted bounding box. Finally, encrypted object will be obtained from the center of encrypted bounding box and encrypted distance vectors.

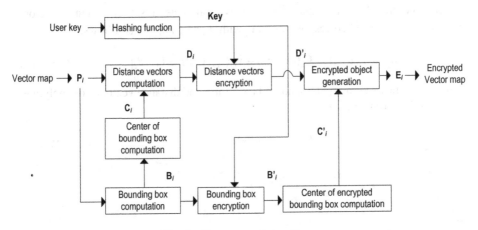

Fig. 2. The proposed algorithm.

A vector map contains number of layers. We consider a layer L contains number of objects of polylines/polygons $L = \{\mathbf{P}_i | i \in [1, |L|]\}$, and a polyline/polygon object contains a series of vertices $\mathbf{P}_i = \{v_{i,j} | j \in [1, |\mathbf{P}_i|]\}$. $|L|$ and $|\mathbf{P}_i|$ are cardinalities of a layer L, and an object $\mathbf{P}_i$. Thus, $v_{i,j}$ indicates j^{th} vertex in i^{th} object of layer L and is defined as two coordinates $v_{i,j} = (x_{i,j}, y_{i,j})$. In order to brief, we define main notation as following: $\mathbf{B}_i = \{(x_{i,min}, y_{i,min}), (x_{i,max}, y_{i,max})\}$ is the bounding box of object $\mathbf{P}_i$; $\mathbf{C}_i = (cx_i, cy_i)$ is the centre of bounding box $\mathbf{B}_i$; $\mathbf{D}_i = \{d_{i,j} | j \in [1, |\mathbf{P}_i|]\}$ is a set of distance vectors of object $\mathbf{P}_i$ with $d_{i,j} = (dx_{i,j}, dy_{i,j})$. $\mathbf{D}'_i$, $\mathbf{B}'_i$ and $\mathbf{C}'_i$ are a set of encrypted distance vectors, encrypted bounding box and the centre of $\mathbf{B}_i$ respectively; $\mathbf{E}_i = \{e_{i,j} | j \in [1, |\mathbf{P}_i|]\}$ is the encrypted object with $e_{i,j} = (ex_{i,j}, ey_{i,j})$. Finally, $E_C(.)$ is encryption function using secret key $\mathbf{K}$.

3.2 Bounding Box, Center of Bounding Box and Distance Vectors Computation

Bounding box $\mathbf{B}_i$ of object $\mathbf{P}_i$ is defined by pairs of coordinates $(x_{i,min}, y_{i,min}), (x_{i,max}, y_{i,max})$:

$$x_{i,min}, y_{i,min} = Min\{v_{i,j}(x_{i,j}, y_{i,j}) | j \in [1, |\mathbf{P}_i|]\} \tag{1}$$

$$x_{i,max}, y_{i,max} = Max\{v_{i,j}(x_{i,j}, y_{i,j}) | j \in [1, |\mathbf{P}_i|]\} \tag{2}$$

And centre $\mathbf{C}_i(cx_i, cy_i)$ of bounding box $\mathbf{B}_i$ is computed by:

$$cx_i = \frac{x_{i,min} + x_{i,max}}{2} \tag{3}$$

$$cy_i = \frac{y_{i,min} + y_{i,max}}{2} \tag{4}$$

From centre $\mathbf{C}_i(cx_i, cy_i)$ and object $\mathbf{P}_i$ we calculate a set of distance vectors $\mathbf{D}_i = \{d_{i,j} | j \in [1, |\mathbf{P}_i|]\}$ corresponding to $\mathbf{P}_i$ with $d_{i,j}$ be compute as follows:

$$d_{i,j}(dx_{i,j}, dy_{i,j}) = \mathbf{C}_i(cx_i, cy_i) - v_{i,j}(x_{i,j}, y_{i,j}) | j \in [1, |\mathbf{P}_i|] \tag{5}$$

Figure 3 shows computed bounding box, centre and distance vectors from polyline/polygon of vector map.

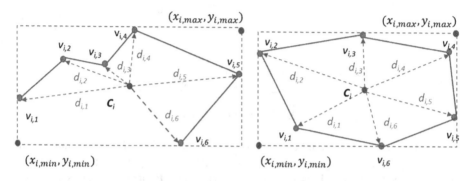

Fig. 3. Bounding box, center and distance vector of polyline/polygon.

3.3   Generate Encrypted Object from Encrypted Bounding Box, Distance Vectors

Bounding box $\mathbf{B}_i$ and distance vectors $\mathbf{D}_i$ will be encrypted by secret key $\mathbf{K}$ and encryption function $E_C(.)$ to obtain encrypted object. Secret key $\mathbf{K}$ is generate by hashing function SHA-512 [14]. And $E_C(.)$ can be used in the encryption algorithms AES, DES, XOR and others. The encryption process of bounding box and distance vectors is described by Eqs. (6), (7) and $\mathbf{B}'_i$, $\mathbf{D}'_i$ are encrypted bounding box, encrypted distance vectors respectively.

$$\mathbf{B}'_i = E_C(\mathbf{B}_i, \mathbf{K}) = \{(x'_{i,min}, y'_{i,min}), (x'_{i,max}, y'_{i,max})\} \tag{6}$$

$$\mathbf{D}'_i = E_C(\mathbf{D}_i, \mathbf{K}) = \{d'_{i,j} | j \in [1, |\mathbf{P}_i|]\} \tag{7}$$

From encrypted bounding box $\mathbf{B}'_i$ we calculate encrypted center $\mathbf{C}'_i(cx'_i, cy'_i)$:

$$cx'_i = \frac{x'_{i,min} + x'_{i,max}}{2} \tag{8}$$

$$cy'_i = \frac{y'_{i,min} + y'_{i,max}}{2} \tag{9}$$

Finally, encrypted object $\mathbf{E}_i = \{e_{i,j} | j \in [1, |\mathbf{P}_i|]\}$ will be obtained from encrypted distance vectors $\mathbf{D}'_i$ and encrypted center $\mathbf{C}'_i(cx'_i, cy'_i)$ with $e_{i,j}$ be computed as follows:

$$e_{i,j}(ex_{i,j}, ey_{i,j}) = \mathbf{C}'_i(cx'_i, cy'_i) - d'_{i,j}(dx'_{i,j}, dy'_{i,j}) \tag{10}$$

4   Experimental Results

We used vector maps with different scales in visualization experiments. The proposed scheme is applied to polylines and polygons in vector map. The data format of vector map data is the shape-file (SHP) format. The shape-file is popular geographical vector data format. We used differential maps of cities as railway, bathymetry, road and census. In comparison with conventional works, the proposed scheme only encrypted features of geometric object. So, it does not alter or expand the size of encrypted file, and it does not have loss data happen. Comparing to previous method of us [11, 12], the current proposed method has lower computation time than previous method but it has higher entropy than previous method. That mean the security of proposed method is higher than previous method.

Table 1 shows the detailed information of maps, computation time and entropy of current method (using AES cipher) and previous method. We show encrypted maps in Sect. 4.1 to evaluate the effect of proposed method, and evaluate the security of its in Sect. 4.2.

Table 1. Detailed information of vector maps in experiments.

Map	# Objects	Proposed method		Previous method	
		Computation time (ms)	Entropy (dB)	Computation time (ms)	Entropy (dB)
Wales railway	5496	61.00	20555	143.65	1565
MS Bay bathymetry	8148	91.28	105860	462.32	1637
California road	15035	106.52	208626	1175	1748
Melbourne census	71872	174.54	1159521	4028	2193
Dresden road	80687	209.26	1315302	6680	2217

4.1   Visualization

In our experiments, we used SHA-512 algorithm to hash user key, and used AES cipher to encrypt bounding boxes, distance vectors. AES algorithm is selected because it is higher security than DES, XOR and others. The encryption process of bounding boxes and distance vectors is described in Fig. 4. The entire content of map is changed after encryption process. The proposed method is originality and unique than previous algorithms because we did not encrypted objects directly. We encrypted features of object to obtain encrypted object. We show original maps beside encrypted maps by the proposed methods from Figs. 5, 6, 7, 8 and 9 to compare differences between themselves and original maps.

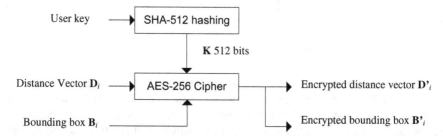

Fig. 4. Bounding boxes and distance vectors encryption process using AES cipher.

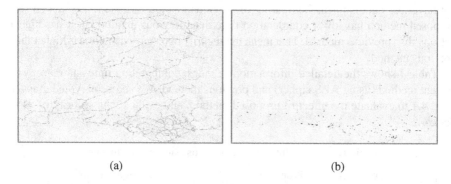

(a)   (b)

Fig. 5. (a) Wales railway map, and (b) Encrypted Wales railway map.

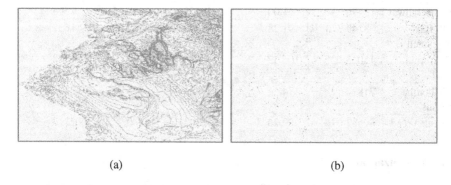

(a)   (b)

Fig. 6. (a) MS Bay bathymetry map, and (b) Encrypted MS Bay bathymetry map.

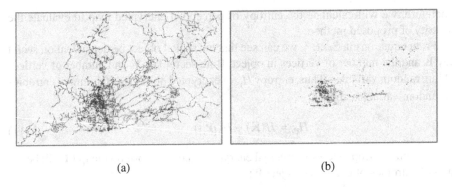

(a)   (b)

Fig. 7. (a) California road map, and (b) Encrypted California road map.

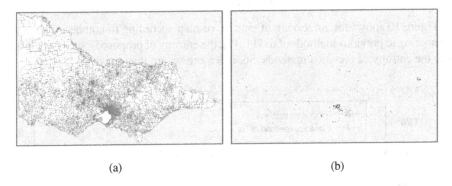

(a)   (b)

Fig. 8. (a) Melbourne census map, and (b) Encrypted Melbourne census map.

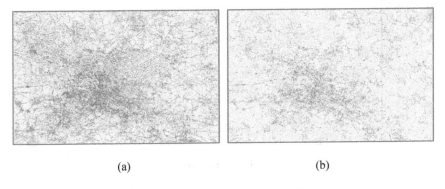

(a)   (b)

Fig. 9. (a) Dresden road map, and (b) Encrypted Dresden road map.

4.2 Security Evaluation

In order to extract information from the perceptual encrypted map, any pirate has to extract all encrypted objects of map without the knowledge of keys. If the randomness of perceptual encryption is high, it will be so difficult to attack encrypted objects.

Therefore, we will calculate the entropy of perceptual encrypted map to evaluate the security of proposed method.

From equations in Sect. 3, we can see that encrypted object be dependent on secret key $\mathbf{K}$ and the number of vertices in object. Both secret key $\mathbf{K}$ and number of vertices $|\mathbf{P}_i|$ are random variables. Thus, entropy $H_{\mathbf{P}i}$ of encrypted object $\mathbf{P}'_i$ is the sum of entropies of random variables above:

$$H_{\mathbf{P}i} = H(\mathbf{K}) + H(|\mathbf{P}_i|) \tag{11}$$

And thus, entropy $H_{\mathbf{M}}$ of perceptual encrypted map from original map $\mathbf{M}$ will be the sum of entropies of encrypted object $\mathbf{P}'_i$:

$$H_{\mathbf{M}} = \sum H_{\mathbf{P}i} \tag{12}$$

Figure 10 shows the increasing of entropy of map according to number of objects. Comparing to previous methods of us [11, 12], the entropy of proposed method is higher than the entropy of previous methods. So, it is more secure than previous methods.

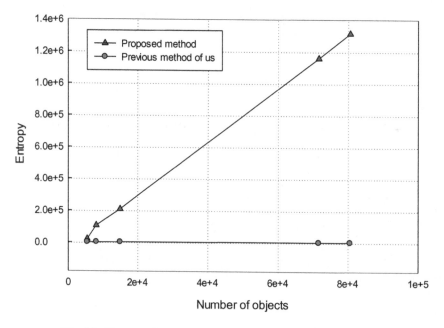

Fig. 10. Entropy of encrypted map according to number of objects.

4.3 Computation Time

Looking in Table 1, we see that the computation time of proposed method is lower than the computation time of previous methods of us. Because the computation time of proposed method is only dependent on the number of objects and AES cipher while the computation time of previous methods is dependent on DCT process, K-mean clustering and randomization process. So, the proposed method is faster than previous methods. Figure 11 shows the computation time of proposed method according to the number of objects in map, and compares it with previous methods.

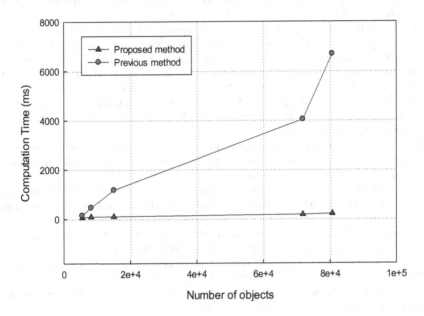

Fig. 11. Computation time of proposed method.

5   Conclusion

In this paper, we proposed a perceptual encryption scheme for vector map security. It is based on encrypting bounding box and distance vectors of object to compute and obtain encrypted object. Experimental results showed that the proposed scheme is very effective with a large volume of vector map dataset. It is also responsive to various formats of vector map data, reduces computation time and has higher security. It can be applied to the security of map service on on/off-lines. Furthermore, my algorithm can be applied to various vector contents such as CAD and 3D content fields.

Acknowledgements. This research was supported by Basic Science Research Program through the National Research Foundation of Korea (NRF) funded by the Ministry of Education (NRF-2014R1A1A4A01006663).

References

1. Foote, K.E., Lynch, M.: Geographic Information Systems as an Integrating Technology Context, Concepts, and Definitions (2014). Last revised

2. Goodchild, M.F.: Twenty years of progress: GIS science in 2010. J. Spat. Inf. Sci. **1**, 3–20 (2010)
3. Bertino, E., Damiani, M.L.: A controlled access to spatial data on web. In: Proceedings of Conference on Geographic Information Science, pp. 369–377 (2004)
4. Chena, S.C., Wangb, X., Rishea, N., Weiss, M.A.: A web-based spatial data access system using semantic R-trees. J. Inform. Sci. **167**, 41–61 (2003)
5. Rybalov, N.B., Zhukovsky, O.I.: Access to the spatial data in the web-oriented GIS. In: Proceedings of Siberian Conference on Control and Communications, pp. 104–107 (2007)
6. Bertino, E., Thuraisingham, B., Gertz, M., Damiani, M.L.: Security and privacy for geospatial data: concepts and research directions. In: Proceedings of the SIGSPATIAL ACM GIS 2008 International Workshop on Security and Privacy in GIS and LBS, pp. 6–19 (2008)
7. Fuguang, M., Yong, G., Menglong, Y., Fuchun, X., Ding, L.: The fine-grained security access control of spatial data. In: Proceedings of the 18th International Conference on Geoinformatics, pp. 1–4 (2010)
8. Wu, F., Cui, W., Chen, H.: A compound chaos-based encryption algorithm for vector geographic data under network circumstance. In: Proceedings of Cardholder Information Security Program, vol. 1, pp. 254–258 (2008)
9. Li, G.: Research of key technologies on encrypting vector spatial data in Oracle spatial. In: Proceedings of International Conference on Industrial Electronics and Computer Science, pp. 1–4 (2010)
10. Dakroury, Y., El-ghafar, I.A., Tammam, A.: Protecting GIS data using cryptography and digital watermarking. J. Comput. Sci. Netw. Secur. **10**, 75–84 (2010)
11. Giao, P.N., Kwon, G.C., Lee, S.H., Kwon, K.R.: Selective encryption algorithm based on DCT for GIS vector map. J. Korea Multimedia Soc. **17**, 769–777 (2014)
12. Giao, P.N., Lee, S.H., Kwon, K.R.: Selective encryption algorithm for GIS vector map using geometric objects. J. Secur. Appl. **9**, 61–72 (2015)
13. Environmental Systems Research Institute: An ESRI White Paper: ESRI Shape-file Technical Description, USA (1998)
14. RSA Laboratories: PKCS #5 v2.1: Password-Based Cryptography Standard (2006)

Efficient Scalar Multiplication
for Ate Based Pairing over KSS Curve
of Embedding Degree 18

Md. Al-Amin Khandaker[1]([✉]), Yasuyuki Nogami[1],
Hwajeong Seo[2], and Sylvain Duquesne[3]

[1] Graduate School of Natural Science and Technology,
Okayama University, Okayama, Japan
khandaker@s.okayama-u.ac.jp, yasuyuki.nogami@okayama-u.ac.jp
[2] Pusan National University, Busan, South Korea
hwajeong@pusan.ac.kr
[3] Université Rennes I, Rennes, France
sylvain.duquesne@univ-rennes1.fr

Abstract. Efficiency of the next generation pairing based security protocols rely not only on the faster pairing calculation but also on efficient scalar multiplication on higher degree rational points. In this paper we proposed a scalar multiplication technique in the context of Ate based pairing with Kachisa-Schaefer-Scott (KSS) pairing friendly curves with embedding degree $k = 18$ at the 192-bit security level. From the systematically obtained characteristics p, order r and Frobenious trace t of KSS curve, which is given by certain integer z also known as mother parameter, we exploit the relation $\#E(\mathbb{F}_p) = p + 1 - t \bmod r$ by applying Frobenius mapping with rational point to enhance the scalar multiplication. In addition we proposed z-adic representation of scalar s. In combination of Frobenious mapping with multi-scalar multiplication technique we efficiently calculate scalar multiplication by s. Our proposed method can achieve 3 times or more than 3 times faster scalar multiplication compared to binary scalar multiplication, sliding-window and non-adjacent form method.

Keywords: KSS curve · Frobenius mapping · Scalar multiplication

1 Introduction

The intractability of Elliptic Curve Discrete Logarithm Problem (ECDLP) spurs on many innovative pairing based cryptographic protocols. Pairing based cryptography is considered to be the basis of next generation security. Recently a number of unique and innovative pairing based cryptographic applications such as identity based encryption scheme [17], broadcast encryption [8] and group signature authentication [7] surge the popularity of pairing based cryptography. In such consequence Ate-based pairings such as Ate [9] and Optimal-ate [20],

© Springer International Publishing AG 2017
D. Choi and S. Guilley (Eds.): WISA 2016, LNCS 10144, pp. 221–232, 2017.
DOI: 10.1007/978-3-319-56549-1_19

twisted Ate [13] and χ-Ate [15] pairings has gained much attention. To make such cryptographic applications practical, these pairings need to be computed efficiently and fast. This paper focuses on such Ate-based pairings.

Pairing is a bilinear map from two rational point $\mathbb{G}_1$ and $\mathbb{G}_2$ to a multiplicative group $\mathbb{G}_3$ [19] typically denoted by $\mathbb{G}_1 \times \mathbb{G}_2 \rightarrow \mathbb{G}_3$. In the case of Ate-based pairing, $\mathbb{G}_1$, $\mathbb{G}_2$ and $\mathbb{G}_3$ are defined as follows:

$$\mathbb{G}_1 = E(\mathbb{F}_{p^k})[r] \cap \mathrm{Ker}(\pi_p - [1]),$$
$$\mathbb{G}_2 = E(\mathbb{F}_{p^k})[r] \cap \mathrm{Ker}(\pi_p - [p]),$$
$$\mathbb{G}_3 = \mathbb{F}_{p^k}^* / (\mathbb{F}_{p^k}^*)^r,$$

$$\alpha : \mathbb{G}_1 \times \mathbb{G}_2 \rightarrow \mathbb{G}_3,$$

where α denotes Ate pairing. In general, pairings are only found in certain extension field $\mathbb{F}_{p^k}$, where p is the prime number, also know as characteristics and the minimum extension degree k is called *embedding* degree. The rational points $E(\mathbb{F}_{p^k})$ are defined over a certain pairing friendly curve of embedded extension field of degree k. Security level of pairing based cryptography depends on the sizes of both r and p^k, where r generally denotes the largest prime number that divides the order $\#E(\mathbb{F}_p)$. The next generation security of pairing-based cryptography needs $\log_2 r \approx 256$ bits and $\log_2 p^k \approx 3000$ to 5000 bits. Therefore taking care of $\rho = (\log_2 p)/(\log_2 r)$, k needs to be 12 to 20. This paper has considered Kachisa-Schaefer-Scott (KSS) [12] pairing friendly curves of embedding degree $k = 18$ described in [10]. Pairing on KSS curve is considered to be the basis of next generation security as it conforms 192-bit security level. Making the pairing practical over KSS curve depends on several factors such as efficient pairing algorithm, efficient extension field arithmetic and efficiently performing scalar multiplication. Many researches have conducted on efficient pairing algorithms [4] and curves [5] along with extension field arithmetic [2]. This paper focuses on efficiently performing scalar multiplication in $\mathbb{G}_2$ by scalar s, since scalar multiplication is required repeatedly in cryptographic calculation. Scalar multiplication is also considered to be the one of the most time consuming operation in cryptographic scene. Moreover in asymmetric pairing such as Ate-based pairing, scalar multiplication in $\mathbb{G}_2$ is important as no mapping function is explicitly given between $\mathbb{G}_1$ to $\mathbb{G}_2$. By the way, as shown in the definition, $\mathbb{G}_1$ is a set of rational points defined over prime field and there are many researches for efficient scalar multiplication in $\mathbb{G}_1$.

Scalar multiplication by s means $(s-1)$ times elliptic additions of a given rational point on the elliptic curve. This elliptic addition is not as simple as addition of extension field, but it requires 3 multiplications plus an inversion of the extension field. General approaches to accelerate scalar multiplication are log-step algorithm such as binary and non-adjacent form (NAF) methods, but more efficient approach is to use Frobenius mapping in the case of $\mathbb{G}_2$ that is defined over $\mathbb{F}_{p^k}$. Frobenious map $\pi : (x, y) \mapsto (x^p, y^p)$ is the p-th power of the rational point (x, y) defined over $\mathbb{F}_{p^k}$. In this paper we also exploited the Frobenious trace t, $t = p + 1 - \#E(\mathbb{F}_p)$ defined over KSS curve. In the previous work on optimal-ate pairing, Aranha et al. [1] derived an important relation: $z \equiv -3p + p^4 \bmod r$, where z is the mother parameter of KSS curve and z is about six times smaller than the size of order r. We have utilized this relation to construct z-adic representation of scalar s which is introduced in Sect. 3. In addition with Frobenius mapping and z-adic representation of s, we applied the multi-scalar multiplication technique to compute elliptic curve addition in parallel in the proposed scalar multiplication. We have compared our proposed method with three other well studied methods named binary method, sliding-window method and non-adjacent form method. The comparison shows that our proposed method is at least 3 times or more than 3 times faster than above mentioned methods in execution time. The comparison also reveals that the proposed method requires more than 5 times less elliptic curve doubling than any of the compared methods.

As shown in the previous work of scalar multiplication on sextic twisted BN curve by Nogami et al. [16], we can consider sub-field sextic twisted curve in the case of KSS curve of embedding degree 18. Let us denote the sub-field sextic twisted curve by E'. It will include sextic twisted isomorphic rational point group denoted as $\mathbb{G}_2'$. In KSS curve, $\mathbb{G}_2$ is defined over $\mathbb{F}_{p^{18}}$ whereas its sub-field isomorphic group $\mathbb{G}_2'$ is defined over $\mathbb{F}_{p^3}$. Important feature of this sextic twisted isomorphic group is, all the scalar multiplication in $\mathbb{G}_2$ is mapped with $\mathbb{G}_2'$ and it can be efficiently carried out by applying skew Frobenious map. Then, the resulted points can be re-mapped to $\mathbb{G}_2$ in $\mathbb{F}_{p^{18}}$. This above mentioned skew Frobenious mapping in sextic twisted isomorphic group will calculate more faster scalar multiplication. However, the main focus of this paper is presenting the process of splitting the scalar into z-adic representation and applying Frobenius map in combination with multi-scalar multiplication technique.

2   Preliminaries

In this section we will go through the fundamental background of elliptic curves and its operations. We will briefly review elliptic curve scalar multiplication. After that pairing friendly curve of embedding degree $k = 18$, i.e., KSS curve and its properties will be introduced briefly.

2.1   Elliptic Curve [21]

Let $\mathbb{F}_p$ be a prime field. Elliptic curve over $\mathbb{F}_p$ is defined as,

$$E/\mathbb{F}_p : y^2 = x^3 + ax + b, \tag{1}$$

where $4a^3 + 27b^2 \neq 0$ and $a, b \in \mathbb{F}_p$. Points satisfying Eq. (1) are known as rational points on the curve.

Point Addition. Let $E(\mathbb{F}_p)$ be the set of all rational points on the curve defined over $\mathbb{F}_p$ and it includes the point at infinity denoted by $\mathcal{O}$. The order of $E(\mathbb{F}_p)$ is denoted by $\#E(\mathbb{F}_p)$ where $E(\mathbb{F}_p)$ forms an additive group for the elliptic addition. Let us consider two rational points $L = (x_l, y_l)$, $M = (x_m, y_m)$, and their addition $N = L + M$, where $N = (x_n, y_n)$ and $L, M, N \in E(\mathbb{F}_p)$. Then, the x and y coordinates of N is calculated as follows:

$$(x_n, y_n) = ((\lambda^2 - x_l - x_m), (x_l - x_n)\lambda - y_l), \tag{2a}$$

where λ is given as follows:

$$\lambda = \begin{cases} (y_m - y_l)(x_m - x_l)^{-1} & (L \neq M \text{ and } x_m \neq x_l), \\[2mm] (3x_l^2 + a)(2y_l)^{-1} & (N = M \text{ and } y_l \neq 0), \end{cases} \tag{2b}$$

λ is the tangent at the point on the curve and $\mathcal{O}$ it the additive unity in $E(\mathbb{F}_p)$. When $L \neq M$ then $L + M$ is called elliptic curve addition (ECA). If $L = M$ then $L + M = 2L$, which is known as elliptic curve doubling (ECD).

Scalar Multiplication. Let s is a scalar where $0 \leq s < r$, where r is the order of the target rational point group. Scalar multiplication of rational points M, denoted as $[s]M$ can be done by $(s - 1)$-times additions of M as,

$$[s]M = \underbrace{M + M + \cdots + M}_{s-1 \text{ times additions}}. \tag{3}$$

If $s = r$, where r is the order of the curve then $[r]M = \mathcal{O}$. When $[s]M = N$, if s is unknown, then the solving s from M and N is known as elliptic curve discrete logarithm problem (ECDLP). The security of elliptic curve cryptography lies on the difficulty of solving ECDLP.

2.2   KSS Curve

KSS curve is a non super-singular pairing friendly elliptic curve of embedding degree 18 [12]. The equation of KSS curve defined over $\mathbb{F}_{p^{18}}$ is given by

$$E : Y^2 = X^3 + b, \quad (b \in \mathbb{F}_p), \tag{4}$$

where $b \neq 0$ and $X, Y \in \mathbb{F}_{p^{18}}$. Its characteristic p, Frobenius trace t and order r are given systematically by using an integer variable z as follows:

$$\begin{aligned} p(z) = (z^8 + 5z^7 + 7z^6 + 37z^5 + 188z^4 + 259z^3 + 343z^2 \\ + 1763z + 2401)/21, \end{aligned} \tag{5a}$$

$$r(z) = (z^6 + 37z^3 + 343)/343, \tag{5b}$$

$$t(z) = (z^4 + 16z + 7)/7, \tag{5c}$$

where z is such that $z \equiv 14 \pmod{42}$ and the co-factor is $\rho = (\log_2 p/\log_2 r)$ is about $4/3$. The order of rational points $\#E(\mathbb{F}_{p^{18}})$ on KSS curve can be obtained by the following relation.

$$\#E(\mathbb{F}_{p^{18}}) = p^{18} + 1 - t_{18}, \tag{6}$$

where $t_{18} = \alpha^{18} + \beta^{18}$ and α, β are complex numbers such that $\alpha + \beta = t$ and $\alpha\beta = p$. Since Aranha et al. [1] and Scott et al. [18] has proposed the size of the characteristics p to be 508 to 511-bit with order r of 384-bit for 192-bit security level, therefore this paper considered $p = 511$-bit.

Frobenius Mapping of Rational Point in $E(\mathbb{F}_{p^{18}})$. Let (x, y) be the rational point in $E(\mathbb{F}_{p^{18}})$. Frobenious map $\pi_p : (x, y) \mapsto (x^p, y^p)$ is the p-th power of the rational point defined over $\mathbb{F}_{p^{18}}$. Some previous work [11] has been done on constructing Frobenius mapping and utilizing it to calculate scalar multiplication. Nogami et al. [16] showed efficient scalar multiplication in the context of Ate-based pairing in BN curve of embedding degree $k = 12$. This paper has exploited Frobenius mapping for efficient scalar multiplication for the case of KSS curve.

2.3 $\mathbb{F}_{p^{18}}$ Extension Field Arithmetic

In context of pairing, it is required to perform arithmetic in higher extension fields, such as $\mathbb{F}_{p^k}$ for moderate value of k [19]. Therefore it is important to construct the field as a tower of extension fields [6] to perform arithmetic operation efficiently. Higher level computations can be calculated as a function of lower level computations. Because of that an efficient implementation of lower level arithmetic results in the good performance of arithmetic in higher degree fields.

In this paper extension field $\mathbb{F}_{p^{18}}$ is represented as a tower of sub field to improve arithmetic operations. In some previous works, such as Bailey et al. [3] explained tower of extension by using irreducible binomials. In what follows, let $(p - 1)$ is divisible by 3 and θ is a quadratic and cubic non residue in $\mathbb{F}_p$. Then for case of KSS-curve [12], where $k = 18$, $\mathbb{F}_{p^{18}}$ is constructed as tower field with irreducible binomial as follows:

$$\begin{cases} \mathbb{F}_{p^3} = \mathbb{F}_p[i]/(i^3 - \theta), \text{where } \theta = 2 \text{ is the best choice,} \\ \mathbb{F}_{p^6} = \mathbb{F}_{p^3}[v]/(v^2 - i), \\ \mathbb{F}_{p^{18}} = \mathbb{F}_{p^6}[w]/(w^3 - v). \end{cases}$$

According to previous work such as Aranha et al. [1], the base extension field is $\mathbb{F}_{p^3}$ for the *sextic twist* of KSS curve.

3   Efficient Scalar Multiplication

In this section we will introduce our proposal for efficient scalar multiplication in $\mathbb{G}_2$ rational point for Ate-based pairing on KSS curve. Before going to detailed procedure, an overview about how the proposed method will calculate scalar multiplication efficiently of $\mathbb{G}_2$ rational point is given.

Overview. At first $\mathbb{G}_1$, $\mathbb{G}_2$ and $\mathbb{G}_3$ groups will be defined. Then a rational point $Q \in \mathbb{G}_2$ will be considered. In context of KSS curve, properties of Q will be obtained to define the Eq. (9) relation. Next, a scalar s will be considered for scalar multiplication of $[s]Q$. After that, as Fig. 1, $(t-1)$-adic representation of s will be considered, where s will be divided into two smaller parts S_H, S_L. The lower bits of s, represented as S_L, will be nearly equal to the size of $(t-1)$ while the higher order bits S_H will be the half of the size of $(t-1)$. Next, z-adic representation of S_H and S_L will be considered. Figure 2, shows the z-adic representation from where we find that scalar s is divided into 6 coefficients of z, where the size of z is about $1/4$ of that of $(t-1)$ as Eq. (5c). Next we will pre-compute the Frobenius maps of some rational points defined by detailed procedure. As shown in Eq. (12), considering 3 pairs from the coefficients we will apply the mult-scalar multiplication in addition with Frobenious mapping, as shown in Fig. 3 to calculate scalar multiplication efficiently. Later part of this section will provide the detailed procedure of the proposal.

Figure 1 shows $(t-1)$-adic representation of scalar s.

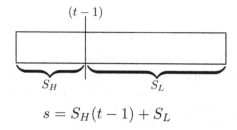

$$s = S_H(t-1) + S_L$$

Fig. 1. $(t-1)$ -adic representation of scalar s.

Figure 2 shows the final z-adic representation of scalar s.

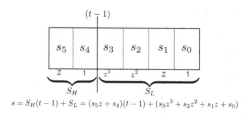

$$s = S_H(t-1) + S_L = (s_5 z + s_4)(t-1) + (s_3 z^3 + s_2 z^2 + s_1 z + s_0)$$

Fig. 2. z-adic and $(t-1)$-adic representation of scalar s.

Figure 3 shows, an example of multi-scalar multiplication process, implemented in the experiment.

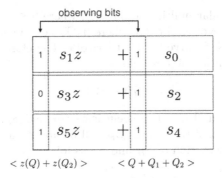

Fig. 3. Multi-scalar multiplication of s with Frobenius mapping.

$\mathbb{G}_1, \mathbb{G}_2$ **and** $\mathbb{G}_3$ **groups.** In the context of pairing-based cryptography, especially on KSS curve, three groups $\mathbb{G}_1, \mathbb{G}_2$, and $\mathbb{G}_3$ are considered. From [14], we define $\mathbb{G}_1, \mathbb{G}_2$ and $\mathbb{G}_3$ as follows:

$$\mathbb{G}_1 = E(\mathbb{F}_{p^k})[r] \cap \mathrm{Ker}(\pi_p - [1]),$$
$$\mathbb{G}_2 = E(\mathbb{F}_{p^k})[r] \cap \mathrm{Ker}(\pi_p - [p]),$$
$$\mathbb{G}_3 = \mathbb{F}_{p^k}^* / (\mathbb{F}_{p^k}^*)^r,$$

$$\alpha : \mathbb{G}_1 \times \mathbb{G}_2 \to \mathbb{G}_3, \tag{7}$$

where α denotes Ate pairing. In the case of KSS curve, $\mathbb{G}_1, \mathbb{G}_2$ are rational point groups and $\mathbb{G}_3$ is the multiplicative group in $\mathbb{F}_{p^{18}}$. They have the same order r.

Let us consider a rational point $Q \in \mathbb{G}_2 \subset E(\mathbb{F}_{p^{18}})$. In the case of KSS curve, it is known that Q satisfies the following relations,

$$[p + 1 - t]Q = \mathcal{O},$$
$$[t - 1]Q = [p]Q. \tag{8}$$

$$[\pi_p - p]Q = \mathcal{O},$$
$$\pi_p(Q) = [p]Q. \tag{9}$$

Thus, these relations can accelerate a scalar multiplication in $\mathbb{G}_2$. Substituting $[p]Q$ in Eq. (8) we find $[t - 1]Q = \pi_p(Q)$.

z-adic representation of scalar s. From the previous work on optimal-ate pairing, Aranha et al. [1] derived the following relation from parameters Eq. (5a), (5b) and (5c) of KSS curve.

$$z + 3p - p^4 \equiv 0 \bmod r. \tag{10}$$

Here z is the mother parameter of KSS curve and z is about six times smaller than the size of order r.

Let us consider scalar multiplication $[s]Q$, where $0 \leq s < r$. From Eq. (5b) we know r is the order of KSS curve where $[r]Q = \mathcal{O}$. Here, the bit size of s is nearly equal to r. In KSS curve t is $4/6$ times of r. Therefore, let us first consider $(t-1)$-adic representation of s as follows:

$$s = S_H(t-1) + S_L, \tag{11}$$

where s will be separated into two coefficients S_H and S_L. Size of S_L will be nearly equal to the size of $(t-1)$ and S_H will be about half of $(t-1)$. Now we consider z-adic representation of S_H and S_L as follows:

$$S_H = s_5 + s_4,$$
$$S_L = s_3 z^3 + s_2 z^2 + s_1 z + s_0.$$

Finally s can be represented as 6 coefficients as follows:

$$s = \sum_{i=0}^{3} s_i z^i + (s_4 + s_5 z)(t-1),$$

$$s = (s_0 + s_1 z) + (s_2 + s_3 z)z^2 + (s_4 + s_5 z)(t-1). \tag{12}$$

Reducing the Number of ECA and ECD for Calculating $[s]Q$. Let us consider a scalar multiplication of $Q \in \mathbb{G}_2$ in Eq. (12) as follows:

$$[s]Q = (s_0 + s_1 z)Q + (s_2 + s_3 z)z^2 Q + (s_4 + s_5 z)(t-1)Q. \tag{13}$$

Let us denote $z^2 Q$, $(t-1)Q$ of Eq. (13) as Q_1 and Q_2 respectively. From Eqs. (9) and (10) we can derive the Q_1 as follows:

$$\begin{aligned} Q_1 &= z^2 Q, \\ &= (9p^2 - 6p^5 + p^8)Q, \\ &= 9\pi^2(Q) - 6\pi^5(Q) + \pi^8(Q). \end{aligned} \tag{14}$$

Using the properties of cyclotomic polynomial Eq. (14) is simplified as,

$$\begin{aligned} Q_1 &= 8\pi^2(Q) - 5\pi^5(Q), \\ &= \pi^2(8Q) - \pi^5(5Q). \end{aligned} \tag{15}$$

And from the Eqs. (8) and (9), Q_2 is derived as,

$$Q_2 = \pi(Q). \tag{16}$$

Substituting Eqs. (15) and (16) in Eq. (13), the following relation is obtained.

$$s[Q] = (s_0 + s_1 z)Q + (s_2 + s_3 z)Q_1 + (s_4 + s_5 z)Q_2. \tag{17}$$

Using $z \equiv -3p + p^4 \pmod{r}$ from Eq. (10), $z(Q)$ can be pre-computed as follows:

$$z(Q) = \pi(-3Q) + \pi^4(Q). \tag{18}$$

Table 1 shows all the pre-computed values of rational points for the proposed method. In this paper pre-computed rational points are denoted such as $< Q + Q_2 >$. Finally applying the multi-scalar multiplication technique in Eq. (17) we can efficiently calculate the scalar multiplication. Figure 3 shows an example of this multiplication. Suppose in an arbitrary index, from left to right, bit pattern of s_1, s_3, s_5 is 101 and at the same index s_0, s_2, s_4 is 111. Therefore we apply the pre-computed points $< z(Q) + z(Q_2) >$ and $< Q + Q_1 + Q_2 >$ as ECA in parallel. Then we perform ECD and move to the right next bit index to repeat the process until maximum length z-adic coefficient becomes zero.

Table 1. Pre-computed values of rational point for efficient scalar multiplication

	$z(Q)$
Q_1	$z(Q_1)$
Q_2	$z(Q_2)$
$Q_1 + Q_2$	$z(Q_1) + z(Q_2)$
$Q + Q_2$	$z(Q) + z(Q_2)$
$Q + Q_1$	$z(Q) + z(Q_1)$
$Q + Q_1 + Q_2$	$z(Q) + z(Q_1) + z(Q_2)$

As shown in Fig. 3, during scalar multiplication in parallel, we are considering Eq. (12) like 3 pair of coefficients of z-adic representation. If we consider 6-coefficients for parallelization, we will need to calculate $2^6 \times 2$ pre-computed points. The chance of appearing each pre-computed point in parallel calculation will be only once which will make the pre-calculated points redundant.

4   Experimental Result Evaluation

In order to demonstrate the efficiency of the proposal, this section shows some experimental result with the calculation cost. In the experiment we have compared the proposed method with three well studied method of scalar multiplication named binary method, sliding-window method and non-adjacent form (NAF) method.

In the experiment the following parameters are considered for the KSS curve $y^2 = x^3 + 11$.

$$z = 65\text{-bit},$$
$$p = 511\text{-bit},$$
$$r = 378\text{-bit},$$
$$t = 255\text{-bit}.$$

The mother parameter z is also selected accordingly to find out $\mathbb{G}_2$ rational point Q.

500 scalar numbers of size (about 377-bit) less than order r is generated randomly in the experiment. Then average number of ECA and ECD for the proposed method and the three other methods is calculated for a scalar multiplication. 13 pre-computed ECA is taken into account while the average is calculated for the proposed method. In case of sliding-window method window size 4-bit is considered. Therefore 14 pre-computed ECA is required. In addition, average execution time of the proposed method and the three other methods is also compared.

Table 2 shows the environment, used to experiment and evaluate the proposed method.

Table 2. Computational environment

	PC	iPhone6s
CPU[a]	2.7 GHz Intel Core i5	Apple A9 Dual-core 1.84 GHz
Memory	16 GB	2 GB
OS	Mac OS X 10.11.4	iOS 9.3.1
Compiler	gcc 4.2.1	gcc 4.2.1
Programming Language	C	Objective-C, C
Library	GNU MP 6.1.0	GNU MP 6.1.0

[a]Only single core is used from two cores.

Analyzing Table 3 we can find that our proposed method requires more than 5 times less ECD than binary method, sliding-window method and NAF method. The number of ECA is also reduced in the proposed method by about 30% than binary method.

In this experiment, execution time may seems slower than other efficient algorithm such as Montgomery reduction. But the main purpose of this execution time comparison is to compare the ratio of the execution time of the proposed method with other well studied methods. The result shows that proposed method is at least 3 times faster than the other methods. Other acceleration techniques

Table 3. Comparative result of average number of ECA and ECD and execution time in [ms] for scalar multiplication

	Average ECA, ECD and execution time [ms] comparison			
	PC		PC	iPhone 6s
Methods	#ECA	#ECD	Execution time	Execution time
Binary	187	376	1.15×10^3	1.3×10^3
Sliding-window	103	376	1.14×10^3	1.10×10^3
NAF	126	377	1.03×10^3	1.13×10^3
Proposed	124	64	3.36×10^2	3.76×10^2

such as Montgomery reduction, Montgomery trick and efficient coordinates can be applied to this proposed method to enhance its execution time.

5   Conclusion and Future Work

In this paper we have proposed an efficient method to calculate elliptic curve scalar multiplication using Frobenious mapping over KSS curve in context of pairing based cryptography. We have also applied $(t - 1)$-adic and z-adic representation on the scalar and have applied multi-scalar multiplication technique to calculate scalar multiplication in parallel. We have evaluated and analyzed the improvement by implementing a simulation for large size of scalar in 192-bit security level. The experimented result shows that our proposed method is at least 3 times efficient in context of execution time and takes 5 times less number of elliptic curve doubling than binary method, sliding-window method and non-adjacent form method. As a future work we would like to enhance its computation time by applying not only Montgomery reduction but also skew Frobenius map in sub-field isomorphic rational point group technique and test the effect of the improvement in some pairing application for practical case.

Acknowledgment. This work was partially supported by the Strategic Information and Communications R&D Promotion Programme (SCOPE) of Ministry of Internal Affairs and Communications, Japan.

References

1. Aranha, D.F., Fuentes-Castañeda, L., Knapp, E., Menezes, A., Rodríguez-Henríquez, F.: Implementing pairings at the 192-bit security level. In: Abdalla, M., Lange, T. (eds.) Pairing 2012. LNCS, vol. 7708, pp. 177–195. Springer, Heidelberg (2013). doi:10.1007/978-3-642-36334-4_11
2. Bailey, D.V., Paar, C.: Optimal extension fields for fast arithmetic in public-key algorithms. In: Krawczyk, H. (ed.) CRYPTO 1998. LNCS, vol. 1462, pp. 472–485. Springer, Heidelberg (1998). doi:10.1007/BFb0055748
3. Bailey, D.V., Paar, C.: Efficient arithmetic in finite field extensions with application in elliptic curve cryptography. J. Cryptology **14**(3), 153–176 (2001). http://dx.doi.org/10.1007/s001450010012
4. Barreto, P.S.L.M., Kim, H.Y., Lynn, B., Scott, M.: Efficient algorithms for pairing-based cryptosystems. In: Yung, M. (ed.) CRYPTO 2002. LNCS, vol. 2442, pp. 354–369. Springer, Heidelberg (2002). doi:10.1007/3-540-45708-9_23
5. Barreto, P.S.L.M., Lynn, B., Scott, M.: Constructing elliptic curves with prescribed embedding degrees. In: Cimato, S., Persiano, G., Galdi, C. (eds.) SCN 2002. LNCS, vol. 2576, pp. 257–267. Springer, Heidelberg (2003). doi:10.1007/3-540-36413-7_19
6. Benger, N., Scott, M.: Constructing Tower extensions of finite fields for implementation of pairing-based cryptography. In: Hasan, M.A., Helleseth, T. (eds.) WAIFI 2010. LNCS, vol. 6087, pp. 180–195. Springer, Heidelberg (2010). doi:10.1007/978-3-642-13797-6_13
7. Boneh, D., Boyen, X., Shacham, H.: Short group signatures. In: Franklin, M. (ed.) CRYPTO 2004. LNCS, vol. 3152, pp. 41–55. Springer, Heidelberg (2004). doi:10.1007/978-3-540-28628-8_3

8. Boneh, D., Gentry, C., Waters, B.: Collusion resistant broadcast encryption with short ciphertexts and private keys. In: Shoup, V. (ed.) CRYPTO 2005. LNCS, vol. 3621, pp. 258–275. Springer, Heidelberg (2005). doi:10.1007/11535218_16

9. Cohen, H., Frey, G., Avanzi, R., Doche, C., Lange, T., Nguyen, K., Vercauteren, F.: Handbook of Elliptic and Hyperelliptic Curve Cryptography. CRC Press, Boca Raton (2005)

10. Freeman, D., Scott, M., Teske, E.: A taxonomy of pairing-friendly elliptic curves. J. Cryptology **23**(2), 224–280 (2010)

11. Iijima, T., Matsuo, K., Chao, J., Tsujii, S.: Construction of frobenius maps of twists elliptic curves and its application to elliptic scalar multiplication. In: Proceedings of SCIS, pp. 699–702 (2002)

12. Kachisa, E.J., Schaefer, E.F., Scott, M.: Constructing brezing-weng pairing-friendly elliptic curves using elements in the cyclotomic field. In: Galbraith, S.D., Paterson, K.G. (eds.) Pairing 2008. LNCS, vol. 5209, pp. 126–135. Springer, Heidelberg (2008). doi:10.1007/978-3-540-85538-5_9

13. Matsuda, S., Kanayama, N., Hess, F., Okamoto, E.: Optimised versions of the ate and twisted ate pairings. In: Galbraith, S.D. (ed.) Cryptography and Coding 2007. LNCS, vol. 4887, pp. 302–312. Springer, Heidelberg (2007). doi:10.1007/978-3-540-77272-9_18

14. Mori, Y., Akagi, S., Nogami, Y., Shirase, M.: Pseudo 8–sparse multiplication for efficient ate–based pairing on barreto–naehrig curve. In: Cao, Z., Zhang, F. (eds.) Pairing 2013. LNCS, vol. 8365, pp. 186–198. Springer, Cham (2014). doi:10.1007/978-3-319-04873-4_11

15. Nogami, Y., Akane, M., Sakemi, Y., Katou, H., Morikawa, Y.: Integer variable chi-based ate pairing. In: Proceedings of the Second International Conference on Pairing-Based Cryptography - Pairing 2008, Egham, UK, 1–3 September 2008, pp. 178–191 (2008). http://dx.doi.org/10.1007/978-3-540-85538-5_13

16. Nogami, Y., Sakemi, Y., Okimoto, T., Nekado, K., Akane, M., Morikawa, Y.: Scalar multiplication using frobenius expansion over twisted elliptic curve for ate pairing based cryptography. IEICE Trans. **92**-A(1), 182–189 (2009). http://search.ieice.org/bin/summary.php?id=e92-a_1_182&category=A&year=2009&lang=E&abst=

17. Sakai, R., Kasahara, M.: Id based cryptosystems with pairing on elliptic curve. IACR Cryptology ePrint Archive 2003, 54 (2003)

18. Scott, M.: On the efficient implementation of pairing-based protocols. In: Chen, L. (ed.) IMACC 2011. LNCS, vol. 7089, pp. 296–308. Springer, Heidelberg (2011). doi:10.1007/978-3-642-25516-8_18

19. Silverman, J.H., Cornell, G., Artin, M.: Arithmetic Geometry. Springer, Heidelberg (1986)

20. Vercauteren, F.: Optimal pairings. IEEE Trans. Inf. Theory **56**(1), 455–461 (2010)

21. Washington, L.C.: Elliptic Curves: Number Theory and Cryptography. CRC Press, Boca Raton (2008)

LRCRYPT: Leakage-Resilient Cryptographic System (Design and Implementation)

Xiaoqi Yu[1], Nairen Cao[2], Gongxian Zeng[1], Ruoqing Zhang[1],
and Siu-Ming Yiu[1(✉)]

[1] Department of Computer Science,
The University of Hong Kong, Hong Kong, China
rpyxqi@gmail.com, naksi@connect.hku.hk,
rockyzhanghku@gmail.com, smyiu@cs.hku.hk
[2] Department of Computer Science,
Georgetown University, Washington, D.C., USA
nc645@georgetown.edu

Abstract. Due to the advancement of side-channel attacks, leakage-resilient cryptography has attracted a lot of attention in recent years. Many fruitful results have been proposed by researchers. Most, if not all, of these results are theoretical in nature. Not much has been done to realize these schemes for practical use. In this work, we design and provide a leakage-resilient cryptographic system $\mathcal{LRCRYPT}$ with programming interfaces for users to build leakage-resilient cryptographic applications. $\mathcal{LRCRYPT}$ consists of a few fundamental building blocks that perform leakage-resilient public-key encryption, leakage-resilient signature, and leakage-resilient secret-key encryption, which can also be extended to many existing leakage resilience cryptographic primitives. We have conducted both a security analysis and a performance evaluation on $\mathcal{LRCRYPT}$. To our knowledge, $\mathcal{LRCRYPT}$ is the first to work in this domain.

1 Introduction

Leakage-resilient Cryptography. Traditionally, cryptographic primitives are considered as mathematical objects with a well-defined interface between the primitives and the user/adversary. The primitives are provably secure in common sense: if an efficient adversary can break a primitive π with significant probability, there exists a simulator that can solve a known hard problem P. By the assumption that P is hard, it implies that there is no efficient adversary for π.

However, the actual interactions between the primitive and the adversary may be influenced by its implementations and physical devices in real-world applications. In such cases, extra information about the primitive may be leaked to the adversary, which accumulatively may lead to the attack on the primitive that is proved secure. Main types of these "side-channel" attacks are elaborated below. The literature dealing with the circumstance that can capture adversaries who execute the attacks through the implementations of a primitive is called Leakage-resilient Cryptography.

© Springer International Publishing AG 2017
D. Choi and S. Guilley (Eds.): WISA 2016, LNCS 10144, pp. 233–244, 2017.
DOI: 10.1007/978-3-319-56549-1_20

Types of Side Channel Attacks. In practice, there are numerous attacks by side-channels, *i.e.* time attacks, power dissipation, cold-boot attacks [15–17]. Followings are some main types of attacks that fall into the broader class of such attacks.

- Power Analysis Attacks: This type of attack is executed by measuring the power consumption of a cryptographic hardware, which is stated in Kocher *et al.* [16].
- Timing Attacks: When the adversary uses the running time of a protocol as extra information, it may achieve partial knowledge of the implementation to derive information about the secret key.
- Fault Injection Attacks: This type of attacks are carried out in the ways that the adversary enforces the device to run an erroneous operation, which might leak information for the secret key.
- Memory Attacks: Proposed by Halderman *et al.* [15], Memory Attacks stem from the property that DRAM will hold the states for some period without the power of refresh. Hence, the adversary can read the content of parts of the cells and retrieve some information about the secret key as the examples presented in Halderman *et al.* [15].

Hardware-Level Countermeasures. In terms of countermeasures, one may try to modify the implementation or secure hardware, which is easy to be restrictedly secure against a certain type of attack. In other words, the hardware-level solutions target a specific side-channel attack, which should be revised once a more efficient side-channel attack is captured.

Software-Level Solutions. On the line of software-level solutions, researchers try to capture many possible side-channel adversaries and extract the details of the hardware and implementation, which is commonly represented as a leakage function f. By the definition of a leakage function family $\mathcal{F}$, the theoretical constructions work under various models and security targets.

Since the detailed models are out of the scope of this paper, we only introduce the main existing models in the followings: computation-leak-information by Micali and Reyzin [15], bounded-memory model considered by [3], continual memory leakage ($\mathcal{CML}$) [18], auxiliary-input model [24].

Difficulties for Practical System. Hardware-level measures are impractical to be integrated into a platform since the difficulties stem from numberous attack types and devices, while software-level solutions seem better to fit the requirements to build a general platform that can be applied in real-world applications. Even so, it is non-trivial to extend an existing cryptographic system to a leakage-resilient one since the difficulties inherent from the complexities of the attack types and various models. Besides, only the schemes that are built under standard models and simple assumptions can be candidate building blocks for such a practical system. To the best of our knowledge, no existing leakage-resilient cryptographic systems are found until now. In this work, we aim to integrate the software-level results to build a practical system that can be easily applied in many cryptographic platforms, which can defend the potential attacks caused by side-channel information.

1.1   Our Results and Techniques

Overview of Results. In this work, we explore the solutions to build a general leakage-resilient cryptographic system that can be applied in various real-world applications. It is easy to find that the main types of cryptographic applications consist of public-key encryption, signature and secret-key encryption. Specifically, our system begins with leakage-resilient public-key encryption, which is implemented with an identity-based encryption. In addition, we extend it to a leakage-resilient signature construction. Furthermore, by applying leakage-resilient secret sharing layer, we design a general method to extend the existing secret-key encryption primitives to a leakage-resilient secret-key encryption. In this paper, we call our system $\mathcal{LRCRYPT}$, whose details are postponed to Sect. 3. In the followings we outline several key observations for the detailed designs.

Leakage-resilient Public-key Encryption ($\mathcal{LRPKE}$): To build a practical leakage-resilient public-key encryption based on the software-level solutions, we hope that the construction is secure based on simple assumption and standard model, along with efficiency compared to the original systems. With regards to these goals, we find that an identity-based hash proof system ($\mathcal{IBHPS}$) in Alwen et al. [4] can be used to construct public-key and identity-based encryption schemes in Bounded Retrieval Model (BRM). In addition, the techniques in Chow et al. [11] showed how to build a leakage-resilient identity-based encryption ($\mathcal{LRIBE}$) from $\mathcal{IBHPS}$. The advantages of these techniques include but not limited to simper security definitions and no need to deal with the leakage details. On a very high level, one can construct a desired $\mathcal{LRIBE}$ by combining an $\mathcal{IBHPS}$ with a randomness extractor (see [14]). Thus we will construct a $\mathcal{LRIBE}$ via $\mathcal{IBHPS}$ as the $\mathcal{LRPKE}$ building blocks since it can be easily applied to construct a general public-key encryption, and can also be extended to a secure signature scheme.

Leakage-resilient Signature ($\mathcal{LRSIG}$) from $\mathcal{LRIBE}$: Provided that IND-CCA secure $\mathcal{IBE}$ implies secure public-key signature [8], we also expand $\mathcal{LRCRYPT}$ to cover the domain of leakage-resilient signature ($\mathcal{LRSIG}$) almost freely.

Leakage-resilient Secret Key Encryption ($\mathcal{LRSKE}$): Compared to traditional cryptography that assumes perfect secrecy of the secret key, leakage-resilient schemes build on the condition that leakage on a fraction of secret key exists. We will apply the secret sharing method on the secret key which will be updated accordingly [13] to avoid a significant fraction of the secret key to be derived by the adversary. Through this abstraction, we can extend it to various secret key encryption constructions. We design a software-level layer that can protect the secret key from being derived from the leaked informations, and be updated efficiently, through which we can achieve a secure $\mathcal{LRSKE}$.

1.2   Our Contributions

In the followings, we outline the contributions of this paper.

- $\mathcal{LRCRYPT}$ is among the first to explore a practical leakage-resilient platform.
- We build a library with programming interfaces for cryptographic applications consisting of $\mathcal{LRPKE}$, $\mathcal{LRSIG}$, $\mathcal{LRSKE}$.
- We build an extended leakage-resilient layer $\mathcal{CLRS}$, which derives from leakage-resilient secret sharing schemes [13], to be applied in other cryptographic primitives.
- As independent interest, we develop a pairing based matrix calculation building block PIM, which can be applied to matrix operations on the group elements and big integers.

2   Preliminaries

Identity-Based Encryption ($\mathcal{IBE}$). $\mathcal{IBE}$ [21] is public-key encryptions based on users' identities, which can solve difficulties of the public-key deployment [5][9]. $\mathcal{IBE}$ scheme consists of four PPT algorithms (Setup, KeyGen, Enc, Dec).

1. $(MPK, MSK) \leftarrow$ Setup(1^λ): The Setup algorithm takes the security parameter λ as input, and output the (MPK, MSK) key pair. MPK is included in public parameter, while MSK is held by the authority as a secret message.
2. $SK_{ID} \leftarrow$ KeyGen(ID, MSK): The KeyGen algorithm is run by the key generator authority to generate the secret key SK_{ID} according to the user's id.
3. $C \leftarrow$ Enc(ID, M): The Enc algorithm outputs the ciphertext C with the input of user ID and plaintext M.
4. $M \leftarrow$ Dec($C SK_{ID}$): Decrypt algorithm with ciphertext C and secret key SK_{ID} outputs plaintext M.

Identity-Based Hash Proof System ($\mathcal{IBHPS}$). In Chow *et al.* [11], they proposed a practical $\mathcal{LRIBE}$ system built from the $\mathcal{IBHPS}$ with a random extractor and designed invalid ciphertext in the encapsulation phase of $\mathcal{IBHPS}$ system. Particularly, they applied this technique to $\mathcal{BBIBE}$ [7], $\mathcal{WIBE}$ [22], $\mathcal{LWIBE}$ [19] respectively. The most encouraging results are that the overhead for $\mathcal{LRIBE}$ is linear of their counterpart in terms of the key calculations such as exponentiation on group elements and pairing operations. $\mathcal{IBHPS}$ consist of five PPT algorithms:

1. $(MPK, MSK) \leftarrow$ Setup(1^λ): Setup generates the master public-key and master secret key of the system with the input of security parameter λ.
2. $SK_{ID} \leftarrow$ KeyGen(ID, MSK): KeyGen outputs a secret key corresponding to the user ID.
3. $(C, k) \leftarrow$ EnCap(ID): The valid encapsulation algorithm creates a valid ciphertext C paired with an encapsulation key.
4. $C \leftarrow$ EnCap*(ID): The invalid encapsulation algorithm outputs an invalid ciphertext to the given *id*.

5. $k \leftarrow DecCap(C, SK_{ID})$: The deterministic decapsulation algorithm recovers the encapsulation key with the input of ciphertext C and secret key SK_{ID}.

Continual-Leakage-Resilient Sharing ($\mathcal{CLRS}$). Following is the description of $\mathcal{CLRS}$.

1. $(sh_1, sh_2) \leftarrow ShareGen(1^\lambda, M)$: The generation algorithm outputs two shares sh_1 and sh_2 with inputs security parameter and message M.
2. $sh'_b \leftarrow Update_b(sh_b)$: The randomized update algorithm updates the current version of share sh_b to sh'_b.
3. $M \leftarrow Reconstruct(sh_1, sh_2)$: The reconstruction algorithm will output the secret message M with inputs of secret shares.

3 System Design

$\mathcal{LRCRYPT}$ is built on the existing arithmetic library GMP [2], pairing-based cryptographic library PBC [20], and Openssl [1]. Based on GMP [2] and PBC [20], we build the $\mathcal{IBHPS}$ layer, which is the basic structures for $\mathcal{LRIBE}$ and hence $\mathcal{LRSIG}$. In addition, $\mathcal{CLRS}$ [13] works as the leakage-resilient secret sharing layer to blind the secret key and efficiently update the secret key of the existing cryptographic primitives. As independent interest, $\mathcal{PIM}$ is designed for the system that utilises matrix based on group elements or the big integer in GMP [2].

Figure 1 depicts the system architecture of $\mathcal{LRCRYPT}$ and shows the interactions between the layers. Based on the basic libraries is our Develop layer, which is the key components of $\mathcal{LRCRYPT}$. Precisely, Develop consists of $\mathcal{LRPKE}$ and $\mathcal{LRSIG}$ both of which are built on $\mathcal{IBHPS}$, $\mathcal{PIM}$, and $\mathcal{LRP}$. Assumed that P is the cryptographic primitives. The topmost one is the Application layer, which provides the programming interfaces of $\mathcal{LRCRYPT}$ for the users.

In $\mathcal{LRIBE}$, we implement the system based on $\mathcal{IBHPS}$, consisting of leakage-resilient $\mathcal{BBIBE}$ [7], leakage-resilient $\mathcal{WIBE}$ [22], and leakage-resilient $\mathcal{LWIBE}$ [19]. After initialisation, users will obtain the corresponding secret keys and call the encryption or decryption algorithms as the normal identity-based encryption system.

To begin with $\mathcal{LRP}$, users first initialise parameters of the $\mathcal{CLRS}$ layer. Following that, a cryptographic encryption primitive, *i.e.* the secret key encryption $\mathcal{DES}$, has to be initialised as well. Then $\mathcal{LRP}$ is called to build $\mathcal{LRDES}$ by adopting the $\mathcal{CLRS}$ as the secret key encapsulation layer that can blind the protected message and update it accordingly.

3.1 Leakage Resilient Public-Key Encryption (LRPKE)

$\mathcal{IBHPS}$ is regarded as a special $\mathcal{IBE}$ in the circumstance that there are many valid secret key SK_{ID} for given identity ID, and also valid and invalid ciphertexts. Even given SK_{ID}, a random valid ciphertext C is indistinguishable from

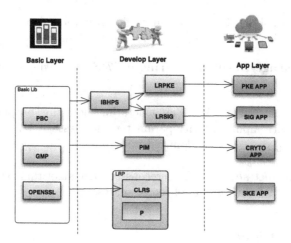

Fig. 1. System architecture

a random invalid one C'. Moreover, a valid ciphertext C decrypts in coincidence with SK_{ID} while an invalid ciphertext C' decrypts to a random value R'. To decrypt a valid ciphertext C, it will output a value R that is indistinguishable from a value that has $|R| - l$ bits of entropy. In this case, $\mathcal{LRIBE}$ via $\mathcal{IBHPS}$ with a randomnessextractor. Luckily, the extractor can be implemented by applying the existing random functions designed in the lower libraries PBC and GMP.

3.2 Leakage-Resilient Signature (LRSIG)

IND-CCA $\mathcal{IBE}$ implies a public-key signature scheme that is existentially unforgeable against a chosen message attack [8]. Therefore, we build a leakage-resilient public-key signature scheme from $\mathcal{LRIBE}$. Intuitively, the master secret key for $\mathcal{IBE}$ scheme $\mathcal{I} = (\mathsf{Setup_I}, \mathsf{KeyGen_I}, \mathsf{Enc_I}, \mathsf{Dec_I})$ is set as secret key of the signature scheme $\mathcal{S} = (\mathsf{Setup_S}, \mathsf{Sign_S}, \mathsf{Ver_S})$, and the public-key for $\mathcal{S}$ is included in the public parameters for $\mathcal{I}$. Supposed that identity $\mathsf{ID} = \mathsf{M}$ (M is set as input message), the decryption key for ID works as the signature σ on a message M. In order to verify a signature σ, the verifier simply chooses a random message $\bar{M}$, then encrypt $\bar{M}$ with the public-key $ID = M$. Then in the Verify process, it tries to decrypt it using the signature on $\bar{M}$ as the decryption key. If decryption succeeds, Verify returns pass, else reject. Hence given $\mathcal{I}$ and $\mathcal{S}$, we can build the leakage-resilient signature scheme LRSIG $\pi = (\mathsf{Setup}, \mathsf{Sign}, \mathsf{Verify})$.

3.3 Leakage-Resilient Primitive ($\mathcal{LRP}$)

Without loss of generality, we assume that the encryption primitive $\mathcal{P} = (\mathsf{Setup_P}, \mathsf{KeyGen_P}, \mathsf{Enc_P}, \mathsf{Dec_P})$. The difference of leakage-resilient cryptography is built on the assumption that some side-channel information will be leaked through implementation and devices, thus we figure out some efficient approaches to limit the probability that the secret key of the encryption scheme to be derived from such dangerous information. Given $\mathcal{CLRS}$ scheme $\mathcal{C} = (\mathsf{Setup}_C, \mathsf{ShareGen}_C, \mathsf{Update}_C, \mathsf{Reconstruct}_C)$ and $\mathcal{P}$, we describe the leakage-resilient encryption scheme $\mathcal{E} = (\mathsf{Setup}, \mathsf{KeyGen}, \mathsf{Enc}, \mathsf{Dec})$ in the followings.

1. $PP \leftarrow \mathsf{Setup}(1^\lambda)$: This algorithm takes security parameter λ as input, and calls two Setup algorithms in both $\mathcal{E}$ and $\mathcal{P}$, then includes the public parameters in both algorithms to the output PP.
2. $sh \leftarrow \mathbf{keygen}(PP)$: This algorithm calls $\mathcal{P}'$s KeyGen to get usk, then it takes this usk as secret share and runs $\mathsf{ShareGen}(1^\lambda, \Phi(usk))$, where Φ is a map from the group usk to the group M and it's not difficult to find its inverse Φ^{-1} in polynomial time. Then output the two shares $sh = (sh_1, sh_2)$ as user's secret key.
3. $C \leftarrow \mathsf{Enc}(P, sh)$: Enc takes plaintext P and secret key sh, then calls Enc_P in the same way, and outputs ciphertext C.
4. $(M, \perp) \leftarrow \mathsf{Dec}(sh_1, sh_2, C)$: This algorithm firstly calls $\mathsf{Reconstruct}(sh_1, sh_2)$ of $\mathcal{CLRS}$ and gets $\Phi(usk)$, then computes usk and runs Dec and outputs the plaintext M or $\perp$ if decryption fails.

3.4 Pairing and Big Integer Based Matrix ($\mathcal{PIM}$)

As independent interest, we abstract the matrix operations over group elements and develop a component called Pairing/Integer Matrix ($\mathcal{PIM}$), which is designed for the matrix and list operations for abundant matrix operations. Precisely, $\mathcal{PIM}$ is built directly on a library of GMP [2] and PBC [20]. $\mathcal{PIM}$ is not only available as an integrated component in $\mathcal{LRCRYPT}$ but also aims to provide other systems with common matrix calculations based on cryptographic group elements and big integers. To our knowledge, we are among the first to demonstrate such a calculation library. $\mathcal{IML}$ [10], which is based on GMP [2] library, cannot be applied to the group elements.

3.5 Programming Interfaces

In $\mathcal{LRCRYPT}$, we provide abundant programming interfaces that allow users to build it in a leakage-resilient cryptographic application. In Table 1, we list the parts the programming interfaces of our system, and complete interface description tion will be found in our *Github* project. In $\mathcal{LRIBE}$ and $\mathcal{LRSIG}$, we can set the parameter $TYPE$ in range $(1, 3)$ as in the subtypes of $\mathcal{IBE}$ types settings as $\mathcal{BBIBE}$, $\mathcal{LWIBE}$, and $\mathcal{WIBE}$.

3.6 Security Parameter and Leakage Parameter

Leakage parameter l is defined as the amount of bits leaked on secret key over the total size of the secret key, in particular, $l = |leakage\ info|/|secret\ key|$. In terms of choice for the curve in $\mathcal{LRCRYPT}$, we initialise the group by

Table 1. Programming interfaces

$\mathcal{LRIBE}$	$(PP, MSK) \leftarrow$ Setup$(1^\lambda, TYPE)$ $TYPE$ ranges from 1–3
	$SK \leftarrow$ KeyGen(PP, MSK, ID)
	$C \leftarrow$ Enc(PP, MSK, SK, M)
	$M \leftarrow$ Dec(PP, MSK, SK, C)
$\mathcal{LRSIG}$	$(PP, MSK) \leftarrow$ Setup$(1^\lambda, SK, \mathsf{TYPE})$ $TYPE$ ranges from 1–3, $MSK = SK$
	$\sigma \leftarrow$ Sign(PP, MSK, M)
	$(\mathsf{accept}, \mathsf{reject}) \leftarrow$ Verify$(\mathsf{PP}, \mathsf{msk}, \sigma)$
$\mathcal{LRP}$	$(PP) \leftarrow$ Setup$(1^\lambda, SK)$
	$sh \leftarrow$ KeyGen(PP)
	$C \leftarrow$ Enc(P, sh)
	$P \leftarrow$ Dec(C, sh)
$\mathcal{PIM}$	$\mathsf{mtr} \leftarrow$ Init$(\mathsf{SIZE\ R}, \mathsf{SIZE\ C}, \mathsf{INFO\ E})$ initialise matrix mtr with size R $*$ C
	Assigning functions
	Arithmetic calculation Add/Sub/Mul/Pow$(\mathsf{mtr_{out}}, \mathsf{mtr_1}, \mathsf{mtr_2})$
	Matrix property calculation Kernel, Xor

A-$TYPE$, which is 512-bit length of the group order. Without loss of generality, we set leakage parameter as $l = c \times \lambda$, where c is denoted as the leakage ratio and $c \in (0, 1)$. In the subtype of $\mathcal{LRIBE}$-$\mathcal{BB}$ and $\mathcal{LRIBE}$-$\mathcal{W}$ [12], the leakage rate is $\frac{1}{3}$, while it is $\frac{1}{9}$ for the $\mathcal{LRIBE}$-$\mathcal{LW}$ type [11]. Assumed that the size of key space is 2^μ, then the system will operate on the message space $M = (0, 1)^\nu$, where ν satisfies $v \le \mu - 2log(1/\epsilon) - 1$. $\mathcal{LRIBE}$-$\mathcal{LW}$ structure is built from the composite order group. We denote length of the composite order $N = 1024$ bits, where $N = p_1 \times p_2 \times p_3(p_1, p_2, p_3$ are all primes).

4 Performance Analysis

In terms of performance evaluation, we mainly focus on the followings:

Running Time: As general, we will record running time of the key algorithms of the system, which is the prominent part of the performance evaluations.

Blowup: In order to achieve leakage-resilience, we need to operate extra operations than their counterparts. Intuitively, the blowup is defined as the ratio of the time cost in the algorithms of leakage-resilient settings over the non-leakage-resilience baseline. Our goal is to build the system that can achieve comparative blowup and leakage-resilience.

4.1 System Analysis

Efficient Pairing Calculation Overhead. Since pairing calculation $\mathsf{e}(\mathsf{g_1}, \mathsf{g_2})$ that maps from group $\mathbb{G}_1$ $\mathbb{G}_2$ to $\mathbb{G}_T$ is time-consuming, we will store the pairing result in private memory after the setup of the system in order to save running time when the number of pairings is relatively large by reading an element instead of calculating the pairing.

Efficient for Large Scale. Although $\mathcal{LRP}$ is not necessarily more efficient than some existing leakage resilient secret key constructions [6], $\mathcal{LRP}$ will outperform its counterpart in terms of large scale. Since we only have to initialise the $\mathcal{CLRS}$ layer once and apply it in the secret key encryptions for multiple times. In this domain, the blowup for leakage-resilient will be significantly lower in average. Therefore, our system achieves significant improvements for large-scale calculations, which is common nowadays.

4.2 Security Analysis

In this section, we demonstrate the security analysis of the main building blocks for $\mathcal{LRCRYPT}$.

Security of Leakage-Resilient Signature: Through the constructions in Sect. 3, we can easily conclude that if there exists an adversary $\mathcal{A}$ that can break the signature scheme π, we can construct a simulator $\mathcal{B}$ that breaks the security of $\mathcal{LRIBE}$ system with non-trivial probability in the defined security model.

$\mathcal{LRSKE}$ from $\mathcal{CLRS}$: Denoted that $\mathcal{P}$ is a cryptographic primitive and usk is the user's secret key in $\mathcal{P}$. At the first step, we recap the $\mathcal{CLRS}$ $\mathcal{C} = ($ShareGen, Update, Reconstruct$)$.

Now we discuss the definition of the security for $\mathcal{LRP}$. Particularly, the security model is a split-state model [23], which means the adversary can only learn the secret information in a split way. Under this model, we design the system of generic leakage resilient cryptographic scheme with $\mathcal{CLRS}$. More precisely, a user in LRP has secret key $\mathsf{sk} = \mathsf{sh} = (\mathsf{sh}_1, \mathsf{sh}_2)$, and the adversary can only get the leakage information of $f(\mathsf{sh}_1)$ and $f(\mathsf{sh}_2)$, where $f \in \mathcal{F}$ is the leakage function the adversary can access. However, the adversary cannot get any information of $f(\mathsf{sh}_1, \mathsf{sh}_2)$ simultaneously. From the results of [23], we can infer that our $\mathcal{LRSKE}$ scheme built in this way is secure in the split-state model. Then we apply this leakage-resilient layer in the secret key primitive. e.g. $\mathcal{DES}$ in our system.

4.3 Implementation Results

We do the implementations in the windows system of Intel(R) Xeon(R) E7-2830 CPU@3.40 GHz configured with GMP and PBC libraries. We build our system with $C/C + +$ program, and output the library $\mathcal{LRCRYPT}$ for development in some cryptographic systems which are sensitive to side-channel attacks. In this section, we will present the implementation results for performance evaluation. In addition, we also maintain our project in $Github$, which will be public in the coming future.

$\mathcal{LRIBE}$ **Results.** With varied parameters, we collect the running time for various subtypes of $\mathcal{LRIBE}$ (Fig. 2), consisting of a four algorithms Setup, KeyGen,

Enc, Dec. $\mathcal{LRIBE\text{-}BB}$ is the simplest version with selectively secure [11] which only consists of constant number of pairing calculations. While $\mathcal{LRIBE}$-W is the compromising one since its complexity of the group multiplication is linear in the size of the identity input *id*. However, the composite version $\mathcal{LRIBE\text{-}LW}$ subtype is most time-consuming. Composite order group operations suffer from the efficiency constraint compared to its counterparts. However, it can not be always transferred to the prime order groups, since the security of the scheme inherits directly from the composite order group.

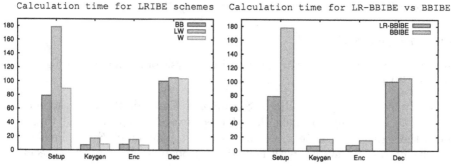

Fig. 2. LRIBE results   **Fig. 3.** LR-BBIBE vs BBIBE

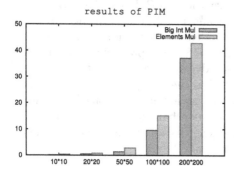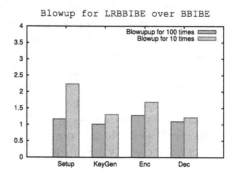

Fig. 4. PIM results   **Fig. 5.** Blowup for LRIBE

LRIBE and IBE Results. In terms of practical requirements, we compare our $\mathcal{LRIBE}$ subtype with the original identity-based encryption scheme in Fig. 3. Specifically, we implement one example by both calling the programming interface of $\mathcal{LRCRYPT}$ and original $\mathcal{BBIBE}$ [7] scheme. As shown in Fig. 5, the curves depict the cost for $\mathcal{LRIBE}$ and $\mathcal{IBE}$ share the similar trend, though running time for $\mathcal{LR\text{-}BBIBE}$ is about 1.3 times of $\mathcal{BBIBE}$[7]. As the increase of running number, the average blowup for Setup decreases since the extra cost for $\mathcal{CLRS}$ will be divided to numerous process, resulting in lowering blowup for each round.

PIM Results. To evaluate the performance of PIM layer, we choose the operations of matrix addition and multiplication with varying dimensions $20 * 20, 50 * 50, 100 * 100$, and execute the calculations for 50, 100, 1000 times to lower the error bar. As discussed in previous sections, we set the bit size of operation element as 128 bits and present the results in Fig. 4.

In the experiments, we compare $\mathcal{PIM}$ results with the existing integer matrix library called IML with large elements, and notice that running time of our system is comparable with results of IML. Moreover, we also compare the results for matrix with big integers and group elements. Without loss of generality, we denoted Mz and Me as a matrix for bit integer and a matrix for group elements respectively.

Acknowledgments. This work was supported in part by NSFC/RGC Joint Research Scheme (N_HKU 72913) of Hong Kong, Seed Funding Programme for Basic Research of HKU (201511159034, 201411159142), and National High Technology Research and Development Program of China (2015AA016008).

References

1. https://www.openssl.org/
2. https://gmplib.org/
3. Akavia, A., Goldwasser, S., Vaikuntanathan, V.: Simultaneous hardcore bits and cryptography against memory attacks. In: Reingold, O. (ed.) TCC 2009. LNCS, vol. 5444, pp. 474–495. Springer, Heidelberg (2009). doi:10.1007/978-3-642-00457-5_28
4. Alwen, J., Dodis, Y., Wichs, D.: Leakage-resilient public-key cryptography in the bounded-retrieval model. In: Halevi, S. (ed.) CRYPTO 2009. LNCS, vol. 5677, pp. 36–54. Springer, Heidelberg (2009). doi:10.1007/978-3-642-03356-8_3
5. Barker, E., Barker, W., Burr, W., Polk, W., Smid, M.: Recommendation for Key Management-Part 1: General (revised). NIST special publication, Citeseer (2006)
6. Belaïd, S., Grosso, V., Xavier-Standaert, F.: Masking and leakage-resilient primitives: one, the other (s) or both? (2014)
7. Boneh, D., Boyen, X.: Efficient selective-ID secure identity-based encryption without random oracles. In: Cachin, C., Camenisch, J.L. (eds.) EUROCRYPT 2004. LNCS, vol. 3027, pp. 223–238. Springer, Heidelberg (2004). doi:10.1007/978-3-540-24676-3_14
8. Boneh, D., Franklin, M.: Identity-based encryption from the weil pairing. In: Kilian, J. (ed.) CRYPTO 2001. LNCS, vol. 2139, pp. 213–229. Springer, Heidelberg (2001). doi:10.1007/3-540-44647-8_13
9. Canetti, R., Halevi, S., Katz, J.: A forward-secure public-key encryption scheme. In: Biham, E. (ed.) EUROCRYPT 2003. LNCS, vol. 2656, pp. 255–271. Springer, Heidelberg (2003). doi:10.1007/3-540-39200-9_16
10. Chen, Z.: https://cs.uwaterloo.ca/~astorjoh/iml.html

11. Chow, S.S., Dodis, Y., Rouselakis, Y., Waters, B.: Practical leakage-resilient identity-based encryption from simple assumptions. In: Proceedings of the 17th ACM Conference on Computer and Communications Security, pp. 152–161. ACM (2010)

12. Conti, M., Di Pietro, R., Mancini, L.V., Mei, A.: (old) Distributed data source verification in wireless sensor networks. Inf. Fusion **10**(4), 342–353 (2009)

13. Dodis, Y., Lewko, A., Waters, B., Wichs, D.: Storing secrets on continually leaky devices. In: IEEE 52nd Annual Symposium on Foundations of Computer Science (FOCS), pp. 688–697. IEEE (2011)

14. Dodis, Y., Reyzin, L., Smith, A.: Fuzzy extractors: how to generate strong keys from biometrics and other noisy data. In: Cachin, C., Camenisch, J.L. (eds.) EUROCRYPT 2004. LNCS, vol. 3027, pp. 523–540. Springer, Heidelberg (2004). doi:10.1007/978-3-540-24676-3_31

15. Halderman, J.A., Schoen, S.D., Heninger, N., Clarkson, W., Paul, W., Calandrino, J.A., Feldman, A.J., Appelbaum, J., Felten, E.W.: Lest we remember: cold-boot attacks on encryption keys. Commun. ACM **52**(5), 91–98 (2009)

16. Kocher, P., Jaffe, J., Jun, B.: Differential power analysis. In: Wiener, M. (ed.) CRYPTO 1999. LNCS, vol. 1666, pp. 388–397. Springer, Heidelberg (1999). doi:10.1007/3-540-48405-1_25

17. Kocher, P.C.: Timing attacks on implementations of Diffie-Hellman, RSA, DSS, and other systems. In: Koblitz, N. (ed.) CRYPTO 1996. LNCS, vol. 1109, pp. 104–113. Springer, Heidelberg (1996). doi:10.1007/3-540-68697-5_9

18. Lewko, A., Rouselakis, Y., Waters, B.: Achieving leakage resilience through dual system encryption. In: Ishai, Y. (ed.) TCC 2011. LNCS, vol. 6597, pp. 70–88. Springer, Heidelberg (2011). doi:10.1007/978-3-642-19571-6_6

19. Lewko, A., Waters, B.: New techniques for dual system encryption and fully secure HIBE with short ciphertexts. In: Micciancio, D. (ed.) TCC 2010. LNCS, vol. 5978, pp. 455–479. Springer, Heidelberg (2010). doi:10.1007/978-3-642-11799-2_27

20. Lynn, B.: PBC: the pairing-based cryptography library. http://crypto.stanford.edu/pbc/

21. Shamir, A.: Identity-based cryptosystems and signature schemes. In: Blakley, G.R., Chaum, D. (eds.) CRYPTO 1984. LNCS, vol. 196, pp. 47–53. Springer, Heidelberg (1985). doi:10.1007/3-540-39568-7_5

22. Waters, B.: Efficient identity-based encryption without random oracles. In: Cramer, R. (ed.) EUROCRYPT 2005. LNCS, vol. 3494, pp. 114–127. Springer, Heidelberg (2005). doi:10.1007/11426639_7

23. Xiong, H., Zhang, C., Yuen, T.H., Zhang, E.P., Yiu, S.M., Qing, S.: Continual leakage-resilient dynamic secret sharing in the split-state model. In: Chim, T.W., Yuen, T.H. (eds.) ICICS 2012. LNCS, vol. 7618, pp. 119–130. Springer, Heidelberg (2012). doi:10.1007/978-3-642-34129-8_11

24. Yuen, T.H., Chow, S.S.M., Zhang, Y., Yiu, S.M.: Identity-based encryption resilient to continual auxiliary leakage. In: Pointcheval, D., Johansson, T. (eds.) EUROCRYPT 2012. LNCS, vol. 7237, pp. 117–134. Springer, Heidelberg (2012). doi:10.1007/978-3-642-29011-4_9

Revocable Group Signatures with Compact Revocation List Using Vector Commitments

Shahidatul Sadiah$^{(\boxtimes)}$ and Toru Nakanishi

Department of Information Engineering,
Hiroshima University, Higashihiroshima, Japan
{d152447,t-nakanishi}@hiroshima-u.ac.jp

Abstract. A group signature allows any group member to anonymously sign a message. One of the important issues is an efficient membership revocation. The scheme proposed by Libert et al. has achieved $O(1)$ signature and membership certificate size, $O(1)$ signing and verification times, and $O(\log N)$ public key size, where N is the total number of members. However the Revocation List (RL) data is large, due to $O(R)$ signatures in RL, where R is the number of revoked members. The scheme proposed by Nakanishi et al. achieved a compact RL of $O(R/T)$ signatures for any integer T. However, this scheme increases membership certificate size by $O(T)$. In this paper, we extend the scheme proposed by Libert et al., by reducing the RL size to $O(R/T)$ using a *vector commitment* to compress the revocation entries, while $O(1)$ membership certificate size remains.

Keywords: Privacy · Group signatures · Revocation · Vector commitments

1 Introduction

In a group signature scheme, a group member is allowed to sign a message anonymously on behalf of the group. There are two types of authorities: A *group manager* (GM) who adds users into the group, and an *opener* who can identify the signer from the signature when necessary. One important function in the group signature scheme is *revocation*, where the user's privilege to sign a message is removed. It is a critical issue, which has been broadly studied.

Recently, Libert et al. proposed a scalable scheme [7] based on the broadcast encryption framework by Naor et al. [10], where $O(1)$ signature size, $O(1)$ signing/verification costs, $O(1)$ membership certificate size, and $O(\log N)$ public key size are achieved. However, the scheme still needs an improvement on the revocation list (RL) size. In the scheme, the RL contains signatures for all subsets of authorized users, which are formed by a subset difference (SD) method. In the worst case, the number of signatures amounts to $2R - 1$. As the signature, an AHO signature with 7 group elements is used. Thus, in case of 128-bit security, the RL size is $900R$ bytes or more. Since the signer needs to fetch the RL for every revocation epoch, the large size will cause delay in mobile environment.

© Springer International Publishing AG 2017
D. Choi and S. Guilley (Eds.): WISA 2016, LNCS 10144, pp. 245–257, 2017.
DOI: 10.1007/978-3-319-56549-1_21

There are studies on reducing the RL size. Nakanishi et al. proposed a scheme [9] with compact RL using an accumulator. In this scheme, since GM accumulates T SD subsets and signs the accumulated value, the number of signatures is reduced by $1/T$ and the RL size is $O(R/T)$. However, the public key size and membership certificate size are increased, when T is increased. The other scheme is proposed by Attrapadung et al. [2], where the RL size is constant by adopting identity based revocation (IBR) method. However, as the trade-off, the membership certificate size and signing cost are $O(R)$ in the worst case.

In this paper, we propose a revocable group signature scheme with a compact RL. Similarly to [9], we partition the subsets into a number of blocks and compress it using a vector commitment [8]. Since the compression is simpler than the accumulator, we can reduce the RL size to $O(R/T)$, and the public key size to $O(T + \log N)$, while maintaining the membership certificate size as $O(1)$.

2   Preliminaries

Here, we show the cryptographic primitives and proof system used in the proposed revocable group signature scheme.

2.1   Bilinear Maps

We use bilinear groups and bilinear map in our system, where $\mathbb{G}$ and $\mathbb{G}_T$ are multiplicative cyclic groups of prime order p, g is a randomly chosen generator of $\mathbb{G}$ and $e : \mathbb{G} \times \mathbb{G} \to \mathbb{G}_T$ is a computable bilinear map, with the following properties:

- **Bilinearity:** for all $u, v \in \mathbb{G}$ and $a, b \in \mathbb{Z}, e(u^a, v^b) = e(u, v)^{ab}$.
- **Non-degeneracy:** $e(g, g) \neq 1_{\mathbb{G}_T}$, where $1_{\mathbb{G}_T}$ is an identity element of $\mathbb{G}_T$.

2.2   Complexity Assumptions

As well as [7], the security of our proposed system is based on DLIN (Decision LINear) assumption [3], the q-SDH (Strong DH) assumption [4], the n-FlexDHE assumption [11], the n-DHE assumption [5], and the q-SFP (Simultaneous Flexible Pairing) assumption [1].

Definition 1 (DLIN assumption). For all PPT algorithm $\mathcal{A}$, the probability

$$\left| Pr\left[\mathcal{A}(g, g^a, g^b, g^{ac}, g^{bd}, g^{c+d}) = 1\right] - Pr\left[\mathcal{A}(g, g^a, g^b, g^{ac}, g^{bd}, g^z) = 1\right]\right|$$

is negligible, where $g \in_R \mathbb{G}$ and $a, b, c, d, z, \in_R \mathbb{Z}_p$.

Definition 2 (q-SDH assumption). For all PPT algorithm $\mathcal{A}$, the probability

$$Pr\left[\mathcal{A}(g, g^a, \ldots, g^{a^q}) = (b, g^{1/(a+b)} \wedge b \in \mathbb{Z}_p)\right]$$

is negligible, where $g \in_R \mathbb{G}$ and $a \in_R \mathbb{Z}_p$.

Definition 3 (n-FlexDHE assumption). For all PPT algorithm $\mathcal{A}$, the probability

$$Pr\left[\mathcal{A}(g, g^{a^1}, \ldots, g^{a^n}, g^{a^{n+2}}, \ldots, g^{a^{2n}}) = (g^\mu, g^{\mu a^{n+1}}, g^{\mu a^{2n}}) \in (\mathbb{G}\backslash\{1_\mathbb{G}\})^3\right]$$

is negligible for some $\mu \in \mathbb{Z}_p^*$, where $g \in_R \mathbb{G}$ and $a \in_R \mathbb{Z}_p$.

Definition 4 (n-DHE assumption). For all PPT algorithm $\mathcal{A}$, the probability

$$Pr\left[\mathcal{A}(g, g^a, \ldots, g^{a^n}, g^{a^{n+2}}, \ldots, g^{a^{2n}}) = g^{a^{n+1}}\right]$$

is negligible, where $g \in_R \mathbb{G}$ and $a \in_R \mathbb{Z}_p$. The n-FlexDHE assumption is stronger than the n-DHE assumption, i.e., the former implies the latter.

Definition 5 (q-SFP assumption). For all PPT algorithm $\mathcal{A}$, the probability

$$Pr\left[\begin{array}{l}\mathcal{A}\left(g_z, h_z, g_r, h_r, a, \tilde{a}, b, \tilde{b}, \{(z_j, r_j, s_j, t_j, u_j, v_j, w_j)\}_{j=1}^q\right) \\ = (z^*, r^*, s^*, t^*, u^*, v^*, w^*) \in \mathbb{G}^7 \wedge e(a, \tilde{a}) = e(g_z, z^*)e(g_r, r^*)e(s^*, t^*)\wedge \\ e(b, \tilde{b}) = e(h_z, z^*)e(h_r, u^*)e(v^*, w^*) \wedge z^* \neq 1_\mathbb{G} \wedge z^* \neq z_j \text{ for all } 1 \leq j \leq q\end{array}\right]$$

is negligible, where $(g_z, h_z, g_r, h_r, a, \tilde{a}, b, \tilde{b}) \in \mathbb{G}^8$ and all tuples $\{(z_j, r_j, s_j, t_j, u_j, v_j, w_j)\}_{j=1}^q$) satisfy the above relations.

2.3   AHO Structure-Preserving Signatures

In the previous system [7], AHO signature [1] is used as the structure-preserving signature, where the knowledge of the signature can be proved by the following Groth-Sahai (GS) proofs. The AHO signature allows us to sign multiple elements to obtain a signature with the constant size.

AHOKeyGen: Select bilinear groups $\mathbb{G}, \mathbb{G}_T$ with a prime order p and a bilinear map e. Select $g, G_r, H_r \in \mathbb{G}$ and $\mu_z, \nu_z, \mu_1, \ldots, \mu_k, \nu_1, \ldots, \nu_k, \alpha_a, \alpha_b \in_R \mathbb{Z}_p$. Compute $G_z = G_r^{\mu_z}, H_z = H_r^{\nu_z}, G_1 = G_r^{\mu_1}, \ldots, G_k = G_r^{\mu_k}, H_1 = H_r^{\nu_1}, \ldots, H = H_r^{\nu_k}, A = e(G_r, g^{\alpha_a}), B = e(H_r, g^{\alpha_b})$. Output the public key as $pk = (\mathbb{G}, \mathbb{G}_T, p, e, g, G_r, H_r, G_z, H_z, G_1, \ldots, G_k, H_1, \ldots, H_k, A, B)$, and the secret key as $sk = (\alpha_a, \alpha_b, \mu_z, \nu_z, \mu_1, \ldots, \mu_k, \nu_1, \ldots, \nu_k)$.

AHOSign: Given a vector of messages $(M_1, \ldots, M_k) \in \mathbb{G}^k$ together with sk, choose $\beta, \epsilon, \eta, \iota, \kappa \in_R \mathbb{Z}_p$, and compute $\theta_1 = g^\beta$, and

$$\theta_2 = g^{\epsilon - \mu_z \beta}\prod_{i=1}^k M_i^{-\mu_i}, \quad \theta_3 = G_r^\eta, \quad \theta_4 = g^{(\alpha_a - \epsilon)/\eta},$$

$$\theta_5 = g^{\iota - \nu_z \beta}\prod_{i=1}^k M_i^{-\nu_i}, \quad \theta_6 = H_r^\kappa, \quad \theta_7 = g^{(\alpha_b - \iota)/\kappa}.$$

Output the signature $\sigma = (\theta_1, \ldots, \theta_7)$.

AHOVerify: Given a vector of messages $(M_1, \ldots, M_k) \in \mathbb{G}^k$ and the signature $\sigma = (\theta_1, \ldots, \theta_7)$, accept these if following equations are hold:

$$A = e(G_z, \theta_1) \cdot e(G_r, \theta_2) \cdot e(\theta_3, \theta_4) \cdot \prod_{i=1}^{k} e(G_i, M_i),$$
$$B = e(H_z, \theta_1) \cdot e(H_r, \theta_5) \cdot e(\theta_6, \theta_7) \cdot \prod_{i=1}^{k} e(H_i, M_i).$$

This signature is existentially unforgeable against chosen-message attacks under the q-SFP assumption [1].

The re-randomization algorithm in [1] allows us to publicly randomize an AHO signature to obtain another signature $(\theta'_1, \ldots, \theta'_7)$ on the vector of the same messages. In the GS proof of the randomized signature, $(\theta'_i)_{i=3,4,6,7}$ can be revealed, but $(\theta'_i)_{i=1,2,5}$ is committed, as in [7].

2.4   GS Proof

To prove the secret knowledge in relations of the bilinear maps, we utilize Groth-Sahai (GS) proofs [6]. We adopt the instantiation based on DLIN assumption. The GS proof needs a common reference string (CRS) $(\boldsymbol{f}_1, \boldsymbol{f}_2, \boldsymbol{f}_3) \in \mathbb{G}^3$ for $\boldsymbol{f}_1 = (f_1, 1, g)$, $\boldsymbol{f}_2 = (1, f_2, g)$ for some $f_1, f_2 \in \mathbb{G}$. For an element $X \in \mathbb{G}$, the commitment is $\boldsymbol{C} = (1, 1, X) \cdot \boldsymbol{f}_1^r \cdot \boldsymbol{f}_2^s \cdot \boldsymbol{f}_3^t$, where $r, s, t \in_R \mathbb{Z}_p^*$. In the perfectly sound proofs, the CRS is $\boldsymbol{f}_3 = \boldsymbol{f}_1^{\xi_1} \cdot \boldsymbol{f}_2^{\xi_2}$ for $\xi_1, \xi_2 \in_R \mathbb{Z}_p^*$. In case of the witness indistinguishability, $\boldsymbol{f}_1, \boldsymbol{f}_2, \boldsymbol{f}_3$ are linearly independent.

For an exponent value $x \in \mathbb{Z}_p$, the commitment is $\boldsymbol{C} = \tilde{\boldsymbol{f}}^x \cdot \boldsymbol{f}_1^r \cdot \boldsymbol{f}_2^s$, where $r, s \in_R \mathbb{Z}_p^*$ and a CRS $\tilde{\boldsymbol{f}}, \boldsymbol{f}_1, \boldsymbol{f}_2$. In the perfectly sound proofs, $\tilde{\boldsymbol{f}}, \boldsymbol{f}_1, \boldsymbol{f}_2$ are linearly independent (we can set $\tilde{\boldsymbol{f}} = \boldsymbol{f}_3 \cdot (1, 1, g)$ for $\boldsymbol{f}_3 = \boldsymbol{f}_1^{\xi_1} \cdot \boldsymbol{f}_2^{\xi_2}$ [7]). In case of the witness indistinguishability, $\tilde{\boldsymbol{f}} = \boldsymbol{f}_1^{\xi_1} \cdot \boldsymbol{f}_2^{\xi_2}$.

Using the GS proof, the prover can prove the set of pairing product equations:

$$\prod_{i=1}^{n} e(A_i, X_i) \cdot \prod_{i=1}^{n} \prod_{j=1}^{n} e(X_i, X_j)^{a_{ij}} = t,$$

for secret variables $X_1, \ldots, X_n \in \mathbb{G}$ and revealed constants $A_1, \ldots, A_n \in \mathbb{G}, a_{ij} \in \mathbb{Z}_p, t \in \mathbb{G}_T$. Additionally we can prove the multi-exponentiation equations:

$$\prod_{i=1}^{m} A_i^{y_i} \cdot \prod_{j=1}^{n} X_j^{b_j} \cdot \prod_{i=1}^{m} \prod_{j=1}^{n} X_j^{y_i \gamma_{ij}} = T,$$

for secret variables $X_1, \ldots, X_n \in \mathbb{G}$, $y_1, \ldots, y_m \in \mathbb{Z}_p$ and revealed constants $T, A_1, \ldots, A_m \in \mathbb{G}, b_1, \ldots, b_n, \gamma_{ij} \in \mathbb{Z}_p$.

2.5   Vector Commitment

We adopt a primitive called vector commitment [8], where a vector of multiple values are committed, and the commitment can be opened at specific coordinate. Generally, the commitment is randomized for hiding. However, as in [7], we utilize the non-randomized version, since we need only the binding property. The public key for the commitments is $pk_{vc} = (g_1, \ldots, g_n, g_{n+2}, \ldots, g_{2n})$, where $g_i = g^{\gamma^i}$ for each $\gamma \in_R \mathbb{Z}_p$. To commit to a vector $\vec{m} = (m_1, \ldots, m_n) \in \mathbb{Z}_p^n$, the committer computes

$$C = \prod_{\kappa=1}^n g_{n+1-\kappa}^{m_\kappa}.$$

A single group element $W_i = \prod_{\kappa=1, \kappa \neq i}^n g_{n+1-\kappa+i}^{m_\kappa}$ provides the evidence that m_i is the i-th component of $\vec{m}$. It satisfies the verification relation $e(g_i, C) = e(g, W_i) \cdot e(g_1, g_n)^{m_i}$. The infeasibility of opening a commitment to two distinct messages for some coordinate i relies on the n-FlexDHE assumption or n-DHE assumption (see the proof sketch of Theorem 1).

3 Syntax and Security of Revocable Group Signatures

As in [7], we define the revocable group signatures.

3.1 Syntax

The algorithms and protocol of the revocable group signature scheme are as follows.

Setup: Given a security parameter $\lambda \in \mathbb{N}$, a maximal number of a group members $N \in \mathbb{N}$ and a partitioning parameter $T \in \mathbb{N}$, this algorithm generates a group public key $\mathcal{Y}$, the group manager's (GM) key $\mathcal{S}_{\text{GM}}$ and the opener's private key $\mathcal{S}_{\text{OA}}$. This algorithm initializes a public state St comprising a set data structure $St_{users} = \phi$ and a string data structure $St_{trans} = \epsilon$.

Join: This interactive protocol is between GM and prospective group's member u. The common input is $\mathcal{Y}$. As a result, the member obtains a membership secret sec_u and a membership certificate cert_u. GM updates St in the database by $St_{user} = St_{user} \cup \{u\}$ and $St_{trans} = St_{trans} \| <u, \text{transcript}_u>$.

Revoke: This algorithm is run by GM. The inputs are $\mathcal{Y}$ and the set of the revoked users, $\mathcal{R}_t$. This algorithm allows GM to generate an update revocation list RL_t for the new revocation epoch t.

Sign: This algorithm is run by u. Given $t, RL_t, \text{cert}_u, \text{sec}_u$, and a message M, this algorithm outputs $\perp$ if $u \in \mathcal{R}_t$, or a signature σ otherwise.

Verify: This algorithm is run by a verifier. Given $\sigma, t, RL_t, M, \mathcal{Y}$, this deterministic algorithm outputs 1 if the signatures is valid and not revoked, or 0 otherwise.

Open: This algorithm is run by an opener. Given $St, \mathcal{S}_{\text{OA}}, M$, and a valid signature σ w.r.t. $\mathcal{Y}$ for revocation epoch t, it outputs $u \in St_{users} \cup \{\perp\}$, which is the identity u as a group member or an opening failure.

3.2   Security

There are three security requirements in the revocable group signature scheme. The first one is *security against misidentification attacks*. This requirement means that an adversary cannot compute a group signature where **Open** identifies outside of the corrupted non-revoked members. The second one is *security against framing attacks*, which means that an honest member is not traced for signatures that the member did not issue, even if everyone (including GM) except the member colludes. The third one is *anonymity*, which implies the anonymity and unlinkability of signatures. The formal definitions are shown in [7].

4   Previous Scheme

In this section, we explain about the revocable group signature proposed by Libert et al. [7], and discuss about the remaining problem. In [7], the approach of the Subset Difference (SD) method is used as in Fig. 1. In a binary tree, group members are assigned to the leaves. Each node v is indexed by an identifier $\text{ID}(v)$ of an integer. When a user becomes a member of the group, the group manager (GM) certifies him with a signature that contains the node IDs of the path from the root to the user's leaf, $(I_1, \ldots, I_\ell)$, where ℓ shows the level of the tree.

In the SD method, non-revoked users are divided into disjoint subsets (subtrees), where a subset S_i is defined by primary node P_i, which is the root node of the subtree, and the secondary node S_i that is a descendant of P_i. The subset S_i consists of the leaves of the subtree rooted by P_i except leaves of the subtree rooted by S_i. The levels of P_i and S_i are denoted as ϕ_i and ψ_i, respectively.

In the example of Fig. 1, the user of the leaf node with $\text{ID}(v) = 8$ is distinguished by the path $(I_1, I_2, I_3, I_4) = (1, 2, 4, 8)$. It is included in subset S_1 rooted by P_1 but not by S_1.

For every revocation, GM renews a revocation list RL that contains signed dataset $R_i = (\phi_i, \psi_i, \text{ID}(P_i), \text{ID}(S_i))$ of all subset entries $i \in \{1, \ldots, m\}$. For signing a group signature, the user retrieves the revocation data for subset S_i that contains his leaf, and proves that $\text{ID}(P_i) = I_{\phi_i}$ and $\text{ID}(S_i) \neq I_{\psi_i}$ to prove the non-revocation. This relation means that his leaf v is connected with P_i on level ϕ_i and not connected to S_i on level ψ_i, which means that u is in the subtree rooted by P_i but not in that by S_i. The proof is done in the Zero-Knowledge Proof fashion for the anonymity.

The problem in this scheme is the size of RL. We have $m \leq 2R - 1$ [7]. Each entry is signed by GM using an AHO signature. Furthermore, an AHO signature contains 7 bilinear group elements. For $R = 10,000$, the size of signatures could be about 8 MB in 128 bit security. The signer needs to fetch the large RL for every revocation epoch, which will cause delay in mobile environment.

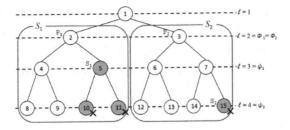

Fig. 1. An example of SD method.

5   Proposed Scheme

5.1   Construction Idea

The proposed scheme is extended from the previous scheme [7]. In the previous scheme, GM signs each RL entry of $(\phi_i, \psi_i, \text{ID}(\text{P}_i), \text{ID}(\text{S}_i))$. Meanwhile, in the proposed scheme, multiple elements of each type in the entry are compressed using a vector commitment [8] and are signed. For example, $\text{ID}(\text{P}_1), \ldots, \text{ID}(\text{P}_n)$ are divided to blocks with T elements as $\text{ID}(\text{P}_1), \ldots, \text{ID}(\text{P}_T)$, and each block of elements is accumulated to the vector commitment. By this accumulation, the number of signed entries in the RL is reduced to m/T.

In [7], the signer only retrieves $(\phi_i, \psi_i, \text{ID}(\text{P}_i), \text{ID}(\text{S}_i))$ of the subtree that contains his leaf v. In the proposed scheme, since we adopt the vector commitment, the signer must show the correct opening of vector commitments. The verification needs the correctness of g_j indicating the opened j-th component. Thus all g_j are signed by GM, and the signer proves the correctness of g_j by the GS proof of the signature of g_j. In addition, we need to prove that g_ϕ and g_ψ are compatible to g_1^ϕ and g_1^ψ respectively, because we need to map g_1^ϕ and g_1^ψ to their public parameter as g_ϕ and g_ψ. Thus, we prepare signatures of (g_1^ϕ, g_ϕ) and (g_1^ψ, g_ψ), and the signer proves the mapping, using the GS proofs of the signatures.

5.2   Construction

Setup(λ, N, T): Given a security parameter $\lambda \in \mathbb{N}$ and the allowed number of users $N = 2^{\ell-1}$ for integer ℓ, and the number of elements for partitioning T, do the following, where step 5 and 6 are added to the previous scheme [7].

1. Select bilinear group $(\mathbb{G}, \mathbb{G}_T)$ of prime order $p > 2^\lambda$, with a generator $g \xleftarrow{R} \mathbb{G}$.
2. Define $\delta_0 = 1$, $\delta_1 = 2$, $\delta_2 = 2$, $\delta_3 = 5$. Generate four key pairs $(sk_{\text{AHO}}^{(d)}, pk_{\text{AHO}}^{(d)})$, $d \in \{0, 1, 2, 3\}$ for the AHO signature in order to sign messages of $\{\delta_d\}_{d=0}^3$ group elements, respectively.
3. Generate a public parameter $pk_{\text{vc}} = (g_1, \ldots, g_n, g_{n+2}, \ldots, g_{2n}) \in \mathbb{G}^{2n-1}$ for n-dimension vector commitment, where $n = \mathbf{max}(\ell, T)$.

4. Generate a CRS for the GS NIWI proof: Select $f = (f_1, f_2, f_3) \in \mathbb{G}^3$, and $\tilde{f} \in \mathbb{G}$, where $f_1 = (f_1, 1, g)$, $f_2 = (1, f_2, g)$, $f_3 = f_1^{\varepsilon_1} \cdot f_2^{\varepsilon_2}$ with $f_1 = g^{\beta_1}$, $f_2 = g^{\beta_2} \xleftarrow{R} \mathbb{G}$ and $\beta_1, \beta_2, \varepsilon_1, \varepsilon_2 \xleftarrow{R} \mathbb{Z}_p^*$. Set $\tilde{f} = f_3 \cdot (1, 1, g)$.

5. Using $sk_{AHO}^{(0)}$, generate an AHO signature on message g_j as $\sigma_{g_j} = (\theta_{j,1}, \ldots, \theta_{j,7})$ for all $1 \leq j \leq T$.

6. Using $sk_{AHO}^{(1)}$, generate an AHO signature on the pair of (g_τ, g_1^τ) as $\tilde{\sigma}_\tau = (\tilde{\theta}_{\tau,1}, \ldots, \tilde{\theta}_{\tau,7})$ for all $1 \leq \tau \leq \ell$.

7. Choose $(U, V) \xleftarrow{R} \mathbb{G}^2$ that, together with generators $f_1, f_2, g \in \mathbb{G}$, will form a public encryption key.

8. Select a strongly unforgeable one-time signature $\Sigma = (\mathcal{G}, \mathcal{S}, \mathcal{V})$.

9. Set $\mathcal{S}_{GM} := (\{sk_{AHO}^{(d)}\}_{d \in \{0,1,2,3\}})$, $\mathcal{S}_{OA} := (\beta_1, \beta_2)$ as GM's and opener's private keys, respectively, and the group public key as

$$\mathcal{Y} := \left(g, N, \ell, T, \{pk_{AHO}^{(d)}\}_{d=0}^3, pk_{vc}, f, \tilde{f}, (U, V), \Sigma, \{\sigma_{g_i}\}_{i=1}^T, \{\sigma_k\}_{k=1}^\ell \right).$$

Join: GM and a joining user u run the following interactive protocol $[\mathsf{J}_{user}(\lambda, \mathcal{Y}),$ $\mathsf{J}_{GM}(\lambda, St, \mathcal{Y}, \mathcal{S}_{GM})]$, which is the same as [7].

1. J_{user} chooses $x \xleftarrow{R} \mathbb{Z}_p$, computes $X = g^x$ and send X to J_{GM}. If $X \in \mathbb{G}$ already appears in the database St_{trans}, J_{GM} halts and returns $\perp$ to J_{user}.

2. J_{GM} assigns to u an available leaf v of identifier $\mathsf{ID}(v)$ in the tree. The corresponding identifiers in the path from the root to v are $I_1 = 1, \ldots, I_\ell = \mathsf{ID}(v) \in \{N, \ldots, 2N - 1\}$. Then J_{GM} does the following.

   a. Commit the vector $(I_1, \ldots, I_\ell)$ as $C_v = \prod_{\kappa=1}^\ell g_{n+1-\kappa}^{I_\kappa}$.

   b. Using $sk_{AHO}^{(2)}$, generate an AHO signature $\sigma_{C_v} = (\vartheta_1, \ldots, \vartheta_7)$ on the pair $(X, C_v) \in \mathbb{G}^2$ to bind C_v to the value X that identifies u.

3. J_{GM} sends $\mathsf{ID}(v)$ and C_v to J_{user} that halts if either of then is found incorrect. Otherwise, J_{user} sends a normal signature sig_u on $X \| (I_1, \ldots, I_\ell)$.

4. J_{GM} checks if the signature is valid. If not, J_{GM} aborts. Otherwise, J_{GM} returns σ_{C_v} to J_{user} and stores $\mathsf{transcript}_u = (X, C_v, \sigma_{C_v}, sig_u)$ in St_{trans}.

5. J_{user} defines the membership certificate as $\mathsf{cert}_u = (\mathsf{ID}(v), X, C_v, \sigma_{C_v}) \in \{N, \ldots, 2N-1\} \times \mathbb{G}^9$. The membership secret sec_u is define as $\mathsf{sec}_u = x \in \mathbb{Z}_p$.

Revoke$(\mathcal{Y}, \mathcal{S}_{GM}, t, \mathcal{R}_t)$: Parse $\mathcal{S}_{GM} := \{sk_{AHO}^{(d)}\}_{d \in \{0,1,2,3\}}$ and do the following.

1. Using the SD method, find a cover of unrevoked users' subsets $S_1, \ldots, S_m$ and let ϕ_i and ψ_i be the level of the primary (P_i) and secondary (S_i) nodes of subset S_i. The ID for these nodes are $\mathsf{ID}(\mathsf{P}_i)$ and $\mathsf{ID}(\mathsf{S}_i)$ respectively. Define the elements of vector of $\vec{\Phi}, \vec{\Psi}, \vec{\mathsf{P}}$, and $\vec{\mathsf{S}}$ are as follows.

$$\vec{\Phi} = (\phi_1, \ldots, \phi_i, \ldots, \phi_m) \qquad \vec{\mathsf{P}} = (\mathsf{ID}(\mathsf{P}_1), \ldots, \mathsf{ID}(\mathsf{P}_i), \ldots, \mathsf{ID}(\mathsf{P}_m))$$

$$\vec{\Psi} = (\psi_1, \ldots, \psi_i, \ldots, \psi_m) \qquad \vec{\mathsf{S}} = (\mathsf{ID}(\mathsf{S}_1), \ldots, \mathsf{ID}(\mathsf{S}_i), \ldots, \mathsf{ID}(\mathsf{S}_m))$$

2. For $\Omega = \lceil m/T \rceil$, partition $S_1, \ldots, S_m$ into Ω sequences with T elements:
$$\vec{S}_1 = (S_1, \ldots, S_T), \vec{S}_2 = (S_{T+1}, \ldots, S_{2T}), \ldots, \vec{S}_\Omega = (S_{(\Omega-1)T+1}, \ldots, S_m).$$
The element of $\vec{\Phi}$ is partitioned as,
$$\vec{\Phi}_1 = (\phi_1, \ldots, \phi_T), \vec{\Phi}_2 = (\phi_{T+1}, \ldots, \phi_{2T}), \ldots, \vec{\Phi}_\Omega = (\phi_{(\Omega-1)T+1}, \ldots, \phi_m),$$
Similarly, the partitions $(\vec{\Psi}_1, \ldots), (\vec{P}_1, \ldots)$, and $(\vec{S}_1, \ldots)$ are obtained.
3. Using the vector commitment, compress the partitions of each elements into:
$$C_{\vec{\Phi}_k} = \prod_{j=1}^{T} g_{n+1-j}^{\phi_{(k-1)T+j}}, \qquad C_{\vec{\Psi}_k} = \prod_{j=1}^{T} g_{n+1-j}^{\psi_{(k-1)T+j}},$$
$$C_{\vec{P}_k} = \prod_{j=1}^{T} g_{n+1-j}^{\mathrm{ID}(P_{(k-1)T+j})}, \qquad C_{\vec{S}_k} = \prod_{j=1}^{T} g_{n+1-j}^{\mathrm{ID}(S_{(k-1)T+j})},$$
for all $1 \le k \le \Omega$.

4. Using $sk_{\mathrm{AHO}}^{(3)}$, generate AHO signatures $\sigma_{\mathrm{RL}_k} = (\Theta_{k,1}, \ldots, \Theta_{k,7})$ on $(t, C_{\vec{\Phi}_k}, C_{\vec{\Psi}_k}, C_{\vec{P}_k}, C_{\vec{S}_k})$ for $1 \le k \le \Omega$, where $t \in \mathbb{Z}_p$ is the epoch number.

Return the revocation list
$$\mathrm{RL}_t = \left(t, \mathcal{R}_t, \{C_{\vec{\Phi}_k}, C_{\vec{\Psi}_k}, C_{\vec{P}_k}, C_{\vec{S}_k}\}_{k=1}^{\Omega}, \{\sigma_{\mathrm{RL}_k} = (\Theta_{k,1}, \ldots, \Theta_{k,7})\}_{k=1}^{\Omega} \right).$$

Sign$(\mathcal{Y}, t, \mathrm{RL}_t, \mathrm{cert}_u, \mathrm{sec}_u, M)$: Return $\perp$ if $u \in \mathcal{R}_t$. Otherwise, to sign $M \in \{0,1\}^*$, generate a one-time signature key pair $(\mathrm{SK}, \mathrm{VK}) \leftarrow \mathcal{G}_\lambda$. Parse cert_u as $(\mathrm{ID}(v_u), X, C_{v_u}, \sigma_{v_u}) \in \{N, \ldots, 2N-1\} \times \mathbb{G}^9$ and sec_u as $x \in \mathbb{Z}_p$. Do the following based on the previous scheme [7], to which step 1, 2 and 3 are added.

1. Using RL_t, find vector commitments $(C_{\vec{\Phi}_k}, C_{\vec{\Psi}_k}, C_{\vec{P}_k}, C_{\vec{S}_k})$ that contains subset S_i, where the user's leaf v_u lies. In commitment $C_{\vec{\Phi}_k}$, assume that the $\tilde{j}$-th component includes ϕ_i, i.e., $i = (k-1)T + \tilde{j}$. This is similar for $C_{\vec{\Psi}_k}, C_{\vec{P}_k}$, and $C_{\vec{S}_k}$. Define $\phi_{k,j} = \phi_i, \psi_{k,j} = \psi_i, P_{k,j} = P_i, S_{k,j} = S_i$. Set $(R_1, R_2, R_3, R_4, \tilde{R}_1, \tilde{R}_2) = (g_1^{\phi_{k,\tilde{j}}}, g_1^{\psi_{k,\tilde{j}}}, g_1^{\mathrm{ID}(P_{k,\tilde{j}})}, g_1^{\mathrm{ID}(S_{k,\tilde{j}})}, g_{\phi_{k,\tilde{j}}}, g_{\psi_{k,\tilde{j}}})$, and set $(\varphi_0, \varphi_{2n}, \tilde{\varphi}_0, \tilde{\varphi}_{2n}) = (g^{\mathrm{ID}(P_{k,\tilde{j}})}, g_{2n}^{\mathrm{ID}(P_{k,\tilde{j}})}, g^{\mathrm{ID}(S_{k,\tilde{j}})}, g_{2n}^{\mathrm{ID}(S_{k,\tilde{j}})})$. Compute GS commitment of all these elements. Then, calculate witnesses for the vector commitments:
$$W_{\vec{\Phi}_k} = \prod_{j=1,j\ne\tilde{j}}^{T} g_{n+1-j+\tilde{j}}^{\phi_{k,j}}, \qquad W_{\vec{\Psi}_k} = \prod_{j=1,j\ne\tilde{j}}^{T} g_{n+1-j+\tilde{j}}^{\psi_{k,j}},$$
$$W_{\vec{P}_k} = \prod_{j=1,j\ne\tilde{j}}^{T} g_{n+1-j+\tilde{j}}^{\mathrm{ID}(P_{k,j})}, \qquad W_{\vec{S}_k} = \prod_{j=1,j\ne\tilde{j}}^{T} g_{n+1-j+\tilde{j}}^{\mathrm{ID}(S_{k,j})},$$
which satisfies the following equalities.
$$e(g_{\tilde{j}}, C_{\vec{\Phi}_k}) = e(R_1, g_n) \cdot e(g, W_{\vec{\Phi}_k}), \quad e(g_{\tilde{j}}, C_{\vec{\Psi}_k}) = e(R_2, g_n) \cdot e(g, W_{\vec{\Psi}_k}), \quad (1)$$
$$e(g_{\tilde{j}}, C_{\vec{P}_k}) = e(R_3, g_n) \cdot e(g, W_{\vec{P}_k}), \quad e(g_{\tilde{j}}, C_{\vec{S}_k}) = e(R_4, g_n) \cdot e(g, W_{\vec{S}_k}). \quad (2)$$
$$e(R_3, g) = e(g_1, \varphi_0), \qquad\qquad e(\varphi_{2n}, g) = e(g_{2n}, \varphi_0). \quad (3)$$
$$e(R_4, g) = e(g_1, \tilde{\varphi}_0), \qquad\qquad e(\tilde{\varphi}_{2n}, g) = e(g_{2n}, \tilde{\varphi}_0). \quad (4)$$

To prove the above opening relations, commit $g_{\tilde{j}}, C_{\vec{\Phi}_k}, C_{\vec{\Psi}_k}, C_{\vec{P}_k}, C_{\vec{S}_k}, W_{\vec{\Phi}_k}, W_{\vec{\Psi}_k}, W_{\vec{P}_k}, W_{\vec{S}_k}$, and compute GS proofs of (1)–(4) as π_{S_i}.

2. To show that $g_{\tilde{j}}$ is correct, re-randomize the AHO signature $\sigma_{g_{\tilde{j}}}$ on $g_{\tilde{j}}$ to $(\theta'_{\tilde{j},1}, \ldots, \theta'_{\tilde{j},7})$, commit $\{\theta_{\tilde{j},i}\}_{i=\{1,2,5\}}$ and compute the GS proofs as follows:

$$A^{(0)} = e(G_z^{(0)}, \theta'_{\tilde{j},1}) \cdot e(G_r^{(0)}, \theta'_{\tilde{j},2}) \cdot e(\theta'_{\tilde{j},3}, \theta'_{\tilde{j},4}) \cdot e(G^{(0)}, g_{\tilde{j}}),$$
$$B^{(0)} = e(H_z^{(0)}, \theta'_{\tilde{j},1}) \cdot e(H_r^{(0)}, \theta'_{\tilde{j},5}) \cdot e(\theta'_{\tilde{j},6}, \theta'_{\tilde{j},7}) \cdot e(H^{(0)}, g_{\tilde{j}}).$$

We denote the above proof by $\pi_{g_{\tilde{j}}}$.

3. To prove that $g_1^{\phi_{k,\tilde{j}}}$ (resp. $g_1^{\psi_{k,\tilde{j}}}$) is mapped to $g_{\phi_{k,\tilde{j}}}$ (resp. $g_{\psi_{k,\tilde{j}}}$), for $\tau \in \{\phi_{k,\tilde{j}}, \psi_{k,\tilde{j}}\}$, re-randomize the AHO signature $\tilde{\sigma}_\tau$ on (g_1^τ, g_τ) to $(\tilde{\theta}'_{\tau,1}, \ldots, \tilde{\theta}'_{\tau,7})$, commit $\{\tilde{\theta}_{\tau,\iota}\}_{\iota=\{1,2,5\}}$, and compute the GS proofs of the following:

$$A^{(1)} = e(G_z^{(1)}, \tilde{\theta}'_{\tau,1}) \cdot e(G_r^{(1)}, \tilde{\theta}'_{\tau,2}) \cdot e(\tilde{\theta}'_{\tau,3}, \tilde{\theta}'_{\tau,4}) \cdot e(G_1^{(1)}, g_1^\tau) \cdot e(G_2^{(1)}, g_\tau),$$
$$B^{(1)} = e(H_z^{(1)}, \tilde{\theta}'_{k_\tau,1}) \cdot e(H_r^{(1)}, \tilde{\theta}'_{\tau,5}) \cdot e(\tilde{\theta}'_{\tau,6}, \tilde{\theta}'_{\tau,7}) \cdot e(H_1^{(1)}, g_1^\tau) \cdot e(H_2^{(1)}, g_\tau),$$

for $\tau \in \{\phi_{k,\tilde{j}}, \psi_{k,\tilde{j}}\}$, where $R_1 = g^\tau$ and $\tilde{R}_1 = g_\tau$ (resp. $R_2 = g^\tau$, $\tilde{R}_2 = g_\tau$) for $\tau = \phi_{k,\tilde{j}}$ (resp. $\tau = \psi_{k,\tilde{j}}$). We denote the above proof by π_{lvl}.

4. To prove that the signer is an unrevoked user of subset S_i with $i = (k-1)T+\tilde{j}$, commit C_v, and do the following, which is the same as [7].

   a. To show that $I_{\phi_{k,\tilde{j}}} = \text{ID}(P_{k,\tilde{j}})$, compute $W_{\phi_{k,\tilde{j}}} = \prod_{l=1,l\neq\phi_{k,\tilde{j}}}^{\ell} g_{n+1-l+\phi_{k,\tilde{j}}}^{I_l}$ that satisfies the equality $e(g_{\phi_{k,\tilde{j}}}, C_v) = e(g_1, g_n)^{I_{\phi_{k,\tilde{j}}}} \cdot e(g, W_{\phi_{k,\tilde{j}}})$. Then, commit $W_{\phi_{k,\tilde{j}}}$, and prove it by the GS proof of this:

   $$e(\tilde{R}_1, C_v) = e(R_3, g_n) \cdot e(g, W_{\phi_{k,\tilde{j}}}).$$

   We denote the above proof by by π_{eq}.

   b. To show that $I_{\psi_{k,\tilde{j}}} \neq \text{ID}(S_{k,\tilde{j}})$, compute $W_{\psi_{k,\tilde{j}}} = \prod_{l=1,l\neq\psi_{k,\tilde{j}}}^{\ell} g_{n+1-l+\psi_{k,\tilde{j}}}^{I_l}$ that satisfies the equality $e(g_{\psi_{k,\tilde{j}}}, C_v) = e(g_1, g_n)^{I_{\psi_{k,\tilde{j}}}} \cdot e(g, W_{\psi_{k,\tilde{j}}})$. Then, commit $W_{\psi_{k,\tilde{j}}}$, and the group elements $(\Gamma, \psi_0, \psi_1, \psi_{2n}) = (g_1^{1/(I_{\psi_{k,\tilde{j}}}-\text{ID}(S_{k,\tilde{j}}))}, g^{I_{\psi_{k,\tilde{j}}}}, g_1^{I_{\psi_{k,\tilde{j}}}}, g_{2n}^{I_{\psi_{k,\tilde{j}}}})$, and compute GS proofs of the following:

   $$e(\tilde{R}_2, C_v) = e(\psi_1, g_n) \cdot e(g, W_{\psi_{k,\tilde{j}}}), \qquad e(\psi_1/R_4, \Gamma) = e(g_1, g_1),$$
   $$e(\psi_1, g) = e(g_1, \psi_0), \qquad\qquad\qquad e(\psi_{2n}, g) = e(g_{2n}, \psi_0).$$

   We denote the above proof by π_{neq}.

5. To prove that $(E_1, E_2, E_3, E_4, E_5) = (t, C_{\overrightarrow{\phi}_k}, C_{\overrightarrow{\psi}_k}, C_{\text{ID}(\overrightarrow{P}_k)}, C_{\text{ID}(\overrightarrow{S}_k)})$ is derived from RL_t, re-randomize AHO signature σ_{RL_k} to $(\Theta'_1, \ldots, \Theta'_7)$ and compute the commitments to $\{E_\tau\}_{\tau=2}^5$ and $\{\Theta_j\}_{j\in\{1,2,5\}}$. Then generate a GS proof π_{RL} proving

$$A^{(3)} = e(G_z^{(3)}, \Theta'_1) \cdot e(G_r^{(3)}, \Theta'_2) \cdot e(\Theta'_3, \Theta'_4) \cdot e(G_1^{(3)}, g^t) \cdot \prod_{\tau=2}^5 e(G_\tau^{(3)}, E_\tau),$$
$$B^{(3)} = e(H_z^{(3)}, \Theta'_1) \cdot e(H_r^{(3)}, \Theta'_5) \cdot e(\Theta'_6, \Theta'_7) \cdot e(H_1^{(3)}, g^t) \cdot \prod_{\tau=2}^5 e(G_\tau^{(3)}, E_\tau).$$

6. Re-randomize AHO signature σ_{C_v} to $(\theta_1', \ldots, \theta_7')$ and compute commitments to $X, \{\theta_j'\}_{j \in \{1,2,5\}}$. Then, generate GS proof π_{C_v} proving:

$$A^{(2)} = e(G_z^{(2)}, \vartheta_1') \cdot e(G_r^{(2)}, \vartheta_2') \cdot e(\vartheta_3', \vartheta_4') \cdot e(G_1^{(2)}, X) \cdot e(G_2^{(2)}, C_v),$$
$$B^{(2)} = e(H_z^{(2)}, \vartheta_1') \cdot e(H_r^{(2)}, \vartheta_5') \cdot e(\vartheta_6', \vartheta_7') \cdot e(H_1^{(2)}, X) \cdot e(H_2^{(2)}, C_v).$$

7. The following steps are the same as in [7]. Using VK as a tag, compute a tag-based encryption of X, denoted as Υ.
8. Generate a GS proof to show the knowledge of X, denoted as π_X, as in [7].
9. Compute a weakly secure Boneh-Boyen signature $\sigma_{\text{VK}} = g^{1/(x+\text{VK})}$ on VK and a commitment to σ_{VK}. Then generate a GS proof $\pi_{\sigma_{\text{VK}}}$ of the verification of σ_{VK}.
10. Compute a one-time signature $\sigma_{ots} = \mathcal{S}(\text{SK}, (M, \text{RL}_t, \Upsilon, \Omega, \text{com}, \Pi))$ where Ω consists of ι-th component for re-randomized $\sigma_{g_{\bar{\jmath}}}, \sigma_{\phi_i}, \sigma_{\psi_i}, \sigma_{\text{RL}_k}, \sigma_{C_v}$ for $\iota = 3, 4, 6, 7$. **com** consists of all commitments, and Π consists of all GS proofs.

Return the signature $\sigma = (\text{VK}, \Upsilon, \Omega, \text{com}, \Pi, \sigma_{ots})$.

Verify$(\sigma, M, t, \text{RL}_t, \mathcal{Y})$: If the one-time signature in σ is verified as invalid or if tag-based encryption is not well-formed, return 0. Then, return 1 if all GS proofs are properly verified. Otherwise, return 0.

Open$(M, t, \text{RL}_t, \sigma, \mathcal{S}_{\text{OA}}, \mathcal{Y}, S_t)$: Return $\perp$ if Verify$(\sigma, M, t, \text{RL}_t, \mathcal{Y}) = 0$. Otherwise, decrypt Υ to get $\hat{X}$, and in the database S_{trans}, find a record $\langle u,$ transcript$_u = (X_u, \text{ID}(v_u), C_{v_u}, \sigma_{v_u}, sig_u) \rangle$ s.t. $X_u = \hat{X}$. If no such record exist in S_{trans}, return $\perp$. Otherwise, return u.

5.3 Security Discussion

Here, due to the page limitation, we only show the proof sketch of the security against misidentification attack. The proofs of security against framing attack and anonymity are similar to the previous scheme [7].

Theorem 1. *The scheme is secure against the misidentification attacks assuming that q-SFP and the n-FlexDHE problems are both hard.*

Proof sketch. This proof is derived from [7]. Assume that the adversary $\mathcal{A}_{\text{mis}}$ outputs a non-trivial signature σ^* that does not open to unrevoked adversarially-controlled group member. Depending on the context of extractable commitments in the forged signature σ^*, similarly to [7], we categorize the followings: (a) the forgery of certificates $\sigma_{v_u}, \sigma_{g_{\bar{\jmath}}}, \sigma_{\phi_i}, \sigma_{\psi_i}, \sigma_{\text{RL}_k}$, (b) the improper opening of $C_{\vec{\Phi}_k}$, $C_{\vec{\Psi}_k}, C_{\vec{P}_k}, C_{\vec{S}_k}$, and (c) $I_{\phi_{k,\bar{\jmath}}} \neq \text{ID}(\text{P}_{k,\bar{\jmath}})$ or $I_{\psi_{k,\bar{\jmath}}} = \text{ID}(\text{S}_{k,\bar{\jmath}})$ due to the improper opening of C_v.

As in [7], if any of the signatures in (a) is forged, it means a forgery against the AHO signature, which contradicts the q-SFP assumption. Therefore, we next consider the forgery where all AHO signatures are correctly issued, but any opening of vector commitments in (b) is done improperly. In this case,

σ^* provides the extracted committed values satisfying Eqs. (1)–(4). Then, we can construct an adversary $\mathcal{A}_{\mathrm{DHE}}$ or $\mathcal{A}_{\mathrm{FlexDHE}}$ against n-DHE or n-FlexDHE problem, using $\mathcal{A}_{\mathrm{mis}}$. The adversary knows the values $\phi, \psi \in \{1, \dots, \ell\}$ s.t. $R_1 = g_1^{\phi}$ and $R_2 = g_1^{\psi}$, since valid AHO signatures σ_{ϕ} and σ_{ψ} on them are issued. Similarly, the correctness of $g_{\tilde{j}}$ in (1) and (2) is assured by the AHO signature $\sigma_{g_{\tilde{j}}}$ on $g_{\tilde{j}}$. Thus, as in proof of [7] (the opening of $\mathrm{ID}(\mathsf{P}_i)$ in C_v), from the improper opening of $C_{\overrightarrow{\Phi}_k}$ or $C_{\overrightarrow{\Psi}_k}$, we can construct $\mathcal{A}_{\mathrm{DHE}}$ which means that $\mathcal{A}_{\mathrm{FlexDHE}}$ exists. On the other hand, in case of improper opening of $C_{\overrightarrow{\mathsf{P}}_k}$, $C_{\overrightarrow{\mathsf{S}}_k}$, the exponents of R_3, R_4 are unknown. Thus, Eqs. (3) and (4) are added for solving the n-FlexDHE assumption as in [7]. In this case, as in the proof of [7] (the opening of $\mathrm{ID}(\mathsf{S}_i)$ in C_v), we can construct $\mathcal{A}_{\mathrm{FlexDHE}}$.

The remaining case is that all the AHO signatures are correctly issued ones and the opening of $C_{\overrightarrow{\Phi}_k}$, $C_{\overrightarrow{\Psi}_k}$, $C_{\overrightarrow{\mathsf{P}}_k}$, and $C_{\overrightarrow{\mathsf{S}}_k}$ is correct, but (c) the opening of C_v is improper which means $I_{\phi_{k,\tilde{j}}} \neq \mathrm{ID}(\mathsf{P}_{k,\tilde{j}})$ or $I_{\psi_{k,\tilde{j}}} = \mathrm{ID}(\mathsf{S}_{k,\tilde{j}})$. Note that $\tilde{R}_1 = g_{\phi_{k,\tilde{j}}}$, $\tilde{R}_2 = g_{\psi_{k,\tilde{j}}}$ are ensured, due to the AHO signature $\sigma_{\phi_{k,\tilde{j}}}$ (resp., $\sigma_{\psi_{k,\tilde{j}}}$) on the pair $(g_1^{\phi_{k,\tilde{j}}}, g_{\phi_{k,\tilde{j}}})$ (resp., $(g_1^{\psi_{k,\tilde{j}}}, g_{\psi_{k,\tilde{j}}})$). In this case, the proof is the same as in [7]. $\square$

6   Efficiency Consideration

This section compares revocable group signature schemes with compact RL and [7]. Comparisons are given in Table 1 in terms of computational costs and the size (measured by the number of group elements) of public keys, signatures, membership certificates and revocation list. Let N be the maximum number of users, R be the number of revoked users, R' be the maximum number of revoked users, and T be the compression parameter.

From Table 1, the proposed scheme reduces the RL size from $O(R)$ to $O(R/T)$, which is the same as the scheme of [9]. In case of $R = 10,000$ and $T = 100$, the proposed scheme reduces the RL from about 8 MB in [7] to about 70 KB in 128-bit security. The advantages against [9] are the reduction from $O(T \log N)$ to $O(T + \log N)$ of the public key size, and from $O(T)$ to $O(1)$ of the membership certificate size. Compared to [2,7], our proposed scheme has a signing time of $O(T)$, due to the W computations of vector commitment. The signing time is a trade-off to the RL size, and T can be set such that the two are balanced. The scheme [2] has a constant RL size and group PK size, but the scheme has $O(R)$ signing time and $O(R')$ membership certificate size. We

Table 1. Comparisons of revocable group signatures schemes.

	Group PK size	Sig size	Membership cert. size	Revocation list size	Signing time	Verifying time	Revocation time
[7]	$O(\log N)$	$O(1)$	$O(1)$	$O(R)$	$O(1)$	$O(1)$	$O(R)$
[9]	$O(T \log N)$	$O(1)$	$O(T)$	$O(R/T)$	$O(T)$	$O(1)$	$O(R \log N)$
[2]	$O(1)$	$O(1)$	$O(R')$	$O(1)$	$O(R)$	$O(1)$	$O(R)$
This work	$O(T + \log N)$	$O(1)$	$O(1)$	$O(R/T)$	$O(T)$	$O(1)$	$O(R)$

consider that our proposed scheme is more efficient in the mobile environment, due to lower user computation time and storage.

7 Conclusion

In this paper, we have proposed a revocable group signature scheme with a compact revocation list, where the vector commitments compress the data in the revocation list. Our future work includes decreasing the overhead in signing.

Acknowledgments. This work was partially supported by JSPS KAKENHI Grant Number 16K00187.

References

1. Abe, M., Fuchsbauer, G., Groth, J., Haralambiev, K., Ohkubo, M.: Structure-preserving signatures and commitments to group elements. In: Rabin, T. (ed.) CRYPTO 2010. LNCS, vol. 6223, pp. 209–236. Springer, Heidelberg (2010). doi:10.1007/978-3-642-14623-7_12
2. Attrapadung, N., Emura, K., Hanaoka, G., Sakai, Y.: Group signature with constant-size revocation list. Comput. J. **58**(10), 2698–2715 (2015)
3. Boneh, D., Boyen, X., Shacham, H.: Short group signatures. In: Franklin, M. (ed.) CRYPTO 2004. LNCS, vol. 3152, pp. 41–55. Springer, Heidelberg (2004). doi:10.1007/978-3-540-28628-8_3
4. Boneh, D., Boyen, X.: Short signatures without random oracles. In: Cachin, C., Camenisch, J.L. (eds.) EUROCRYPT 2004. LNCS, vol. 3027, pp. 56–73. Springer, Heidelberg (2004). doi:10.1007/978-3-540-24676-3_4
5. Camenisch, J., Kohlweiss, M., Soriente, C.: An accumulator based on bilinear maps and efficient revocation for anonymous credentials. In: Jarecki, S., Tsudik, G. (eds.) PKC 2009. LNCS, vol. 5443, pp. 481–500. Springer, Heidelberg (2009). doi:10.1007/978-3-642-00468-1_27
6. Groth, J., Sahai, A.: Efficient non-interactive proof systems for bilinear groups. In: Smart, N. (ed.) EUROCRYPT 2008. LNCS, vol. 4965, pp. 415–432. Springer, Heidelberg (2008). doi:10.1007/978-3-540-78967-3_24
7. Libert, B., Peters, T., Yung, M.: Group signatures with almost-for-free revocation. In: Safavi-Naini, R., Canetti, R. (eds.) CRYPTO 2012. LNCS, vol. 7417, pp. 571–589. Springer, Heidelberg (2012). doi:10.1007/978-3-642-32009-5_34
8. Libert, B., Yung, M.: Concise mercurial vector commitments and independent zero-knowledge sets with short proofs. In: Micciancio, D. (ed.) TCC 2010. LNCS, vol. 5978, pp. 499–517. Springer, Heidelberg (2010). doi:10.1007/978-3-642-11799-2_30
9. Nakanishi, T., Funabiki, N.: Revocable group signatures with compact revocation list using accumulators. In: Lee, H.-S., Han, D.-G. (eds.) ICISC 2013. LNCS, vol. 8565, pp. 435–451. Springer, Cham (2014). doi:10.1007/978-3-319-12160-4_26
10. Naor, D., Naor, M., Lotspiech, J.: Revocation and tracing schemes for stateless receivers. In: Kilian, J. (ed.) CRYPTO 2001. LNCS, vol. 2139, pp. 41–62. Springer, Heidelberg (2001). doi:10.1007/3-540-44647-8_3
11. Izabachène, M., Libert, B., Vergnaud, D.: Block-wise p-signatures and non-interactive anonymous credentials with efficient attributes. In: Chen, L. (ed.) IMACC 2011. LNCS, vol. 7089, pp. 431–450. Springer, Heidelberg (2011). doi:10.1007/978-3-642-25516-8_26

The Quantum-Safe Revolution

Jean-Charles Faugère[1] and Ludovic Perret[2][✉]

[1] Inria, Paris Center, Sorbonne Universités, UPMC Univ Paris 06, Équipe PolSys,
LIP6, 75005 Paris, France
`jean-charles.faugere@inria.fr`
[2] CNRS, UMR 7606, LIP6, 75005 Paris, France
`ludovic.perret@lip6.fr`

Abstract. This paper is a position paper based on an invited talk at
WISA'16 in Korea. We argue that Quantum-Safe Cryptography (QSC)
will likely have a deep impact on the practice of IT professionals. We
detail also in the second part a classical candidate for quantum-safe cryptography: multivariate cryptography. Finally, we conclude by presenting
HFEBoost a real-life deployment of multivariate cryptography.

1 Introduction

The goal of *Quantum-Safe* (or *post-quantum*) cryptography[1] is to design cryptographic primitives which are secure against a classical and quantum adversary.
This is a classical academic topic mainly motivated by Shor's milestone quantum algorithm [55]. Indeed, although no classical polynomial-time algorithm has
been found for the number theoretic cryptographic problems used in practice –
such as integer factorization (FACT), e.g., in RSA, and discrete logarithm (DLOG),
e.g., in the Diffie-Hellman key-exchange – Shor's algorithm allows to solve DLOG
and FACT in polynomial-time on a quantum computer.

Quantum-Safe Cryptography (QSC) is an active cryptographic topic which
started soon after Shor's algorithm. Today, it is commonly admitted that the
most promising quantum-safe cryptosystems include [7, 24]: Quantum-Key Distribution (QKD, [4]), code-based cryptosystems [46], hash-based cryptosystems
[13, 34], isogeny-based cryptography [28, 36], lattice-based [40] cryptosystems and
finally multivariate-based cryptosystems [20].

Among this list, QKD is different from the others techniques. It is not based
on the hardness of an algorithmic problem but rather on a physical assumption.
It can be also mentioned that finding isogenies between supersingular curves
[28, 36] is the youngest algorithmic problem introduced in QSC; the first paper
[36] by Di Feo and Jao dates of 2011.

The status of quantum-safe cryptography is currently completely changing.
It is quickly moving from a purely academic theme to a topic of major industrial interest. As such, this can be considered as a revolution. This new industrial
interest is mainly driven by the fact that quantum-safe cryptography has received

---

[1] We prefer to use quantum-safe cryptography in this document.

© Springer International Publishing AG 2017
D. Choi and S. Guilley (Eds.): WISA 2016, LNCS 10144, pp. 258–266, 2017.
DOI: 10.1007/978-3-319-56549-1_22

recently much attention from the standardization and policy spectrum. The trigger event is the announcement in August 2015 by the National Security Agency (NSA) of preliminary plans for a transition to quantum resistant algorithms[2]:

> *"Currently, Suite B cryptographic algorithms are specified by the National Institute of Standards and Technology (NIST) and are used by NSA's Information Assurance Directorate in solutions approved for protecting classified and unclassified National Security Systems (NSS). Below, we announce preliminary plans for transitioning to* **quantum resistant** *algorithms."*

This was quickly followed by an announcement of NIST which detailed the transition process. NIST, which has the authority to establish the security standards of the US government, released in January 2016 a call to select standards for quantum-safe public-key cryptosystems: public-key exchange, signature and public-key encryption [14,45]. With historical perspective, for example with the Advanced Encryption Standard, it seems likely that the quantum-safe standards derived from this process will be widely endorsed around the world.

In parallel of the US process, Europe is also at the forefront of quantum-safe standardization with an industry specification group (ISG) on QKD[3] and a more recent ISG on quantum-safe cryptography[4]; the latter focusing more on algorithmic techniques. It can be emphasized the ISG-QSC already organized four "Quantum-Safe Cryptography" workshops[5]. We also mention that the International Standardization Organization (ISO SC 27/WG 2) is currently in a study period on quantum-safe cryptography. Industry-based think-tank such as the Cloud Security Alliance is also contributing to raise awareness on QSC with an industry group dedicated[6] to quantum-safe security. This group released for instance a glossary of terms used in QSC. To complete the world tour, we mention that Asia recently started a dedicated forum on quantum-safe cryptography[7].

Since January 2016, NIST has engaged the international community to submit their proposals for quantum-safe public-key exchange, quantum-safe signature and quantum-safe public-key encryption. It seems that the intention of NIST is not to take a single winner for each category but to select a certain number of admissible candidates. NIST will receive candidates until November, 2017 and envision a study period of 5 years to select candidates.

At this stage, it is really difficult to anticipate possible winners. What is clear is that the new standards will have different features that the currently deployed cryptography. In any case, QSC will likely have a deep impact on the practice of IT professionals [38,42].

Among quantum-safe candidates, it is probably fair to say that multivariate cryptography is not the most popular. Until the mid 2000's, multivariate

---

[2] https://www.nsa.gov/ia/programs/suiteb_cryptography/.

[3] https://portal.etsi.org/tb.aspx?tbid=723&SubTB=723.

[4] https://portal.etsi.org/tb.aspx?tbid=836&SubTB=836.

[5] http://www.etsi.org/news-events/events/949-etsi-iqc-4.

[6] https://cloudsecurityalliance.org/group/quantum-safe-security/.

[7] http://cps.cqu.edu.cn/.

cryptography was developing very rapidly, producing many interesting and versatile design ideas such as C* [39], HFE [48], SFLASH [16], UOV [37], TTM [41], TTS [59], Rainbow [19]. However, some of them were successfully cryptanalysed [8,9,25,26,31,39,56]. The biggest surprise was probably the break of SFLASH in 2007 [21], shortly after it was chosen by the NESSIE European Consortium [44] as one of the three recommended public-key signature schemes. As a consequence, the confidence in multivariate cryptography declined, and so did the research in this area as well.

Now, several years later, there have emerged new important reasons for renewal of the interest in multivariate cryptography. After an intense period of activity, it appears that few schemes resisted to the taste of time: typically, UOV [37] and variants of HFE such as the *minus variant* (HFE-,[48]) and the *vinegar variant* (HFEv,[49,51]). Historically, multivariate cryptography has been always more successful in the design of (short) signature schemes. Typically, QUARTZ [49] is a multivariate signature scheme also submitted to NESSIE [44], but not selected (SFLASH has probably be chosen instead). QUARTZ has a public-key of 71 KBytes for a security level initially estimated of 82 bits. The main feature of QUARTZ is to provide very short signatures, i.e. 128 bits for the parameters proposed initially [49].

A challenge for QSC in general is now to show that it can be used at large scale on various devices. We describe below a project, called HFEBoost[8], that we developed together with a startup WASSA[9] and SATT LUTECH[10] which is an accelerating technology transfer unit from UPMC. The goal was to develop a simple quantum-safe key-transport application using multivariate cryptography on a Android smartphone. The application has been tested in a real-life scenario by French military.

2   Multivariate Public-Key Cryptography (MPKC) and HFEBoost

Multivariate cryptography is commonly defined as the set of cryptographic schemes using the computational hardness of solving a set of non-linear equations:

Polynomial System Solving over a Finite Field (PoSSo_q)
Input. $p_1(x_1, \ldots, x_n), \ldots, p_m(x_1, \ldots, x_n) \in \mathbb{F}_q[x_1, \ldots, x_n]$.
Goal. Find – if any – a vector $(z_1, \ldots, z_n) \in \mathbb{F}_q^n$ such that:

$$p_1(z_1, \ldots, z_n) = 0, \ldots, p_m(z_1, \ldots, z_n) = 0.$$

It is well-known that PoSSo_q is a NP-hard problem [30]. As a consequence, it is unlikely that it can be solved in quantum polynomial-time [3].

---

[8] http://www-polsys.lip6.fr/Links/hfeboost.html.
[9] http://www.wassa.fr.
[10] http://www.sattlutech.com/en/.

Most basic cryptographic primitives can be constructed in multivariate cryptography: hash-function [10], stream-cipher [5,6], Zero-Knowledge authentication scheme [32,43,53,54], asymmetric encryption, for instance [1,2,27,39,48], and signature [19,35,37,48] among others. Few more advanced cryptographic primitives can also be constructed in multivariate cryptography. We mention for instance a threshold ring signature [50], a group signature [60], a fully-homomorphic scheme [1], ...

Historically, the first multivariate scheme – known as C^* – has been proposed by Matsumoto and Imai [39]. C^* permits to perform public-key encryption as well as signature. Unfortunately, this scheme has been completely broken by Patarin [47]. However, the general principle inspired a whole generation of researchers that proposed improved variants of the Matsumoto-Imai (MI) principle, e.g. [16,19,37,48,49]. The Hidden Field Equations (HFE) cryptosystem [48] is probably one of the most popular in MPKC. In HFE, the public-key $\mathbf{p} = (p_1, \ldots, p_n) \in \mathbb{F}_q[x_1, \ldots, x_n]^n$ is obtained from a particular univariate $\mathbb{F}_{q^n}[X]$:

Definition 1. *Let $D > 0$ be an integer, and q be prime. A polynomial $F \in \mathbb{F}_{q^n}[X]$ has a HFE-shape if it has the following structure:*

$$F = \sum_{\substack{0 \leqslant i \leqslant j < n \\ q^i + q^j \leqslant D}} A_{i,j} X^{q^i + q^j} + \sum_{\substack{0 \leqslant i < n \\ q^i \leqslant D}} B_i X^{q^i} + C, \tag{1}$$

with $A_{i,j}, B_i, C \in \mathbb{F}_{q^n}, \forall i, j, 0 \leqslant i, j < n$.

From now on, we always assume that q is a prime. The special structure (1) allows to have only quadratic polynomials in its (multivariate) $\mathbb{F}_q$-representation. Namely, let $(\theta_1, \ldots, \theta_n) \in (\mathbb{F}_{q^n})^n$ be a basis of $\mathbb{F}_{q^n}$ over $\mathbb{F}_q$ and $\varphi : V = \sum_{i=1}^n v_i \theta_i \in \mathbb{F}_{q^n} \longrightarrow \varphi(V) = (v_1, \ldots, v_n) \in \mathbb{F}_q^n$. We can now define a set of multivariate polynomials $\mathbf{f} = (f_1, \ldots, f_n) \in (\mathbb{F}_q[x_1, \ldots, x_n])^n$ derived from $F \in \mathbb{F}_{q^n}[X]$:

$$F(\varphi^{-1}(x_1, \ldots, x_n)) = \varphi^{-1}(f_1, \ldots, f_n)$$

$$F\left(\sum_{i=1}^n \theta_i x_i\right) = \sum_{i=1}^n \theta_i f_i.$$

The polynomials $f_1, \ldots, f_n \in \mathbb{F}_q[x_1, \ldots, x_n]^n$ are the components of $F \in \mathbb{F}_{q^n}[X]$ over $\mathbb{F}_q$. In Algorithm 1, we describe the HFE public-key encryption. The very same (secret-key, public-key) pair can be used to construct a digital signature. A signature $\mathbf{s} \in \mathbb{F}_q^n$ is valid for a given digest $\mathbf{d} \in \mathbb{F}_q^n$ if $\mathbf{p}(\mathbf{s}) = \mathbf{d}$. We generate a signature $\mathbf{s} \in \mathbb{F}_q^n$ by applying the decryption process to $\mathbf{d} \in \mathbb{F}_q^n$.

The decryption (resp. signature generation) step in HFE is then essentially equivalent to find the roots of a polynomial as in (1). We recall below the classical complexity result for finding the roots of an univariate polynomial with the Cantor-Zassenhaus algorithm [57, Corollary 14.16]:

Algorithm 1. Hidden Field Equations (HFE) Public-Key Encryption [48]

PARAMETERS. size of the field q, number of variables n, and degree of the univariate polynomial D.
Plaintext space: $\mathbb{F}_2^n$. Ciphertext space: $\mathbb{F}_2^n$.

KEYGEN. We randomly select a polynomial $F \in \mathbb{F}_{q^n}[X]$ of degree D with a HFE-shape as in (1) and $\mathbf{f} = (f_1, \ldots, f_n) \in (\mathbb{F}_q[x_1, \ldots, x_n])^n$ such that $F\left(\sum_{i=1}^n \theta_i x_i\right) = \sum_{i=1}^n \theta_i f_i$. We also randomly select $(\mathbf{S}, \mathbf{T}) \in \mathrm{GL}_n(\mathbb{F}_q) \times \mathrm{GL}_n(\mathbb{F}_q)$.

PRIVATE-KEY. $F \in \mathbb{F}_{q^n}[X]$ and $(\mathbf{S}, \mathbf{T}) \in \mathrm{GL}_n(\mathbb{F}_q) \times \mathrm{GL}_n(\mathbb{F}_q)$.
PUBLIC-KEY. It is given by:

$$\mathbf{p} = (g_1, \ldots, g_n) = \big(f_1((x_1, \ldots, x_n)\,\mathbf{S}), \ldots, f_n((x_1, \ldots, x_n)\,\mathbf{S})\big)\mathbf{T}. \qquad (2)$$

DECRYPT.

1: Input $\mathbf{c} \in \mathbb{F}_q^n$

ENCRYPT.

2: Compute $C' = \varphi^{-1}(\mathbf{c}\,\mathbf{T}^{-1})$
3: Compute the roots $\underline{Z} \in \mathbb{F}_{q^n}$ of:

1: Input $\mathbf{m} \in \mathbb{F}_q^n$
2: Output $\mathbf{c} = \mathbf{p}(\mathbf{m}) \in \mathbb{F}_q^n$.

$$F(\underline{Z}) - C' = 0. \qquad (3)$$

4: Output $\varphi(Z) \cdot \mathbf{S}^{-1}$

Theorem 1. *Let $F \in \mathbb{F}_p[X]$ be an univariate polynomial of degree $\leq D$. We can find all the roots of F using an expected number of $\tilde{O}(D\log(p))$ operations over $\mathbb{F}_p$.*

In HFE, we have that $p = q^n$. Assuming that q is a constant, the roots of $F \in \mathbb{F}_{q^n}[X]$ can be found in $\tilde{O}(nD)$. As a consequence, a HFE polynomial has to be chosen of moderate degree for being efficiently solvable. To fix the ideas on the degree that can be considered in practice, we provide below some timings of the roots finding function Roots of MAGMA (v. 2.21) [11] applied on a random HFE-polynomial $F \in \mathbb{F}_{2^n}[X]$ of degree D. We have performed the experiments on a MacBook Air, Intel dual-core i5 1.6 GHz with 4 GB of RAM. The timings are obtained by taking the average time of Roots on 100 calls.

D	129	257	513	1025	1280	2049	4097	8193	16385	32769
$n = 128$	0.1 s	0.21 s	0.55 s	1.55 s	6.63 s	7.36 s	13.82 s	30.28 s	61.47 s	132.09 s

Over the years, the security of HFE has been thoroughly investigated, for instance [9,12,15,17,18,22,23,25,26,33]. The major observation is that the complexity of the best attacks against HFE are all exponential in $O(\log_q(D))$. We have then only one parameter which allows to control the security and efficiency of the scheme.

The challenge in HFE is to find parameters which permit security and efficiency. To do so, we have designed a variant HFE- that we have called HFEBoost. It is a careful choice of the parameters with a particular, somewhat sparse, secret univariate polynomial. The Android application has been tested during real experiments performed by French army. The goal was to test the next generation of communication systems. Our application was only a small part of these experiments. Anyway, the application has been deployed on the smartphones (Samsung Galaxy S5) of around 100 participants (military, national security, DGA, ...) and experimented in various operational scenarios. The experiments were performed through a home-made 4G network deployed on a dedicated site.

For a security level of 80 bits, HFEBoost has a public-key of 130 Kbytes. The first lesson learned is that no problem has been reported regarding the size of the public-key and its transmission on the 4G channel. The time for performing a key-transport is currently 0.7 s on a Galaxy S5. The key-transport can be performed in ≈ 0.18 s on Mac book pro laptop. The application is still a proof-of-concept and performances could be improved (typically, by using special 64 bits instructions available now in the Galaxy S6). Still, the second lesson learned is that smartphones are now very powerful. Probably the biggest information is that MPKC could be used in real-life applications.

Acknowledgment. We would like to thank the attendees of WISA'16 for preliminaries comments on the "quantum-safe revolution" as well as the PC-Chairs for inviting us to write on this topic (and in particular S. Guilley for his comments/feedbacks on this paper).

References

1. Albrecht, M.R., Farshim, P., Faugère, J.-C., Perret, L.: Polly cracker, revisited. In: Lee, D.H., Wang, X. (eds.) ASIACRYPT 2011. LNCS, vol. 7073, pp. 179–196. Springer, Heidelberg (2011). doi:10.1007/978-3-642-25385-0_10
2. Barkee, B., Can, D.C., Ecks, J., Moriarty, T., Ree, R.F.: Why you cannot even hope to use Gröbner bases in public key cryptography: an open letter to a scientist who failed and a challenge to those who have not yet failed. J. Symbolic Comput. **18**(6), 497–501 (1994)
3. Bennett, C.H., Bernstein, E., Brassard, G., Vazirani, U.V.: Strengths and weaknesses of quantum computing. SIAM J. Comput. **26**(5), 1510–1523 (1997)
4. Bennett, C.H., Brassard, G.: Quantum cryptography: public key distribution and coin tossing. Theor. Comput. Sci. **560**, 7–11 (2014)
5. Berbain, C., Gilbert, H., Patarin, J.: QUAD: a practical stream cipher with provable security. In: Vaudenay, S. (ed.) EUROCRYPT 2006. LNCS, vol. 4004, pp. 109–128. Springer, Heidelberg (2006). doi:10.1007/11761679_8
6. Berbain, C., Gilbert, H., Patarin, J.: QUAD: a multivariate stream cipher with provable security. J. Symb. Comput. **44**(12), 1703–1723 (2009)
7. Bernstein, D.J., Buchmann, J., Dahmen, E. (eds.): Post-Quantum Cryptography. Mathematics and Statistics Springer-11649; ZDB-2-SMA. Springer, Heidelberg (2009)
8. Bettale, L., Faugère, J.-C., Perret, L.: Hybrid approach for solving multivariate systems over finite fields. J. Math. Crypt. **3**(3), 177–197 (2010)

9. Bettale, L., Faugère, J.-C., Perret, L.: Cryptanalysis of HFE, Multi-HFE and variants for odd and even characteristic. Des. Codes Crypt. **69**(1), 1–52 (2013)

10. Billet, O., Robshaw, M.J.B., Peyrin, T.: On building hash functions from multivariate quadratic equations. In: Pieprzyk, J., Ghodosi, H., Dawson, E. (eds.) ACISP 2007. LNCS, vol. 4586, pp. 82–95. Springer, Heidelberg (2007). doi:10.1007/978-3-540-73458-1_7

11. Bosma, W., Cannon, J.J., Playoust, C.: The Magma algebra system I: the user language. J. Symbolic Comput. **24**(3–4), 235–265 (1997)

12. Bouillaguet, C., Fouque, P.-A., Joux, A., Treger, J.: A family of weak keys in HFE and the corresponding practical key-recovery. J. Math. Crypt. **5**(3–4), 247–275 (2012)

13. Buchmann, J., Dahmen, E., Szydlo, M.: Hash-based digital signature schemes. In: Bernstein, D.J., Buchmann, J., Dahmen, E. (eds.) Post-Quantum Cryptography, pp. 35–93. Springer, Heidelberg (2009)

14. Chen, L., Jordan, S., Liu, Y.-K., Moody, D., Peralta, R., Perlner, R., Smith-Tone, D.: Report on post-quantum cryptography. Reasearch report NISTIR 8105, NIST (2003)

15. Courtois, N.T., Daum, M., Felke, P.: On the security of HFE, HFEv- and Quartz. In: Desmedt, Y.G. (ed.) PKC 2003. LNCS, vol. 2567, pp. 337–350. Springer, Heidelberg (2003). doi:10.1007/3-540-36288-6_25

16. Courtois, N.T., Goubin, L., Patarin, J.: SFLASHv3, a fast asymmetric signature scheme. Cryptology ePrint Archive, Report 2003/211 (2003). http://eprint.iacr.org/2003/211

17. Daniels, T., Smith-Tone, D.: Differential properties of the HFE cryptosystem. In: Mosca, M. (ed.) PQCrypto 2014. LNCS, vol. 8772, pp. 59–75. Springer, Cham (2014). doi:10.1007/978-3-319-11659-4_4

18. Ding, J., Hodges, T.J.: Inverting HFE systems is quasi-polynomial for all fields. In: Rogaway [53], pp. 724–742 (2011)

19. Ding, J., Schmidt, D.: Rainbow, a new multivariable polynomial signature scheme. In: Ioannidis, J., Keromytis, A., Yung, M. (eds.) ACNS 2005. LNCS, vol. 3531, pp. 164–175. Springer, Heidelberg (2005). doi:10.1007/11496137_12

20. Ding, J., Yang, B.-Y.: Multivariate public key cryptography. In: Bernstein, D.J., Buchmann, J., Dahmen, E. (eds.) Post-Quantum Cryptography, pp. 193–241. Springer, Heidelberg (2009)

21. Dubois, V., Fouque, P.-A., Shamir, A., Stern, J.: Practical cryptanalysis of SFLASH. In: Menezes, A. (ed.) CRYPTO 2007. LNCS, vol. 4622, pp. 1–12. Springer, Heidelberg (2007). doi:10.1007/978-3-540-74143-5_1

22. Dubois, V., Gama, N.: The degree of regularity of HFE systems. In: Abe, M. (ed.) ASIACRYPT 2010. LNCS, vol. 6477, pp. 557–576. Springer, Heidelberg (2010). doi:10.1007/978-3-642-17373-8_32

23. Dubois, V., Granboulan, L., Stern, J.: An efficient provable distinguisher for HFE. In: Bugliesi, M., Preneel, B., Sassone, V., Wegener, I. (eds.) ICALP 2006. LNCS, vol. 4052, pp. 156–167. Springer, Heidelberg (2006). doi:10.1007/11787006_14

24. ETSI ISG QSC. Quantum-Safe Cryptography (QSC); Quantum-safe algorithmic framework. http://www.etsi.org/deliver/etsi_gr/QSC/001_099/001/01.01.01_60/gr_QSC001v010101p.pdf

25. Faugère, J.-C.: Algebraic cryptanalysis of HFE using Gröbner bases. Reasearch report RR-4738, INRIA (2003)

26. Faugère, J.-C., Joux, A.: Algebraic cryptanalysis of Hidden Field Equation (HFE) cryptosystems using Gröbner Bases. In: Boneh, D. (ed.) CRYPTO 2003. LNCS, vol. 2729, pp. 44–60. Springer, Heidelberg (2003). doi:10.1007/978-3-540-45146-4_3

27. Fellows, M., Koblitz, N.: Combinatorial cryptosystems galore! In: Mullen, G.L., Shiue, P.J.-S. (eds.) Finite Fields: Theory, Applications, and Algorithms, vol. 168. Contemporary Mathematics, pp. 51–61. AMS (1994)

28. De Feo, L., Jao, D., Plût, J.: Towards quantum-resistant cryptosystems from supersingular elliptic curve isogenies. J. Math. Crypt. 8(3), 209–247 (2014)

29. Fischlin, M., Buchmann, J., Manulis, M. (eds.): PKC 2012. LNCS, vol. 7293. Springer, Heidelberg (2012)

30. Garey, M.R., Johnson, D.S.: Computers and Intractability: A Guide to the Theory of NP-Completeness. W.H. Freeman (1979)

31. Goubin, L., Courtois, N.T.: Cryptanalysis of the TTM cryptosystem. In: Okamoto, T. (ed.) ASIACRYPT 2000. LNCS, vol. 1976, pp. 44–57. Springer, Heidelberg (2000). doi:10.1007/3-540-44448-3_4

32. Gouget, A., Patarin, J.: Probabilistic multivariate cryptography. In: Nguyen, P.Q. (ed.) VIETCRYPT 2006. LNCS, vol. 4341, pp. 1–18. Springer, Heidelberg (2006). doi:10.1007/11958239_1

33. Granboulan, L., Joux, A., Stern, J.: Inverting HFE is quasipolynomial. In: Dwork, C. (ed.) CRYPTO 2006. LNCS, vol. 4117, pp. 345–356. Springer, Heidelberg (2006). doi:10.1007/11818175_20

34. Hülsing, A.: Practical forward secure signatures using minimal security assumptions. PhD thesis, Darmstadt University of Technology 2013, pp. 1–101 (2013)

35. Hülsing, A., Rijneveld, J., Samardjiska, S., Schwabe, P.: From 5-pass MQ -based identification to MQ-based signatures. IACR Cryptology ePrint Archive 2016:708 (2016)

36. Jao, D., De Feo, L.: Towards quantum-resistant cryptosystems from supersingular elliptic curve isogenies. In: Yang [59], pp. 19–34 (2011)

37. Kipnis, A., Patarin, J., Goubin, L.: Unbalanced oil and vinegar signature schemes. In: Stern, J. (ed.) EUROCRYPT 1999. LNCS, vol. 1592, pp. 206–222. Springer, Heidelberg (1999). doi:10.1007/3-540-48910-X_15

38. Mailloux, L.O., Lewis, C.D., Riggs, C., Grimaila, M.R.: Post-quantum cryptography: what advancements in quantum computing mean for it professionals. IT Prof. 18(5), 42–47 (2016)

39. Matsumoto, T., Imai, H.: Public quadratic polynomial-tuples for efficient signature-verification and message-encryption. In: Barstow, D., Brauer, W., Brinch Hansen, P., Gries, D., Luckham, D., Moler, C., Pnueli, A., Seegmüller, G., Stoer, J., Wirth, N., Günther, C.G. (eds.) EUROCRYPT 1988. LNCS, vol. 330, pp. 419–453. Springer, Heidelberg (1988). doi:10.1007/3-540-45961-8_39

40. Micciancio, D., Regev, O.: Lattice-based cryptography. In: Bernstein, D.J., Buchmann, J., Dahmen, E. (eds.) Post-Quantum Cryptography, pp. 147–191. Springer, Heidelberg (2009)

41. Moh, T.-T.: A public key system with signature and master key functions. Commun. Algebra 27(5), 2207–2222 (1999)

42. Mosca, M.: Cybersecurity in an era with quantum computers: will we be ready? Cryptology ePrint Archive, Report 2015/1075 (2015). http://eprint.iacr.org/2015/1075

43. Nachef, V., Patarin, J., Volte, E.: Zero-knowledge for multivariate polynomials. Cryptology ePrint Archive, Report 2012/239 (2012). http://eprint.iacr.org/2012/239

44. NESSIE. New european schemes for signatures, integrity, and encryption (2003). https://www.cosic.esat.kuleuven.be/nessie/, Accessed Sept 2014

45. NIST. Proposed submission requirements and evaluation criteria for the post-quantum cryptography standardization process (DRAFT). http://csrc.nist.gov/groups/ST/post-quantum-crypto/documents/call-for-proposals-draft-aug-2016.pdf

46. Overbeck, R., Sendrier, N.: Code-based cryptography. In: Bernstein, D.J., Buchmann, J., Dahmen, E. (eds.) Post-Quantum Cryptography, pp. 95–145. Springer, Heidelberg (2009)

47. Patarin, J.: Cryptanalysis of the Matsumoto and Imai public key scheme of Eurocrypt 1988. In: Coppersmith, D. (ed.) CRYPTO 1995. LNCS, vol. 963, pp. 248–261. Springer, Heidelberg (1995). doi:10.1007/3-540-44750-4_20

48. Patarin, J.: Hidden Fields Equations (HFE) and Isomorphisms of Polynomials (IP): two new families of asymmetric algorithms. In: Maurer, U. (ed.) EUROCRYPT 1996. LNCS, vol. 1070, pp. 33–48. Springer, Heidelberg (1996). doi:10.1007/3-540-68339-9_4

49. Patarin, J., Courtois, N., Goubin, L.: QUARTZ, 128-bit long digital signatures. In: Naccache, D. (ed.) CT-RSA 2001. LNCS, vol. 2020, pp. 282–297. Springer, Heidelberg (2001). doi:10.1007/3-540-45353-9_21

50. Petzoldt, A., Bulygin, S., Buchmann, J.A.: A multivariate based threshold ring signature scheme. Appl. Algebra Eng. Commun. Comput. $24(3$–$4)$, 255–275 (2013)

51. Petzoldt, A., Chen, M.-S., Yang, B.-Y., Tao, C., Ding, J.: Design principles for HFEv- based multivariate signature schemes. In: Iwata, T., Cheon, J.H. (eds.) ASIACRYPT 2015. LNCS, vol. 9452, pp. 311–334. Springer, Heidelberg (2015). doi:10.1007/978-3-662-48797-6_14

52. Rogaway, P. (ed.): CRYPTO 2011. LNCS, vol. 6841. Springer, Heidelberg (2011)

53. Sakumoto, K.: Public-key identification schemes based on multivariate cubic polynomials. In: Fischlin et al. [29], pp. 172–189 (2012)

54. Sakumoto, K., Shirai, T., Hiwatari, H.: Public-key identification schemes based on multivariate quadratic polynomials. In: Rogaway [53], pp. 706–723 (2011)

55. Shor, P.W.: Polynomial-time algorithms for prime factorization and discrete logarithms on a quantum computer. SIAM J. Comput. $26(5)$, 1484–1509 (1997)

56. Thomae, E., Wolf, C.: Cryptanalysis of enhanced TTS, STS and all its variants, or: why cross-terms are important. In: Mitrokotsa, A., Vaudenay, S. (eds.) AFRICACRYPT 2012. LNCS, vol. 7374, pp. 188–202. Springer, Heidelberg (2012). doi:10.1007/978-3-642-31410-0_12

57. von zur Gathen, J., Gerhard, J.: Modern Computer Algebra, 3rd edn. Cambridge University Press, Cambridge (2013)

58. Yang, B.-Y. (ed.): PQCrypto 2011. LNCS, vol. 7071. Springer, Heidelberg (2011)

59. Yang, B.-Y., Chen, J.-M., Chen, Y.-H.: TTS: high-speed signatures on a low-cost smart card. In: Joye, M., Quisquater, J.-J. (eds.) CHES 2004. LNCS, vol. 3156, pp. 371–385. Springer, Heidelberg (2004). doi:10.1007/978-3-540-28632-5_27

60. Yang, G., Tang, S., Yang, L.: A novel group signature scheme based on MPKC. In: Bao, F., Weng, J. (eds.) ISPEC 2011. LNCS, vol. 6672, pp. 181–195. Springer, Heidelberg (2011). doi:10.1007/978-3-642-21031-0_14

New Integral Characteristics of KASUMI Derived by Division Property

Nobuyuki Sugio[1]([✉]), Yasutaka Igarashi[2]([✉]), Toshinobu Kaneko[2]([✉]), and Kenichi Higuchi[2]

[1] NTT DOCOMO, INC., Tokyo, Japan
sugio@nttdocomo.com
[2] Tokyo University of Science, Tokyo, Japan
yasutaka@rs.noda.tus.ac.jp, kaneko@ee.noda.tus.ac.jp

Abstract. Integral cryptanalysis is one of the most powerful attacks on symmetric key ciphers. Todo proposed a novel technique named the *division property* to find efficient integral characteristics. In this paper, we apply this technique to the symmetric key block cipher KASUMI which was developed by modifying MISTY1. It has been used worldwide in the 3-rd generation mobile communication networks. As a result, we found new 4 and 5-round integral characteristics of KASUMI with FL and 6-round characteristics of KASUMI without FL for the first time. We show that 6-round KASUMI with FL is attackable with 2^{57} data complexity and 2^{58} encryptions. The attack of 6-round KASUMI by integral cryptanalysis is the best in terms of time complexity.

Keywords: Integral cryptanalysis · Division property · Symmetric key cipher · KASUMI

1 Introduction

The symmetric key ciphers are widely used in our livelihoods, such as e-mail, IC cards, and mobile phones etc. The symmetric key cipher KASUMI was proposed by European Telecommunications Standards Institute (ETSI), and was standardized by the 3-rd Generation Partnership Project (3GPP) in 2000 [1]. KASUMI has been used in the 3-rd generation mobile communication networks all over the world. It is a 64-bit block cipher algorithm supporting secret key length of 128 bits, which was developed by modifying MISTY1. MISTY1 achieves a provable security against differential cryptanalysis [2] and linear cryptanalysis [11] with round function FO.

The security of symmetric key ciphers are evaluated by finding out the strength against various cryptanalytic methods. Many methods, such as higher order differential attack [15,16], impossible differential attack [6,9], meet-in-the-middle attack [7], related key attack [3,5] etc., were used to evaluate the security of KASUMI. The best single key attack is the meet-in-the-middle attack on the

© Springer International Publishing AG 2017
D. Choi and S. Guilley (Eds.): WISA 2016, LNCS 10144, pp. 267–279, 2017.
DOI: 10.1007/978-3-319-56549-1_23

full-round KASUMI proposed by Jia, which needs 2^{32} chosen plaintexts and $2^{125.5}$ encryptions [7]. In the related-key situation, Biham et al. firstly proposed related-key rectangle attack on the full-round KASUMI, which needs $2^{54.6}$ chosen plaintexts and $2^{76.1}$ encryptions [3]. Dunkelman et al. introduced practical-time related-key attack on the full-round KASUMI with 2^{26} data complexity and 2^{32} encryptions by using sandwich attack [5].

Integral cryptanalysis, which was introduced by Knudsen and Wagner in [8], is one of the most powerful cryptanalytic methods on symmetric key ciphers. It is very important for an attacker to discover integral characteristics of a target cipher. Todo proposed a novel technique named the *division property* to find integral characteristics efficiently, and applied it to the Feistel-type and SPN-type block ciphers [17]. Todo improved this method for MISTY1. As a result, Todo discovered new integral characteristic propagating 6-round output, and showed that the full-round MISTY1 was attackable faster than exhaustive search [18]. KASUMI is a modified version of MISTY1. The key-dependent linear functions FL of KASUMI have 1-bit left rotations additionally, and they are different from those of MISTY1. Consequently, Attackers don't apply this cryptanalytic technique illustrated in [18] to KASUMI straightforwardly. There is an open question whether integral cryptanalysis by the division property is useful to attack on KASUMI or not.

Our contribution: In this paper, we apply integral cryptanalysis by the division property to KASUMI, and show that new 4 and 5-round integral characteristics of KASUMI with FL and 6-round characteristics of KASUMI without FL exist. We analyzed all the propagations through FL function which has 1-bit left rotations and is different from that of MISTY1. Table 4 shows the results. We show that 6-round KASUMI with FL is attackable with 2^{57} data and 2^{58} encryptions. It is 2^{27} times faster than Multidimensional Zero-Correlation attack [19]. This result means that KASUMI has more than one round security margin against integral cryptanalysis, since the recommended number of rounds is eight.

The remainder of this paper is organized as follows. Section 2 illustrates integral cryptanalysis and the definition of division property. Section 3 shows the main structure and components of KASUMI. Section 4 explains the results of integral characteristics derived by the division property. Section 5 illustrates integral cryptanalysis on 6-round KASUMI, and consider the results. Section 6 summarizes this paper.

2   Cryptanalytic Method

2.1   Square Attack and Integral Cryptanalysis

Daemen et al. illustrated a new attack on the block cipher SQUARE, which is called *Square attack*. It works as well for other SQUARE-like ciphers such as AES [13]. We briefly outline it as follows. Considering a bijective S-box which has an m-bit input, attackers prepare 2^m inputs, and get the outputs corresponding to the inputs. If the XOR summation of all the outputs becomes zero, we say that it is balanced with 2^m inputs, which is called the *saturation property* in [10]. Let $\{Y\}$ be an output set which has 2^m elements. Daemen et al. defined four types of properties for the set $\{Y\}$ as follows [4].

- ALL ($\mathcal{A}$): Every value appears the same times in the set $\{Y\}$.
- BALANCE ($\mathcal{B}$): The XOR summation of all the elements of the set $\{Y\}$ becomes 0.
- CONSTANT ($\mathcal{C}$): All elements of the set $\{Y\}$ are arbitrary fixed values.
- UNKNOWN ($\mathcal{U}$): Otherwise.

Knudsen and Wagner proposed integral cryptanalysis [8] by generalizing Square attack [4]. In integral cryptanalysis, we regard the XOR summation of all the outputs as an integral. If an integral of all the elements of set $\{Y\}$ becomes 0 regardless of the value of secret key, we say that the block cipher has an integral property.

Attackers first prepare N chosen plaintexts for an integral characteristic of a reduced-round block cipher, and get the corresponding ciphertexts. Then, they guess the keys which are inserted in the last several rounds, and calculate the XOR summation of N intermediate values which are decrypted from ciphertexts. Finally, they evaluate whether the XOR summation of N intermediate values becomes 0 or not. If the XOR summation does not become 0, they can discard the guessed round key from candidates of the correct key.

2.2 Division Property

Todo redefined four types of integral property: ALL ($\mathcal{A}$), BALANCE ($\mathcal{B}$), CONSTANT ($\mathcal{C}$) and UNKNOWN ($\mathcal{U}$), which was introduced as the *division property* in [17]. We give a brief summary of the division property. See [17] for details to better understand the concept of division property.

In this paper, we use the following notations. For any $a \in GF(2)^n$, the i-th bit of a is expressed as $a[i]$, and the hamming weight w of a is calculated as $w(a) = \sum_{i=1}^{n} a[i]$.

Definition 1 (Bit product function). *A bit product function π_u and $\pi_{\boldsymbol{u}}$ are used to evaluate the division property of a set. Let $\pi_u : GF(2)^n \to GF(2)$ be a function for any $u \in GF(2)^n$. Let $x \in GF(2)^n$ be an input, and let a bit product function $\pi_u(x)$ be the product of $x[i]$ satisfying $u[i] = 1$, i.e., it is defined as follows.*

$$\pi_u(x) := \prod_{i=1}^{n} x[i]^{u[i]} \tag{1}$$

Let $\pi_{\boldsymbol{u}} : GF(2)^{n_1} \times GF(2)^{n_2} \times \cdots \times GF(2)^{n_m} \to GF(2)$ be a function for any $\boldsymbol{u} \in GF(2)^{n_1} \times GF(2)^{n_2} \times \cdots \times GF(2)^{n_m}$. Let $\boldsymbol{x} \in GF(2)^{n_1} \times GF(2)^{n_2} \times \cdots \times GF(2)^{n_m}$ be an input, and $\pi_{\boldsymbol{u}}(\boldsymbol{x})$ is defined as

$$\pi_{\boldsymbol{u}}(\boldsymbol{x}) := \prod_{i=1}^{m} \pi_{u_i}(x_i). \tag{2}$$

Definition 2 (Division Property). *Let* $\{X\}$ *be a set whose elements take a value of* $\boldsymbol{x} \in GF(2)^{n_1} \times GF(2)^{n_2} \times \cdots \times GF(2)^{n_m}$. *Let* $\boldsymbol{k}$ *be an m-dimensional vector, and let* k_i *be the i-th component of vector* $\boldsymbol{k}$ *which takes an integer between 0 and* n_i. *When a set* $\{X\}$ *has the division property* $\mathcal{D}^{n_1, n_2, \ldots, n_m}_{\boldsymbol{k}^{(1)}, \boldsymbol{k}^{(2)}, \ldots, \boldsymbol{k}^{(q)}}$, *it fulfills the following conditions.*

$$\bigoplus_{\boldsymbol{x} \in \{X\}} \pi_{\boldsymbol{u}}(\boldsymbol{x}) = \begin{cases} unknown \ (W(\boldsymbol{u}) \succeq \boldsymbol{k}^{(j)}, \ 1 \le j \le q) \\ 0 \qquad\qquad (Otherwise) \end{cases} \tag{3}$$

where $W(\boldsymbol{u}) = (w(n_1), w(n_2), \cdots, w(n_m))$, *and* $\boldsymbol{k}' \succeq \boldsymbol{k}$ *satisfies* $k_i' \ge k_i$ *for all i.*

The correspondence between integral property and division property is as follows. Assuming that the elements of set $\{X\}$ take a value of $x \in GF(2)^n$, and the set $\{X\}$ has the division property $\mathcal{D}^n_k$. When $k = n$, we have ALL property. When $k = 2$, we have BALANCE property. When $k = 1$, we have UNKNOWN property, respectively.

A bit product function $\pi_{\boldsymbol{u}}(\boldsymbol{x})$ expresses the monomial of degree d ($1 \le d \le n_1 + n_2 + \cdots + n_m$) on $GF(2)$. If a set $\{X\}$ has the division property $\mathcal{D}^{n_1, \ldots, n_m}_{\boldsymbol{k}}$, where the i-th component of vector $\boldsymbol{k}$ is $k_i = (d_i + 1)$, the XOR summation $\bigoplus_{\boldsymbol{x} \in \{X\}} f(\boldsymbol{x})$ for any function $f(\cdot)$ of degree $d = \sum_{i=1}^{m} d_i$ always becomes 0. Thus, the division property enables us to estimate the degree of the outputs. In the above case, we say the set $\{X\}$ has an integral property of function $f(\cdot)$.

When we search for integral characteristics by the division property, we calculate propagation characteristics for a target cipher. The rules are summarized as follows. They are proved in [18].

Rule 1 (Substitution). Let F be a function which consists of m S-boxes. Let d_i be the algebraic degree of the i-th n_i-bits S-box. The input and the output take a value of $GF(2)^{n_1} \times GF(2)^{n_2} \times \cdots \times GF(2)^{n_m}$, and $\{X\}$ and $\{Y\}$ denote the input set and the output set, respectively. Assuming that input set $\{X\}$ has the division property $\mathcal{D}^{n_1, n_2, \ldots, n_m}_{\boldsymbol{k}^{(1)}, \boldsymbol{k}^{(2)}, \ldots, \boldsymbol{k}^{(q)}}$, the division property of the output set $\{Y\}$ has $\mathcal{D}^{n_1, n_2, \ldots, n_m}_{\boldsymbol{k}'^{(1)}, \boldsymbol{k}'^{(2)}, \ldots, \boldsymbol{k}'^{(q)}}$ calculated as follows.

$$k_i'^{(j)} = \left\lceil \frac{k_i^{(j)}}{d_i} \right\rceil \quad \text{for } 1 \le i \le m, \ 1 \le j \le q$$

Rule 2 (Copy). Let F be a copy function, where the input x takes a value of $GF(2)^n$ and the output is calculated as $(y_1, y_2) = (x, x)$. Assuming that the input set $\{X\}$ has the division property $\mathcal{D}^n_k$, the division property of the output set $\{Y\}$ has $\mathcal{D}^{n,n}_{\boldsymbol{k}'^{(1)}, \boldsymbol{k}'^{(2)}, \ldots, \boldsymbol{k}'^{(k+1)}}$ calculated as follows.

$$\boldsymbol{k}'^{(i+1)} = (k - i, i) \ \text{for } 0 \le i \le k$$

Rule 3 (Compression by XOR). Let F be a compressing function by an XOR, where the input (x_1, x_2) takes a value of $GF(2)^n \times GF(2)^n$ and the output is calculated as $y = x_1 \oplus x_2$. Assuming that the input set $\{X\}$ has the division property $\mathcal{D}^{n,n}_{k^{(1)},k^{(2)},\ldots,k^{(q)}}$, the division property of the output set $\{Y\}$ has $\mathcal{D}^{n}_{k'}$ calculated as follows.

$$k' = \min\{k_1^{(1)} + k_2^{(1)}, k_1^{(2)} + k_2^{(2)}, \ldots, k_1^{(q)} + k_2^{(q)}\}$$

If the minimum value of k is larger than n, the propagation characteristic of the division property is aborted.

Rule 4 (Split). Let F be a split function, where the input x takes a value of $GF(2)^n$ and the output is calculated as $x = y_1 \| y_2$, where (y_1, y_2) takes a value of $GF(2)^{n_1} \times GF(2)^{n-n_1}$. Assuming that the input set $\{X\}$ has the division property $\mathcal{D}^n_k$, the division property of the output set $\{Y\}$ has $\mathcal{D}^{n_1,n-n_1}_{k'^{(1)},k'^{(2)},\ldots,k'^{(k+1)}}$ calculated as follows.

$$\boldsymbol{k'^{(i+1)}} = (k - i, i) \text{ for } 0 \leq i \leq k$$

where $(k - i)$ is smaller than or equal to n_1, and i is smaller than or equal to $n - n_1$.

Rule 5 (Concatenation). Let F be a concatenation function, where the input (x_1, x_2) takes a value of $GF(2)^{n_1} \times GF(2)^{n_2}$ and the output is calculated as $y = x_1 \| x_2$. Assuming that the input set $\{X\}$ has the division property $\mathcal{D}^{n_1,n_2}_{k^{(1)},k^{(2)},\ldots,k^{(q)}}$, the division property of the output set $\{Y\}$ is $\mathcal{D}^{n_1+n_2}_{k'}$ calculated as follows.

$$k' = \min\{k_1^{(1)} + k_2^{(1)}, k_1^{(2)} + k_2^{(2)}, \ldots, k_1^{(q)} + k_2^{(q)}\}$$

3   KASUMI

KASUMI is a Feistel type 64-bit block cipher supporting secret key length of 128 bits. KASUMI was selected as an international standard cipher by the 3-rd Generation Partnership Project (3GPP), and it has been used worldwide in mobile communication networks. KASUMI was developed by modifying MISTY1 [12] which achieves a provable security against differential cryptanalysis [2] and linear cryptanalysis [11] with round function FO. The recommended number of rounds is eight.

Figure 1 shows the main structure and components of KASUMI. The round functions FO_i $(1 \leq i \leq 8)$ are 32-bit bijective functions. The input is divided into two 16-bit data, which are transformed by bitwise XOR operations denoted by the symbol $\oplus$ and sub-functions FI_{ij} $(1 \leq j \leq 3)$. FI_{ij} are 16-bit bijective functions. The input is divided into left 9-bit data and right 7-bit data, which are transformed by bitwise XOR operations and substitution tables S7 and S9. The algebraic degrees of S7 and S9 are three and two, respectively. The key dependent linear functions FL_i $(1 \leq i \leq 8)$ are composed of bitwise AND operation denoted by the symbol $\cap$, OR operation denoted by the symbol $\cup$, XOR operations, and 1-bit left circular rotations denoted by the symbol $\lll_1$.

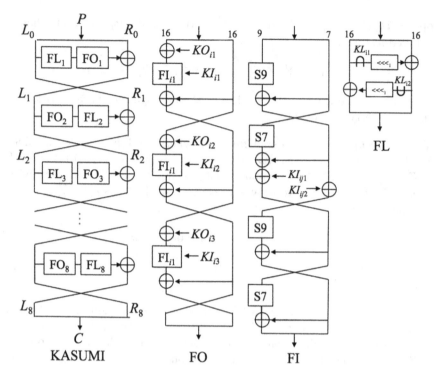

Fig. 1. Main structure and components of KASUMI

3.1 Notations Used in This Paper

We use the following notations for intermediate values during the KASUMI encryptions process.

- The left 32-bit value of i-th round output $(0 \leq i \leq 8)$ is denoted by L_i, and the right 32-bit value is denoted by R_i, respectively.
- Let Z be a intermediate variable. $Z[j]$ denotes j-th bit of Z, and $Z[j - l]$ denotes bits from j to l of Z. The most significant bit of Z is $Z[31]$, and the least significant bit is $Z[0]$.

4   Results of New Integral Characteristics of KASUMI

4.1 Division Properties of S-boxes

Tables 1 and 2 show the division properties propagating through the substitution tables S7 and S9 of KASUMI. The division properties of input set $\{X\}$ and output set $\{Y\}$ are denoted as $\mathcal{D}_k^n$ and $\mathcal{D}_{k'}^n$ $(n = 7, 9)$, respectively.

Since the degree of S7 is three, it is expected that the division property of output $\mathcal{D}_{k'}^7$ has $\mathcal{D}_2^7$ corresponding to the input $\mathcal{D}_6^7$. The result is that the division

Table 1. The division property of S7

$\mathcal{D}_k^7$	$\mathcal{D}_1^7$	$\mathcal{D}_2^7$	$\mathcal{D}_3^7$	$\mathcal{D}_4^7$	$\mathcal{D}_5^7$	$\mathcal{D}_6^7$	$\mathcal{D}_7^7$
$\mathcal{D}_{k'}^7$	$\mathcal{D}_1^7$	$\mathcal{D}_1^7$	$\mathcal{D}_1^7$	$\mathcal{D}_2^7$	$\mathcal{D}_2^7$	$\mathcal{D}_4^7$	$\mathcal{D}_7^7$

Table 2. The division property of S9

$\mathcal{D}_k^9$	$\mathcal{D}_1^9$	$\mathcal{D}_2^9$	$\mathcal{D}_3^9$	$\mathcal{D}_4^9$	$\mathcal{D}_5^9$	$\mathcal{D}_6^9$	$\mathcal{D}_7^9$	$\mathcal{D}_8^9$	$\mathcal{D}_9^9$
$\mathcal{D}_{k'}^9$	$\mathcal{D}_1^9$	$\mathcal{D}_1^9$	$\mathcal{D}_2^9$	$\mathcal{D}_2^9$	$\mathcal{D}_3^9$	$\mathcal{D}_3^9$	$\mathcal{D}_4^9$	$\mathcal{D}_4^9$	$\mathcal{D}_9^9$

property of output has $\mathcal{D}_4^7$. The deterioration of the division property of S7 is slower than that of any function $f(\cdot)$ of degree three. The same case occurs in S7 of MISTY1 [18]. The division property of S9 is the same that of any function $f(\cdot)$ of degree two.

4.2 Division Properties of FI Function

We searched for the division properties of FI function in the same manner described in [18]. The differences between FI function of KASUMI and that of MISTY are the number of rounds and S-boxes. FI function has 16-bit input and 16-bit output, and we divided them into 7-bit, 2-bit, and 7-bit respectively. The elements of input set $\{X\}$ and output set $\{Y\}$ take a value of $GF(2)^7 \times GF(2)^2 \times GF(2)^7$. The division properties of input set $\{X\}$ are $\mathcal{D}_k^{7,2,7}$, where $k = (k_1, k_2, k_3)$, $0 \le k_1, k_3 \le 7$ and $0 \le k_2 \le 2$ except for $k = 0$. The symbol '0' expresses all the elements of vector k are zero. The following expression shows an example of the division property propagating through FI function.

$$\mathcal{D}_{[3,2,5]}^{7,2,7} \xrightarrow{FI} \mathcal{D}_{[(0,0,4),(0,1,3),(0,2,2),(1,0,1),(1,1,0),(2,0,0)]}^{7,2,7}$$

4.3 Division Properties of FO Function

The division properties of FO function are generated by combining those of FI function with the propagation rules recursively. The elements of input set $\{X\}$ and output set $\{Y\}$ take a value of $GF(2)^7 \times GF(2)^2 \times GF(2)^7 \times GF(2)^7 \times GF(2)^2 \times GF(2)^7$. The division properties of input set $\{X\}$ are $\mathcal{D}_k^{7,2,7,7,2,7}$, where $k = (k_1, k_2, k_3, k_4, k_5, k_6)$, $0 \le k_1, k_3, k_4, k_6 \le 7$ and $0 \le k_2, k_5 \le 2$ except for $k = 0$. The following expression shows an example of the division property propagating through FO function. We show the vectors $k'^{(q)}$, $(1 \le q \le 56)$ as follows (Table 3).

$$\mathcal{D}_{[4,2,7,3,1,6]}^{7,2,7,7,2,7} \xrightarrow{FO} \mathcal{D}_{k'^{(1)},k'^{(2)},\dots,k'^{(56)}}^{7,2,7,7,2,7}$$

4.4 Division Properties of FL Function

The FL function of KASUMI has 1-bit shift rotations, and it is different from that of MISTY1. Since the division properties of FL explained in [18] aren't applicable to KASUMI, we newly mounted a division property including 1-bit shift rotations.

Table 3. An example of the division property propagating through FO function

The vectors $\boldsymbol{k}'^{(q)}$, $1 \leq q \leq 56$
(000004),(000013),(000022),(000102),(000111),(000120),(000200),(001003),
(001012),(001021),(001101),(001110),(002002),(002011),(002100),(003020),
(004001),(004010),(010003),(010012),(010101),(010110),(011002),(011011),
(011100),(012020),(013001),(013010),(020021),(020100),(021020),(022001),
(022010),(027000),(100002),(100011),(100020),(100100),(101001),(101010),
(106000),(110001),(110010),(115000),(124000),(200001),(200010),(203000),
(212000),(221000),(302000),(311000),(320000),(401000),(410000),(500000)

We abbreviate $\boldsymbol{k}'^{(i)} = (k_1, k_2, k_3, k_4, k_5, k_6)$ as $(k_1 k_2 k_3 k_4 k_5 k_6)$ for simplicity.

Table 4. Integral characteristics by the division property on KASUMI

Rounds	FL	Division property of the input $\mathcal{D}_{\boldsymbol{k}}^{7,2,7,7,2,7,7,2,7,7,2,7}$	Characteristics of the output
4*	✓	$\boldsymbol{k} = (0,0,5,7,2,7,7,2,7,7,2,7)$	$(\mathcal{U},\mathcal{B},\mathcal{B},\mathcal{U},\mathcal{U},\mathcal{U})$
4*	✓	$\boldsymbol{k} = (0,1,4,7,2,7,7,2,7,7,2,7)$	$(\mathcal{U},\mathcal{B},\mathcal{B},\mathcal{U},\mathcal{U},\mathcal{U})$
4*	✓	$\boldsymbol{k} = (0,2,3,7,2,7,7,2,7,7,2,7)$	$(\mathcal{U},\mathcal{B},\mathcal{B},\mathcal{U},\mathcal{U},\mathcal{U})$
5	✓	$\boldsymbol{k} = (5,2,7,7,2,7,7,2,7,7,2,7)$	$(\mathcal{U},\mathcal{U},\mathcal{U},\mathcal{U},\mathcal{U},\mathcal{U},\mathcal{B},\mathcal{B},\mathcal{B},\mathcal{B},\mathcal{B},\mathcal{B})$
6		$\boldsymbol{k} = (6,1,7,7,2,7,7,2,7,7,2,7)$	$(\mathcal{U},\mathcal{U},\mathcal{U},\mathcal{U},\mathcal{U},\mathcal{U},\mathcal{U},\mathcal{B},\mathcal{B},\mathcal{U},\mathcal{U},\mathcal{U})$
6		$\boldsymbol{k} = (6,2,6,7,2,7,7,2,7,7,2,7)$	$(\mathcal{U},\mathcal{U},\mathcal{U},\mathcal{U},\mathcal{U},\mathcal{U},\mathcal{U},\mathcal{B},\mathcal{B},\mathcal{U},\mathcal{U},\mathcal{U})$
6		$\boldsymbol{k} = (6,2,7,7,2,7,7,2,7,7,2,7)$	$(\mathcal{U},\mathcal{U},\mathcal{U},\mathcal{U},\mathcal{U},\mathcal{U},\mathcal{B},\mathcal{B},\mathcal{B},\mathcal{U},\mathcal{U},\mathcal{U})$

The 4-round characteristics denote the output of FO4[31-0]. The symbol '✓' means KASUMI includes FL. The symbol '$\mathcal{U}$' is UNKNOWN, and '$\mathcal{B}$' is BALANCE.

4.5 New Integral Characteristics of KASUMI

We searched for integral characteristics of reduced-round KASUMI by analyzing the transition of division property. We discoverd new 4 and 5-round integral characteristics of KASUMI with FL and 6-round characteristics of KASUMI without FL for the first time. Table 4 shows the results. One of the 6-round characteristics is as follows.

$$\mathcal{D}_{[6,2,7,7,2,7,7,2,7,7,2,7]}^{7,2,7,7,2,7,7,2,7,7,2,7} \xrightarrow{6R} (\mathcal{U},\mathcal{U},\mathcal{U},\mathcal{U},\mathcal{U},\mathcal{U},\mathcal{B},\mathcal{B},\mathcal{B},\mathcal{U},\mathcal{U},\mathcal{U}), \qquad (4)$$

where the symbol '$\mathcal{U}$' is UNKNOWN and '$\mathcal{B}$' is BALANCE. Therefore, integral property of 16 bits of 6-round output $R_6[31 - 16]$ is 0. The division property for 6-round characteristic (4) needs 2^{63} chosen plaintexts whose one bit of the upper 7 bits is constant and other 63 bits are active, which is half of the full code book. Other 6-round characteristics shown in Table 4 need 2^{62} chosen plaintexts. Unfortunately, we could not discover integral characteristics through more than 7 rounds.

5   Integral Cryptanalysis of Reduced-Round KASUMI

5.1   Key Recovery of 6-Round KASUMI with FL

We explain the attack of 6-round KASUMI with FL by using 4-round characteristics described in Table 4. These characteristics mean that an integral property of FO4[24-16] is BALANCE. We show one of the characteristics as follows.

$$\mathcal{D}_{[0,0,5,7,2,7,7,2,7,7,2,7]}^{7,2,7,7,2,7,7,2,7,7,2,7} \xrightarrow{4R} (\mathcal{U}, \mathcal{B}, \mathcal{B}, \mathcal{U}, \mathcal{U}, \mathcal{U}) \qquad (5)$$

We derive the following equation to recover the key by using above characteristic.

$$\bigoplus_{C_R, C_L \in \{C\}} FL4^{-1}(FL6(FO6(C_R; KO_6); KL_6) \oplus C_L; KL_4)[24 - 16] = 0 \qquad (6)$$

where $\{C\}$ refers to the set of ciphertexts corresponding to plaintexts, and 32-bit values C_R, C_L are right and left part of ciphertext, and $FL4^{-1}$ denotes an inverse of FL function. There are $96 + 18 + 9 = 123$ bits key in Eq. (6). If the 18 bits key $KL_{62}[15, 7 - 0]$ and $KL_{42}[15, 7 - 0]$ are all one, we can regard Eq. (6) as follows.

$$\bigoplus_{C_R \in \{C\}} FO6(C_R; KO_6)[24 - 16] \oplus \bigoplus_{C_L \in \{C\}} C_L[24 - 16] = 0 \qquad (7)$$

There are 50 bits key ($KO_6 = \{KO_{61}, KI_{61}[8-0], KO_{62}, KI_{62}[8-0]\}$) in Eq. (7). Therefore, we can reduce the complexity for key recovery by assuming the 18 bits key ($KL_{62}[15, 7 - 0]$ and $KL_{42}[15, 7 - 0]$) as all one.

We apply linearizing method [14] to determine KO_6. This method expands Eq. (7) as boolean polynomials over $GF(2)$, and linearizes by treating every higher order variables with new independent variables. The number of unknown variables L is 494 by using REDUCE version 3.6. Since the nine linearized equations are derived from one set of Eq. (7), we need $\lceil \frac{494}{9} \rceil = 55$ sets of Eq. (7) to recover the key KO_6. A set of expression (5) needs 2^{53} chosen plaintexts whose upper 9 bits and 2 bits of $L_0[22 - 16]$ are constant, and others are active. If we prepare 2^{55} chosen plaintexts whose upper 9 bits are arbitray constant and others are active, we can generate $\binom{7}{5} \times 2^2 = 84$ sets of expression (5) by reusing plaintexts. Thus, the necessary number of chosen plaintexts is $D = 2^{55}$. The time complexity for the attack is estimated as summation of the following steps.

- Preparation of ciphertexts
- Derivation of mod 2 frequency distribution table (MFDT)
- Key recovery

The complexity for preparation of ciphertexts is $T_E = 2^{55}$ encryptions. We prepare 32-bit mod 2 frequency distribution table (MFDT) which counts the number of appearance of C_R, and 9-bit MFDT for $C_L[24 - 16]$ in order to reduce total time complexity. Because the values which appear even times are 0 by XOR summation, we have only to calculate C_R and $C_L[24 - 16]$ which appear odd times. The complexity for derivation of MFDT is $T_{MFDT} = \frac{55 \times 2 \times 2^{53}}{12 \times 6} \approx 2^{53.7}$ encryptions[1]. The complexity for key recovery by using MFDT is estimated as follows.

$$T_{KR} = 2^{32} \times (494 + 1) \times \left\lceil \frac{494}{9} \right\rceil \times \frac{1}{6} \approx 2^{44.2} \tag{8}$$

The total complexity for attack is $T = T_E + T_{MFDT} + T_{KR} \approx 2^{55.5}$ encryptions. The success provability for the attack is 2^{-18}.

We can improve the above success provability up to almost 1. We firstly divide Eq. (6) into nine 1-bit equations. If both $KL_{62}[j]$ and $KL_{42}[j]$ ($j = 0, 1, \ldots, 7, 15$) are one, Eq. (6) is rewrite as follows.

$$\bigoplus_{C_R \in \{C\}} FO6(C_R; KO_6)[i] \oplus \bigoplus_{C_L \in \{C\}} C_L[i] = 0 , \ (16 \leq i \leq 24) \tag{9}$$

We can recover the key KO_6 by solving above 1-bit equation separately. We need 494 sets of Eq. (9) to recover the key. If we prepare a set of 2^{57} chosen plaintexts whose upper 7 bits are arbitray constant and others are active, we can generate $\binom{9}{5} \times 2^4 = 2016$ sets of 4-round characteristics described in Table 4 by reusing plaintexts. Namely, the necessary number of chosen plaintexts is $D = 2^{57}$. The time complexity is $T = T_E + T_{MFDT} + T_{KR} = 2^{57} + 2^{56.8} + 2^{50.5} \approx 2^{58}$ encryptions. The success provability is $1 - (\frac{3}{4})^9 \approx 0.925$.

5.2 Key Recovery of 7-Round KASUMI Without FL

We describe the attack of 7-round KASUMI without FL by using the following 6-round integral characteristic.

$$\mathcal{D}^{7,2,7,7,2,7,7,2,7,7,2,7}_{[6,2,6,7,2,7,7,2,7,7,2,7]} \xrightarrow{6R} (\mathcal{U},\mathcal{U},\mathcal{U},\mathcal{U},\mathcal{U},\mathcal{U},\mathcal{U},\mathcal{B},\mathcal{B},\mathcal{U},\mathcal{U},\mathcal{U}) \tag{10}$$

We can recover 50 bits key existing in 7-round by solving the following equation.

$$\bigoplus_{C_R \in \{C\}} FO(C_R; KO_7)[24 - 16] \oplus \bigoplus_{C_L \in \{C\}} C_L[24 - 16] = 0 \tag{11}$$

where $KO_7 = \{KO_{71}, KI_{71}[8-0], KO_{72}, KI_{72}[8-0]\}$. The 6-round characteristic (10) needs 2^{62} chosen plaintexts whose 1 bit of $L_0[31-25]$ and 1 bit of $L_0[22-16]$ are constant and others are active. We prepare a 32-bit MFDT which counts the number of appearance of C_R, and a 9-bit MFDT for $C_L[24 - 16]$ in order to reduce time complexity. Since 9-bit equation is derived from one set of Eq. (11), we need $\lceil \frac{50}{9} \rceil = 6$ sets of Eq. (11) to remove all false keys. If we prepare 2^{63} chosen plaintexts whose 1 bit of upper 7 bit is constant and others are active, we can generate 7 kinds of different 6-round characteristic denoted in expression (10) by reusing plaintexts. The seven sets of 6-round characteristic (10) is enough to determine the key KO_7. Thus, the necessary number of data is 2^{63}. The time is $T = T_E + T_{MFDT} + T_{KR} = 2^{63} + 2^{59.8} + \sum_{i=0}^{5} \frac{2^{50} \times 2^{32} \times 2^{-9i}}{7} \approx 2^{79.2}$ encryptions.

---

[1] We regard that a complexity for one MFDT look-up equals a complexity for one S-box look-up.

5.3   Discussion

In this section, we compare integral cryptanalysis of KASUMI by the division property to the previous results. Table 5 shows the main results of KASUMI in single key attack scenario. Although the integral cryptanalysis is not the best attack of KASUMI, it is more efficient cryptanalytic method than previous 6-round attacks in terms of time complexity. This attack aims at KASUMI which simply starts from the 1-st round, and it is 2^{27} times faster than Multidimensional Zero-Correlation attack [19].

Todo showed that the full-round MISTY1 was attackable faster than exhaustive search [18]. Although KASUMI is a modified version of block cipher MISTY1, the maximum attack rounds is six. This result means KASUMI has more than one round security margin against integral cryptanalysis by the division property, because the recommended number of rounds is eight.

The odd-round functions of KASUMI start from FL then FO, and the even-round start from FO then FL, respectively. Some results, such as [6,9,15,19], accept attackers to analyze a target cipher which starts from 2-nd round. In future work, we are going to search integral characteristics which start from 2-nd round.

Table 5. Summary of the attacks on KASUMI with FL

Rounds	Data	Time	Method	Source
5	$2^{28.9}$ CP	$2^{31.2}$ Enc.	Higher order differential	[16]
6(2–7)	$2^{60.8}$ CP	$2^{65.4}$ Enc.	Higher order differential	[15]
6(2–7)	2^{55} CP	2^{100} Enc.	Impossible differential	[9]
6	$2^{62.8}$ KP	2^{85} Enc.	Multidimensional zero-correlation	[19]
6	2^{57} CP	2^{58} Enc.	Integral by division property	**Section** 5.1
7(2–8)	$2^{52.5}$ CP	$2^{114.3}$ Enc.	Impossible differential	[6]
7	2^{62} KP	$2^{115.8}$ Enc.	Impossible differential	[6]
7(2–8)	$2^{62.1}$ KP	$2^{110.5}$ Enc.	Multidimensional zero-correlation(WK)	[19]
8	2^{32} CP	$2^{125.5}$ Enc.	Meet-in-the-middle attack	[7]

CP refers to the number of chosen plaintexts. KP refers to the number of known plaintexts. Enc shows the number of encryptions. WK denotes the weak key setting.

6   Conclusion

In this paper, we searched for integral characteristics of KASUMI by the division property, and showed that new 4 and 5-round integral characteristics of KASUMI with FL and 6-round characteristics without FL exist. 6-round KASUMI with FL is attackable with 2^{57} data and 2^{58} encryptions. It is the best attack on 6-round KASUMI in terms of time complexity. Since the recommended number of rounds is eight, This result means that KASUMI has more than one round security margin against integral cryptanalysis by the division property.

References

1. 3GPP. Specification of the 3GPP confidentiality and integrity algorithms; document 2: KASUMI specification. 3rd Generation Partnership Project Technical Specification 35.202

2. Biham, E., Shamir, A.: Differential Cryptanalysis of the Data Encryption Standard. Springer-Verlag, Heidelberg (1993)

3. Biham, E., Dunkelman, O., Keller, N.: A related-key rectangle attack on the full KASUMI. In: Roy, B. (ed.) ASIACRYPT 2005. LNCS, vol. 3788, pp. 443–461. Springer, Heidelberg (2005). doi:10.1007/11593447_24

4. Daemen, J., Knudsen, L., Rijmen, V.: The block cipher square. In: Biham, E. (ed.) FSE 1997. LNCS, vol. 1267, pp. 149–165. Springer, Heidelberg (1997). doi:10.1007/BFb0052343

5. Dunkelman, O., Keller, N., Shamir, A.: A practical-time related-key attack on the KASUMI cryptosystem used in GSM and 3G telephony. In: Rabin, T. (ed.) CRYPTO 2010. LNCS, vol. 6223, pp. 393–410. Springer, Heidelberg (2010). doi:10.1007/978-3-642-14623-7_21

6. Jia, K., Li, L., Rechberger, C., Chen, J., Wang, X.: Improved cryptanalysis of the block cipher KASUMI. In: Knudsen, L.R., Wu, H. (eds.) SAC 2012. LNCS, vol. 7707, pp. 222–233. Springer, Heidelberg (2013). doi:10.1007/978-3-642-35999-6_15

7. Jia, K., Rechberger, C., Wang, X.: Green cryptanalysis: meet-in-the-middle key-recovery for the full KASUMI cipher. International Association for Cryptologic Research (IACR), Cryptology ePrint Archive: Report 2011/466

8. Knudsen, L., Wagner, D.: Integral cryptanalysis. In: Daemen, J., Rijmen, V. (eds.) FSE 2002. LNCS, vol. 2365, pp. 112–127. Springer, Heidelberg (2002). doi:10.1007/3-540-45661-9_9

9. Kühn, U.: Cryptanalysis of reduced-round MISTY. In: Pfitzmann, B. (ed.) EUROCRYPT 2001. LNCS, vol. 2045, pp. 325–339. Springer, Heidelberg (2001). doi:10.1007/3-540-44987-6_20

10. Lucks, S.: The saturation attack — a bait for twofish. In: Matsui, M. (ed.) FSE 2001. LNCS, vol. 2355, pp. 1–15. Springer, Heidelberg (2002). doi:10.1007/3-540-45473-X_1

11. Matsui, M.: Linear cryptanalysis method for DES cipher. In: Helleseth, T. (ed.) EUROCRYPT 1993. LNCS, vol. 765, pp. 386–397. Springer, Heidelberg (1994). doi:10.1007/3-540-48285-7_33

12. Matsui, M.: New block encryption algorithm MISTY. In: Biham, E. (ed.) FSE 1997. LNCS, vol. 1267, pp. 54–68. Springer, Heidelberg (1997). doi:10.1007/BFb0052334

13. NIST: Advanced encryption standard (AES). National Institute of Standards and Technology (NIST), Federal Information Processing Standard (FIPS) Publication 197 (2001)

14. Shimoyama, T., Moriai, S., Kaneko, T., Tsujii, S.: Improving higher order differential attack and its application to Nyberg-Knudesens designed block cipher. IEIEC Trans. Fundam. **E82–A**(9), 1971–1980 (1999)

15. Saito, T.: A single-key attack on 6-round KASUMI. International Association for Cryptologic Research (IACR), Cryptology ePrint Archive: Report 2011/584

16. Sugio, N., Aono, H., Hongo, S., Kaneko, T.: A study on higher order differential attack of KASUMI. IEICE Trans. Fundam. **E90–A**(1), 14–21 (2007)

17. Todo, Y.: Structural evaluation by generalized integral property. In: Oswald, E., Fischlin, M. (eds.) EUROCRYPT 2015. LNCS, vol. 9056, pp. 287–314. Springer, Heidelberg (2015). doi:10.1007/978-3-662-46800-5_12
18. Todo, Y.: Integral cryptanalysis on full MISTY1. International Association for Cryptologic Research (IACR), Cryptology ePrint Archive: Report 2015/682
19. Yi, W., Chen, S.: Multidimensional zero-correlation linear cryptanalysis of the block cipher KASUMI. J. IET Inf. Secur. 1–7 (2015)

On Pseudorandomness in Stateless Sources

Maciej Skorski$^{(\boxtimes)}$

University of Warsaw, Warsaw, Poland
`maciej.skorski@gmail.com`

Abstract. Some authors suggest to estimate the number of unbiased bits extractable from a stateless physical source by Shannon entropy, which can be justified asymptotically by the Asymptotic Equipartition Property. We show that this estimate, refereed to as the *AEP heuristic*, involves a heavy error term and makes the extracting process insecure.

Suppose one wants to obtain k almost uniform bits from i.i.d samples $X_1, \ldots, X_n$. While the AEP heuristic gives $k \approx \mathbf{H}(X)$ where H is the Shannon Entropy, we show that *pseudoentropy* of this sequence equals

$$k = H(X) - \Theta\left(\sqrt{n \log(1/\epsilon)}\right)$$

where ϵ is a user-defined security parameter that bounds distinguishing probability (typically $\epsilon = 2^{-80}$).

Implications of our result are as follows.
(a) AEP heuristic is *provably insecure* in the information-theoretic sense
(b) AEP heuristic is not *provably secure* in the computational setting
(c) AEP heuristic is secure if the error term is addressed.
Our proof uses tools from large deviation theory and hypothesis testing.

Keywords: Pseudoentropy · Stateless sources · Asymptotic Equipartition Property

1 Introduction

1.1 True Random Number Generators

Design. True Random Number Generators utilize physical phenomena to produce nearly unbiased bits. They are typically made [Sun09] of the following building blocks

(a) randomness source (weak source)
(b) harvesting mechanism (gathering data)
(c) post-processing algorithm (extractor)

An optional but recommended component is the entropy estimator, used to ensure that the extractor is fed with enough entropy [BL05]. This design can be illustrated as shown in Fig. 1.

A full version is available on the ePrint archive.

This work is supported by National Science Center, Poland project no.: 2015/17/N/ST6/03564.

© Springer International Publishing AG 2017
D. Choi and S. Guilley (Eds.): WISA 2016, LNCS 10144, pp. 280–291, 2017.
DOI: 10.1007/978-3-319-56549-1_24

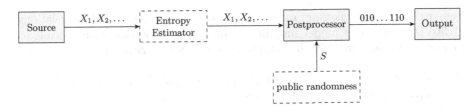

Fig. 1. The mathematical model of the typical TRNG design.

Data provided by the underlying randomness source is not truly random (this is impossible to achieve in practice) but is assumed to have certain amount of randomness. Examples of randomness source are radiation, thermal noise or data gathered from sensors of mobile devices. The purpose of the harvesting mechanism is to collect the data from the underlying physical process (e.g. sensors of a mobile device). Sometimes extra preprocessing steps are taken to smooth the data (for example transforming data series to reduce internal correlations [LPR11,KMZ09]). Finally, a special algorithm (extractor) is applied to convert collected randomness into a shorter sequence which is (almost) unbiased.

Provable Security. The extractor is considered secure if no attacker (of bounded size if computational security is considered) can distinguish the produced values and truly random values with probability bigger than ϵ, where nowadays typically $\epsilon = 2^{-80}$. Generic extractors can guarantee quality of their output, provided that sufficient entropy (measured with an appropriate notion) is provided on input. On the other hand, if the source has been transformed into almost uniform bits, it must be indistinguishable from a high min-entropy distribution. Roughly speaking, if we want extract k bits with security ϵ then we have the following conditions on the input distribution (see Lemma 2 for concrete statements).

- **Necessary:** ϵ-closeness to a distribution of min-entropy k.
- **Sufficient:** ϵ-closeness to a distribution of min-entropy $k + 2\log(1/\epsilon)$

Therefore, the main concern is the quality of the randomness source, and good estimates on source entropy are critical. This is emphasized by standards for designing and testing TRNGs [AIS99,BK12,BRS+10].

Source Model. Theoretically, the most general source model would be a Markov chain. However, simpler models are preferred in security analysis. Indeed, while there are general and popular tools that can be used to analyze chains and in particular to estimate entropy (like Maurer's Universal Tests [Mau92,Cor99]), lot of applied literature focus on the i.i.d model.

Stateless source: produces iid samples $X_1, \ldots, X_n$ with distribution μ.

First, sometimes it is possible to enforce this assumption may be enforced by implementing a reset state into the hardware [BL05]. Second, there are many evidences in empirical works [LRSV12,VSH11,KMZ09,HBF09] that other sources seem to follow this assumption (sometimes after correcting autocorrelations slightly). Finally, this model simplifies a lot the security analysis and leads to concrete bounds, contrarily to asymptotic results for Markov chains.

Extractors. Most popular extractors in applied and theoretical literature are independent hash functions [BST03, VSH11, BKMS09].

AEP Extraction Heuristic. The Asymptotic Equipartition Property [Sha48] in the simplest form states that for any i.i.d. symbols $X_1, \ldots, X_n$, there is a set T_n of so called "typical" elements such that

(a) Almost all elements are typical: $\Pr[X_1, \ldots, X_n \in T_n] \to 1$ when $n \to \infty$.
(b) Typical elements occur (roughly) equally likely: $\Pr[(X_1, \ldots, X_n) = x] \approx 2^{-n\mathbf{H}(X_1)}$

where $\mathbf{H}(\cdot)$ is the Shannon Entropy. Essentially, the AEP states that almost every sequence occurs with probability (roughly) bounded by $2^{-nH(X)}$. This result is very important for cryptography, because the upper bound on the probability mass function determines how many (almost) random bits can we extract. In theory, if every element of X appears with the probability at most 2^{-k}, we can extract almost k truly random bits. Denoting the number of extractable bits by $\mathbf{H}_{\text{ext}}$, we can rewrite the AEP as $\lim_{n\to\infty} \frac{1}{n}\mathbf{H}_{\text{ext}}(X_1, \ldots, X_n) = H(p)$. We stress that this is possible only because we are conditioning on *typical sets*. For any single n, we cannot bound the probability mass function by the Shannon entropy on the whole set. Putting this in simple words, we have the following result

> *AEP Heuristic*: for i.i.d. samples, the extractable entropy per sample approaches the source Shannon entropy. The heuristic estimate is given by $\mathbf{H}_{\text{ext}}(X_1, \ldots, X_n) \approx n\mathbf{H}(X_1)$.

This justifies the use of Shannon Entropy as an entropy estimator in the i.i.d asymptotic regime. Interestingly, quantitative versions of this fact find applications in theoretical cryptography, in constructions of PRGs from OWFs [Hol06, HILL88].

In applied literature some authors also follow this rule, using the Shannon entropy as an estimate on the number of extractable bits [Mul, LRSV12, HWGP11]. However, there is still an inherit error due to the approximation in the AEP, which may affect the estimate. This motivates the following question:

> **Question:** For i.i.d sources, how many samples do we need to extract a k-bit key which is ϵ-indistinguishable from uniform?

1.2   Our Results

Summary and Related Works. We answer the question showing that the AEP heuristic involves an error of $n^{\frac{1}{2}}\log^{\frac{1}{2}}(1/\epsilon)$.

Answer: If the security level is ϵ, one needs to assume

$$k < n\mathbf{H}(X_1) - \Omega\left(n^{\frac{1}{2}}\log^{\frac{1}{2}}(1/\epsilon)\right)$$

Also, the sufficient condition is

$$k > n\mathbf{H}(X_1) - O\left(n^{\frac{1}{2}}\log^{\frac{1}{2}}(1/\epsilon)\right).$$

Note that this bound clearly shows that the AEP heuristic is insecure, unless the error term is taken into consideration.

Related Works. The AEP is well known and quantitative lower bounds on extractable entropy appear in theoretical works [Hol06, RW05]. Also, a very special case (i.i.d. bits) of our upper bound was studied in [Sko15]. Our improvements over these prior works are twofold:

- We prove lower as well as upper bounds and show that the deviation from Shannon entropy is the same up to a constant. To our knowledge, no upper bounds are known even for information-theoretic security.
- our bounds hold in computational, not information-theoretic, settings and thus are more relevant to applications like TRNGs.

Techniques. To obtain lower and upper bounds on the extractable entropy, we use bounds on multinomial distribution derived from so called theory of types. Types are basically frequencies of occurring symbols in the sequence and determine probabilities, similarly like in a coin tossing experiment the number of heads/tails determine the probability. To estimate advantages of distinguishers, we carefully estimate tail probabilities in the region defined by multidimensional boxes.

Negative Results. Our first result shows how to distinguish a series of iid samples from distributions of pseudoentropy k, if there is a gap between k and the Shannon entropy of order $\Omega\left(\log^{\frac{1}{2}}(1/\epsilon)n^{\frac{1}{2}}\right)$.

Theorem(Informal) 1 (Pseudoentropy of IID Sources, Upper Bounds). *If X has k bits of pseudorandomness against attackers with time n and advantage at most ϵ, then*

$$\cdot\quad k < n\mathbf{H}(X) - c\left(n^{\frac{1}{2}}\log^{\frac{1}{2}}(1/\epsilon),\right)$$

where c is a constant dependent on the source.

Note that to achieve information-theoretic security, we cannot extract more than min-entropy which is even smaller than pseudoentropy.

Corollary 1 (The entropy gap is necessary for information-theoretic security). *If k is as above, then the extractor output is not ϵ-indistinguishable from the uniform distribution.*

Remark 1 (The error may be heavy). Note that the error we calculated is quite heavy - for typical settings where $\epsilon = 2^{-80}$ and $n > 256$ (say we want a 128-bit key and the source compression below 50%) it is bigger than 100 bits.

Positive Results. We show an analogous lower bound on pseudoentropy.

Theorem(Informal) 2 (Pseudoentropy of IID Sources, Lower Bounds).
If X has k bits of pseudorandomness against attackers with time n and advantage at most ϵ, then

$$k > n\mathbf{H}(X) - C\left(\log^{\frac{1}{2}}(1/\epsilon), n^{\frac{1}{2}}\right)$$

where C is a constant dependent on the source.

The proof appears in Theorem 2 and uses large deviation tools and some basic ideas from hypothesis testing.

2   Preliminaries

2.1   Information-Theoretic Divergence Measures

Definition 1 (Variational (Statistical) Distance). *We say that discrete random variables X_1 and X_2, taking values in the same space, have the statistical distance at least ϵ if their probability mass functions are at most ϵ-away in terms of the ℓ_1 norm, that is*

$$\mathrm{SD}(X_1, X_2) \leqslant \sum_x |\mathbf{P}_{X_1}(x) - \mathbf{P}_{X_2}(x)| \leqslant \epsilon.$$

Definition 2 (Kullback-Leibler Divergence).

$$\mathrm{KL}\left(X_1 \| X_2\right) = \sum \mathbf{P}_{X_1}(x) \log \frac{\mathbf{P}_{X_1}(x)}{\mathbf{P}_{X_2}(x)}$$

These two information metrics are related by the following result.

Lemma 1 (Pinsker's Inequality). *We have*

$$2\left(\mathrm{SD}(X_1, X_2)\right)^2 \leqslant 2\mathrm{KL}\left(X_1 \| X_2\right)$$

2.2   Entropy

Definition 3 (Min-Entropy). *The min-entropy of a random variable X is defined as $\mathbf{H}_\infty(X) = \min_x \log \frac{1}{\mathbf{P}_X(x)}$.*

Definition 4 (Colision-Entropy). *The collision-entropy of a random variable X is defined as $\mathbf{H}_2(X) = -\log\left(\sum_x (\mathbf{P}_X(x))^2\right)$.*

Definition 5 (Shannon-Entropy). *The Shannon-entropy of a random variable X is defined as $\mathbf{H}X = -\sum_x \mathbf{P}_X(x) \log \mathbf{P}_X(x)$.*

For bit sources we abuse the notation and write $H(p) = p\log(p^{-1}) + q\log q^{-1}$.

2.3   Computational Entropy

Definition 6 (Computational Distance). *We say that X and Y are (s, ϵ)-close if $|\mathbf{E}f(X) - \mathbf{E}f(Y)| \leqslant \epsilon$ for all boolean circuits f[1] of size s.*

---

[1] In this definition it doesn't matter if the circuit is deterministic or randomized, as we can always hardcode the choice of internal coins that achieves best advantage.

Definition 7 (HILL Entropy). *We say that X has k bit of HILL entropy of quality (s, ϵ) if there exists Y of min-entropy k such that $|\mathbf{E}D(x) - \mathbf{E}D(Y)| < \epsilon$ for every circuit D of size s.*

Metric entropy is weaker than HILL. However it is known [BSW03] that it can be converted with loss of a factor of roughly $1/\epsilon^2$.

Definition 8 (Metric Entropy). *We say that X has k bit of Metric entropy of quality (s, ϵ) if for every circuit D of size s there exists Y of min-entropy k such that $|\mathbf{E}D(x) - \mathbf{E}D(Y)| < \epsilon$.*

2.4   Extractors

Extractors are functions which process weak sources into distributions that are close (in the information-theoretic sense) to the uniform distribution. In general, they need some amount of auxiliary randomness called *seed*.

Definition 9 (Seeded extractors). *A deterministic function* $\mathrm{Ext} : \{0,1\}^n \times \{0,1\}^d \to \{0,1\}^k$ *is a (k, ϵ)-extractor for X if we have*

$$\mathrm{SD}\left(\mathrm{Ext}(X, U_d), U_d; U_k, U_d\right) \leqslant \epsilon$$

Typically we don't know the true source distribution. Fortunately, there are simple and generic extractors that achieve theoretically best possible output lengths.

Definition 10. *A family $\mathcal{H}$ of functions from n to k bits is pair-wise independent if for every $x_1 \neq x_2$ we have $\Pr[h(x_1) = h(x_2)] = 2^{-k}$ where h is chosen from $\mathcal{H}$ at random. An example of such a family can be obtained by taking pars (A, B) where A is any binary matrix with n columns and m rows, and B is any binary vector of length n.*

Lemma 2 (Efficient Generic Extractors [HILL99]). *There exist extractors that achieve $k = m - 2\log(1/\epsilon)$ bits from every source that has min-entropy m. They can be constructed from any family of independent hash functions as* $\mathrm{Ext}(X), H = H(X)$ *where H is a random member of $\mathcal{H}$.*

Remark 2 (Relaxing weak sources for seeded extractors). The definition of the weak source can be relaxed at least in two ways:

(a) X needs to be only close to a distribution with entropy k
(b) The entropy notion can be relaxed to less restrictive collision entropy.

In particular, both are true with respect to Lemma 2.

Lemma 3 (A necessary conditions for extracting). *Let Ext be any function such that $\mathrm{SD}\left(\mathrm{Ext}(X, S); U_k|S\right) \leqslant \epsilon$. Then X is ϵ-close to a distribution of min-entropy at least k.*

Definition 11 (Smooth Entropy). *We say that X has k-bits of ϵ-smooth min-entropy if X is ϵ-close to Y such that $\mathbf{H}_\infty(Y) \geqslant k$.*

2.5   Useful Auxiliary Results

We need two facts about multinomial distributions. The first observation is that probability mass function is determined only by frequencies of symbols in the input. The second result provides good bounds that the empirical frequency falls into a given set.

Lemma 4 (Multinomial Bounds in Terms of Entropy [CK82]). *Let $X = (X_1, \ldots, X_n)$ be a sequence of i.i.d. random variables, distributed according to a distribution μ over a finite set $\mathcal{X} = \{a_1, \ldots, a_m\}$. Let $x \in \mathcal{X}^n$, and let k_i counts how many times the element a_i appears in the sequence x, for $i = 1, \ldots, m$. Let $\overline{\mu}_x$ be the* empirical frequency distribution *defined by $\overline{\mu}_x(a_i) = \frac{k_i}{m}$. Then we have*

$$\Pr(X = x) = 2^{-n\mathbf{H}(\overline{\mu}_x) - n\mathrm{KL}(\overline{\mu}_x \| \mu)} \tag{1}$$

and

$$\frac{1}{(n+1)^m} 2^{n\mathbf{H}(\overline{\mu}_x)} \leqslant \binom{n}{k_1, \ldots, k_m} \leqslant 2^{n\mathbf{H}(\overline{\mu}_x)} \tag{2}$$

Theorem 1 (Sanov's Theorem [CK82]). *Let X be as in Lemma 4. Let A be any subset of probability distributions on $\mathcal{X}^n$. Then we have the following bound*

$$(n+1)^{-|\mathcal{X}|} 2^{-\mathrm{KL}(\mu^* \| \mu)} \leqslant \Pr_{x \sim X}[\overline{\mu}_x \in A] \leqslant (n+1)^{|\mathcal{X}|} 2^{-\mathrm{KL}(\mu^* \| \mu)} \tag{3}$$

where $\nu = \mu^*$ minimizes $\mathrm{KL}(\nu \| \mu)$ over $\nu \in A$.

3   Results

3.1   Lower Bounds on Pseudoentropy

Theorem 2 (Pseudoentropy of an IID Sequence, Upper Bounds). *Let X be as in Lemma 4. Then for n large enough, that is when $\epsilon = (n+1)^{-\Omega(m)}$, we have*

$$\mathbf{H}_{s,\epsilon}^{\mathrm{Metric}}(X) = \mathbf{H}(X) - O\left(n^{\frac{1}{2}} \log^{\frac{1}{2}}(1/\epsilon)\right)$$

with any $s > n$. The constant under $O(\cdot)$ depends on the distribution μ.

Proof (Proof of Theorem 2). Suppose not, then

$$\mathbf{E}D(X) - \mathbf{E}D(Y) \geqslant \epsilon.$$

for some D of size n and all Y of min-entropy k. We can rewrite it as

$$\Pr[D(X) = 1] - 2^{-k}|D| \geqslant \epsilon$$

which is equivalent to

$$\Pr[D(X) = 1] - 2^{n \log m - k} \Pr[D(U) = 1] \geqslant \epsilon$$

We can assume that D we chose achieves best possible advantage within the given time. Now the most important part of the proof: we note that D can actually implement best possible, in the information-theoretic sense, distinguisher: the maximum likelihood ratio test. Given x, it can check if $\Pr[X = x] \geqslant 2^{-k}$ in time $O(n)$ (as the left-hand side probability depends only on μ which is known to the attacker, and on the empirical frequency of x). If this is the case, then it makes sense to output 1 because then $\Pr[X = x] \cdot 1 > 2^{-k}D(x)$. Otherwise, we have $\Pr[X = x] \leqslant 2^{-k}$ for all other x' of the same type as x and the distinguisher should return 0. In particular we get the following result.

Claim. If D is optimal for time $O(n)$, then it is a function of the sequence type.

This means that D simply checks if the input belongs to some set A of probability measures on $\mathcal{X}$. Now Theorem 1 gives us

$$(n + 1)^m 2^{-n\mathrm{KL}(\nu_1\|\mu)} - 2^{n\log m - k}(n + 1)^{-m} 2^{-n\mathrm{KL}(\nu_2\|\mu)} \geqslant \epsilon \qquad (4)$$

where ν_1 minimizes $\mathrm{KL}(\nu\|\mu)$ and ν_2 minimizes $\mathrm{KL}(\nu\|U_{\mathcal{X}})$ over A. Note that $\mathrm{KL}(\nu_2\|U_{\mathcal{X}}) > \mathrm{KL}(\nu_1\|U_{\mathcal{X}})$, which gives us

$$(n + 1)^m 2^{-n\mathrm{KL}(\nu\|\mu)} - 2^{n\log m - k}(n + 1)^{-m} 2^{-n\mathrm{KL}(\nu\|\mu_{\mathcal{X}})} \geqslant \epsilon \qquad (5)$$

where $\nu = \nu_1$. Essentially, we have two inequalities

(a) $(n + 1)^m 2^{-n\mathrm{KL}(\nu\|\mu)} > 2^{n\log m - k}(n + 1)^{-m} 2^{-n\mathrm{KL}(\nu\|\mu_{\mathcal{X}})}$
(b) $(n + 1)^m 2^{-n\mathrm{KL}(\nu\|\mu)} > \epsilon$

From the first inequality, we conclude that

$$k + n \sum_i \nu(a_i) \log(\mu(a_i)) - 2m \log(n + 1) > 0 \qquad (6)$$

The second inequality implies

$$\mathrm{KL}(\nu\|\mu) \leqslant \frac{m \log(n + 1) + \log(1/\epsilon)}{n},$$

which by Lemma 1 gives us

$$\mathrm{SD}(\nu, \mu) \leqslant \sqrt{\frac{m \log(n + 1) + \log(1/\epsilon)}{2n}}.$$

This, under assumption that $\epsilon = (n + 1)^{-\Omega(m)}$, means

$$\mathrm{SD}(\nu, \mu) = O\left(n^{-\frac{1}{2}} \log^{\frac{1}{2}}(1/\epsilon)\right) \qquad (7)$$

Combining this with Eq. 6 and the definition of KL-divergence we obtain

$$k > n \sum_i (\mu(a_i) - \nu(a_i)) \log(\mu(a_i)) - n \sum_i \mu(a_i) \log(\mu(a_i))$$

$$\geqslant n\mathbf{H}(\mu) - O\left(\log^{\frac{1}{2}} n \log^{\frac{1}{2}}(1/\epsilon)\right) \qquad (8)$$

which finishes the proof.

3.2   Attacks on Pseudoentropy

Theorem 3 (Pseudoentropy of an IID Sequence, Upper Bounds). *Let X be as in Lemma 4. Then for n large enough, that is when $\epsilon < (n+1)^{-2m}$ and $\frac{n}{\log n} > m$, we have*

$$\mathbf{H}^{\text{Metric}}_{O(n),\epsilon}(X) = \mathbf{H}(X) - \Omega\left(\log^{\frac{1}{2}}(1/\epsilon)n^{\frac{1}{2}}\right)$$

where the constant under Ω depends on μ.

Remark 3 (Proof outline). To distinguish between X and high-entropy distributions, we first distinguish between X and the uniform distribution. For this we compare frequencies of input symbols against threshold. Since these frequencies follow binomial distributions and are concentrated around means - by setting threshold between the expected frequencies we are able to distinguish these two distributions (this strategy is called *likelyhood ratio test*). We set the threshold so that the acceptance probability of X is much bigger than for U:

$$\Pr[\text{Accept}(X) = 1] \gg 2^{n-k} \cdot \Pr[\text{Accept}(U) = 1]$$

Next we use the fact that high min-entropy distributions can be bounded by the uniform distribution. Namely, if Y has min-entropy k and is n-bit long then

$$\mathbf{E}f(U) \geqslant 2^{k-n} \cdot \mathbf{E}f(Y)$$

for every function f. By combining the last two inequalities we get

$$\Pr[\text{Accept}(X) = 1] \gg \Pr[\text{Accept}(Y) = 1].$$

This implies

$$\Pr[\text{Accept}(X) = 1] - \Pr[\text{Accept}(Y) = 1] > \Pr[\text{Accept}(X) = 1],$$

and the result follows then by choosing the parameters so that $\Pr[\text{Accept}(X) = 1] \gg \epsilon$. The actual proof is merely handling binomial estimates.

Proof. Define $I_+ = \{i : \mu(a_i) > 1/m\}$, $I_- = \{i : \mu(a_i) < 1/m\}$, $m_+ = \sum_{i \in I_+} \mu(a_i)$ and $m_- = \sum_{i \in I_-} \mu(a_i)$. Let A be the set of empirical probabilities having the following type: for every $i \in I_+$ the symbol a_i appears with frequency

$$\nu(a_i) \geqslant \mu(a_i)(1 + \delta/m_+) \quad \forall i \in I_+$$
$$\nu(a_i) \leqslant \mu(a_i)(1 - \delta/m_-) \quad \forall i \in I_-. \tag{9}$$

Note that this is simply a multidimensional box. Let U be uniform over $\mathcal{X}^n$ and $U_{\mathcal{X}}$ be uniform over $\mathcal{X}$. Then by Theorem 1 we obtain that for some ν_1, ν_2

$$\Pr[X \in D] - \Pr[Y \in D] \geqslant \Pr[X \in D] - 2^{n \log m - k} \Pr[U \in D]$$
$$\geqslant (n+1)^{-m} 2^{-n\text{KL}(\nu_1\|\mu)} - 2^{n-k} m(n+1)^m 2^{-n\text{KL}(\nu_2\|U)} \tag{10}$$

where ν_1 minimizes $\mathrm{KL}\,(\nu\|\mu)$ and ν_2 minimizes $\mathrm{KL}\,(\nu\|U_\mathcal{X})$ over $\nu \in A$. These points are different in general, however note that if $\nu = \nu_2$ then $\mathrm{KL}\,(\nu_1\|\mu) \leqslant \mathrm{KL}\,(\nu\|\mu)$ and therefore $2^{-n\mathrm{KL}(\nu_1\|\mu)} \geqslant 2^{-n\mathrm{KL}(\nu\|\mu)}$. This means that for some ν (actually for $\nu = \nu_2$) we have

$$\Pr[X \in D] - \Pr[Y \in D] \geqslant (n+1)^{-m}2^{-n\mathrm{KL}(\nu\|\mu)} - 2^{n-k}m(n+1)^m 2^{-n\mathrm{KL}(\nu\|U)} \tag{11}$$

We will show that this is bigger than ϵ. To this end, we show for any $\nu \in A$

(a) $(n+1)^{-m}2^{-n\mathrm{KL}(\nu\|\mu)} > 2\epsilon$.
(b) $(n+1)^{-m}2^{-n\mathrm{KL}(\nu\|\mu)} > 2 \cdot 2^{n-k}m(n+1)^m 2^{-n\mathrm{KL}(\nu\|U)}$

We want

$$-\mathrm{KL}\,(\nu\|\mu) > \log m - k - \mathrm{KL}\,(\nu\|U) + O\left(\frac{m\log n}{n}\right) \tag{12}$$

Note that

$$\begin{aligned}
\mathrm{KL}\,(\nu\|\mu) - \mathrm{KL}\,(\nu\|U) + n\log m &= \mathbf{H}(\mu) - \sum_i (\nu(a_i) - \mu(a_i))\log\mu(a_i) \\
&= \mathbf{H}(\mu) - \sum_{i\in I_+} (\nu(a_i) - \mu(a_i))\log\mu(a_i) \\
&\quad - \sum_{i\in I_-} (\nu(a_i) - \mu(a_i))\log\mu(a_i) \\
&\geqslant \mathbf{H}(\mu) + \Omega(\delta)
\end{aligned}$$

where the constant depends on μ. Thus (b) is satisfied when $k > \mathbf{H}(\mu) + \Omega(\delta)$ and $\delta \gg \frac{m\log n}{n}$.

For the specific ν where all the constraints in its definition are achieved, we have

$$\begin{aligned}
\mathrm{KL}\,(\nu\|\mu) &= \sum_i (\mu(a_i) + \mu(a_i)\delta_i)\log(1+\delta_i) \\
&= \sum_i (\mu(a_i) + \mu(a_i)\delta_i)(\delta_i + O(\delta_i^2)) \\
&= \sum_i a_i\delta_i + O\left(\sum_i \mu(a_i)\delta_i^2\right) \\
&= 0 + O(\delta^2) \tag{13}
\end{aligned}$$

where $\delta_i = \delta/m^+$ for I_+ and $\delta_i = -\delta/m_-$ for $i \in I_-$. Since (a) is equivalent to

$$n\mathrm{KL}\,(\nu\|\mu) < \log(1/\epsilon) - \frac{m}{\log(n+1)} \tag{14}$$

we see that (a) is satisfied if $\delta = O(\log^{\frac{1}{2}}(1/\epsilon)n^{-\frac{1}{2}})$, provided that $\epsilon < (n+1)^{-2m}$. We set

$$\delta = \Theta(\log^{\frac{1}{2}}(1/\epsilon)n^{-\frac{1}{2}}) \tag{15}$$

with an appropriate constant. To make (a) and (b) satisfied simultaneously it remains to check if $\log^{\frac{1}{2}}(1/\epsilon)n^{-\frac{1}{2}} \gg n^{-1}m\log n$ which is equivalent to $n\log(1/\epsilon) \gg m^2\log^2 n$. As we assumed $\epsilon < (n+1)^{-2m}$, it suffices if $mn\log(n+1) \gg m^2\log^2 nn$, which is $n/\log n \gg m$.

4 Open Problems

One interesting problem we leave for future work is to derive a corresponding lower bound on the extraction rate. The difficulty is in the choice of the set A in Eq. 10. Here we define it to be a complement of a box around the mean point, and this simple set is enough conclude our bounds. For this we would need to optimize the choice of A which seems to be a bit hard optimization problem with no explicit solutions.

References

[AIS99]   Functionality classes and evaluation methodology for deterministic random number generators. Technical report AIS 20, Bonn, Germany, December 1999

[BK12]   Barker, E.B., Kelsey, J.M.: Sp 800-90a. Recommendation for random number generation using deterministic random bit generators. Technical report (2012)

[BKMS09] Bouda, J., Krhovjak, J., Matyas, V., Svenda, P.: Towards true random number generation in mobile environments. In: Jøsang, A., Maseng, T., Knapskog, S.J. (eds.) NordSec 2009. LNCS, vol. 5838, pp. 179–189. Springer, Heidelberg (2009). doi:10.1007/978-3-642-04766-4_13

[BL05]   Bucci, M., Luzzi, R.: Design of testable random bit generators. In: Rao, J.R., Sunar, B. (eds.) CHES 2005. LNCS, vol. 3659, pp. 147–156. Springer, Heidelberg (2005). doi:10.1007/11545262_11

[BRS+10] Bassham, L.E., III, Rukhin, A.L., Soto, J., Nechvatal, J.R., Smid, M.E., Barker, E.B., Leigh, S.D., Levenson, M., Vangel, M., Banks, D.L., Heckert, N.A., Dray, J.F., Vo, S.: Sp 800-22 rev. 1a. A statistical test suite for random and pseudorandom number generators for cryptographic applications. Technical report, Gaithersburg, MD, United States (2010)

[BST03]   Barak, B., Shaltiel, R., Tromer, E.: True random number generators secure in a changing environment. In: Walter, C.D., Koç, Ç.K., Paar, C. (eds.) CHES 2003. LNCS, vol. 2779, pp. 166–180. Springer, Heidelberg (2003). doi:10.1007/978-3-540-45238-6_14

[BSW03]   Barak, B., Shaltiel, R., Wigderson, A.: Computational analogues of entropy. In: Arora, S., Jansen, K., Rolim, J.D.P., Sahai, A. (eds.) APPROX/RANDOM -2003. LNCS, vol. 2764, pp. 200–215. Springer, Heidelberg (2003). doi:10.1007/978-3-540-45198-3_18

[CK82] Csiszar, I., Korner, J.: Information Theory: Coding Theorems for Discrete Memoryless Systems. Academic Press Inc., Cambridge (1982)

[Cor99] Coron, J.-S.: On the security of random sources. In: Imai, H., Zheng, Y. (eds.) PKC 1999. LNCS, vol. 1560, pp. 29–42. Springer, Heidelberg (1999). doi:10.1007/3-540-49162-7_3

[HBF09] Holcomb, D.E., Burleson, W.P., Kevin, F.: Power-up sram state as an identifying fingerprint and source of true random numbers. IEEE Trans. Comput. **58**(9), 1198–1210 (2009)

[HILL88] Impagliazzo, R., Levin, L.A., Luby, M.: Pseudo-random generation from one-way functions. In: Proceedings of 20th STOC 1988, pp. 12–24 (1988)

[HILL99] Hastad, J., Impagliazzo, R., Levin, L.A., Luby, M.: A pseudorandom generator from any one-way function. SIAM J. Comput. **28**(4), 1364–1396 (1999)

[Hol06] Holenstein, T.: Pseudorandom generators from one-way functions: a simple construction for any hardness. In: Halevi, S., Rabin, T. (eds.) TCC 2006. LNCS, vol. 3876, pp. 443–461. Springer, Heidelberg (2006). doi:10.1007/11681878_23

[HWGP11] Hartung, D., Wold, K., Graffi, K., Petrovic, S.: Towards a biometric random number generator - a general approach for true random extraction from biometric samples. BIOSIG **2011**, 267–274 (2011)

[KMZ09] Krhovjak, J., Matyas, V., Zizkovsky, J.: Generating random and pseudorandom sequences in mobile devices. In: Schmidt, A.U., Lian, S. (eds.) MobiSec 2009. LNICSSITE, vol. 17, pp. 122–133. Springer, Heidelberg (2009). doi:10.1007/978-3-642-04434-2_11

[LPR11] Lauradoux, C., Ponge, J., Röck, A.: Online entropy estimation for nonbinary sources and applications on iPhone. Technical report, Inria, June 2011

[LRSV12] Lacharme, P., Röck, A., Strubel, V., Videau, M.: The linux pseudorandom number generator revisited. Cryptology ePrint Archive, Report 2012/251 (2012). http://eprint.iacr.org/

[Mau92] Maurer, U.: A universal statistical test for random bit generators. J. Cryptol. **5**, 89–105 (1992)

[Mul] Muller, S.: CPU time jitter based non-physical true random number generator

[RW05] Renner, R., Wolf, S.: Simple and tight bounds for information reconciliation and privacy amplification. In: Roy, B. (ed.) ASIACRYPT 2005. LNCS, vol. 3788, pp. 199–216. Springer, Heidelberg (2005). doi:10.1007/11593447_11

[Sha48] Shannon, C.E.: A mathematical theory of communication. Bell Syst. Tech. J. **27** (1948)

[Sko15] Skorski, M.: How much randomness can be extracted from memoryless Shannon entropy sources? In: Kim, H., Choi, D. (eds.) WISA 2015. LNCS, vol. 9503, pp. 75–86. Springer, Cham (2016). doi:10.1007/978-3-319-31875-2_7

[Sun09] Sunar, B.: True random number generators for cryptography. In: Koç, Ç.K. (ed.) Cryptographic Engineering, pp. 55–73. Springer, US (2009)

[VSH11] Voris, J., Saxena, N., Halevi, T.: Accelerometers and randomness: perfect together. In: WiSec 2011, pp. 115–126. ACM (2011)

Algebraic Degree Estimation for Integral Attack by Randomized Algorithm

Haruhisa Kosuge[✉] and Hidema Tanaka[✉]

National Defence Academy of Japan, Yokosuka, Japan
{ed16005,hidema}@nda.ac.jp

Abstract. Integral attack is a powerful method to recover some round keys of block ciphers by exploiting the characteristic that a set of outputs after several rounds encryption has (*integral distinguisher*). Recently, Todo proposed a new algorithm to construct integral distinguisher with division property. However, the existence of integral distinguisher which holds in additional rounds can not be denied by the algorithm. On the contrary, our approach is to obtain the number of rounds which integral distinguisher does not hold. The approach is based on algebraic degree estimation. We execute a random search for a term which has a degree equals the number of all inputted variables. We propose two algorithms and apply them to PRESENT and RECTANGLE. Then, we confirm that there exists no 8-round integral distinguisher in PRESENT and no 9-round integral distinguisher in RECTANGLE. From these facts, it is infeasible to attack more than 11-round and 13-round of PRESENT and RECTANGLE, respectively.

Keywords: Chosen plaintext attack · Integral attack · Algebraic normal form · Algebraic degree

1 Introduction

1.1 Background

Integral attack was proposed by Knudsen et al. in FSE2002 [2]. Attackers can recover some round keys based on integral distinguisher which is obtained by 2^n chosen plaintexts, where n must be less than the block length N. A set of chosen plaintexts is encrypted for multiple rounds to make a set of outputs. If there exist bits which are always 0 in an integrated value of the set of outputs, we can define integral distinguisher. Integral distinguisher can be constructed by algebraic degree estimation which is commonly used in higher order differential attack [3]. Algebraic degrees can be estimated by using *algebraic normal form* (ANF).

Recently, Todo proposed an algorithm to construct integral distinguisher by *division property* [4]. Division property is based on algebraic degree estimation considering small bijective functions such as bijective S-box. However, the algorithm can not deny the existence of integral distinguisher which holds in

© Springer International Publishing AG 2017
D. Choi and S. Guilley (Eds.): WISA 2016, LNCS 10144, pp. 292–304, 2017.
DOI: 10.1007/978-3-319-56549-1_25

additional rounds, since algebraic degrees are overestimated. For example, the algorithm regard algebraic degrees of all output bits of S-box as 3 in PRESENT, though there is an output bit which has a degree 2. The algorithm can obtain 6-round integral distinguisher [4], however, Wu et al. showed 7-round integral distinguisher using the fact [6]. Because of the output bit with degree 2, algebraic degree of intermediate values increase unevenly when a round function of PRESENT is iterated [6].

1.2 Contribution

We take an approach to analyze the number of rounds which integral distinguisher does not hold. Then, we can obtain the number of rounds which integral attack is definitely invalid. The idea follows *provable security against integral attack* proposed by Todo et al. [5] which is based on *bit-based division property*. On the other hand, our approach is based on algebraic degree estimation. We can properly obtain integral distinguisher of block ciphers whose algebraic degrees increase unevenly such as PRESENT. As a practical approach, we propose two different strategies of randomized algorithm which search for a term which has a degree n in the ANF.

We apply them to PRESENT [1] and RECTANGLE [9]. As a result, we confirm that there is no 8-round integral distinguisher in PRESENT and no 9-round integral distinguisher in RECTANGLE. In other word, attackers may be able to construct 7-round and 8-round integral distinguisher, respectively. Using these facts and a key recovery technique proposed by Zhang et al. [8], we estimate the number of rounds in integral attack scenario. Then, we confirm that it is infeasible to attack more than 11-round and 13-round of PRESENT and RECTANGLE. Hence, we conclude that full-round PRESENT (31-round) and RECTANGLE (25-round) are secure enough for integral attack.

Conventionally, attack results are used for security evaluation. Our approach is different from existing evaluation methods. We consider the number of rounds which can not be attacked. This parameter is directly related to security margin of block ciphers. To obtain the parameter, we search for integral distinguisher by estimating algebraic degrees.

2 Preliminaries

2.1 Algebraic Normal Form

Let f be a boolean function of n variables ($f : \mathbb{F}_2^n \to \mathbb{F}_2$). The algebraic normal form (ANF) of f is written as

$$f(x_0, x_1, ..., x_{n-1}) = \bigoplus_{I \subseteq \{0,1,...,n-1\}} a_I \prod_{i \in I} x_i, \tag{1}$$

where $\prod_{i \in I} x_i$ is an AND product of all variables whose indexes are elements of I, and variable x_i and coefficient a_I are elements of $\mathbb{F}_2$. Let $deg(f)$ be an algebraic degree of f and it is defined as the maximum $|I|$, s.t., $a_I = 1$.

2.2 PRESENT and RECTANGLE

PRESENT [1] and RECTANGLE [9] are 64-bit lightweight block ciphers based on SP-network which has three layers in each round: AddRoundkey, SBoxLayer and Player. Both ciphers has two variations of key lengths, 80-bit and 128-bit. PRESENT and RECTANGLE iterate 31 rounds and 25 rounds, respectively. In AddRoundKey, a 64-bit round key RK is XORed. Then, a 4-bit Sbox S is applied to each 4-bit of 64-bit block in parallel in SBoxLayer. Finally, a linear permutation $\pi : \mathbb{F}_2^{64} \rightarrow \mathbb{F}_2^{64}$ is employed in PLayer. S-boxes of PRESENT and RECTANGLE are bijective permutation, s.t., $S : \mathbb{F}_2^4 \rightarrow \mathbb{F}_2^4$. See the details of specifications in [1,9].

2.3 Integral Distinguisher

Attackers choose n bits $X = (x_0, x_1, ..., x_{n-1}) \in \mathbb{F}_2^n$ as variables in plaintext, where n must be less than block length N (plaintext length). In 2^n chosen plaintexts, the value of X takes every possible element of $\mathbb{F}_2^n$. We denote intermediate value (an element of $\mathbb{F}_2$) of encryption process by the ANF $f(X)$ as shown in Eq. (1). We define *integral* of intermediate value as an XOR summation for all chosen plaintexts. If $deg(f) < n$ for any round key values, an integrated value has following property.

$$\bigoplus_{X \in \mathbb{F}_2^n} f(X) = 0 \tag{2}$$

If an integrated value is 0 (*balanced*), we can define integral distinguisher. In this way, construction of integral distinguisher depends on $deg(f)$.

3 Algebraic Degree Estimation

As well as the algebraic degree, existence of bijective components is an important factor of integral distinguisher [2]. Let F be a bijective function, s.t., $F : \mathbb{F}_2^n \rightarrow \mathbb{F}_2^n$. If a boolean function f is a composition of F and f' ($f = f' \circ F$), we can rewrite Eq. (1) as

$$\begin{aligned} f(X) &= f'(F(X)) \\ &= f'(X') \\ &= \bigoplus_{I \subseteq \{0,1,...,n-1\}} a'_I \prod_{i \in I} x'_i, \end{aligned} \tag{3}$$

where $X' = (x'_0, x'_1, ..., x'_{n-1})$. Note that we suppose all coefficient values depending on round key values are 1 in order to estimate the maximum algebraic degree for all possible round key values. From Eqs. (2) and (3), we have

$$\bigoplus_{X' \in \mathbb{F}_2^n} f'(X') = 0, \tag{4}$$

if $deg(f') < n$ with respect to X' for any round key values. Therefore, we estimate an algebraic degree of f' instead of f to obtain integral distinguisher. Note that vectors of $X' \in \mathbb{F}_2^n$ are input bits for intermediate rounds and we regard these vectors as a set $\mathbb{X}'$. Also we use a notation x_i^r for i-th bit of r-th round.

3.1   Reduction of the Number of Terms

We truncate redundant terms from th ANF of a round function to estimate algebraic degrees. In iteration of a round function, we repeat substitution and expansion of polynomials. In the ANF of a round function, some terms are not required to be considered for algebraic degree estimation. As an example, we have $x_0^r = x_0^{r-1} \oplus x_2^{r-1} \oplus x_3^{r-1} \oplus x_1^{r-1}x_2^{r-1}$ in the round function of PRESENT. A term of x_2^{r-1} is redundant to estimate algebraic degree, because $deg(x_2^{r-1}) \le deg(x_1^{r-1}x_2^{r-1})$ and $deg(x_0^r) = max\{deg(x_0^{r-1}), deg(x_2^{r-1}), deg(x_3^r),$ $deg(x_1^{r-1}x_2^{r-1})\}$. Since the term x_2^{r-1} does not affect an increase of the algebraic degree even after some iteration of the round function, we can truncate x_2^{r-1}. Also, constant term is redundant for algebraic degree estimation, and we can neglect it.

We use the above truncation technique to express the ANF of the round functions. Let π_p and π_r be linear permutations of P-Layer of PRESENT and RECTANGLE, respectively [1,9]. We express the ANF of the round function of PRESENT for $0 \le j \le 15$ as

$$
\begin{aligned}
x_{\pi_p(4j+3)}^r &= x_{4j}^{r-1}x_{4j+1}^{r-1}x_{4j+2}^{r-1} \oplus x_{4j}^{r-1}x_{4j+1}^{r-1}x_{4j+3}^{r-1} \oplus x_{4j}^{r-1}x_{4j+2}^{r-1}x_{4j+3}^{r-1} \\
x_{\pi_p(4j+2)}^r &= x_{4j}^{r-1}x_{4j+1}^{r-1}x_{4j+3}^{r-1} \oplus x_{4j}^{r-1}x_{4j+2}^{r-1}x_{4j+3}^{r-1} \\
x_{\pi_p(4j+1)}^r &= x_{4j}^{r-1}x_{4j+1}^{r-1}x_{4j+2}^{r-1} \oplus x_{4j}^{r-1}x_{4j+1}^{r-1}x_{4j+3}^{r-1} \oplus x_{4j}^{r-1}x_{4j+2}^{r-1}x_{4j+3}^{r-1} \\
x_{\pi_p(4j)}^r &= x_{4j}^{r-1} \oplus x_{4j+3}^{r-1} \oplus x_{4j+1}^{r-1}x_{4j+2}^{r-1}.
\end{aligned} \tag{5}
$$

Also, ones of RECTANGLE ($0 \le j \le 15$) is:

$$
\begin{aligned}
x_{\pi_r(4j+3)}^r &= x_{4j+1}^{r-1}x_{4j+2}^{r-1} \oplus x_{4j+2}^{r-1}x_{4j+3}^{r-1} \oplus x_{4j}^{r-1}x_{4j+1}^{r-1}x_{4j+3}^{r-1} \\
x_{\pi_r(4j+2)}^r &= x_{4j+1}^{r-1} \oplus x_{4j+3}^{r-1} \oplus x_{4j}^{r-1}x_{4j+3}^{r-1} \\
x_{\pi_r(4j+1)}^r &= x_{4j+1}^{r-1} \oplus x_{4j}^{r-1}x_{4j+2}^{r-1} \oplus x_{4j}^{r-1}x_{4j+3}^{r-1} \\
x_{\pi_r(4j)}^r &= x_{4j+1}^{r-1}x_{4j+3}^{r-1} \oplus x_{4j+2}^{r-1}x_{4j+3}^{r-1} \oplus x_{4j}^{r-1}x_{4j+1}^{r-1}x_{4j+2}^{r-1}.
\end{aligned} \tag{6}
$$

While we iterate a round function, the number of terms increases, and it can be counted by Algorithm 1. If we combine similar terms, the number of all possible terms is 2^n at most. However, we do not combine them, and the number is not therefore upper bounded. Let $x_l^\gamma = f'(X')$ ($1 \le \gamma, 0 \le l \le N-1$) be an output value. Functions $\{c_0, c_1, ..., c_{N-1}\}$ ($c_i : \mathbb{Z}^N \to \mathbb{Z}$) calculate the number of terms included in an output bit from ones of input bits. For example in PRESENT, we can derive c_0 from Eq. (5) as

---

Algorithm 1. Counting algorithm for the number terms.

---

   procedure CountTerms($\mathbb{X}', x_l^\gamma$)
        for all $x_i^\tau \in \mathbb{X}'$ **do** $t_i^\tau = 1$ ▷ Set 1 for only variable bits.
        end for
        for all $x_i^\tau \notin \mathbb{X}'$ **do** $t_i^\tau = 0$
        end for
        for $r = 1 \to \gamma + 1$ **do**   ▷ γ rounds iteration.
           for $i = 0 \to N - 1$ **do**
               $t_i^r = c_i(t_0^{r-1}, t_1^{r-1}, ... t_{N-1}^{r-1})$ ▷ $c_i : \mathbb{Z}^N \to \mathbb{Z}$
           end for
        end for
        return t_l^γ
   end procedure

$$x_0^r = x_0^{r-1} \oplus x_3^{r-1} \oplus x_1^{r-1} x_2^{r-1}$$
$$\Rightarrow t_0^r = c_0(t_0^{r-1}, t_1^{r-1}, ..., t_{63}^{r-1})$$
$$= t_0^{r-1} + t_3^{r-1} + t_1^{r-1} \times t_2^{r-1}, \tag{7}$$

where $t_i^r \in \mathbb{Z}$ is the number of terms included in x_i^r.

We search for a term which has the highest degree among t_l^γ terms. Therefore, the search cost increases depending on t_l^γ. To show the effectiveness of the above truncation technique, we compute t_l^γ for $1 \leq \gamma \leq 4$ and $0 \leq l \leq 63$ by two methods in PRESENT and RECTANGLE (see Table 1). The column "#terms (before truncation)" shows the results using the ANF of the actual round functions of the ciphers [1,9]. And "#terms (after truncation)" shows ones using the ANF of Eqs. (5) and (6). Note that we input $\mathbb{X}' = \{x_0^0, x_1^0, ..., x_{63}^0\}$ to CountTerm in Algorithm 1 for simplicity, and we show only maximum and minimum number of terms among all 64 bits. From Table 1, we succeed to reduce the search cost by the truncation technique, which enables us to estimate algebraic degrees in additional rounds.

3.2 Combinatorial Method to Express Terms

We can express intermediate values by the ANF, using the structure of a round function. Here, we repeat substitution and expansion of polynomials from plaintext side to ciphertext side. The number of terms is calculated by Algorithm 1, and it is hard to store all the terms in a memory if γ is large. To reduce the required memory, we generate terms in the ANF in our original method, and check their degrees one by one. The terms are generated by the following calculation from ciphertext side to plaintext side.

In r-th round, we denote p_i^r as any of all terms in x_i^r, e.g., $p_1^1 = x_0^0$ or $x_1^0 x_2^0$ when $x_1^1 = x_0^0 \oplus x_1^0 x_2^0$ ($r = 1$). Then p_i^r can be expressed as an AND product of a subset of $\{p_0^{r-1}, p_1^{r-1}, ..., p_{N-1}^{r-1}\}$, and this subset is given by a round function. We define *selection-term set* as such subset, and it is written as $\mathbb{S}_i^{r-1}[k]$, where it corresponds with k-th term of the ANF to output i-th bit

Table 1. Comparison of the number of terms in ANF of PRESENT and RECTANGLE.

	Rounds	# terms (before truncation)		# terms (after truncation)	
		Max	Min	Max	Min
PRESENT	1	$2^{3.00}$	$2^{2.00}$	$2^{1.58}$	$2^{1.58}$
	2	$2^{10.71}$	$2^{4.80}$	$2^{6.33}$	$2^{3.90}$
	3	$2^{33.72}$	$2^{9.76}$	$2^{20.60}$	$2^{7.99}$
	4	$2^{93.32}$	$2^{25.28}$	$2^{63.39}$	$2^{15.99}$
RECTANGLE	1	$2^{2.80}$	$2^{2.00}$	$2^{1.58}$	$2^{1.58}$
	2	$2^{8.29}$	$2^{6.16}$	$2^{5.49}$	$2^{3.90}$
	3	$2^{22.65}$	$2^{16.11}$	$2^{15.40}$	$2^{11.00}$
	4	$2^{59.61}$	$2^{43.21}$	$2^{40.76}$	$2^{29.35}$

$(0 \le k \le \kappa_i - 1, 0 \le i \le N - 1)$. For example in PRESENT, we can derive p_0^r by using selection-term sets derived from Eq. (5) as

$$x_0^r = x_0^{r-1} \oplus x_3^{r-1} \oplus x_1^{r-1} x_2^{r-1}$$

$$\Rightarrow p_0^r = \prod_{p_i^{r-1} \in \mathbb{S}_0^{r-1}[0]} p_i^{r-1} \text{ or } \prod_{p_i^{r-1} \in \mathbb{S}_0^{r-1}[1]} p_i^{r-1} \text{ or } \prod_{p_i^{r-1} \in \mathbb{S}_0^{r-1}[2]} p_i^{r-1}.$$

$$(\mathbb{S}_0^{r-1}[0] = \{p_0^{r-1}\}, \ \mathbb{S}_0^{r-1}[1] = \{p_3^{r-1}\}, \ \mathbb{S}_0^{r-1}[2] = \{p_1^{r-1}, p_2^{r-1}\}) \quad (8)$$

Let us attempt to express a term p_l^γ in $x_l^\gamma = f'(X')$. By choosing $k_l \in \mathbb{Z}(0 \le k_l \le \kappa_l)$ of $\mathbb{S}_l^{\gamma-1}[k_l]$, we can express it as $p_l^\gamma = \prod_{p_{l'}^{\gamma-1} \in \mathbb{S}_l^{\gamma-1}[k_l]} p_{l'}^{\gamma-1}$. Also, each $p_{l'}^{\gamma-1} \in \mathbb{S}_l^{\gamma-1}[k_l]$ can be expressed as an AND product of each selection-term set (subset of $\{p_0^{\gamma-2}, p_1^{\gamma-2}, ..., p_{N-1}^{\gamma-2}\}$) by choosing $k_{l'}$ in $\mathbb{S}_{l'}^{\gamma-2}[k_{l'}]$. In this way, we can express p_l^γ as an AND product of a set of terms. We define such set as *AND-product-term set*, and we denote $\mathbb{P}^r$, s.t., $p_l^\gamma = \prod_{p_i^r \in \mathbb{P}^r} p_i^r$ $(0 \le r \le \gamma)$, and it can be expressed as an OR summation of selection-term sets.

For example in PRESENT, we fix $p_0^\gamma = \prod_{p_{l'}^{\gamma-1} \in \mathbb{S}_0^{\gamma-1}[2]} p_{l'}^{\gamma-1} = p_1^{\gamma-1} p_2^{\gamma-1}$ from Eq. (8). Then, we choose a combination of $\{k_1, k_2\}$ in $\mathbb{S}_1^{\gamma-2}[k_1](p_1^{\gamma-1} = \prod_{p_{l''}^{\gamma-2} \in \mathbb{S}_1^{\gamma-2}[k_1]} p_{l''}^{\gamma-2})$ and $\mathbb{S}_2^{\gamma-2}[k_2](p_2^{\gamma-1} = \prod_{p_{l''}^{\gamma-2} \in \mathbb{S}_2^{\gamma-2}[k_2]} p_{l''}^{\gamma-2})$. Since $0 \le k_1 \le 2$ and $0 \le k_2 \le 2$, there are 3×3 possible combinations, and the AND-product-term set is written as $\mathbb{P}^{\gamma-2} = \mathbb{S}_1^{\gamma-2}[k_1] \cup \mathbb{S}_2^{\gamma-2}[k_2]$.

Fixing a combination of selection-term sets, we can uniquely obtain $\mathbb{P}^{r-1}$ from $\mathbb{P}^r$. In the repetition, we will find $p_i^{r'} \in \mathbb{P}^{r'}$ which is also $p_i^{r'} \in \mathbb{X}'$. Since we supposed $p_i^{r'}$ as an input variable, then $p_i^{r'}$ equals $x_i^{r'}$. This fact means that an objective term p_l^γ includes $x_i^{r'}$. In the end, all elements of AND-product-term set correspond with elements of $\mathbb{X}'$. In the end, we can express p_l^γ as an AND product of subset of $\mathbb{X}'$. In this way, p_l^γ can be uniquely obtained by choosing a combination of selection-term sets in each round. If it is written as $p_l^\gamma = \prod_{x_i' \in \mathbb{X}'} x_i'$, we have $deg(p_l^\gamma) = n$ and therefore $deg(f') = n$.

4   Proposal Algorithms

We can express terms by using a combination of selection-term sets (see Sect. 3.2), and the number of all terms is computed by Algorithm 1. However, it is still an open problem to determine the number of terms with the highest degree except for brute force search. Therefore, we propose a random search to take T $(1 \leq T \leq t_l^\gamma)$ times of trials for checking the degrees of terms. The value of t_l^γ, which equals the number of all terms, is the maximum number of trials given by Algorithm 1, and t_l^γ times of trials is the same as brute force search. When t_l^γ is so large, we cannot help but limit the value of T considering our computational resources. Among T terms, if we can find a term which has a degree n, we can determine "$deg(f') = n$", otherwise, we can not determine it ("$deg(f') =$?"). Note that we express x_l^γ is *unbalanced* if $deg(f') = n$ in $x_l^\gamma = f'(X')$, otherwise, x_l^r is *uncertain*.

We propose *simple randomized algorithm* in which we choose selection-term sets randomly. However, there is a bias in distribution of terms with the highest degree when a cipher has simple linear layer. In such case, it is impossible to execute uniformly random search when $T \ll t_l^\gamma$. As a solution, we propose *partitioned randomized algorithm* which improves the uniformness of the random search. In partitioned randomized algorithm, we obtain all possible AND-product-term sets $\mathbb{P}^{\gamma-\gamma'}$ $(0 \leq \gamma' \leq \gamma)$, and we use all $\mathbb{P}^{\gamma-\gamma'}$ as start points of the random search. For each start point, we execute the simple randomized algorithm the same number of times T' $(T' < T)$. Note that we apply the above algorithms to all output bits of γ-th round to construct integral distinguisher.

4.1   Simple Randomized Algorithm

The simple randomized algorithm is shown in Algorithm 2. We input $\{p_l^\gamma\}$ to $\mathbb{P}^\gamma$ and repeat RandomRound for γ times to make $\mathbb{P}^0$. If RandomRound does not output ϕ for every round, we can determine x_l^r is unbalanced. If the number of terms already checked excesses T, x_l^γ is uncertain.

In RandomRound, we use a notation $p_i^{r\,(j)}$, where j is an index, e.g., $\mathbb{P}^r = \{p_0^{r\,(0)}, p_0^{r\,(1)}, p_2^{r\,(0)}\}$. Suppose that j selection-term sets have p_i^r, and OR summation of these term sets becomes an AND-product-term set $\mathbb{P}^r$. As mentioned in Sect. 3.2, p_i^r is any of all terms. Therefore, $\mathbb{P}^r$ has any j terms in the ANF of x_i^r. To give different index to each element, $p_{i'}^{r-1\,(j'+1)}$ becomes an element of $\mathbb{P}^{r-1}$, if $p_{i'}^{r-1\,(j')} \in \mathbb{P}^{r-1}$ in RandomRound.

We use random numbers k_R to choose selection-term sets, where $k_R \in \mathbb{Z}$ $(0 \leq k_R \leq \kappa_i - 1)$. We check variables $\forall x_i^{r-1} \in \mathbb{X}'$ $(x_i^{r-1} = p_i^{r-1})$ are also elements of $\mathbb{P}^{r-1}$. If at least one variable $x_i^{r-1\,(0)}$ is not in $\mathbb{P}^{r-1}$, p_l^γ does not include $x_i^{r-1\,(0)}$. Therefore, the degree of p_l^γ must be less than n. In this case, $\mathbb{P}^{r-1} = \phi$ (empty set) is outputted, and ϕ is outputted from RandomRound thereafter. If $\mathbb{P}^0 \neq \phi$ is outputted, the degree of this term is n and we can determine x_l^r is unbalanced, otherwise, we take another term.

Algorithm 2. Simple Randomized Algorithm.

---

procedure SimpleSearch($T, \mathbb{X}', p_l^\gamma$)
  for $count = 0 \to T - 1$ **do**   ▷ T is the maximum number of trials.
    $\mathbb{P}^\gamma \Leftarrow \{p_l^{\gamma^{(0)}}\}$ ▷ Reset $\mathbb{P}^\gamma$ as $\{p_l^{\gamma^{(0)}}\}$.
    for $r = \gamma \to 1$ **do**
      $\mathbb{P}^{r-1}$=RadomRound($\mathbb{X}', \mathbb{P}^r$)
    end for
    if $\mathbb{P}^0 \neq \phi$ **then return** "x_l^r is unbalanced."   ▷ ϕ is an empty set.
    end if
  end for
  return "x_l^r is uncertain."
end procedure
procedure RandomRound($\mathbb{X}', \mathbb{P}^r$)
  for all $p_i^{r(j)} \in \mathbb{P}^r$ **do**   ▷ $p_i^{r(j)}$ corresponds to $\mathbb{S}_i^{r-1}[k_R]$(k_R: random number).
    for all $p_{i'}^{r-1(0)} \in \mathbb{S}_i^{r-1}[k_R]$ **do**
      if $p_{i'}^{r-1(j')} \in \mathbb{P}^{r-1}$ **then** $\mathbb{P}^{r-1} \Leftarrow \mathbb{P}^{r-1} \cup \{p_{i'}^{r-1(j'+1)}\}$
      end if
    end for
  end for
  $flag \Leftarrow 1$
  for all $x_i^{r-1} \in \mathbb{X}'$ **do**   ▷ If $\exists x_i^{r-1} \in \mathbb{X}'$ not in $\mathbb{P}^{r-1}$, then the degree is not n.
    if $p_i^{r-1(0)} \notin \mathbb{P}^{r-1}$ **then** $flag \Leftarrow 0$
    end if
  end for
  if $flag = 1$ **then return** $\mathbb{P}^{r-1}$
  else return ϕ ▷ Since the degree of this term is not n, substitute ϕ for $\mathbb{P}^{r-1}$.
  end if
end procedure

4.2 Partitioned Randomized Algorithm

The partitioned randomized algorithm is shown in Algorithm 3. We obtain all possible $\mathbb{P}^{\gamma-\gamma'}$ ($0 \leq \gamma' \leq \gamma$) by brute force search, and the result is given by a function RecursiveSearch. The value of γ' is the number of rounds which we can execute brute force search, and it is determined as follows. Let $\mathcal{BF}(\mathbb{P}^{\gamma-\gamma'})$ be a set of all possible $\mathbb{P}^{\gamma-\gamma'}$. We use $\mathbb{P}^{\gamma-\gamma'} \in \mathcal{BF}(\mathbb{P}^{\gamma-\gamma'})$ as a start point of RandomRound of Algorithm 2. We can obtain $|\mathcal{BF}(\mathbb{P}^{\gamma-\gamma'})|$ by CountTerms of Algorithm 1. We execute RandomRound for T' times from each start point, where $T' = \lfloor T/|\mathcal{BF}(\mathbb{P}^{\gamma-\gamma'})| \rfloor$. Using $|\mathcal{BF}(\mathbb{P}^{\gamma-\gamma'})|$, we can decide the value of γ'. To set as many start points as possible, we decide the value of γ' as the maximum integer satisfying $T > |\mathcal{BF}(\mathbb{P}^{\gamma-\gamma'})|$. With respect to PRESENT and RECTANGLE, "#terms (after truncation)" of Table 1 shows $|\mathcal{BF}(\mathbb{P}^{\gamma-\gamma'})|$ where $\gamma' \in \{1, 2, 3, 4\}$ for any γ.

In RecursiveSearch, two procedures are repeated: (i) Make each element $p_i^{r(j)} \in \mathbb{P}^r$ correspond to $\mathbb{S}_i^{r-1}[k]^{(j)} \in \mathbf{S}^{r-1}$ (recursion in the same round). (ii) Make $\mathbb{P}^{r-1}$ from $\mathbf{S}^{r-1}$ (recursion for a next round). Note that $\mathbf{S}^{r-1}$ is a set of

---

Algorithm 3. Partitioned Randomized Algorithm.

---

procedure PartitionedSearch($T, \gamma', \mathbb{X}', x_l^{\gamma}$)

     $\mathbb{P}^{\gamma} \Leftarrow \{p_l^{\gamma(0)}\}$

     $T' = T/\text{CountTerms}(\{x_0^{\gamma-\gamma'}, x_1^{\gamma-\gamma'}, .., x_{N-1}^{\gamma-\gamma'}\}, x_l^{\gamma})$

     global $deg(f') \Leftarrow 0$ ▷ $deg(f')$ is a global variable.

     RecursiveSearch($T', \gamma', \mathbb{X}', \mathbb{P}^{\gamma}, \phi$)

     if $deg(f') = n$ **then return** "x_l^r is unbalanced."

     else return "x_l^r is uncertain."

     end if

end procedure

procedure RecursiveSearch($T', \gamma', \mathbb{X}', \mathbb{P}^r, \mathbf{S}^{r-1}$)

     if $deg(f') \neq n$ **then**   ▷ If $deg(f') = n$, then the resursion stops.

        if $\mathbb{P}^r \neq \phi$ **then**

           for all $p_i^{r(j)} \in \mathbb{P}^r$ **do**

              $\mathbb{P}^r \Leftarrow \mathbb{P}^r \backslash \{p_i^{r(j)}\}$

              for $k = 0 \rightarrow \kappa_i - 1$ **do**

                 RecursiveSearch($T', \gamma', \mathbb{X}', \mathbb{P}^r, \mathbf{S}^{r-1} \cup \{\mathbb{S}_i^{r-1}[k]^{(j)}\}$)

              end for   ▷ Try every possible selection terms by recursion.

          end for

        else

           for all $\mathbb{S}_i[k]^{(j)} \in \mathbf{S}^{r-1}$ **do**

              for all $p_{i'}^{r-1(0)} \in \mathbb{S}_i^{r-1}[k]$ **do**

                 if $p_{i'}^{r-1(j')} \in \mathbb{P}^{r-1}$ **then** $\mathbb{P}^{r-1} \Leftarrow \mathbb{P}^{r-1} \cup \{p_{i'}^{r-1(j'+1)}\}$

                 end if

              end for

           end for

           if $r > \gamma - \gamma'$ **then** RecursiveSearch($T', \gamma', \mathbb{X}', \mathbb{P}^{r-1}, \phi$)

          else

             for $count = 0 \rightarrow T' - 1$ **do**

                $\dot{\mathbb{P}}^{r-1} \Leftarrow \mathbb{P}^{r-1}$ ▷ $\mathbb{P}^{r-1} = \mathbb{P}^{\gamma-\gamma'}$.

                for $r' = r - 1 \rightarrow 1$ **do**

                   $\dot{\mathbb{P}}^{r'-1} \Leftarrow \text{RandomRound}(\mathbb{X}', \dot{\mathbb{P}}^{r'})$ ▷ See Algorithm 2

                end for

                if $\dot{\mathbb{P}}^0 \neq \phi$ **then** $deg(f') \Leftarrow n$

                end if

             end for

          end if

        end if

     end if

end procedure

---

selection-term sets, and we use a notation $\mathbb{S}_i^{r-1}[k]^{(j)} \in \mathbf{S}^{r-1}$ for the same reason as $p_i^{r(j)}$. By repeating procedure (i), we can try all possible selection-term sets in $(r-1)$-th round recursively. If there is no more selection-term sets ($\mathbb{P}^r = \phi$), then we advance to procedure (ii). In procedure (ii), $\mathbb{P}^{r-1}$ is constructed by $\mathbb{S}_i^{r-1}[k]^{(j)} \in \mathbf{S}^{r-1}$ and $\mathbb{P}^{r-1}$ becomes an input for next recursion. However, we check if $r > \gamma - \gamma'$ in advance to procedure (ii). If $r \leq \gamma - \gamma'$, we execute

RandomRound (see Algorithm 2) for T' times. In Algorithm 3, $deg(f')$ is a global variable as used in C/C++ language. In RecursiveSearch, if n is substituted for $deg(f')$ at least once, RecursiveSearch does not repeat anymore and PartitionedSearch returns "x_l^r is unbalanced".

4.3 Application to PRESENT and RECTANGLE

By using Algorithms 2 and 3, we obtain algebraic degrees of output bits of PRESENT and RECTANGLE. From the attack scenario of integral attack, 63 is the maximum number of variables. By setting 63 variables, we can construct integral distinguisher which holds in the maximum number of rounds. Therefore, we set all possible conditions for 63 variables. Let $x_c^0 \in \{x_0^0, x_1^0, .., x_{63}^0\}$ be a constant bit in plaintext. As mentioned in Sect. 3, we consider bijective components F to obtain $\mathbb{X}'$. Elements of $\mathbb{X}'$ are input bits for intermediate rounds, and the maximum number of rounds they exist directly affects the number of rounds which integral distinguisher does not hold. In PRESENT, elements of $\mathbb{X}'$ are input bits from 1st round to 3rd round. In RECTANGLE, they are from 1st round to 4th round.

First, we set $T = 2^{22}$ considering our computer environment (CPU: Intel Core i7-3770 3.40 GHz and memory: 16Gbyte), since we can check all 64 output bits for all 64 possible x_c^0 in a month. Note that $t_l^\gamma \gg 2^{22}$ for any l when $\gamma > 5$ in both ciphers. Next, we consider correspondence of algorithms to ciphers. As mentioned in Sect. 4, we propose Algorithm 3 for improving uniformness of random search which is effective for ciphers with simple linear layer. Therefore, we apply Algorithm 3 to RECTANGLE since it has a more simple P-Layer. As for PRESENT, we use Algorithm 2, since it has a more complex P-Layer.

The above experimental results show that all 64 output bits of 8th round has degree 63 for all x_c^0 in PRESENT. Also in RECTANGLE, we find that all 64 output bits of 9th round has degree 63 for all x_c^0. Hence, we confirm that there is no 8-round integral distinguisher in PRESENT and no 9-round integral distinguisher in RECTANGLE. While we set $T = 2^{22}$, we could find them in 2^{13} times of trials at most, and both experiments are ended in an hour. To evaluate effectiveness of the algorithms, we switch the algorithms to apply. As a result, we find that both experiments needs 2^{20} times of trials (about 100 h). Therefore, the above results supports our conjecture.

As an additional experiment, we obtain the number of unbalanced bits in 7th round of PRESENT and 8th round of RECTANGLE. We use Algorithm 2 for PRESENT and Algorithm 3 for RECTANGLE, and we set $T = 2^{22}$. Let μ be the number of unbalanced bits in a round ($0 \leq \mu \leq 64$). Table 2 shows μ for all x_c^0 in PRESENT and RECTANGLE. The number of uncertain bits is $64-\mu$. Therefore, the number of balanced bits can be $64 - \mu$ at most. In other words, there is a possibility that attackers can exploit $64-\mu$ bits as integral distinguisher. When μ is small, integral distinguisher is more advantageous for attackers. In PRESENT, there are 9 possible x_c^0 to have $\mu = 45$ from Table 2. On the contrary, we have $\mu = 6$ for all x_c^0 in RECTANGLE. Hence, integral distinguisher of PRESENT depends on a position of a constant bit, and attackers should consider it.

Table 2. Results on PRESENT and RECTANGLE.

	x_c^0	μ	x_c^0	μ	x_c^0	μ	x_c^0	μ	x_c^0	μ	x_c^0	μ	x_c^0	μ	x_c^0	μ
PRESENT (7th round)	x_0^0	45	x_8^0	50	x_{16}^0	46	x_{24}^0	48	x_{32}^0	46	x_{40}^0	46	x_{48}^0	50	x_{56}^0	50
	x_1^0	47	x_9^0	50	x_{17}^0	46	x_{25}^0	48	x_{33}^0	45	x_{41}^0	48	x_{49}^0	50	x_{57}^0	50
	x_2^0	48	x_{10}^0	49	x_{18}^0	46	x_{26}^0	47	x_{34}^0	48	x_{42}^0	47	x_{50}^0	51	x_{58}^0	50
	x_3^0	49	x_{11}^0	47	x_{19}^0	46	x_{27}^0	47	x_{35}^0	45	x_{43}^0	47	x_{51}^0	49	x_{59}^0	50
	x_4^0	45	x_{12}^0	45	x_{20}^0	47	x_{28}^0	46	x_{36}^0	47	x_{44}^0	45	x_{52}^0	52	x_{60}^0	51
	x_5^0	49	x_{13}^0	45	x_{21}^0	47	x_{29}^0	46	x_{37}^0	47	x_{45}^0	48	x_{53}^0	50	x_{61}^0	48
	x_6^0	49	x_{14}^0	45	x_{22}^0	46	x_{30}^0	48	x_{38}^0	46	x_{46}^0	45	x_{54}^0	52	x_{62}^0	51
	x_7^0	50	x_{15}^0	45	x_{23}^0	47	x_{31}^0	47	x_{39}^0	47	x_{47}^0	46	x_{55}^0	51	x_{63}^0	48
RECTANGLE (8th round)	x_0^0	6	x_8^0	6	x_{16}^0	6	x_{24}^0	6	x_{32}^0	6	x_{40}^0	6	x_{48}^0	6	x_{56}^0	6
	x_1^0	6	x_9^0	6	x_{17}^0	6	x_{25}^0	6	x_{33}^0	6	x_{41}^0	6	x_{49}^0	6	x_{57}^0	6
	x_2^0	6	x_{10}^0	6	x_{18}^0	6	x_{26}^0	6	x_{34}^0	6	x_{42}^0	6	x_{50}^0	6	x_{58}^0	6
	x_3^0	6	x_{11}^0	6	x_{19}^0	6	x_{27}^0	6	x_{35}^0	6	x_{43}^0	6	x_{51}^0	6	x_{59}^0	6
	x_4^0	6	x_{12}^0	6	x_{20}^0	6	x_{28}^0	6	x_{36}^0	6	x_{44}^0	6	x_{52}^0	6	x_{60}^0	6
	x_5^0	6	x_{13}^0	6	x_{21}^0	6	x_{29}^0	6	x_{37}^0	6	x_{45}^0	6	x_{53}^0	6	x_{61}^0	6
	x_6^0	6	x_{14}^0	6	x_{22}^0	6	x_{30}^0	6	x_{38}^0	6	x_{46}^0	6	x_{54}^0	6	x_{62}^0	6
	x_7^0	6	x_{15}^0	6	x_{23}^0	6	x_{31}^0	6	x_{39}^0	6	x_{47}^0	6	x_{55}^0	6	x_{63}^0	6

5 Discussion

Table 3 shows integral distinguisher shown in previous works. These results show the number of rounds in which integral distinguisher holds γ and balanced bits β when the number of chosen plaintexts is 2^n. Our result shows the number of uncertain bits $64 - \mu$, and it may be less than β. Since $\gamma = 7$ in PRESENT and $\gamma = 8$ in RECTANGLE at most, our results are consistent with previous works.

From the above, we estimate the number of rounds which integral attack is invalid by supposing that we can use 7-round and 8-round integral distinguisher in PRESENT and RECTANGLE (128-bit key length), respectively. In [8], Zheng et al. proposed a technique to reduce the time complexity for key recovery, and

Table 3. Previous results on PRESENT and RECTANGLE.

	γ	β	n	Reference
PRESENT	3.5	16	4	[7]
	5	16	32	[10]
	6	64	60	[4]
	7	1	16	[6,8]
	7	19[a]	63	Our result
RECTANGLE	7	22	36	[8]
	8	6[a]	63	Our result

[a] The number of uncertain bits ($64 - \mu \le \beta$).

it is the most effective technique for the two ciphers. Using the technique, we can attack $(\gamma + 4)$-round PRESENT and $(\gamma + 5)$-round RECTANGLE. Therefore, it is infeasible to attack more than 11-round ($\gamma = 7$) PRESENT and 13-round ($\gamma = 8$) of RECTANGLE.

6 Conclusion

We propose randomized algorithms to obtain algebraic degrees of intermediate outputs which support for constructing integral distinguisher. By demonstrating the algorithms in PRESENT and RECTANGLE, we confirm that there exists no 8-round integral distinguisher in PRESENT and no 9-round integral distinguisher in RECTANGLE. From these facts, we confirm that we can not attack more than 11-round and 13-round, respectively. Hence, we conclude that both ciphers are secure enough for integral attack considering the specifications of the number of rounds. The number of rounds which integral distinguisher does not hold helps designers to decide security margin. The proposal algorithms enables them to obtain such security parameter by algebraic degree estimation.

Acknowledgment. This work was supported by JSPS KAKENHI Grant Number 24560491.

References

1. Bogdanov, A., Knudsen, L.R., Leander, G., Paar, C., Poschmann, A., Robshaw, M.J.B., Seurin, Y., Vikkelsoe, C.: PRESENT: an ultra-lightweight block cipher. In: Paillier, P., Verbauwhede, I. (eds.) CHES 2007. LNCS, vol. 4727, pp. 450–466. Springer, Heidelberg (2007). doi:10.1007/978-3-540-74735-2_31
2. Knudsen, L., Wagner, D.: Integral cryptanalysis. In: Daemen, J., Rijmen, V. (eds.) FSE 2002. LNCS, vol. 2365, pp. 112–127. Springer, Heidelberg (2002). doi:10.1007/3-540-45661-9_9
3. Knudsen, L.R.: Truncated and higher order differentials. In: Preneel, B. (ed.) FSE 1994. LNCS, vol. 1008, pp. 196–211. Springer, Heidelberg (1995). doi:10.1007/3-540-60590-8_16
4. Todo, Y.: Structural evaluation by generalized integral property. In: Oswald, E., Fischlin, M. (eds.) EUROCRYPT 2015. LNCS, vol. 9056, pp. 287–314. Springer, Heidelberg (2015). doi:10.1007/978-3-662-46800-5_12
5. Todo, Y., Morii, M.: Bit-based division property and application to simon family. IACR Cryptology ePrint Archive 2016, 285 (2016). http://eprint.iacr.org/2016/285
6. Wu, S., Wang, M.: Integral attacks on reduced-round PRESENT. In: Qing, S., Zhou, J., Liu, D. (eds.) ICICS 2013. LNCS, vol. 8233, pp. 331–345. Springer, Cham (2013). doi:10.1007/978-3-319-02726-5_24
7. Z'aba, M.R., Raddum, H., Henricksen, M., Dawson, E.: Bit-pattern based integral attack. In: Nyberg, K. (ed.) FSE 2008. LNCS, vol. 5086, pp. 363–381. Springer, Heidelberg (2008). doi:10.1007/978-3-540-71039-4_23
8. Zhang, H., Wu, W., Wang, Y.: Integral attack against bit-oriented block ciphers. In: Kwon, S., Yun, A. (eds.) ICISC 2015. LNCS, vol. 9558, pp. 102–118. Springer, Cham (2016). doi:10.1007/978-3-319-30840-1_7

9. Zhang, W., Bao, Z., Lin, D., Rijmen, V., Yang, B., Verbauwhede, I.: RECTAN-
GLE: A bit-slice ultra-lightweight block cipher suitable for multiple platforms.
Cryptology ePrint Archive, Report 2014/084 (2014). http://eprint.iacr.org/

10. Zhang, W., Su, B., Wu, W., Feng, D., Wu, C.: Extending higher-order integral: an
efficient unified algorithm of constructing integral distinguishers for block ciphers.
In: Bao, F., Samarati, P., Zhou, J. (eds.) ACNS 2012. LNCS, vol. 7341, pp. 117–134.
Springer, Heidelberg (2012). doi:10.1007/978-3-642-31284-7_8

Applications of Soft Computing in Cryptology

Stjepan Picek[1,2]([✉])

[1] ESAT/COSIC and iMinds, KU Leuven, Kasteelpark Arenberg 10,
Bus 2452, 3001 Leuven-Heverlee, Belgium
stjepan@computer.org
[2] LAGA, UMR 7539, CNRS, University of Paris 8, Saint-Denis, France

Abstract. Soft computing offers a number of interesting options how to solve many real world problems where security and cryptology domains are not exceptions. There, machine learning and various optimization techniques can play a significant role in finding new, improved solutions. Sometimes those methods are used to solve the problem itself, while sometimes they just represent a helper tool in a larger task. A more in-depth understanding of such techniques is always beneficial. Moreover, the research topics belonging to the intersection of the soft computing and the cryptology are rather demanding since usually neither of those two communities devotes much attention to the other area. In this paper, we briefly discuss three well-known applications of soft computing to the cryptology area where we identify main challenges and offer some possible future research directions.

Keywords: Soft computing · Machine learning · Evolutionary computation · Cryptology · Side-channel attacks · PUFs

1 Introduction

Informally speaking, soft computing encompasses methods that are tolerant of imprecision, uncertainty, and approximation. Such methods can obtain good solutions for various difficult problems with a relatively low solution cost and a high degree of robustness. On the basis of the previous definition, we can immediately observe that a plethora of methods can actually belong under the umbrella of soft computing. However, in this paper, we focus on machine learning (ML) and evolutionary computation (EC) techniques. Such methods are used with great success on many real world, difficult problems where some of those problems also belong to the cryptology domain.

Cryptographic problems represent an interesting objective for soft computing since there researchers often deal with objectives where there exist no deterministic algorithms or algorithms that can compute an exact solution in a polynomial time. Naturally, using soft computing techniques is not always straightforward. Although some of those methods (e.g., evolutionary algorithms) are perceived as black-box solvers, that does not mean one will always obtain good solutions without some expert knowledge of the problem (especially if it is difficult,

D. Choi and S. Guilley (Eds.): WISA 2016, LNCS 10144, pp. 305–317, 2017.
DOI: 10.1007/978-3-319-56549-1_26

e.g., NP-hard problem). Therefore, since we talk about an interdisciplinary area, the best results can naturally be expected when combining specific domain knowledge from both areas. However, this is often not the case. For instance, the cryptography community often uses soft computing techniques but regards them as black-box solvers that are consequently not used in an optimal way or utilizing their full potential. On the other hand, the soft computing community will work on cryptography problems but without a deeper understanding of the implications related with the problem at hand.

In this paper, we concentrate on three applications of ML and EC to the area of cryptology. Namely, we discuss the evolution of cryptographic primitives, side-channel analysis, and attacks on Physical Unclonable Functions (PUFs). For the first problem we discuss how to use evolutionary computation methods, for the second problem we use machine learning techniques, and finally, for the third problem, both ML and EC are used. Note that we do not go into details about cryptographic problems, but rather we discuss the implications for soft computing techniques. Furthermore, we aim to avoid discussions about any specific soft computing technique, but we give more general insights into the presented problems.

The rest of this paper is organized as follows. We start in Sect. 2 with background information about machine learning and evolutionary computation techniques. In Sect. 3, we discuss how to use evolutionary computation to evolve various cryptographic primitives in the form of Boolean functions and S-boxes. Section 4 discusses how to use machine learning techniques to conduct side-channel analysis. Next, Sect. 5 discusses utilizing machine learning or evolutionary computation techniques to attack PUFs. Then, in Sect. 6 we give a short discussion on possible future research directions as well as some other applications of soft computing in cryptography. Finally, Sect. 7 concludes the paper.

2   Background

In this section, we discuss machine learning and evolutionary computation techniques. Note that those areas are often overlapping so we do not aim to give a single (best) definition or classification for each term presented here.

2.1   Machine Learning

Machine learning (ML) is a subfield of computer science that evolved from the study of pattern recognition and computational learning theory in artificial intelligence. Generally speaking, all algorithms extract certain information from data, but with machine learning, algorithms also learn a model to discover something about the data in the future [1]. Machine learning is therefore a term encompassing a number of methods that can be used for clustering, classification (binary or multi-class), regression, feature selection, and other knowledge discovering methods [2,3]. One commonly used definition of machine learning from T.

Mitchell, states that "The field of machine learning is concerned with the question of how to construct computer programs that automatically improve with experience." [2]. Or to state it more formally, a computer program is said to learn from experience E with respect to some task T and some performance measure P, if its performance on T, as measured with P, improves with experience E [2].

Therefore, we use ML techniques to discover a function $y = f(x)$ that best predicts the value of y associated with the each value of x [1]. Since the definition given here is quite general, this immediately gives us an intuition that many methods can fit under machine learning. Indeed, today there is a plenitude of methods that are considered as machine learning techniques. All those methods can be classified in several ways where a common classification method divides the techniques into supervised and unsupervised machine learning methods. In supervised machine learning, the algorithm is provided with a set of data instances and data labels in a training phase. The goal of this phase is to "learn" the relationship between the instances and the labels in order to be able to reliably map new instances to the labels in the testing phase. On the other hand, in unsupervised machine learning, an algorithm does not know the labels a priori and needs to infer the relationships between the data and the unlabeled classes (commonly referred to as clusters), i.e., to group the data into clusters according to some distance measure.

In Fig. 1 we give a depiction of a machine learning process. There, one starts with raw data that are obtained from a device, e.g., an oscilloscope used in the side-channel analysis. Then, one needs to process/prepare the data for machine learning process. After that, feature selection/construction/transformation phase is conducted with a goal of selecting more important features or constructing new, high-level features from the original features [4]. Next, one needs to select the machine learning method to use (or a number of methods) and tune the parameters for that method. As a final step, one verifies that the model is correct on some new data.

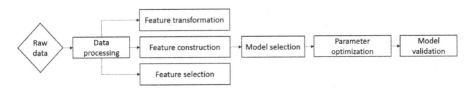

Fig. 1. Machine learning process

We emphasize that the process just described is not a straightforward one. Moreover, the "No Free Lunch" theorem for supervised machine learning shows that there exists no single model that works best for every problem [5]. Therefore, to find the best model for any problem, numerous algorithms and parameter combinations should be tested. Naturally, not even then we can be sure that we found the best model, but at least we should be able to estimate the possible trade-offs between the speed, accuracy, and complexity of the obtained models.

2.2   Evolutionary Computation

Evolutionary Computation (EC) techniques are optimization methods based on a set of solution candidates which are iteratively refined. Moreover, they belong to the metaheuristics area, i.e., they are general-purpose algorithms that can be applied to solve many optimization problems. Finally, they could be regarded as upper level general methodologies that are used as a guiding strategy in designing underlying heuristics to solve specific optimization problems [6]. One possible classification of optimization methods is given in Fig. 2. We see that metaheuristics as well as the specific heuristics belong to the heuristic algorithms area. The main difference is that specific heuristics area represents methods that are custom-made to solve a certain problem [6] while metaheuristics can be applied to many different classes of problems.

Similar to the machine learning area, EC encompasses a number of different methods where one well known family of algorithms is Evolutionary Algorithms (EAs). Evolutionary algorithms are a subclass of EC where algorithms draw inspiration from natural evolution (e.g., mutation, selection, survival of the fittest) [7]. Again similar to the machine learning area, for optimization methods there exists "No Free Lunch" theorem that shows when averaged over all optimization problems, all optimization algorithms behave the same, i.e., there exists no single best algorithm for all optimization problems [8]. Therefore, to select the most appropriate algorithm for a specific problem, we often need experience and some knowledge about the problem.

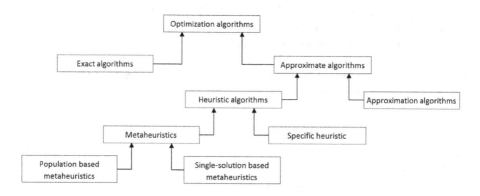

Fig. 2. Classification of optimization techniques

In Figs. 3a and b we depict two problem space landscapes one often encounters. The first one is the best case scenario where all solutions are leading to the optimal solution (i.e., maximal value marked with a black circle). On the other hand, the second landscape is called needle-in-a-haystack and it presents one of the most difficult landscapes since there are no information leading the search. Many cryptographic problems will have the characteristics of a needle-in-a-haystack landscape and will therefore be hard to solve with EC techniques (or any optimization technique).

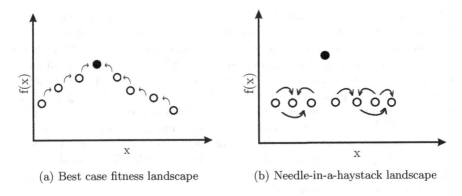

(a) Best case fitness landscape   (b) Needle-in-a-haystack landscape

Fig. 3. Examples of fitness landscapes

Here, we briefly discuss the similarities between machine learning and evolutionary computation techniques. As one can imagine, many problems can be stated in various ways and therefore one can use different approaches when solving them. Accordingly, often we can use interchangeably machine learning and evolutionary computation but also we can use them together to obtain even better results. We elaborate this with several examples.

There exists so-called Evolutionary Machine Learning area where evolutionary computation can be used to solve various supervised or unsupervised problems. In the same area also belongs neuroevolution where EC is used to optimize the weights of the artificial neural networks. Furthermore, the task of feature construction or selection given in Fig. 1 can be also addressed with EC. Finally, EC can be used to evolve a set of learners that are then used to solve a problem.

Moreover, an interesting application of evolutionary computation methods to the machine learning area is called hyperheuristic. There, EC is used to find solutions not in the problem space, but in the heuristic/parameter space. Therefore, EC can be used to do automatic parameter optimization (see Fig. 1) or to select more suitable heuristic techniques.

On the other hand, machine learning can be also used to enhance the search performance of evolutionary computation. This combination is often called Machine Learning Evolutionary Computation (MLEC) where ML is used to improve the performance of various stages of evolutionary computation methods (e.g., better selection procedure or better initialization of the starting population) [9].

3   Design of Cryptographic Primitives

We start with the evolution of cryptographic primitives in the form of Boolean functions and S-boxes. Both of those primitives are intended to introduce nonlinearity into symmetric ciphers. However, Boolean functions are in general used to add nonlinearity to stream ciphers while S-boxes are commonly used in block ciphers (note that S-boxes are also used in stream ciphers but then the output size of an S-box is strictly smaller than the input size of an S-box [10]). Boolean functions are mostly used in a conjunction with Linear Feedback Shift Registers (LFSRs) where two most used models are called filter generator and combiner generator. In a filter generator, the output is obtained by a nonlinear combination of a number of positions in one longer LFSR while in combiner generators, several LFSRs are used in parallel and their output is the input for a Boolean function [11]. However, correlation-immune, low Hamming weight Boolean functions can be also used to reduce the cost of masking countermeasures either by applying leakage squeezing method [12,13] or with Rotating S-box masking [14]. For more information about Boolean functions and their role in cryptography, we refer interested readers to [11].

What is in common to all those applications is that it is possible to (easily) evaluate cryptographic properties of Boolean functions where those properties make them more or less appropriate for such usages. Because it is possible to evaluate those properties, evolutionary computation can be used in a function optimization role. Furthermore, there are several EC encodings that lend themselves naturally to the encoding of Boolean functions such as bitstring encoding (when talking about the truth table representation of Boolean function), integer encoding (when using the Walsh-Hadamard representation), or a tree-based encoding (when using combinatorial representation of Boolean functions).

The EC community is exploring the evolution of cryptographic Boolean functions from late 1990s. As far as we are aware, the first paper investigating the evolution of Boolean functions with good cryptographic properties is done by [15] where the authors experiment with genetic algorithms to evolve Boolean functions with high nonlinearity. From that time, a number of papers appeared that investigated how to evolve Boolean functions with a certain set of cryptographic properties. For an overview of such papers, we refer interested readers to [16]. We note that the majority of those papers report results that can compete with algebraic constructions of Boolean functions and therefore we can conclude EC is a viable candidate when designing Boolean functions for cryptography. However, we note that there exist one possible serious drawback when using EC for the evolution of Boolean functions – the cost of evaluation. Indeed, if a certain cryptographic property is expensive to calculate for a single individual in one iteration of the EC algorithm, then the cumulative cost of calculating that property for all individuals during the whole evolution process can become infeasible.

Since S-boxes ((m, n)-functions) are vectorial Boolean functions, the evolution of S-boxes seems to be a natural extension of the evolution of Boolean functions. Indeed, many properties are calculated in the same way but here we calculate those properties for all non-zero linear combinations of the output functions. This is currently a problem for EC methods since except for small size S-boxes (e.g., 4×4 S-boxes), EC cannot reach optimal values of cryptographic properties [17]. Therefore, for the evolution of S-boxes, EC cannot compete with algebraic methods and we are still waiting for some new insight how to circumvent the problems observed. However, one possible research direction that could be of interest is the evolution of hardware-friendly S-boxes (i.e., S-boxes with small area or low power consumption) since there algebraic constructions cannot account for such implementation based properties.

4   Side-Channel Analysis

Attacks that do not aim at the weaknesses of the ciphers, but on their actual implementations on cryptographic devices are called implementation attacks. When considering usability, strength or cost, such attacks are among the most powerful known attacks against cryptographic devices. One type of implementation attack where the device operates within its specification and the attacker just reads hidden signals is called side-channel attack (SCA) [18]. As such, side-channel attacks represent one extremely powerful category of attacks on cryptographic devices with profiled side-channel attacks in a prominent place as the most powerful among them. There, within the profiling phase the attacker estimates leakage models for targeted intermediate computations, which are then exploited to extract secret information from the device in the actual attack phase. Note that profiled attacks have a clear connection with the supervised learning algorithms from ML domain. There, in the learning phase, the attacker trains an ML algorithm to recognize the output value (class) on the basis of the input data (called attributes or features). Later, that ML model is used to classify new data for which the attacker does not know the classes. Naturally, feature selection can be used to select features having more relevant information, which is especially important if the number of features is too large since the time complexity for ML methods grows with the number of features.

Profiled SCA has many variations since the results can differ substantially with the respect to the number of classes, features, instances, levels of noise, ML algorithms that are used, and parameter tuning. Up to now, ML methods such as Support Vector Machines (SVMs) [19] or Random Forest (RF) [20] have been investigated on several datasets (e.g., DPAcontest v2 [21] and DPAcontest v4 [21]) with very good results when compared with for instance, template attack, which is the most powerful attack from the information theoretic point of view [22]. Several examples of such research are [23–28]. Besides the classification, it is also possible to conduct clustering where the attacker does not know classes for any values but rather tries to group them into a number of clusters. In the context of binary classification, unsupervised attacks on exponentiations are a well explored topic ranging from the usage of custom algorithms [29], over cross-correlation [30–32], to clustering algorithms [33,34].

5   Attacks on PUFs

As a final example we present here how both machine learning and evolutionary computation techniques can be used to attack Physical Unclonable Functions (PUFs). PUFs use inherent manufacturing differences within physical objects to give each of those physical objects a unique identity [35]. First, we give a

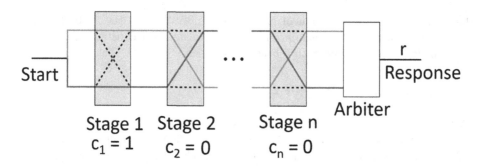

Fig. 4. n-bit Arbiter PUF

depiction of an n-bit Arbiter PUF in Fig. 4. It consists of two signals (top and bottom) that are fed through a number of stages. In each stage, there are two identical layout multiplexers, which receives the signals as inputs. Since each of those multiplexers has a little bit different delay characteristics in the transistors (due to the process variations), the delay introduced by multiplexers will differ for two signals. If the challenge bit c_i for a stage k equals 1, then the multiplexers switch the top and bottom signal, while if the challenge bit is 0, the signals are not switched. An arbiter in the end decides which of the two signals is faster (i.e., comes first) and the results equals 1 if the top signal is faster, and 0 if the bottom signal is faster.

Here, it is possible to attack such a structure with the aforesaid soft computing techniques where the main idea is to model the delay vector $\boldsymbol{w}$. The response of a PUF is determined by the delay difference between the top and bottom signals where that difference equals the sum of differences of individual stages. The delay difference for each stage depends on the corresponding challenge bit c_i. The expressions that are used to calculate the delay difference ΔD are the following:

$$\phi_i = \prod_{l=1}^{k}(-1)^{c_l}, \text{ for } 1 \leq i \leq k. \tag{1}$$

$$\Delta D = \boldsymbol{w}^T \boldsymbol{\phi}^T.$$

$$r = \begin{cases} 1 & \text{if } \Delta D < 0 \\ 0 & \text{if } \Delta D > 0 \end{cases}$$

where c is the challenge and ϕ the feature vector. To obtain the delay vector, one can use regression techniques from the ML area where the output value y of a mapping $y = f(x)$ is a real number or to use function optimization (i.e., evolutionary computation) where one looks for a delay vector that will minimize the error between the predicted and the observed behavior. Some examples of successful applications of soft computing techniques when attacking PUFs can be found in [35–38]. We note that similarly as with the SCA scenario, here it is again hard to obtain a guarantee on the performance of soft computing techniques.

6   Discussion

In previous sections we gave several examples where soft computing techniques are used in cryptology. We omitted details about the algorithms used since the idea here is to give a motivation about the problems and general techniques how to solve them. This is especially important since the soft computing methods used up to now gave good results but they are certainly not the only ones that would produce good results for the presented problems. However, what all problems and approaches have in common is that the results obtained are usually experimentally validated but not mathematically proven. Indeed, it is hard to give the worst case behavior of such methods although some efforts in that direction exist such as the Provably Approximately Correct Learning (PAC Learning) [39]. We note that the difficulties when proving the optimality of such solutions (or algorithms) are also the reason why often it is easier to use soft computing techniques to attack than to construct new designs. Indeed, to confirm that something is a valid attack one just needs to be able to show the attack succeeded, while to prove that some cryptographic primitive is secure often there are no automatic tools or a unified way to proceed. Therefore, to increase the confidence in experimental results, one needs to approach the investigation in a rigorous way with enough information provided to make the experiments reproducible. Moreover, since claiming that something was done successfully can be misleading, such results should be accompanied with a rigorous statistical analysis. Indeed, it is not the same if something is found once out of 100 times, or 90 times out of 100 times.

From the selection of algorithms perspective, it is always good to use several algorithms that preferably belong to different families in order to explore what paradigm is working the best. A proper tuning procedure should be of course a mandatory step. Although there are methods that are quite successful even without extensive tuning, the best results will in general be obtained with properly tuned algorithms. One way how to possibly speed-up the tuning phase could be to use algorithms that do not have parameters to be tuned (e.g., Naive Bayes [40] and $P3$ algorithm [41]). However, such methods are usually either less powerful or much slower in obtaining high quality solutions. When working with the evolutionary computation techniques, we emphasize the importance of the choice of a proper encoding of solutions and objective function.

We note that here we present only several, relatively well researched cryptographic topics that use soft computing techniques. However, there are many more examples such as hardware Trojan detection [42], design of short addition chains [43], or finding fault injection parameters [44] to name a few. We emphasize that when extending the search to the security area, the number of applications grows rapidly. Finally, by simply looking the scenarios where random search is used, one can get an impression where soft computing could be also used. Naturally, often such techniques will not present the core of the research, but only a helper tool.

Finally, we emphasize that many mitigating factors (e.g., noise, large number of classes, the imbalance between the number of measurements belonging to each class, etc.) are also encountered in other research areas. However, often it seems those areas handle such problems more successfully where there is a number of techniques one can employ to deal with any of the aforesaid problems (as well as many other) but such techniques at least for now seem to elude the cryptographic community.

7   Conclusions

In this paper, we discuss the advantages and drawbacks when using soft computing techniques and tackling several real-world problems from the cryptography domain. Although here we focus on successful applications that does not mean soft computing represents some sort of "magic solver". Indeed, there are many problems that cannot (at least for now) be solved with such techniques and any attempts up to now did not bring any positive results. Moreover, a number of difficulties also stem from the fact that we do not always have a good approach of evaluating our designs. Sometimes, the objective functions used are too expensive to be applied in the evolution process or even worse they do not describe the problem sufficiently well. However, the results obtained up to now bring confidence that soft computing will find its place as a viable assortment of techniques when dealing with difficult problems in cryptography, but also generally in the security domain.

Acknowledgments. This work has been supported in part by Croatian Science Foundation under the project IP-2014-09-4882. In addition, this work was supported in part by the Research Council KU Leuven (C16/15/058) and IOF project EDA-DSE (HB/13/020).

The author would like to thank Annelie Heuser and Domagoj Jakobovic for their helpful suggestions when preparing this paper.

References

1. Leskovec, J., Rajaraman, A., Ullman, J.: Mining of Massive Datasets. Cambridge University Press, Cambridge (2014)
2. Mitchell, T.M.: Machine Learning, 1st edn. McGraw-Hill Inc., New York (1997)
3. Bishop, C.M.: Pattern Recognition and Machine Learning (Information Science and Statistics). Springer-Verlag New York Inc., Secaucus (2006)
4. Tran, B., Xue, B., Zhang, M.: Genetic programming for feature construction and selection in classification on high-dimensional data. Memet. Comput. **8**(1), 3–15 (2016)
5. Wolpert, D.H.: The lack of a priori distinctions between learning algorithms. Neural Comput. **8**(7), 1341–1390 (1996)

6. Talbi, E.G.: Metaheuristics: From Design to Implementation. Wiley Publishing, New Jersey (2009)
7. Holland, J.H.: Adaptation in Natural and Artificial Systems: An Introductory Analysis with Applications to Biology, Control, and Artificial Intelligence. The MIT Press, Cambridge (1992)
8. Wolpert, D.H., Macready, W.G.: No free lunch theorems for optimization. IEEE Trans. Evol. Comput. **1**(1), 67–82 (1997)
9. Zhang, J., Zhan, Z., Lin, Y., Chen, N., Gong, Y., Zhong, J., Chung, H., Li, Y., Shi, Y.: Evolutionary computation meets machine learning: a survey. IEEE Comput. Intell. Mag. **6**(4), 68–75 (2011)
10. Carlet, C.: Vectorial Boolean functions for cryptography. In: Crama, Y., Hammer, P.L. (eds.) Boolean Models and Methods in Mathematics, Computer Science, and Engineering, 1st edn., pp. 398–469. Cambridge University Press, New York (2010)
11. Carlet, C.: Boolean functions for cryptography and error correcting codes. In: Crama, Y., Hammer, P.L. (eds.) Boolean Models and Methods in Mathematics, Computer Science, and Engineering, 1st edn., pp. 257–397. Cambridge University Press, New York (2010)
12. Carlet, C., Guilley, S.: Correlation-immune Boolean functions for easing counter measures to side-channel attacks. In: Niederreiter, H., Ostafe, A., Panario, D., Winterhof, A. (eds.) Algebraic Curves and Finite Fields. Cryptography and Other Applications, pp. 41–70. De Gruyter, Berlin (2014)
13. Carlet, C., Guilley, S.: Side-channel Indistinguishability. In: Proceedings of the 2nd International Workshop on Hardware and Architectural Support for Security and Privacy, HASP 2013, pp. 9:1–9:8. ACM, New York (2013)
14. Carlet, C., Danger, J.L., Guilley, S., Maghrebi, H.: Leakage squeezing of order two. In: Galbraith, S., Nandi, M. (eds.) Progress in Cryptology - INDOCRYPT 2012. LNCS, vol. 7668, pp. 120–139. Springer, Heidelberg (2012). doi:10.1007/978-3-642-34931-7_8
15. Millan, W., Clark, A., Dawson, E.: An effective genetic algorithm for finding highly nonlinear boolean functions. In: Han, Y., Okamoto, T., Qing, S. (eds.) ICICS 1997. LNCS, vol. 1334, pp. 149–158. Springer, Heidelberg (1997). doi:10.1007/BFb0028471
16. Picek, S., Jakobovic, D., Miller, J.F., Batina, L., Cupic, M.: Cryptographic Boolean functions: one output, many design criteria. Appl. Soft Comput. **40**, 635–653 (2016)
17. Picek, S., Cupic, M., Rotim, L.: A new cost function for evolution of S-boxes. Evol. Comput. **24**(4), 695–718 (2016)
18. Mangard, S., Oswald, E., Popp, T.: Power Analysis Attacks: Revealing the Secrets of Smart Cards (Advances in Information Security). Springer-Verlag New York Inc., Secaucus (2007)
19. Vapnik, V.N.: The Nature of Statistical Learning Theory. Springer-Verlag New York Inc., New York (1995)
20. Breiman, L.: Random forests. Mach. Learn. **45**(1), 5–32 (2001)
21. TELECOM ParisTech SEN research group: DPA contest, 2nd edn. (2009–2010). http://www.DPAcontest.org/v2/
22. Chari, S., Rao, J.R., Rohatgi, P.: Template attacks. In: Kaliski, B.S., Koç, K., Paar, C. (eds.) CHES 2002. LNCS, vol. 2523, pp. 13–28. Springer, Heidelberg (2003). doi:10.1007/3-540-36400-5_3
23. Heuser, A., Zohner, M.: Intelligent machine homicide. In: Schindler, W., Huss, S.A. (eds.) COSADE 2012. LNCS, vol. 7275, pp. 249–264. Springer, Heidelberg (2012). doi:10.1007/978-3-642-29912-4_18

24. Hospodar, G., Gierlichs, B., De Mulder, E., Verbauwhede, I., Vandewalle, J.: Machine learning in side-channel analysis: a first study. J. Cryptograph. Eng. **1**, 293–302 (2011). doi:10.1007/s13389-011-0023-x
25. Lerman, L., Bontempi, G., Markowitch, O.: Power analysis attack: an approach based on machine learning. Int. J. Appl. Cryptol. **3**(2), 97–115 (2014)
26. Lerman, L., Poussier, R., Bontempi, G., Markowitch, O., Standaert, F.-X.: Template attacks vs. machine learning revisited (and the curse of dimensionality in side-channel analysis). In: Mangard, S., Poschmann, A.Y. (eds.) COSADE 2014. LNCS, vol. 9064, pp. 20–33. Springer, Cham (2015). doi:10.1007/978-3-319-21476-4_2
27. Lerman, L., Bontempi, G., Markowitch, O.: A machine learning approach against a masked AES - reaching the limit of side-channel attacks with a learning model. J. Cryptograph. Eng. **5**(2), 123–139 (2015)
28. Lerman, L., Medeiros, S.F., Bontempi, G., Markowitch, O.: A machine learning approach against a masked AES. In: Francillon, A., Rohatgi, P. (eds.) CARDIS 2013. LNCS, vol. 8419, pp. 61–75. Springer, Cham (2014). doi:10.1007/978-3-319-08302-5_5
29. Walter, C.D.: Sliding windows succumbs to big Mac attack. In: Koç, Ç.K., Naccache, D., Paar, C. (eds.) CHES 2001. LNCS, vol. 2162, pp. 286–299. Springer, Heidelberg (2001). doi:10.1007/3-540-44709-1_24
30. Messerges, T.S., Dabbish, E.A., Sloan, R.H.: Power analysis attacks of modular exponentiation in smartcards. In: Koç, Ç.K., Paar, C. (eds.) Cryptographic Hardware and Embedded Systems. LNCS, pp. 144–157. Springer, Heidelberg (1999). doi:10.1007/3-540-48059-5_14
31. Clavier, C., Feix, B., Gagnerot, G., Roussellet, M., Verneuil, V.: Horizontal correlation analysis on exponentiation. In: Soriano, M., Qing, S., López, J. (eds.) ICICS 2010. LNCS, vol. 6476, pp. 46–61. Springer, Heidelberg (2010). doi:10.1007/978-3-642-17650-0_5
32. Witteman, M.F., Woudenberg, J.G.J., Menarini, F.: Defeating RSA multiply-always and message blinding countermeasures. In: Kiayias, A. (ed.) CT-RSA 2011. LNCS, vol. 6558, pp. 77–88. Springer, Heidelberg (2011). doi:10.1007/978-3-642-19074-2_6
33. Heyszl, J., Ibing, A., Mangard, S., Santis, F.D., Sigl, G.: Clustering algorithms for non-profiled single-execution attacks on exponentiations. In: Smart Card Research and Advanced Applications - 12th International Conference, CARDIS 2013, Berlin, Germany, November 27–29, 2013, 79–93. Revised Selected Papers (2013)
34. Specht, R., Heyszl, J., Kleinsteuber, M., Sigl, G.: Improving non-profiled attacks on exponentiations based on clustering and extracting leakage from multi-channel high-resolution EM measurements. In: Mangard, S., Poschmann, A.Y. (eds.) COSADE 2014. LNCS, vol. 9064, pp. 3–19. Springer, Cham (2015). doi:10.1007/978-3-319-21476-4_1
35. Becker, G.T.: The gap between promise and reality: on the insecurity of XOR Arbiter PUFs. In: Güneysu, T., Handschuh, H. (eds.) CHES 2015. LNCS, vol. 9293, pp. 535–555. Springer, Heidelberg (2015). doi:10.1007/978-3-662-48324-4_27
36. Hospodar, G., Maes, R., Verbauwhede, I.: Machine learning attacks on 65 nm Arbiter PUFs: accurate modeling poses strict bounds on usability. In: 2012 IEEE International Workshop on Information Forensics and Security (WIFS), pp. 37–42, December 2012
37. Rührmair, U., Sehnke, F., Sölter, J., Dror, G., Devadas, S., Schmidhuber, J.: Modeling attacks on physical unclonable functions. In: Proceedings of the 17th ACM Conference on Computer and Communications Security, CCS 2010, pp. 237–249. ACM, New York (2010)

38. Rührmair, U., Sölter, J., Sehnke, F., Xu, X., Mahmoud, A., Stoyanova, V., Dror, G., Schmidhuber, J., Burleson, W., Devadas, S.: PUF modeling attacks on simulated and silicon data. IEEE Trans. Inf. Forensics Secur. **8**(11), 1876–1891 (2013)

39. Valiant, L.G.: A theory of the learnable. Commun. ACM **27**(11), 1134–1142 (1984)

40. Friedman, N., Geiger, D., Goldszmidt, M.: Bayesian network classifiers. Mach. Learn. **29**(2), 131–163 (1997)

41. Goldman, B.W., Punch, W.F.: Parameter-less population pyramid. In: Proceedings of the 2014 Annual Conference on Genetic and Evolutionary Computation, GECCO 2014, pp. 785–792. ACM, New York (2014)

42. Saha, S., Subhra Chakraborty, R., Shashank Nuthakki, S., Anshul, Mukhopadhyay, D.: Improved test pattern generation for hardware trojan detection using genetic algorithm and Boolean satisfiability. In: Güneysu, T., Handschuh, H. (eds.) CHES 2015. LNCS, vol. 9293, pp. 577–596. Springer, Heidelberg (2015). doi:10.1007/978-3-662-48324-4_29

43. Picek, S., Coello Coello, C.A., Jakobovic, D., Mentens, N.: Evolutionary algorithms for finding short addition chains: going the distance. In: Chicano, F., Hu, B., García-Sánchez, P. (eds.) EvoCOP 2016. LNCS, vol. 9595, pp. 121–137. Springer, Cham (2016). doi:10.1007/978-3-319-30698-8_9

44. Picek, S., Batina, L., Buzing, P., Jakobovic, D.: Fault injection with a new flavor: memetic algorithms make a difference. In: Mangard, S., Poschmann, A.Y. (eds.) COSADE 2014. LNCS, vol. 9064, pp. 159–173. Springer, Cham (2015). doi:10.1007/978-3-319-21476-4_11

Parallel Implementations of LEA, Revisited

Hwajeong Seo[1], Taehwan Park[2], Shinwook Heo[2], Gyuwon Seo[2], Bongjin Bae[2],
Zhi Hu[3], Lu Zhou[4], Yasuyuki Nogami[5], Youwen Zhu[6], and Howon Kim[2(✉)]

[1] Institute for Infocomm Research (I2R), Singapore, Singapore
hwajeong84@gmail.com
[2] Pusan National University, Geumjeong, Republic of Korea
{pth5804,shinwookheo,wkdfekf1,bongjinbae704,howonkim}@pusan.ac.kr
[3] Central South University, Changsha, China
huzhi_math@csu.edu.cn
[4] University of Luxembourg, Luxembourg, Luxembourg
happyeveryday5588@126.com
[5] Okayama University, Okayama, Japan
yasuyuki.nogami@okayama-u.ac.jp
[6] Nanjing University, Nanjing, China
zhuyw@nuaa.edu.cn

Abstract. In this paper we revisited the parallel implementations of
LEA. By taking the advantages of both the light-weight features of LEA
and the parallel computation abilities of ARM-NEON platforms, performance is significantly improved. We firstly optimized the implementations on ARM and NEON architectures. For ARM processor, barrel
shifter instruction is used to hide the latencies for rotation operations.
For NEON engine, the minimum number of NEON registers are assigned
to the round key variables by performing the on-time round key loading
from ARM registers. This approach reduces the required NEON registers
for round key variables by three registers and the registers and temporal
registers are used to retain four more plaintext for encryption operation.
Furthermore, we finely transform the data into SIMD format by using
transpose and swap instructions. The compact ARM and NEON implementations are combined together and computed in mixed processing
way. This approach hides the latency of ARM computations into NEON
overheads. Finally, multiple cores are fully exploited to perform the maximum throughputs on the target devices. The proposed implementations
achieved the fastest LEA encryption within 3.2 cycle/byte for Cortex-A9
processors.

Keywords: Lightweight Encryption Algorithm · ARM · NEON ·
OpenMP · Parallel implementation

This work was partly supported by Institute for Information & communications Technology Promotion(IITP) grant funded by the Korea government(MSIP)
(No.10043907, Development of high performance IoT device and Open Platform with
Intelligent Software) and partly supported by the MSIP(Ministry of Science, ICT and
Future Planning), Korea, under the ITRC(Information Technology Research Center) support program (IITP-2016-H8501-16-1017) supervised by the IITP(Institute
for Information & communications Technology Promotion).

© Springer International Publishing AG 2017
D. Choi and S. Guilley (Eds.): WISA 2016, LNCS 10144, pp. 318–330, 2017.
DOI: 10.1007/978-3-319-56549-1_27

1   Introduction

In WISA'13, Lightweight Encryption Algorithm (LEA) was announced by the Attached Institute of ETRI [7]. The LEA algorithm follows ARX architecture which shows high speed in software and hardware implementations and security against timing attacks. In ICISC'13, LEA implementations on high-end ARM-NEON and GPGPU platforms are introduced [16]. The works present efficient techniques for SIMD and SIMT based parallel computations. In [11], LEA block cipher is implemented in web languages such as JavaScript. The results show that the LEA has high performance over web-browsers as well. In FDSE'14, Van Nguyen et al. implemented the NFC protocols with LEA block cipher [17]. In WISA'15, low-end 8-bit AVR processor is also evaluated [12]. The author presented speed and size optimized techniques on 8-bit processors and compared the performance with representative ARX block ciphers including SPECK and SIMON. The work proves that LEA is the most optimal block cipher for embedded applications. Recently, block cipher competition is held by Luxembourg University (FELICS Triathlon). Many light-weight block ciphers are submitted and finally LEA achieved the most efficient block ciphers for Internet of Things by considering three factors including RAM, ROM and execution timing [8]. As listed above, many works prove that LEA is the most promising block cipher for both high-end computers and low-end microprocessors. In this paper, we re-visit previous results for parallel computations. We found that there are large room to improve the parallelism on ARM-NEON processors. Several new techniques are employed and performance is significantly improved. Furthermore, presented techniques are not limited to LEA block cipher implementations. The methods can be easily applied to the other ARX block ciphers such as SIMON and SPECK with simple modifications.

The remainder of this paper is organized as follows. In Sect. 2, we recap the basic specifications of LEA block cipher, FELICS triathlon and target ARM-NEON platform. In Sect. 3, we present the compact parallel implementations of LEA block cipher on ARM-NEON platform. In Sect. 4, we evaluate the performance of proposed methods in terms of clock cycles. Finally, Sect. 5 concludes the paper.

2   Related Works

2.1   LEA Block Cipher

In 2013, Lightweight Encryption Algorithm (LEA) was announced by the Attached Institute of ETRI [7]. The LEA block cipher only performs simple Addition-Rotation-eXclusive-or (ARX) without S-box operations. These lightweight features are appropriate for high performance on both software and hardware environments.

2.2 FELICS Triathlon

In 2015, the open-source software benchmarking framework named Fair Evaluation of Lightweight Cryptographic Systems (FELICS) was proposed. This is similar to SUPERCOP benchmark framework but the system is particularly targeting for embedded processors, which are widely used in IoT and M2M services. Total three different platforms including 8-bit AVR, 16-bit MSP and 32-bit ARM were selected and three different metrics such as execution time, RAM and code size were evaluated. The implementations are tested in three different scenarios including cipher operation, communication protocol and challenge-handshake authentication protocol. In the FELICS Triathlon, more than one hundred different implementations of block and stream ciphers are submitted by researchers from different countries. After the competition, LEA won first triathlon and HIGHT won second triathlon (See Table 1). The other block ciphers including SPECK and Chaskey also show the competitive performance [2,8]. The one interesting observation is all of high-ranking players follow the ARX architecture. Unlike traditional Substitution-Permutation-Networks (SPN), the round function involves only three simple operations including modular addition, rotation with fixed offsets and bit-wise exclusive-or. The ARX operations are relatively fast and cheap for both hardware and software implementations than traditional SPN architecture. Furthermore the operations are performed in constant time, which is immune to timing attacks.

Table 1. First and second winners of FELICS triathlon (Block size/Key size)

Rank	First triathlon	Second triathlon
1	LEA (128/128)	HIGHT (64/128)
2	SPECK (64/96)	Chaskey (128/128)
3	Chaskey (128/128)	SPECK (64/128)

2.3 ARM-NEON Processor

Advanced RISC Machine (ARM) is an instruction set architecture (ISA) design by ARM for high-performance 32-bit embedded applications. Although ARM cores are usually larger and more complex than AVRs and MSPs, most ARM designs also have competitive features in terms of low power consumptions and high code density. The ARM family has developed from the traditional ARM1 to advanced Cortex architectures in these days. They provide large number of pipeline stages and various caches, SIMD extensions and simple load/store architecture. Most instructions of the ARM are computed in a single cycle except memory access and some arithmetic instructions. Particularly, the inline barrel shifter instruction allows the shifted/rotated second operand before the main operation. The load and store-multiple instructions copy any number of general-purpose registers from/to a block of sequential memory addresses. Their 32-bit wise instructions mainly used for ARX architectures are described in Table 2.

Table 2. Instruction set summary for ARM

Mnemonics	Operands	Description	Cycles
ADD	Rd, Rr	Add without carry	1
EOR	Rd, Rr	Exclusive OR	1
ROL	Rd, Rr,#imm	Rotate left through carry	1
ROR	Rd, Rr,#imm	Rotate right through carry	1

Table 3. Instruction set summary for NEON

Mnemonics	Operands	Description	Cycles
VADD	Qd,Qn,Qm	Vector addition	1
VEOR	Qd,Qn,Qm	Vector exclusive-or	1
VSHL	Qd,Qm,#imm	Vector left shift	1
VSRI	Qd,Qm,#imm	Vector right shift with insert	2

NEON is a 128-bit SIMD architecture for the ARM Cortex-A series. One of the biggest difference between traditional ARM processors and new ARM-NEON processors is NEON features. The NEON engine offers 128-bit wise registers and instructions. Each register is considered as a vector of elements of the same data type and this data type can be signed/unsigned 8-bit, 16-bit, 32-bit, or 64-bit. The detailed instructions for ARX operations are described in Table 3. This feature provides a more precise operation in various word sizes, which allows us to perform multiple data in single instruction. With this features, the NEON engine can accelerate data processing by at least 3X that provided by ARMv5 and at least 2X that provided by ARMv6 SIMD instructions. This nice structure can boost previous implementations by converting single instruction single data model to SIMD. In CHES 2012, NEON-based cryptography implementations including Salsa20, Poly1305, Curve25519 and Ed25519 were presented [4]. In order to enhance the performance, the authors provided novel bit-rotation, integration of multiplication and reduction operations exploiting NEON instructions. In CT–RSA'13, ARM–NEON implementation of Grøstl shows that 40% performance enhancements than the previous fastest ARM implementation [6]. In HPEC 2013, a multiplicand reduction method for ARM-NEON was introduced for the NIST curves [5]. In CHES 2014, the Curve41417 implementation adopts 2-level Karatsuba multiplication in the redundant representation [3]. In ICISC 2014, Seo et al. introduced a novel 2-way Cascade Operand Scanning (COS) multiplication for RSA implementation [13,14]. In ICISC 2015, Seo et al. introduced a efficient modular multiplication and squaring operations for NIST P-521 curve [15]. Recently, Ring-LWE implementation is also accelerated by taking advantages of NEON instructions [1].

Particularly for LEA block ciphers, in [7], LEA implementation exploits multiple load/store, rotate instructions on ARM processor and shows higher performance than AES implementations [9]. In [16], first LEA implementation on NEON engine is suggested, which is highly accelerating the performance of LEA encryption with SIMD instructions. For performance enhancements, interdependency between each instruction set is removed and multiple plaintext/round keys are performed in parallel way. Surprisingly, parallel implementations of LEA are not studied actively. By considering the importance of LEA block cipher, we need to further study on parallel implementations of LEA. In this paper, we suggested the several new techniques to improve the LEA block cipher in parallel way. The proposed methods are not limited to LEA but they can be applied to the other ARX block ciphers including SPECK and SIMON with simple modifications.

3   Proposed Parallel Implementations of LEA

3.1   Optimizations of ARM Implementation

LEA block cipher can be efficiently implemented on the 32-bit ARM processor, because the platform provides 32-bit wise addition, bit-wise exclusive-or and rotation within single clock cycle, which are main ARX operations for LEA block cipher described in Table 4. In order to further improve the performance, we combine the bit-wise exclusive-or and rotation operations with barrel shifter technique. This operation provides cost-free rotation by inserting inline rotation into second operand. The bit-wise exclusive-or instruction needs two operands. The second operand should be rotated before it is inputted to next operation. We perform inline barrel shifter to conduct rotation operation on second operand. The optimized operations are described in Table 5. Particularly, the source codes describe the first and second rounds of LEA encryption with/without inline barrel shifter instructions. Without inline barrel shifter, whole intermediate results are rotated before next round computations. Unlike traditional approach, we perform rotation operations with inline barrel shifter for second operand of bit-wise exclusive-or operation. This approach reduces the independent rotation computations and improves performance by number of rotation operations. For register level optimization, we assigned 4 registers for plaintext, 4 registers for round keys and remaining registers are used for temporal registers in encryption procedures.

Table 4. 32-bit instructions over 32-bit ARM, where R8 and R3 represent destination and source registers

Addition	Exclusive-or	Right rotation by 31
ADD R8, R8, R5	EOR R8, R8, R5	ROR R8, #31

Table 5. Different implementations with, without inline barrel shifter in source code level, where %0, %1, r4-r7 and r8-r11 represent round-key pointer, plaintext pointer, round-key and plaintext

With inline barrel shifter	Without inline barrel shifter
ldmia %1, {r8-r11}	ldmia %1, {r8-r11}
//round 1	//round 1
ldmia %0!, {r4-r7}	ldmia %0!, {r4-r7}
eor r11, r11, r5	eor r11, r11, r5
eor r7, r7, r10	eor r7, r7, r10
add r11, r11, r7	add r11, r11, r7
eor r10, r10, r5	eor r10, r10, r5
eor r6, r6, r9	eor r6, r6, r9
add r10, r10, r6	add r10, r10, r6
eor r9, r9, r5	eor r9, r9, r5
eor r4, r4, r8	eor r4, r4, r8
add r9, r9, r4	add r9, r9, r4
	ror r11, #3
	ror r10, #5
	ror r9, #23
//round 2	//round 2
ldmia %0!, {r4-r7}	ldmia %0!, {r4-r7}
eor r8, r8, r5	eor r8, r8, r5
eor r7, r7, r11, ror#3	eor r7, r7, r11
add r8, r8, r7	add r8, r8, r7
eor r11, r5, r11, ror#3	eor r11, r5, r11
eor r6, r6, r10, ror#5	eor r6, r6, r10
add r11, r11, r6	add r11, r11, r6
eor r10, r5, r10, ror#5	eor r10, r5, r10
eor r4, r4, r9, ror#23	eor r4, r4, r9
add r10, r10, r4	add r10, r10, r4
	ror r8, #3
	ror r11, #5
	ror r10, #23

3.2 Optimizations of NEON Implementation

The basic 32-bit wise ARX operations of LEA block cipher are established with NEON instructions (See Table 6). We further optimize the register usages in order to reduce the memory accesses where the NEON architecture has 16 128-bit Q registers. The previous implementations used 8 registers for plaintext,

Table 6. 32-bit instructions over 128-bit ARM-NEON, where `q1` and `q0` represent destination and source registers

Addition	Exclusive-or	Right rotation by 9
`vadd.i32 q1, q1, q0`	`veor q1, q1, q0`	`vshl.i32 q1, q0, #9`
		`vsri.32 q1, q0, #23`

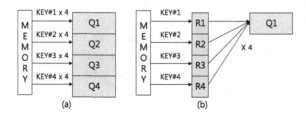

(a)   (b)

Fig. 1. Managements of round keys (a) previous approach, (b) proposed approach

4 registers for round keys and 4 registers for temporal registers [16]. Particularly, the four identical round keys are saved into memory and loaded to `Q` registers for LEA computations. However this approach requires multiple memory access operations to get duplicated round key pairs and target platforms consumes large amounts of memory to store the duplicated round keys. In our approach, we store the round keys in memory without duplication. The one round key is loaded to the ARM's `R` registers and then this variable is duplicated to the NEON registers in each time with `vdup` instruction. The detailed descriptions are drawn in Fig. 1. For previous approach, duplicated round keys are directly loaded to the NEON registers (`Q1-Q4`). However, proposed approach loads non-duplicated round keys into ARM registers (`R1-R4`) and then each time they are duplicated into the NEON register (`Q1`). The approach reduces the required number of `Q` registers for round keys by 3 registers and required memory storages for round keys are also reduced by 75%. The obtained 3 registers are used to handle the 3 more plaintext in parallel way. In our implementations, 12 registers are assigned for plaintext and only one register is used for round keys. The remaining 3 registers are used for temporal registers.

In order to exploit the SIMD instruction, traditional data format should be realigned to meet the SIMD architecture. Previous implementations use transpose and move operations to align the data into 4 32-bit packed alignments for single 128-bit register [16]. However, two or three move operations are easily replaced into one 64-bit wise swap instruction. In our approach, we used the transpose and swap instructions, which optimizes the 2/3 move instruction into 1 swap instruction for 64-bit wise swap operation. The detailed descriptions are available in Fig. 2. Firstly sequentially aligned four packets ({1-1, 1-2, 1-3, 1-4},

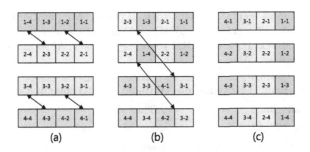

Fig. 2. Register alignments (a) transposing the registers, (b) swapping the registers, (c) aligned registers

{2-1, 2-2, 2-3, 2-4}, {3-1, 3-2, 3-3, 3-4}, {4-1, 4-2, 4-3, 4-4}) are transposed, which output the packets in ({1-1, 2-1, 1-3, 2-3}, {1-2, 2-2, 1-4, 2-4}, {3-1, 4-1, 3-3, 4-3}, {3-2, 4-2, 3-4, 4-4}) order. After then 64-bit swap operations are performed to get the results in ({1-1, 2-1, 3-1, 4-1}, {1-2, 2-2, 3-2, 4-2}, {1-3, 2-3, 3-3, 4-3}, {1-4, 2-4, 3-4, 4-4}) order.

3.3 Parallel Computations of ARM and NEON

ARM processor and NEON engine are independent processing modules and perform the computations independently. This feature can be utilized to improve the performance by hiding the latency of ARM operations. As we can see in Fig. 3(a), sequential approach performs the NEON and ARM operations in sequential order so processing time are exactly the sum of NEON and ARM execution time. However, the proposed approach in Fig. 3(b) hides the ARM operation timing into NEON operation by mixing the program codes. The detailed program codes are written in Table 7. The proposed approach mixed the ARM and NEON instructions each time and processing timing for ARM operations are hidden into NEON operations. Finally, we performed the 12 LEA encryptions in NEON engine and 1 additional LEA encryption within reduced execution timing. This approach hides the computation timing for ARM processor and optimizes the performance.

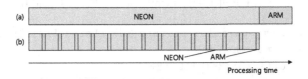

Fig. 3. Comparison of processing time (a) sequential approach, (b) parallel approach

Table 7. Different implementations with/without parallel computations in source code level, where q12, (q3, q7, q11), (r2-r5), (r6, r7) and r10 represent NEON round key register, NEON plaintext registers, ARM round key register, ARM plaintext registers, ARM temporal register

With parallel computations	Without parallel computations
//ARM--NEON	//NEON
vdup.32 q12, r3	vdup.32 q12, r3
eor r7, r3, r7, ror#23	veor q3, q3, q12
veor q3, q3, q12	veor q7, q7, q12
eor r10, r5, r6, ror#3	veor q11, q11, q12
veor q7, q7, q12	//ARM
add r7, r7, r10	eor r7, r3, r7, ror#23
veor q11, q11, q12	eor r10, r5, r6, ror#3
	add r7, r7, r10

3.4 Thread Level Optimization with OpenMP

Recent ARM-NEON processors have multiple cores and each core can perform independent work loads in parallel way. In order to exploit the full capabilities of multiple processing, we used SIMT programming library, namely OpenMP. Our target device has four physical cores, which can lead to theoretically 4 times of performance improvements. We re-scheduled previous our implementations using OpenMP programming to support parallel functions. The detailed program codes are described in Table 8. The id variables are critical data and defined as private. The PLAINTEXT is defined as shared variables. The PLAINTEXT is indexed by id variables, which ensures that each thread accesses to different data. We assigned each encryption operation into single thread so the four different LEA encryptions are performed in four different cores. As we can see in Fig. 4, 1 encryption (ARM) and 12 encryptions (NEON) in each core are performed simultaneously. Total 52 (13×4) parallel encryptions are performed in 4 different cores.

Table 8. Parallel Implementation of LEA in OpenMP

```
#pragma omp parallel private(id) shared(PLAINTEXT)
    #pragma omp for
        for(id=0;id<TOTAL;id++)
            Encryption(ROUNDKEY,PLAINTEXT[id]);
```

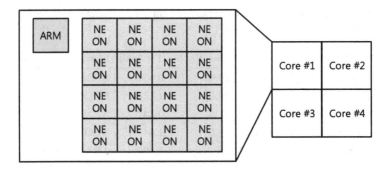

Fig. 4. Detailed architectures of parallel encryptions in multiple cores

4   Results

For performance evaluation, we selected the Cortex-A9 board, which is 32-bit processor with L1 cache and L2 cache. The board is widely used in commercial products such as Galaxy/Apple Smart-phones, PandaBoard/Odroid development platforms. Particularly, our target platform supports quad-core operated at 1.4 GHz. The program codes are written in assembly language and compiled with NDK android library. The performance is measured in system time function. The comparison results are drawn in Table 9. The previous LEA implementation on ARM instruction sets achieved the 20.06 cycle/byte [7]. In this paper, we improve the performance by taking advantages of barrel shifter instruction. The technique does not impose rotation overheads and enhances the performance by 13.8% for ARM platform. In terms of NEON instruction, the previous parallel LEA implementation achieved the 10.06 cycle/byte [16]. The previous work presented several techniques such as efficient ARX instructions in NEON and pipelined implementations. In this paper, we further improve the performance by suggesting the compact round key access techniques. The method reduces the required registers for round keys and increases the number of plaintext for encryption in each round. Second, ordinary format is efficiently converted into SIMD format with transpose and swap instructions. With these techniques, NEON implementation is improved by 15.5%. The both implementations are finely integrated together, which hides the latency for ARM instruction. The results show 20.4% performance enhancements.

The performance is accelerated again by exploiting the full multiple cores in the platforms. Our target platform is quad-core architecture so it improves the performance by increasing the number of threads. Interestingly, the performance decreases when the number of threads is larger than the number of cores, because many number of threads requires a number of context-switching procedures and this causes performance bottleneck (See Fig. 5). Finally, fully parallelized LEA

Table 9. Comparison of LEA implementations on ARM/NEON architectures, c/b: cycle/byte, Gbps: Giga bit per second

Method	Speed(c/b)	T(Gbps)	Instruction
Hong et al. [7]	20.06	0.558	ARM
Seo et al. [16]	10.06	1.113	NEON
Proposed method ver 1	17.3	0.647	ARM
Proposed method ver 2	8.5	1.317	NEON
Proposed method ver 3	8	1.400	ARM–NEON

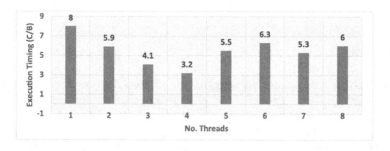

Fig. 5. Performance evaluation of multiple-thread encryptions

implementations achieved the 3.2 cycle/byte with 4 threads. This is the highest performance reported ever[1].

5   Conclusion

In this paper, we presented new parallel implementation methods for LEA block cipher on representative SIMD platform, namely ARM-NEON. We firstly optimized the both ARM and NEON implementations after then both methods are finely integrated into processing order. The results are accelerated again by taking advantages of multiple cores. Finally, we achieved performance enhancement up-to 8 cycle/byte with single core implementation, which is 20.4% faster than previous parallel implementation on identical target platforms. By enabling the features of multiple cores, we achieved 3.2 cycle/byte which improved again the our single core results by 60%.

The proposed methods improved the LEA block cipher on ARM-NEON platforms. For this reason, there are many future works remained. First, we can directly improve the other ARX block ciphers such as SPECK and SIMON. Recent works by [10] does not consider the any methods proposed in this paper so we expect high performance enhancements with proposed methods. Second, we

---

[1] For reproduction of results, the source codes will be public domain in following address. (https://github.com/solowal/WISA2016_LEA).

only explore the ARM-NEON platform. However, INTEL and AMD processors also provide SIMD instructions such as AVX and SSE. These SIMD instructions are very similar to NEON instructions so we can directly apply the proposed techniques to other SIMD instruction sets. Furthermore, these platforms support multiple cores and multiple threads. We can further explore the strong features of OpenMP on these platforms.

References

1. Azarderakhsh, R., Liu, Z., Seo, H., Kim, H.: NEON PQCryto: fast and parallel ring-LWE encryption on ARM NEON architecture
2. Beaulieu, R., Shors, D., Smith, J., Treatman-Clark, S., Weeks, B., Wingers, L.: The SIMON and SPECK lightweight block ciphers. In: Proceedings of the 52nd Annual Design Automation Conference, p. 175. ACM (2015)
3. Bernstein, D.J., Chuengsatiansup, C., Lange, T., Schwabe, P.: Kummer strikes back: new DH speed records. In: Sarkar, P., Iwata, T. (eds.) ASIACRYPT 2014. LNCS, vol. 8873, pp. 317–337. Springer, Heidelberg (2014). doi:10.1007/978-3-662-45611-8_17
4. Bernstein, D.J., Schwabe, P.: NEON crypto. In: Prouff, E., Schaumont, P. (eds.) CHES 2012. LNCS, vol. 7428, pp. 320–339. Springer, Heidelberg (2012). doi:10.1007/978-3-642-33027-8_19
5. Faz-Hernández, A., Longa, P., Sánchez, A.H.: Efficient and secure algorithms for GLV-based scalar multiplication and their implementation on GLV-GLS curves. In: Benaloh, J. (ed.) CT-RSA 2014. LNCS, vol. 8366, pp. 1–27. Springer, Cham (2014). doi:10.1007/978-3-319-04852-9_1
6. Holzer-Graf, S., Krinninger, T., Pernull, M., Schläffer, M., Schwabe, P., Seywald, D., Wieser, W.: Efficient vector implementations of AES-based designs: a case study and new implemenations for Grøstl. In: Dawson, E. (ed.) CT-RSA 2013. LNCS, vol. 7779, pp. 145–161. Springer, Heidelberg (2013). doi:10.1007/978-3-642-36095-4_10
7. Hong, D., Lee, J.-K., Kim, D.-C., Kwon, D., Ryu, K.H., Lee, D.-G.: LEA: a 128-bit block cipher for fast encryption on common processors. In: Kim, Y., Lee, H., Perrig, A. (eds.) WISA 2013. LNCS, vol. 8267, pp. 3–27. Springer, Cham (2014). doi:10.1007/978-3-319-05149-9_1
8. Mouha, N., Mennink, B., Herrewege, A., Watanabe, D., Preneel, B., Verbauwhede, I.: Chaskey: an efficient MAC algorithm for 32-bit microcontrollers. In: Joux, A., Youssef, A. (eds.) SAC 2014. LNCS, vol. 8781, pp. 306–323. Springer, Cham (2014). doi:10.1007/978-3-319-13051-4_19
9. Osvik, D.A., Bos, J.W., Stefan, D., Canright, D.: Fast software AES encryption. In: Hong, S., Iwata, T. (eds.) FSE 2010. LNCS, vol. 6147, pp. 75–93. Springer, Heidelberg (2010). doi:10.1007/978-3-642-13858-4_5
10. Park, T., Seo, H., Kim, H.: Parallel implementations of SIMON and SPECK. In: 2016 International Conference on Platform Technology and Service (PlatCon), pp. 1–6. IEEE (2016)
11. Seo, H., Kim, H.: Low-power encryption algorithm block cipher in JavaScript. J. Inf. Commun. Convergence Eng. 12(4), 252–256 (2014)
12. Seo, H., Liu, Z., Choi, J., Park, T., Kim, H.: Compact implementations of LEA block cipher for low-end microprocessors. In: Kim, H., Choi, D. (eds.) WISA 2015. LNCS, vol. 9503, pp. 28–40. Springer, Cham (2016). doi:10.1007/978-3-319-31875-2_3

13. Seo, H., Liu, Z., Großschädl, J., Choi, J., Kim, H.: Montgomery modular multi-plication on ARM-NEON revisited. In: Lee, J., Kim, J. (eds.) ICISC 2014. LNCS, vol. 8949, pp. 328–342. Springer, Cham (2015). doi:10.1007/978-3-319-15943-0_20

14. Seo, H., Liu, Z., Großschädl, J., Kim, H.: Efficient arithmetic on ARM-NEON and its application for high-speed RSA implementation. IACR Cryptology ePrint Archive **2015**, 465 (2015)

15. Seo, H., Liu, Z., Nogami, Y., Park, T., Choi, J., Zhou, L., Kim, H.: Faster ECC over $\mathbb{F}_{2^{521}-1}$ (feat. NEON). In: Kwon, S., Yun, A. (eds.) ICISC 2015. LNCS, vol. 9558, pp. 169–181. Springer, Cham (2016). doi:10.1007/978-3-319-30840-1_11

16. Seo, H., Liu, Z., Park, T., Kim, H., Lee, Y., Choi, J., Kim, H.: Parallel implemen-tations of LEA. In: Lee, H.-S., Han, D.-G. (eds.) ICISC 2013. LNCS, vol. 8565, pp. 256–274. Springer, Cham (2014). doi:10.1007/978-3-319-12160-4_16

17. Nguyen, H., Seo, H., Kim, H.: Prospective cryptography in NFC with the light-weight block encryption algorithm LEA. In: Dang, T.K., Wagner, R., Neuhold, E., Takizawa, M., Küng, J., Thoai, N. (eds.) FDSE 2014. LNCS, vol. 8860, pp. 191–203. Springer, Cham (2014). doi:10.1007/978-3-319-12778-1_15

Multi-precision Squaring
for Public-Key Cryptography
on Embedded Microprocessors, a Step Forward

Hwajeong Seo[1], Taehwan Park[2], Shinwook Heo[2], Gyuwon Seo[2],
Bongjin Bae[2], Lu Zhou[3], and Howon Kim[2(✉)]

[1] Institute for Infocomm Research (I2R), Singapore, Singapore
hwajeong84@gmail.com
[2] Pusan National University, Busan, Republic of Korea
{pth5804,shinwookheo,wkdfekf1,bongjinbae704,howonkim}@pusan.ac.kr
[3] University of Luxembourg, Luxembourg, Luxembourg
happyeveryday5588@126.com

Abstract. Multi-precision squaring is one of the most performance-critical operations for implementations of public-key cryptography, e.g. RSA, ECC as well as Diffie-Hellman key exchange protocols. In this paper, we propose novel techniques to push the speed limits of multi-precision squaring on embedded processors. The method reduces the number of memory access operations and improves the previous Sliding Block Doubling method by 4.1% on 8-bit RISC processor.

Keywords: Multi-precision multiplication · Public key cryptography · RSA · DSA · ECC · Diffie-Hellman · Embedded processor

1 Introduction

Multi-precision arithmetic is a performance-critical component of public-key cryptographic algorithms. Particularly, the multiplication and squaring operations impose the high overheads on resource-constraint embedded processors [7,8,10,11,13]. In order to improve the performance, a number of studies have performed on the optimizations of operations on the target platforms [9,12,18,20–22,25–27].

There are several optimizations to implement multiplication on embedded processors, ranging from classic Operand Scanning (OS) method to some sophisticated methods (e.g. Hybrid Scanning (HS) multiplication [2] and Operand

This work was partly supported by Institute for Information & communications Technology Promotion (IITP) grant funded by the Korea government (MSIP) (No. 10043907, Development of high performance IoT device and Open Platform with Intelligent Software) and partly supported by the MSIP (Ministry of Science, ICT and Future Planning), Korea, under the ITRC (Information Technology Research Center) support program (IITP-2016-H8501-16-1017) supervised by the IITP (Institute for Information & communications Technology Promotion).

© Springer International Publishing AG 2017
D. Choi and S. Guilley (Eds.): WISA 2016, LNCS 10144, pp. 331–340, 2017.
DOI: 10.1007/978-3-319-56549-1_28

Caching (OC) method [5]). The operand scanning method loads all operands in a row and computes partial products at once [14]. An alternative way to implement multiplication is Product Scanning (PS) method. This method computes all partial products in a column, eliminating needs to reload intermediate results [1]. However, the operand scanning method needs a number of accumulator registers, while the product scanning method requires a number of memory-access to get the operands. The hybrid scanning method combines the useful features of both operand-scanning and product-scanning [2]. By adjusting the width of row and column, the number of operand and intermediate result access are optimized. In CHES 2011, the operand caching method, which reduces the number of `load` operations by caching the operands, was presented in [5]. Later, Seo and Kim optimized operand caching method in [17,19] proposed the Consecutive Operand Caching (COC) method, which has continuous operand caching process.

In terms of efficient multi-precision squaring operation, most of the proposed multiplication methods can be used to squaring. However, it is inefficient since all partial products and loading both operands are unnecessary for squaring operation. For this reason, squaring dedicated methods have been suggested. In [16], Carry Catcher (CC) method, which removes carry propagation generating carry values to the most significant byte position in most word-to-word multiplication by introducing storages for saving carry values, was used for squaring. In 2012, Lazy Doubling (LD) method was proposed in [6]. In this technique, the byte-wise multiplication results, which are required to be added twice to intermediate results, are doubled after they are collected to the accumulation registers at the end of each column computation. In INDOCRYPT'13, Sliding Block Doubling (SBD) method, the squaring algorithm executes doubling operation by delaying the operation to the end of process [23]. The doubling process is conducted on fully accumulated intermediate results with 1-bit shift operation. The basic multiplication and squaring methods can be accelerated again by using asymptotically faster integer multiplication, namely Karatsbua technique [4,24].

In this paper, we revisited the previous SBD squaring technique and presented new optimizations for further pushing the speed limits. The proposed technique delays the least and most significant parts, which reduce the number of memory accesses for these parts. Finally we achieve the record-setting results on 8-bit AVR platform, which outperform the previous SBD results by 4.1%. The remainder of this paper is organized as follows. In Sect. 2, we recap the previous squaring methods. In Sect. 3, we present novel methods for multi-precision squaring on AVR microcontroller. Thereafter, we will show the our experiment results in Sect. 4. Finally, in Sect. 5, we conclude the paper.

2   Related Works

Throughout the paper, we will use the following notations. Let A be one operand with a length of m-bit that are represented by multiple-word arrays. The operand is written as follows: $A = (A[n-1], ..., A[2], A[1], A[0])$, whereby $n = \lceil m/w \rceil$, and w is the word size. The result of squaring $C = A \cdot A$ is twice length of A, and represented by $C = (C[2n-1], ..., C[2], C[1], C[0])$. For clarity, we describe the method using a squaring structure and triangle forms. The squaring structure describes order of partial products from top to bottom and each point in triangle form represents a squaring $A[i] \times A[j]$. The rightmost corner of the triangle represents the lowest indices $(i, j = 0)$, whereas the leftmost represents corner the highest indices $(i, j = n-1)$. The lowermost side represents result indices $C[k]$, which ranges from the rightmost corner $(k = 0)$ to the leftmost corner $(k = 2n-1)$. Particularly, the squaring structure is described in triangle form and consists of three parts including red dotted middle part, light and dark gray parts. The red part represents the multiplication, which is computed once. The other parts including light and dark gray parts can be computed with one multiplication and doubling.

Figure 1 describes Yang et al.'s method [15]. The method requires a number of registers for intermediate results. First, duplicated partial products are computed using operand scanning. After then the intermediate results are doubled. Lastly, remaining partial products are computed. When we accumulate the partial products in ascending order, this process generates carry values. In order to handle carry values, carry-catcher method is introduced, which stores carry values into additional registers and then updates the carry values to the intermediate results at the end of computations. In Fig. 2, Carry Catcher (CC) based squaring was introduced by [16]. This method follows hybrid-scanning and doubles partial product results before they are added to results. This method is

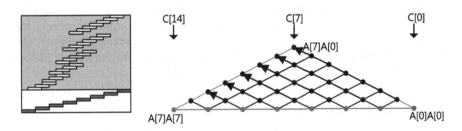

Fig. 1. Yang et al.'s squaring [15] (Color figure online)

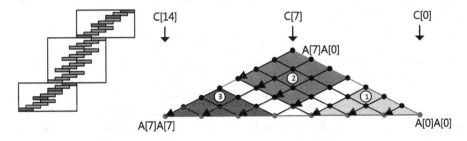

Fig. 2. Carry catcher squaring [16]. (Color figure online)

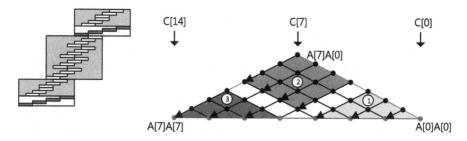

Fig. 3. Lazy doubling squaring [6] (Color figure online)

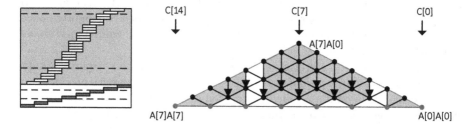

Fig. 4. Sliding block doubling squaring [23]. (Color figure online)

inefficient because all products should be doubled, before it added to the inter-mediate results. In Fig. 3, the Lazy-Doubling (LD) method is described [6]. This method follows hybrid scanning structure. The inner loop is computed in operand scanning way, and then carry catcher method is used for removing consecutive carry updates. In Fig. 4, Sliding Block Doubling (SBD) method performs the "1-bit left shifting" operation at the end of duplicated partial products. The SBD method exploits product-scanning technique to compute duplicated partial products. After then the intermediate results are doubled.

3   Proposed Method

We introduce a novel method to implement multi-precision squaring method for microprocessors named Sliding Middle Block Doubling (SMBD). The previous SBD method computes the whole duplicated partial products in first stage, which requires $2n$ times of `load` and `store` instructions for the intermediate results [23]. However, the proposed SMBD method performs the middle part of duplicated partial products first and then the remaining parts are computed with doubling process. The technique allows us to reduce the number of intermediate result access. Similar as SBD, we also adopted product scanning method to perform the partial products. The detailed SMBD procedures are as follows. Firstly, the whole computations are divided into three parts including middle (M), right (R) and left (L) parts. Second, in Fig. 5, black dots in middle part (M) are computed in the first stage. And then the black dots in right section (R) is computed and

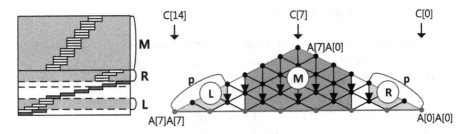

Fig. 5. Sliding middle block doubling squaring (Color figure online)

then doubled together. After then the partial products colored in red located in right section (R) are performed. In the middle part (M), intermediate results are doubled and red dots are performed. Finally, on the left section (L), the partial products are computed and doubled, computing the red dots. The size of sub-sections is determined by block size (p). The ideal value of size p is the half of general purpose registers in processors, because we need to maintain both variables including operand values and intermediate results in order to compute sections (L, R) without additional memory accesses. Compared with previous SBD method, we can reduce memory load and store by size of right and left sections. The example for 8-limb computations are given in Fig. 5. Firstly, the block located at the upper middle part (M) of the triangle form are executed in product scanning method from $A[4] \times A[0]$ to $A[7] \times A[3]$. The block located at the right section (R) is computing partial products from $A[0] \times A[1]$ to $A[2] \times A[1]$ by following "product scanning" technique. After computing right part, we doubled the intermediate results, using 1-bit left shift operation. Simultaneously red dots are performed from $A[0] \times A[0]$ to $A[5] \times A[5]$. After then, the block located at the left section (L) is computing partial products from $A[6] \times A[5]$ to $A[7] \times A[6]$ by following "product scanning" technique and then doubled, while, remaining partial products including $A[6] \times A[6]$ and $A[7] \times A[7]$ are computed[1].

4   Results

ATmega128 is representative RISC 8-bit embedded processor clocked at 7.37 MHz. It has a 128 kB EEPROM chip, 4 kB RAM chip and 32 registers [3]. Among general purpose registers, 6 registers ($R_{26} \sim R_{31}$) serve as the special pointers for indirect addressing and 2 registers ($R_0 \sim R_1$) store results of multiplication. The remaining 24 registers are available for arithmetic operations. One arithmetic instruction incurs one clock cycle, and memory instructions or 8-bit multiplication incurs two processing cycles. The detailed descriptions for instructions are given in Table 1. The most expensive operations in resource constrained device belongs to memory access (e.g. load and store) and multiplication.

---

[1] Pseudo code of sliding middle block doubling is available in Appendix A, and the triangle form in 160-bit is depicted in Fig. 6 in Appendix B.

Table 1. Instruction set summary for AVR

Mnemonics	Operands	Description	Operation	#Clock
ADD	Rd, Rr	Add without carry	Rd ← Rd + Rr	1
ADC	Rd, Rr	Add with carry	Rd ← Rd + Rr + C	1
MUL	Rr1, Rr2	Multiply	R1, R0 ← Rr1 × Rr2	2
LSL	Rd	Logical shift left	C|Rd ← Rd<<1	1
LSR	Rd	Logical shift right	Rd|C ← 1>>Rd	1
LD	Rd, X	Load indirect	Rd ← (X)	2
ST	Z, Rr	Store indirect	(Z) ← Rr	2

Table 2. Comparison of computation complexity with previous works

Algorithms	mul	load	store	add	shift
CC [16]	$\frac{n^2}{2}$	$5n$	$2n$	$\frac{6n^2}{2}$	–
LD [6]	$\frac{n^2}{2}$	$\frac{15}{4}n - 26$	$2n$	$\frac{3n^2}{2}$	–
SBD [23]	$\frac{n^2}{2}$	$3n$	$4n$	$\frac{3n^2+4n}{2}$	$2n$
SMBD	$\frac{n^2}{2}$	$3n - 2p$	$4n - 2p$	$\frac{3n^2+4n}{2}$	$2n$

Table 3. Comparison of clock cycle with related works in unrolled 160-bit version

Instruction	add	mul	ld	st	mov	Other cycles	Total cycles
CPI	1	2	2	2	1		
Yang [15]	909	210	468	280	n/a	284	3009
CC [16]	1265	210	100	40	n/a	100	2065
LD [6]	804	210	51	40	n/a	103	1509
SBD [23]	671	210	58	81	n/a	87	1456
Proposed SMBD	**676**	**210**	**41**	**68**	**19**	**63**	**1396**

We analyze the computation complexity of several squaring methods in terms of these basic instructions in Table 2. The number of multiplication is identical in all methods, but the proposed SMBD method requires $3n - 2p$ load instruction. Specifically, the whole operands and intermediate results are loaded once and number of memory load is reduced by $2p$ times since the left and right corner sections are computed at the end of the whole computations. For store instruction, whole intermediate results are stored twice into the memory and $2p$ times of memory access are reduced. The practical example for instruction in clock cycle is given in Table 3. As we explored in Table 2, SMBD requires the small number of memory accesses. This method improved the previous INDOCRYPT'13 results by 4.1% [23]. Particularly, total $4p$ times of memory access operations are

Table 4. Comparison of squaring in clock cycle on 8-bit AVR processors

Method	160-bit	192-bit	224-bit
CC [16]	2065	2909	3897
LD [6]	1509	2107	2785
SBD [23]	1456	2014	n/a
Proposed SMBD	**1396**	**1958**	**2685**

optimized from SBD method. In Table 4, we compared the results in different operand lengths. The SMBD method achieved the highest performance among them.

5   Conclusion

This paper introduced novel methods to enhance the performance critical squaring operation on RISC microcontrollers. Particularly, we propose the SMBD methods for multi-precision squaring. This method reduces a number of load and store instructions by optimizing the computation orders. Based on these proposed method, we set the record-setting result for squaring operation. In order to illustrate our solution, we implemented them on 8-bit ATmega128 platform. Using SMBD method on ATmega128, we achieved an execution time of 1396 clock cycles for 160-bit squaring. This result improves the best reported solution by a factor of 4.1% comparing with the previous result in INDOCRYPT'13 [23].

There are several future works. First, the proposed method is generic squaring algorithm and the method can be optimized further by taking advantages of asymptotically faster integer multiplication method, namely Karatsuba algorithm [4,24]. The previous Karatsuba squaring work accelerates the performance by using SBD based squaring technique, which can be improved directly with SMBD technique [24]. Second, the proposed method can be used for PKC implementations to enhance the performance. The proposed works can optimize the performance of ECC and RSA with simple modifications. We hope the proposed methods can help to further enhance the lightweight efficient implementation of PKC on embedded controllers.

A   Appendix: Pseudo Code: Sliding Middle Block Doubling

Input: word size n, size of left and right block p, where $n \geq p$, Integers $a \in [0, n), c \in [0, 2n)$.
Output: $c = a^2$.
$R_A[n - 1, ..., 0] \leftarrow M_A[n - 1, ..., 0]$.
$ACC \leftarrow 0$.
for $i = p$ **to** $n - 1$

$\mathbf{for}\ j = 1\ \mathbf{to}\ \lceil \frac{i}{2} \rceil$
$\quad ACC \leftarrow ACC + R_A[i - j] \times R_A[j].$
$\mathbf{end\ for}$
$M_C[i] \leftarrow ACC_0.$
$(ACC_1, ACC_0) \leftarrow (ACC_2, ACC_1).$
$ACC_2 \leftarrow 0.$
$\mathbf{end\ for}$
$\mathbf{for}\ i = n\ \mathbf{to}\ 2n - 1 - p$
$\quad \mathbf{for}\ j = n - 1\ \mathbf{to}\ \lceil \frac{i}{2} \rceil$
$\qquad ACC \leftarrow ACC + R_A[i - j - n] \times R_A[j].$
$\quad \mathbf{end\ for}$
$\quad M_C[i] \leftarrow ACC_0.$
$\quad (ACC_1, ACC_0) \leftarrow (ACC_2, ACC_1).$
$\quad ACC_2 \leftarrow 0.$
$\mathbf{end\ for}$
$ACC \leftarrow 0.$
$\mathbf{for}\ i = 0\ \mathbf{to}\ p - 1$
$\quad \mathbf{for}\ j = 1\ \mathbf{to}\ \lceil \frac{i}{2} \rceil$
$\qquad ACC \leftarrow ACC + R_A[i - j] \times R_A[j].$
$\quad \mathbf{end\ for}$
$\quad M_C[i] \leftarrow ACC_0.$
$\quad (ACC_1, ACC_0) \leftarrow (ACC_2, ACC_1).$
$\quad ACC_2 \leftarrow 0.$
$\mathbf{end\ for}$
$ACC \leftarrow 0.$
$\mathbf{for}\ i = 0\ \mathbf{to}\ 2n - 1$
$\quad \mathbf{if}\ i > 2n - 1 - p$
$\qquad \mathbf{for}\ j = n - 1\ \mathbf{to}\ \lceil \frac{i}{2} \rceil$
$\qquad\quad ACC \leftarrow ACC + R_A[j - i + n] \times R_A[i - n].$
$\qquad \mathbf{end\ for}$
$\quad \mathbf{end\ if}$
$\quad \mathbf{if}\ i \% p == 0$
$\qquad R_C[i + p, ..., i] \leftarrow M_C[i + p, ..., i].$
$\qquad R_C[i + p, ..., i] \leftarrow R_C[i + p, ..., i] \ll 1.$
$\quad \mathbf{end\ if}$
$\quad ACC \leftarrow ACC + R_C + R_A[i \% n] \times R_A[i \% n].$
$\quad M_C[i] \leftarrow ACC_0.$
$\quad M_C[i + 1] \leftarrow ACC_1.$
$\mathbf{end\ for}$
$\mathbf{Return}\ c.$

B   Appendix: Triangle Form for SMBD Squaring

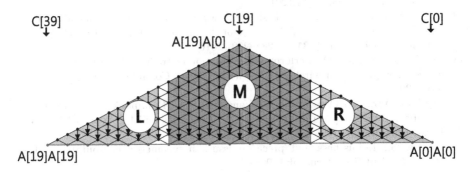

Fig. 6. Sliding middle block doubling where $p = 12$ in 160-bit (Color figure online)

References

1. Comba, P.G.: Exponentiation cryptosystems on the IBM PC. IBM Syst. J. **29**(4), 526–538 (1990)
2. Gura, N., Patel, A., Wander, A., Eberle, H., Shantz, S.C.: Comparing elliptic curve cryptography and RSA on 8-bit CPUs. In: Joye, M., Quisquater, J.-J. (eds.) CHES 2004. LNCS, vol. 3156, pp. 119–132. Springer, Heidelberg (2004). doi:10.1007/978-3-540-28632-5_9
3. Hill, J.L., Culler, D.E.: Mica: a wireless platform for deeply embedded networks. Micro IEEE **22**(6), 12–24 (2002)
4. Hutter, M., Schwabe, P.: Multiprecision multiplication on AVR revisited. J. Cryptogr. Eng. **5**(3), 201–214 (2015)
5. Hutter, M., Wenger, E.: Fast multi-precision multiplication for public-key cryptography on embedded microprocessors. In: Preneel, B., Takagi, T. (eds.) CHES 2011. LNCS, vol. 6917, pp. 459–474. Springer, Heidelberg (2011). doi:10.1007/978-3-642-23951-9_30
6. Lee, Y., Kim, I.-H., Park, Y.: Improved multi-precision squaring for low-end RISC microcontrollers. J. Syst. Softw. **86**(1), 60–71 (2013)
7. Liu, Z., Huang, X., Hu, Z., Khan, M.K., Seo, H., Zhou, L.: On emerging family of elliptic curves to secure Internet of Things: ECC comes of age (2016)
8. Liu, Z., Seo, H., Großschädl, J., Kim, H.: Efficient implementation of NIST-compliant elliptic curve cryptography for sensor nodes. In: Qing, S., Zhou, J., Liu, D. (eds.) ICICS 2013. LNCS, vol. 8233, pp. 302–317. Springer, Cham (2013). doi:10.1007/978-3-319-02726-5_22
9. Liu, Z., Seo, H., Großschädl, J., Kim, H.: Reverse product-scanning multiplication and squaring on 8-bit AVR processors. In: Hui, L.C.K., Qing, S.H., Shi, E., Yiu, S.M. (eds.) ICICS 2014. LNCS, vol. 8958, pp. 158–175. Springer, Cham (2015). doi:10.1007/978-3-319-21966-0_12
10. Liu, Z., Seo, H., Großschädl, J., Kim, H.: Efficient implementation of NIST-compliant elliptic curve cryptography for 8-bit AVR-based sensor nodes. IEEE Trans. Inf. Forensics Secur. **11**(7), 1385–1397 (2016)

11. Liu, Z., Seo, H., Hu, Z., Hunag, X., Großschädl, J.: Efficient implementation of ECDH key exchange for MSP430-based wireless sensor networks. In: Proceedings of the 10th ACM Symposium on Information, Computer and Communications Security, pp. 145–153. ACM (2015)

12. Liu, Z., Seo, H., Kim, H.: A synthesis of multi-precision multiplication and squaring techniques for 8-bit sensor nodes: state-of-the-art research and future challenges. J. Comput. Sci. Technol. **31**(2), 284–299 (2016)

13. Liu, Z., Seo, H., Xu, Q.: Performance evaluation of twisted Edwards-form elliptic curve cryptography for wireless sensor nodes. Secur. Commun. Netw. **8**(18), 3301–3310 (2015)

14. Menezes, A.J., van Oorschot, P.C., Vanstone, S.A.: Handbook of Applied Cryptography. CRC Press Series on Discrete Mathematics and Its Applications. CRC Press, Boca Raton (1996)

15. Schirra, S.: Robustness and precision issues in geometric computation. Max-Planck-Institut für Informatik (1998)

16. Scott, M., Szczechowiak, P.: Optimizing multiprecision multiplication for public key cryptography. Cryptology ePrint Archive, report 2007/299 (2007). http://eprint.iacr.org

17. Seo, H., Kim, H.: Multi-precision multiplication for public-key cryptography on embedded microprocessors. In: Lee, D.H., Yung, M. (eds.) WISA 2012. LNCS, vol. 7690, pp. 55–67. Springer, Heidelberg (2012). doi:10.1007/978-3-642-35416-8_5

18. Seo, H., Kim, H.: Implementation of multi-precision multiplication over sensor networks with efficient instructions. J. Inf. Commun. Converg. Eng. **11**(1), 12–16 (2013)

19. Seo, H., Kim, H.: Optimized multi-precision multiplication for public-key cryptography on embedded microprocessors. Int. J. Comput. Commun. Eng. **2**(3), 255 (2013)

20. Seo, H., Kim, H.: Multi-precision squaring on MSP and ARM processors. In: 2014 International Conference on Information and Communication Technology Convergence (ICTC), pp. 356–361. IEEE (2014)

21. Seo, H., Kim, H.: Study of modular multiplication methods for embedded processors. J. Inf. Commun. Converg. Eng. **12**(3), 145–153 (2014)

22. Seo, H., Lee, Y., Kim, H., Park, T., Kim, H.: Binary and prime field multiplication for public key cryptography on embedded microprocessors. Secur. Commun. Netw. **7**(4), 774–787 (2014)

23. Seo, H., Liu, Z., Choi, J., Kim, H.: Multi-precision squaring for public-key cryptography on embedded microprocessors. In: Paul, G., Vaudenay, S. (eds.) INDOCRYPT 2013. LNCS, vol. 8250, pp. 227–243. Springer, Cham (2013). doi:10.1007/978-3-319-03515-4_15

24. Seo, H., Liu, Z., Choi, J., Kim, H.: Optimized Karatsuba squaring on 8-bit AVR processors. Secur. Commun. Netw. **8**(18), 3546–3554 (2015)

25. Seo, H., Liu, Z., Nogami, Y., Choi, J., Kim, H.: Improved modular multiplication for optimal prime fields. In: Rhee, K.-H., Yi, J.H. (eds.) WISA 2014. LNCS, vol. 8909, pp. 150–161. Springer, Cham (2015). doi:10.1007/978-3-319-15087-1_12

26. Seo, H., Liu, Z., Nogami, Y., Choi, J., Kim, H.: Montgomery multiplication and squaring for optimal prime fields. Comput. Secur. (2015)

27. Seo, H., Shim, K.-A., Kim, H.: Performance enhancement of TinyECC based on multiplication optimizations. Secur. Commun. Netw. **6**(2), 151–160 (2013)

A Secure and Privacy Preserving Iris Biometric Authentication Scheme with Matrix Transformation

Abayomi Jegede[1,2(✉)], Nur Izura Udzir[1], Azizol Abdullah[1], and Ramlan Mahmod[1]

[1] Faculty of Computer Science and Information Technology,
Universiti Putra Malaysia, UPM Serdang,
43400 Seri Kembangan, Selangor, Malaysia
abayomi.jegede@ymail.com,
{izura,azizol,ramlan}@upm.edu.my
[2] Department of Computer Science, University of Jos, Jos, Nigeria

Abstract. Biometric authentication is the use of unique human features to provide secure, reliable, friendly and convenient access to an environment or a computer installation. However, the use of biometrics as a means of authentication exposes legitimate users to security threats, privacy attacks and loss of identity. This paper proposes and implements a novel non-invertible transformation technique known as matrix transformation. Matrix transformation is a simple but powerful and effective method to achieve template revocability and prevent the recovery of original biometric data from secured templates. The approach provides a high level template security and user privacy. It is also robust against replay attack, cross matching and loss of identity.

Keywords: Authentication · Biometric · Non-invertible transformation · Security · Privacy

1 Introduction

Biometrics can be defined as an "automated recognition of individuals based on their behavioural and biological characteristics" [1]. A biometric authentication system uses physiological characteristics (such as face, fingerprint and iris) and behavioural characteristics such as gait, keystroke dynamics, signature [23] to identify clients before they are allowed access to a physical environment or a computer installation. Biometrics are more convenient, reliable and universal [24] than other means of authentication such as passwords, PINs, tokens and chips. Biometrics provide secure authentication, but the biometric traits are not secret. Attacks against stored biometric data can lead to a compromise in the security of the authentication system and violation of privacy of legitimate users. Biometric cryptosystems (or template protection systems) address these problems by combining random, secret information with a biometric data before it is stored in the database. This is in contrast to conventional biometric systems which store templates directly in the database.

© Springer International Publishing AG 2017
D. Choi and S. Guilley (Eds.): WISA 2016, LNCS 10144, pp. 341–352, 2017.
DOI: 10.1007/978-3-319-56549-1_29

The iris a very suitable means of identification because of its uniqueness among individuals [6]. No two humans have the same pattern of iris structure, even in the case of identical twins [11]. The iris also provides a reliable means of authentication because it is a well-protected internal organ, which makes it difficult for its structure to be altered [37]. The information in iris patterns is believed to be very stable throughout life, unlike fingerprints and facial patterns. Moreover, the iris cannot be easily altered by people trying to fake their identity, as in the case of modification of face through plastic surgery or tampering in case of fingerprint or palmprint patterns. However, a recent study showed that iris patterns experience minimal changes over time [14]. Factors such as aging and severe eye diseases also increase intra-class variation between the iris patterns, which has a negative impact on the recognition accuracy.

Cancelable biometric techniques apply different transformations to a given biometric data, which makes it possible to obtain multiple versions of a transformed template from the same biometric data [31]. This provides unlinkability among templates of a user enrolled in multiple databases and helps prevent cross matching attack. Templates can also be revoked or updated in the event of loss or compromise. The cancelable biometric technique provides secure authentication in the sense that templates are never decrypted during authentication. Rather, the authentication involves a comparison between reference and probe templates in the transformation domain. Cancelable biometrics are in two main categories: non-invertible transforms and biometric salting [35]. Non-invertible transforms is one-way and irreversible while biometric salting allows the recovery of the original template if both the transformed template and the transformation parameters are known.

2 Related Work

Non-invertible transformation techniques such as grid morphing, block permutation [31], blind deconvolution [7, 22], block re-mapping, texture warping [12, 20], GRAY-COMBO [43] and Log-Polar transform [30] have been proposed for image-level transformation of fingerprint, face and iris biometric data. Feature level transformation of fingerprint minutiae have also been achieved via cartesian, polar and surface folding (functional) transforms [32, 33]. Revocable biotokens [4, 5], pseudo-random permutations [17], and Gaussian distribution [25] were also used to transform real-value face vectors. Another approach to feature-level transformation is the use of partial Hadamard matrix to create renewable and non-invertible fingerprint templates [42]. Biometric features obtained from ECG signals can be protected using a technique known as Pulse active transform [38], while techniques such as BIN-COMBO [43], user-specific secret permutations [34] and alignment-free adaptive bloom filter [36] have been applied on binary iris features. A number of improvements have been proposed for existing non-invertible transformation techniques. User-dependent multi-state discretization [41] was used to address stolen-token scenario and improve the performance of the original fingerprint Biohash [40] algorithm. The use of different dimensions of iris codes in different applications, bit permutation and key binding were also proposed as remedies for correlation attacks on secured iris codes [29]. Another improvement is the use of spiral cube technique [28] to enhance the security of face templates created using random projection [18] method.

3 Proposed Approach

The security of the previous approaches rely on the secrecy of the user specific key or the complexity of the feature transformation algorithm. For example, user-specific secret permutation is secured as long as the permutation key remains secret. Moreover, pseudorandom permutation depends on the complexity of the pseudo-random ordering of the scheme, while spiral cube relies on the difficulty of computing the projection matrix. This paper proposed a one-way and irreversible transformation technique known as matrix transformation. The main significance of this study is the proposal of an approach which does not rely solely on the complexity of the matrix transformation algorithm or the secrecy of the transformation key. The research also presents a scenario to demonstrate the security of stored biometric data and privacy of legitimate users even if an attacker compromises the authentication system.

Matrix transformation creates a non-invertible binary feature vector from a reference biometric vector by multiplying (or permuting) it with a transformation matrix. The original feature vector cannot be recovered from the transformed vector because the inverse of the transformation key is undefined. This prevents stolen templates from being used for replay and cross-matching attacks. It also provides resistance against image reconstruction attack which can lead to severe privacy violation and loss of identity. Studies have shown that it is possible for to recover original face images [2, 13] and fingerprint images [8, 26] from stolen binary templates. Such biometric images can be used to create multiple templates which the attacker can use to impersonate the victim. This implies that the victim has lost his biometric modality forever as fingerprint, face or iris patterns cannot be changed unlike password or PIN.

4 Methodology

4.1 Iris Image Processing and Feature Extraction

The first step is the use of segmentation to isolate the iris from other structures within its vicinity such as pupil, sclera, eyelids and eye lashes. This is accomplished by detecting the inner and outer boundaries of the iris. It also involves detecting the eyelids and the eye lashes that can interrupt the circular contour of the limbus boundary. Next, normalization is used to transform the segmented iris structure from cartesian coordinates to pseudo-polar coordinates. Normalization is usually carried out using the rubber sheet [10] model. Normalization addresses variations in pupil size which can also affect the size of the iris. It ensures that irises of different individuals are mapped into a common domain, since the size of the pupil can vary across the subjects. Feature extraction is carried out by breaking the 2D normalised iris image into a number of 1D signals. A convolution operation is then applied to the 1D signals using 1D Gabor wavelets. A Log-Gabor filter is defined as

$$G(f) = exp\left(\frac{-(log(f/f_0))^2}{2(log(\sigma/f_0))^2}\right) \tag{1}$$

where f_0 is the frequency and σ is the bandwidth of the filter [15]. The frequency response determines whether a given frequency value is quantized as 0 or 1. Feature extraction produces a binary template which represents the iris image. The total number of bits in the template is 2 times the product of the angular resolution, the radial resolution, and the number of filters used. This paper used the procedures described in [27] to carry out segmentation, normalization and feature extraction.

4.2   Enrolment and Authentication

The implementation process begins with the computation of the non-invertible matrix that will be used as the transformation key. A non-invertible matrix is created from two permutation matrices [16] in Galois Field [3] of two elements. A permutation matrix is a square matrix obtained from an $n \times n$ identity matrix by a permutation of rows [19]. The computation of a non-invertible matrix is done by first creating a $n \times n$ general permutation matrix, P. Note that a total of $n!$ elementary permutation matrices can be obtained from a general permutation matrix of dimension, n. Next, two elementary permutation matrices, p_1 and p_2 are obtained by interchanging any pair of rows of P. An XOR operation is performed on the elementary permutation matrices to obtain a non-invertible matrix, P'. In other words, $P' = p_1$ XOR p_2. The flowchart in Fig. 1 illustrates the processes involved in the computation of transformation matrix.

Combining two elementary permutation matrices (from a given set of $n!$ elementary permutation matrices) to obtain a non-invertible matrix yields a total of $\binom{n!}{2} = $

$$n!_{C_2} = \frac{(n!)!}{(n!-2)2!} = \frac{n!(n!-1)\ldots(n!-2+1)}{2!}$$ non-invertible matrices. This provides a

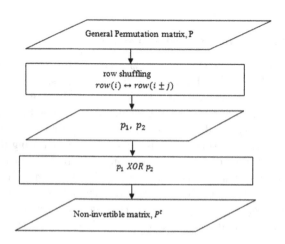

Fig. 1. Computation of transformation matrix

large number of non-invertible transformation matrices which can be used in different applications involving the same set of users. Using different transformation matrices for different applications minimizes the correlation among transformed templates of the same subject which are stored in different databases.

Enrolment is performed by multiplying the transformation matrix, P^t and a reference iris feature vector, X in order to obtain a non-invertible feature vector, X^t. That is, $X^t = P^t * X$. Authentication requires the provision of a probe feature vector, Y which is also used to multiply the same transformation matrix in order to obtain a non-invertible feature vector, Y^t. In other words, $Y^t = P^t * Y$. Intra-class variation between transformed iris templates belonging to the same subject is addressed using Hamming distance error correction, $Hamming\ (X^t, Y^t)$ and threshold value, ρ.

Authentication succeeds if the value of the hamming distance is less than a given threshold. Biometric templates belonging to the same subject have smaller hamming distances compared to templates obtained from different subjects. The flowchart in Fig. 2 illustrates the enrolment and authentication phases of the proposed matrix transformation technique.

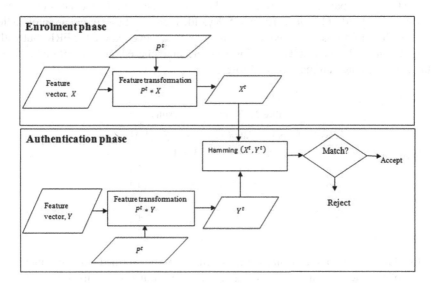

Fig. 2. Enrolment and authentication

5   Results and Discussion

5.1   Performance Evaluation

The performance of the scheme was evaluated using 7 iris images of 15 subjects obtained from CASIA iris image database version 1.0 [9]. The enrolment set consists of 4 images per subject, while the verification set is made up of 3 images of each subject. The recognition accuracy is reported in terms of false acceptance rate (FAR) and false rejection rate (FRR). False rejection occurs if the hamming distance between a pair of transformed templates of the same subject is larger than the threshold. The computation of false rejection rate involves 12 comparisons for each class and a total of 180 comparisons for the entire dataset. The formula below is used to calculate false rejection rate for each class

$$FRR = (no\ of\ false\ reject/number\ of\ comparisons) \times 100\% \qquad (2)$$

False acceptance is a situation whereby the hamming distance between a pair of templates of different subjects is less than the threshold. This implies $12 * 14$ or 168 comparisons for each class and a total of $15 * 168$ or 2,520 comparisons for the entire dataset. The false acceptance rate for each class is calculated based on the formula

$$FAR = (no\ of\ false\ accept/number\ of\ comparisons) \times 100 \qquad (3)$$

The range for intra-class variation for CASIA Near Infra Red iris database lies between 10 and 20% [21]. Thus a successful authentication requires that the hamming distance between a pair of transformed templates is at most 20%. However, preliminary tests using threshold of between 10 and 25% yielded low FAR (≈ 0), but an intolerable FRR. The threshold was increased to 30% in order to achieve reasonable FRR, but with an increase in FAR. The results of performance accuracy based on different dimensions of the iris codes are summarized in Table 1.

Table 1. Summary of results

Length of iris template (bits)	FRR (%)	FAR (%)
64	32.64	31.66
128	38.86	21.10
256	39.47	14.12
512	60	4.52
1024	61.10	1.13

High false rejection rate occurs as the dimension of transformed templates increases because of the increase in intra-class variation among transformed iris codes of long dimensions. A reduction in false acceptance rate is observed as the dimension of transformed iris codes increases. This is because the correlation among the bits in the transformed templates of different subjects reduces as the length of the templates increases. Performance results obtained also depend on the threshold value. Using a higher threshold increases the correlation among transformed templates of same subjects. It also increases the collision among transformed templates of different users. This results in an increase in false acceptance rate and a reduction in false rejection rate. The Receiver Operating Characteristic (ROC) curve in Fig. 3 illustrates the relationship between the FRR and FAR.

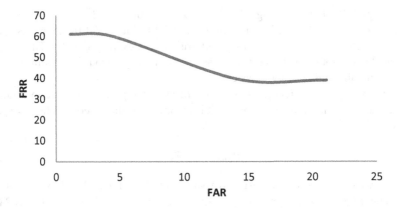

Fig. 3. ROC curve for FRR and FAR

5.2 Security Analysis

The security of the scheme is analyzed to determine its robustness to guessing, key exhaustion and template inversion attacks. This involves the computation of key length, key space, entropy and theoretical analysis of reversibility.

Key length is defined as $K_l = n^2$, where n = dimension of the transformation matrix. The values of n used are 64, 128, 256, 512 and 1024. This translates to key lengths of 2^{12}, 2^{14}, 2^{16}, 2^{18} and 2^{20} bits respectively. That is, 4096 bits, 16,384 bits, 65,536 bits, 262,144 bits and 1,048,576 bits for 64-bit, 128-bit, 256-bit, 512-bit and 1,024-bit templates respectively. These keys are long enough to prevent guessing attack.

The key space consists of all keys (of a particular dimension) that can be used for feature transformation. With respect to matrix transformation, the key space implies the number of transformation matrices that can be computed from a set of elementary permutation matrices. The larger the key space, the more robust the scheme is to brute force attack. Key space is expressed as

$$K_s = n!_{C_2} = \frac{(n!)!}{(n! - 2)2!} = \frac{n!(n! - 1)\ldots(n! - 2 + 1)}{2!} \tag{4}$$

The values of n used for the experiments are 64, 128, 256, 512 and 1024. Thus the range of the key space of the proposed matrix transformation scheme lies between $\gg 64!$ and $\gg 1024!$ ($\gg$ is the symbol for much greater than). The large key space prevents key exhaustion or brute force attack.

The entropy of the key generated by the proposed scheme is calculated to determine its robustness against key guessing attack. Entropy is measured in bits. It is expressed as

$$H = \log_2 N^K \tag{5}$$

where N is the possible symbols used to create the key and K is the key length [39]. The values of key length computed are $2^{12}2^{14}$, 2^{16}, 2^{18} and 2^{20}.

$H = \log_2 2^{4096}$, $\log_2 2^{16384}$ $\log_2 2^{65536}$, $\log_2 2^{262144}$, and $\log_2 2^{1048576}$

$\therefore H = 4096$ bits, 16,384 bits, 65,536 bits, 262,144 bits and 1,048,576 bits for 64 bit 128-bit, 256-bit, 512-bit and 1,024-bit iris templates respectively. This is prohibitively large enough to prevent an attacker from carrying out a random guessing attack against the authentication system.

The probability of correct guess is an estimate of the probability that an impostor will guess a transformation key correctly. It is computed as the inverse of the key space. That is,

$$P_{guess} = 1/K_s \tag{6}$$

where K_s is the key space. The respective values of P_{guess} for 64-bit, 128-bit, 256-bit, 512-bit and 1,024-bit templates are $\ll 1/64!$, $1/128!$, $1/256!$, $1/512!$ and $1/1024!$.

Feature transformation is defined as $Y = kX$, where k is transformation key, X is the biometric feature vector and Y is the transformed vector. Conversely, $X = Y/k$. However, k^{-1} is undefined, and X cannot be computed. For example, consider a 4×4 general permutation matrix, $P = \begin{bmatrix} 0 & 0 & 0 & 1 \\ 0 & 0 & 1 & 0 \\ 0 & 1 & 0 & 0 \\ 1 & 0 & 0 & 0 \end{bmatrix}$. Two elementary permutation

matrices, p_a and p_b are obtained by interchanging the first and second rows as well as

third and fourth rows of P. That is, $p_a = \begin{bmatrix} 0 & 0 & 1 & 0 \\ 0 & 0 & 0 & 1 \\ 0 & 1 & 0 & 0 \\ 1 & 0 & 0 & 0 \end{bmatrix}$ and

$p_b = \begin{bmatrix} 0 & 0 & 0 & 1 \\ 0 & 0 & 1 & 0 \\ 1 & 0 & 0 & 0 \\ 0 & 1 & 0 & 0 \end{bmatrix}$. The transformation matrix or key, k is computed by the

operation p_a xor p_b. Hence, $k = \begin{bmatrix} 0 & 0 & 1 & 1 \\ 0 & 0 & 1 & 1 \\ 1 & 1 & 0 & 0 \\ 1 & 1 & 0 & 0 \end{bmatrix}$. Now consider a one dimensional

column vector, $X = \begin{bmatrix} 1 \\ 0 \\ 0 \\ 1 \end{bmatrix}$. The transformed template Y is computed by the multi-

plication operation, $Y = kX$. That is, $Y = \begin{bmatrix} 0 & 0 & 1 & 1 \\ 0 & 0 & 1 & 1 \\ 1 & 1 & 0 & 0 \\ 1 & 1 & 0 & 0 \end{bmatrix} \cdot \begin{bmatrix} 1 \\ 0 \\ 0 \\ 1 \end{bmatrix} = \begin{bmatrix} 1 \\ 1 \\ 1 \\ 1 \end{bmatrix}$.

Figure 4 shows that attempts to compute X from the values of Y and k using either the left array division or right array division produced invalid results. Moreover, the inverse of k is a matrix of infinite values. Thus it is computationally infeasible to obtain an original biometric template from its transformed version even if the transformation parameters are known.

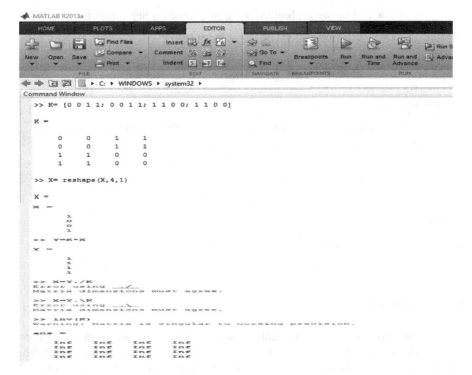

Fig. 4. Analysis of reversibility

5.3 Privacy Analysis

The large key space of between $\gg 64!$ and $\gg 1024!$ ($\gg$ means 'much greater than') implies that matrix transformation can compute between $\gg 64!$ and $\gg 1024!$ protected templates from an instance of biometric data. The possibility of generating such a large number of protected templates from a single biometric input facilitates template renewability and diversity. Unlinkability is also guaranteed because it is computationally challenging for an attacker to match $64!$, $128!$, $256!$, $512!$ or $1024!$ protected templates. This prevents privacy attacks such as record multiplicity and cross matching.

Table 2 shows that matrix transformation has lower recognition accuracy (minimum FRR and FAR of 36.10% and 0.75% respectively) than existing techniques However, the proposed approach has much higher security than existing schemes. Guessing an elementary permutation matrix will require a minimum of between $64!$ and $1024!$ random guesses which is sufficiently large enough to prevent key exhaustion attack. The large size of the transformation key (between 4096 bits and 1,048,576 bits) also prevents guessing attack. Security analysis show that an increase in the dimension of biometric templates provides better security and privacy but with a negative impact on recognition accuracy of the proposed scheme.

Table 2. Comparison between our approach and existing techniques

Method	Modality	Performance (%)			Security analysis			
		FRR	FAR	EER	Key length (bits)	Key space	Entropy	Pr (guess)
Bin-combo [43]	iris code				560	2^{560}	560	0
User-specific permutation [34]	iris code	3.821	0			38!		1.91×10^{-45}
Multi-state discretization [41]	Fingerprint			3.42	250	2^{250}	250	5.52×10^{-76}
Spiral cube [28]	Face					100^{200}		$\ll 0$
Hadamard transform [42]	Fingerprint			3.00/9.12				
Pulse active transform [38]	ECG signal			0.1538/0.2388				
Bloom filter [36]	iris code	2.05	0.01					
Matrix transform	iris code	36.10	0.75		4096 to 1,048,576	$\gg 64!$ to $\gg 1024!$	4096 to 1,048,576	$\ll 7.88 \times 10^{-90}$ to $\ll 0$

6 Conclusion

This research proposed and implemented a secure and privacy preserving authentication scheme which uses the human iris as a means of identifying legitimate users. The approach provides template security, diversity, revocability and unlinkability. Overall, the scheme is robust against replay attack, privacy attack and loss of identity. A future work will address the low recognition accuracy of the proposed approach by integrating a key binding scheme with the matrix transformation technique. This will result in a hybrid scheme which uses better error correction techniques to provide improved recognition accuracy, security and privacy.

References

1. ANSI: Biometrics. http://www.iso.org/iso/iso_technical_committee.html?commid=313770
2. Adler, A.: Images can be regenerated from quantized match score data. In: Proceedings of Canadian Conference on Electrical and Computer Engineering, pp. 469–472. IEEE, New York (2004)
3. Benvenuto, C.J.: Galois field in cryptography. https://www.math.washinghton.edu/~morrow/333_12/papers/juan.pdf
4. Boult, T.: Robust distance measure for face recognition supporting revocable biometric tokens. In: Proceedings of 7th International Conference on Automatic Face and Gesture Recognition, pp. 560–566. IEEE, New York (2006)
5. Boult, T., Scheirer, W., Woodworth, R.: Revocable fingerprint biotokens: accuracy and security analysis. In: Proceedings of IEEE Conference on Computer Vision and Pattern Recognition. IEEE, New York (2007)
6. Bowler, K., Hollingsworth, K., Flynn, P.: Image understanding for iris: a survey. Comput. Vis. Image Underst. **110**(2), 281–307 (2007)

7. Campisi, P., Egiazarian, K.: Blind Image Deconvolution: Theory and Applications. CRC Press, Boca Raton (2007)
8. Cappelli, R., Lumini, A., Maio, D., Maltoni, D.: Can fingerprints be reconstructed from ISO templates? In: 9th International Conference on Control, Automation, Robotics and Vision. IEEE, New York (2006)
9. CASIA-IrisV1. http://biometrics.idealtest.org/
10. Daugman, J.: How iris recognition works. IEEE Trans. Circuits Syst. Video Technol. **14**(1), 21–30 (2004)
11. Daugman, J., Downing, C.: Epigenetic randomness, complexity and singularity of human iris patterns. In: Proceedings of the Royal Society (London) Biological Sciences, vol. 268, pp. 1737–1740. The Royal Society, London (2001)
12. Färberböck, P., Hämmerle-Uhl, J., Kaaser, D., Pschernig, E., Uhl, A.: Transforming rectangular and polar iris images to enable cancelable biometrics. In: Campilho, A., Kamel, M. (eds.) ICIAR 2010. LNCS, vol. 6112, pp. 276–286. Springer, Heidelberg (2010). doi:10.1007/978-3-642-13775-4_28
13. Feng, Y.C., Yuen, P.C.: Vulnerabilities in binary face template. In: 2012 IEEE Computer Society Conference on Computer Vision and Pattern Recognition Workshop, pp. 105–110. IEEE, New York (2012)
14. Fenker, S.P., Bowyer, K.W.: Experimental evidence of a template aging effect in iris biometrics. In: Proceedings of IEEE Workshop on Applications of Computer Vision, pp. 232–239. IEEE, New York (2011)
15. Field, D.J.: Relations between the statistics of natural images and the response properties of cortical cells. J. Opt. Soc. Am. **4**(12), 2379–2394 (1987)
16. Fuzhen, Z.: Matrix Theory. Springer, New York (2011)
17. Grassi, M., Faundez-Zanuy, M.: Protecting DCT templates for a face verification system by means of pseudo-random permutations. In: Cabestany, J., Sandoval, F., Prieto, A., Corchado, J.M. (eds.) IWANN 2009. LNCS, vol. 5517, pp. 1216–1223. Springer, Heidelberg (2009). doi:10.1007/978-3-642-02478-8_152
18. Goel, N., Bebis, G., Nefian, A.: Face recognition experiments with random projection. In: Proceedings of the SPIE, vol. 5779, pp. 426–437 (2005)
19. Grinshpan, A.: Linear Algebra: Permutation Matrices. http://www.math.drexel.edu/~tolya/permutations.pdf
20. Hämmerle-Uhl, J., Pschernig, E., Uhl, A.: Cancelable iris biometrics using block re-mapping and image warping. In: Samarati, P., Yung, M., Martinelli, F., Ardagna, C.A. (eds.) ISC 2009. LNCS, vol. 5735, pp. 135–142. Springer, Heidelberg (2009). doi:10.1007/978-3-642-04474-8_11
21. Hao, F., Anderson, R., Daugman, J.: Combining cryptography with biometrics effectively. IEEE Trans. Comput. **55**(9), 1081–1088 (2006)
22. He, Y., Yap, K.H., Chen, L., Chau, L.P.: A novel hybrid model framework to blind color image deconvolution. IEEE Trans. Syst. Man Cybern. Part A Syst. Humans **38**(4), 867–880 (2008)
23. Jain, A.K., Flynn, P.J., Ross, A.A.: Handbook of Biometrics. Springer, Heidelberg (2008)
24. Jain, A.K., Nandakumar K., Nagar A.: Biometric template security. EURASIP J. Adv. Sig. Process. Spec Issue Biometrics (2008). Springer-Verlag, Berlin Heidelberg
25. Jeong, M., Teoh, A.B.J.: Cancellable face biometrics system by combining independent component analysis coefficients. In: Sako, H., Franke, K.Y., Saitoh, S. (eds.) IWCF 2010. LNCS, vol. 6540, pp. 78–87. Springer, Heidelberg (2011). doi:10.1007/978-3-642-19376-7_7
26. Li, S., Cot, A.C.: Attacks using reconstructed fingerprint. In: 2011 IEEE International Workshop on Information Forensics and Security. IEEE, New York (2011)

27. Masek, L.: Recognition of Human Iris for Biometric Identification. Upublished MSc Thesis. University of Western Australia (2003)

28. Moujahdi, C., Ghouzali, S., Mikram, M., Rziza, M., Bebis, G.: Spiral cube for biometric template protection. In: Elmoataz, A., Mammass, D., Lezoray, O., Nouboud, F., Aboutajdine, D. (eds.) ICISP 2012. LNCS, vol. 7340, pp. 235–244. Springer, Heidelberg (2012). doi:10. 1007/978-3-642-31254-0_27

29. Ouda, O., Tusamura, N., Nakaguchi, T.: Securing BioEncoded IrisCodes against correlation attacks. In: 2011 IEEE International Conference on Communications. IEEE, New York (2011)

30. Plesca, C., Morogan, L.: Efficient and robust perceptual hashing using log-polar image representation. In: 2014 10th International Conference on Communications. IEEE, New York (2014)

31. Ratha, N.K., Connell, J.H., Bolle, R.M.: Enhancing security and privacy in biometrics-based authentication systems. IBM Syst. J. **40**(3), 614–634 (2001)

32. Ratha, N.K, Connell, J.H., Bolle, R.M., Chikkerur, S.: Cancellable biometrics: a case study in fingerprints. In: Proceedings of 18th International Conference on Pattern Recognition, pp. 370–373. IEEE, New York (2006)

33. Ratha, N.K., Connell, J.H., Bolle, R.M., Chikkerur, S.: Generating cancellable fingerprints templates. IEEE Trans. Pattern Anal. Mach. Intell. **29**(4), 561–572 (2007)

34. Rathgeb, C., Uhl, A.: Secure iris recognition based on local intensity variations. In: Campilho, A., Kamel, M. (eds.) ICIAR 2010. LNCS, vol. 6112, pp. 266–275. Springer, Heidelberg (2010). doi:10.1007/978-3-642-13775-4_27

35. Rathgeb, C., Uhl, A., Wild, P.: Iris-Biometrics: From Segmentation to Template Security. In: Jajodia, S. (ed.) Advances in Information Security. Springer, New York (2013)

36. Rathgeb, C., Breitinger, F., Busch, C., Baier, H.: On the application of bloom filters to iris biometrics. IET Biometrics **3**(4), 207–218 (2014)

37. Ross, A.: Iris recognition: the path forward. Computer **43**, 30–35 (2010)

38. Safie, S.I., Nurfazira, H., Azavitra, Z., Soraghan, J.J., Petropoulakis, L.: Pulse active transformation: a non-invertible transformation with application to ECG biometric authentication. In: 2014 IEEE Region 10 Symposium. IEEE, New York (2014)

39. Shannon, C.E.: A Mathematical Theory of Communication. Bell Syst. Tech. J. **27**(3), 379–423 (1948)

40. Teoh, A.B.J., Ngo, D.C.L., Goh, A.: Biohashing: two factor authentication featuring fingerprint data and tokenised random number. Pattern Recognit. **37**(11), 2245–2253 (2004)

41. Teoh, A.B.J., Yip, W.K., Toh, K.A.: Cancellable biometrics and user-dependent discretization in biohash. Pattern Anal. Appl. **13**, 301–307 (2010)

42. Wang, S., Hu, J.: A Hadamard Transformed-based method for the design of cancellable fingerprint templates. In: 2013 6th International Congress on Image and Signal Processing. IEEE, New York (2013)

43. Zuo, J., Ratha, K., Connell, J.H.: Cancelable iris biometric. In: Proceedings of 19th International Conference on Pattern Recognition. IEEE, New York (2008)

Exploration of 3D Texture and Projection for New CAPTCHA Design

Simon S. Woo[1,2(✉)], Jingul Kim[1,3], Duoduo Yu[1], and Beomjun Kim[1]

[1] Computer Science Department, University of Southern California,
Los Angeles, CA, USA
{simonwoo,jingulki,duoduoyu,beomjun}@usc.edu
[2] Information Sciences Institute, Marina Del Rey, CA, USA
simonwoo@isi.edu
[3] Korea Army Academy at Yeongcheon, Yeongcheon, Republic of Korea

Abstract. Most of current text-based CAPTCHAs have been shown to be easily breakable. In this work, we present two novel 3D CAPTCHA designs, which are more secure than current 2D text CAPTCHAs, against automated attacks. Our approach is to display CAPTCHA characters onto 3D objects to improve security. We exploit difficulty for machines in rotating 3D objects to find a correct view point and in further recognizing characters in 3D, both tasks that humans can easily perform. Using an offline automated computer vision attack, we found that 82% of the new text reCAPTCHA characters were successfully detected, while approximately 60% of our 3D CAPTCHAs were detected only if characters were focused and zoomed from the direct view point. When CAPTCHAs are presented in slightly different views, the attack success rates against our approaches are reduced to almost 0%.

Keywords: CAPTCHA · Authentication · 3D

1 Introduction

The Completely Automated Public Turing test to tell Computers and Humans Apart (CAPTCHA) [27] is a type of challenge and response test to distinguish humans from machines. Although CAPTCHAs must be easy for humans to solve, they must be difficult for a bot to pass in a reasonable amount of time. Currently, the most widely used form of a CAPTCHA, 2D text CAPTCHA, presents a CAPTCHA as a combination of random characters, symbols, and numbers in a 2D space. Due to its simplicity and ease of use, 2D text CAPTCHAs have been widely deployed in many websites to prevent access from automated bots. However, 2D text CAPTCHA is vulnerable and even easily breakable by Optical Character Recognition (OCR) software or automated offline post-processing attacks such as segmentation attacks [8,20] that segment and recognize each character separately. There have been attempts to add more background noise, dots, and lines across characters to make recognition difficult. However, automated character recognition technology is getting better every day. Therefore,

© Springer International Publishing AG 2017
D. Choi and S. Guilley (Eds.): WISA 2016, LNCS 10144, pp. 353–365, 2017.
DOI: 10.1007/978-3-319-56549-1_30

there is a fundamental limitation to 2D text CAPTCHAs, which can be easily broken by improved OCR applications and segmentation attacks.

In order to overcome the fundamental limitations of 2D text CAPTCHA, audio based CAPTCHAs [2] have been proposed. However, [18] shows that an automatic speech recognition (ASR) system can defeat audio reCAPTCHA with a significantly high probability of success. Also, moving-image object recognition (or video) based CAPTCHAs [12,22,24] have been proposed, where characters are moving or streaming as a video and users enter animating 2D characters. However, [28] provides an effective attack against these types of CAPTCHAs.

In this work, we address the weakness of the current text CAPTCHA mechanisms from a fundamentally different direction. We either place or project 2D text CAPTCHAs on the surface of a 3D object, and then randomize the viewpoint of the 3D object. Thus, users need to rotate objects first to get the right view points, and the identify characters. We explore two different approaches to place 2D text CAPTCHA onto 3D objects. The first approach is to *embed* CAPTCHA characters as a part of textures in a 3D object using *UV* mapping [5]. The second approach is to *project* a 2D text CAPTCHA onto a 3D object. The first approach explores various texture rendering techniques on the surface of a 3D object to improve security and usability. The second approach projects an individual CAPTCHA character from a specific view point towards uneven surfaces of a 3D object using ray-tracing.

While humans can easily perform the object rotation and character recognition task in 3D, bots require additional complex algorithms to identify the correct shape of a 3D object and pin-point the coordinates that CAPTCHA characters are placed on. Then, bots have to perform character recognition and segmentation to recognize characters displayed on the 3D objects. Although significant progress has been made in 3D shape identification and character recognition research [7,11,16,26], we demonstrate that a series of object recognition, rotation, and CAPTCHA recognition tasks in 3D are still challenging given the current bots' capabilities.

2   Related Work

Many types of CAPTCHAs have been proposed using video, audio, game, puzzle, cognitive task, etc. Due to space limitations, we mainly surveyed research that is directly relevant to our approaches.

Text-based CAPTCHAs are widely used due to their simplicity, where humans have to type displayed characters. The reCAPTCHA [2] is the most popular text CAPTCHA. Recent research in [9] addresses the importance of correctly configuring 2D text CAPTCHA parameters to maximize usability and security. They performed an extensive evaluation and user study, and provided new insights and details on the factors to improve usability and security of 2D text CAPTCHA. However, their focus was to mainly evaluate existing 2D text CAPTCHA systems. Much research including [8,20] has shown that it is very easy to break 2D text CAPTCHAs with text recognition and segmentation attacks. Therefore, 2D text CAPTCHAs have a fundamental limitation that can be defeated by the improved OCR and segmentation attacks. Hollow CAPTCHAs were proposed as alternatives, which use contour lines to form connected hollow characters and further aim to make segmentation and recognition difficult in a 2D space. However, [14] successfully broke a whole family of hollow CAPTCHAs.

Another popular CAPTCHA is an image based CAPTCHA that requires a user to classify and choose specific images. The Asirra CAPTCHA [13] is an image classification-task-CAPTCHA that for example, distinguishes a cat image from a dog image. However, the automated machine classification algorithm proposed by [15] can easily break this approach. Also, Sketcha [23] asks a user to rotate images to specific directions or positions. This is similar to our approach as users have to perform a rotation task. However, rotation in Sketcha is performed in a 2D space using rather simple image sets, which can be potentially defeated by a 2D image classification algorithm. The new reCAPTCHA (No CAPTCHA reCAPTCHA) includes an object classification task as well, where it asks a user to select all of the "cake", "cat", or "sushi", etc. images. However, [25] shows that new image based reCATPCHA can be broken with more than 70% accuracy using off-the-shelf deep learning package. In addition, animated CAPTCHAs, also known as moving-image (video) object recognition CAPTCHAs, have been proposed. However, [28] demonstrated a way to break animated CAPTCHAs with computer vision and motion tracking techniques using classifiers. Further, they proposed the new CAPTCHA based on an emerging image concept in [19]. However, it is still in the 2D domain. In fact, CAPTCHA characters can be displayed in a 3D space. However, recent work [21] demonstrated the step-by-step approach to break 3D characters with offline processing techniques. They claimed to decode the 3D text CAPTCHA with 92% accuracy.

3   3D CAPTCHA Design

We explore two types of 3D CAPTCHAs: *3D Texture CAPTCHA* and *3D Projection CAPTCHA*. In *3D Texture CAPTCHA*, we embed CAPTCHA characters directly to the surface of a 3D model as a part of textures using *UV* [5] mapping, where *UV* maps 2D textures to a 3D model. This allows adding various textures, backgrounds, and noise effects from the 2D text CAPTCHAs onto a 3D object. Users have to identify the surfaces that CAPTCHA characters are located. In the second 3D Projection approach, we project a 2D text CAPTCHA to a 3D model. In particular, we projected the 2D text CAPTCHA image from a specific view point towards a 3D object. Therefore, users have to identify a correct projection view point, in order to recognize CAPTCHA characters. Users can rotate a randomly placed 3D object in a 3D space to locate CAPTCHAs in a direct view. Once, users are able to locate the CAPTCHA, they can read and enter the CAPTCHA characters similar to 2D text-based CAPTCHAs.

3.1 2D Character Generation

Similar to current 2D text CAPTCHAs, we randomly generated 2D characters as an image file. The characters are read from left-to-right direction. We used the similar character sets recommended in [9] for lowercase letters, uppercase letters, digits, and non-confusable letters. In addition, font color, dot size, number of dots, number of lines, and line width can be used as configurable parameters. However, we did not consider these additional parameters. Instead, we capture those lines and dots as a part of texture in a 3D model. Since the font and color of CAPTCHA characters do not impact the usability and security according to [9], we only used the one font and one color for convenience in this work.

3.2 3D Object Generation

First, we created simple 3D models first using Unity [3] such as cube, circular cone, cylinder, triangular pyramid, hexagonal pyramid, etc. as base objects. Then, we combined and concatenated multiple 3D base objects to construct more complex synthetic shapes and polygons. Especially, we generated synthetic shapes to have irregular convex or concave surfaces to ensure that CAPTCHA characters are not easily detectable and recognizable. Also, this allows that a character can span over multiple surfaces so that it requires to rotate multiple times to completely recognize a character.

Further, these synthetic shapes are advantageous since these are new models that do not exist in the real world. Therefore, it is very difficult to train machine learning algorithms to perform meaningful prediction and classification because of a lack of a training set on the newly created 3D models. In addition, Unity provides more than 1,000 free 3D models to use. We collected freely available 3D object models that Unity provides such as a car, a piano, a chair, etc. Therefore, our 3D models include models that exist in real life as well as syntactically created objects. Some samples of syntactically generated 3D models and 3D models from real life are as the Figs. 1 and 4 respectively.

3.3 Approach1: 3D Texture CAPTCHA

We placed the generated 2D text CAPTCHAs to different 2D textures, where different types of fractal lines or background noise effects can be added to the texture. This has much more stronger impact than adding dots or lines in current 2D text CAPTCHAs. For texture mapping, we have following two different base texture sizes, (1) 1024×1024 and (2) 2048×2048 resolution (in pixels), in order to capture the granularity of a texture in a 3D model. Based on our empirical experiments on configuring different texture and model sizes, above two different texture resolution sizes suffice most of our needs. Once we generated a combined texture and CAPTCHA characters in 2D, we applied a UV mapping [5] to map a 2D texture in (u,v) coordinate onto a 3D object in (x,y,z) coordinate. The UV mapping assigns pixels in 2D image to surface on the polygon, by copying a triangle shaped piece of the 2D image map onto a triangle on a 3D object.

Fig. 1. Examples of 3D Texture CAPTCHAs

The texturing and UV mapping is a one-way transformation. Hence, after this step, it is nearly impossible to simply separate CAPTCHA characters from a 3D model. Figure 1 shows examples of 3D models with UV mapped textured from the previous step. Therefore, finally we created a 3D object with CAPTCHA characters embedded in its texture.

3.4   Approach 2: 3D Projection CAPTCHA

In this approach, we project CAPTCHA characters onto a 3D object as shown in Fig. 3. The main idea is to project a 2D text CAPTCHA from a specific angle. Hence, viewing from a slightly different view point (angle) would blur or occlude projected CAPTCHA characters. In Fig. 3, the projection point is shown as a red light source, which projects the 2D text CAPTCHA image toward a 3D object. Before projecting a 2D text CAPTCHA, we preprocessed the generated 2D text CAPTCHA image to be 64×64 pixels so that the 2D CAPTCHA can be smaller than the 3D object size. Further, we varied the alpha channel value [1] of 2D text CAPTCHA, where alpha channel value or compositing controls the transparency of the image from background. We set CAPTCHA characters to be transparent, while setting opaque for other background in the image as shown in Fig. 2. In Fig. 2, the left figure is the original 2D text CAPTCHA image. The right figure is the generated image from changing the alpha channel value so that background is black (opaque) while all characters are white (transparent). This alpha compositing functions a filter so that a light only passes through the character parts while the rest of opaque parts are completely blocked. Certainly, other background effects such as dots and lines can be added before this step similar to 3D Texture CAPTCHA to improve usability and security. Next, we placed a 3D object in (x, y, z) coordinate as shown at the center in Fig. 3. In addition, various lighting effect such as directional lights, point lights, and spot lights with different color can be added from any 3D space coordinate, and further projected into the 3D object to make CAPTCHA recognition difficult. Furthermore, we can add and configure different shading effects at this step. Some examples of finally generated 3D Projection CAPTCHAs are shown in Fig. 4.

Fig. 2. Alpha channel value changed before Projection

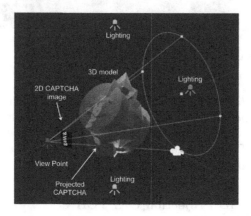

Fig. 3. 2D text CAPTCHA Projection onto a 3D model with different light sources (Color figure online)

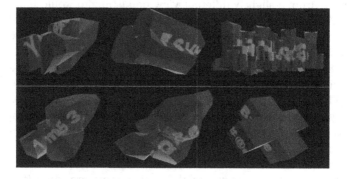

Fig. 4. Examples of 3D Projection CAPTCHAs

3.5   Final 3D CAPTCHA Generation

Finally, we generated 3D Texture and Projection CAPTCHAs by compiling objects, models, and textures we defined in the previous steps with the Unity 3D Web Player. The Unity Web Player [3] generates a binary to be completely played in the web browsers after installing the plugin. We developed the web-based user interface to move and rotate a 3D object in 360° in (x, y, z) direction with a mouse click. Following Figs. 5(a) and 6(a) show the generated 3D Texture and Projection CAPTCHAs, respectively. Also, we present screen captures of object rotations to identify the CAPTCHAs in each approach in Figs. 5 and 6. In the

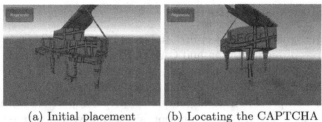

(a) Initial placement   (b) Locating the CAPTCHA

Fig. 5. 3D Texture CAPTCHAs to locate "SF@OyW"

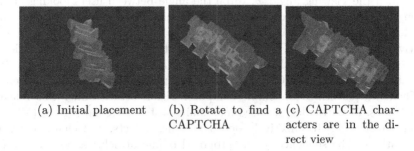

(a) Initial placement   (b) Rotate to find a (c) CAPTCHA char-
                           CAPTCHA   acters are in the di-
                                             rect view

Fig. 6. 3D Projection CAPTCHAs to locate "HNe6"

first 3D Texture approach, users have to rotate the piano object multiple times to locate CAPTCHA characters "SF@OyW" as shown in in Fig. 5(b).

In the second projection approach, users have to rotate a 3D object to view from a projection point as well as they need to adjust the precise viewing angle to recognize all CAPTCHA characters, "HNe6", as shown in Fig. 6(a)–(c). Furthermore, in the second approach, if users view from a slightly different angle such as in Fig. 6(b), the CAPTCHA characters appear blurred. Once users locate the CAPTCHAs, we provide a text box to enter CAPTCHA characters similar to reCAPTCHA.

4 Potential Attacks to 3D CAPTCHAs

We analyzed and conducted the following five realistic attacks against 3D CAPTCHAs: (1) Off-The-Shelf OCR attack, (2) Computer Vision Attack, (3) Client Side Code Attack, (4) Brute-Force based Incremental Object Rotation Attack, and (5) CAPTCHA relay attack for human solvers. The first attack is using OCR. Although OCR is getting better, current OCR technology focuses mainly on 2D object and character recognition. We tried the commercial OCR [6] to our 3D models and the 2D OCR performed extremely poorly against our systems. The 2D OCR by itself is useless to attack our systems. Therefore, we do not present the result with the OCR attack alone. Other more serious attacks are discussed in the following sections:

4.1   Computer Vision Attack

A bot has to recognize a 3D object first and rotate the object. Then, a bot should perform a series of segmentation and CAPTCHA recognition attacks similar to attack 2D text CATPCHAs. Currently, we are not aware of any approaches that can intelligently rotate objects, and detect characters in an automated way. Hence, in order to provide meaningful quantitative comparisons with computer vision attack, we relaxed our assumption significantly. We rotated an object and presented parts or all of CAPTCHA characters to be in the direct or near direct view so that the CAPTCHA recognition algorithm can directly attack. We defined the viewing angle, θ, to be the angle between users looking at the screen and the surface where the CAPTCHA characters were located in a 3D model. Therefore, $\theta = 0°$ was the direct view towards the CAPTCHA characters, effectively making 3D CAPTCHAs to the 2D text CAPTCHAs. We varied θ from $-45°$ to $45°$ so that all or part of CAPTCHA characters were shown. If θ is greater than $\pm 45°$, then CAPTCHA characters would not be seen to users.

Then, we performed an offline computer vision attack under this relaxed assumptions. In particular, we used maximally stable extremal regions (MSER) region detector [11] to effectively detect regions, objects, and characters with modifications. The sequence of the proposed offline attack was as follows: (1) detect regions containing CATPCHAs, (2) segment out characters from a 3D model, and (3) perform optical character recognition (OCR). In particular, we used the Canny Edge Detector [10] to further segment the CAPTCHA characters after detecting the MSER region. Also, we filtered character candidates using connected component analysis. For the 3D Texture CAPTCHA, we used 6 different models and 2 different textures, and randomly generated characters. Also, in order to improve CAPTCHA detections, we zoomed-in the area where CAPTCHAs were located for offline processing. This scenario is the optimistic scenario, where a bot already figured out the 3D object rotation and CAPTCHA area identification, and further it could focus on the region that to improve CAPTCHA segmentation after removing noise.

Figures 7(a) and (b) are the examples of CAPTCHA characters presented in the direct view for 3D Texture and Projection CAPTCHA, respectively. The identified MSER region is shown in the first figure of Fig. 7(a). The second figure in Fig. 7(a) is the final CAPTCHA region detected by the proposed attack, and it cannot recognize the text. Next, we carried out the same attack to 3D Projection CAPTCHAs with 17 different models, where algorithms attempted to identify the CAPTCHA character region with MSER detector and the Canny detector in Fig. 7(b). However, in Fig. 7(b), it cannot not successfully identify the correct region and further is not able to carry out CAPTCHA recognition, even if the CAPTCHA is presented in the near direct view. On the other hand, we applied the same attack to the new text-based reCATPCHA. As shown in Fig. 7(c), the off-the-shelf computer vision algorithm can successfully detecting the CAPTCHA "12028".

In Fig. 8, we provide the average CAPTCHA character recognition success rate from the proposed attacks. We consider an attack is successful only if all the

(a) Attack on 3D Texture CAPTCHA: MSER Region Detection and Recognition Failure

(b) Attack on 3D Projection CAPTCHA: MSER Region Detection and Recognition Failure

(c) Attack on New Text reCAPTCHA: MSER Region Detection and Recognition Failure

Fig. 7. Computer vision attack on each approach

given CAPTCHA characters are correctly recognized from the viewing angle, θ. For example, it is possible that only 2 characters are visible if $\theta = -30°$, while 5 characters can be shown if $\theta = 0°$. In order to compare, we manually rotated objects to be at $\pm 45°, \pm 30°, \pm 15°$ and $0°$ from the direct view point, and captured those images, and inputted those images into our proposed attacks. The detection results are shown in Fig. 8. From 50 manually rotated and captured images, overall on average 48.9% and 31.5% of all of given CAPTCHAs were successfully detected for 3D Texture and Projection CAPTCHAs, respectively. At $\theta = 0°$, we zoomed and focused the CAPTCHA region area to improve detection. Then, the detection success rate increased to 60% and 64.7% for 3D Texture and Projection CATPCHAs, respectively. This demonstrates that even viewing from the precise and best angle, a computer vision algorithm does not achieve the high success rate as found in the 2D text CAPTCHAs. Also, it was interesting to observe that, if angle was improved from $\pm 30°$ to $\pm 15°$, the detection rate was not improved at all. This is due to the fact that our CATPCHAs span over multiple surfaces and require to have multiple views to locate all CAPTCHA characters. Hence, our design is resistant to current 2D text CAPTCHA attack in several different ways. If $\theta \neq 0°$, 3D Projection CAPTCHA was more difficult to detect than 3D Texture approach. However, if $\theta = 0°$, then 3D Texture CAPTCHA was slightly more difficult to detect than 3D Projection CAPTCHA.

Also, we obtained 50 different new text-based reCAPTCHA and performed the same attack. We found out that 82.9% of new text reCAPTCHA were completely detectable with the simple automated computer vision attacks. The reCATPCHAs detection success rate was much higher than ours in the most

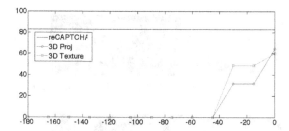

Fig. 8. Viewing angle (θ) vs. Detection success rate with automated computer vision attacks(%)

optimum scenario: only if a machine can perfectly rotate, identify, and focus on the CAPTCHA area in a 3D model (finding $\theta = 0°$) as humans do, then it can achieve the highest success rate. Therefore, for the same attack, our approach is much stronger than the new text reCAPTCHA.

4.2 Client Side Code Attack and Binary Analysis

Although the WebGL [17] provides the similar 3D graphic capabilities, we specifically did not use the WebGL due to the potential client side code attack. Since WebGL relies on the client side JavaScript to render 3D object, textures, and further CAPTCHAs, it is possible to parse the WebGL that describes 3D objects, 2D textures, and extract the 2D text CAPTCHAs. On the other hand, Unity generates a Web Player binary that includes all 3D objects, textures, and CAPTCHAs from the backend and only plays through the web browser. Therefore, it is difficult to reverse engineer and parse the CAPTCHAs from the generated binary. Although it is not impossible to decompile and obfuscate the Unity script using a tool such as [4], we generate a new CAPTCHA and texture information from the backend and the client-side web player calls backend code to retrieve the detailed CAPTCHA and 3D information. Hence, even though attackers are able to decompile the binary, the CAPTCHA, 3D models, and textures information are not stored in the client side. Our approach is much more robust against the client side code attack compared to other 3D development platforms that heavily use client side code such as the WebGL.

4.3 Brute-Force Based Incremental Object Rotation Attack

It is possible that the automated system can incrementally rotate a 3D object until to detect the characters regions with high probability and try to identify characters with OCR types of applications. This Brute-force approach might take a lot of iterations but does not require any intelligence in understanding unseen synthetic 3D objects. If attackers have enough computing power, this Brute-Force based Incremental Object Rotation Attack can be a serious to our system.

Table 1. Human behavior modeling on 3D CATPCHAs

Modeling parameters	Avg	Median	std
Num. of clicks	3.31	2	0.0878
Click distance in pixels	150.26	126.5	0.0035

However, first, our textures and uneven surface make accurate detection difficult as we use different background noise and lighting effect as we observed from computer vision attack. Second, we measured the average time, and the number of clicks needed to solve CAPTCHAs from 90 participants as shown in Table 1. In order for this attack to be successful, a bot has to completely mimic human behavior and we observed that humans are not incrementally rotating objects. Therefore, our defense is to compare the average solving time and human click behavior with this attack, where each rotation requires a mouse click. Therefore, (1) if it takes far longer or shorter to solve or (2) significantly exceeds the number of clicks usually needed for humans, we can classify this as an attack and reject. Using gathered statistic on typical human behaviors on solving 3D CAPTCHA as a prior information, we believe we can easily mitigate and reject the brute-force based incremental object rotation attacks.

5   Conclusion and Future Work

We present two different 3D CAPTCHA mechanisms using 3D objects, projection, and texture techniques. Although our concept is simple, we provide much stronger protection against various existing attacks, which can easily break current 2D text CAPTCHAs. The future work is to conduct user study to evaluate the usability and security trade-offs among different CAPTCHA mechanisms.

Acknowledgements. We would like to thank Ulrich Neumann, Michael Zyda, and Jelena Mirkovic for providing helpful comments and feedback.

References

1. Alpha compositing. http://en.wikipedia.org/wiki/Alpha_compositing
2. reCAPTCHA. https://www.google.com/recaptcha/intro/index.html
3. Unity. http://unity3d.com/
4. Unity 3D obfuscator. http://en.unity3d.netobf.com/unity3d_decompiler
5. UV mapping. http://en.wikipedia.org/wiki/UV_mapping
6. AABBYY OCR software. http://www.abbyy.com/
7. Aldoma, A., Tombari, F., Stefano, L., Vincze, M.: A global hypotheses verification method for 3D object recognition. In: Fitzgibbon, A., Lazebnik, S., Perona, P., Sato, Y., Schmid, C. (eds.) ECCV 2012. LNCS, vol. 7574, pp. 511–524. Springer, Heidelberg (2012). doi:10.1007/978-3-642-33712-3_37

8. Bursztein, E., Martin, M., Mitchell, J.: Text-based CAPTCHA strengths and weaknesses. In: Proceedings of the 18th ACM Conference on Computer and Communications Security, pp. 125–138. ACM (2011)

9. Bursztein, E., Moscicki, A., Fabry, C., Bethard, S., Mitchell, J.C., Jurafsky, D.: Easy does it: more usable CAPTCHAs. In: Proceedings of the 32nd Annual ACM Conference on Human Factors in Computing Systems, pp. 2637–2646. ACM (2014)

10. Canny, J.: A computational approach to edge detection. IEEE Trans. Pattern Anal. Mach. Intell. **6**, 679–698 (1986)

11. Chen, H., Tsai, S.S., Schroth, G., Chen, D.M., Grzeszczuk, R., Girod, B.: Robust text detection in natural images with edge-enhanced maximally stable extremal regions. In: 2011 18th IEEE International Conference on Image Processing (ICIP), pp. 2609–2612. IEEE (2011)

12. Cui, J.-S., Mei, J.-T., Zhang, W.-Z., Wang, X., Zhang, D.: A CAPTCHA implementation based on moving objects recognition problem. In: 2010 International Conference on e-Business and e-Government (ICEE), pp. 1277–1280. IEEE (2010)

13. Elson, J., Douceur, J.R., Howell, J., Saul, J.: Asirra: a CAPTCHA that exploits interest-aligned manual image categorization. In: ACM Conference on Computer and Communications Security, pp. 366–374 (2007)

14. Gao, H., Wang, W., Qi, J., Wang, X., Liu, X., Yan, J.: The robustness of hollow CAPTCHAs. In: Proceedings of the 2013 ACM SIGSAC Conference on Computer & Communications Security, pp. 1075–1086. ACM (2013)

15. Golle, P.: Machine learning attacks against the asirra CAPTCHA. In: Proceedings of the 15th ACM Conference on Computer and Communications Security, pp. 535–542. ACM (2008)

16. Lowe, D.G.: Object recognition from local scale-invariant features. In: The Proceedings of the Seventh IEEE International Conference on Computer Vision 1999, vol. 2, pp. 1150–1157. IEEE (1999)

17. Marrin, C.: WebGL specification. Khronos WebGL Working Group (2011)

18. Meutzner, H., Nguyen, V.-H., Holz, T., Kolossa, D.: Using automatic speech recognition for attacking acoustic CAPTCHAs: the trade-off between usability and security. In: Proceedings of the 30th Annual Computer Security Applications Conference, pp. 276–285. ACM (2014)

19. Mitra, N.J., Chu, H.-K., Lee, T.-Y., Wolf, L., Yeshurun, H., Cohen-Or, D.: Emerging images. ACM Trans. Graph. (TOG) **28**, 163 (2009). ACM

20. Mori, G., Malik., J.: Recognizing objects in adversarial clutter: breaking a visual CAPTCHA. In: 2003 IEEE Computer Society Conference on Computer Vision and Pattern Recognition, 2003, Proceedings, vol. 1, pp. 1–134. IEEE (2003)

21. Nguyen, V.D., Chow, Y.-W., Susilo, W.: Breaking a 3D-based CAPTCHA scheme. In: Kim, H. (ed.) ICISC 2011. LNCS, vol. 7259, pp. 391–405. Springer, Heidelberg (2012). doi:10.1007/978-3-642-31912-9_26

22. NuCaptcha - most secure and usable CAPTCHA. http://www.nucaptcha.com/

23. Ross, S.A., Halderman, J.A., Finkelstein, A.: Sketcha: a CAPTCHA based on line drawings of 3D models. In: Proceedings of the 19th International Conference on World Wide Web, pp. 821–830. ACM (2010)

24. Shirali-Shahreza, M., Shirali-Shahreza, S.: Motion CAPTCHA. In: 2008 Conference on Human System Interactions, pp. 1042–1044. IEEE (2008)

25. Sivakorn, S., Polakis, I., Keromytis, A.D.: I am robot: (deep) learning to break semantic image CAPTCHAs. In: IEEE European Symposium on Security and Privacy (EuroS&P) (2016)

26. Vedaldi, A., Fulkerson, B.: VLFeat: an open and portable library of computer vision algorithms (2008). http://www.vlfeat.org/
27. Ahn, L., Blum, M., Hopper, N.J., Langford, J.: CAPTCHA: using hard AI problems for security. In: Biham, E. (ed.) EUROCRYPT 2003. LNCS, vol. 2656, pp. 294–311. Springer, Heidelberg (2003). doi:10.1007/3-540-39200-9_18
28. Xu, Y., Reynaga, G., Chiasson, S., Frahm, J.-M., Monrose, F., van Oorschot, P.C.: Security and usability challenges of moving-object CAPTCHAs: decoding codewords in motion. In: USENIX Security Symposium, pp. 49–64 (2012)

A Study on Feature of Keystroke Dynamics for Improving Accuracy in Mobile Environment

Sung-Hoon Lee[1,2(✉)], Jong-Hyuk Roh[2], Soohyung Kim[2], and Seung-Hun Jin[2]

[1] Informaion Security Engineering, University of Science and Technology, 217 Gajeong-ro,
Yuseong-gu, Daejeon 34113, Korea
sunghoon1130@etri.re.kr
[2] Electronics and Telecommunications Research Institute, 217 Gajeong-ro, Yuseong-gu,
Daejeon 34129, Korea
{jhroh,lifewsky,jinsh}@etri.re.kr

Abstract. User behavior-based authentication, while providing convenience to the user, is not widely used in the real world due to its low accuracy. Keystroke dynamics is one of the user behavior-based authentication methods, and it has been studied for about 40 years. Conventional keystroke dynamics has used key timing features for the personal computer (PC) environment. Since the smartphone equipped with advanced sensors (e.g., accelerometer, gyroscope, and touchscreen sensor) was released, sensor-based features have been used to improve the accuracy of classifying users with key timing features. In this paper, we analyze the keystroke dynamics features in the literature and evaluate each feature to find efficient features. Based on tapping data collected from 12 participants, we evaluate the effectiveness of several features from the empirical data of a six-digit PIN. Our experimental results show that the feature Up-Up (UU), the time difference between releasing a key and the next key, and the min, max, and mean features extracted from motion sensor data have the best accuracy and efficiently classify each user.

Keywords: Keystroke dynamics · User behavior · Mobile sensor · User pattern

1 Introduction

Recently, the popularity of smartphones has raised concerns over mobile technology security. Our sensitive and private data are being stored on smartphones, and user authentication is the only way to protect the data. Compared to the personal computer (PC) environment, there are many methods (e.g., PINs, passwords, and biometric (face/finger) recognition) for authentication in smartphones. Biometrics tries to recognize users by the physiological or behavioral features of the person.

This work was supported by Institute for Information & communications Technology Promotion (IITP) grant funded by the Korea government (MSIP) (No. B0126-16-1007, Development of Universal Authentication Platform Technology with Context-Aware Multi-Factor Authentication and Digital Signature).

D. Choi and S. Guilley (Eds.): WISA 2016, LNCS 10144, pp. 366–375, 2017.
DOI: 10.1007/978-3-319-56549-1_31

There are several biometrics technologies currently available. Behavior-based authentication, such as keystroke dynamics, has been studied in the computer environment since [1] studied keyboard typing patterns in 1970. They characterized the time intervals between sequential keys. After the smartphone was released, researchers strived to improve the authentication accuracy by using smartphones equipped with various sensors (e.g., accelerometer, gyroscope, and touchscreen sensor). The past works focused on classifiers to improve accuracy, not features. On the other hand, there has been little intensive study of the features of key tapping patterns.

In this paper, we analyze the key timing- and sensor-based features used in the literature to find efficient features in the mobile environment. To this end, we collect datasets targeting the Android smartphone from 12 participants and extract not only five types of key timing-based features (i.e., DU, UD, UU, DD, and Tot) but also sensor-based features from an accelerometer, gyroscope, and touchscreen sensor.

The remainder of the paper is structured as follows. In Sect. 2, we briefly introduce some previous work and the features they used in keystroke dynamics. In Sect. 3, we describe key timing- and sensor-based features. In Sect. 4, we compare and evaluate each feature and present new features with the evaluated data. Finally, we present our conclusions.

2   Related Works

Buchoux and Clarke [2] studied several classifiers, including a distance-based classifier, for keystroke analysis on window mobile environments. They collected a dataset from 16 users with a simple PIN number and obtained a 20.63% false-rejection rate (FRR) and 53.13% false-acceptance rate (FAR) with a Mahalanobis distance classifier on average. Kambourakis et al. [3] obtained a 26% error equal rate (EER) using keystroke dynamics features related with speed and distance.

Saevanee and Bhatarakosol [4] obtained an accuracy of 99% by using a touch pressure-related feature, and they claimed that the feature of touch pressure is more discriminative than conventional key timing-based features.

The researchers in [5] extracted features from accelerometers, touch pressure, and touch size and utilized them with the conventional key timing feature. They analyzed four-digit and eight-digit PINs from 80 participants and obtained a 3.65% EER. They applied an outlier-removal process to all the collected raw data, because some participants intentionally failed to tap smoothly.

The researchers in [6] extracted 11 features: RMS, RMSE, Min, Max, AvgDeltas, NumMax, NumMin, TTP, TTC, RCR, and SMA. A performance analysis on a dataset of 20 subjects reached a 4.94% EER with a combination of key timing-based and sensor-based features.

The researchers in [7] extracted a total of 35 features (e.g., mean, min, max, variance, first quartile, second quartile, and third quartile) from an accelerometer. They obtained an FAR of 0.9% and an FRR of 20.9% from the Manhattan Distance, Random Forest (RF), and SVM classifier.

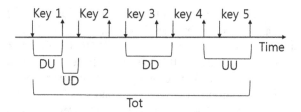

Fig. 1. Key timing-based features extracted from tapping time interval (adapted from [8])

3   Tapping Pattern Feature

We describe the key timing-based feature and sensor-based feature extracted from key time data and sensor data while a user is tapping one PIN. The key timing-based feature is extracted from the time data between the tapping of keys, and it is used for both conventional keystroke and mobile keystroke environments. The sensor-based feature is extracted from smartphone-embedded sensor data, such as accelerometer, gyroscope, and touchscreen sensor data, and it is used with the key timing-based feature in mobile environments.

Table 1. Key timing-based features

Feature	Description
DU	Difference between time at which a key is pressed and released. It represents how long the user holds down the key, referred to as dwell time [9]
UD	Difference between time at which a key is released and time at which the next key is pressed, referred to as flight time [9]
DD	Difference between time at which a key is pressed and time at which next key is pressed
UU	Difference between time at which a key is released and time at which next key is released
Tot	Difference between time at which the first key is pressed and time at which the last key is released

3.1   Key Timing-Based Feature

Tapping keys provides the instant at which each key is pressed (down, D) and released (up, U), as shown Fig. 1. From this basic information, the key timing-based feature is extracted and used to model the user's own unique keystroke pattern for classifying the genuine user. Five types of key timing features, including the total time feature, are described in Table 1.

Four types of key timing features are constructed with combinations of D and U, and the total time feature is extracted from the difference between the time at which the first key is pressed and the time at which the last key is released.

3.2 Sensor-Based Feature

Sensor data, such as accelerometer, gyroscope, and orientation data, is useful to monitor three-dimensional device movement or positioning or changes in the ambient environment near a device [10]. Sensors are divided into two categories: motion sensors, including accelerometers and gyroscopes, and position sensors, including orientation sensors. The motion sensors are used to extract the tapping behavior of a user in keystroke dynamics.

Touchscreen sensors, like touch size, touch pressure, and touch coordinates (x, y), are also utilized with other keystroke features. These features are extracted at Touch-Down and Touch-Up: there are two features per key for touch size and touch pressure and four features per key for touch coordinates (i.e., x, y coordinates data at Touch-Down and Touch-Up). Almost all smartphones provide APIs of touch size and touch coordinates, but some of them do not provide touch pressure APIs.

Recent works have been using both motion sensors and touchscreen sensors to improve accuracy with conventional keystroke timing features, as shown in Table 2. There are a number of sensor-based features extracted from sensor data compared to key timing features. The extracted sensor-based features are summarized in Table 3.

Table 2. Sensor-based keystroke dynamics works. Touch sensors are divided into Pressure (P), Size (S), and x-y Coordinates (C), and Motion sensors are divided into Accelerometer (A) and Gyroscope (G).

Sensor	Ref.								
	Z [5]	T [11]	C [12]	J [13]	H [7]	G [6]	D [14]	B [2]	M [15]
Touch									
P	√	√	√	√					√
S	√	√			√				√
C				√			√	√	
Motion									
Acc	√				√	√			√
Gyr						√			

4 Experiment

This section presents a study on our dataset on the keystroke dynamics of the smartphone. To collect the dataset from users, we developed a data-collection application on Android. With the dataset, we extracted features and evaluated them with several classifiers, like J48, Naïve Bayes (NB), Multi-layer Perceptron (MP), and RF on WEKA [16].

Table 3. Sensor-based features for keystroke dynamics

Ref.	Touch-based extracted feature	Motion-based extracted feature
Z [5]	Pressure, Size value at D/U	Min, Max, Mean from Acc at DU Acc value at D/U
T [11]	Pressure, size value	
C [12]	Pressure value	
J [13]	Pressure, x-y Coordinates value	
H [7]		Min, Max, Mean, Variance, first quartile, second quartile, and third quartile from Acc
G [6]		Root mean square, Min, Max, Mean, Number of Local Maxima and Minima, Mean Delta, Sum of Positive values, Sum of Negative values, Standard Deviation from Acc and Gyr
D [14]	Offset value to the center of a key tapped	
B [2]	x-y Coordinates value at D/U	
M [15]	Pressure, Size value at D/U	Min, Max, Mean, Variance from Acc

4.1 Data Collection

For collecting the dataset, we invited graduate students and researchers to our institution to participate in this study. Our six-digit PIN number was 766240. We collected data from 12 participants for four weeks, with data collected twice daily (one in the daytime and one at night), with each datum comprising five taps. When collecting the dataset, we divided users' postures, because the users' tapping patterns differed each day. The postures were as follows:

- Table (tab): tapping one PIN with smartphone on the table
- Normal (nor): tapping one PIN while seated or standing
- Moving (mov): tapping one PIN while walking

The application of conventional research [7, 17] to the real world is limited, since it does not distinguish postures. Our dataset adds more flexibility to authenticate a user by collecting posture data.

Our collected dataset consisted of the following data entries: 1406 Normal, 1413 Table (from 12 participants), and 1035 Moving (from eight participants). The raw data were saved as seven files: key time, accelerometer, gyroscope, gravity, orientation, touch size, and touch coordinates (x, y), except pressure data. Our test phone was a Samsung Galaxy S4, which does not provide pressure data, so the pressure data was not stored.

4.2 Key Timing-Based Feature Analysis

Key timing-based features have five categories that 21 features are extracted from DU, UD, UU, and DD at the process of tapping one PIN, 766420, and one Tot feature was extracted. Therefore, 22 features in total were extracted per tapping.

After extracting the features, we evaluated the accuracy of each feature, and the result is shown in Fig. 2. The top classified feature was UU, and the Moving posture was more accurate than the other postures. The DU feature showed relatively low accuracy, because the DU feature is not affected by other keys and almost all participants tap with similar periods between touch-down and touch-up for one key.

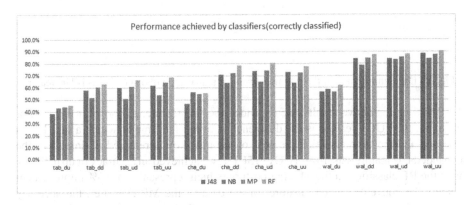

Fig. 2. Accuracy achieved by classifiers (correctly classified)

We assume each user has an inherent tapping rhythm between the two sequential keys. Other features, especially UU, had inherent keystroke patterns for each user, because they represent the time related between a key and the next key. For this reason, DU is the worst feature, and UU is the best feature. RF is the most accurate of the classifiers, and NB is the worst.

A sample UU feature graph is shown in Fig. 3, and the UU feature graphs on Moving are the most discriminative. The graphs of Users 2 and 3 in the Table dataset are quite similar. The accuracy of our Table dataset is relatively low compared to the Normal and Moving datasets.

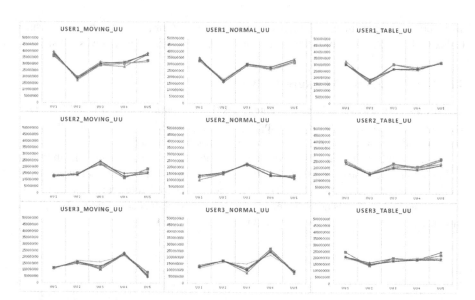

Fig. 3. UU feature graph of three sample users. Y-axis is time (ns) and X-axis is UU feature

Based on the above results, we expanded the UU feature, as shown in Fig. 4. For example, the 2UU1 feature is the difference between the time at which a first key is released and the time at which the next of the next key is released. Using all of the expanded UU feature sets, from 1UU1 to 5UU1, we achieved an accuracy of up to 90.9% with the RF classifier on the Moving posture, which represented a 0.5% improvement against the conventional UU feature. In the case of the MP classifier, the accuracy decreased by 0.7%, and we obtained an accuracy of 86.9%. It is believed to be because the expanded UU feature already includes characteristics of conventional UU features and the length of the PIN is too short to expand the number of feature sets. If a 10-digits PIN or more in length were used to our experiment, the result may be changed. We will leave this to future work.

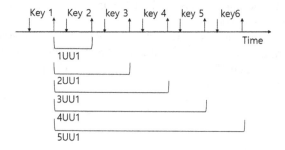

Fig. 4. Expanded UU feature

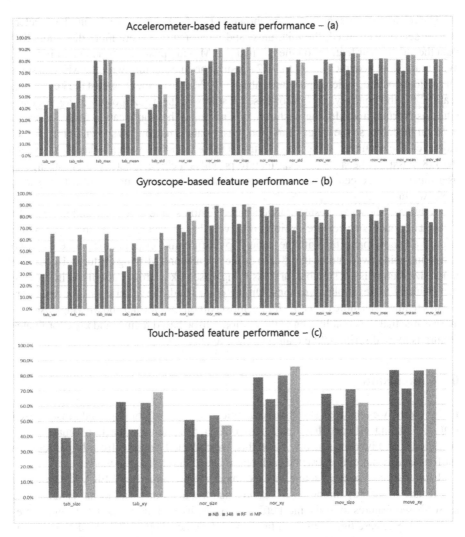

Fig. 5. Accuracy achieved by classifiers (correctly classified)

5 Sensor-Based Feature Analysis

As mentioned above and summarized in Table 3, many sensor-based features are used to study keystroke dynamics on mobile devices. Some works used features from motion-based sensors, accelerometers and gyroscopes, or touch-based sensors. Compared to the key timing feature, the sensor-based feature, especially the motion sensor, can be extracted to various types, such as min, max, mean, std, and var. In order to find sufficient features, we extracted the sensor-based features of each position from an accelerometer, gyroscope, and touch sensor.

The results of our experiment are shown in Fig. 5. When features from the accelerometer sensor were used, the min, max, and mean features were more discriminative than the std and var features on the Normal and Moving postures, as shown in Fig. 5-a. We obtained an accuracy of up to 91.2% using the max feature with the MP classifier on Normal posture, which represented about a 10% improvement against the key timing feature. On the contrary, the sensor-based features of the Table posture were not classified as Normal and Moving postures. It is assumed that the location of the phone is fixed on the table, so the range of motion sensor data is narrow, as shown in Fig. 5-a, b. However, the accuracy of the max feature is more than 80% with all classifiers except the J48 classifier, because the max feature provides a characteristic of how strongly a user touches the screen. The result of the gyroscope-based feature is almost the same, as shown in Fig. 5-b.

Figure 5-c shows the result of touch-based features, like touch size and x-y coordinates. The touch size feature exhibits relatively lower accuracy than the x-y feature. Almost all participants tap with the same grip posture, like gripping the phone with two hands and using two thumbs in the case of the Normal and Moving postures. Hence, the touch size feature is not suitable for classifying a user's keystroke pattern and improving the accuracy of keystroke dynamics. On the other hand, the accuracy of the x-y coordinates feature was more than 80% for the most part on the Normal and Moving postures. We assume that the combination of the motion sensor-based feature and x-y coordinates feature is more discriminative than separated features.

6   Conclusion

In this paper, we analyzed keystroke dynamics features, key timing- and sensor-based features, to find efficient features for mobile environments, especially smartphones equipped with advanced sensors. To do this, we collected a dataset from 12 participants for four weeks and then extracted each feature used in related past works.

In order to analyze each feature, an experiment was performed on WEKA. We found the UU feature of the key timing-based features and the min, max, and mean feature of the sensor-based features to be the most efficient to classify each user. The UU feature represents the key release time between a first key and the next key, so it showed higher accuracy than the other key timing-based features. We also expanded the UU feature and obtained slightly higher accuracy. Among the sensor-based features, the min, max, and mean features showed higher accuracy than the others on the Normal and Moving postures. In the case of the Table posture, neither the key timing- nor the sensor-based features represented users' unique keystroke patterns. This challenge is left as future work.

We used several classifiers to find efficient features on WEKA. The classifiers are also important to improve the accuracy of determining whether a tapping user is the true owner or an imposter who happens to mimic the tapping of the true owner on a mobile device. In future work, keystroke dynamics classifiers may be analyzed to find which classifier is suitable to this area.

References

1. Gaines, R.S., Lisowski, W., Press, S.J., Shapiro, N.: Authentication by keystroke timing: Some preliminary results. Report R-2526-NSF, Rand Corp (1980)
2. Buchoux, A., Clarke, N.L.: Deployment of keystroke analysis on a smartphone. In: Proceedings of the 6th Australian Information Security Management Conference, Perth, Western Australia, pp. 40–47. SECAU - Security Research Centre (2008)
3. Kambourakis, G., Damopoulos, D., Papamartzivanos, D., Pavlidakis, E.: Introducing touchstroke: keystroke-based authentication system for smartphones. Security and Communication Networks (2014)
4. Saevanee, H., Bhatarakosol, P.: User authentication using combination of behavioral biometrics over the touchpad acting like touch screen of mobile device. In: Proceedings of the International Conference on Computer and Electrical Engineering, pp. 82–86 (2008)
5. Zheng, N., Bai, K., Huang, H., Wang, H.: You are how you touch: user verification on smartphones via tapping behaviors. In: William, M. (ed.) Department of Computer Science, pp. 1–13. WM-CS (2012)
6. Giuffrida, C., Majdanik, K., Conti, M., Bos, H.: I sensed it was you: authenticating mobile users with sensor-enhanced keystroke dynamics. In: Dietrich, S. (ed.) DIMVA 2014. LNCS, vol. 8550, pp. 92–111. Springer, Cham (2014). doi:10.1007/978-3-319-08509-8_6
7. Ho, G.: Tapdynamics: Strengthening user authentication on mobile phones with keystroke dynamics. Technical report, Stanford University (2014)
8. Pisani, P.H., Lorena, A.C.: Emphasizing typing signature in keystroke dynamics using immune algorithms. Appl. Soft Comput. **34**, 178–193 (2015)
9. Moskovitch, R., Feher, C., Messerman, A., Kirschnick, N., Mustafić, T., Camtepe, A., Lohlein, B., Heister, U., Moller, S., Rokach, L., Elovici, Y.: Identity theft, computers and behavioral biometrics. In: ISI 2009, Richardson, TX, USA, 8–11 June 2009
10. Android Developers, Develop > API Guides > Location and Sensors - Sensors overview. https://developer.android.com/guide/topics/sensors/sensors_overview.html
11. Trojahn, M., Ortmeier, F.: KeyGait: framework for continuously biometric authentication during usage of a smartphone. In: 3rd International Conference on Mobile Services, Resources, and Users, pp. 114–119 (2013)
12. Ting-Yi, C., Cheng-Jung, T., Jyun-Hao, L.: A graphical-based password keystroke dynamic authentication system for touch screen handheld mobile devices. J. Syst. Softw. **85**(5), 1157–1165 (2012)
13. Jain, L., Monaco, J.V., Coakley, M.J., Tappert, C.C.: Passcode keystroke biometric performance on smartphone touchscreens is superior to that on hardware keyboards. Int. J. Res. Comput. Appl. Inf. Technol. **2**, 29–33 (2014)
14. Draffin, B., Zhu, J., Zhang, J.: KeySens: passive user authentication through micro-behavior modeling of soft keyboard interaction. In: Memmi, G., Blanke, U. (eds.) MobiCASE 2013. LNICST, vol. 130, pp. 184–201. Springer, Cham (2014). doi:10.1007/978-3-319-05452-0_14
15. de Mendizabal-Vazquez, I., de Santos-Sierra, D., Guerra-Casanova, J., Sanchez-Avila, C.: Supervised classification methods applied to keystroke dynamics through mobile devices. In: IEEE International Carnahan Conference on Security Technology, pp. 1–6 (2014)
16. Hall, M., Frank, E., Homes, G., Pfahringer, B., Reutemann, P., Wittern, I.H.: The WEKA data mining software: an update. SIGKDD Explor. **11**(1), 10–18 (2016)
17. Giot, R., El-Abed, M., Rosenberger, C.: Greyc keystroke: a benchmark for keystroke dynamics biometric systems. In: Proceedings of the IEEE International Conference on Biometrics: Theory, Applications and Systems (BTAS), USA (2009)

Geocasting-Based Almanac Synchronization Method for Secure Maritime Cloud

Donghyeok Lee[1,2] and Namje Park[1,2(✉)]

[1] Department of Computer Education, Teachers College, Jeju National University,
61 Iljudong-ro, Jeju-si, Jeju 690-781, Korea
{bonfard,namjepark}@jejunu.ac.kr
[2] Elementary Education Research Institute, Jeju National University,
61 Iljudong-ro, Jeju-si, Jeju 690-781, Korea

Abstract. A number of recent maritime accidents strongly imply the need of distributed smart surveillance. The maritime cloud, proposed as communications infrastructure of e-Navigation, is one of the most optimal infrastructure systems in the smart surveillance environment. To maintain the safe maritime environment, security in the distributed smart surveillance environment is critical, but research on security of the maritime cloud, which will be adopted as major communications infrastructure in the smart surveillance system, is still in the fledging stage. In this regard, this paper suggested a safe synchronization method of Almanac, which is necessary to provide unimpeded maritime cloud service. Almanac plays a role of a telephone directory and it should be shared in the latest version in communicating between vessels or a vessel and land. In other words, synchronization of Almanac between offshore and vessels is required to safely deliver major video information collected by the distributed smart camera. The method proposed in this paper enables geocasting based synchronization between vessels, which is suitable for maritime conditions, and does not expose information in the course of synchronization even in the case of broadcasting through an unsafe channel. In addition, the method ensures integrity based on block ID and supports delta update, thereby minimizing bandwidth and boosting performance.

Keywords: Maritime cloud · Geocasting · Synchronization · Almanac

1 Introduction

Since the late 1990s when smart cameras popularized, the video surveillance industry has started to employ smart cameras. Smart cameras not only collect and save video information but carry out various tasks such as intelligent image processing and pattern recognition algorithm. Thanks to these features, smart cameras can be utilized in a range of sectors. In line with the advancement of network technologies, sensor network, and wireless communications technologies, the smart camera industry developed a new camera system, which is called a distributed smart camera. This camera system enables connection of a smart camera and a number of cameras over network, connecting the entire network as a single virtual smart camera. In other words, the system combines a

© Springer International Publishing AG 2017
D. Choi and S. Guilley (Eds.): WISA 2016, LNCS 10144, pp. 376–387, 2017.
DOI: 10.1007/978-3-319-56549-1_32

separate video image taken by each camera to analyze an event or conduct a task, which makes the system view as a virtual smart camera. Distributed smart camera can be an extremely useful means in the field of smart surveillance.

In general, smart surveillance, the state-of-the-art technology, recognizes the surveillance target from video information through computer, analyzes behaviors of the target, and gives an alarm to the surveillance if any behavior corresponding to the surveillance purpose is detected so as to take appropriate action. When IoT (Internet of Things) arrived in reality, the need for distributed smart surveillance system, which carries out collection and integrated processing of smart surveillance video information through distributed camera, will increase day by day. In the distributed smart surveillance environment, even trained surveillance staff has a limit in handling and responding data and in particular, it is almost impossible for them to monitor and respond to case by case in a large-scale environment. Therefore, video information required for maritime smart surveillance should be comprehensively collected and controlled based on cloud, and relevant infrastructure is also needed [1–3].

In response to the demand, International Maritime Organization (IMO) has recently proposed the maritime cloud. This infrastructure facilitates offshore centers to collect video information from on-board distributed smart camera, thus allowing effective utilization of distributed smart surveillance system through server. Maritime cloud is a major communications-based technology in e-Navigation. This is different from general storage cloud and aims to support smooth information exchange between various systems in the maritime domain, and a number of communications links. Research on the maritime cloud is in the initial stage and, in particular, there have been lack of studies on information security. The maritime cloud provides basic functions like confidentiality and integrity, but it is still vulnerable to a range of attacks including impersonation attack, information disturbance, authority seizure, service rejection attack, message tapping attack, message hacking attack, access to illegal information, and insider attack (Fig. 1).

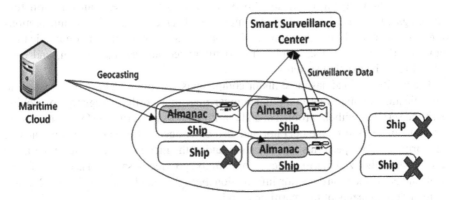

Fig. 1. Maritime cloud-based Smart Surveillance environment

Those problems also affect the distributed smart surveillance environment, which is based on the maritime cloud, with vulnerability of security being exposed. Smart cameras may have sensitive information of which security is critical, so safe transmission and reception of video information should be ensured. Compromising security of the distributed smart surveillance system can be connected to safety of vessels, offshore, and even the general public. Therefore, study on the safe distributed smart surveillance environment is highly required. This paper proposed a method for synchronization of almanac on the maritime cloud, major communications infrastructure to build a safe distributed smart camera environment. The method features geocasting-based synchronization, which enables synchronization even when disconnected with server, and low bandwidth through delta update-based minimized information delivery. Meanwhile, data security is assured with all data in the course of transmission being encrypted, and data integrity can be checked through block ID.

2 Related Work

2.1 Maritime Cloud

2.1.1 Overview of Maritime Cloud

Maritime cloud is a communications system that enables effective, safe, stable and unimpeded information exchange between authorized parties concerned with maritime, through available communications systems. It was proposed to give explanation on infrastructure that supports smooth delivery of information in accordance with IMO's strategies. Communications infrastructure to facilitate smooth delivery of information between parties concerned as per IMO's e-Navigation strategies was required, while increasing the need for maritime cloud to provide reliable and mutually operable service. The maritime cloud is significant in that efficient and sustainable communications infrastructure is well established [14–16].

Maritime cloud is utilized as a communications means in the e-Navigation structure and enables smooth transmission of information among a number of communications links. In addition, the infrastructure allows parties concerned to exchange information through gateway, in order to mitigate complexity of selecting specific communications system or channel. Using this communications infra enables smooth communication between different systems, simple shift to future technology and system, and easy utilization of the existing systems.

The maritime cloud has three major components: maritime identity registry to safe authentication in maritime communications; maritime portfolio registry to provide maritime services without problems; and maritime message service (MMS), a message hub that can be used by the operator and also other agents. Based on the components, the maritime cloud performs identification and authentication when a maritime actor accesses an authorized maritime actor community, provides a safe data access environment, and offers location detection information through smooth roaming. Figure 2 shows the major components of the maritime cloud.

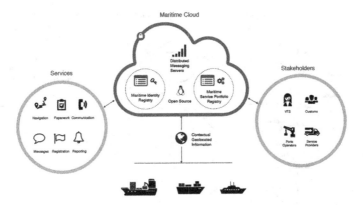

Fig. 2. The major components of the maritime cloud

As an integral component of maritime portfolio registry, Almanac is the offline version of part disclosed from maritime identity registry and maritime portfolio registry and plays a role of a telephone directory by name and business sector. Through Almanac, users can perform automatic search for MMSI number for digital selective calling (DSC) and email addresses, telephone numbers, and other contacts of VHS operating channels or VTS center ports, and adjacent MRCC or other vessels that need to contact. Basically, Almanac is a digital publication that can be downloaded and includes registered identifiers, contact information, service instances, and open key for encryption. This Almanac enables registered parties to communicate each other without online access to central registry, providing high availability.

2.1.2 Geocasting in the Maritime Cloud

Vessels on the maritime cloud can realize unimpeded roaming between communications links by using maritime messaging service, which is an international interoperability service. Leveraging Almanac, vessels can use a number of services in a faraway port and MSI service providers can broadcast MSI geocast to vessels in the MSI service coverage, through MMS. In other words, the maritime cloud enables commercialized data links to provide geocast MSI service, and users may make or hear a broadcast logically in the area adjacent to them, regardless of communications link used to make or hear the broadcast (Fig. 3).

This paper aims to utilize geocasting for efficient synchronization of Almanac. Even though disconnected with the maritime cloud for some reasons, synchronization can be achieved based on data from adjacent vessels through geocasting.

2.2 Existing Data Synchronization Methods

In the cloud environment, data synchronization is a widely-used element technology, which aims to synchronize data of different pieces of equipment through information exchanges. There have been many studies on synchronization methods including synchronization between PDA and PC; HotSync [4] running on Palm OS for

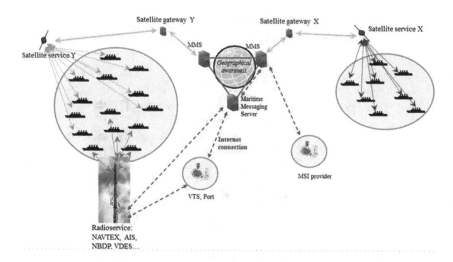

Fig. 3. Geocasting in Maritime Cloud

synchronization between devices; and Active Sync [5] operating based on Windows CE. However, these methods are dependent on a single platform and inefficient in the cloud environment as the entirety of data is transmitted in the event of synchronization. To overcome the drawbacks, studies on various subjects like similarity overlapping check, delta update, and multi device synchronization have been conducted [6–10]. This section examines the synchronization method based on SyncML [11] and Rsync [12] as a major synchronization method applicable to the cloud environment and Uppoor's research [13] supporting P2P-though-synchronization.

3   Proposal of New Synchronization Method

This section examines technical requirements for designing a data synchronization method and offers a method for safe synchronization of Almanac data.

3.1   Overview of the Proposed Method

The proposed method is about safe synchronization of Almanac data based on geocasting in the maritime cloud environment and aims to synchronize Almanac data in the maritime cloud service and Almanac data retained by each vessel to be completely identical. Vessels in a specific geological scope are subject to synchronization and unauthorized vessels are excluded from synchronization even if they are in the applicable scope. In short, authorized vessels are entitled to synchronization of Almanac data (Fig. 4).

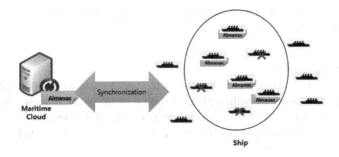

Fig. 4. Overview of proposed method

3.2 Technical Requirements

This section analyzes technical requirements in aspects of efficiency and security to design the maritime cloud synchronization method.

3.2.1 Minimized Bandwidth

Bandwidth for synchronization should be minimized. The format for information delivery should be concise as much as possible and an amount of data to be delivered in the course of implementing protocol should be minimized, and the method should not be designed such a way to waste data bandwidth more than necessary on the vessel side for synchronization.

3.2.2 Delta Update

When changing data, update for the changed part only should be available. In particular, if it is large-volume data, the entirety of the data should not be delivered for synchronization. This will lead to an increase in bandwidth and speed of synchronization, resulting in low efficiency. In the event that data is partially changed, relevant detection algorithm is required and after detecting the changed part, the corresponding part should be updated.

3.2.3 Consideration of Distributed Environment

In designing a synchronization method, a distributed environment should be considered. Even in the server-offline state, synchronization should be possible only with data on the other vessel and safe synchronization can be assured. For example, it should be confirmed that there was no original data forgery or impersonation attack on the other side. In addition, data should be identical among vessels and all vessels should maintain unified data.

3.2.4 Assurance of Integrity

Almanac data should not be damaged. Damaged data can cause a problem with receiving the maritime cloud service and directly affect the safety of vessels. If Almanac data is revised, the changed part should be detected and immediately updated so that accurate original copy can be maintained.

3.2.5   Data Encryption

Data should be protected safely in the course of synchronization. To prevent exposure of original data to a person with malice, it should be designed in such a way that an unauthorized vessel should not be able to identify original data even if it acquires data in the process of synchronization, data synchronization must be restricted to an authorized group of vessels.

3.2.6   Real-Time Synchronization

Synchronization should be carried out in real time. In this context, real time means completing synchronization within a specific time range set by policy, and if necessary, immediate update should be available.

3.3   Procedure of Implementing the Proposed Method

This section describes detailed procedure of implementing the proposed method for Almanac synchronization.

3.3.1   Abbreviations

This dissertation provides abbreviations and their definitions in Table 1 to explain the proposed method.

Table 1. Notation

Abbreviation	Explication
K_S	Pre-shared Secret Key
K_T	Temporary Key
M	Transferring Message
B_i	Block Data
$H(\cdot)$	Hash Function
$E(\cdot)$	Encryption

3.3.2   Extracting of Block ID

In the block ID extracting stage, data is split into blocks and ID corresponding to each block is extracted. Figure 5 illustrates block ID extracting process. First is to split original data by block in certain size. Block size can be changed, and in case of changeable-sized block, ID and size should be managed together. After then, a hash value for each split block is set to be a block ID.

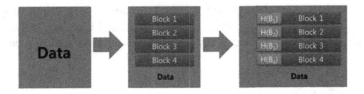

Fig. 5. Block ID extraction

Handling original data in the unit of block is to raise efficiency and detect partial changes. In case part of data is changed, only the changed part should be synchronized and there is no need to synchronize the entire data. To identify which part is changed in data, block ID is used. If block 3 is changed, a hash value of block 3, which is a block ID, will be changed. In this case, the user compares the changed block ID with his block ID and if they are different, it is confirmed that block 3 is changed and implement synchronization for the corresponding data.

If the size of original data is small enough, the data may not be split in the unit of block, and in this case, the original data can be considered as a single block. As more blocks are created by reducing the block size, the amount of data to be transmitted for synchronization, efficiency of partial data synchronization increases. However, the number of block IDs to be handled will increase and extra cost for creation of each hash value shall be borne. Therefore, appropriate block size should be determined.

3.3.3 Data Transmission

In the data transmission stage, block IDs are distributed to authorized vessels, based on geocasting. Here, it is assumed that secret key K_S between maritime cloud server and authorized vessels are shared in advance. For each block ID, encryption is implemented with ephemeral key K_T, which is based on K_S and nonce, as a key, and this value and nonce are set to message M to implement geocasting for authorized vessels. The vessel that received information can create K_T based on K_S that was shared in advance. Then, decoding of each value for message M is implemented to acquire all block IDs, and the user should compare these block IDs and saved block IDs and identify block ID showing difference [17–19].

If part of data is changed, block ID will also change. In other words, in case received block ID is different from block ID on the vessel side, synchronization for the relevant block is required. Data transmission procedure is as follows.

1. The server creates key K_T based on nonce and KS that was shared in advance.
2. The server implements encryption for each block ID.
3. The server delivers all of the encrypted block IDs and nonce to the client through geocasting.
4. The client (vessel) creates key K_T based on nonce and KS that was shared in advance.
5. Extract each block ID by implementing decoding.
6. Determine whether or not each block ID is identical to saved block ID in the vessel.

In the course of geocasting, message M is safe even if it is exposed to many unspecified individuals. It is because all data is encrypted, and decoding is available for authorized vessels possessing secret key K_S. Figure 6 illustrates the data transmission process.

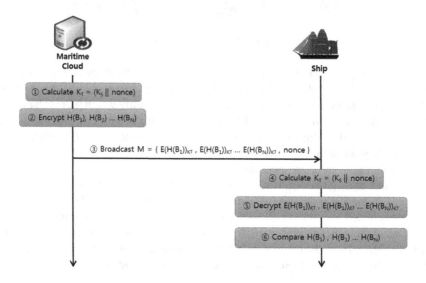

Fig. 6. Data transmission

3.3.4   Data Synchronization

The data synchronization stage includes detection of changes in data based on block ID and reception of data for the changed part. Request of client for data is made by block ID and the server encrypts the requested block and delivers it to the client. Integrity of data can be checked by comparing a hash value and block ID, and when the checking is completed, the client saves the received block data, and then synchronization is completed eventually. Data synchronization procedure is as follows:

1. The client shall compare block IDs to detect which block is changed.
2. The client shall request the server for nonce and a set of blocks in which changes were made.
3. The server sets K_T as a key for requested block and transmit the encrypted actual data to the vessel.
4. The client shall check that the hash value of the received data and block ID are identical.
5. The client shall save the received block data.

Request for data can be made not only to the server side of the maritime cloud but also other vessels in the authorized group. If communications between vessels is available, synchronization is possible even when communication is disconnected from the server. Figure 7 shows synchronization between vessels. Even in the case where a vessel deliberately sends wrong information, the abnormality can be easily identified because the block

ID value and the hash value of actual data will be different. The vessel completes synchronization by saving data when the block ID and hash value are the same.

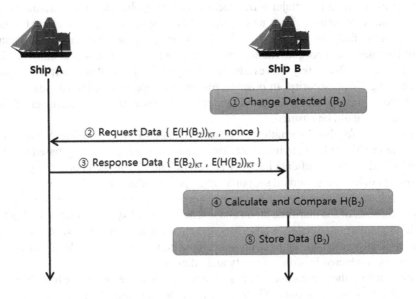

Fig. 7. Synchronize data between vessels

4   Analysis of Efficiency

4.1   Efficiency of Transmission

The proposed method supports delta update, which enables saving bandwidth and efficient transmission of synchronization information. Based on block ID, information on a specific block can be updated, and thanks to this feature, it does not need to update all files for synchronization. Meanwhile, synchronization speed is enhanced. It is not that the entire data is updated but that data is partially updated for the changed block, resulting in saving of synchronization of bandwidth and time to complete synchronization.

4.2   Availability

Even in the case where data communication is disconnected from the server, request for data synchronization can be made to adjacent vessels. This is the greatest advantage of this method, which allows synchronization only through geocasting between vessels even in loss of communication with the server, ensuring availability.

5   Conclusion

The maritime cloud is a major infrastructure system applicable to a distributed smart surveillance environment. As a newly proposed concept, the maritime cloud has been studied in the fledging stage. Before the development of the maritime cloud, security should be taken into account. The security issue greatly affects not only communications availability but also safety of vessels. In addition, the distributed smart surveillance requires high-level security. In other words, information of distributed smart camera should be safely delivered to the server and safety against exposure and damage of video information should be ensured.

In this regard, this dissertation proposes a method of synchronizing Almanac data for a safe maritime cloud environment. The method features geocasting-based synchronization and assurance of data integrity and confidentiality in the course of synchronization. In addition, the method supports delta update, enhancing efficiency.

To achieve the objective of this paper, Sect. 2 provides overview of concept and major elements of the maritime cloud and research trend of synchronization technology in cloud computing. Section 3 describes technical requirements before proposing the synchronization method, along with synchronization procedure in detail. In Sect. 4, analysis is conducted in terms of safety and efficiency.

Research on the maritime cloud is still in the initial stage, and there have been lack of studies on its security issue. Since security in the maritime cloud greatly affects the safety of vessels, research on the security should be actively conducted.

Acknowledgments. This paper is extended and improved from accepted paper of GST2015, WISA 2016 conference. This research was supported by Basic Science Research Program through the National Research Foundation of Korea(NRF) funded by the Ministry of Education(NRF-2016R1D1A3A03918513).

References

1. Gae Il., A., Kwangil, L., Ho, C.B.: Analysis of cyber-security threat on maritime cloud proposed as maritime communication framework. In: Conference Proceedings of Korea Information Science Society, pp. 892–893, December 2015
2. https://imo.amsa.gov.au/iala-aism/e-nav/enav16/9-24.pdf
3. https://www.iho.int/mtg_docs/com_wg/SNPWG/SNPWG17/SNPWG17-9.3_An overview of the Maritime Cloud – input to IMO e-nav CG.PDF
4. HotSync, P.: Palm developer online documentation (2002)
5. Lee, D., Park, N.: Geocasting-based synchronization of Almanac on the maritime cloud for distributed smart surveillance. J. Supercomputing, 1–16 (2016)
6. Yan, H., Irmak, U., Suel, T.: Algorithms for low-latency remote file synchronization. In: INFOCOM 2008, The 27th Conference on Computer Communications. IEEE, pp. 156–160 (2008)
7. Xu, D., Sheng, Y., Ju, D., Wu, J., Wang, D.: High effective two-round remote file fast synchronization algorithm. Jisuanji Kexue yu Tansuo **5**(1), 38–49 (2011)
8. Park, N., Bang, H.-C.: Mobile middleware platform for secure vessel traffic system in IoT service environment. Secur. Commun. Netw. **9**(6), 500–512 (2016)

9. Lee, J., Jung, H., Lee, S.: Forensic investigation procedure for real-time synchronization service. J. Korea Inst. Inform. Secur. Cryptology **22**, 1363–1374 (2012)

10. Agarwal, S., Starobinski, D., Trachtenberg, A.: On the scalability of data synchronization protocols for PDAs and mobile devices. IEEE Netw. **16**, 22–28 (2002)

11. Tridgell, A.: Efficient algorithms for sorting and synchronization. Ph.D. thesis, The Australian National University (1999)

12. Uppoor, S., Flouris, M.D., Bilas, A.: Cloudbased synchronization of distributed file system hierarchies. In: Proceedings of IEEE International Conference on Cluster Computing Workshops and Posters (CLUSTER WORKSHOPS2010), pp. 1–4, September 2010

13. Ha, B.H., Park, K.H., Ju, H.T., Woo, J.J.: Design and implementation of a session handler module for SyncML data synchronization clients. KIPS Trans. Part C **12C**(5), 741–748 (2005)

14. Jung, H.M., Ko, Y.W., Park, J.M., Kong, J.S.: A file synchronization system using similarity-based deduplication. J. KIISE Comput. Practices Lett. **18**(7), 548–552 (2012)

15. Jang, J.R., La, H.J., Kim, S.D.: Architectural tactics for efficient data synchronization of mobile applications in multi-device environments. J. KISS Softw. Appl. **39**(11), 833–847 (2012)

16. Park, N., Hu, H., Jin, Q.: Security and privacy mechanisms for sensor middleware and application in Internet of Things (IoT). Int. J. Distrib. Sens. Netw. **2016**, 1–3 (2015). Article 2965438

17. Park, N., Kwak, J., Kim, S., Won, D., Kim, H.: WIPI mobile platform with secure service for mobile RFID network environment. In: Shen, H.T., Li, J., Li, M., Ni, J., Wang, W. (eds.) APWeb 2006. LNCS, vol. 3842, pp. 741–748. Springer, Heidelberg (2006). doi:10.1007/11610496_100

18. Park, N., Kim, M.: Implementation of load management application system using smart grid privacy policy in energy management service environment. Cluster Comput. **17**, 653–664 (2014)

19. Park, N., Kang, N.: Mutual authentication scheme in secure internet of things technology for comfortable lifestyle. Sensors **16**(1), 1–16 (2016)

The Vessel Trajectory Mechanism for Marine Accidents Analysis

Seung-hee Oh[✉], Byung-gil Lee[✉], and Byungho Chung[✉]

ICT Convergence Security Laboratory, Information Security Department,
Electronics and Telecommunications Research Institute, Daejeon, Republic of Korea
{seunghee5,bglee,cbh}@etri.re.kr

Abstract. In this paper, we provide a mechanism to be able to save time and human resources to predict the time of occurrence of accidents at sea this time of the incident are not clear and to extract the suspected vessel-related accidents at sea. The proposed mechanism, it save such amount of data and time to trajectory extraction by managing separate the control area in a grid pattern, and is characterized as possible through trajectory analysis for a particular area. It also can be reduced 30 times faster than existing marine accident analysis time using the playback function in VTS operating system, so it is effective in saving human resource and time.

Keywords: Marine accident · Vessel trajectory · VTS

1 Introduction

The vessel is a next number of transportation of motor vehicles. These days, large quantities of material are being exported and imported through the vessels. Increasing movement of vessels through the seas, and thus various types of marine accidents are also increasing. Although it is the best way to prevent vessel accidents in advance, it is also important to quickly and accurately process when the marine accident occurred [1–3].

The large scale of marine accident is easy to check the time of the accident and accident areas, but the marine accident, such as fishing nets damage or fish farms damage are in many cases unknown of the accident area and the date (including exact time). The existing method mainly to analyze all the data collected in the Vessel Traffic Service (VTS) system is used in order to determine such a marine accident which has unknown accident date, time and area. Therefore, existing method requires a lot of time and human resources to solve the marine accident. In this paper, we propose the vessel trajectory mechanism that can efficiently and speedly support of the marine accident analysis.

This paper is organized as follows. Section 2 introduces existing analysis mechanism of marine accidents. In Sect. 3, we proposes preprocessing mechanism of vessel trajectory for efficient vessel trajectory extraction. In Sect. 4, vessel trajectory mechanism is proposed and in Sect. 5, comparison with existing playback method is conducted. Finally, conclusions and possible extensions of this work for future research are drawn in Sect. 6.

© Springer International Publishing AG 2017
D. Choi and S. Guilley (Eds.): WISA 2016, LNCS 10144, pp. 388–396, 2017.
DOI: 10.1007/978-3-319-56549-1_33

2   The Existing Analysis Methods of Marine Accidents

A service implemented by a competent authority, VTS is designed to improve the safety and efficiency of navigation, safety of life at sea and the protection of the marine environment. VTS is governed by SOLAS(International Convention for the Safety of Life at Sea) Chap. 5 Regulation 12 together with the Guidelines for VTS [IMO Resolution A.857(20)] adopted by the International Marine Organization (IMO) on 27 November 1997 [4].

Figure 1 shows the various types of information stored at VTS center. The VTS is installed on the port or coastal and collects the radar images through marine surveillance radar, Automatic Identification System (AIS) static and dynamic information of vessel, and Closed-Circuit TeleVision (CCTV) image through interworking CCTV. The VTS center most of the data that can be analyzed marine accidents is collected [5] (Fig. 2).

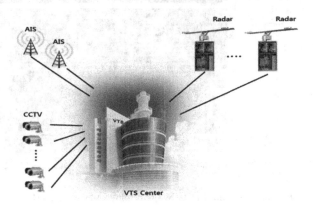

Fig. 1. The information stored at VTS center

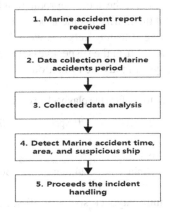

Fig. 2. Marine accident process flow

In most cases, in order to analyze the data collected by the VTS center uses a playback function of operation console of VTS system. The playback function is a method to determine the time of the accident and incident information, importing historical data stored within the marine traffic control systems at a faster speed than the actual play. The Fig. 3 shows the example of playback function GUI in VTS operation system of Kongsberg Norcontrol IT.

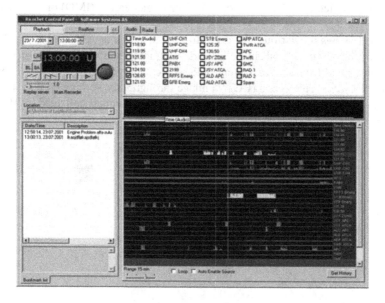

Fig. 3. Norcontrol IT C-Scope Replay Control Panel [6]

However, this method has a disadvantage in that it consumes a lot of time to confirm the exact time of an accident, even if the speed reproduction by applying in most cases, except when exactly identified the marine accident occurrence time.

If you see an accident damaged fishing nets one week later, these time as shown in Table 1 are required in order to confirm the suspect vessel and the exact date/time of the incident in the existing VTS system playback functions.

Table 1. Maximum required time to confirm the playback results (A week source data reference).

Playback speed	1 Speed	10 Speed	20 Speed	30 Speed	50 Speed
Analysis time	7 days	16 h	8 h	5 h	3 h
		48 min	24 min	36 min	22 min

Even applying the maximum playback speed of 50 speed playback of the current VTS system takes a time of at least 3 h 22 min for the accident analysis. Moreover, in reality, it is very difficult to check visually verify when executing the recording playback speed increased by more than 10 speed. Therefore it takes more time to the real event analysis in current VTS system.

3   Proposed Preprocessing Mechanism of Vessel Trajectory

The proposed preprocessing mechanism of vessel trajectory helps quickly and accurately analyze the marine accidents especially damage fishing nets or damage fishing farms. The proposed mechanism regularly collects and manages information of radar track and AIS track to take advantage of when you extract a suspect vessel and analyze marine accidents.

Figure 4 shows how to collect the track information in the VTS system and how to manage and provide to the vessel traffic controller the AIS track and radar track information.

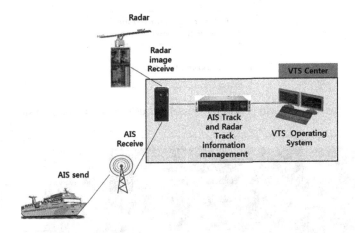

Fig. 4. Track information collecting and management

Each AIS track and radar track are generated every 3 s in normal VTS system. Therefore, the one day track number of each vessel are 28,800 AIS track and 28,800 radar track. To manage and extract the track information from number of vessels needs more efficient approach.

The mechanism proposed after checking where it belongs among the pre-defined grid area before storing the target information in order to facilitate the analysis of large target information is stored with latitude and longitude information. In Fig. 5, it is the flowchart of selecting vessel lists from proposed preprocessing mechanism.

The proposed mechanism, when the track information of the vessel arrives, extracts the location information (latitude, longitude) by parsing the received track messages. Then, the extracted location information updates the vessel information table after adding the grid positions of the controlled region. This preprocessing mechanism improves the processing speed when the accidents occurred in the future, to extract a list of vessels that transit the requested area.

Figure 6 shows the example dividing controlled area by grid based on the latitude and longitude in the VTS center.

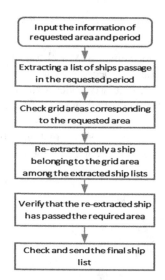

Fig. 5. Flowchart of selecting vessel lists using proposed mechanism

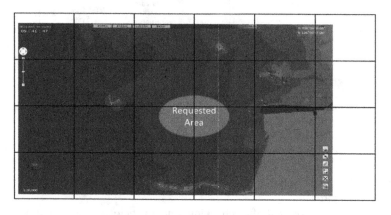

Fig. 6. The example of divided control area of Gunsan VTS center

4   Proposed Trajectory Extraction Mechanism for Analysis of Marine Accidents

In Sect. 3, we suggested the preprocessing mechanism for extraction faster from stored track information including vessel detail information, longitude, latitude using virtual grid. In this section, we propose the mechanism that can make quickly confirm the exact time of marine accident date and time. Our proposed mechanism is more useful when use it together with existing playback method. When you do not know the date and time of marine accident, we suggest to check the vessels trajectory before applying playback function as like Fig. 7.

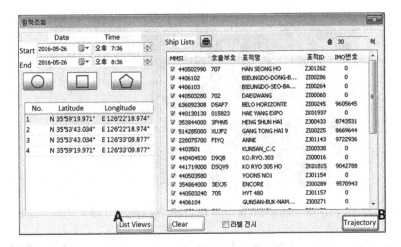

Fig. 7. Trajectory query popup window

In the case of fishing nets damage accident, it is possible to find out the location information that has been installed of fishing net. The proposed trajectory information extraction mechanism has an advantage of offering to select a desired area other than the control information for the entire controlled area. Therefore, it makes to shorten the time of extraction information and verification, because of checking only selected area.

Figure 7 shows a popup window for area-based trajectory query. First, select the shape to be displayed in the area to request in the popup window with the start date and end date. Then, after selecting the shape for drawing among circle, rectangle, and polygons, you directly drag on the electronic chart in the VTS operating system drawn by selecting the desired area. The shapes for area-based trajectory query can be selected from circles, squares and polygons. After you select start date, end date and desired area, press the button "List Views" (A) to request vessels trajectory list. It is provided with a list of vessels which request time there is a past history of the desired area [7].

Select one or more vessels appeared on the vessels list window, and then click "Trajectory" button (B) is that Fig. 8 shows the example of the vessel is passed by vessels trajectory appear as red dots. Figure 8 shows the screen of the VTS operating system and red dots on the electronic chart displays the vessel trajectory which passed the selected area during requested date. When the mouse pointed one certain red dot, it shows the date and time of trajectory. So you can search out the suspicious period using vessel trajectories and it makes reduce the period for checking playback function. The less time you need to check the playback has the effect of reduced processing time of marine accident.

Our proposed trajectory extraction mechanism can be confirmed by checking the VTS operation system screen directly to one or more suspicious vessels by vessels trajectory. The suggested approach is in progress the analysis of marine accidents rapidly and efficiently, it can be saved through human resource as well as time resources.

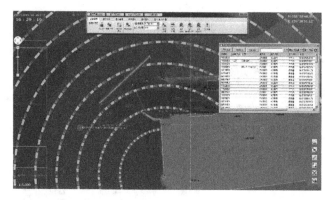

Fig. 8. Display vessel trajectories in VTS operating system (Color figure online)

5   Analysis of the Proposed Trajectory Extraction Mechanism

We analyze the proposed mechanism using the example situation in this section. In this paper, we utilize the recorded data that are collected using simulated virtual target the Gunsan VTS center in Republic of Korea. The example of request condition for vessel list in the selected area in Gunsan VTS center is shown as Table 2. We have performed the request to date only the period change to the same area 1 day, 2 days, 3 days and 7 days.

Table 2. Request condition for vessel list in the selected area

```
== [2016/05/15-14:00:51] ==
Request Period:
[2015-08-24 00:00:24:622] ~ [2015-08-25 00:00:24:288]
ZoneType [3] -> means Rectangle
Index [1], Latitude [36.055699], Longitude [126.282004]
Index [2], Latitude [35.903019], Longitude [126.282005]
Index [3], Latitude [35.903019], Longitude [126.676133]
Index [4], Latitude [36.055699], Longitude [126.676133]
```

Table 3 shows the time required to extract a list of vessels to analyze the passage for 1 day, 2days, 3 days and 7 days in the selected area. The processing time it takes to receive the results of the analysis vessels list passage during the requested period for a particular area is represented differently depending on the regional marine traffic control through traffic volume characteristics. This is only one of the example, the processing result time will always be treated differently.

Table 3. Request processing time of vessel list in the selected area

Request period	Analysis and extraction time of vessel list (seconds)
1 Day	126.114
2 Days	304.344
3 Days	602.593
7 Days	1600.759

The first row in Table 2 means query request time. We provide 3 types of zone shape which are Circle, Rectangle, and Polygon and ZoneType [3] means Rectangle. Index [1–4] show the four points of the drawing rectangle.

To find out the exact time of the marine accident takes more time than Table 3 results because our proposed mechanism used with existing playback method. Also it can be used alone to confirm the suspicious vessel but we recommend it uses together with playback method for accuracy.

This example has more vessel trajectories than normal situation on the VTS system because we made almost 2,000 virtual vessels to give strong adverse condition at the same time. However, to apply the proposed mechanism approximately reduces the analysis time about more than 30 times faster than using only 10-speed playback method.

6   Conclusions

In this paper, we proposed two mechanisms for analyzing marine accident in particularly accident time unknown cases. One is preprocessing mechanism to store track information of vessels and it helps when extracts the information about appointed area and time condition. The other is vessel trajectory extraction mechanism to confirm suspicious vessels and it is useful when uses the case such as fishing net damages before applying existing playback method.

Our proposed two mechanisms can complementary the disadvantage that it takes a lot of time used an existing playback method, these help quickly and efficiently determine the accident date/time and suspect vessels especially the time unknown marine accident. It has an advantage that it can choose the request area. Therefore it reduce the processing time to find out unnecessary area.

We are still interest of reducing the processing time so that we are studying on the method to use index value applied to the request of trajectory list.

Acknowledgement. This work was supported by ETRI through Maritime Safety & Maritime Traffic Facilities Management R&D Program of the MPSS (Ministry of Public Safety and Security)/KIMST (2009403, Development of next generation VTS for maritime safety).

References

1. Smierzchalski, R., Michalewicz, Z.: Modeling of ship trajectory in collision situations by an evolutionary algorithm. IEEE Trans. Evol. Comput. **4**, 227–241 (2000)

2. Zhu, F.: Mining ship spatial trajectory patterns from AIS database for marine surveillance. In: 2011 2nd IEEE International Conference on Emergency Management and Management Sciences (ICEMMS), pp. 772–775, August 2011
3. Accident damage fishing nets attention needed. http://www.haewoon.or.kr/ksa/bbs/selectBoardArticle.do?nttId=17659&bbsId=B_000735&menuNo=700039
4. Wikipedia, "Vessel traffic service". https://en.wikipedia.org/wiki/Vessel_traffic_service
5. Oh, S.H., Choi, J., Cho, K., Lee, B.G.: The efficient trajectory extraction mechanism for marine accidents. In: Korea Information Processing Society 2015 Conference, vol. 22, No. 2, pp. 30–32, October 2015
6. "C-Scope Logging and Replay", Kongsberg Norcontrol IT brochure
7. Oh, S.H., Lee, B.G., Chung, B.: The extraction mechanism of ship list and vessel trajectory based on the requested region for VTS. In: The 2016 International Conference on Information and Knowledge Engineering, July 2016

Author Index

Printed in the United States
By Bookmasters